HINTS & TIPS TO MAKE LIFE EASIER

READER'S DIGEST

HINTS & TIPS TO MAKE LIFE EASIER

PRACTICAL
SOLUTIONS for
EVERYDAY
PROBLEMS

Reader's Digest

The Reader's Digest Association (Canada) Ltd., Montreal

CANADIAN STAFF

PROJECT EDITOR
Andrew Jones

DESIGNER
Cécile Germain

COPY EDITOR
Gilles Humbert

RESEARCHERS
Alison Fripp-Coderre
Melanie Kindrachuck

PICTURE RESEARCHERS
Rachel Irwin
Alexis Lipsitz

PRODUCTION MANAGER
Holger Lorenzen

COORDINATOR
Susan Wong

ART DIRECTOR
John McGuffie

MANAGING EDITOR
Alice Philomena Rutherford

EDITORIAL DIRECTOR, BOOKS AND HOME ENTERTAINMENT
Deirdre Gilbert

U.S. STAFF

PROJECT ART EDITOR
Virginia Wells Blaker

EDITOR
Nancy Shuker

SENIOR RESEARCH EDITORS
Eileen Einfrank
Maymay Quey Lin

RESEARCH EDITORS
Linda Ingroia
Barbara Guarino Lester
Willard Lubka

SENIOR ASSOCIATE EDITORS
Jeffrey Akellian
Alexis Lipsitz

ASSOCIATE EDITOR
Tracy A. O'Shea

SENIOR ASSOCIATE ART EDITOR
Tomaso Milian

ASSOCIATE ART EDITORS
Antonio Mora
Andrew Ploski

EDITORIAL/RESEARCH ASSISTANTS
Claudia Kaplan
Valerie Sylvester

CONTRIBUTORS

PROJECT EDITOR
Pamela Thomas

CONTRIBUTING EDITORS
Edward S. Barnard
Harvey Loomis
Cinda Siler

WRITER/CONSULTANTS
Ann Arnott
Barbara Bedway
Eleanor Berman
Thomas Christopher
Susan Cohen
Cynthia L. Cooper
Marian Faux
Wendy B. Murphy
David "Dré" Soloman
Charles Wardell
Carol Weeg
Charles A. Wills

CONSULTANTS
JoAnne Baldini
Charles Davis
Philip Englander
Martha Faghani
Sandra Rose Gluck
Jenifer Lang
Timothy J. Leffert, D.C.
Reuben N. Lubka, M.D.
Ruth L. Perles

RESEARCHER
Paula M. Phelps

COPY EDITORS
Erin Clermont
Virginia Croft

PROOFREADER
Julee Binder Shapiro

INDEXER
Rose M. Bernal

ILLUSTRATORS
Kirsten Soderlind, chief
Steve Fuller

PHOTOGRAPHER
Steven B. Mays

*Cover illustrations
by Nancy L. Hoffmann
for The Stock Illustration Source, Inc.*

READER'S DIGEST GENERAL BOOKS

**EDITOR-IN-CHIEF,
BOOKS AND HOME ENTERTAINMENT**
Barbara J. Morgan

EDITOR, U.S. GENERAL BOOKS
David Palmer

EXECUTIVE EDITOR
Gayla Visalli

MANAGING EDITOR
Christopher Cavanaugh

The acknowledgments that appear on page 416 are hereby made a part of this copyright page.
Copyright © 1997 The Reader's Digest Association, Inc.
Copyright © 1997 The Reader's Digest Association (Canada) Ltd.

Canadian Cataloging in Publication Data

Main entry under title:

Hints & tips to make life easier: practical solutions to everyday problems

ISBN 0-88850-611-2

1. Home economics—Handbooks, manuals, etc. 2. Life skills—Handbooks, manuals, etc. I. Reader's Digest Association (Canada). II. Title: Hints and tips to make life easier.

HQ2037.H55 1997   640   C97-900834-4

Printed in Canada

For information on this and other Reader's Digest products or to request a catalogue, please call our 24-hour Customer Service hotline at 1-800-465-0780.

You can also visit us on the World Wide Web at http://www.readersdigest.ca

This book is made up of over 4,000 hints and tips arranged under more than 1,000 alphabetized topic headings. If you are looking for hints on a particular subject, simply turn to that heading. (All headings are printed in blue type.) For example, if you want to learn easy ways to bake a pie, look under "Pies & Pie Crusts."

Sometimes, however, you won't find particular topic in the alphabetical listing, or you'll want to find additional topics under more general categories, such as "Decorating," "Computers," or "Diet & Nutrition." To make locating a topic easy, we have provided this "Quick Look-It-Up Guide," which lists 34 general category heads and the specific topics related to them. If you still can't find a topic or want greater detail ("Vinegar," for example, is mentioned under many headings), refer to the comprehensive index that begins on page 406.

Quick Look-It-Up Guide

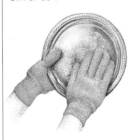

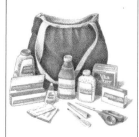

About This Book

Do you feel that there are simply not enough hours in the day to accomplish everything? Do you wonder where you'll find the energy to go to work, fix the meals, mow the lawn—and exercise regularly? Do you worry that you can never save up enough money to pay off the mortgage, educate your children, put away for retirement—and still enjoy vacations? In short, do you wish that life was just a bit less difficult?

With *Reader's Digest Hints & Tips to Make Life Easier,* you have the perfect tool for taking the hassle out of everyday living. Featuring more than 4,000 practical hints and tips, each one a cogent nugget of knowledge, this book is bursting with fresh ideas to help you cope with life's conundrums—from the tiny ("What should I do with this leftover tomato paste?") to the terrifying ("My mother must go into a nursing home, but how are we going to manage it?").

Boxes, charts, and illustrations amplify many subjects. For example, "Easy Does It" boxes provide details to such subjects as "Birthdays" (creative last-minute gifts) and "First-Aid Kits" (essential contents of one), while "Right Stuff" boxes highlight commercial products specially designed to ease your way (ergonomic snow shovels, disposable cameras, and the latest computer software, to name a few). In addition, photographs, illustrated charts, and annotated documents clarify complicated concepts and provide facts at a glance.

Safeguarding your health, managing your money, maintaining your house and car, enjoying your garden, keeping yourself organized, eating wisely and well, developing warm relationships, even dealing with knotty legal problems—these topics, and many more, are covered in *Reader's Digest Hints & Tips to Make Life Easier.* Take a few minutes to browse though this book. You'll quickly realize that life can be easier, and now you have the means to make it so.

—*The Editors*

ACCESSORIES TO AWNINGS

ACCESSORIES

Display your favorite brooch pinned to a ribbon on a hat, suspended from a long chain, or attached to a scarf.

To simplify your life, wear matching pants, skirts, jackets, and sweaters in a deep, neutral color like black, navy, gray, or burgundy and change your "look" with colorful blouses, scarves, and jewelry.

Spruce up plain pumps by attaching a clip earring to each shoe. A dab of florist's clay under the clip prevents it from falling off or marring the shoe leather.

Be selective. Too many accessories—a bold necklace, a bright scarf, and a fancy belt all worn together—create a cluttered look. Highlight one accessory at a time.

Office to evening. Swap your tailored blouse for a silk camisole; trade your opaque pantyhose for a sheer pair; and change from comfortable work shoes into glamorous higher heels.

Raid your husband's closet. Borrow his shirts to top leggings; wear his suspenders with jeans; or use his tie as a funky belt.

Explore secondhand shops for garments with vintage buttons or trim. Sew trimming onto a plain blouse or jacket to create a custom garment for less money.

ACCOUNTING

Track your investments. Keep detailed records of the transactions you've made through a broker and compare them with the monthly brokerage report. Discuss any discrepancies with your broker right away, since it is easier to clear up errors as soon as they become evident.

Streamline your checkbook. Don't bother balancing your checkbook to the last penny. When entering a transaction, round your checks "up" to the next dollar. After a year's time you'll likely end up within $20 of your actual balance—and the difference will be in your favor.

ACNE

Don't scrub too hard. Using harsh exfoliators and applying too much friction when you wash your face can increase the possibility of acne eruptions.

 Dry a blemish overnight by dabbing it with witch hazel or calamine lotion. Both work just as well as alcohol-based products but are gentler on your skin.

Hands off. Never pick or pop a blemish with your bare fingers. You'll risk spreading bacteria.

Avoid the sun. Although exposure to sunlight seems to clear up acne, the results are temporary. A week or two later the oil-producing sebaceous glands go into high gear, often increasing breakouts.

RIGHT STUFF — A TOOL FOR PAINLESS HOME ACCOUNTING

Managing money is easier with software such as Intuit's Quicken or Microsoft Money. These programs automate bank account and credit card records, budgeting, bill paying, investment tracking, loan payments, tax planning, expenditure analysis, home inventories, and such complex financial calculations as interest rates. Professional-quality reports, charts, and graphs can be easily generated. And connecting to on-line banking services allows you to make account transactions conveniently from your computer.

ADDRESS BOOKS

Write the names in ink and the addresses and phone numbers in pencil. That way, when family members or acquaintances move, you can erase the old information and add the new. Your address book will be up-to-date without any messy cross-outs.

 Make a copy of your address book. Photocopy the up-to-date pages, then store this duplicate in a safe place; it will come in handy if the original is lost.

Quick reference. List often-used addresses on the first page of your book. Put those who provide similar services in one place, like your family's doctors under "D".

Use index cards, stored in a small file box, for addresses and phone numbers. You'll have room for personal notes, such as the dates of birthdays and anniversaries. For quick access, put emergency phone numbers on red cards placed at the beginning of the file. Discard outdated cards.

Save old address books. Browsing through old address books brings back memories of friends and acquaintances, and serves as an information resource.

AEROBIC EXERCISE

Gauge your fitness. Without straining yourself, cover as much distance as possible by running and/or walking for 12 minutes. If you manage to do 1.6 km (1 mi) or more in those 12 minutes, you're in pretty good shape.

How often? Exercise aerobically at least three times a week for maximum benefits. Just as important: try to sustain your aerobic pace for at least 20 minutes.

Make workouts fun. Jog in a pretty park; watch television as you pedal a stationary bicycle; listen to a book on tape as you take a brisk walk, away from traffic.

Set goals that are specific, measurable, and easily attainable. For example, add five minutes each week to your jogging time. Celebrate when you achieve a goal.

How hard? Exercise at a level that brings your heart to within 65 to 80 percent of its maximum capacity. A quick way to judge if you are at the right level: If your breathing is so labored that talking causes discomfort, you're pushing too hard. Conversely, if you are able to sing, quicken the rate of exercise.

AGING GRACEFULLY

Stay involved socially. Keep a job you enjoy. If you have retired, become a volunteer, entertain friends at home, take courses, or join a club. Don't cut yourself off from other people.

Exercise regularly to stay fit and to boost your energy level. Ease into it: begin by walking 1.6 km (1 mi) three times a week. Aim toward more vigorous activities like jogging, swimming, or tennis.

Maintain your proper weight. Studies show that your optimum weight should remain fairly constant from the age of 25 through old age. Avoid gaining or losing too much weight.

THE AEROBIC ADVANTAGE

The sustained movement of the body's large muscles causes the heart, circulatory system, and lungs to work harder. Done regularly, such aerobic activity lowers blood pressure, reduces the risk of coronary disease, and gives one an overall sense of well-being.

ACTIVITY	CALORIES PER HOUR	CARDIOVASCULAR BENEFIT
Aerobic dance	360–480	Excellent
Bicycling (19 km/h [12 mph])	410–600	Excellent
Golf (walking with clubs)	300–360	Fair
Jogging (8 km/h [5 mph])	600–700	Excellent
Jumping rope	800	Excellent
Skiing (cross-country)	700–1,020	Excellent
Skiing (downhill)	500–600	Fair to good
Swimming (crawl)	275–750	Excellent
Tennis (singles)	400–480	Good
Walking	300–480	Good to excellent

Keep learning. Don't let age become an excuse for not staying intellectually fit. Take music lessons; become computer literate; take a college course.

Accept your age. Trying to compensate for your years by dressing or acting like a younger person only undermines what you have to offer: experience, wisdom, and a seasoned perspective.

AIR BAGS

Air bag alert. Never put a baby, a child, or even a small adult in the front seat of a vehicle that is fitted with air bags. Studies have shown that the force of an inflating air bag can cause serious injury and even death to children or small adults.

Air bags and seat belts work in tandem to protect passengers involved in frontal crashes. The air bag softens the impact of the crash; the shoulder and lap belts hold passengers at a safe distance from the air bag. For optimum protection, use both.

Driver's precaution. If your car has air bags, drive with your hands on the rim of the steering wheel, not in the center, where the air bag could knock them into your face. Never drive with anything sticking out of your mouth, such as a lollipop or cigarette, which might be jammed down your throat by the air bag.

AIR CONDITIONERS

Install the air conditioner in the window that receives the least sunlight. If it must go in a sunny spot, try to add some shade, such as a canopy or awning.

Filter upkeep. Dirty air filters should be replaced or cleaned. Check at the start of each cooling season and every 30 days during periods of heavy use. To wash, put the filter in a sink and wipe with a damp cloth and mild detergent.

The cooling capacity of an air conditioner is measured in British thermal units (Btu's). The number of Btu's that will be right for you depends on the size of the space in square meters / square feet (length multiplied by width). But several other factors can affect Btu requirements. Therefore a well-informed salesperson, calculator in hand, should ask you the following questions:

◗ *How big is the space in square meters / square feet?*

◗ *Are you also going to use the air conditioner to cool the kitchen, the bedroom, or some other space?*

◗ *How thick are the walls? Are they made of masonry? Are they insulated or uninsulated?*

◗ *In which compass direction does the longest outside wall face?*

◗ *How high are the ceilings? Is the space on the top floor? Is the ceiling insulated?*

◗ *Does the space receive direct sunlight? Are the windows well shaded?*

◗ *Will the air conditioner be used mainly at night?*

Let the filter dry before reinstalling. Vacuuming effectively cleans some filters.

Make energy efficiency, not price, the top priority when buying an air conditioner. Although the air conditioner may be more expensive, the long-term savings on electric bills will more than offset any extra expense.

Buy a timer for your air conditioner. Set it to turn on the air a half hour before you get home so that you'll be greeted by cool air when you walk through the door.

Don't fool the system. Keep appliances that produce heat away from the unit's thermostat. Otherwise, they will "fool" the system into making the space cooler than necessary.

Close off unused rooms. Use your air conditioner to cool only the spaces you use regularly. Your rooms will cool more quickly, and you'll save money on utility bills.

End-of-season maintenance. Run the air conditioner's fan for several hours on a clear day at season's end. This removes moisture from the unit's interior, thus protecting it from damage.

AIR FRESHENERS

Freshen closet air with a pomander ball, made by inserting whole cloves into an unpeeled orange, lemon, lime, or apple. (Poke holes in the peel with a nail first to keep the cloves from breaking.) Tie pretty ribbons around the pomander ball, leaving long enough ends for hanging.

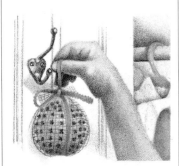

Instant air spray. Mix 250 mL (8 oz) of water with 10 or more drops of an essential oil—rosemary, eucalyptus, pine, lavender, or any of the citruses—in a spray bottle. Add 10 or more drops if you want a stronger scent. Essential oils, found at cosmetics or health-food stores, actually kill airborne bacteria and evaporate cleanly, leaving no sticky residue.

Revive a musty closet by placing an open pan of charcoal briquettes on the floor. Once a month replace the briquettes, which absorb moisture and odors.

For a sweeter-smelling house, squeeze a few drops of fresh lemon juice into the dustbag of your vacuum cleaner before you start it up.

AIR TRAVEL

Meal choices. Airlines offer as many as 20 different menus—from Asian, kosher, and vegetarian to low-cholesterol or low-calorie. Any special order, however, must be requested at least 24 hours in advance. Once you are

AIRPLANE COMFORT

▶ *Book ahead for a good seat. Generally, the roomiest ones in economy are on the bulkhead row (it faces the wall between classes). Next best are seats on the exit row, where the seats in front don't recline.*

▶ *Wear loose, nonconstricting clothes and bring a sweater or jacket and warm socks—even in summer. Cabin temperatures go down as the plane gains altitude.*

▶ *Bring your own inflatable neck pillow for your head and use the airline pillow for back support.*

▶ *Elevate your feet, using your carry-on bag as a footrest. Resist removing your shoes since your feet may swell.*

▶ *Combat the cabin's dry air with lip balm, skin moisturizer, and eyedrops. Wear glasses instead of contact lenses. Drink plenty of water and fruit juice; avoid alcohol, caffeine, carbonated beverages, and salty foods.*

▶ *On a long flight, walk up and down the aisle every hour to avoid stiffness and swollen feet. Also, do stretching exercises and tense and relax your muscles in your seat.*

in the air, give the flight attendant a note with your name, meal type, and seat number.

Too much sunshine forces you to fly with your window shade down during the day. To avoid the sunny side when traveling eastbound, ask for an A, B, or C seat. Going west, request D, E, or F.

AIRFARES

Dig for good deals. Airlines and travel agents don't always volunteer information on low fares. Ask questions: Is it cheaper to fly on a different day or at a different time of day? Are any seasonal or promotional sales coming up?

Early-bird specials. For normal low rates, make your plane reservations two to three weeks in advance. To take advantage of special promotions, you may have to book even further ahead. Don't worry; if the price is low enough, you will save even if your plans

change and you have to pay a fee to switch your reservation.

Save with consolidators, which buy up blocks of airline tickets and sell them at a discount. Many consolidators sell to the public. Look for ads in the Sunday travel sections of big-city newspapers.

Charter flights offer the convenience of nonstop flights to popular vacation spots and often save money as well. You can buy "air only" or a tour package. The drawbacks are limited schedules and tight seating. You are dealing with a tour operator, not an airline, so use a travel agent to have the best chance of a refund should you need it.

AIRLINE HASSLES

A canceled flight means long lines for rebooking at the airport. To avoid the crowds, find a pay phone and call the airline's toll-free reservation number to book the next flight out.

Tight connections when the first leg of your flight arrives late can be stressful. Ask the gate attendant to alert your connecting gate—and relax.

Missed connections. When the airline is at fault and you are seriously inconvenienced, don't wait for your carrier's next flight. Under "Resolution 735d," you can request an earlier flight on another carrier "if necessary." Explain why you must get to your destination without delay. If you are held up more than several hours and the delay is not weather-related, you can also ask for a meal voucher.

To avoid weather delays, fly early in the day—fewer thunderstorms occur at that time—and take nonstop flights. If you must change planes in winter, book through warmer hubs like Dallas, Atlanta, or Las Vegas rather than Chicago, Denver, or Detroit. Never book the last flight of the day; if it is canceled, you're stuck.

Getting bumped. If you are denied a seat because the airline overbooked and are rescheduled on a later flight that gets you to your destination one to two hours late, the airline must pay you the lesser of the price of a one-way ticket or $200; more than two hours late, up to $400. There is no payment if you are rescheduled within an hour of your original arrival time.

Bump insurance. On crowded flights, check in at the gate at least 45 minutes before departure time to avoid being bumped. Early arrival will also give you the first chance to volunteer to be rescheduled when you have extra time. Your reward for getting on the next flight: a free ticket for future use.

AIRLINE TICKETS

Pay with a credit card. It protects you if your airline gets into financial trouble or cancels a flight. Don't deal with charters, smaller airlines, or consolidators that won't accept credit cards.

Photocopy your ticket. A copy makes replacing a lost ticket easy and quick. You'll still pay a service fee, but the ticket will be reissued immediately. Without a copy—or the ticket number—you must buy a new ticket at current fares and wait as long as six months to get a refund for the lost ticket.

"Ticketless" electronic tickets are now offered by many airlines, eliminating worry about lost tickets. Present the reservation number and a photo ID at the check-in counter to get a boarding pass.

 Avoid the crush. Weekdays from 7:30 to 9:30 A.M. and 5:30 to 7:30 P.M. are rush hours at major airports—and Monday mornings and Friday evenings are particularly hectic. To avoid flight delays and getting stuck in heavy traffic, schedule flights for other times.

AIRPORTS

Avoid missed flights—If your winter holiday in the sun is threatened because a blizzard is forecast for the day of your flight and you live far from the airport, book you

and your family into the airport hotel the night before.

Luggage tags can be tip-offs to burglars who roam airports watching for names and addresses of families leaving home for an extended period of time. Use tags that cover your name, or put your business address on the tag.

Curbside check-in, if it is available, is worth the tip to the attendant to save hauling heavy luggage across the airport or standing in long check-in lines. Wherever you check in, be sure tags to the correct airport are attached to each of your bags before they are taken away.

Time-saver. Before walking through the metal detector, place any keys, coins, or metal jewelry into your carry-on to avoid setting off the alarm.

Beware of thieves who snatch cameras and computers from airport X-ray machines. Team up with a travel companion to protect each other's possessions. Have your friend pass through the metal detector first, then feed bags or equipment into the X-ray machine. Your friend can guard your possessions as they emerge.

Check the rates for airport limousines and cabs in a destination city before you arrive. (Ask your travel agent.) Settle on the fare with the driver before your luggage is put in the trunk.

ALCOHOLIC BEVERAGES

A splash of liqueur can jazz up a hot drink. Try hazelnut liqueur in coffee, cinnamon schnapps in apple cider, or amaretto in tea.

Cooking with wine or liquor can add rich flavor to many foods. Don't serve such dishes to people who can't drink, however, because you can't be sure that all the alcohol will have evaporated.

Meltdown. Use large ice cubes instead of shaved ice when making cocktails. Smaller pieces melt fast and dilute drinks too rapidly.

Weight watchers should avoid alcoholic drinks altogether, because they add empty calories to the daily quota while stimulating an appetite for high-fat, sweet, or salty foods.

 Party strategy. To stay convivial without overindulging at a cocktail party, dilute your drinks with mixers or alternate a nonalcoholic drink with an alcoholic one throughout the evening.

ALLERGIES

Mysterious food allergy? To track down an unknown allergen, keep a food journal for a week. Record what you eat and how you feel afterward. See if a certain food triggers problems and if avoiding the food gives relief.

Natural air cleaners. Philodendrons, ferns, and dracaenas filter many allergens from the air naturally. For maximum benefits, have one plant for every 9.3 m² (100 ft²) of space.

Better vacuuming. If you're allergy prone, invest in a vacuum cleaner with a HEPA (high-efficiency particulate air) filter. Standard vacuum cleaners aggravate allergies because dust particles are agitated during vacuuming and then escape through the filter.

ALLOWANCES

Start early. Children entering elementary school are old enough to begin managing small amounts of money.

Pay early. Set a specific day when money gets distributed, preferably at the beginning of the week. That way, children will need to plan ahead for how they'll spend it on the weekend.

No strings. Don't link an allowance to a child's chores, behavior, or school grades. Children don't learn to manage money when it is given as a reward or rescinded as punishment.

Set clear rules. Decide before you start giving an allowance just what it should be used for. If part of it is to be given to savings, church, or charity, be sure your child understands. If you want to set limits on how much can be spent on candy or other treats, make those restrictions clear.

ALTERATIONS

Iron a garment before you begin to alter it. A wrinkle may cause a crooked hem or some other flaw in the alteration.

A quick hem fix. Instead of stitching, use iron-on fusing tape (available at sewing centers) to hold a hem in place.

 Measure twice. Before making any alterations, verify your measurements a second time. With complicated alterations, ask someone else to check your measurements.

Adjustable Balloon Pants

Putting elastic in the legs is an easy way to alter pants so that your child can grow into them. Simply buy a pair 10 cm (4 in.)

1 *Turn your child's pants inside out. Using small sewing or nail scissors, make a slit where the hem meets the inside leg seam. Make sure that the slit does not extend past the hem.*

longer than needed. Turn them into "balloon pants." Then when the altered pants become too short, simply remove the elastic and let down the hem.

2 *Cut two elastic strips, 6 to 12 mm (¼–½ in.) wide and long enough to fit around your child's ankle. Attach a safety pin to the end of the elastic, then thread the elastic through the hem.*

3 *Overlap the two ends of the elastic and secure them with a couple of whip stitches. Push the elastic inside the hem and finish the seam.*

ALTITUDE SICKNESS

Know the symptoms. Altitude sickness feels like flu and includes throbbing headaches, nausea, fatigue, shortness of breath, heart palpitations, and sleep disturbances. If symptoms persist for more than 48 hours, see a physician or immediately descend to a lower elevation.

Drink lots of water. Even if you don't develop symptoms, drink more water than usual when you venture to a higher elevation.

Exercise moderately. Many people head to high elevations to ski, hike, climb, or mountain bike. Alternate any vigorous exercise with rest for the first two or three days until your body has a chance to acclimate. Stop exercising immediately if you feel dizzy.

Avoid caffeine and alcohol. Both exacerbate the symptoms, especially headache and nausea.

Eat right. When visiting higher elevations, load up on foods high in carbohydrates, such as pastas, breads, crackers, cereals, fruits, and vegetables. Keep salt intake to a minimum.

AMMONIA

For easier oven cleaning, place a bowl of ammonia inside the oven overnight. In the morning, wipe away grease and clean as usual. This method, however, is not recommended for use on self-cleaning ovens.

Gold dust. Clean gilt picture frames by rubbing them with a slice of fresh white bread lightly moistened with ammonia.

Garbage detail. Keep raccoons and other marauders out of your garbage cans by wiping the pails with ammonia or spraying the garbage bags with a mixture of ammonia and water.

To force blooms on woody stems such as cherry or dogwood, slit the ends and place in a bucket with 5.6 L (1 ¼ gal) warm water and a cotton ball drenched in sudsy ammonia. Place the bucket in a plastic garbage bag, knot it closed, and set in a warm corner until the buds begin to open.

A

AMUSEMENT PARKS

Plan your day. Before you go to an amusement park, call for a brochure and map of the park. Figure out where to start and how to work your way around the main attractions.

Timing. Try to arrive early on the least crowded days: nonholiday Mondays and Tuesdays. Other weekdays are better than weekends and major holidays.

Food strategy. Pack a lunch and snacks to avoid food lines as well as save money. Use disposable containers so that you can lighten your load after you eat.

Safety first. Show children the lost-and-found section of the park and explain to them how to seek help from security personnel.

Easy ID. Have children carry identification cards with their name, address, and telephone number. Pin the information to the inside of their clothes or put it in a zippered pocket.

ANGER

Be tolerant of other people's behavior. No one is perfect—including you—and constant disapproval of others takes a toll on your friendships and your health.

Distract yourself. If you find yourself waiting in a long line or

TREAT ANGER WITH HUMOR

◗ *Look for the humor. Don't let the little absurdities of life control you and get you all steamed up. Try to see the ridiculousness of what often turns out to be a harmless situation. Humor can defuse many a volatile moment.*

◗ *Laugh at yourself. Taking yourself too seriously can result in tunnel vision—an inability to see that your reaction to a situation is over the top.*

◗ *Forgive with a smile. Dwelling on past affronts or being consumed by vengeful thoughts takes a toll on physical and emotional health. Studies show that people who forgive are quickly freed of active anger.*

stuck in traffic, don't go ballistic. Instead, focus your mind on one of your favorite places, memories of wonderful meals, or the plans for your next vacation.

Count to 10. Taking a few seconds to defuse potentially explosive emotions works as a distraction and gives you time to consider the consequences of your actions.

ANIMAL BITES

View wildlife from a distance and teach children to do so as well. Nondomestic animals in the wild, your yard, a cage, or anywhere else should be considered dangerous—no matter how cute or "tame" they appear. Touching such animals invites nasty bites.

Once bitten. Bite wounds should be promptly flushed with water and covered with a clean cloth to control bleeding. See your doctor or go to an emergency room immediately. If you know, tell the doctor what kind of animal bit you and note any strange sensations like dizziness. The incident should be reported to the police

as soon as possible. If and when the culprit is found, it should be tested for rabies.

Protect cats and dogs. Vaccinate family pets, even those that stay indoors, against rabies. Call your vet or the local animal protection agency to find out how and where to get vaccinations.

Report roamers. Promptly report any animals—such as raccoons, foxes, or skunks—behaving oddly in the vicinity of your home to your local humane society or the police department.

Be pooch-wise. After asking permission to pet a dog, approach the animal slowly. Avoid sudden movements near a dog's head and always place your hand palm up when reaching to pet it. Steer clear of chained dogs. Don't bother a dog that is eating, sleeping, or caring for pups.

Curb dog attacks. Stand still and speak firmly and calmly. Don't stare directly into a dog's eyes or turn your back. Let the dog sniff you. If it lunges, hold out objects for the dog to bite, such as your jacket or purse. If you fall or are knocked down, curl into a ball, cover your face and neck, and don't move.

ANNIVERSARIES

A milestone party. For a 25th or 50th wedding anniversary, grown children, close friends, or the happy couple can host a celebration. Include the original wedding party as well as new friends. Photocopy a picture of the bride and groom at their wedding to use for the invitations. Blow up other pictures from the wedding to serve as decorations.

GIFT MOTIFS

Each major wedding anniversary is associated with a symbolic motif. Use these motifs creatively when you give an anniversary gift. For example, for a fifth anniversary (wood), instead of purchasing an ordinary wooden bowl, plant a tree in honor of the marriage; for the 20th (china), forgo the porcelain dishes and take a trip to China.

ANNIVERSARY	MOTIF
First	Paper
Second	Cotton
Third	Leather
Fourth	Linen
Fifth	Wood
Sixth	Iron
Seventh	Copper
Eighth	Bronze
Ninth	Pottery
Tenth	Tin
Eleventh	Steel
Twelfth	Silk
Thirteenth	Lace
Fourteenth	Ivory
Fifteenth	Crystal
Twentieth	China
Twenty-fifth	Silver
Thirtieth	Pearl
Thirty-fifth	Coral or Jade
Fortieth	Ruby
Forty-fifth	Sapphire
Fiftieth	Gold
Fifty-fifth	Emerald
Sixtieth	Diamond

Create a "memory book." Ask each guest at an anniversary party to contribute ahead of time a poem, an anecdote, or a tribute to the couple, which you can collect into a scrapbook and present at the party. Or pass around a blank writing album at the party and ask guests to inscribe a favorite memory of the couple.

Create a video remembrance. Find the family's old Super-8 home movies and pick the choice scenes. Then interview friends and family on a video camera. Ask well-wishers who live far away to send a video or audio message. Take the film and tapes to a video or photography store that will splice together all the pieces and provide background music.

Renew your vows. You can do it as part of a regular service in many faiths. Or you can pick a setting that the two of you like—in a park, aboard a boat, at your favorite restaurant. Surround yourself with family and friends and reread the wedding service.

ANNUALS

To stifle weeds in your annual bed, apply a pre-emergent herbicide such as trifluralin in early spring. The herbicide will prevent weeds from sprouting without harming your flower seedlings.

Buy small. When shopping for annual seedlings, look for stocky, compact plants with no flower buds. At the prebud stage, annuals will root in your garden faster and yield bigger, healthier, more drought-resistant plants.

Natural calendar. You can tell when it is safe to start planting cold-sensitive annuals, such as geraniums and impatiens, by looking around your garden or yard. If the lilacs are in full bloom and the oak leaves are at least an inch long, the danger of frost is most likely past.

Prolific flowers. If you let marigolds, poppies, sweet alyssum, petunias, and Johnny-jump-ups go to seed at the end of the blooming season, they will come up again next spring.

A quick trim. To keep annuals flowering, you need to deadhead, or pinch back, wilted blossoms before they go to seed. The simplest way to deadhead a row of annuals is with hedge clippers.

ANSWERING MACHINES

Avoid "telephone tag." When you call people who aren't available, leave a message that suggests a good time for them to call you back. Then make sure you are available when they call.

Memory prod. To remind yourself of something you need to do, call your answering machine and leave yourself a message.

 Smart answer. Never record a greeting that tells callers you are not home or, even worse, are away on an extended trip. Such messages are invitations to would-be burglars. Be general, as in "Hello, I can't come to the phone right now."

Clean swipe. If the sound quality of the cassette on your machine has deteriorated, remove the tape and gently wipe the tape heads with a cotton swab dampened in rubbing alcohol.

ANTILOCK BRAKE SYSTEMS (ABS)

Practice first. Get a feel for how an ABS works by practicing before you drive in wet or icy weather. You should apply pressure to the brakes firmly and not let up until you have come to a stop. If you are used to pumping conventional brakes in slippery conditions to prevent the wheels from locking, you'll need to change this habit.

Steering lesson. ABS modulates the brakes as often as 15 times per second, preventing the locking that makes you skid when driving with conventional brakes. With an ABS, you can steer your car out of danger as you apply the brakes. This, too, takes practice, especially if you are not accustomed to having control during a skid.

To identify ABS in a borrowed or rented car, look for a light on the dashboard that says ABS when you first start the ignition.

ANTIQUE SHOPPING

Buyer beware. Before buying an expensive antique, consult collectors' guidebooks listing the prices of similar items sold at auction within the last year (most public libraries have such books). Also check prices at other antique stores. If the item is very costly, consult an appraiser.

Look for repairs. Alterations or repairs usually reduce the value of an antique. For example, on furniture, check for such clues as legs made of wood different from the rest of the piece, new screws, or machine-cut braces.

 Is it an antique? True antiques are at least 100 years old and are made by hand, not machine. Good design determines value, not age. Unattractive pieces are not desirable just because they are old.

Get a written record of the sale when you buy any valuable antique. The bill provided by the dealer should describe the piece, its age and condition, the materials used in its manufacture, and the name of the artisan. If you dis-cover you've been sold a fake, this bill of sale is your only proof of a fraudulent sale.

Ask for a provenance, a document that includes the names of all of the item's previous owners, when you buy an expensive antique. This is the dealer's warranty that the article is genuine.

Appraise your appraiser. Before you trust an appraiser's opinion, be sure you have chosen a specialist in the kind of items you want to purchase—Oriental rugs, for example, or American quilts.

ANTIQUING FURNITURE

Easier than refinishing. You needn't strive for perfection when antiquing furniture. The goal of antiquing is to create an "aged" look, not a flawless finish.

Age wooden furniture instantly by distressing it. Create a random pattern of dents by banging surfaces with a piece of wood studded with nails, a ring of keys, a chain, stones, or other blunt or jagged objects. Sand away any splinters or rough spots.

Antiquing Furniture the Easy Way

Turn a new piece of furniture into an instant heirloom with an antiquing kit (available at craft stores). Simply choose the finish you prefer (we used a crackling kit) and follow the easy instructions. Most projects can be completed in a weekend.

1 On a porous surface (concrete, terra-cotta, etc.), start with a primer coat. Then apply two coats of your base color. (Let the first coat dry before applying the second.)

Smooth sharp edges with sandpaper. Particularly on a new piece, make sure all the corners and edges are slightly rounded so that the furniture gives the appearance of years of loving use.

Explore color. When antiquing, select any color of the rainbow—and any shade or tint of that color—for the base coat. Choose hues that were commonly used in historic periods and styles. Experiment on scrap wood.

ANTISEPTICS

Kill germs and prevent infection by rinsing cuts and scrapes with sterile saline solution or hydrogen peroxide diluted with water.

Improvise. In a pinch, you can use an antiseptic mouthwash instead of an antiseptic ointment on a cut or scrape.

 OLD SAW **First line of defense.** Always wash cuts and abrasions with warm, soapy water to remove any dirt and debris.

ANXIETY

To calm jangled nerves, slowly sip a cup of hot chamomile tea. Steep the tea for at least 15 minutes to reap the full benefit of the herb's natural sedative.

Take a breather. To calm yourself, sit quietly, close your eyes, and slowly inhale and exhale, focusing on your breathing. Do this for at least 10 minutes.

Distract yourself. When anxiety strikes, involve yourself in an activity to take your mind off the problem. Distancing yourself from your worries may help you to see the problem in a fresh light.

Take baby steps. If a specific activity prompts a panic attack, break it down into manageable parts. By separating the task into stages and completing each stage at your own pace, you'll gradually overcome your fear.

APARTMENT LIVING

Noises off. To muffle the sounds coming from your apartment, cover the floors wall to wall with deep pile carpeting, place rubber padding under noisy appliances, and line adjoining walls with book shelves or soft wall hangings.

Double duties. Plan your apartment so that space is used to maximum effect. Equip your den with a sofa bed so that your everyday TV room can easily convert into a guest room. Or arrange your dining area so that it can be used both as a formal dining room and a home office.

A few favorite things. If you must move from a large home into a smaller apartment, avoid crowding your new space. Be ruthless: store, give away, or sell your "big house" accoutrements. Take only your favorite possessions, and, of course, what you need most.

2 *With a clean foam brush, apply the crackle undercoat. If, after drying, the finish appears dull, add a second coat of the undercoat.*

3 *Apply the crackle top coat with a sponge. Dab on the top coat using even pressure. Don't cover the same area twice or it will ruin the effect.*

4 *Using a clean sponge, apply a light coat of the antiquing medium. For a dramatic effect, apply a second coat. If desired, apply a matte-finish sealer.*

A

APPETITE

Don't skip meals. Whether you want to stimulate your appetite or curb it, eating at least three to five small meals a day will benefit you. Several regular meals keep dieters from getting too hungry and bingeing; similarly regular smaller meals keep light eaters from feeling overwhelmed by too much food.

Exercise before meals. Walk, jog, or perform some form of exercise before meals. Paradoxically, invigorating exercise both sparks the appetite and curbs it.

Dine with others. Appetite is stimulated by social contact. If you must eat alone, treat yourself. Make a favorite dish, put on some relaxing music, and serve yourself on your good china.

Trick for eating less. Serve yourself on a smaller-than-average plate. You'll have the illusion of eating heartily while eating less.

Start with soup. A clear soup, which has few calories, goes a long way toward filling you up before you get to the richer courses of lunch or dinner.

APPETIZERS & FINGER FOODS

Natural servers. Short on serving platters? Simply hollow out a cantaloupe (for fruit salad), a cabbage head (for vegetable dip), an eggplant (for eggplant "caviar"), or a loaf of bread (for seafood salad).

 Serve finger foods at standup parties, where guests must balance a drink and a napkin and cannot manage silverware as well.

Pair fruit slices with cheese instead of crackers on a cheese board. Apple and pear slices

AN APPETIZER PANTRY

Stock up on foods that have a long shelf life so that you'll never be at a loss for something to serve when unexpected guests arrive. Here are a few suggestions:

▶ *Nuts. Almonds, cashews, and pecans are a treat served plain or roasted at 230°C (450°F) for 15 minutes with a little butter and coarse salt.*

▶ *Olives. Whether in cans or jars, green or ripe, pitted, unpitted, or stuffed, olives make a tasty accompaniment to cocktails.*

▶ *Smoked oysters, sardines, shrimp, and caviar come in tins or jars that can be opened and served in a minute.*

▶ *Garbanzo beans. To make a quick hummus, drain the beans and place them in a blender or food processor with a garlic clove, 5 mL (1 tsp) of dried minced onion, 30 mL (2 tbsp) of lemon juice, salt, and pepper. Blend until smooth and serve with pita slices or crackers.*

▶ *Crackers and breads. Crackers can be kept in the cupboard. Freeze cocktail rye and pita bread and defrost in a 150°C (300°F) oven as you need them.*

marry nicely with blue cheeses, cheddars, and Gruyères.

Something for everyone. At a party, balance it out: along with the sinfully rich hors d'oeuvres, offer low-fat options like raw vegetables or air-popped popcorn.

The numbers game. At a large gathering, if you are serving only appetizers, estimate about 8 to 10 "bite-size" pieces per person. They may be supper for many guests.

Just for starters. When you serve hors d'oeuvres before a large dinner, keep them to a minimum so that you don't spoil the main event. Figure three to five pieces per person. Keep the cocktail hour to no more than 45 minutes.

APPLES

Measuring up. 450 g (1 lb) of apples equals two large, three medium, or four small apples, or about (2½ cups) of apple slices.

A 20 cm (9 in.) apple pie requires 900 g to 1.5 kg (2–3 lb) of apples.

To prevent a shriveled shell on baked apples, cut a horizontal strip of peel from the fruit's midsection before baking.

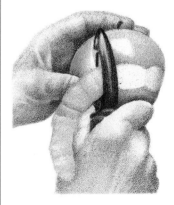

Odor absorber. Keep in mind that an apple's thin skin absorbs odors, so store apples away from pungent foods like onions or garlic to keep the flavor pure.

Brown out. To keep cut apples from turning brown, toss or dip the cut pieces in lemon juice or salted water.

APPRAISALS

Check the credentials and references of any appraiser, whether you need an evaluation of a piece of jewelry, a family heirloom desk, or a house you want to buy. Be aware that only certain real-estate appraisers are required by law to be licensed; otherwise, the occupation is largely unregulated.

How to find an appraiser. Check your Yellow Pages to find a reputable appraiser in your area who specializes in the field that you need. The Appraisal Institute of Canada (204-783-2224) is also a good resource; visit their website at http://www.realworks.com/aicanada.

Appraisal schedule. Jewelry, fine art, antiques, and other collectible objects may appreciate in value every two to three years. Have such items reappraised regularly, and alter your insurance policy to cover any increase in their worth.

When buying a house, hire an appraiser who is approved by your mortgage lender. If you hire an unapproved appraiser, you may run the risk of having to pay for two appraisals.

AQUARIUMS

Natural stress reducer. Invest in an aquarium to find a respite from life's worries. Studies show that the calming sights and sounds of an aquarium can lower blood pressure and reduce heart rate.

For a first aquarium, choose freshwater fish, which are less expensive and easier to maintain than marine fish. Try a mix of nonaggressive tropical fish, such as guppies, tetras, barbs, and small catfish.

Live plants, such as Amazon sword, Java fern, and elodea, absorb chemical waste products in the aquarium that can be toxic to fish. If you see any decaying plant life, however, remove the offender; it pollutes the water.

Water temperature. To keep the aquarium water at a consistent and healthy temperature for your fish, place the aquarium out of direct sunlight and away from any air conditioners, open windows, or drafty doorways.

To add new fish to your aquarium, use a net. Water from the store contains waste products that will pollute your tank.

YOUR FIRST AQUARIUM

A beginner's aquarium kit includes a 38 L (8.3 gal) tank, a cover with a built-in light to reduce evaporation and keep out dust, a heater to keep the water warm enough for tropical fish, a water thermometer, a filter with a built-in air pump to keep the water clean and aerated, a water conditioner, aquarium salt, pH and ammonia testers to make sure that chemicals are at proper levels, gravel to collect waste products, and a gravel cleaner.

EVERYDAY ESSENTIAL OILS

PURPOSE	ESSENTIAL OIL/FRAGRANCE
Soothing fragrances	Chamomile, rose, jasmine, lavender, clary sage, geranium, sandalwood, vanilla, musk, nutmeg
Energizing fragrances	Eucalyptus, pine, lemon, citrus, bergamot, peppermint, rosemary, cinnamon
Aphrodisiacs	Clary sage, geranium, sandalwood, ylang-ylang, lavender
Spirit lifters	Neroli, bergamot, rosemary
Mental stimulants	Clary sage, juniper berry, pine, peppermint
Muscle relaxants	Jasmine, vanilla, musk, eucalyptus, peppermint

ARCHITECTS

Before shopping for an architect, write a description of the job you want done, including your wishes to use existing furniture or artifacts and your preferences with regard to color. Collect photos of houses or clip pictures from home furnishing magazines of designs that appeal to you. The more detailed your description, the better you'll be able to convey your ideas to your architect.

Home base. Choose an architect from among those who work frequently in your area. A local architect will know about zoning laws and ordinances, as well as other potential problems in your community. This could save you disappointment and dollars.

Talk to two or three candidates before making a choice. Ask your architect for references from former clients, and check with local contractors and builders who have worked with him in the past.

Don't begin the job until 95 percent of the decisions have been made. If changes occur during construction, the alterations can cost twice as much and add months to the construction time.

Clarify payment up front. You may simply want the architect to design a plan that a contractor can carry out, or, on a large project, you may want the architect to oversee the builder and all the various contractors. Research your options and nail down fees, costs, and payment procedures before the architect begins work.

AROMATHERAPY

Dilute essential oils with a "carrier oil" such as mineral oil, vitamin E oil, or safflower oil. Applying concentrated essential oils directly to the skin may cause an allergic reaction. Dilute according to the directions on each bottle of oil or do a test patch on your arm with a solution of equal parts essential oil and carrier oil. If you have an allergic reaction, dilute the essential oil, or avoid it completely.

Spread a subtle scent throughout your home by dabbing a few drops of oil onto a cool lightbulb. When the light is on, the heat of the bulb will cause the oil to evaporate, sending the fragrance wafting through the house.

For a more intense scent, use a light ring; these are available where potpourri and essential oils are sold. The rings come in metal, ceramic, or disposable cardboard styles. Just fill the groove with oil, place the ring over a lightbulb, and turn on the light.

A quick pick-me-up. Moisten a tissue with a few drops of an invigorating oil and keep it in a plastic bag in your purse. When you need a lift, simply pull out the tissue and hold it to your nose.

ART DISPLAY

Movable feast. Line a hallway with two long rows of molding, available at most home stores. Use it as a shelf on which to set pictures and photographs. If the rows line one wall, space them far enough apart to display prints and photographs of different sizes. The molding is the only thing that is nailed down, so you can change whatever is perched on the shelf as often as you like.

 Visual tricks with pictures. Vertical arrangements of pictures can make a room seem higher; horizontal displays, wider. Hanging pictures lower can help a low-ceilinged room appear more spacious.

Eye-level guide. Hang your art so that the eye of the viewer looks into the main point of interest. In the living room or dining room, hang art low enough to accommodate seated viewers. Hang hallway pictures a bit higher.

Use picture glass, which is lighter in weight and clearer than window glass, to protect watercolors, pastels, and prints from dust and dirt. Never hang art where the sun will hit it directly; there is no protection from the fading caused by the sun's ultra-violet rays.

ART SUPPLIES

Keep chalk from breaking by wrapping masking tape around the middle. This also keeps chalk from smudging your fingers.

No more smudges! Protect charcoal or chalk drawings by spraying them with hair spray or art fixative available at art supply stores.

Recycle an old easel by using it as a display stand for a favorite painting or photograph. The easel-plus-painting becomes a work of art in itself.

Buy in bulk. Many art supply companies sell paints, canvas, brushes, and other supplies by volume. You can save money and time by ordering direct.

Pen revival. Give new life to a dried-out marker by dipping the tip into an acetone-based nail polish remover. Replace the cap and let the marker sit for a couple of hours before using.

Store artist's brushes in a ceramic toothbrush stand. The individual holes let you separate the brushes by size—making it a snap to find the right one.

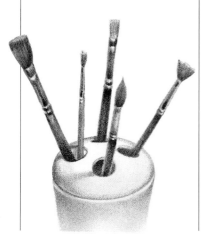

DEVICES FOR ARTHRITIS SUFFERERS

Many products are available to make everyday chores less painful for those with arthritis. The bottle opener not only unscrews caps easily but can press open the tabs on aluminum cans. The jar opener "pops" vacuum-packed tops, which often require a strong twist. The scissors are specially designed to help pained fingers trim fabric and paper with ease. These ingenious products—and many others—can be ordered by mail. Just write to the Arthritis Society, 250 Bloor St. E., Suite 901, Toronto, Ont. M4W 3P2 or call 1-800-321-1433 for a catalog. Visit their website at http://www.arthritis.ca.

ARTHRITIS

See your doctor if joint pain, swelling, or stiffness lasts for more than two weeks. Seeking medical help for arthritis soon after the onset of symptoms may greatly reduce the risk of any permanent joint injury.

If your knee feels hot and sore, place an ice pack in a plastic bag around it. Repeat three times a day for 20 minutes. You should notice a reduction in pain and an improvement in range of motion.

Exercise may be your most important weapon against the effects of arthritis. Physical activity strengthens the muscles and prevents the joints from stiffening further. Ask your doctor about an exercise program specifically tailored to your needs.

Take off the weight. Extra weight puts extra pressure on arthritic joints, particularly hips and knees. Losing weight should make you feel better almost immediately.

Easier opening. People with arthritic hands often have trouble grasping the small knobs and thin handles on drawers, cabinets, and household appliances. To make access easier, tie strips of soft fabric into loops and attach them to handles or knobs.

 Make dressing easier by replacing hard-to-manage snaps, buttons, and zippers with strips of hook-and-eye tape (Velcro). In addition, avoid sweaters and shirts that must be pulled on over your head.

A good support. Buy a sheet of ¾-inch plywood from a lumber yard and slip it between your box springs and mattress to relieve a stiff, arthritic back.

ARTICHOKES

Rules of the heart. The rounder the artichoke, the bigger its heart; the smaller the artichoke, the more tender its leaves.

A good soak. Before cooking them, tenderize artichokes, deepen their color, and prevent them from turning brown by soaking them for an hour in 1 L (4 cups) of cold water mixed with 30 mL (2 tbsp) of lemon juice.

Don't cook artichokes in aluminum or cast-iron pots, which can discolor both the pots and the artichokes. Instead, pick a stainless steel, enamel-coated, or Teflon-lined pan.

Don't throw out the stems! Peel and cook them in boiling water until very tender. Serve them warm, dipped in melted butter or lemon juice, or cold, dipped in salad dressing or as part of a salad.

ASPIRIN

Caffeine fix. Caffeine increases the effectiveness of aspirin. If you have a headache, take two aspirin with a caffeinated soft drink or a cup of coffee. Speedy relief will be on the way.

Aspirin powder alert. A single dose of powdered aspirin equals two tablets. Because many people take aspirin powder to treat chronic pain, they can easily overdose—leading to hallucinations and slurred speech. To be safe, stick to tablets or caplets.

 An aspirin a day. Aspirin acts as a blood thinner, reducing the risk of heart attack. That's why many doctors recommend that heart patients take one aspirin each day. Check with your own physician before starting an aspirin regimen.

Avoid aspirin during pregnancy. Aspirin, especially if taken during the last trimester of pregnancy, can possibly injure the baby and cause the mother to bleed excessively during childbirth.

Aspirin allergies. If you notice that your nose runs, you sneeze more often, and you have difficulty breathing when you take aspirin, you are probably allergic to salicylate, the primary ingredient in aspirin. (You are also proba-bly allergic to oranges, raspberries, and spices such as cinnamon— these foods all contain large amounts of salicylate.) For relief, switch to acetaminophen.

ATHLETE'S FOOT

Cover your feet when using public showers, locker rooms, and swimming pools to prevent exposure to athlete's foot. Flip-flops or beach shoes work well.

Dry feet thoroughly after showering or swimming to avoid athlete's foot. Pay special attention to the areas around the nails and between the toes.

Wear loose-fitting shoes when you are suffering from athlete's foot. The fungus that causes athlete's foot thrives in moist, dark places, and tight shoes promote fungal growth. In addition, change your socks twice a day.

Sandals with no socks are an ideal shoe to wear if you have athlete's foot because the increased air circulation keeps the fungus under control. The best remedy of all: Go barefoot.

Antifungal creams and ointments can alleviate athlete's foot.

Preparing Artichokes

1 Wash artichokes thoroughly in cold water. Using a chef's knife, cut off the stem, creating a flat bottom for the artichoke to stand on.

2 Slice 1.2 to 2.5 cm (½–1 in.) from the artichoke's prickly top cone. The cooked artichoke is easier to eat when sharp leaves are trimmed.

3 Using kitchen scissors, trim the prickly tips from the surrounding leaves.

If one product fails to work, try another. Brands vary; another may work better for you.

Dust feet often with a moisture-absorbent powder to avoid athlete's food. Use cornstarch, talcum powder, baby powder or a medicated foot powder.

ATTICS

Increase the storage capacity of your attic. Add shelves, use stacking boxes, and install wooden rods (or metal pipes) for hanging clothes. Store light but bulky articles in hammocks or sturdy bags strung to rafters.

Attic inventory. To keep track of what's in your attic, take an inventory and post the list near the entrance. If you add or remove anything, record it on your inventory list.

Treasure hunt. Take a look through your attic for antiques and collectibles, including old magazines, prints, toys, and baseball cards. Before you sell any item to a dealer, check current collectibles price lists at your local library.

AUCTIONS

Come early to examine items at the presale exhibition. If you see something you like, ask the attendant or auctioneer what it is likely to bring in—this is often a good estimate of the item's true worth.

Stay late. Some of the best bargains may be snagged after most of the bidders have given up and gone home.

Don't get into a bidding war and pay more than the item is worth. Decide in advance what your top bid will be and stick to it.

Moving and storage auctions often provide furniture bargains. Movers hold auctions periodically to clear unclaimed goods out of their warehouses. Check newspaper classified ads or contact local movers for dates.

Business bankruptcy auctions can yield unexpected good buys. A closeout auction by a restaurateur, for example, may include a car or a computer along with the kitchen supplies. Since most bidders come for the restaurant items, extras like the car and computer attract only low bids.

AUTOMATIC TELLER MACHINES (ATM'S)

Save time by choosing the least-busy hours to visit your ATM. Avoid lunch hours, paydays—generally Thursdays and Fridays—and Monday mornings.

 Safety first. Never use an ATM alone at night, when most ATM crimes take place. If you must get cash after dark, choose a well-lighted ATM in full public view on a well-trafficked street.

Don't deposit cash in an ATM if you can avoid it. If the envelope is lost, you can't replace the money.

4 After preparing the artichokes for cooking, rub all the cut surfaces with lemon juice to keep cut edges from turning brown.

5 Submerge artichokes in a large pot of water. Cover the pot, bring the water to a boil, and allow the artichokes to simmer for 35 to 40 minutes, or until a few leaves can be pulled easily from the base.

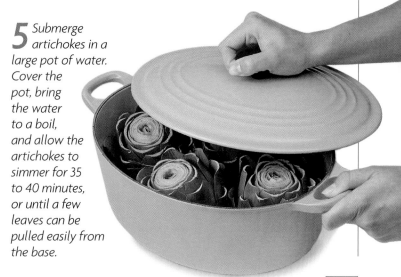

AVOCADOS

To soften a hard avocado (but not really ripen it), place it in a microwave at medium power for no more than 45 seconds, rotating the avocado every 15 seconds.

Easy pulp removal. To simplify avocado preparation, lay a wire rack over a bowl. Cut the ripe avocado in half, remove the pit, and press each half through the rack. Mashed pulp is released from the skin quickly and with little mess.

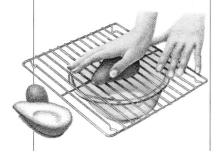

Keep it green. Spritz the pulp with fresh lemon juice as soon as you've removed it from the skin to prevent it from turning brown.

AWNINGS

Mildew removal. Although mildew is caused by dampness, hosing off your awning once a week is the best protection. Hosing gets rid of pollen, which breeds mildew by holding moisture. Hose early on a clear day so that the awning will dry quickly. Avoid using harsh detergents; they break down the awning's waterproof coating.

Power wash an awning no more than once a year. Strong water pressure can weaken the fabric by forcing open the weave.

To remove bird droppings, spray the spot with a penetrating oil such as WD-40, wait a couple of minutes, then gently rub the area with a soft brush. Rinse with plain water. If any stain remains, use a mild detergent and rinse.

B

BABY CARRIERS TO BUTTONS

BABY CARRIERS

Sling carriers are perfect for newborns and infants who can't hold up their heads yet. The sling cradles a baby like a hammock and perfectly positions the child for breast-feeding. It also leaves your hands free. Older babies like the security of the sling carrier but often prefer facing outward.

Use a back carrier when your baby reaches about seven months of age or can sit up on his own. Babies can be carried in backpacks until they are about three years old. The frame and belt work together to transfer the baby's increasing weight to your hips, reducing strain on your back.

BABY CLOTHES

Avoid fussy closures. Pass up clothing with too many buttons, snaps, or other fasteners. Get overalls and "stretchies" with snaps at the crotch that can be unbuttoned or unsnapped easily for fast changes.

Resist tiny sizes. Babies grow quickly, so buy 3- or 6-month size clothes for newborns and a size ahead for older babies. Most 6-month-old babies wear 9- or 12-month size clothes, 1-year-olds wear size 2, and so on.

Consider used clothing. Scout garage sales and consignment shops for used clothes. Since babies outgrow most outfits quickly, you can find many items with little wear and tear.

Garment safety check. Babies can swallow loose snaps and buttons; check carefully for dangling fasteners. To help keep them in place, close all snaps and buttons before doing your baby's laundry.

BABY SHOWERS

Boy or girl? If the parents-to-be know the gender of their unborn baby—and agree to have the

THE BOTTOM LINE ON DIAPERS

The bottom line is go ahead, use disposable diapers.

▶ *Disposables are used once, then thrown away, while cloth diapers must be laundered, folded, and stored.*

▶ *Disposable diapers are more absorbent than cloth.*

▶ *Over the two or three years that your baby will wear diapers, using disposables saves time and energy, which more than compensates for their higher cost.*

▶ *As far as the environment is concerned, studies show that cloth and disposable diapers rank about equal.*

A NEW KIND OF BABY BAG

Here's a chic and convenient solution to toting all of baby's paraphernalia. Instead of an old-fashioned diaper bag, consider equipping Mommy and Daddy with a fisherman's or photographer's vest with loads of pockets to hold all of baby's necessities. Stock it with diapers, bottles, a pacifier, and a couple of small toys or books, leaving hands free to take care of baby.

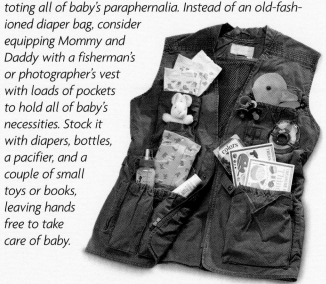

information made public—inform the guests on the shower invitation so that they can select appropriate presents.

Use baby accessories as party decorations. Fill baby bottles with flowers; create place cards by attaching name tags to pacifiers; wrap silverware in cloth bibs; provide baby rattles to shake during toasts. At the party's end, present the favors to the new parents.

Make room for Daddy. Plan a shower for an expectant or new daddy. Invite his male pals and ask them to provide advice as well as appropriate new daddy essentials, such as an alarm clock or matching daddy/baby shirts.

Host a grandparents shower. Have a shower for new grandparents, attended by the new parents, friends, and family members. Presents can include children's books, baby toys, a supply of baby necessities, and bits of advice from other grandparents—all things new grandparents can use.

Double duty. Use the wrapping paper from your shower presents and other baby gifts to line the new baby's dresser drawers.

BABY STROLLERS

No tipping. Don't hang packages over a stroller's handles; this can cause the stroller to tip over. Place your packages low on the back of the stroller or directly over the rear wheels.

For newborns, avoid lightweight "umbrella" strollers. These strollers provide little head and back support for infants. Instead, choose a convertible carriage-stroller, which operates like a small carriage but can be converted to a stroller, by reversing the handle, when the baby is able to sit up alone.

BABYSITTERS

Prepare the sitter. Have a new babysitter arrive early for a get-acquainted session with you and your children. Give a tour of the house and point out the location of the medicine cabinet and first-aid kit. Provide instructions regarding the kids: bedtime routines, and emergency procedures. For quick reference, put emergency numbers at the top of your written instructions.

 Interview potential sitters before hiring them. Ask about previous experience and whether they've had training in first aid or CPR. Ask for references— and check them. Introduce the sitter to your child and note the interaction.

Provide treats for your children when you go out. Let them eat popcorn or watch a favorite movie on the VCR. For younger children, make a tape of a favorite story to be played before nap or bedtime, and add a confident reassurance at the end.

Establish a babysitting co-op to exchange babysitting "duties" with other parents in an organized way. Devise a schedule that fixes certain times for parents to be available for sitting. Once the co-op is running smoothly, expand it to include other arrangements, such as chauffeuring and toy swaps.

BACK PAIN PREVENTION

To lift a heavy object, use your thigh muscles instead of your back and arms. Keeping your back straight, squat and then raise the object as you stand up. Never bend at the waist or lock your knees when doing heavy lifting.

Belt alert. The wide leather belts used by professional weightlifters don't protect your back from the strain of lifting heavy objects. Instead, they put pressure on your abdomen, which can raise your blood pressure.

Chair support. When you sit for extended periods, make sure that the chair supports the curve of your lower back. If it doesn't, place a small pillow behind your lower back. At least once an hour, get up, stretch, and walk around.

Exercise regularly. Strengthening the muscles of the back will help to prevent injuries. Try brisk walking, swimming, or yoga at least three times a week.

Slim down. Extra weight can aggravate an existing back problem or create a new one. If you are overweight, see your doctor about a weight-loss program.

If the shoe fits. Shoes act as shock absorbers. Wear ones with soft, cushioned soles, or ask your doctor about shoe inserts.

High heels aggravate back problems. Heels higher than 4.5 cm (1¾ in.) push your weight forward, forcing your spine into unnatural positions as you walk.

Save Your Back in Just 20 Minutes a Day

This simple routine—done every day—can keep your back strong and prevent problems than can complicate your life. If your back has been injured or you suffer from any other health problems, consult your doctor before beginning this. Before exercising, warm up by doing a cardiovascular activity (such as walking or jumping rope) for 10 to 15 minutes.

Knee-to-Shoulder Stretch. Lie on the floor with both knees bent and your feet flat on the floor. Slowly pull one knee to your chest, hold it for 10 seconds, and then release. Repeat the exercise 5 times with each leg.

Chair Stretch. Sit upright in a sturdy straight-backed chair. Slowly bend forward toward the floor, head first, until you begin to feel a slight pull in your back. Hold the stretch for 10 seconds. Repeat 5 times.

Cat Stretch: Step 1. On your hands and knees, press your back toward the floor; lift your head toward the ceiling for greater stretch. Hold.

Cat Stretch: Step 2. Slowly, in a single motion, arch your back, bringing your chin to your chest; hold for 2 to 3 seconds. Repeat 5 times.

Toting techniques. When carrying heavy items, use two tote bags rather than one to distribute the weight evenly between both sides of your body. Avoid lugging heavy briefcases or bags on one side.

BACK PAIN TREATMENT

Get help fast. If your back pain was caused by a fall or an acute injury or is accompanied by numbness in your arms or legs, contact your doctor immediately. This could be serious.

Treat back pain with ice immediately after an injury and for the next 48 hours to prevent swelling. Apply ice packs for 15 minutes as often as every hour. The third day, use moist heat—a heating pad or hot-water bottle—to relax muscles around the injury.

Get out of bed! For back injuries, short periods of bed rest are more effective than long ones. By staying in bed too long, muscles may start to weaken. Once back pain lessens a bit, start walking. Slowly ease into other activities.

The anti-inflammatory agents in aspirin, ibuprofen, and naproxen can reduce the swelling and pain associated with minor back pain.

Get a massage. A professional masseuse can provide temporary relief from muscle pain and ease tension by kneading painful areas.

Listen to your body. A muscle spasm—an intense, violent contraction—is nature's way of immobilizing you to prevent further damage. Relax; give your body a breather and a chance to heal.

Half Curl. Lie on the floor with a pillow supporting your head and upper back. Keeping your knees bent, feet flat on the floor, and arms straight, reach for your knees until your shoulders lift off the pillow. (For a harder exercise, cross your arms over your chest while you lift your shoulders.) Repeat 5 times.

Shoulder Squeeze. Sit upright in a sturdy straight-backed chair. Look straight ahead and pull your shoulder blades backward. Hold for 5 seconds, then relax. Repeat 5 times.

The Hydrant. On your hands and knees, pull one knee into your chest. In a sweeping motion, push your leg back so that your thigh is parallel to the floor and the sole of your foot is toward the ceiling. Return the knee to the chest. Repeat 5 times for each leg.

The Twist. Sit on the floor, legs straight in front of you. Bend your left leg and cross it over your right. Bring your right arm across your left thigh. Use both arms to twist your upper body until you feel a stretch. Hold for 10 seconds, release, and repeat with the other leg.

BACKPACKING

Work out to improve physical fitness before backpacking in the wilderness. Make sure you are able to walk 8 to 9.6 km (5–6 mi) a day—with a pack on your back. Gradually increase its load.

Borrow or rent equipment before buying. Experiment with different gear on a trial basis to determine your needs and preferences more accurately.

Include at least three people in your backpacking team. In the event of an accident, one person can stay with the injured party while the other goes for help. Also, notify a family member or friend of your hiking route and your expected time of return.

Check all equipment and supplies thoroughly before your trip. Most important: Inspect water bottles, tent linings, knife blades, stove, zippers, batteries, and matches.

Smart planning. Use a contour map, which reveals the topography of the landscape through illustrated concentric rings which are much like the rings of a tree trunk. The smaller the ring, the higher the elevation.

Set a leisurely pace at the start of each day on the trail. This

EASY DOES IT

BACKPACKING BASICS

For strenuous hikes—whether overnight or just for the day, take food, make sure you have a supply of clean water, and carry the following items in your backpack:

- *First-aid kit, including pain relievers, bandages, and elastic wraps for sprains*
- *Clothing that keeps you warm and dry*
- *Flashlight, including extra batteries and bulbs*
- *Waterproof matches and a fire starter, such as paraffin blocks*
- *Map, detailed and up-to-date*
- *Sunglasses and sunscreen with an SPF of at least 15*
- *Pocketknife equipped with multiple tools*
- *Compass*
- *Plastic zipper bags to tote food, garbage, paper goods, and medicine; to keep cameras, batteries, and maps dry*

warms up the body, stretching muscles and increasing blood flow. Set distance goals each day.

Take periodic rests and replenish your body with water and snacks. Stop at a scenic spot— a lake, a waterfall, or a ridge with far-reaching vistas.

BACKPACKS

Spread the weight. Buy a backpack with wide shoulder straps, which ease the burden by more evenly distributing the weight.

To organize your backpack, put the frequently used items in the most accessible pockets. Stow seldom-used gear farthest inside.

Repack items in the same place every time. This helps you keep track of your backpack's contents and avoid prolonged searches.

Travel trick. Tuck your backpack inside a durable carryall before checking it at the airport. This protects the backpack's loose ends—straps, buckles, and flaps—

from being damaged by carousels and luggage handlers.

Use both shoulders. Even the small all-purpose backpacks that children carry to school are liable to cause pain in the lower back if slung across only one shoulder.

BAD BREATH

It's not just a garnish. Munch a sprig or two of fresh parsley after a meal to sweeten your breath.

Switch toothpaste. Research suggests that toothpastes containing hydrogen peroxide may be more effective at controlling the germs that cause bad breath than ordinary fluoride toothpaste.

Chronic bad breath may be a symptom of periodontal disease or an underlying medical problem such as sinusitis. If dental hygiene fails to eliminate the problem, talk to your dentist or doctor.

Carry protection. Always keep breath mints in your purse or pocket. Should you find yourself in a close conversation with someone who has bad breath, eat a mint yourself and then offer one to your friend. More often than not, the person will get the hint.

BAKING

Hot air. Don't crowd pans near oven walls. Proper air circulation is vital to good baking. When using two oven racks, space them 15 cm (6 in.) apart and stagger the pans so none is directly above another.

No-stick solution. Lay a piece of aluminum foil in the center of a cake pan before you fill it with batter to keep the finished cake from sticking in the middle.

Even distribution. You can keep raisins, dates, and other dried fruit from sinking to the bottom of muffins and cakes by rolling them in the cake flour before folding them into the batter.

Cake sticking to the pan? Simply rest the pan on a damp cloth for a few minutes as soon as the cake comes out of the oven.

Improvised cooling racks. A rack from the oven, set on supports to allow air to circulate under it, can handle cake layers, a dozen muffins, and large cookies. For baked goods that cool in the pan, such as a pie, use a metal stovetop grate set on the counter.

 Glass vs. metal. Baked goods cook faster in glass than in metal, so if you are using a glass pie or cake pan, reduce the oven temperature given in a recipe by 14°C (25°F).

Freezer taboo. Don't freeze pastries that hold cream fillings. Moisture from the filling seeps out and makes the pastry soggy.

BAKING SODA

Carpet deodorizer. Keep your carpet smelling fresh and clean with baking soda. Just sprinkle the soda liberally over the entire carpet and let it sit for an hour. Then vacuum it up.

Soothe a sunburn or relieve itching by adding a cup of baking soda to your bathwater. For best results, make sure the water is warm, not hot.

Clean up spills. Pour baking soda directly over messy liquid spills. Let the spill sit undisturbed until the baking soda has absorbed the liquid, then vacuum.

Fire extinguisher. Keep a box of baking soda near the stove to quash grease fires. Putting water on a grease fire will make it worse; reach for the baking soda instead.

Stop black spot, a common fungus, from attacking your roses. Spray the bushes with a mixture of 20 mL (4 tsp) baking soda per 3.8 L (1 gal) of water.

Combat silverfish with a 50-50 combination of baking soda and sugar. Sprinkle the mixture near baseboards, radiators, and wherever it is needed.

BAKING PAN SUBSTITUTION CHART

You may not always have the baking pan that a recipe calls for, so check the chart below for some pan substitutions. Pan capacity (volume) can be calculated by pouring water to the inside rim using a liquid measure. Remember that baking times will be reduced when batter/dough is divided into smaller or shallower pans.

PAN SIZE	PAN CAPACITY	SUBSTITUTE PAN	SUBSTITUTE CAPACITY
8½" x 4½" (20 x 11 cm) loaf pan	6 cups (1.5 L)	Two 2¾" x 1⅜" (7 x 3.5 cm) muffin tins	6 cups (12 half-cup muffins or 1.5 L)
9" x 5" x 3" (22 x 12 x 7 cm) loaf pan	8 cups (2 L)	Two 8" x 4" x 2½" (20 x 10 x 6 cm) loaf pans	8 cups (2 L)
9" x 2" (22 x 5 cm) round cake pan	8 cups (2 L)	One 8" x 2" (20 x 5 cm) square pan	8 cups (2 L)
10" x 3¼" (25 x 9.5 cm) Bundt pan	12 cups (3 L)	One 10" x 4" (25 x 10 cm) tube pan	12 cups (3 L)
13" x 9" x 2" (33 x 22 x 5 cm) pan	14 cups (3.5 L)	Two 9" x 2" (22 x 5 cm) round cake pans	16 cups (4 L)
15" x 10" x 1" (38 x 25 x 2.5 cm) jelly roll pan	10 cups (2.5 L)	Two 8" x 1½" (20 x 4 cm) round pans	10 cups (2.5 L)

THE FOOD PYRAMID

The food pyramid is a visual guide to what U.S. Department of Agriculture researchers see as a healthful diet. Built on a broad base of carbohydrates, the plan includes eating plenty of grains, fruits, and vegetables. Proteins are important but in more modest amounts than most Americans are used to. Fats, sugar, alcohol, and salt should be limited.

Fats, sugar, alcohol, and salt. Eat these sparingly. Fats should make up less than 30 percent of your daily calories. Sugar and alcohol represent "empty," nonnutritive calories. You normally get enough salt (500 milligrams or more) naturally from other foods in your diet.

Protein. Eat 2–3 servings of meat, poultry, fish, eggs, dried beans and peas, and nuts per day as well as 2–3 servings of dairy products including milk, yogurt, or cheese. (A serving equals 90–120 mL [3–4 oz].) Choose lean meats and low-fat dairy products.

Vegetables and fruits. Eat 3–5 servings of vegetables daily (about 250 mL [1 cup] of leafy greens or 125 mL [½ cup] of cooked vegetables) and 2–4 servings of fresh fruit or fruit juice.

Grains. Eat 6–11 servings of grains (preferably whole grains) a day, such as cereals, breads, pasta, or rice.

BALANCED DIET

Eating a variety of foods is healthier than sticking to a limited menu. Essential vitamins and minerals come from different sources, so vary your choices, especially when selecting among proteins, fruits, and vegetables.

Teach kids about healthful eating early. Consult your pediatrician on the best time to start your children on low-fat milk and other low-fat dairy products. Have snacks like raisins, carrot sticks, apples, popcorn, and pretzels around the house instead of cookies and ice cream or chips and dips.

Limiting fat. Government guidelines suggest that you keep fat to under 30 percent of your total calories. The American Cancer Society believes that it should be even lower, at 20 percent. The trick? Combine small amounts of healthful but high-fat foods—certain oils, cheeses, and nuts—with large portions of low-fat ones, like raw vegetables and grains, to reach a proper balance.

Reward yourself—occasionally. If you regularly avoid including fat in your diet, let yourself go every now and then, and treat yourself to a hamburger or a bite of Brie.

Be skeptical of nutrition news. If you read about a nutrition study suggesting yet another perfect food, think twice before running out to stock up. Ask critical questions. How many people were in the study? Was it sponsored by a product manufacturer? Wait for substantial corroborating studies before making lifestyle changes.

Fresh, frozen, or canned? Although fresh fruits and vegetables have long been considered tops nutritionally, frozen and canned products are not to be overlooked. In some cases, food flash-frozen or canned straight from the fields is more nutritious than fresh. Long-stored or overcooked fresh veggies can rapidly lose vitamins and minerals.

Fortify yourself. More and more, processed foods are being beefed up with vitamins and minerals. Look for calcium-fortified juice as well as grain products packed with extra folic acid.

BALANCING CAREER, HOME & LEISURE

 Schedule family time just as you would a doctor's appointment or business lunch. Be present at important occasions by reserving dates far in advance for birthdays, special school activities, Little League games, and holidays.

Reduce your housework. Hire a cleaning person to help out once a month; instead of cooking, have dinner delivered; aim for a "tidy" house instead of a "spotless" one.

Have some fun. Make a list of 10 things that bring you enjoyment, such as gardening, knitting, or dancing. Do one item every day, even if only for a few minutes.

Share your career with your family. Talk about your professional projects, ask their opinion about work issues, include them in company events at which they can meet your coworkers; take your spouse or a child along on a business trip.

Counter on-the-job stress by using your lunch hour to take a walk, read a book, or meet with an old friend. Use daily breaks to relax and refresh your spirit. You'll be more effective.

Make the ordinary extraordinary. Turn daily routines into creative adventures, such as having a picnic during your lunch break or taking an evening stroll as a family instead of staring at the TV.

BANANAS

Bananas in the refrigerator? Yes, you can store bananas in the refrigerator—either in a sealed plastic container or wrapped in newspaper. The peel will turn brown, but the flesh inside will be unaffected. The cold slows down the ripening process, so that the fruit keeps longer.

Mash overripe bananas, add a teaspoon of lemon juice per banana, and freeze the puree in an airtight container. Frozen banana puree will last six months and tastes delicious in milkshakes, cakes, and quick breads.

To ripen bananas quickly, put them in a brown paper bag with an apple or two. Close the bag for even faster ripening.

BANKRUPTCY

Pay off one credit card. If you plan to file for bankruptcy, try to pay the balance on one major card. A credit card that is paid off before you file bankruptcy papers will be exempt from the procedures and can then be used to help you reestablish credit.

 Head off bankruptcy. Learn to recognize the signs that you are carrying too much debt—making only the minimum payments on your charge accounts each month, charging essentials like food and gas, or nearing the credit limit on your credit cards. If these situations apply to you, develop a budget and a debt repayment plan.

Consult a lawyer. Before filing for bankruptcy, get good legal advice. Laws governing what property is exempt in a bankruptcy filing vary from province to province. Also, a lawyer can help you understand the different types of individual bankruptcy and determine the one most advantageous for your situation.

To rebuild a credit rating after filing for bankruptcy, take out a savings passbook loan at a bank. (You are borrowing against your savings.) The bank will report the loan to a credit bureau, and the punctual payments you make will be reported in your file.

BASEMENTS

Why is the basement damp? To find out, secure 30 cm (12 in.) squares of aluminum foil to the floor and walls with a waterproof tape. After several days, check the squares. If water beads on top of the foil, the problem is condensation from excessive moisture in the air. If moisture has collected between the foil and the walls or floor, groundwater is seeping through the concrete.

Wet basement? Check the gutters. Clogged gutters and downspouts are the most frequent cause of basement water. Rain or snow pouring off the roof over clogged gutters can puddle around the foundation and seep in through cracks in the concrete.

Poor drainage is the second most likely cause of a wet basement. The ground around the house should slope away from the foundation at least 8.3 cm per meter (1 in. per foot). Use splash blocks to help direct downspout drains away from the foundation.

New house reminder. Don't be alarmed by dampness in the basement of a brand-new house. It can take two years for a new basement to dry out completely.

BASKETS

Gift baskets. Fill a pretty basket with homemade jellies, jams, bread, and vinegar to make a charming—and useful—present for a hostess or a friend who has helped you out. A colorful ribbon is all the wrapping you will need.

To clean a basket, use mild soap and warm water. Clean the nooks and crannies with a soft paintbrush or old toothbrush; rinse well; and hang it to dry in a well-ventilated place. To clean a colored basket, test the bottom first; if water causes the dyes to run, settle for a good dusting.

Store baskets out in the open where they can add texture and warmth to a room. Hang them from a high kitchen ceiling with hooks or set them on top of a cabinet or bookshelf.

BATHING

Not too hot, not too cold. Set your shower to the desired temperature and put a dot of nail polish on the knob and the wall behind it. For the perfect shower, simply line up the dots.

Bath or shower? It's a good idea to take a quick shower after a bath. Although a warm bath is a delightful way to unwind, it does not cleanse as well as a shower because soap residue does not completely rinse away.

A rosy experience. For a soothing bath, toss fresh rose petals into the water. The oils from the fragrant petals will leave your skin velvety smooth.

Winter warm-up. Add 30 mL (2 tbsp) of ground ginger to the bathwater to give your bath zing. The ginger will intensify your feeling of warmth—so add a little at a time until you're comfortable.

Summer refresher. Cool off by adding 125 mL (1 cup) of lemon juice to your bath. The lemon juice gives the water a clean, fresh scent in addition to toning and tightening your skin.

To soothe dry skin, add bath oil to the bathwater. If you don't have any bath oil, improvise by using 30 mL (2 tbsp) of vegetable or olive oil instead.

Timing is everything. Add bath oil to the bath only after you've soaked for 5 to 10 minutes in the warm bathwater. This "presoak" period allows your skin's pores to open and absorb the water. Then when you add the oil, it will create a barrier and lock the moisture into your skin.

Make bathing easier for sick or frail individuals by providing a bath seat that is specially designed for invalids. Available from medical supply stores, it allows them to sit comfortably in the tub while bathing or showering. A plastic lawn chair placed in the shower works almost as well.

BATHING SUITS

Longevity. Your bathing suit will last longer if you rinse it in cold water after swimming to remove any salt or chlorine residues.

Hand-wash your bathing suit or wash it in the gentle cycle of your machine using a mild soap. Avoid twisting or wringing the suit, which could break delicate fibers or destroy elasticity.

WHERE TO USE BASKETS

Tucked around the house, baskets of every shape, size, and color make charming organizers that enhance any decor, from farmhouse to formal. Below are just a few ideas for using baskets:

- *To separate mittens from scarves in the hall closet*
- *At a party to hold crudités or crackers*
- *On a hall table to sort his mail from hers*
- *In the bathroom to hold lipsticks and blushes*
- *On a desk to sort correspondence and hold supplies*
- *At the buffet table to hold silverware and napkins*
- *At the end of a bed as a linen chest*
- *Beside the bed to hold magazines and books for reading*
- *In the living room as a toy chest for nightly pickups*
- *Under the coffee table to sort magazines, books, and newspapers*
- *Next to your favorite chair as a mending basket*

SHAVER'S HAVEN

A fog-free mirror with a light allows a man to shave in the shower while his beard is still soft from the warm water. A bonus waterproof, battery-powered radio makes sure he doesn't miss the news—or his favorite music—during his ablutions. Attached with an adhesive strip, the mirror is also a cinch to install.

Audition. Sit, stand, jump, and mimic swimming motions when trying on a swimming suit to make sure the suit stays in place.

Suiting up. If you like two-piece suits but your bust and hip measurements differ greatly, look in catalogs. Many popular mail-order companies sell tops and bottoms separately—letting you choose the best-fitting sizes for each.

BATHROOM SAFETY

Grab bars. Minimize the risk of falling by installing sturdy horizontal grab bars or rails in the bath or shower area, near the toilet, and in dressing or sitting areas.

Shower doors made of ordinary glass can produce dangerous shards if they are accidentally broken. Replace them with shatterproof glass or plastic doors.

Prevent scalding. Plumbing suppliers sell a variety of valves and other devices that detect and shut off excessively hot water in faucets and showerheads. These devices help prevent scalding injuries, particularly for children, elderly people, or anyone with a disease such as diabetes that can reduce the ability to sense temperature changes.

Shock safety. The possibility of an appliance or frayed electrical cord accidentally contacting water in the bathroom and exposing people to potentially deadly electricity surges makes a ground fault interrupter (GFI) a must. GFI's are electrical outlets that cut off the power supply when a surge occurs. To identify a GFI outlet, look for a red reset button on the front. If there's no button, call an electrician; the cost for installing a GFI is usually less than $150.

BATHROOMS

A picnic basket, colorfully painted, is a decorative solution to keeping a hair dryer, a curling iron, and other awkwardly shaped appliances out of sight in the bathroom until they are needed.

 Firm footing. Use nonskid rugs and bath mats in the bathroom, especially if the floor is tiled or polished. Put antislip stickers on the shower or tub floor. If you install a new tub, choose one with a flat rather than a curved bottom.

An exhaust fan with exterior ventilation can remove the excess humidity from a bathroom that causes mildew. Fans are rated by their capacity to exchange air, represented by a CFM (cubic feet per minute) rating. To determine your CFM rating, multiply the square feet of your bathroom (its length times its breadth) times 1.07. If your ceiling is high, select a fan with a larger CFM rating than is indicated.

Upgrade the lighting to give your bathroom a major face-lift. Downlights recessed in the ceiling shed pools of diffused light, appropriate for illuminating a counter or washbasin. Rows of clear round bulbs placed on either side of the mirror provide good lighting for applying makeup.

Color-code your towels so that each family member can easily keep track of his or her own. The results are colorful, and, since each family member can quickly identify his towel, the likelihood of passing infections is reduced.

Stretch your budget for bathroom decorating by using colorful ceramic tiles. Because they are often pricier than regular bathroom tiles, you may want to buy just a few and arrange them as a focal point in a limited space, such as the wall behind your sink.

BATTERIES

Weaker batteries drain power from stronger ones if they are used simultaneously. Replace all batteries at the same time when you are changing a battery in a multiple-battery appliance.

Store batteries in the refrigerator in an airtight plastic bag to keep out moisture. Most batteries will hold their charge slightly longer when kept chilled. On the other hand, if you plan to use the batteries in the near future, storing them in a dry place at room temperature will do just fine.

Invest in rechargeable batteries. Despite the initial cost for the recharger and the slightly more expensive batteries, you'll save in the long run. Keep a steady supply by recharging one set of batteries while the others are in use.

Use alkaline batteries, not rechargeables or heavy duties, when duration of the power supply is the key factor. Alkalines last more than twice as long as the other batteries.

Keep batteries protected. If you carry them in a pocket or purse, their terminals come into contact with metal objects—coins or keys—and lose their charge.

COOKING DRIED BEANS AND PEAS

Packaged dried beans and peas are economical and easy to cook. They've already been picked over and cleaned, so all you have to do is soak and simmer them.

▶ *To soak dried beans the quick way, cover them with cold water, bring to a boil, boil for two minutes, remove from the heat, and let them stand for one hour. Drain and rinse. To cook, cover the beans again with water, bring to a boil, reduce the heat, and simmer until tender.*

▶ *If you prefer your beans on the creamy side, cook them with the lid on; if you prefer a firmer bean, cook them with the lid off.*

▶ *Dried beans are overcooked if their skins burst when you blow on them. Since dried beans differ from batch to batch, test for doneness the old-fashioned way: by tasting.*

BEACHES

If you're caught in a riptide, don't fight it. These fast-moving undercurrents will pull you out quickly. Go with it (it won't be far) or try swimming parallel to the beach. When you're free of the rip, swim back to shore.

Swim and condition. Apply 90 mL (3 oz) of hair conditioner after each swim. The conditioner will prevent the sun and salt from drying out your hair, and will work as a sort of natural hot oil treatment. Inexpensive brands work just as well as expensive ones.

Beach shoes, made to wear in the water, help protect feet on hot sand, in rocky wading areas, or where pinching crabs or jellyfish are prevalent. Children in particular need to wear something on their feet.

 Swim only in areas with lifeguard supervision. Don't swim at unmanned beaches with strong currents or rock-strewn waters.

Watch out for pollution. Wait a day after a heavy rainstorm before swimming at an urban-area beach. The runoff from streets and other sources is likely to cause a dangerous level of contamination.

BEANS

Double duty. Dried beans can be stored and used as decoration at the same time. Place various kinds of colored beans, such as navy beans, yellow or green peas, or French beans, in clear jars and then arrange the jars attractively on your kitchen shelves.

Delay salting beans during the cooking process until they have reached the desired texture. Salt in the water slows cooking and toughens the beans.

Add lemon juice or tomato juice to a bean recipe after the beans have cooked. Acidic ingredients tend to toughen beans if they are added during cooking.

Warm bean salad. For maximum flavor, add dressing to bean salad while the beans are still warm. Prepare the dressing while the beans are cooking, quickly combine the cooked beans with the dressing, then let the salad cool to the temperature you desire.

BEATING THE BLUES

Go for a walk. Physical activity, especially aerobic exercise like jogging, swimming, or brisk walking, is a great way to perk up a blue mood. Exercise releases endorphins, a group of proteins produced by the brain that are thought to elevate mood.

Keep busy. If you've just experienced a bad stint at work or had a fight with a close friend, fill up your schedule. Immerse yourself in a favorite activity, find a new hobby, plan a vacation, or take an evening course.

Socialize. Isolating yourself from others when you feel blue can make things seem worse. Make a date to go out with friends, do some volunteer work, write a letter, or telephone a relative or an old friend.

Listen to music. Music can have a profound effect on the emotions. If you're feeling down, put on some of your favorite upbeat music. Sing along at the top of your lungs or dance around the living room. At the same time, avoid sad songs or music that reminds you of a loss.

Express your creativity. Try painting, sculpting, knitting, embroidery, cooking, or any other art or craft—even if you've never

done it before. Focusing on something new will help you forget your worries.

BEDROOMS

An attractive trunk at the end of a bed does double furniture duty. As a bench, it gives you a place to sit while you put on your shoes; as a storage chest, it holds extra blankets or pillows.

Snappy bed making. If you buy matching bedskirt, fitted bottom sheet, top sheet, duvet cover, pillowcases, and pillow shams, making the bed is a simple matter of smoothing the sheet, spreading out the comforter, and plumping the pillows.

Freshen up. To quickly refresh bedspreads or curtains between expensive seasonal dry cleanings, place in the dryer with a sheet of fabric softener and tumble on the air-only setting for approximately 20 minutes.

BEDS

Invest in a trundle bed for your kids. A trundle bed allows children to share a bedroom or have sleepovers without permanently giving up floor space. Also, it is safer than a bunk bed.

Create a makeshift bassinet for your newborn with a large, lined wicker basket. For the mattress, use a folded baby quilt. In an emergency a dresser drawer also works as a fine crib.

Instead of a headboard, hang a dramatic quilt or an attractive Oriental rug at the head of your bed. Hang the quilt or rug from a decorative curtain rod.

Protect your walls from being gouged or scraped by sharp bed frames by padding the corners of the frame with carpet scraps.

B

UNDERBED STORAGE DRAWER

A shallow drawer with a top, this under-the-bed storage unit keeps out-of-season clothes, extra linens, or personal records dust-free and out of the way. A handle and four wheels make retrieval quick; just grab the handle and the whole unit rolls right out. And with a pair of these under your bed, there is little room for dust balls.

BEDTIME

Bedtime hours. Each child has a different sleep need. If your child functions well on eight hours of sleep a night, it's useless to insist on nine. If your child awakens earlier than you do in the morning, provide a quiet activity such as coloring, as well as a snack to keep her occupied. Set an alarm clock for the hour when she can wake you up.

Bed check. Soft bedding can cause infants who sleep on their stomachs to suffocate. To test if a mattress is firm enough, place a 5 kg (10 lb) weight (a large bag of flour or sugar will do) where the baby would sleep. If the weight makes a deep depression, the mattress is potentially unsafe.

Maintain a routine. Keep bedtime at the same hour every night to help establish regular sleep habits. Avoid physical play near bedtime; your child will be too stimulated to go to sleep easily.

Gradually reduce napping to encourage your baby to sleep for longer periods during the night. If, for example, the baby usually takes a 3-hour nap, wake her up after 2½ hours, then 2 hours, and then 1 hour. To make up for lost nap time, the child will sleep longer at night.

Limit television viewing. Children can become overexcited by many of the programs on TV. Encourage your child to turn off the TV and read quietly in bed for a while to calm down before it's time for lights out.

 Security blankets. Don't discourage your baby from thumb sucking or holding a favorite blanket or stuffed toy; these habits can help him fall asleep more easily. He will grow out of them after a while.

BED-WETTING

Check with your doctor if nighttime wetting persists beyond preschool to make sure there's no underlying emotional or physical cause, such as an allergic reaction to cow's milk. Treatment for enuresis, the medical term for bed-wetting, involves a combination of bladder-stretching exercises, a reward system, and nighttime alarms that go off when a child wets the bed.

Keep bedding dry. Make up a bed with two sets of bedding (including two rubber sheets) so that only the top set needs to be stripped off during the night.

Self-help. Place a potty chair near your child's bed and keep a sleeping bag and dry pajamas close by so that your child can get back to sleep in a dry place.

Use your imagination. Help your child visualize staying dry all night. Talk about the pleasures of feeling dry, in control, and grown-up.

Restrict fluid intake. Try not to give your child sweet juices or soda during the evening hours before bedtime. But if a child is thirsty, by all means give her water—not doing so may fix the child's mind on water and increase the chance of nighttime wetting.

BEEF

Don't buy packaged beef that is swimming in excess liquid. It has been stored too long or has been frozen and thawed.

Keep bacteria at bay. Always thaw frozen beef in the refrigerator or in the microwave, never at room temperature.

Freezer storage. Wrapped in airtight plastic or freezer wrap, ground beef can be kept frozen for three months. Solid cuts of meat will freeze well for approximately six months.

Dry or moist heat? Cook tender cuts of beef using dry-heat methods, which include broiling, frying, and roasting. Tenderize tougher cuts by cooking with

READING AT BEDTIME

Reading to a child at bedtime not only is a pleasure for grown-ups and kids but offers many long-term benefits:

▶ *Listening to books read aloud permits children to enjoy stories that would be too difficult for them to read on their own.*

▶ *Studies show that children who have been read to regularly from early childhood learn to read easily and remain good readers throughout their school years.*

▶ *Being read to promotes a child's desire to read books independently as well as fosters improvement of a child's reading skills.*

When you shop for beef, price and availability often guide your purchase. The chart below helps demystify beef cuts and uses and advises on the types of preparations for each cut of beef. Keep in mind that loin and rib cuts are more tender cuts of meat, while chuck, round, and flank are tougher cuts.

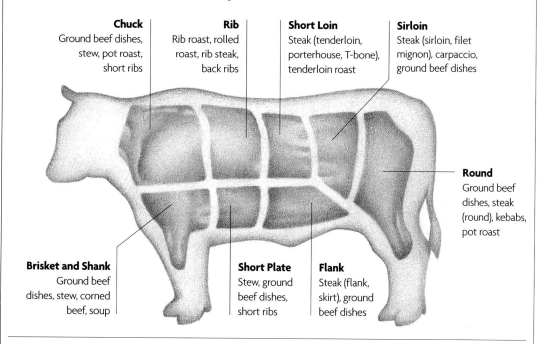

Chuck
Ground beef dishes, stew, pot roast, short ribs

Rib
Rib roast, rolled roast, rib steak, back ribs

Short Loin
Steak (tenderloin, porterhouse, T-bone), tenderloin roast

Sirloin
Steak (sirloin, filet mignon), carpaccio, ground beef dishes

Round
Ground beef dishes, steak (round), kebabs, pot roast

Brisket and Shank
Ground beef dishes, stew, corned beef, soup

Short Plate
Stew, ground beef dishes, short ribs

Flank
Steak (flank, skirt), ground beef dishes

moist-heat methods, which include braising and stewing.

Is it done? Just because beef has browned doesn't necessarily mean that it has been cooked to a safe internal temperature. The best test of doneness is to look at the beef juices, which should have turned from red to almost yellow.

Remove a roast from the oven a few minutes before the desired temperature is reached. The meat continues to cook after it is removed from the oven, and the internal meat temperature generally increases about 3°C (5°F).

BEEPERS

Give beepers to your on-the-go, never-on-time kids so that you can always let them know when to call in or come home.

Carry a beeper when you absolutely must be available. For example, a husband with a pregnant wife may want to be on a pager so that he won't miss the big moment.

Be selective when giving out the number of your pager. Otherwise, you run the risk of being constantly on call, never having a private minute, or blocking urgent calls from important people.

Be wary of special deals when subscribing to a beeper service provider. Some companies offer free beepers and additional service at no cost if you make a long-term commitment. Hidden costs may become evident only after you have signed up.

BEER

Store beer upright. The flavor diminishes when it is on its side and the beer is exposed to air in the bottle.

A cook's aid. Don't forget beer when making marinades, soups, and breads. Substitute beer equally for the water, wine, or stock called for in a recipe. But remember, you cannot substitute beer for milk.

 Foam control. For minimal foam, hold a bottle or can of ice-cold beer close to the glass and pour it slowly down the side. For maximum foam, hold a bottle or can of warm beer high above the glass and pour it into the center.

Serve nonalcoholic beer at parties to accommodate guests who are driving and others who don't wish to partake of an alcoholic beverage.

BELTS

Resize a belt that is too small by simply adding another hole. With a pen, make a dot where you want to position the hole. Place a sharp awl on the dot and give it a few taps with a hammer.

Keep metal buckles bright and shiny with a coat of clear nail polish. Doing this will also help prevent scratches.

Easy storage. To hang belts, install a row of strong cup hooks or simple clothing hooks inside your closet or on the closet door.

Wrap a gold chain belt around a plain black leather or suede belt for a dressy look, or slip a ribbon or scarf around the gold chain to add color.

Accentuate a small waist with a wide belt or two thin ones worn together. A short-waisted woman can make her torso seem longer by wearing a belt in the same color as her top.

BERRIES

Turn around. When you store berries in the refrigerator, turn the basket on its side to relieve pressure on the berries lying at the bottom. Or remove the berries and store them in a covered bowl.

Chill berries before washing them if possible, since cold berries are less likely to bruise or bleed during washing than those at room temperature.

EASY BERRY DESSERTS

Summer signals the arrival of fresh strawberries, raspberries, blueberries, and blackberries. Here are a few quick and delicious ideas for serving them:

▶ *Just plain! Nothing is better than fully ripe, freshly picked berries. They require neither sugar nor cream (although some diehards insist on one or the other).*

▶ *For drama and great flavor, fill a crystal bowl with heaps of berries, add a splash of champagne, sauterne, orange liqueur, or orange juice and toss with 15 or 30 mL (1 or 2 tbsp) of sugar to taste. Serve by itself or over vanilla ice cream, a chocolate brownie, or shortcake.*

▶ *Wash and dry several large, plump strawberries. Dip the bottoms of the berries, stems still attached, into a dish of melted semisweet chocolate. Refrigerate the chocolate-coated berries on a wax-paper-lined cookie sheet for 15 minutes to set the coating, and then serve.*

▶ *Make a fresh raspberry sauce in the blender or food processor, adding just enough sugar to thicken it, and serve over other fresh berries. For variation, drop in 15 mL (1 tbsp) of crème de cassis.*

▶ *Extra berries lying around? Toss them into cake or cupcake batter or stir into a container of plain yogurt. Top off a chocolate pudding with a sprinkling of fresh berries.*

Freeze and store berries for up to nine months. To freeze, wash fresh berries, pat dry, and lay flat on paper towels on a cookie sheet. Put the cookie sheet in the freezer until the berries are hard (about an hour). Transfer frozen berries to an airtight container.

 Sweet time. Don't sugar berries until just before eating, as sugar can discolor or soften the fruit.

BICYCLES

The best bike. A 10- or 12-speed all-terrain bicycle, sometimes called a hybrid, is ideal for general riding on all kinds of surfaces.

Sizing it up. Try this simple test to see whether a bicycle with a crossbar is the right size for you. Straddle the bike with your feet flat on the ground. You should have 5 to 7.5 cm (2–3 in.) clearance between your groin and the crossbar of the bicycle.

Seat adjustment. The seat should be high enough so that your leg is just shy of being fully extended when your foot is at the lowest point of the pedaling cycle. If your seat is uncomfortable, try a wider model or cushioned gel seats.

Hand saver. Store a pair of lightweight surgical gloves in your repair kit to keep your hands clean when you need to make some messy bike repair.

BICYCLING

Good riding form. Bend forward at the hips, not the waist, and keep your back straight. Relax your neck and shoulder muscles. Bend your elbows slightly to absorb jolts with minimum shock.

Wear cycling shoes, which have hard soles that make pedaling more efficient. (The soft cushions on regular sneakers absorb pressure, making pedaling more difficult.) Aim for a steady rhythm.

Better braking. Use both brakes at once, applying a bit more force on the front one. Use pulses rather than prolonged pressure on steep hills to prevent the brake pads from overheating. If you must brake hard, stay low and sit as far back as you can to keep the rear wheel on the road.

Prepare your body. Drink at least 450 mL (1 pt) of water and eat a nutritious high-carbohydrate snack a half hour or so before beginning a long-distance ride. This helps prevent dehydration and increases your energy.

The Two-Minute Bicycle Check

To prevent potential accidents, perform this quick check before each ride.

1 Straddling your front wheel, grab the handlebar and attempt to rotate it. Nothing should move.

2 Spin the front wheel; it should turn freely. Press both your tires to check for sufficient pressure.

3 Squeeze the front brake. It should grip the metal rim of the wheel snugly. Now try to roll the bike forward; the rear wheel should come off the ground. Do the same with the rear brake, rolling the bike backward to force the front wheel off the ground.

4 Attempt to wiggle the crank; it should not move. Spin the pedals; they should spin freely. Jiggle your seat; it should not rotate.

5 Finally, lift your bike 10 cm (4 in.) off the ground and drop it. Nothing should fall off.

BIRD FEEDERS

Position your feeder near a natural perch, such as a shrub, tree, or fence. This gives birds a place to wait while others are eating. Make sure the feeder is positioned high enough to discourage predators.

Taste test. Place several kinds of feeds, such as millet, corn, thistle, peanuts, or bread crumbs, in separate shallow containers on an outdoor table in your yard. Observe the preferences of each bird. Then fill your feeder to attract the species you most want to watch.

Red alert. Adding a touch of red to your nectar feeder attracts hummingbirds. Use ribbons, colored tape, dabs of paint, or a flower, but don't put red food coloring in the sugar water. The dyes can be unhealthy to the birds.

Pinecone feeders. Tie string to the stemless end of a pinecone, spread on some peanut butter, and then sprinkle it with birdseed or bread crumbs. Suspend the pinecone from a tree limb.

BIRDHOUSES

Home security. Tack wire mesh around the birdhouse entrance hole to keep predators from gnawing their way inside.

Custom habitats. Birds can be very particular about choosing a home. Finches, for example, prefer birdhouses with round entrance holes that are approximately 5 cm (2 in.) in diameter, while robins like rectangular homes that have one side open.

A warmer nest. If you live in a cold climate, buy or build a wooden birdhouse, not a plastic or metal one. Wood provides better insulation, keeping the birds toasty on chilly nights.

A safe house. Don't build a birdhouse with chemically treated wood. And in early spring, scoop out the used nest and scrub inside the birdhouse with soap and water. Because old nests breed disease and bacteria, you may be saving the lives of future tenants.

The right height. Place birdhouses supported by poles at least 1.8 m (6 ft) off the ground, to keep four-footed predators at bay.

BIRD-WATCHING

Getting started. Participate in an outing organized by a local bird-watching group. Or ask an enthusiastic bird-watching pal to let you tag along on the next trek.

To get the best views of your favorite birds, you'll need binoculars. Which ones to choose? The best models are under continual evaluation at Cornell University. Write to The Living Bird Quarterly (Laboratory of Ornithology, Cornell University, 159 Sapsucker Woods Rd., Ithaca, NY 14850). Include a self-addressed, stamped envelope, and the magazine will send you assessments of the latest models.

Pause frequently and listen for calls and for movements. Determine where the noise originates and then use binoculars to pinpoint the bird.

RIGHT STUFF

KEEPING SQUIRRELS OUT OF THE BIRD FEEDER

Foil those relentless rascals that raid the food you leave out for birds. One type of product you can use features a hot pepper chemical called capsicum that you dilute with vegetable oil, then mix in with the birdseed. Another way to keep squirrels away: these cleverly designed feeders, which seal off the feeding slot when animals weighing more than birds step on the perch.

BACKYARD BIRDS

Birdhouses and feeders aren't the only attractions that draw birds to your yard. Create a bird-friendly environment with the following landscaping suggestions:

▶ *A border of trees, shrubs, and hedges that bear fruit, berries, nuts, or seeds*

▶ *Flower beds for orioles and nectar-loving birds, such as hummingbirds*

▶ *A source of water—a birdbath, a garden pool, or just an outdoor faucet dripping into a shallow dish*

▶ *Privacy in a neglected corner of yard with piles of brush and thick shrubs for nesting places*

▶ *A patch of dirt where birds can take dust baths*

The waiting game. Settle in one spot and let birds come to you. Seek out habitats that offer food and water—a marsh, a glade with blossoming trees, or a flowery field abuzz with insects.

Follow the birds' schedules. Birds that live inland are most active in the early morning and late afternoon—the best times to go looking for them. Plan to do some birding in springtime, which offers the double bill of migration and courtship.

Wear bright colors, which won't scare off most birds but will alert hunters to your presence when your bird-watching overlaps with hunting season.

BIRTH ANNOUNCEMENTS

Pattern of tiny feet. Get a copy of the impressions made of your baby's feet and hands after birth, or make them yourself with a dusting of charcoal. Have the impressions photocopied onto the front of plain white cards. Inside the card, write or type the baby's name, birth date, height, and weight.

Little diaper announcements can be made by cutting triangles from construction paper. Fold each triangle as you would a diaper, then, on the inside, write the pertinent birth information. Secure each triangle with a pink or blue diaper pin and mail in envelopes that are one size larger.

Use paper dolls. Find paper dolls in appropriate baby motifs. Take them to a copy center, and have them copied in color and duplicated onto sturdy paper. Cut out the dolls, and handwrite the birth information on the back.

BIRTH CERTIFICATES

To speed the request for an official copy of your birth record, contact the civil registry in the city or province where you were born to find out the current fee and preferred method of pay-

ment. Then send in your request, making sure to print or type your full name. You should also include your birth date, sex, parents' names, mother's maiden name, and the county or city where you were born.

A search abroad. Find information on a foreign birth record by contacting the embassy of your birth country in Canada. A directory of foreign diplomatic missions can be found at the public library. If you were born on an airplane or ship, your birth record will be in the country that was the next port of call.

Name changes. If you change your name by court order—rather than through marriage or divorce —amend your birth certificate to reflect your new name.

Searching for your roots. To chart your genealogical roots, write for the birth certificates of your parents, grandparents, aunts, and uncles. Old birth certificates are often held in provincial or county historical archives.

Adult adoptees may be able to view their original birth certificates in some provinces by filing a petition in court. In an adoption, new birth certificates are issued with the names of the adopting parents and the child's new name.

OLD SAW **Keep a certified original** of each family member's birth certificate in a secure place, such as a safe-deposit box. But store several copies in a file at home for convenience. Not only will you need birth certificates to register children for school, but you may also need them to apply for Social Insurance numbers, passports, driver's licenses, marriage licenses, and government benefits.

BIRTHDAY PARTIES

Baby pictures. Create an invitation to a milestone birthday using a baby picture or a photocopy of the honoree's birth certificate.

Computer magic. Personalize a birthday party invitation by composing it yourself on a computer. If you have a color printer, all the better. Fold the finished invitation twice (if it is on 8 ½ x 11-inch paper), seal it with a colorful sticker, and address it as though it were an envelope.

Pick a theme. Relate the theme to a bygone era in the honoree's life (a 1970's disco party), a favorite hobby (a 19th-hole party for a golfer), or just a current fad (a mystery party). Organize the invitations, food, decorations, and possibly even some silly games to carry out the overall theme.

Grand openings. Hold the attention of guests during gift opening by playing spin the bottle to select whose gift will be opened next. (The honoree must supply a kiss to the gift giver.) Be sure each guest presents his own gift.

Instant keepsake. With an instant camera, take a photograph of each birthday party guest together with the celebrant. Include the photo in a bag of favors, or later in a thank-you note from the honoree.

BIRTHDAYS

Start a date-of-birth newspaper file. In plastic wrap, store away the newspaper published on the day a baby is born to parents you know well. Present the paper to the child on a special occasion, such as a 10th birthday, a Sweet Sixteen party, or college graduation.

Never forget a birthday. Sign up with a birthday reminder service, which gently jogs your memory by mail, telephone, or E-mail, a week or so before an important birthday. Some services also recommend gifts or automatically send flowers. Look for advertisements in your local newspaper or search on-line under "Birthday Reminder Services."

Marking time. Watch your child grow up—literally—by creating a height chart. Use an out-of-the-way wall or heavy paper that you can roll up and store until the following year. On each birthday, mark your child's height and take photographs during the measuring process to put into a scrapbook.

Make middle-aged milestones merry occasions by giving gag gifts that tweak the aging process, such as magnifying glasses or a cane, or "artifacts" from the honoree's youth, like Elvis records or love beads.

BLANKETS & COMFORTERS

Read the label. Most blankets and comforters sold today are washable—even those made of

---

LAST-MINUTE BIRTHDAY GIFTS

It's down to the wire, and you still haven't found that perfect birthday gift. Don't sweat it; here are some winning ideas to keep you in good stead with the celebrant.

▶ *Couch Potato Basket. Your favorite videophile will appreciate a basket filled with gourmet popcorn and other munchies, movie-theater candies, a video guide, and a couple of favorite flicks. Line the basket with the Sunday paper entertainment pages featuring splashy movie ads.*

▶ *Chocoholics Cache. Candy stores often prepackage these or will create them to order. If you prefer to make your own, line an old-fashioned cookie tin with doilies and fill it with the honoree's favorite chocolates.*

▶ *Leisure Treats. Give gift certificates for such personalized services or activities as a massage, a beauty makeover, a day at an amusement park, a singing lesson, an exercise class—even dinner at a favorite restaurant.*

▶ *At Your Service. Give a gift of your expertise, labor, or time: a day of home fix-its, a week of home-cooked meals, the lawn mowed, babysitting, piano lessons, tax advice. Give your present as an "IOU" on a gift card.*

wool. Follow the washing instructions on the label carefully.

Make the right choice. Blankets are available in thermal and conventional styles. Thermal blankets are made of cotton or synthetics, have an open weave, and are designed for cooler summer nights or warm climates. Conventional blankets are generally made of wool, wool blends, or synthetics and have a tighter weave for greater warmth.

Layer blankets. Several light blankets will keep you warmer than one heavy blanket. Each layer can increase your warmth by approximately 3 percent.

Use a duvet cover to protect a down comforter from dirt and stains. Wash the cover regularly in the washing machine. Have the comforter cleaned by an experienced dry cleaner once a year.

To fluff up a down comforter, place it in the dryer together with three or four loose tennis balls, which help redistribute the feathers. Spin it on the *Air Only* setting for 15 to 20 minutes.

BLEACH

Wear rubber gloves when handling bleach, and be sure there is good ventilation in any room where you are using it. Remember that, for all its many ordinary household uses, bleach is still a powerful chemical.

 Never mix bleach with any other commercial cleaner, especially products containing ammonia. Bleach and ammonia, when combined, create a lethal gas.

Kill weeds between the flagstones on your terrace or walkway by dowsing them with a solution made of 5 percent

HANDHELD BLENDERS

In recent years several manufacturers have come out with lightweight machines that, for everyday blending, function as well as a mixer or food processor—and are simpler to clean and store. Best of all, you don't have the hassle of transferring the food to the blender; instead, you take the blender right to the soup pot (for creamed soup) or the frosty glass (for a fruit smoothie). In addition to blending soups and shakes, these handy machines whip creams and puddings, puree sauces, and chop everything from fresh, tender herbs to raw carrots and even nuts.

bleach and 95 percent boiling water. If the weed problem is serious, raise the percentage of bleach in the solution.

Add 15 mL (1 tbsp) of bleach to the water container of your dehumidifier to keep it from developing a musty odor and to make your room smell especially fresh and clean.

Clean porcelain teapots and cups by filling them with warm water, adding a few drops of bleach, and letting them soak for an hour or two. When stains are gone, wash thoroughly with soap and water.

BLENDERS

A clean machine. To clean your blender in a jiffy, partly fill the container with a solution of warm water and liquid soap, secure the lid, and then run the motor for a few seconds. Drain the container, rinse it thoroughly, and set aside to dry thoroughly.

Take it easy. Avoid long, uninterrupted use of your blender. It's not meant to be run continuously for more than two or three minutes at a stretch. Such misuse can overheat the motor and possibly cause a complete breakdown.

Protect the blades. When making frozen drinks in a blender, add liquid with the ice. The blender's blades will become bent and dull if they are used as ice crushers.

Retire an old blender to the workshop. Use it to mix paint or for other messy "blending" jobs. The blender's container makes a handy pitcherlike receptacle.

BOATING

Anchor alert. Tie a brightly colored piece of plastic ribbon or tape to the chain extension of your anchor line a few feet above the anchor. When you hoist the anchor, the ribbon will signal that the anchor is about to surface, enabling you to prevent the metal chain and the anchor itself from banging against the boat.

Distribute the weight evenly when you load a small boat. If it is kept in balance, the boat will glide much more smoothly through the water, making paddling or rowing easier.

Boating shoes. Wear shoes with soft, nonslip soles, both to keep you from slipping and to protect the boat. Formal "boat shoes" are not necessary; your trusty sneakers will work just fine.

Wear sunglasses with ultraviolet-filter lenses when boating on sunny days. The harsh reflection of sun against water can damage your eyes.

Boating etiquette. If you are invited to be a guest on a boat, offer to help in any way you can. Even if you're a novice, ask questions. If you can't swim, let your captain know before setting out.

BOATS

Think hard before buying an old or neglected boat in need of repair. You may save money on the purchase price of a fixer-upper, but the task of bringing such a boat back to life often requires a lot of time and skill as well as expensive materials.

Glue outdoor carpet to the floor of your canoe, rowboat, or other small boat to prevent items such as tackle boxes from sliding back and forth.

It's a snap. To keep the snaps that hold down boat covers and canvases from sticking, apply a light coating of petroleum jelly to the snaps every couple of weeks.

Install foam pipe insulation along the gunwales of your canoe to keep your paddles from banging as you stroke. The insulation, which comes with a slit along its length, is simple to apply.

PORTABLE LIGHTS FOR BOATS

These battery-operated bow lights—one held in place with a suction cup, the other by a clamp—come in handy when you're out in a small boat or dinghy at night. Portable stern lights are also available, which, combined with the bow lights, help to alert other boats to your position and heading. The lights come in handy on larger boats as well, where they can be stowed and used as backups in case the built-in lights fail.

BODY LANGUAGE

Signal concentration. To indicate that you are concentrating on what another person is saying, strike a "thinker's pose." Cross your arms, then place the fingers of one hand on your chin, with the thumb pointing down, and the index finger pointing up.

To gain someone's trust or to provide reassurance, pat that person's arm gently or put a hand on his shoulder. In a business situation, physical contact may not be welcomed by another person, especially one of the opposite sex. In this situation, smile reassuringly or shake hands firmly.

Street smarts. When walking along urban streets, especially those that might be dangerous, keep your back straight, your shoulders back, and your head up. Walk briskly. This demeanor projects alertness and makes you less likely to be a target for crime.

Show interest. In a job interview, project interest and enthusiasm by sitting up straight in your chair and looking directly into the interviewer's eyes. In a less formal situation, lean forward to indicate that you're interested in what the other person is saying.

Don't show your hand. After being dealt strong hands, card players often extend and touch

BODY SPEAK

Body language—the physical expression of thoughts and feelings—can sometimes convey messages more eloquently than the spoken word. Here are a few common movements that can help you easily decipher what others may be thinking, as well as master your own telltale body language.

BODY LANGUAGE	WHAT IT MAY MEAN
Crossed legs or arms	May indicate discomfort or defensiveness
Picking dust or lint from clothes	May indicate a lack of interest or an objection to what is being said
Frequent fingering of a collar or touching the neck	May show lying, shyness, or nervousness
Blushing	May indicate shyness or embarrassment
Hands behind the head, leaning far back in a chair	May signal arrogance; an "I'm in charge" attitude
Hands on hips, legs astride	A "don't-mess-with me" pose
Darting eyes	May indicate shyness or lying
Fidgeting with a button or twisting a ring around a finger	May indicate discomfort or shyness
Open arms	May indicate a receptive attitude
Mirroring the behavior of someone else	A sign of interest or physical attraction

their index fingers together while keeping the remaining fingers entwined. Beware of an opponent who strikes this pose—and try not to do it yourself.

BOOKS

Store your books out of direct sunlight. Sunlight will fade the spines of the books, making them appear drab and dirty, and will rot the cloth and cause the spine to weaken or break.

Let them breathe. Avoid storing books in glass cabinets or other enclosed spaces that prevent air from properly circulating; a lack of air encourages the growth of mildew. Never store books in a damp basement or garage.

Buy books on-line. An easy way to purchase bestsellers as well as hard-to-find hardcovers and trade paperbacks is through www.Amazon.com, a site on the Internet that features over one

million titles. You can order with a credit card, and your books will be shipped to your door.

Too many books? An amusing way to get rid of books you no longer want or need is to hold a "Book Swap Party." Invite other bibliophiles to bring their unwanted books, then let everyone trade.

Don't toss those old books! Make them into a unique coffee table instead. Pile several books into stacks of equal size and top with a finished sheet of glass. Make sure the stacks properly support the glass.

Books are not scrapbooks. Never store newspaper clippings inside a book. The chemicals found in newspaper ink can damage the paper in a fine book.

Remove stale, musty odors from a book by placing it in a brown paper bag with a piece of crumpled newspaper. Change the paper every few days until the odor is gone. Or, fan out the pages of the book and sprinkle talcum powder, baking soda, or cornstarch on them. After several hours, brush off the powder.

BOOKSHELVES

When building a bookcase, make sure shelves are at least 20 cm (8 in.) deep and 23 cm (9 in.) high to accommodate books of average or small size, such as standard novels and paperbacks. For larger art books, shelves should be 30 cm (12 in.) deep with 33 cm (13 in.) of clearance.

Transform a plain wall with ordinary windows into an attractive architectural feature by constructing interlocking bookshelves above, below, and on either side of the windows. Fill with books, but save cubbyholes to display cherished objects.

Filter out noise. In an apartment building where noisy neighbors can be an ongoing problem, erect floor-to-ceiling bookshelves on the walls separating the apartments to help screen out noise.

Make a mini-library. Look for nooks in your house—on a wide landing, under a staircase, in the corner of a room—to build a small bookcase. Look for unique places, such as a spare kitchen cabinet for cookbooks.

Encourage a child to appreciate books by giving him his own bookcase. Put a small one in his bedroom, or clear a shelf on your bookcase and reserve that place especially for his books.

BOOTS

Keep from tracking mud into your entryway by storing a stack of plastic grocery bags near the door. Simply place each boot into a bag and knot the handles.

Break in stiff hiking boots by standing them on their toes and using your body weight to bend the heel of the boot over the toe. Repeat this process as needed.

Sizing. Feet tend to swell over the course of the day, so make sure your boots are big enough, especially when you are buying new ones. Shop for new boots in the late afternoon or evening. Bring thick socks with you to ensure that you get the right fit. If your heel can slide 6 mm (¼ in.) in any direction, try a smaller size.

Help little ones find their boots quickly in the classroom by painting bright dots on the heels.

BOWLING

Be mentally focused when it's your turn to bowl. Stand straight, relax, and erase all other thoughts from your mind. Try to visualize yourself making the approach, gracefully releasing the ball, and watching the ball roll down the lane directly into the headpin.

Ask a friend to videotape you. Use the tape to evaluate your approach and to correct any snags in your swing.

Avoid overthrowing on your release of the ball. Ideally, the momentum of the heavy ball swinging downward does most of the work.

Aim for quality, not just quantity, when practicing by concentrating on specific aspects of your game. For example, strive for a smooth release one day; on your next trip to the lanes, try to add more speed to the ball.

BRAINSTORMING

Get comfortable. Create a relaxed atmosphere for your brainstorming sessions, where participants can feel comfortable and confident formulating new ideas and concepts. Choose a neutral location rather than anyone's "turf." Holding your meetings outside the normal environment is helpful (which is why executive gatherings are often held at out-of-town conference centers). Have a ready supply of refreshments, and make sure restrooms and telephones are close by.

Prepare! Prevent last-minute distractions by having supplies—paper, easels, markers, index cards, pencils—ready in advance. Set up the room beforehand so that brainstorm participants can concentrate on the task at hand.

Define boundaries. Describe brainstorming rules at the outset and post them on the wall. Criticism is OUT; adventurous ideas are IN; jumping off from previous ideas is IN; fun and laughter are IN; and above all, negativism is OUT. Judging or dominating: OUT.

Break the ice. Start with a fun exercise to build enthusiasm. Divide the group into twos, say, and ask each pair to interview each other briefly and then introduce their partner to the group.

 Clarify the goal. Establish a clear problem statement or overall goal before the meeting begins. Hand out the statement three or four days before the event to give people time to focus yet retain fresh ideas and enthusiasm.

Mix and match. Deliberately invite people whose problem-solving styles vary, whose backgrounds are diverse, and who do different types of jobs. Invite someone unexpected, like a mailroom worker or a person from outside the organization.

BRASS

Homemade remedies. Make your brass pieces sparkle by rubbing them with a damp cloth dipped in ketchup. Clean tough spots by brushing them hard with an old toothbrush and a small dab of toothpaste. For extremely tarnished brass, rub the item with half a lemon dipped in salt, or polish it with a paste made with equal parts of salt, vinegar, and flour. When the tarnish has disappeared, rinse the object thoroughly, and buff it with soft cloth.

Don't wax brass that is used for cooking or eating. However, for most other brass items, especially those used outdoors, apply a light coat of paste wax to help keep it from tarnishing. For more delicate pieces, use lemon oil instead.

BREAD

Shelf life. While fresh bread generally keeps five to seven days, its shelf life depends largely on weight. The lighter the bread, the more quickly moisture evaporates; thus, a thus roll turns stale faster than a bagel.

Fresh bread. To keep bread and rolls fresh for more than a day, put them in one heavy-duty or two regular plastic bags and store the bags in the freezer. Slice a whole loaf before freezing it, so that you can easily remove just the amount you need.

To restore dried-out rolls or slices of bread, wrap them in a damp towel and put them in a microwave oven, on high, for 30 seconds or until the bread is soft and warm. Or sprinkle the bread lightly with water, wrap it in aluminum foil, and heat in a 175°C (350°F) oven for 10 to 15 minutes.

Don't toss stale bread. Use it to make bread crumbs, croutons, or French toast. Crumble the bread or cut it into croutons and place in an airtight plastic container to store in the freezer. For French toast, wrap whole slices in plastic wrap and store in your freezer.

To make quick work of preparing bread cubes for croutons or bread desserts, cut frozen sliced bread into cubes using a serrated bread knife.

BREAD BAKING

Rolling in dough. If dough sticks to the rolling pin, put the pin in the freezer for about 10 minutes (or until very cold), then roll out the dough with ease.

If your bread burns, remove the charred marks with a grater. Then brush the bare spots with egg yolk and return the loaf to the oven for two minutes or until brown.

If your dough is slow to rise, wrap an electric heating pad set on *Low* in aluminum foil. Place the dough bowl on the heating pad until the dough has risen.

To test if yeast dough has risen enough to bake, lightly press two fingers into the top of the dough. If the slight dent remains in the dough, it is ready for the next step in the recipe.

Sticky fix. Humidity can alter dough even when it is being prepared in a bread machine. Test the dough for stickiness while the bread machine is on the kneading cycle. Open the cover and touch the dough. If it sticks to your finger, add 15 mL (1 tbsp) of flour, allow the kneading to continue for about 30 seconds, then check again. If necessary, repeat the process until the dough feels malleable but not sticky.

For a crisp crust, spray the oven with water three times during the first 10 minutes of baking, or place a pan filled with water in the oven bottom while the bread is baking.

For a soft crust, brush the dough with milk right before baking or with butter just after baking.

Crackers. If your yeast bread turns out too dense, cut the loaf into thin slices and toast in a 135°C (275°F) oven until dry. These crispy "crackers"—which look like melba toast—are great with soups or dips.

Revive dried out quick breads, such as banana bread or muffins, by poking a few holes in the bread, drizzling fruit juice or rum over it, wrapping it in plastic wrap, and refrigerating it for two days.

A BAKER'S HELPER

For big baking jobs, you need some extra help in the kitchen. Whether moving dough for a long braided bread onto a baking stone or taking bread loaves from a hot oven to a cooling rack, you'll find that this aluminum-bladed giant spatula is just the right size. The heavy lifter is also great for transferring a rolled pie crust to a pan and for quickly and easily moving cookies and scones from baking pans. Available through King Arthur Flour Baker's Catalogue: (800) 827-6836.

BREAKFAST

Sugar-coated fib. If your kids love sugared cereals but you want them to eat healthy ones, mix their favorite sugar-coated cereal with a more nutritious kind.

For an instant breakfast, use your blender. Milk or yogurt, bananas, and blueberries make a fine shake to start the day. Add apple juice, peaches, or strawberries.

Skipping breakfast? The jury's still out on whether eating a good breakfast has an effect on your mental acuity in the late morning. Studies show that people differ in their need for breakfast. Eating a nutritious breakfast, however, certainly makes it easier to turn down offers of fattening sweet rolls and doughnuts.

Breakfast food for dinner? No law says you can't have cereal or eggs at dinnertime—especially if you come home late and are tired. Breakfast food is just as nutritious and often less caloric than a meat-and-potatoes dinner.

BRIDAL SHOWERS

Ask before you plan. The bride and groom may need one type of gift—kitchen utensils or linens, for example—more than another, so ask the couple for their preferences before you plan a shower. For a surprise shower, find out what they want from relatives and close friends.

Treasures from Mom. The mother of the bride (or future mother-in-law) can create an especially nostalgic basket of goodies that the bride can proudly take to her new home: a recipe box containing Mom's favorite recipes, a sampling of Mom's trusty health and beauty lotions and salves, and of course, a framed picture of the bride's happy parents.

Don't leave the men out. Many bridal showers are now coed affairs. Plan a party that will be as entertaining to the men as it is to the women. An outdoor event is often a winner; if the weather permits, have a barbecue.

Christmas in June. Host a "Holiday Shower." Give each guest a different holiday and ask them to bring a gift that will help the newlyweds celebrate in style in the years ahead. An antique crèche makes a wonderful Christmas heirloom, while a picnic basket stocked with pretty plates, glasses, and a checkered cloth will enhance future summer holiday celebrations.

BROILING

Decrease smoke and grease when broiling by adding a cup of water to the pan's drip tray before putting it into the oven.

Lean and clean. Before broiling, remove excess fat from meats and the skin from poultry, then provide moisture by basting the meat with a low-calorie salad dressing. Broiling in this way boosts flavor, reduces fat and calories, and makes cleanup easier by reducing grease splatters.

Add vegetables to your broiling repertoire. Traditional candidates for broiling are eggplants, mushrooms, tomatoes, peppers, onions, and zucchinis.

Put a slice of stale bread in the broiling pan to absorb grease. The bread reduces the temperature of the grease, which in turn cuts the amount of smoke and splatters.

Make broiling pan cleanup a snap by sprinkling powdered laundry detergent on top of any burned or greasy areas. Cover the areas with a damp paper towel and let the pan sit. After a few hours you can clean the problem areas easily with a damp sponge.

BRUNCH

An entertaining meal. A combination of breakfast and lunch, brunch begs to be served informally and easily expands for extra last-minute guests. Serve breakfast dishes (an egg casserole or pecan waffles, for example), luncheon dishes (chicken salad, fruit and cheese), or a combination.

A frugal fete. Generally, dishes served at brunch are less costly than the elaborate multiple courses served for a dinner. Therefore, brunch is a gracious way for people on a budget to entertain.

Family affairs. Because brunch is served during the middle of the day and brunch food is often less sophisticated than dinner-party fare, brunch is an ideal way to entertain families with children. The adults can chat, the kids can play, and when nap time arrives, the party can break up naturally.

Brunch from the freezer. The next time you whip up waffles, make extras to serve at your next brunch. Place them in plastic freezer bags and freeze. At your next brunch, simply toast the frozen waffles and serve.

BUFFETS

Not enough dinnerware? If you don't have a large enough set of china, flatware, or glasses to serve all your guests, don't hesitate to combine what you do have. Mix and match at random, or place one set of dishes and utensils at one end of the table and another at the opposite end.

Serve "one-utensil" dishes. Your guests will have an easier time eating off their laps if they don't have to cut food with a knife and fork. Serve casseroles or stews that can be easily eaten with only one utensil.

Lap naps. Provide guests with oversize napkins (or even tea towels) to protect their laps and as many small tables as you can round up. Pull out any TV tables you own and clear end tables and coffee tables.

Replenish serving dishes regularly. A buffet should look abundant, so plan carefully so that you don't run short. Use two dishes for each item on the menu. That way, one can be on the table for guests to dip into while the other is in the kitchen being refilled.

A dessert buffet is an easy way to entertain, especially during the Christmas holidays or for a birthday or anniversary celebration. Most desserts—cookies, cakes, pies, and puddings—can be prepared in advance.

Potluck buffet. Host a buffet and ask each guest to bring a favorite dish. (You may want to assign types of dishes so that you don't end up with four desserts and no main dishes.) You can provide the beverages and a pretty buffet table.

PLANNING A BUFFET TABLE

When you plan to entertain a large number of people in your home, a buffet is the easiest way to do it.

▶ Arrange the buffet table in a logical way. If space permits, allow for two "lanes of traffic" to your buffet table by serving each dish twice, on opposite sides of the table. This way, guests can reach the food quickly and easily.

▶ Wrap utensils in napkins so that both can be picked up at the same time.

▶ Serve beverages and desserts at another table or bar in a location that does not interrupt the flow of the food table.

Napkins and cutlery

Plates

Bread

Salad

Main dish

Vegetable

Potatoes, rice, noodles

Potatoes, rice, noodles

Vegetable

Main dish

Salad

Bread

Plates

Napkins and cutlery

BURNOUT

The "super" complex. If you find you're taking on twice as much as you can reasonably do, you are on your way to suffering burnout. Analyze your priorities and don't let feelings of responsibility for others prevent you from taking care of yourself first.

Find a confidant. Lighten your burden by finding someone you can trust to talk to about the stresses you feel. A confidant can be a spouse, a friend, or a professional counselor or therapist. (It is wise not to discuss personal or professional problems with colleagues or coworkers.) Airing problems with a trusted confidant can help you avoid burnout.

Beware of serious problems brought on by burnout. If you are suffering from depression, abusing alcohol or other drugs, or engaging in compulsive behavior of any kind, seek help. Consult your employee assistance program, a counselor or therapist, or a religious leader to find out where to get the support you need.

BURNS

Cool a minor burn. Put the burned area under cold running water and hold it there for 5 to 15 minutes or until the pain lessens. If the burn exceeds 5 cm (2 in.) or is on the face, call a doctor.

Apply moisturizer to a burn after it has cooled completely to prevent the skin from drying out. Never put butter on a burn because it can trap heat in the affected area, making the burn even more serious.

Bandage the burn. Cover it loosely with a sterile gauze bandage to keep it clean. Change the bandage daily. If you notice any swelling or redness indicating infection, call your doctor.

Leave blisters alone because they help protect against infection. If they do break, wash the area with soap and water, dab on an antibiotic cream, and cover with a bandage.

For a serious, deep burn, one that leaves the skin charred or white, get prompt medical help. Do the same for a superficial burn that covers a particularly large area of the body or is a chemical or electrical burn.

BUS TRAVEL

Reserve early. Like airlines, bus lines give discounts for planning ahead. The best rates are for tickets purchased 21 days in advance; same-day tickets are the costliest.

Make a seat card. Using a felt-tip pen on a piece of stiff paper, write THIS SEAT IS OCCUPIED. If you get off the bus to stretch, boarding passengers will know the seat is taken. Never leave a book, camera, or other valuable to save a seat.

For a smooth ride, take a seat toward the middle of the bus but still in view of the driver. It's a good idea to bring along your own provisions and refreshments. Many stops have no food service, and bus-station cafés often are closed in the evening.

BUSINESS CARDS

Gimmicks can help you stand out among competitors. Create a magnetic version of your card if your business would benefit from having your telephone number on customers' refrigerators (if you are a plumber or locksmith, for example). Or print helpful information on the back of the card, such as a map to your store or quick-reference facts or tips that might be useful to your customers.

Double duty. When someone gives you a business card, record the date and place that you received it on the back. Add any pertinent information—shared business interests, reasons to follow up, or common acquaintances. These notes will jog your memory when you want to follow up at a later date.

Don't leave home without one. Some of the best business contacts occur in unexpected situations. Keep cards in your glove compartment, wallet, purse, datebook—anywhere that keeps this tool within easy reach.

Project quality. To have your cards make a good impression, use a sturdy, attractive stock, and be sure the printing job is clear.

Writing a proper and effective business letter reflects well on you and your employer and is more likely to produce the response you desire from your reader. The chart below shows the basic elements of a good business letter.

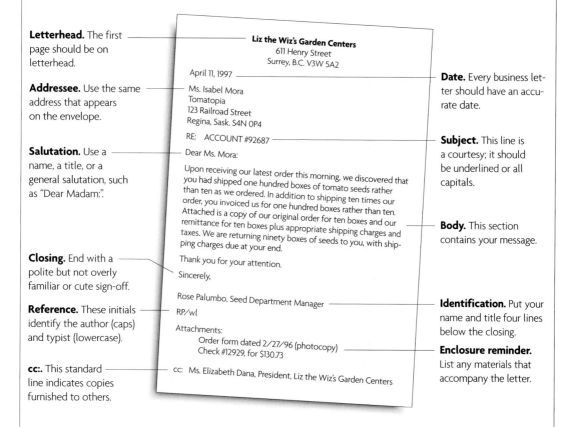

Letterhead. The first page should be on letterhead.

Addressee. Use the same address that appears on the envelope.

Salutation. Use a name, a title, or a general salutation, such as "Dear Madam:".

Closing. End with a polite but not overly familiar or cute sign-off.

Reference. These initials identify the author (caps) and typist (lowercase).

cc:. This standard line indicates copies furnished to others.

Date. Every business letter should have an accurate date.

Subject. This line is a courtesy; it should be underlined or all capitals.

Body. This section contains your message.

Identification. Put your name and title four lines below the closing.

Enclosure reminder. List any materials that accompany the letter.

Letter text:

Liz the Wiz's Garden Centers
611 Henry Street
Surrey, B.C. V3W 5A2

April 11, 1997

Ms. Isabel Mora
Tomatopia
123 Railroad Street
Regina, Sask. S4N 0P4

RE: ACCOUNT #92687

Dear Ms. Mora:

Upon receiving our latest order this morning, we discovered that you had shipped one hundred boxes of tomato seeds rather than ten as we ordered. In addition to shipping ten times our order, you invoiced us for one hundred boxes rather than ten. Attached is a copy of our original order for ten boxes and our remittance for ten boxes plus appropriate shipping charges and taxes. We are returning ninety boxes of seeds to you, with shipping charges due at your end.

Thank you for your attention.

Sincerely,

Rose Palumbo, Seed Department Manager

RP/wl

Attachments:
      Order form dated 2/27/96 (photocopy)
      Check #12929, for $130.73

cc: Ms. Elizabeth Dana, President, Liz the Wiz's Garden Centers

---

A smart design. The look of a business card reflects the image of your company. Logos should match the company stationery. Use unimposing easy-on-the-eye type styles and sizes.

When in Rome. Show sensitivity to the people you do business with. If you interact with people who speak another language, print cards with the reverse side translated into their native tongue.

BUSINESS LETTERS

Keep letters to a single page whenever possible. In business, time is money. Show respect for your reader's time by writing succinctly. In a long letter, use bulleted points to break up the text and create a crisp presentation.

Read business letters aloud before sending them to identify words and phrases that may sound pretentious, unclear, or stilted. Try to make your letter sound as though you were talking in person to the recipient.

Be clear. The key point should appear in the first sentence and should be clear and to the point. If you wait to announce your reason for writing until the last paragraph, you're likely to lose, confuse, or annoy your reader.

Watch your spelling! Misspellings detract from your credibility—and make your employer look bad as well. Don't rely on your computer spell-checker alone; use a dictionary. Above all, spell the name and address of the recipient correctly.

Watch your grammar! Grammar is as important as spelling. If you feel at all unsure about your ability to express the language properly, ask someone to read over your letter for you.

Save copies. Every business letter is a written record containing information you may possibly need in the future. Make a copy of every business letter you send and keep it filed for as long as you may need it.

BUTTER & MARGARINE

Baking with butter. Although you can substitute margarine for butter in most recipes, stick with butter when preparing certain pastries, such as puff pastry, croissants and shaped butter cookies, as well as when you are making certain candies such as toffee.

Make measuring butter easier. Remember that one stick of butter equals 125 mL (½ cup or 8 tbsp). Before you remove the marked butter wrapper, trace the measurement lines (which measure 1 tbsp) into the stick of butter with a knife.

Nonfat buttered popcorn. For movie-house flavor with virtually no added fat or cholesterol, lightly coat freshly popped corn with butter-flavored, no-stick cooking spray. Add a sprinkling of salt if desired.

Flavored butters. With a wooden spoon, blend 60 mL (¼ cup) minced dill, parsley, basil, chives, tarragon, or rosemary and 7.5 mL (1½ tsp) lemon juice into 1 stick softened butter. For a citrus flavor, use 30 mL (2 tbsp) lemon, lime, or orange juice and 10 mL (2 tsp) of the grated fruit rind.

Use unsalted butter to grease baking pans. Salted butter may prevent some baked goods from being easily removed.

Never substitute whipped butter or margarine for regular when you are baking. They contain as much as 45 percent air. If you use whipped, your butter measurements may be wrong, and your baked creation may fail.

BUTTONS

Make buttons stay on longer by dabbing a bit of clear nail polish over the threads to strengthen their hold.

Lose fewer buttons through wear and tear by replacing the thread with dental floss. Floss is stronger and keeps the buttons in place longer.

Dress up kids' clothes by sewing unusual and colorful buttons found in specialty shops onto their sweaters, dresses, and coats. Allow an artistic child to create her own button design on a sweatshirt, then you sew them on.

Decorate a picture frame with colorful buttons. Simply attach the buttons to the frame with a hot-glue gun. Use either a standard picture frame or a framed mirror to create a work of art.

A new pin. Transform an interesting button into a pretty pin. To fashion into a pin, simply secure the button with a hot-glue gun to a pin backing (available at most craft shops) or even a large, utilitarian safety pin.

 Recycle buttons. Before tossing out old clothes, cut off and save the buttons. You never know when that particular style or color may come in handy.

Pick up antique buttons in vintage-clothing stores or flea markets. Use them to replace plain buttons on vests, jackets, and dresses, and to create a unique look. Remember, too: antique buttons can be valuable.

An improvised hold. Prevent a drawstring from pulling through its casing by sewing a big button onto each end of the string.

Button games. Substitute buttons for misplaced poker chips or use unusual buttons as replacements for board-game pieces.

RIGHT STUFF

BUTTON COVERS

Transform your look in minutes with practical, ingenious button covers. For example, dress up a sporty blouse (right) with faux pearl covers without sewing a stitch. Just pop the cover clasp over the button and snap shut. Reverse the order to remove. You'll find button covers in a variety of styles in most notions shops.

CACTI TO CUTS AND SCRAPES

CACTI

Hand saver. To pick up thorny cacti, grasp the plants with a pair of barbecue tongs, kitchen tongs, or even tweezers. The tool should fit the size of the plant.

Painless cleanup. Tongs also serve to remove leaves and wind-blown trash from around the base of a thorny cactus, such as a prickly pear, without scratching your hands.

Water-wise window box. In hot regions, keeping a summertime window box watered is a twice-daily chore. The solution is to plant a desert scape of miniature button, catclaw, and barrel cacti in the box instead of flowers. These plants thrive in the heat and drought found outside a south-facing window.

CAKE DECORATING

When frosting or glazing a cake, keep the cake plate clean by placing pieces of wax or parchment paper around the outer edge before laying the cake down and frosting. When finished, just remove the protective strips.

Flavor plain icing by adding a little grated citrus peel, almond extract, coffee, or fruit juice to the basic recipe.

Spaghetti designs. Make squares, stars, or smiley faces on cakes using drained, cooked spaghetti.

Let cut strands sit in food coloring, dry them, then place on the cake in whatever design your imagination fancies!

For a quick design, place a paper template or doily over the cake and sprinkle with cocoa powder, confectioners' sugar, or cinnamon. Gently remove the pattern to reveal your handiwork.

Make your own cake-decorating tool with a sealable plastic storage bag. Place the icing in the bag and seal it. Squeeze the bag contents to one corner and cut a small opening in the corner. (Enlarge the hole as needed.) Practice your design on the side of the icing bowl or another test surface before working on the cake.

Decorate with candy. Ice a cake in the flavor of your choice. Then make designs on the top and sides using inexpensive "penny candy," candy canes (for Christmas), or chocolate kisses (wrapped or unwrapped). For serious chocoholics, consider chocolate truffles or chocolate-covered cherries.

CACTI AS HOUSEPLANTS

The dry atmosphere of most Canadian homes in winter is hard on the majority of houseplants, but well suited for cacti. Providing you can give them a bright, sunny window, and don't overwater them during their dormant period (usually winter) cacti thrive indoors.

CACTUS	SIZE AND SHAPE	FLOWER AND BLOOM TIME
Golden barrel (*Echinocactus grusonii*)	Barrel-shaped; up to 15 cm (6 in.) with yellow spines	Yellow in summer on large plants
Rat's-tail (*Aporocactus flagelliformis*)	Slender weeping stems, good in hanging baskets	Bright pink in early spring
Bishop's cap (*Astrophytum myriostigma*)	Blue-green spineless with 4–8 ribs; may reach 15 cm (6 in.)	Yellow, spring to summer
Bunny ears (*Opuntia microdasys*)	Flat pads with yellow or white spines; up to 30 cm (12 in.) tall	Yellow in spring
Old man (*Oreocereus celsianus*)	Columnar with long white hairs; can reach 1.8 m (6 ft)	Crimson in summer on mature plants
Peanut (*Echinopsis chamaecereus*)	Creeping, candlelike stems and white spines; up to 15 cm (6 in.)	Bright red, late spring to summer

CAKES

Use a strand of dry spaghetti instead of a toothpick to test whether or not a cake is completely baked. The spaghetti is long enough to keep your hand cool while you test, and thin enough not to damage the cake.

Improvise. If a cake breaks into pieces as you remove it from the pan, place the pieces in a large bowl and add layers of fresh fruit, pudding, nuts, and whipped cream to make an English trifle.

Use dental floss or thread to split a cake layer into two layers. Stick toothpicks into the outside of the cake halfway between the top and the bottom. Circle the cake with a 50 cm (20 in.) length of floss, resting it on the toothpicks. Cross the floss ends into opposite hands, and pull to cut cleanly through the cake.

Patchwork cake. For a dinner party, ask several guests to make a square cake (of an agreed-upon size) and to decorate the top. Arrange the cakes side by side in a patchwork design and finish it with a border of plain icing.

CALCIUM

Women need extra calcium, especially if they have a family history of hip fractures or vertebrae problems. To make sure you are getting enough, take calcium supplements; the recommended

RIGHT STUFF

NO MORE LOPSIDED CAKES

These baking strips help make cake baking almost foolproof. Looking like space-age belts, Magi-Cake Strips are first soaked in water, then placed around the outside edge of a batter-filled cake pan and secured with straight pins. Although the strips increase baking time by a few minutes, they prevent a host of traditional cake-baking problems, like burned edges and cracking. Best of all, each layer comes out perfectly flat, making lopsided layer cakes a thing of the past. You can find the strips at kitchen stores.

dosage is 1,200 to 1,500 mg a day to slow the bone loss connected with osteoporosis.

Small doses. Your body will absorb supplements best if you take two 600 mg doses per day rather than one 1,200 mg dose.

Do weight-bearing exercises, such as walking, jogging, rope-jumping, or weight-lifting. Done on a regular basis, these exercises help the body absorb calcium and keep bones strong. Improvise at home by regularly lifting soup cans or sacks of sugar.

 OLD SAW **Dairy products boost calcium** in your diet but will add fat if you aren't careful. Stick to skim or 1 percent milk, low-fat or non-fat yogurt and cottage cheese, reduced-fat hard cheeses, and low-fat frozen yogurt.

Try calcium-fortified foods for an easy way to add calcium to your diet. Orange juice, tofu, and many breakfast cereals are now available with added calcium.

CALENDARS

Family schedule. Keep track of the family's goings-on by mounting a large calendar in the kitchen next to a box of colored markers. Use a different color for each family member.

Red flag. Use bright red markers to highlight key dates on the calendar, such as birthdays, anniversaries, school vacations, and special occasions that you absolutely don't want to forget. If your family is large, assign each member a different color so his special events stand out.

Use your home computer as a calendar. Print out the day's or week's activities and post the schedule in a central location.

CALLUSES, CORNS, & BUNIONS

Stick to comfortable shoes. Shoes that rub against your feet can allow corns and calluses to develop. For regular use, wear low-heeled shoes that are roomy enough so that you can wiggle your toes.

Pad calluses and corns. Pads or moleskin that take the pressure off corns and calluses are available without a prescription. However, avoid medicated corn pads, which can damage the healthy tissue underneath the corn.

Soften corns and calluses by soaking your feet in 7.5 L (1.7 gal) of warm water with 15 mL (1 tbsp) of Epsom salts for 15 minutes. Then rub off the top layers of dead skin with a pumice stone and apply moisturizing lotion.

Consult a podiatrist about bunions, hard bumps at the big toe joint that cause pain. Foot doctors can prescribe orthotic devices to cushion painful bunions.

To ease bunion pain, apply ice for 15 minutes, then soak the foot in warm water for 15 minutes. Repeat three times a day.

CALORIE COUNTING

Use a small kitchen scale to take the guesswork out of servings measured in grams or ounces, such as pasta, meat, and fish. Translate the weight value into calories with a calorie counter.

Fat count. Fats and oils contain more than twice the calories per gram as carbohydrates (9 versus 4), which explains why a small potato may have fewer calories than the butter you put on it. Cutting down on fats is the easiest way to cut calories without decreasing the volume of food you eat.

CALORIE COUNTING 1-2-3

To quickly figure how many calories you should consume to maintain your present weight—or to achieve your ideal weight—use the following calculations.

▶ *Multiply your ideal weight in kilograms by 33 (or in pounds by 15) to find the number of calories you need to keep that weight. If your ideal weight is 56.8 kg (125 lb), you should consume 1,875 calories daily to keep your weight.*

▶ *If you are overweight, subtract 500 calories from the total number of calories for each 450 g (1 lb) per week you wish to lose. For example, if you wish to weigh 56.8 kg (125 lb) but presently weigh 59 kg (130 lb), cut your caloric intake to 1,375 in order to lose 450 g (1 lb) per week. It will take you approximately 5 weeks to lose the 2.25 kg (5 lb).*

▶ *If you wish to gain weight, add 500 calories to the number of calories needed to maintain your ideal weight. For example, if your ideal weight is 56.8 kg (125 lb) but you weigh 54.4 kg (120 lb), consume 2,375 calories per day (1,875 plus 500). It will take you 5 weeks to gain the extra weight.*

Drink water when you're thirsty instead of high-calorie juice, soft drinks, or beer. Drinking several of these beverages a day can add hundreds of extra calories.

CAMCORDERS

To stabilize your camera, sit astride a chair and prop your elbows on the chair back. Or lean on the hood or trunk of a car with its engine off.

Buying advice. Experiment with different camcorders in the store before choosing a particular model. Make handling ease a high priority. Also, try each camcorder's features and play back the tapes to compare the results.

Maintenance. Periodically have your camcorder cleaned by a professional. The small, quick-turning mechanisms within cameras, especially in smaller models, are easily damaged by dirt.

Keep your camcorder stored in its case to keep dust and grime to a minimum. When you're outdoors and have no time to disassemble it between shots, slip it into a heavy-duty plastic bag.

RIGHT STUFF

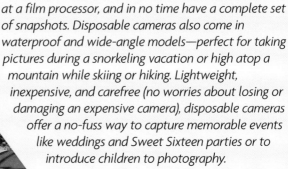

Have you ever arrived at an important event and realized that you've forgotten your camera? For not much more than the cost of a roll of film, you can buy a disposable camera, take your pictures, drop off the entire "package" at a film processor, and in no time have a complete set of snapshots. Disposable cameras also come in waterproof and wide-angle models—perfect for taking pictures during a snorkeling vacation or high atop a mountain while skiing or hiking. Lightweight, inexpensive, and carefree (no worries about losing or damaging an expensive camera), disposable cameras offer a no-fuss way to capture memorable events like weddings and Sweet Sixteen parties or to introduce children to photography.

CAMERA ACCESSORIES

A blower brush and lens paper will safely clean lenses, viewfinders, and other delicate camera mechanisms. Available at most camera shops, both are inexpensive and worth the investment.

Freeze or refrigerate film to keep it from deteriorating. If the roll has been taken out of the original wrapping, use a waterproof plastic bag to protect it from moisture.

A single zoom lens can do the work of several lenses of different focal lengths. One zoom is less expensive and easier to carry.

Buy rolls of film that have 36 exposures rather than 24. The cost per roll is more, but the price per picture is less. What's more, you'll save time by having to change your film less often.

CAMERAS

Check the battery before you take your camera to an important event. Always have a spare on hand to avoid the disappointment of missing a once-in-a-lifetime photograph.

Change the camera battery once a year. Make it part of an annual event such as preparing for the Christmas holidays, planning for your summer vacation, or changing your clocks.

Buy a used camera if you are just learning about photography and want to experiment with an elaborate 35mm model. Used cameras usually cost about half the price.

Camera scams. Be wary of discount camera stores that offer extraordinary deals on cameras and equipment. Often the cut-rate prices exclude necessary items such as straps and cases or apply only to shoddy products.

Down time. If you don't plan on using your camera for a month or more, finish and develop the roll of film in it. Images on undeveloped film tend to lose some of their sharpness with time.

CAMPING

Keep nighttime safety in mind when you select a campsite. Remove small rocks that someone could stumble over in the dark. Place a warning marker or rope off any areas that could be hazardous, such as ledges, logs, or riverbanks.

Trial run. Set up the tent in the backyard before you take children on a camping trip. This lets the kids become acquainted with the experience and gives you an opportunity to test your gear.

Dry soggy boots. Plant two sturdy sticks in the ground and place damp boots upside down on the ends. This also helps to keep pesky insects from climbing into your footgear.

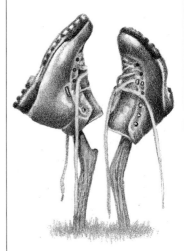

Test the ground before you pitch a tent. Does it slope too much? Are there any ruts or roots to cause you discomfort while you sleep? If so, keep looking.

Check out your gear. Before you leave on a camping trip, be sure that your tent is in good repair and that all your other equipment is working. Don't be caught short when you are far from help late at night.

Take a lightweight headlamp in addition to a flashlight. The headlamp will free your hands, allowing you to work more efficiently around the camp in the dark.

Improvise a campsite lantern by puncturing three or four holes in the sides of an open-topped tin can and standing a candle on the can's bottom. A few drops of hot wax will hold the candle in place.

CANDLES & CANDLESTICKS

Wobbly candle? Steady it with double-sided cellophane tape wrapped around the bottom. The tape will stick to the candle and its holder and is invisible, even in glass candleholders.

Buy dripless candles. They cost a little more, but they save hours of your time cleaning wax off candleholders and tablecloths.

In case of emergency. The longest-burning candles are the short, fat "emergency candles" sold in hardware stores. They burn for as long as 50 hours.

To light an autumn table, use a varied collection of small pumpkins and gourds as candleholders. Cut holes just big enough to insert a candle in the top of each fruit, leaving the seeds and pulp inside to weight it down. Arrange the fruits, of varying shapes and colors, as the centerpiece.

Extend the life of ornamental candles by chilling them in the refrigerator for several hours before lighting them.

For a sparkling effect, fill a shallow glass bowl halfway with water and float in it several small, round candles designed for the purpose. Add a few flower petals or large blooms to the water, and place the bowl, candles lighted, on the buffet or dining table.

Light a party pathway with traditional Mexican paper luminaria. Fill small paper bags with just enough sand to keep them from blowing over, insert a small votive candle into the sand, and set the bags with lighted candles along the walkway to the party.

Quick candle centerpieces can be easily improvised for holiday tables. A cluster of red, green, and white candles, varied in height and girth, can be decorated with fresh evergreens and foil stars for Christmas; several slender white tapers set among potted lilies are perfect for Easter; red, and white candles banded with ribbons set off fireworks on a Canada Day picnic table.

CAMP COOKING

One of the keys to a successful camping trip is hearty, easy-to-prepare food. To make sure the culinary side of your camping trip goes well, keep the following tips in mind.

▶ *Plan menus ahead of time. Store the foods for each meal in protective plastic bags, label each meal's bag, and pack the bags chronologically for easy access.*

▶ *Sample the foods you plan to eat on the trip at home. After a day of hiking, the campsite is no place to discover that you don't like a particular canned or freeze-dried stew.*

▶ *Enjoy nature's bounty by including edible native plants in your campfire dishes. For example, spruce up a salad with dandelion greens or wild onions. Consult a field guide to make sure you are choosing foods that are not poisonous.*

▶ *Take along healthy snacks that won't spoil if kept unrefrigerated for a day or two, including beef jerky, sliced carrots, bagels, crackers, trail mix, dried fruit, hard salami, hard cheeses, and nuts.*

▶ *Never cook inside the tent. Stoves can create lethal levels of carbon monoxide. On rainy days, set up your stove right outside the tent under an awning—but make sure that the tent is well ventilated.*

C

CAR BATTERIES

Replace a car battery before it loses too much power. (Check six months before its warranty expires, which is about the time batteries start to fade.) A weak battery causes the car's charging system to work overtime and its starter motor to overheat.

Always buy the biggest and longest-lasting battery you can fit into your car. A powerful battery saves wear and tear on the vehicle's starting, charging, and electrical systems.

Cranking power. Replace an old battery with one of the same or greater CCA rating (cold-cranking amp rating), which reflects the temperature at which a battery can be charged for 30 seconds at −18°C (0°F).

Beware the battery scam. Check for the temperature at which the CCA is rated. It should say "0°F" (Fahrenheit) next to the CCA rating. A cheap battery may appear to have an appropriate CCA rating when in fact the rating was taken at 0°C (Celsius), which is actually 32°F. In other words, the battery is not guaranteed to function properly at lower temperatures.

A battery that won't start may still have plenty of juice. The problem may be a loose cable connection, which you can readily take care of yourself. Check the cable connections and tighten any loose ones with a wrench. Try again to start the car. If the battery still won't turn over, you should call for help.

Jump-starting a car battery with the ignition turned on is the most frequent cause of car computer failure. Turn off the ignition and remove the key before connecting jumper cables to your battery.

Because the battery is dead, you may forget the key is turned on.

Dirty battery terminals can adversely affect the electronic equipment in your car, including the computer, which in turn affects the digital dashboard displays as well as the cellular phone if you have one.

CAR BUYING

Keep an open mind. If you can settle on two or three choices of automobile makes and models rather than just one, you will have more opportunity to negotiate a good price. When salespeople realize you'll be just as happy to go elsewhere, they'll try harder to get your business.

High-demand cars. If the car you want is a popular model, try to buy it through a buying club or an auto broker. Either is likely to get you a better price than you'll be able to negotiate yourself.

Test-drive at least three cars before making a decision on which one to buy. Be sure the demonstration models have the same engine, transmission, and options that you are considering.

RIGHT STUFF

A CAR EMERGENCY KIT

The jack, lug wrench, and spare tire that come with your car will certainly help you change a tire, but there are many emergencies they can't handle. With this compact kit, you're a one-person maintenance crew. You can jump-start your battery, siphon gas from another car, tape a leaking hose or belt, signal for help, light flares to let other cars know your position on the road, fix a flat, and ask for a tow. And you won't even get your hands dirty—plastic gloves are included.

Financing sense. Unless the manufacturer is offering a special low rate, you should shop around for a car loan. Many banks also offer special car loans that offer "buy back" clauses or lower monthly car payments.

When to close the deal. Approach the salesperson near closing time on a Saturday, particularly the last Saturday of the month. Why? Many salespeople get bonuses for particular weekly and monthly sales records, and your sale may put that person over the top.

Delivery. Make a careful daytime inspection of a new car before you accept it. At night you won't be able to see imperfections such as in the paint or the upholstery.

CAR CLEANING

Car-wash savvy. Put your car through brushless car washes. The spinning cloths and brushes used in many car washes can damage your car's paint. After having your car washed inside and out, put baking soda in the ashtray to make the interior smell fresh.

Family home project. Get everyone in on the washing of the car. Even toddlers can help dry the sides of the car and the hubcaps with soft rags. Car washing goes much faster with many hands.

 To preserve the shine on your car and to provide maximum surface protection, wax the car at least twice a year—in the late spring and in the late fall. Use a product that cleans, polishes, and waxes in one step.

Saving surfaces. A silicone-based protective spray will keep dashboards, vinyl interiors, and

HOW TO WASH A CAR

The easiest way to keep your car looking good and to protect its finish is to wash it yourself occasionally. Follow these steps.

◗ *Park the car in the shade and let the motor cool before you start to work. The cool temperature prevents water spotting as the car dries. Vacuum the inside.*

◗ *Use a washing product that is pH-balanced (the bottle will say so), or add 15 mL (1 tbsp) of baking soda to 3.8 L (0.8 gal) of washing solution to neutralize acid rain, a country-wide problem. (Acid rain mottles the surface of newer cars, which have a clear-coat finish.)*

◗ *Start at the top and work down. Rinse the vehicle first with cool water to wash away loose dirt and soften the stuck-on dirt. Don't use a high-pressure spray; it will push grit, road salt, and grime up into cracks and crevices, where it will remain.*

◗ *Wash one panel at a time. Use back-and-forth motions, not circular ones. And keep rinsing as you work to carry away the dirt and abrasive sand. Use a clean mitt or sponge and rinse it often.*

◗ *For the final rinse, remove the spray nozzle and hose the car with a medium flow of water. The large sheets of water created make drying easier. Wipe the car dry carefully with a clean, soft cloth.*

tires from cracking or dulling prematurely. Such products guard surfaces against the harmful effects of ozone, oxygen, and ultraviolet rays.

CAR LEASING

Comparison shop. Leasing companies differ widely. The larger ones often give the best deals because they are less strict about charging for "normal wear and tear" and offer free perks such as oil changes, wiper refills, minor repairs, road service and towing, and loaner cars during repairs.

Rule of thumb. If you want to keep a car for more than 42 months, you should buy it. For a

shorter amount of time, leasing may make more sense.

 Trade up. Leasing may allow you to drive a more expensive car than you could buy with the same monthly payments.

Leasing terms are negotiable. Haggle over leasing terms in the same way that you would over the selling price of a new car. Pin down mileage allowances, the term "excess wear and tear," the maintenance schedule, and whether or not you pay a penalty if you terminate.

C

CAR MAINTENANCE

 Home inspections. Before you get in your car each day, walk around it and carefully look it over. You may spot a tire that needs air or a dragging tailpipe that should be fixed before it causes trouble.

Tune-ups. Today's cars don't need a full tune-up every 16,000 km (10,000 mi). An annual computerized engine analysis, done at your local garage or car dealership, can pinpoint any problems. Older cars (those produced before 1980) still need regular tune-ups.

Motor oil. Change petroleum-based oil every 4,800 km (3,000 mi) or every three months, whichever comes first. If you use synthetic oil in your car, you can go 12,000 km (7,500 mi) or six months between oil changes.

Wax test. To know when it's time to rewax the finish on your car, flick a few drops of water on the hood and watch how they puddle. If they don't bead, the wax is thin and needs replenishing.

CAR RENTALS

Before you drive off the lot, take time to familiarize yourself with your rental car. Which side is the gas tank on? Are there remote release levers for the tank cap or trunk? Does the ignition lock, and is there a special trick to removing the key? Does the car have air bags or operate with an antilock brake system (ABS)? Adjust the driver's seat and the rearview mirrors. Test the light, signals, horn, windshield wipers, air conditioner, heater, and radio. Refuse to accept the car if these items do not function properly.

Discounts. If your company, automobile club, or another affiliation qualifies you for a rental-car discount, be sure that it is applied to the total bill before you sign your name on the charge slip.

Insurance savings. You may not need to buy the rental company's optional insurance. Check the

CAR MAINTENANCE

Keeping a car in good running condition helps it last longer. Besides checking the fluids listed below, you should also routinely change the air filter (every 24,000 km [15,000 mi]) and check the belts and hoses (at every oil change).

Antifreeze. Have the reservoir checked at least once a year—before winter in cold parts of the country.

Power steering fluid. Have it checked at least twice a year and before any long trip.

Transmission fluid. Check every 3 months; replace every 40,000 km (25,000 mi) on front-wheel-drives, every 80,000 km (50,000 mi) on rear-wheel-drives.

Brake fluid. Have it checked at every oil change. It should be flushed and replaced every 2 years or 39,000 km (24,000 mi), whichever comes first.

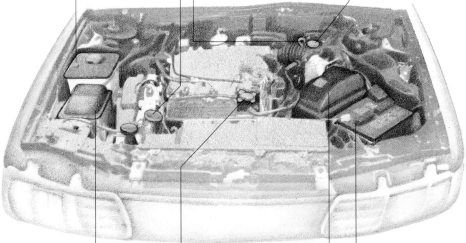

Windshield wiper fluid. Check the level monthly; refill as needed with commercial washer fluid to prevent freeze-ups.

Oil. Change it every 4,800 km (3,000 mi) or 3 months.

Air filter. Replace it every 24,000 km (15,000 mi). A clogged filter can lead to stalling and poor gas mileage.

Battery. If your battery is not permanently sealed, check the level of the battery fluid several times a year. If necessary, fill with distilled water.

policies for your own car as well as your homeowners insurance. You may already be covered.

Refill the gas tank yourself before you return a rental car; it's considerably cheaper than having the rental company charge you for refilling.

CAR SECURITY

Security hardware. Alarms, steering wheel clubs, steering wheel braces, and ignition interrupters might not stop the professional car thief—who may use a tow truck to carry off your car—but such devices will slow down and likely discourage the amateur.

Seasonal alert. Car thieves are most active during the summer months, particularly July and August. They cut back in winter, with February the slowest month.

Hot items. Air bags and engine computers are top targets of thieves who break into cars. You can protect your air bag with a steering wheel cap, but there is no way to secure the computer beyond keeping your car locked and in a safe place.

Smart vanity. The personalized car license plates sold by many provincial motor vehicle departments can actually help protect your car from being stolen. A catchy word on a license plate is easier to spot and to remember than a series of numbers. Thieves are reluctant to take a car that can be so quickly identified.

High-risk cars. Some makes and models of cars, usually luxury-class cars, are more popular with thieves than others. Check with

HOW MUCH IS YOUR CAR WORTH?

How do you arrive at a fair price to ask for your car? It's not as mysterious as you might think. Just follow the steps listed below.

▶ *Look up your car's value in the* CANADIAN RED BOOK, *issued by the Canadian Automobile Dealers Association (1-905-829-5133). This gives you the wholesale or trade-in value of the car's make, model, and year, as well as allowances for accessories, mileage, and condition.*

▶ *Check the retail prices of comparable cars in dealers' and private ads in the newspaper.*

▶ *Pick a price higher than wholesale and slightly under retail. Determine an asking price and then the minimum amount you will accept.*

your insurance company before you buy a new car to be sure you aren't asking for a security problem with your choice.

CAR SELLING

For the best price, sell your old car yourself rather than trading it in on a new car. To make any money, the car dealer has to buy at wholesale prices and sell at retail. By selling the car yourself, you will get a price that is closer to that of retail.

Advertise the car in your local newspaper on Saturday and Sunday, when most people look for new cars. Describe the car truthfully, giving model and year, body style, color, mileage, and a negotiable price.

Tune it up. Since prospective buyers will want to test-drive the car, make sure to get an engine tune-up. Check to see if the lights, windshield wipers, turn signals, horn, and window controls all work properly.

Clean it up. Wash and wax the body and touch up with body paint any nicks or scratches, especially those that may occur

around door and trunk locks. Vacuum and dust the interior and replace badly soiled or worn mats. Oil squeaky hinges.

Road test. Insist on riding with the prospective buyer for the road test. Don't give a stranger an easy opportunity to steal your car.

Payment. Accept only cash or a certified check. Then notify your provincial motor vehicle department and insurance company of the sale so that you won't be held responsible for the new owner's mishaps or misdemeanors.

C

CAREER ADVANCEMENT

Continue your education. Just putting in time doesn't always lead to pay raises and promotions. Make yourself more valuable by expanding your skills. Take courses and attend training sessions. Read trade literature and stay up-to-date. Study new technologies and techniques.

Toot your own horn. Keep notes of your accomplishments and any kudos you receive. Place these notes in a file, which will come in handy during your annual performance reviews.

Be computer literate. If you're still mystified by the technology, it's time to get a book, hire a tutor, or take a basic course. Learn to work comfortably on a computer—it's much easier than most "computerphobes" think.

Use a diary. Carry a message pad and a pen in your pocket at all times. Make a note when you say you'll make a call or promise to write a memo or agree to carry out a task. Refer to your notes as part of your daily routine; they can help you become known as a dependable employee who follows through and delivers.

Use your creativity. Take part in formal and informal brainstorming sessions about such subjects as

EASY DOES IT

AN OUNCE OF PREVENTION

The following exercises, which reduce pressure on the nerves in your wrists, may help keep carpal tunnel at bay. Do them often throughout the day to avoid stiffening up.

▶ *Lift your arms until they are straight in front of you. Flex your hands as if you were pressing them flat against a wall. Hold for five seconds.*

▶ *Arms in front of you, let your hands dangle loosely from your wrists. Hold for five seconds.*

▶ *Clench your hands into tight fists. Keeping your arms straight in front of you, bend your wrists so that your fists are pointing toward the floor. Hold for five seconds.*

promoting new products, improving service, and solving office problems. Show enthusiasm and insight in addressing long- and short-term organizational goals.

 Show responsibility. A promotion usually means taking greater responsibility, so look for opportunities to prove you can handle it. Volunteer to organize a new project or to manage the details of an ongoing project that is making life difficult for your boss.

CAREER SELECTION

Assess yourself. Take an inventory of your interests, skills, physical needs, and personality traits to help you choose a career path. Consult with a career counselor and take a battery of aptitude assessment tests.

Research job market trends and find out which fields are expected to expand in the future. Libraries, on-line services, and job counselors are among the best sources for up-to-date information on these trends.

Practical experience helps you judge how well you'll like a particular profession. Get an internship or a summer job in the field you're considering. Investigate human service careers by doing volunteer work, write for the student newspaper if you want to be a reporter, or agree to be treasurer of an organization if you want to pursue accounting or business.

Make a plan. A plan of action can give a young person a strong start toward achieving career goals. The plan should include completing the necessary education, working with the college placement office, attending career fairs and recruitment events, and networking with professionals.

CARPAL TUNNEL SYNDROME

Pain in your wrist doesn't necessarily indicate carpal tunnel syndrome. True carpal tunnel starts with feelings of numbness and tingling in the thumb, middle, and index fingers and eventually leads to persistent wrist pain. If you experience these symptoms, see your doctor.

Take frequent breaks to give your hands and wrists a chance to rest. You need these moments of relief when you perform repetitive motion tasks for extended periods of time.

Not just computer users suffer repetitive motion strains. Musicians, artists, doctors—any one who must use repetitve motion—needs to take precautions.

CARPET CARE

Remove indentations caused by furniture with a steam iron. Hold the hot iron over the area and let the steam penetrate to loosen the fibers; as they cool, fluff them up with your fingers.

To lift chewing gum from a carpet, first rub the gum with an ice cube, then scrape it off with a blunt knife. Dab the area with a rag dipped in cleaning fluid.

To repair a small burn or stain in pile carpeting, simply snip off the affected tufts with nail scissors. For a deeper problem, cut out the piece and use it as a pattern to cut a plug from a leftover carpet scrap. Dab glue around the edges of the replacement plug, align its fibers with the rest of the rug, and set it in place.

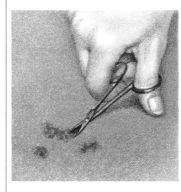

Treat spills immediately. Blot up as much as you can with clean towels, then pour club soda on the spot. Let the soda sit a few minutes, then blot it up with a clean sponge. Repeat if necessary.

CARPETING

Stair strategy. Buy an extra 45 cm (18 in.) of runner carpeting and fold it under on the bottom step. As the runner begins to show wear along the outside edge of each tread, untack and unfold 5 cm (2 in.) from the bottom step and move the runner up all the way to the top. Snip off the extra length at the top before retacking the runner. You can do this two or three times before you have to replace it.

Create a geometric floor design using two colors of carpet tiles. Work out a pattern on graph paper first, then lay the tiles according to the manufacturer's directions.

Cozy cover-up. Cover worn places or stains in the carpet with attractive throw rugs. They will make the room look cozier and save the cost of new carpeting.

CARPET FIBERS

No carpet fiber is perfect; each has different characteristics. Choose carpeting according to where you want to use it and what your budget requires. Stairs and hallways take the most abuse and benefit most from dense, durable carpeting. Bedrooms generally have the lightest traffic. The best carpets of any fiber are densely made with the tufts very close together. Bend a corner of the carpet over; the less of the backing you can see, the better.

FIBER	CHARACTERISTICS	PRICE RANGE	PROS AND CONS
Acrylic	Natural looking; most woollike in in appearance and feel of all the man-made fibers.	Moderately inexpensive	Only moderately durable. Resists water-soluble stains but is susceptible to oily stains. Resists moisture and mildew.
Nylon	Takes color well and comes in a wide range of clear shades. Considered the strongest carpeting fiber.	Wide price range	Very durable. Conceals and resists soil; resists water-soluble stains. Unaffected by mildew. Resists shedding and pilling. Look for a brand with static control.
Olefin	Colorfast in a limited range of shades. Used indoors for kitchens and basements and outdoors on walks and patios.	Inexpensive	Very durable. Resists soil and stains. Resists moisture and mildew. Resistant to static.
Polyester	Comes in a wide range of colors and has a soft and luxurious appearance.	Inexpensive	Only moderately durable. Resists water-soluble stains but susceptible to oily stains. Needs frequent cleaning.
Wool	Comes in a wide range of colors and textures and has a soft and luxurious appearance.	Expensive	Very durable and crush resistant. Resists soil but susceptible to staining.

CARPOOLING

Avoid disagreements among fellow riders by establishing rules from the start. For example, come to a consensus on what type of music, if any, will be played on the car stereo, how gasoline and other expenses will be paid for, or who will drive when the regular driver is ill.

Obtain car insurance that covers potential injury all passengers when you drive. Your policy may cover only family members.

Ask to be dropped off several blocks from your home so that you can walk the last leg of your journey. This is the perfect opportunity to get some exercise and unwind from a busy day.

CATS

Introduce a scratching post to help keep your cat's claws in good shape and to protect your furniture. If he resists using it, rub catnip on it to make it more enticing.

Don't allow cats to play with string unsupervised. They often swallow the string, which then gets caught inside their intestines. Also watch that your cat doesn't swallow thread, dental floss, paper ribbon, or holiday tinsel.

Bury citrus rinds in the soil of your houseplants to keep cats from digging. Orange, grapefruit, lemon, or lime rinds are all unpopular with felines.

Honk first. Beware of cats napping next to a warm car engine in the winter. Honk or bang on the car hood to alert any animals.

 Dogs and cats. Probably the best way to have a dog and cat in the same household is to raise them together from the time they are very young.

Coat a pill for kitty with a little butter or vegetable oil to make it go down more easily. Pinch the cat's jaw to open it, push the pill to the back of his throat, and hold his mouth shut until he swallows.

Avoid feeding your cats too much magnesium-rich fish. Even though cats love the flavor, fish can cause urinary problems, especially among male cats. Treat them to fish only occasionally.

Choose an appropriate breed. As with dogs, different breeds of cats have different personalities.

For example, Himalayan and Persian cats tend to be gentle and placid (although their long hair requires a lot of grooming), while Siamese and Abyssinian cats are busy, active animals. American Shorthairs are generally independent sorts, while Burmese cats prefer human company.

Accustom your cat to a baby. Before bringing a newborn home from the hospital, give the cat a piece of the baby's clothing. When the baby arrives in the house, the cat, though curious, will be less likely to bother or harm the baby.

To remove the smell of urine that has permeated wood, upholstery, or carpeting, use products such as Natural Magic Pet Deodorizer, Nature's Miracle, and Natural World's Non-Toxic Pet Stain and Odor Remover. Available through your local pet shop, these products destroy the pungent smell of cat urine by oxidizing odor-producing bacteria.

CD-ROM'S

Problems with your CD-ROM? If a disc is malfunctioning, grime on its surface may be causing your CD-ROM drive's laser to misread it. Remove the disc from the drive

---

RECOGNIZING YOUR CAT'S MOODS

Although cats don't speak, their faces can express their emotions and desires quite clearly. To understand more easily what your cat is up to, watch for the following clues.

HAPPY CAT	**HUNTING CAT**	**FRIGHTENED CAT**	**ANGRY CAT**

Ears straight up, relaxed whiskers, normal pupils, eyes half closed	Ears up and forward, whiskers forward, large pupils, eyes wide or in slits	Ears flattened, whiskers foward, very large pupils, eyes wide open	Ears up but curved back, whiskers forward, pupils and eyes in slits

LAST-MINUTE CENTERPIECES

When you're having friends over to dinner on the spur of the moment, you probably won't have time to create a lavish centerpiece. Below are a few ideas for quick and easy table toppers.

▶ *Arrange colorful vegetables in a basket. Use fresh green, red, and yellow peppers, beautiful carrots, a lavish eggplant, even a cabbage or a cauliflower. An edible arrangement is both attractive and practical.*

▶ *Pile seasonal fruit in a crystal or glass bowl. Select a dozen or more of a single fruit, such as apples, oranges, peaches, pears, or even lemons—whatever is in season.*

▶ *If it's summer and your herb garden is overflowing, make a lush bouquet of fresh herbs such as rosemary, basil, mint, lemon verbena, or lavender—whatever herbs are handy— and place it in a simple jar or kitchen pitcher.*

and carefully wipe the shiny side with a lightly moistened dust- and lint-free cloth. Be sure the surface is completely dry before returning the disc to the drive.

Play audio CD's. Music CD's will play just fine in your CD-ROM drive; both Windows and Mac operating systems include audio-CD player software. If your stereo system's receiver has a spare audio-in plug, you can connect your computer sound output to it—a great way to enhance game play and multimedia CD-ROM's.

You can use powered speakers with your computer system to enhance the sound, but make sure to buy speakers that are magnetically shielded. Otherwise, emissions from the speakers may distort your monitor's picture.

CELLULAR TELEPHONES

Limit incoming calls to your cellular telephone to keep charges to a minimum. Give your number out only to family, good friends, and close business associates.

Store frequently used numbers in the cell phone's automatic dialing device. This prevents you from being needlessly charged for a key-punching mistake. Also, you won't have to take your eyes off the road if you're driving.

Make calls at off-peak hours to keep costs down. Also, let the person you call know that you are on a cellular phone; that way, he may realize the expense and will try to keep the conversation brief.

Report billing errors quickly. Pirating of telephone numbers, particularly in congested areas, is on the increase. If you don't require international dialing, don't sign up for it. That way, if crooks obtain your number, the calling charges will be limited.

CENTERPIECES

Seasonal displays that you can make yourself can save money and time. Use a Christmas wreath during the holiday season, colored leaves and small gourds in autumn, wildflowers in summer, and tulips, forsythia, and pussywil-

lows in spring. A bonus is that many of these items can be gathered from your garden.

Go for simplicity. When creating your own centerpieces, focus on a single item: place a huge bouquet of daffodils in a simple vase, pile succulent pears in a wooden bowl, or fill a pitcher with fresh-picked Queen Anne's lace.

Conversation stopper. When creating a centerpiece for a dinner party, make sure it is not so tall as to intrude on guests' ability to converse across the table. Consider instead tiny individual bouquets at each place.

Use everyday objects creatively for designs. For a Mediterranean dinner theme, for example, tier three colorful imported tomato cans (the bottom two unopened; the top one empty). In the top can, arrange clipped sunflowers, dahlias, chrysanthemums, or other bright blooms that accentuate the colors on the cans.

Groupies. Place a single blossom in each of several various-sized crystal or glass bud vases. Or group 10 or 12 candles (none whose flame is at eye level) in the center of the table on a platter or in a flat-bottomed basket. Spread fresh flower petals or fragrant potpourri around the candles.

CHAIRS

Virtue in diversity. A disparate group of wooden chairs can make an interesting dining-room set. By painting or staining them the same color and then covering each seat with the same fabric, they will appear to be intriguing members of the same furniture family. If the seats are not upholstered, add matching seat pillows.

Short of chairs? Add a fitted cushion to almost any low and sturdy storage piece—a trunk, a blanket chest, or a footlocker—and gain seating. A one-drawer file cabinet or the shelf under a window can work just as well.

Nice and easy. Freshen a tired easy chair with an inexpensive one-size-fits-all slipcover, now available at many furniture or home-improvement stores. The fit may be generous, but the fabrics are attractive and have the added benefit of being washable.

CHANUKAH

Decorate for a party with a lighted menorah in the front window. Hang six-pointed Stars of David, made from construction paper in the traditional blue and white holiday colors, from the ceiling. Cut out menorahs from gold construction paper and use as place cards.

 A gift a day. Instead of having your children buy gifts, help them make a small present—a drawing, a beaded necklace, even a homemade dreidel (a decorative spinning top)—for each of the eight days of the holiday.

Host a treasure hunt. Fill colorful velvet pouches with the traditional wrapped coins of chocolate called Chanukah gelt. Hide them and give out written clues so that your kids and their friends can hunt for them.

Create a tradition. The third night of Chanukah, called the Third Candle of Tzedakah, marks the Jewish mandate of tzedakah, or acts of righteousness. On this day, host a party and ask guests to bring new toys, canned food or clothing to be distributed to needy families in the community. Hold the party every year.

CHARITABLE DONATIONS

Check before you give. Some so-called charities exist to support the fund-raisers who call or send mailings to you. To find out if a charity is legit and just how much of your donation it spends on charitable works, contact the Canadian Center For Philanthropy (416-515-0764). The Center publishes a newsletter, *Front & Center*, a *Directory of Foundations* and an annual *Resource Guide* providing information on national charities.

Give appreciated stock instead of cash as a charitable donation. Not only will you get an income-tax deduction for the stock's current value, but you also avoid paying tax on the capital gain.

When you donate clothing and furniture, be sure that the organization gives you a receipt for the fair market value of the goods so that your donation is eligible for a tax deduction.

Re-covering an upholstered seat on a straight chair

Replacing the fabric on many chair seats is a snap and no costlier than the fabric and some staples.

1 Upend the chair and unscrew the padded seat board at the corners. Remove the seat board and turn upside down on a flat surface.

2 With a screwdriver and long-nose pliers, remove the tacks or staples securing the fabric and liner, if any, to the seat.

3 Using the old fabric as a pattern, cut the new cover. Also cut new padding if necessary. Center the padding and new fabric on the seat board.

Keep a record of all the cash contributions you make and ask for a receipt from the organization. Even canceled cheques made out to a legitimate charity may not qualify as tax-deductible without a receipt.

CHEESE

To inhibit mold growth on cheese, wrap the cheese in a vinegar-dampened paper towel, then seal it inside a plastic bag. Remoisten the cloth with vinegar as needed.

Make it last. You can preserve expensive Parmesan by grating the cheese completely, then storing it in an airtight plastic container in the freezer. No need to thaw it; use the grated Parmesan straight from the freezer.

Great grating. Put a semisoft cheese such as Gouda or Tilsit in the freezer for about 10 minutes before grating, slicing, chopping, or shredding it. When very cold, such cheeses are easier to handle.

Cool cooking. To prevent cheese from turning rubbery when it is added to a sauce, keep the cooking temperature low until the cheese has blended with the other ingredients.

Instead of grated cheese, top off a salad or soup with thick, luscious shavings of Parmesan, Romano, or another hard cheese. Make shaving extra easy by using a vegetable peeler.

Healthy alternatives. Don't let a recipe that calls for high-fat cheese keep you from making a favorite dish. You can substitute less fatty but equally flavorful cheeses. Try feta cheese instead of Parmesan over pasta; goat cheese instead of Monterey Jack on enchiladas; and low-fat cream cheese instead of regular cream cheese as a spread.

CHEQUING ACCOUNTS

Use "top-stub" cheques, or cheques with a recording stub attached to each cheque. These may cost a few dollars more than regular cheque books, but they allow you to balance your account with greater facility— and thus avoid steep fees if you accidentally bounce a cheque.

Keep it simple. Plain cheques in a vinyl cheque book cost less than those with elaborate paintings in a faux leather cheque book. So long as your name and address are printed on it, a plain cheque is just as valid as a fancy one.

Use direct deposit. Save time by having pay cheques deposited directly in your account. Many government payments qualify for direct deposit free of charge, and many employers offer it for payroll cheques as well.

4 Use a staple gun to attach the new fabric tautly over the padding to the underside of the seat board. Miter the corners as neatly as you can.

5 If your chair has a liner, you can staple it over the edges of the cover fabric for a neat finish. Or just turn the cover edges under and staple.

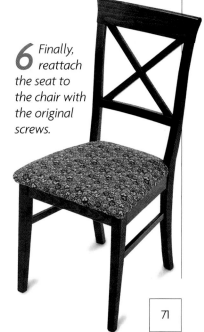

6 Finally, reattach the seat to the chair with the original screws.

CHICKEN LEFTOVERS

Nothing is more comforting than a simple, unadorned roast chicken. Switch gears the next night by transforming leftovers into the taste-tempting meals below.

▶ *Chicken Salad. Toss shredded chicken in a bowl with salad greens, scallions, celery, chopped avocado, olives, or grated cheese. Dress with a simple vinaigrette.*

▶ *Chicken Pasta. Mix chicken, peas, and mushrooms into a simple white sauce. Serve over your favorite pasta.*

▶ *Chicken Pizza. Slice a focaccia round in half, drizzle on oil, and add chicken slices, herbs, tomato sauce, and some grated Parmesan cheese. Broil until the cheese is bubbly.*

▶ *Chicken Stir-fry. Cube chicken pieces, then stir-fry with garlic, broccoli, mushrooms, bok choy, and garlic in a tangy soy sauce. Serve over rice.*

▶ *Chicken Soup. Add cubed chicken pieces, leftover vegetables, and noodles to a good-quality canned chicken broth for an almost-homemade soup.*

CHEWING GUM

No scissors needed. You can remove chewing gum from hair with peanut butter. Apply an ample amount of peanut butter and gently rub it throught the hair until the gum comes out out. Follow up with a thorough shampoo.

First impressions. Although some social mores have changed, it is still considered impolite to chew gum in public. Never do it in any situation where you want to make a professional impression.

Airplane etiquette. Chewing gum when you're airborne not only is acceptable but helps prevent painful ear blockage due to changes in air pressure. Keep a couple of sticks handy to chew during takeoff and landing in order to "pop" your ears.

CHICKEN

Healthy choice. Pick skinless, boneless breast meat as a low-fat way to enjoy chicken. Beware of overcooking, however; because it is so lean, this meat cooks in about 10 minutes and can dry out quickly if it is not watched.

Milky way. Soak chicken breasts, in milk, yogurt or buttermilk for three to four hours before cooking. The milk bath not only gives the chicken a soothing flavor, it improves the texture as well.

Try marinades spiced with soy sauce, curry powder, orange juice, or herb-flavored vinegar and oil. Bottled salad dressing also works well. Chicken absorbs flavors easily, so it needs to marinate for only an hour or two to take in added flavor.

Don't thaw chicken on the kitchen counter, or harmful bacteria may proliferate on the counter and in the meat. To inhibit bacteria from growing, thaw poultry either in your refrigerator, which takes a day or two, or in your microwave, which takes about a half hour.

Deboning trick. Chicken is easier to skin and bone when it is partially frozen.

Microwave cooking. When roasting chicken in a microwave oven, arrange the pieces in a ring with the fat side facing out to assure more even cooking.

CHILD CARE CENTERS

Research several centers. At each center you consider, meet the director and ask many questions, such as: Do the children play outside every day? Are toys available for both active and quiet play? Are parent-teacher conferences scheduled regularly? Are parents encouraged to spend time at the center?

Check out the playground. Look carefully at the swings and other equipment. They should be sturdy and well maintained. For safety's sake, playground equipment should be set in earth or sand rather than a nonresilient surface like concrete.

Check out the staff. The head teachers, at least, should have degrees in early childhood education; the entire staff should be experienced in caring for infants. Ask about staff turnover. A stable staff often indicates a well-run center with dedicated caregivers.

Avoid overcrowded facilities. Experts recommend one caregiver for every three infants and a maximum of six infants; one caregiver for every four toddlers and a maximum of 12 toddlers; one caregiver for every eight preschoolers which is the maximum number.

Prepare your child. Talk to your child about what the day will be like at the center, and arrange a visit in advance so that your child can familiarize herself.

CHILDPROOFING YOUR HOME

Gain perspective. Survey every room in your house from a child's point of view. Get down on the floor to see what dangers lie within the child's reach. Babies and toddlers, for example, might be exposed to sharp edges on a chair or become fascinated by an electrical socket that is out of your normal range of vision.

Hide the hardware. Vocal commands are not enough to protect children from dangerous objects, as well as harmful cleaners and drugs. Avoid needless risk by locking up hazardous objects and substances in places children cannot reach. Attach childproof safety locks to accessible cabinets.

Decorate for safety. Children love to turn beds, sofas, and chairs into play platforms. Prevent accidents by positioning furniture away from drapery cords, appliances, lamps, and windows.

Fence in the playground. Outdoor play areas for toddlers should be inaccessible to the street or to hazards like yard tools, mowers, chemicals, or swimming pools.

CHILD SAFETY SEATS

Test-fit before you buy. Child safety seats for cars come in many shapes and sizes, and not all products will fit in all cars. Before you invest in one, especially if you drive a compact car, test-fit it to check how well the size and shape will work in your vehicle. Most stores will let you try a seat out before you purchase it.

Throw your weight around. A child seat should be belted and fastened tightly so that it won't move or shift as the car takes corners. Lean forward with your knee on the car seat while you pull the seat belt taut and snap it to get a snug fit.

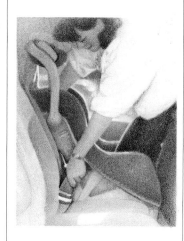

Pedal safely. Small children should be carried on bicycles only in proper safety seats and when wearing a well-fitted helmet. In some regions it is illegal to transport a child under one year of age on a bicycle. Check with the local police about your community's laws and consult a bicycle shop for information about the best equipment to use for carrying children on bicycles.

CHILDREN'S CHORES

Chores are a part of being in a family. Start early; even toddlers can be taught appropriate ways to help out around the house. **Add to their responsibilities as they get older.**

AGES 2–3	AGE 4	AGE 5	AGE 6	AGES 7–9	AGES 10–12
Put toys in bin	Bring in paper	Take out garbage	Load and unload dishwasher	Wipe off table after eating	Empty trash cans
Brush teeth	Set table	Pick up toys	Keep room tidy	Fold and hang up clothes	Vacuum
Fill pets' bowls	Pull weeds in garden; water flowers with a hose	Put clothes away	Make own snacks or lunch	Straighten up bathroom	Help plan and cook meals
Put clothes in hamper	Sort or help fold laundry	Put groceries away	Clean mirrors and windows	Arrange own play dates	Organize parts of garage and closets
Fold napkins	Decorate thank-you notes	Tear up lettuce for salad	Answer telephone and learn to dial	Help with yardwork	Do laundry

CHILDREN'S PARTIES

Keep it short. Children get excited about parties but also quickly become tired and bored—even if you've planned a half-dozen party games. An hour and a half to two hours is plenty of party time for youngsters.

Keep it small. The number of young guests at a children's party should not exceed the honoree's age.

Keep it simple. Don't bring out the antique porcelain and the best linen. Instead, serve food on paper plates and drinks in plastic cups. Use paper tablecloths and mats. Better yet, use butcher's paper and let the kids design their own decorations with crayons and colored markers.

Serve plain, familiar foods such as pizza, hamburgers, or hot dogs. For a birthday party, serve the celebrant's favorite flavor of cake and ice cream.

Include adults. Supervision is necessary for parties with younger children. For children under age six, the ratio of adults to children should be 1 to 3.

Activity parties. Older children prefer parties that have a central activity such as ice skating, in-line skating, or swimming or that involve visiting an exciting place like a zoo, an amusement park, a museum, or a rock concert.

Theme parties can be great fun for slightly older children. For example, try planning Treasure Hunt. Make a pirate's treasure chest from an old jewelry box, fill it with pennies and other treats, and hide it in the yard. Draw a map for the kids to find it. Or try a Western hoedown. Place a chuck-wagon in the yard, serve hamburgers, baked beans, and trail mix, and teach the kids to square dance.

CHOCOLATE

Chocolate keeps well, especially if it is wrapped tightly in plastic wrap. A "bloom," a gray, dusty-looking coating, may develop if it is refrigerated or if it is a bit old. Don't worry; the chocolate has not "gone bad"—it's still good for eating or cooking.

Zip, melt, decorate. Use a heavy-duty sealable plastic storage bag as a tool for decorating cakes and other pastries with melted chocolate. Place sweet chocolate chunks inside the bag and close it tightly. Immerse the bag in a bowl of very hot water until the chocolate melts—which happens quickly. Remove the bag, snip a tiny hole in one corner, and begin designing!

Melting chocolate? Microwave it. All you need for this easy, no-fuss technique is a small microwave-safe bowl. Place a 28 g (1 oz) square of chocolate in the bowl and microwave on high for one to two minutes, or until the chocolate is shiny and smooth.

White chocolate is misnamed chocolate—it does not always contain cocoa butter and never contains cocoa powder. It should be handled a little differently than dark chocolate, because it is softer at room temperature and sets more quickly. In optimum conditions, white chocolate stays fresh about a year; under the same conditions, dark chocolate lasts twice as long.

Hidden asset. White chocolate's quick-setting properties can save a too-thin buttercream or pastry cream filling. Stir in melted white chocolate, a little bit at a time, until the mixture is thickened.

THEME PARTIES FOR GROWN-UP KIDS

Getting in touch with the kid in you is a great way to celebrate—and relive—days gone by, as well as reconnect with old friends. Here are some ideas for grown-up parties:

▶ *Design festivities around a particular decade. A fifties jitterbug party; a sixties "hippie" party; a seventies "Saturday Night Fever" party. Ask guests to dress in appropriate clothes and provide music from the decade. For a fifties party, play spin the bottle. For a sixties party, get out the lava lamp, tarot cards, and Twister game.*

▶ *Treat a group of friends to a day at an amusement park. Ride the scariest roller coasters and dine on junk food.*

▶ *Host a "Come as the Person You Would Most Like to Be" party. Have guests dress up in the costume or outfit of the person—celebrity, athlete, friend—they most admire.*

RIGHT STUFF

CHOLESTEROL TEST KIT

Test your cholesterol level with a convenient home kit. The kit measures total cholesterol without breaking out levels of high-density lipoproteins (HDL), the good cholesterol that helps clean arteries, and low-density lipoproteins (LDL), the bad cholesterol that clogs arteries. Knowing your total cholesterol count, however, can alert you to a problem.

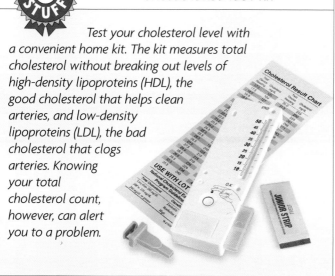

CHOKING

Keep high-risk objects out of the reach of little ones. Hazardous items include toys with small or easily-detached parts, balloons, jewelry, marbles, hardware fasteners, paper clips, tacks, coins, crayon or chalk fragments, buttons, and bottle tops.

 Chew your food. The most common cause of choking is inhaling an unchewed piece of meat. It often occurs when the victim is talking or laughing while eating, eating on the run, or eating while intoxicated.

Foods that cause choking include hot dogs (the biggest single cause of choking among children), seeds, nuts, hard candy, gum, popcorn, fruit pits, grapes, and bones. Cut up children's food into small bites. Don't allow them to run around with food in their mouths or to eat lying down.

Clutching the throat is a typical distress symbol for choking.

Encourage a breathing victim to cough, which may expel the obstruction. If the victim can't speak or cough, apply the Heimlich maneuver.

To perform the Heimlich maneuver on a conscious victim, stand behind him, your arms around his waist. Place one fist, thumb against the abdomen, just above the navel. Hold the fist with your other hand and give a quick, upward thrust. Repeat until the obstruction is expelled.

CHOLESTEROL

Genes influence cholesterol levels. If a history of heart disease runs in your family, monitor your cholesterol levels vigilantly. See your doctor, and use the home cholesterol test regularly. Also, follow a diet and exercise routine that helps keep cholesterol levels down.

Cut fat. To help lower elevated blood cholesterol, restrict your intake of fat to 20 percent of your daily calories. In fact, some nutrition experts recommend that you reduce fat to only 10 percent of calories.

CHOPPING FOOD

For lots of chopping, use a food processor. Keep it out on the countertop, where it can save you time and effort on a daily basis. When preparing dishes with many different types of foods to be chopped, first chop any solids, which leave no mess, and then soft ingredients, which require cleaning the work bowl afterward.

Butcher block reprieve. Research shows that wood is a better chopping surface than plastic in inhibiting bacteria growth. Bacteria don't incubate on wooden boards, while they grow rapidly on plastic boards at room temperature.

When chopping, mincing, or dicing, hold the knife's handle in one hand with your thumb against the blade and place your other hand over the top of the knife. Keeping the blade of the knife on the board, chop using a vertical pivoting motion.

To remove odors and dirt from a wooden cutting board, make a paste of baking soda and water, rub it into the board, then rinse, and allow the board to dry.

To clean a butcher block, let it sit for several hours or overnight coated with coarse salt, which absorbs fats and oils. When you brush off the salt, the oils and fats are discarded with the crystals.

Shiftless. To prevent a cutting board from shifting as you chop, place a damp paper towel or folded dishcloth under it.

CHRISTMAS DECORATIONS

Create a Southern centerpiece. Place a pineapple, a symbol of hospitality, on a plate or tray. Surround it with apples and magnolia leaves or evergreens. Not only is it pretty, but it's fragrant as well.

No poinsettias? Use red chrysanthemums. Or make a centerpiece of white tulips or narcissus, evergreens, and cranberries. Or create "snowballs" out of bunches of white roses with short stems.

A touch of the past. Check out antiques shops and flea markets for vintage wood, glass, or metal ornaments. Complete the old-fashioned look by hanging them on the tree with big Victorian-style bows of green and gold.

A wreath of a different color. Use nontraditional materials to decorate wreaths—toys (wooden soldiers, little dolls, small musical instruments), chocolate kisses, kitchen utensils, lemons and limes, even miniature furniture—whatever you have on hand. Attach with florist's wire or ribbon.

Pillows as decorations. Wrap sofa pillows with ribbon to look like packages. Place a sprig of holiday greenery at each knot. Or wrap pillows in bright fabric and tie the ends with ribbon to resemble a piece of wrapped candy.

Berry alert. If children or pets are around; remove mistletoe or holly berries which are poisonous. Replace with cranberries.

Sweeten the air. Before a Christmas party, place a few drops of vanilla extract on foil and heat in a 175°C (350°F) oven for a few minutes. Or simmer cinnamon sticks in a pan of water on the stove or toss a few into the fireplace.

A festive bathroom. Place a small wreath on the bathroom mirror so that guests will be framed with Christmas greenery.

No fireplace? Have your children draw their own festively decorated fireplace on a large sheet of paper to mount on the wall. Pin real Christmas stockings to the "mantel."

Lighten up. For easy holiday sparkle, put silver or crystal candlesticks on a mirror and watch the lights reverberate around the area when the candles are lit.

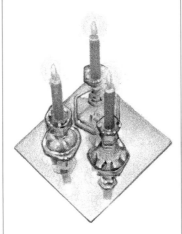

CHRISTMAS GIFTS

Give a gift of time. Instead of spending lots of money on holiday presents, consider offering a generous dose of your time. Alternatives to store-bought gifts can include completing an annoying chore for a busy spouse, baking favorite cookies for Mom, or teaching a child to play the piano.

Recycle old Christmas cards by cutting them up and using them as gift tags for next year's presents.

Make a donation to a charity in someone's name. A card will be sent to that person acknowledging the gift. This is a great gift for an office exchange or for the person who has everything.

Teacher's pet. Best bets for gifts for your children's teachers: pens and markers, tote bags, gift certificates to bookstores or video stores, whimsical pencil or paper clip cases, or hand-stenciled stationery (done jointly by you and your child.)

Expect the unexpected. Have some "emergency" gifts on hand to prevent those embarrassing times when a gift is given and you have none in return. Buy a few generic gifts—a tin of cookies, a box of stationery, pretty candleholders—wrap them, and reach into your ready-wrapped secret stash to give away.

CHRISTMAS RITUALS

A good deed. Each year, include a charitable act as part of your holiday ritual. It could be something big, like giving a tree to a hospital children's ward or collecting food supplies for needy families. Or it could be a something small, like shoveling an elderly neighbor's walk or visiting a sick friend. Encourage your children to join you and participate.

Santa rituals. In addition to leaving a plate of cookies and a glass of milk for Santa, have your child think up additional tokens Santa might need, like water for his reindeer. Follow up on the fantasy. Create snowy footprints and hoofprints (using flour) from the chimney to the tree. Leave a couple of gifts in the fireplace, as if they had slipped out of Santa's bag. Make sure "Santa" eats the cookies—and leaves a thank-you note for your child.

A ritual instead of a gift. Start a yearly tradition with friends and family by celebrating Christmas with a tree-decorating party, a caroling outing, a sledding party, or a recipe exchange party in place of giving presents.

Candleholders for carolers. Save old plastic coffee can lids. When you're ready to go out caroling, create holders for the candles by cutting three 5 cm (2 in.) slits in the lids that intersect in a star shape. Then, simply push the candle through.

Look for gifts in unusual places. Buy mementos and holiday ornaments when you travel; stock up on one-of-a-kind crafts and preserves from state fairs and church bazaars; and buy handmade pottery and jewelry from art fairs. Or instead of buying something new, give a family heirloom.

CHRISTMAS SHOPPING MADE EASY

Try these tips to avoid last-minute holiday hassle:

▶ *Shop year-round for the best bargains. Keep a list of gifts you've bought so you won't duplicate your efforts.*

▶ *Mail out-of-town gifts early. Mailing your gifts in November by third-class mail saves not only money but time spent in long lines at the post office in December.*

▶ *Shop by catalog or on-line so you don't have to deal with crowded stores, gift wrapping, and mailing. Also, most brand-name catalogs offer services 24-hours a day.*

▶ *Keep the names of your gift and card recipients on file on your computer, and update the list during the year. When Christmas comes, just print out the list for easy reference.*

CHRISTMAS TREES

Second time around. At the end of the holidays, cut up your tree or have it shredded. Use the evergreen mulch on perennial beds, in window boxes, or beneath shrubs.

A thirsty tree. Cut off at least 5 cm (2 in.) from the bottom of the tree trunk to allow the tree to better absorb water. Water the tree every day it is up, and mist it occasionally.

A ready-made feeder. Adorn small trees and shrubs in your yard with pinecones and strings of cranberries and popcorn. It not only looks pretty, but birds can pick off the goodies.

Tree by the sea. Save the seashells you collected on the beach in the summer for a seashore theme tree. Sand dollars strung up with shiny red ribbon are particularly beautiful.

CITRUS FRUITS

To increase the juice you can extract from a lemon, lime, or other citrus fruit, lay the fruit on a hard surface, press down on it, and roll it back and forth several times before you cut it.

Zest saver. When grating citrus zest, solve the dilemma of the peel sticking to the grater by placing a piece of plastic wrap, waxed paper, or parchment paper over the utensil before you begin. The tiny citrus bits will remain on the plastic or paper—and will be a cinch to transfer to your recipe.

Ice surprise. Place small strips of citrus peel in individual ice cube holders, fill with water, and freeze. The cubes perk up drinks visually and add flavor as they melt.

Year-round juice. When lemons and limes are at their peak—and least expensive—buy enough to make a large batch of each kind of juice. Freeze the juices in ice cube trays. Whenever fresh citrus juice is called for, thaw one cube for each 30 mL (2 tbsp) you need.

CLEANERS FROM THE PANTRY

Save a spray bottle from a commercial cleaning product, wash it thoroughly, and use it as the dispenser for homemade solutions of vinegar and water, ammonia and water, or bleach and water.

MAKE YOUR OWN CLEANERS

Some common kitchen staples can make effective as well as inexpensive and environmentally safe alternatives to commercial cleaning products. The list below suggests some of the basic "green" cleaners from your pantry shelf.

Drain cleaner	Pour 125 mL (½ cup) baking soda and 185 mL (¾ cup) white vinegar down the drain. After the mixture stops bubbling, flush it with boiling or very hot tap water.
Grease cutter	Scrub with a mixture of 1 part lemon juice, 1 part water, and 2 parts white vinegar.
Laundry brightener	Add lemon juice to the wash water.
Linen whitener	Soak yellowed linens in sour milk; launder as usual.
Marble cleaner	Mix salt and lemon juice to form a thin paste. With a soft cloth, polish the marble.
Oven cleaner	Mix baking soda with water to make a thick paste. Spread liberally over baked-on grease; let sit overnight; scrub with a plastic scrubber; rinse with water.
Room deodorizer	Dab vanilla extract onto a lightbulb.
Scouring powder	Mix baking soda and water to create a thick paste.
Silver polish	Rub with half a raw potato dipped in baking soda.
Wallpaper cleaner	Rub a piece of stale white bread over the paper to remove fingerprints and other oily marks.
Window cleaner	Mix 125 mL (½ cup) white vinegar and 1 L (4 cups) water.

Give it time. Many homemade cleaners take longer to work than their commercial counterparts. Relax; in the end, they get the job done without exposing you to harmful chemicals or requiring any more elbow grease.

CLOCKS

Fail-safe. Pick an electric alarm clock with a battery-powered backup system. If you keep fresh batteries in the backup, the alarm will sound even if a power outage occurs while you are asleep.

Sound bytes. People with failing eyesight can buy an alarm clock that announces the time (the voice is recorded) as well as sounding a get-up call.

Good turn. Upending a disabled electric clock for a few days just might fix it. Oil in the clock that has settled at the bottom may move into the internal mechanisms, lubricating them and making the clock run again.

Cover the bright LED display on your digital clock with a piece of cheesecloth or other gauzy material. The fabric will deflect the light so that you can sleep but allow you to read the time when you wake up.

Windup clocks last longer if you treat them gently. When you wind a clock, make short turns with the key, and stop before the spring becomes fully taut. When resetting the time, always move the hands clockwise.

CLOSET ORGANIZATION

Wardrobe efficiency. If you arrange your clothes by category—blouses, skirts, jackets, pants, and dresses—and by purpose—work versus leisure, for example—you can pick out what you want to wear in half the time.

Hooks are handy in both the bathroom and the bedroom for hanging up bathrobes, pajamas, and towels. Just don't overdo it. Most clothes will wrinkle and become misshapen on a hook.

Double duty. Hang accessories such as hats, evening bags, necklaces, or scarves on the wall of your bedroom. Getting such items out of your closet will allow more room. What's more, these accessories can make delightful displays.

Fold and store most knits on a shelf. Hanging sweaters and other knits on conventional hangers damages the weave and causes the garments to lose their shape.

Towel trick. Your towels will look neat and attractive—and take up less space in the linen closet—if instead of folding them, you roll them up like a jelly roll and stack them. Guest towels look especially pretty rolled in a decorative basket in the bath.

CLOTHES STORAGE

Before you store clothes at the end of a season, weed out your wardrobe. Discard or give away those clothes you have outgrown, you dislike, or you simply never wear. Make sure all items are clean and mended. When you get them out again in six months, they will seem like new.

Moth watch. Wash or have clothes dry-cleaned before you store them for a season. It's the stains, particularly from food, that attract the moths, not the fabric.

Protect woolens and silks with cedar chips, which repel moths. Place cedar chips in pairs of old pantyhose and either hang them in the closet or put them in the storage box.

Store clothes in clear bags and boxes. It's a waste of time to have to open bags and boxes to find out what is inside. However, avoid using dry cleaner's bags, which often cause discoloration. Clothes are better off stored in vented garment bags.

MAXIMIZING CLOSET SPACE

A little organization goes a long way in a closet, as the before-and-after pictures below illustrate. With the addition of shelves, dividers, and extra poles, this closet keeps clothes tidy and lets you see at a glance where everything is.

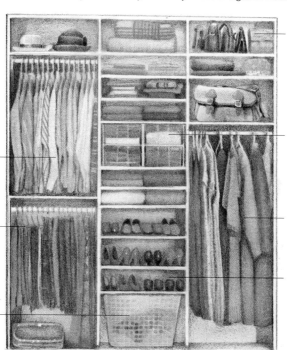

The top shelves hold infrequently used items, like blankets and out-of-season purses and hats.

Special partitions keep each sweater separate, so that you can remove one without dumping the pile.

Full-length coats and long dresses hang in this area.

Shoe shelves keep shoes organized and make vacuuming the closet floor easier.

Blouses and jackets stay wrinkle-free in this short hanging space.

Skirts and pants are hung below the blouses, making good use of what was previously dead space in the closet.

A hamper for dirty clothes fits into the bottom of the closet.

CLUTTER

Get rid of the excess. How many cooking pots do you actually use? How many baking pans? Pencil holders? Cookie jars? Earrings? Separate infrequently used items into boxes labeled "Toss," "Sell," "Give Away," or "Store for Future Use." Then take care of each box.

Organize daily. Whether it takes 5 minutes or 15, spend a little time each day picking up and organizing the clutter left from the day, especially newspapers and junk mail. That way, things don't pile up and become unmanageable.

File, file, file. Set up a simple filing system for all your papers—bills, receipts, guarantees, directions to a friend's country house, clippings, and instruction manuals. File often and weed out as you go. Don't hold on to old papers that are no longer useful.

Take it with you. Every time you go out of the house, take something with you that needs to go—the dry cleaning, garbage, recycled newspapers, or contributions to the compost pile. This will save you many separate trips.

Mount it. When possible, hang small appliances, gadgets, and utensils on the wall or from the ceiling. The items are then easy to find and easy to put away. Ceiling hooks and Peg-Board equipped with appropriate hardware are especially useful both in the kitchen and in the workshop.

A tidy toy box. Use built-in closet shelves at child's-eye level, a colorful wooden chest, or a wicker or plastic laundry basket to tuck away toys, and a designated bookshelf for children's books. Even toddlers can learn to put away their clutter.

COFFEE

Freeze coffee to keep it fresh. To go one step further, transfer the beans or ground coffee from the original bag into several well-sealed small plastic containers. This reduces the coffee's exposure to air and moisture, which rob it of freshness and flavor.

Use distilled water to make coffee (many coffee connoisseurs suggest chilling it first). It gives the coffee a purer flavor, particularly in communities with hard or chlorinated water, and prevents the accumulation of mineral deposits in your coffeemaker.

Add a pinch of salt to your ground coffee before brewing a pot, to reduce bitterness and enhance flavor.

To remove coffee stains from a cup, fill the cup with water, add a denture-cleaning tablet, soak for a few hours, and then rinse.

Flavored coffee. Give your coffee a special touch by adding one teaspoon of ground cinnamon or a grating of orange peel to the coffee before you brew it. The aroma is as good as the taste.

 Garden trick. Put coffee grounds into the planting holes of acid-loving plants such as rhododendrons, azaleas, and blueberries to enhance their growth.

If you love coffee but want to cut down on caffeine, make a pot of half regular coffee and half decaffeinated. The brew will have good flavor with less punch. Many restaurants are happy to serve a half-and-half coffee mixture.

Use your coffee pot daily? If so, clean it once a month with equal parts of white vinegar and water. For electric percolators, run the solution through the cycle two or three times, or until it comes out clean. For other pots, let the vinegar solution sit in the pot for an hour, then wash the pot as usual.

RIGHT STUFF

COFFEE CARAFES

Keep fresh-brewed coffee hot—without the bitter taste produced when it is re-heated or sits on a hot plate—by using a thermal carafe. Enjoy the first pot all morning long. A thermos is energy-efficient as well; no need to use the stove or microwave for reheating.

C

Filters in a pinch. Fit a fairly thick paper towel or a two-ply paper napkin into the cone as a substitute filter.

COLDS & FLU

Eat foods high in vitamin C, such as oranges and strawberries, or take vitamin supplements. Vitamin C may help you get rid of a cold more quickly, although there is no proof that it prevents colds.

 Drink liquids. Drinking at least eight glasses of water or juice a day will help prevent dehydration if you have a fever and will thin mucus in the nose and throat. Hot tea or broth (including chicken soup) helps open a stuffy nose. Caffeinated beverages make bronchial passages dilate, which makes breathing easier.

Wash your hands regularly with soap and water to avoid catching cold and flu viruses. Encourage children to do the same. Also, try to avoid touching your eyes, nose, and mouth; if you have come in contact with a virus, touching these areas will increase the likelihood of your becoming ill.

Get a flu shot between mid-October and mid-November for protection during the flu season. Flu shots are especially recommended for people over 65, adults and children with a chronic illness such as diabetes or asthma. (But don't get a shot if you are allergic to eggs, because the serum contains egg protein.)

Vaporize sore throats and congestion. Use a cool-mist vaporizer at night to ease a sore throat. Standing in a steamy shower can open clogged sinuses and keep a cold from becoming sinusitis.

Use saline nose drops to help clear nasal congestion. (Make your own by boiling a pinch of salt in 60 mL [¼ cup] water; store it in a medicine bottle with a dropper.) If you use commercial decongestant nose drops or sprays, limit their use to three or four days.

COLLECTION AGENCIES

Take the initiative. If you have to miss a payment on a debt, talk to the creditor right away. You may be able to work out an extended payment plan before the matter is turned over to a collection agency.

Legal limits. Collection agents are not supposed to call you before 8 A.M. or after 8 P.M. If you inform the agent that your lawyer is handling the case, the bill collector may not call you in person.

Resist pressure. Don't agree to a repayment schedule that you can't afford. Be honest with creditors about your finances, and come up with a realistic plan for paying off your debt. You'll rebuild your credit quicker if you make your payments on time.

COLLEGE SELECTION

Don't rely on college-ranking lists in national magazines in making your choice; they can be helpful, but can reflect the magazine editors' priorities—not necessarily yours or your youngster's. In addition, colleges often manipulate statistics to make themselves look attractive and competitive.

Seek out students to interview when you visit a college. Undergraduates are likely to be more candid about what they like and dislike about the school. Better yet, try to spend a few days living on campus and attending classes.

Consider community colleges, two-year schools designed to offer a convenient, inexpensive start toward a four-year college degree. They are located throughout the country and offer more education choices at far lower cost than traditional colleges.

Keep a journal. If you're visiting several colleges, list the pros and cons of each campus while you are actually there. Often the quality of a place is different on paper than in reality. Compare your lists to help determine your choices.

WHEN BILL COLLECTORS GET TOUGH

Each province in Canada has its own laws dealing with fair debt collection practices. Before contacting your provincial consumer protection agency for help, try taking the following steps:

▶ *Write a letter to the bill collection agency saying you will not or cannot pay the debt and that you want the agency to leave you alone.*

▶ *Send the letter by certified mail, return receipt requested, to be certain the agency receives it.*

▶ *If the collection agency persists in harassing you after receiving the letter, keep careful notes about any offending contacts. Then notify your consumer protection agency.*

COLOR IN THE GARDEN

Create a color theme. To give your garden a unified look, find a color scheme that you like, then repeat the colors in various hues and shades using different varieties of plants.

Family harmony. A sure way to ensure a comfortable mixture of colors in a flower bed is to plant several varieties of the same flower. Different colors of roses, for example, almost always blend well with one another.

Tone it down. If the color of new shrub blossoms proves to be too garish, surround the plant with a silver-foliaged ground cover, such as artemesia 'Silver King'. The subtle grays will temper the harsher colors of the shrubs.

Perk up somber plantings by adding a dash of the complementary color for contrast. A foundation planting of all-green shrubs can be enlivened with a single clump of scarlet geraniums. One orange-colored blossom adds vibrancy to a whole garden of blue, and one yellow flower electrifies a bed of purple blossoms.

Coping with the blues. Blue and purple color schemes in the garden are dramatic but tend to fade against green surroundings. For a stronger effect, plant blue flowers in direct sunlight and add white or yellow flowers to the scheme.

Rehearse with annuals. When you are plotting a color scheme for your landscape, try out your designs with fast-blooming annuals first. When you know you like the color harmony, then invest in permanent plantings of trees, shrubs, perennials, and bulbs.

COMMUTING

Bike it! More and more people are discovering the benefits of riding a bicycle to work. In many communities, organizations for cyclists have sprung up, providing routing information and other kinds of support. If enough people in your company bike to work, lobby for a bike rack. In many urban centers, parking garages will provide bike-parking facilities for a nominal fee.

Stagger your hours. One way to reduce the hassle of commuting, especially in a car, is to get your employer to arrange alternative work hours. Come in and leave earlier, or arrive and leave later, in order to travel when the roads are relatively uncrowded.

Books-on-tape are the easiest way to catch up on your reading while commuting, even if you drive. Select from a wide range of novels, biographies, self-help, and meditation tapes, then just put on your head phones and enjoy yourself. Some bookstores and libraries lend books-on-tape to customers. Or consider swapping tapes with fellow commuters.

Everyone into the pool. Car pooling is still an efficient way of getting to work from the 'burbs. Some cities have special parking lots outside city limits where you can park before you pool.

COLOR IN THE GARDEN

To achieve color harmony in the garden, refer to a color wheel. A traditional artist's aid, the wheel arranges colors in the way that they occur in the natural spectrum. Complementary colors, or those found opposite each other, such as blue and orange, give a pleasing effect. Triad schemes, or 3 colors occurring equidistant from each other, like red, orange, and yellow, also work well.

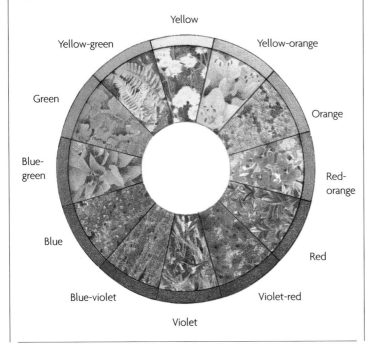

Yellow

Yellow-green · Yellow-orange

Green · Orange

Blue-green · Red-orange

Blue · Red

Blue-violet · Violet-red

Violet

EASY-OPEN COMPACT DISCS

With this little gadget, known as the EZ-CD, you'll never have to struggle again when you remove new compact discs from their seemingly impenetrable wrapping. A small blade shielded by two flaps does the magic as you guide the opener along the edge of the disc's container. Even those resilient metallic strips can't stop EZ-CD.

Be prepared for breakdowns. Keep you car well maintained, and make sure the tools you need in case of an emergency are in the trunk and the spare tire is fully infated at all times. Join an auto club for roadside help. Carry a cellular telephone to use to call for assistance and to alert your family or the office in case of trouble.

COMPACT DISCS

Clean discs the right way. To effectively remove dust and dirt, use a static-free cloth, repeatedly wiping the disc from its center to its outer edges.

Discs scratched and skipping? Try a commercial restoration kit, which contains a supersensitive sandpaper-like material that smoothes out indentations.

Remove the foam that some manufacturers use to cushion compact discs in their packaging. Over time, the material can cause discs to discolor and deteriorate.

A remedy for warped discs. Using a hair dryer, heat the disc until it becomes pliable, then place it on a flat surface between two sheets of wax paper. Pile two or three heavy books on top and let sit for several hours. Repeat the process if the disc is only partially flattened.

Don't bother to invest in a high-priced CD player. As a general rule, even cheaper models, though lacking in many features, produce decent-quality sound, especially in smaller spaces.

COMPLIMENTS

Compliments as ice-breakers. Paying a compliment is a nice way to begin a conversation with a stranger. Compliments are especially effective when you want to make a positive impression with a member of the opposite sex. Be honest, and don't gush.

 Ask for advice. In doing so, you are paying someone the highest kind of compliment—you are trusting in her good judgment.

Receiving a compliment gracefully is as important as giving one. A simple thank you is appropriate; and returning the compliment with a comment like "You are so nice to say that" will enhance the warm feelings. It is rude to refute a compliment because it implies that the giver's taste is faulty.

Be honest. A compliment should always be genuine. Even if you are asked if you like a friend's new sofa—and you don't—compliment some aspect that you do appreciate, such as the color or the way it looks in the room.

COMPOSTING

A sweet formula. Add two parts brown and dry materials (leaves, sawdust, or pine needles, for example) to the compost heap for each part green and juicy materials (vegetable peels, grass clippings, and fresh manures). Mix both parts together well. This combination allows your compost to decay quickly and remain free from unpleasant odors.

Discourage varmints from your compost heap by adding only vegetable refuse such as peelings, coffee grounds, grass clippings, and the like. Piling on meat scraps, bones, or dairy products is an invitation to dogs, cats, and rodents.

Easy air. The micoorganisms that turn garbage into compost need air to work. Turn the heap with a fork every few days, or let it aerate itself by building the heap on top of a 15 cm (6 in.) pile of brush around a cylinder of wire mesh. As the materials decompose, they heat up; this creates a draft up the cylinder, which continually draws in fresh air through the brush.

Save time transporting compost by composting in place. Bury vegetable refuse from the kitchen under the paths of your vegetable garden. By next spring the refuse will be composted, and the enriched paths can become your planting beds while the old beds can become your paths.

COMPUTER ACCESSORIES

An antiglare screen can ease eyestrain by reducing glare from natural or artificial light. These screens are available in sizes to fit most monitors. Also, experiment with your monitor's brightness and contrast controls to find a comfortable setting for your eyes.

A wrist rest—a foam or plastic strip placed along the lower edge of your keyboard—makes typing more comfortable and may help prevent carpal tunnel syndrome. A similar rest is available for the mouse pad.

A mouse pad improves the mouse's traction, making it easier to control, and helps prevent grease and grime from building up in the mouse's mechanism. Many experts consider a mouse pad to be essential.

 A surge protector, which shuts off the power to your computer when there are electrical surges or spikes, is an essential accessory that you shouldn't skimp on.

More surge protection. A UPS (or uninterruptable power supply) is an even better investment than a conventional surge protector. If you lose household power, a UPS will supply your system with enough power—typically 10 minutes' worth—for you to save your work and shut down your computer normally. A high-quality UPS will also protect your computer's circuitry from power spikes and guard your modem's phone line from "line noise."

COMPUTER BUYING

Know what you need. It's not in your best interest to expect a computer store salesperson to guide you to the best computer for your needs at the best price. Study before you buy: talk with knowledgeable friends, coworkers, or family members or ask advice from a local Macintosh or PC users group.

Computer magazines can be good sources of information for the first-time computer buyer. While many are written for technical types, *Home PC* and *Family PC* (mainly but not exclusively oriented toward Windows PCs) and *Mac Home Journal* (just for the Macintosh) often have articles with useful information for first-time buyers and novice home users. These are available at bookstores and computer stores.

Factor in extra costs. Computers aimed at the home user usually come complete with monitor, keyboard, modem, and a "bundle" of software. Make sure the bundled software includes the programs you'll want or need, or ask the salesperson if you can pick and choose. If software does not come with your computer or the bundled software does not suit your needs, don't forget to figure in the additional cost.

Order direct. Some of the biggest PC makers, including Dell

EXTERNAL BACKUPS

Until recently, backing up all the material on your hard drive was a time-consuming job involving a stack of floppy disks or tapes. Now simple external drives make the chore faster and easier. Iomega's Zip drives and drives from several manufacturers using the SyQuest mechanism are good choices. Each connects to the computer externally and stores data on cartridges—more like super-diskettes—that can be removed and kept in a safe place. The Zip drives are smaller and more portable, making them ideal for moving large files between a computer at work and one at home. SyQuest drives offer several storage capacities.

MAC VS PC

One decision you must make when buying a home computer is which of two leading operating systems you prefer: Macintosh (Mac) or PC with Windows. Consider the following to make that choice easier.

▶ *Macs and PC's speak different languages, and the software written for one won't work on the other without the use of special translating software.*

▶ *About 85 percent of home computers in North America are Windows-running PC's; 10 to 15 percent are Macs.*

▶ *If you're buying a computer chiefly for your children, think about matching the system they use in school.*

▶ *If you or your spouse uses a computer on the job and often brings work home, you may want to have compatible systems at home and on the job.*

▶ *If you think you will want to add hardware such as a scanner or an extrernal drive, a Mac comes equipped with a connector port that makes hooking up devices simpler.*

and Gateway 2000, ship custom-configured systems directly from the factory to the user. You can get a computer system tailored to your needs without paying for extras that you may never use.

Use a credit card. Buying a computer with a credit card gives you some protection. If your computer arrives damaged, if you experience long delays in shipping (sadly, a frequent occurrence), or if you get poor service from the seller, you can have the credit card company withhold payment until the situation is resolved.

Beware of used computers. Although cheaper, a pre-owned computer can be more difficult to evaluate than a used car. It is hard to determine how much wear and tear the machine has endured. Also, computer technology advances so quickly that a system that may not be more than a few months old may not be capable

of running the latest software. Still, if the machine suits your needs and you know what you are doing, a used computer can be a great buy.

To check for a fair price for a used computer on the web, download an up-to-date index of used computer prices from United Computer Exchange's website at http://www.uce.com. The site lists computers for sale across North America. For a fee, UCE will match up users and sellers.

Make sure you are insured. A computer is a very expensive tool. Check that it is covered under your homeowners insurance policy. If not, it pays to invest in insurance to cover your system if it is damaged or stolen.

COMPUTER CARE

For a clean screen, spray household glass cleaner onto a soft, lint-free cloth and wipe the dirt

away. You can also use a commercial wet-dry screen-cleaning kit, available at most computer stores.

Blow dust away with a freon-free can of compressed air, available at most computer, electronics, and photography stores. It's a clean, efficient way to get rid of dust, pollen, and other airborne pollutants that collect inside your computer's case. Open the case carefully, following the instructions that came with your computer, spray the dust away, then close the case.

Set up in a safety zone. Install your computer system in a low-traffic area. Be sure it is located in a place that is not subject to extremes of heat and cold, excess dust, or direct sunlight. Check that no magnetic items are located near or on top of your computer. Try to ensure that the computer's electrical source does not share a circuit with another major household appliance. Finally, don't eat or drink near your computer.

An unwieldy mouse may be behaving badly because the ball is dirty. To clean the ball, remove the plastic ring that holds it in place (consult the directions that came with your mouse). Wash the ball in warm soapy water and, using a clean pencil eraser, clean the interior of the mouse case. Make sure the case and the ball are completely dry, then reassemble the mouse.

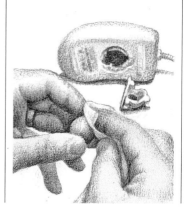

C

COMPUTER COMFORT

A good chair. Avoid the temptation to use an old kitchen chair with your new computer setup. Your computer chair should provide support to your lumbar (lower back) region. It's also helpful if the chair can quickly be adjusted to the optimum height for each member of the family who uses the computer.

Keyboard level. Desks designed for computers have a special lower-than-desktop-level shelf for holding the keyboard at a comfortable typing height. If your desk doesn't have such a shelf, you can buy an inexpensive keyboard holder at computer or office supply stores. One model is metal and attaches to an ordinary desk with screws. It folds out of sight when not in use.

Sitting at the computer, your posture is best when your feet are flat on the floor, and your forearms make a 90-degree angle to your torso as they touch the keyboard. You should face the monitor directly, not looking far up or down, which can put a strain on your neck. Some people are most comfortable looking down at a very slight (15-degree) angle.

Control glare by using task lamps to read papers near your computer that don't reflect on the screen. Line up the computer monitor so that window light doesn't hit the screen.

Glasses check. A computer screen, which sits about 60 cm (2 ft) from your eyes, presents a mid-distance vision problem for many people who wear glasses for reading or for distance. If you have trouble reading text on your computer monitor, ask your ophthalmologist about mid-distance glasses.

COMPUTER PRINTERS

Experiment with settings. Most programs that print give you the option of printing at several different resolutions, ranging from low to high print quality. You can cut down on ink usage if you use the low-quality setting for drafts. Just remember to change the setting for the final document.

Use the right paper. Documents printed on plain paper by some inkjet printers may run or smear, especially if the paper gets wet. Computer, office-supply, and stationery stores carry specially coated paper for use in inkjets. For maximum savings, print out drafts on plain paper and use special paper for your final output.

Jammed paper is the most likely cause of printer failure. Unplug the printer and then open the top cover to pull the paper out from under the platen.

Smeared or streaked print suggests that the printer is dirty. On an inkjet or dot-matrix printer, clean the rollers, platens, and print head (under the ink cartridge on an inkjet) with an alcohol-dampened swab. Also clean the guide rails on a dot-matrix printer. You can clean the corona wire on a laser printer.

Save money on ink cartridges. If you have a black or color inkjet printer that uses a cartridge, you can refill it with ink instead of buying a new one every time the old one runs dry—usually for a substantial savings. You'll find refill kits for the most common inkjet printer models at computer and office-supply stores.

COMPUTER SOFTWARE

Word-processing programs let you create, edit, store, and print documents, from simple letters to book-length manuscripts. Many programs include a dictionary, a thesaurus and even spell- and grammar-checking features. Today's programs often have page-layout functions—the capability to add graphics to your documents, for example—found only in professional desktop-publishing programs a few years ago.

Spreadsheet programs manipulate numbers, typically to show how hypothetical scenarios will affect future financial decisions. To determine how much to save for your children's college education, for example, you can factor in several different projections for your income, as well as different numbers for rising tuitions and inflation rates.

Databases are record-keeping programs, useful for keeping track of everything from the inventory of a home-based business to a mailing list for the PTA.

Integrated programs, such as ClarisWorks and Microsoft Works, combine word-processing, spreadsheet, database, and even graphics and communications functions. While they may not offer the high-end features found in "standalone" versions of each type of program, integrated programs are less expensive and often easier to learn and use, making them a smart choice for people who use home computers.

Personal publishing programs are home-based cousins of the professional desktop-publishing programs used to create books. Personal publishing programs allow you to make your own greeting cards, stationery, invitations, and flyers.

COMPUTER UPGRADES

Memory and speed upgrades allow you to use more sophisticated software on your existing computer for far less money than the cost of a new computer. Different products are designed to increase the memory of Macs and PC's, so discuss options with your computer dealer. Also discuss adding an accelerator board, which will speed up your computer.

A grade up. If you register new software when you buy it, the manufacturer will offer you upgrades with new features and fewer bugs at reasonable prices as soon as the new programs are ready. You can also trade in your old operating system for the latest version.

Replacements. You can have a newer, faster modem put in your old computer. You can also replace an aging (one- or two-year old) CD-ROM player with a new, faster one, or even a model that handles multiple discs.

COMPUTER JARGON

Computers have spawned a whole vocabulary that can be intimidating to the novice. If you are buying a computer, you need to know the terms below (they appear in every ad). Modems, which connect your computer to telephone lines, are controlled by an expansion card; all you'll see is a phone jack at the back of the CPU.

RAM. The "workspace" in which your computer runs its programs. The more RAM installed in your computer, the more programs you can keep open at the same time and (depending on other factors) the more efficiently your computer will operate.

Hard drive. Where your computer stores its operating system, software, and files. Most modern computers have hard disks that are of 1 gigabyte (1,000 megabytes) or larger in size.

Monitor. The screen that displays what's going on. Screen sizes are measured diagonally.

Mouse. A hand-held device that controls movement of an on-screen cursor, necessary for today's "point and click" operating systems and software.

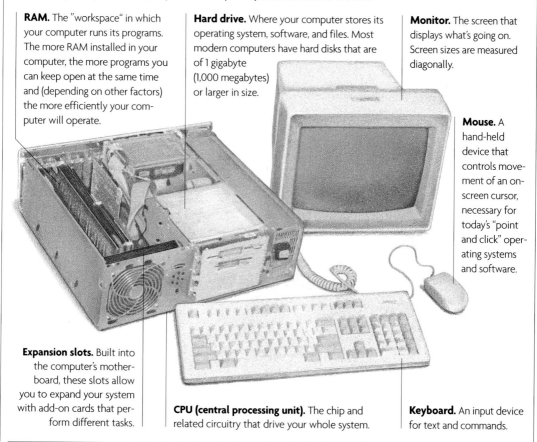

Expansion slots. Built into the computer's motherboard, these slots allow you to expand your system with add-on cards that perform different tasks.

CPU (central processing unit). The chip and related circuitry that drive your whole system.

Keyboard. An input device for text and commands.

CONDIMENTS

Horseradish sauce makes a delicious entree out of cold steak. Simply mix prepared horseradish with sour cream (use the fat-free kind if you like) and serve it with thin slices of the leftover meat.

The salsa story. Salsa, the tomato-based condiment so popular in Tex-Mex cooking, is good for more than dipping tortilla chips. Serve a spicy salsa with cold meat salads, grilled chicken, or fish. If you don't like cilantro, the strong-flavored parsley look-alike used in many salsas, just check the ingredients list on salsa jars; many use other herbs instead.

Sweet relishes like chutney and piccalilli complement chicken, pork, and lamb dishes. Try mixing chutney with a little reduced-fat mayonnaise for a delicious sandwich spread. Or spread on hamburgers for a sweet treat.

Use mustard to add bite to a white sauce. After the sauce is made, add a pinch of dry mustard and blend well with a whisk.

CONSUMER COMPLAINTS

Stay cool. You'll get better results if you clearly state the problem, stick to the facts, and hold your temper. Have at hand the bill of sale that gives the details of your purchase, together with any guarantees.

Be specific about what you want—a free repair, a replacement product, or your money back. You are more likely to get satisfaction.

Keep notes. Get the name and telephone number of each person you speak with. Record what action they promised to take and by what date. If they don't follow through, get back in touch.

Climb the executive ladder when you don't get results. Ask for a supervisor, then a manager. As a last resort, write to the president of the company.

Further recourse. If the company isn't responsive, report the problem to the state consumer protection agency. If the business has a city license, complain to the department that grants it. Also call the Better Business Bureau so that other consumers will know the company's record.

CONTACT LENSES

Lost a lens? Cover the nozzle of a vacuum cleaner hose with a nylon stocking, then carefully vacuum the area. The lens will be sucked up against the stocking.

Carry lens-cleaning solution with you at all times in case your contacts need cleaning. Putting them in your mouth or rinsing them under tap water can lead to a serious eye infection.

Aerosols first. Apply hair spray and spray perfume or deodorant before inserting lenses. Aerosols can leave a sticky film on contacts that can't be removed.

Beware of fumes. Remove contact lenses and wear glasses when you work around household cleaners, pesticides, solvents, or paint. Fumes from these products can get caught between the lens and your eye—leading to serious eye irritation.

CONTAINER GARDENING

Safe haven. Fruits and vegetables grown in containers on a sunny porch or patio are safe from many

---

RIGHT STUFF

THROWAWAY LENSES

Have you ever forgotten to disinfect your lenses? Are you amazed at what you spend on cleaning solutions? Try the new disposable contacts. You can get lenses that are meant to be tossed after a week or just one day of wear. Disposables are pricey, but you'll save on the cost of cleaning and storage solutions and will experience very little deposit buildup—which means clearer vision and fewer infections.

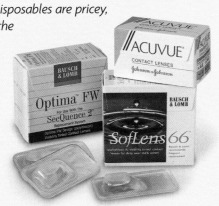

garden pests, such as deer, moles, and woodchucks. Grow strawberries in hanging baskets; cucumbers, zucchini, and tomatoes in tubs; and salad greens in window boxes. For the best results, use dwarf or bush varieties.

Thirst quenchers. To avoid having to water container plants every day during the dog days of summer, add water-absorbent soil polymers—available at garden centers and through garden catalogs—to your potting mix. The granules absorb up to 400 times their weight in water and then release it gradually. They can cut your watering chores in half.

Revive tired houseplants with a summer outdoors. Start them in a heavily shaded spot; after a week, move them into brighter light. If a plant's foliage shows signs of browning or bleaching, however, move it back into more shade.

CONTESTS

Respond early and often. Enter a contest as many times as the rules permit to increase your chances of winning. Also spread out the dates on which you send in your separate entry forms.

Follow the rules to the letter. You'll be disqualified immediately if you don't.

Be persevering. Contests that require entrants to fill out long forms or to write a short essay praising a product are bound to discourage other contestants—and increase your odds.

Small pond. Look for contests that are held only in summer, when many people are on vacation and aren't likely to enter.

Lightweight Potting

You can plant a large and handsome container with lightweight materials and make it a cinch to move from a sunny window in winter to the patio for summer and back again in the fall.

1 Start with a good-looking plastic pot. Make a drainage area at its bottom with Styrofoam peanuts from a mail-supply store.

2 Cover the peanuts with a circle of geotextile mulch, which allows water and air—but not potting soil—to pass through.

3 Add lightweight potting soil, available from garden centers, and arrange the plants. Fill up the pot with more soil.

4 Finally, water the new transplants. You should have little trouble moving the full container from spot to spot; its total weight is less than 13.6 kg (30 lb).

RIGHT STUFF

VERSATILE NONSTICK PAN LINERS

Teflon-coated nonstick pan liners save time and reduce fat calories, too. If you use Du Pont's Teflon Bakeware Liners or Thermohauser's Magic Sheets, made of Teflon-coated fiberglass, you don't need to grease the baking pans. The sheets can be cut to fit any size pan, so they can be used for cookies, cakes, muffins, pizzas, and even casseroles and roasts. Plus, they go from freezer to oven (or microwave) with no problem. The liners can be reused, requiring only a quick wipe for cleanup. Du Pont's liners are available in kitchen stores nationwide; Thermohauser's Magic Sheets are available by mail from the Baker's Catalogue (800-827-6836).

COOKIES

Reserve a handful of the raisins, nuts, or chocolate chips called for in a cookie recipe. When you get to the last of the dough, mix in the ingredients you held back so there will be some goodies in even the very last cookies.

OLD SAW

Store cookies which contain no preservatives (that is, homemade cookies), in an airtight cookie tin. You can buy attractive ones in cookware stores.

Instant blondies. Buy a roll of commercial chocolate chip cookie dough, and spread the dough on a cookie sheet about 5 cm (2 in.) deep. Bake for 45 minutes in a preheated 175°C (350°F) oven. Let cool and cut into bars. Dress up your blondies by sprinkling extra chocolate chips or nuts on top before you bake.

Soft and chewy. If you like your cookies on the soft and chewy side, take the cookie sheet out of the oven halfway through the baking process, rap it briskly on the counter, and return it to the oven to finish baking. The rapping releases the carbon dioxide gas produced by the baking soda in the recipe. Instead of rising, the cookies will collapse and stretch out, making them chewy rather than crisp.

Cook the last small batch of cookies on a small cookie sheet. If you don't have one, substitute an upside-down pie tin or cake pan. A small batch of cookies on a large cookie sheet draws so much heat that the bottoms of the cookies often burn.

COOKING FOR ONE

Salad bar savings. Make use of the supermarket salad bar, where single servings of cut-up fruit, mixed salad greens, carrot sticks, and other raw vegetables allow you to have a variety of fresh produce without any spoilage or waste. No muss or fuss, either: the foods are already washed, peeled, and ready to eat.

Add variety to solo dining by cooking one or two main dishes in big batches. Freeze half of each and then alternate eating each dish for a week or so. As you repeat the process week after week, you will build up a large and varied stock of meals in the freezer.

Roast a chicken or a cut of beef and use it all week in other dishes. From the leftovers you can make casseroles, stir-fries, salads, soups, or sandwiches.

Buy small. Look for individual servings of such food items as fruit juices, canned tuna, cottage cheese, pies, soft drinks, and prepared frozen dinners. You may pay more per serving, but you will save money in the long run because you won't have to throw out spoiled leftovers.

COOKING MEASUREMENTS

Fill measuring spoons or cups away from the mixing bowl. Measuring over the bowl is risky: if you accidentally pour out too much, you may have to start from scratch with your recipe. A better place is over the sink for easy

When things go wrong in the kitchen, keep a cool head and use the guide below to help salvage the meal. Remember, these things can happen even to the best cooks, who are never too proud to improvise a fix.

Too Salty 	For boiled vegetables, rinse with freshly boiled unsalted water.
	For soups and sauces, add a sliced raw potato to absorb salt; discard the potato later.
	For stews, add a pinch or two of brown sugar, which cuts the salt without adding sweetness.
Too Much Fat	Put the dish in the refrigerator until the fat congeals, then spoon out the fat.
	Skim the fatty surface of a liquid with a paper towel or salad greens, which attract the denser fat components.
Burned Food	Quickly transfer unburned food (avoid scraping the pan bottom) to a new pot. Set the new pot in cold water to stop the cooking and kill any burned flavor.
	To absorb burned flavor, put a damp towel over the pot for a few minutes. For drier foods such as rice or couscous, lay fresh white bread on top.
Boil-overs	Just before a boil-over, pull the pot away from the heat, then whisk the pot liquid to break the bubbles.
	Grease the pot or pan rim to prevent liquid from bubbling over the top.
Food That Sticks	For drained rice or noodles, simply run hot water over them in a colander.
	For fried foods, set the skillet in a larger pan of cold water, then gently pry up the food with a thin, flexible spatula.

cleanup. Remember to measure dry ingredients before liquid.

Measure oil first in a recipe that also includes sticky ingredients like honey or molasses. The oil left coating the measuring cup or spoon helps the sticky stuff to slide right out.

 For accuracy, always measure dry ingredients with a set of measuring cups (including metric and imperial containers), leveling off the top of the measure with a knife. Always measure liquid in a glass measuring cup, resting the cup on a firm, level surface when taking the reading.

COOKING MISTAKES

In cooking disasters, the problem is often more visual than gustatory—a collapsed cheese soufflé, for example, may not be beautiful but is still quite tasty. Call it an "after the fall" soufflé and serve it. A sense of humor can turn a cooking disaster into a rich anecdote that saves the meal.

To prevent curdling, add acid-based foods, such as lemon, lime, and vinegar, before adding eggs and cream to a dish.

Break eggs individually into a small bowl before adding them to a dish. This way, you can check the freshness of each egg. Separate eggs into whites and yolks individually too, so that you don't ruin a whole batch of egg whites with some yolk from the last egg you separate.

Cake repair. If your cake layers turn out uneven, don't despair. Match the low side of one cake layer to the high side of the other, and use plenty of icing to hide any imperfections around the cake's sides.

COOKING OILS

A healthy alternative to butter: delicious extra virgin olive oil. Serve with crusty French or Italian bread. Pour a small amount of oil onto a plate and let guests dip their bread in it.

Stir-fry with peanut oil, which can be heated to a higher temperature than other oils without smoking or burning. Stir-fried foods depend on quick cooking at a high temperature.

A few drops of oil in a pan do the job of expensive cooking sprays. Simply spread the oil very thin with a pastry brush.

Refrigerate nut and seed oils if you don't plan to use them for a few months. Your refrigerated oils may solidify, but this won't affect their quality. It is not necessary to refrigerate olive or vegetables oils, as they don't turn rancid as rapidly as nut and seed oils do.

CORN

Buy corn in the husk. A grass-green color and a damp husk are signs that the corn is fresh. The silk should be light to amber brown, with no black. Feel for plump kernels through the husk rather than tearing it back.

 Quick cooking is the secret to heavenly corn on the cob. Steamed or boiled, fresh-picked corn needs about three minutes; supersweet corn, five to seven minutes.

Winter corn. Try the fresh "supersweet" corn grown in Florida and shipped all over the country year-round. Bred for sweetness and a shelf life of two weeks, winter corn lacks the moisture of locally grown corn at its late-summer peak. But it easily surpasses frozen or canned corn for flavor.

A fast shave. Use a tube pan to shave kernels off the cob. Insert the small end of the ear into the hole of the pan. It will hold the cob in place as you work. The pan conveniently collects the kernels.

To remove corn silk, rub a damp vegetable brush or paper towel along the rows. The strands will come right off.

Use sugar, not salt, in the corn cooking water. Salt will toughen the corn; sugar keeps it tender.

COUPONS & REBATES

Sort your coupons into folders of envelopes under categories like cleaning products, cereals, soups, condiments, and personal-care items. You'll be able to get your hands on the coupons you need quickly and easily.

Swap coupons with friends and neighbors. Not your brand of cereal? Trade the cereal coupon for a coupon for something you use. Some coupon savers even use the Internet to find swap partners.

Circle expiration dates or underscore them with a colored marker so you will use the earlier coupons first.

Look for rebate offers. Many manufacturers offer rebates on certain products when you mail in the store receipt, so file receipts and watch for rebate offers in supermarket advertising.

Refund coupons found on packages are seldom for less than $1, so using a first class stamp to mail one in is still a good investment.

Buy extras when you see coupons on non-perishable products that you use regularly. You can save as much as 40 percent.

Prime times for grocery coupon offers are during major holiday periods. May and October are the best months for beauty and health-care products.

CREAM

Use the right cream for the job. Light whipping cream is ideal for making foams, while heavy cream, which tends to turn lumpy, is essential for making stiffly whipped cream. Half-and-half, as its name suggests, is a combination of milk and cream and works best in your coffee.

Chill the bowl and beaters for 10 minutes in the freezer before you whip cream. Also helpful, especially in summer, is to place the cream in the freezer for a few minutes before whipping—but take care not to let the cream freeze or you won't be able to whip it. Watch carefully at the end so you don't make butter.

Add sugar to whipped cream only toward the end of the whipping process. Sugar decreases the volume of whipped cream slightly. Be sure to use confectioners' sugar, which stabilizes the stiffened cream.

Use leftover whipped cream as soon as possible. If the cream has not been sweetened, it can be used in any dish that calls for cream, such as homemade soup or scalloped potato casserole.

CREDIT CARDS

Negotiate for a no-fee card. Many banks offer them to customers with checking and savings accounts. Or tell the issuer of your card that you have received an offer for a no-fee card and you're thinking of switching. Ask your issuer if it will match the offer. These days issuers are likely to accommodate you. So just ask.

A two-card strategy. Two credit cards should meet most consumers' needs. Use a low-interest-rate card for big-ticket items on which you'll carry a balance; carry a second, no-fee card for smaller purchases that you will pay off in full each month.

EASY DOES IT

Even though most of us never see it, everyone has the right to dispute the accuracy and completeness of the information contained in our credit report.

▶ *If you find an error in your report, photocopy the report and spell out the errors on it. Return the annotated copy along with an explanatory letter to the credit agency.*

▶ *The law requires the agency to respond to a consumer complaint. If the agency can't prove you wrong within a specified period of time, it must remove the disputed information from your report.*

▶ *Follow up on the corrections. If you have successfully challenged mistakes in your credit report, always request a complete corrected copy and ask the bureau to send corrected copies to the many smaller credit bureaus with whom they do business as well.*

Know your billing cycle; you can then use your card on days that will give the longest use of the money without interest. For example, you can get six to eight weeks of free credit by buying just after the billing date and paying in full just before the due date.

Say no to insurance offers. Avoid insurance products offered by a credit card issuer. The terms are generally not nearly as good as you could secure by working through a professional insurance broker.

Correct errors quickly. If a mistake turns up on your billing statement, contact the bank that issued your card immediately. You must report a disputed charge to the card issuer in writing within 60 days of the date postmarked on the billing statement. The creditor has 90 days or two billing periods, whichever comes first, either to fix the mistake or to explain why it believes the bill to be correct. You are not required to pay the charge in question until the dispute has been settled.

CREDIT RATING

Check your credit report every year, especially before applying for a major loan or a new job. To check your credit rating, notify either of the two major credit bureaus, Equifax Canada (1-800-256-5717) or Trans Union (1-905-525-0060), in writing. You will have to provide them with two copies of signed identity papers (such as a driver's license) and your addresses for the past five years, along with your name, phone number, and date of birth.

To remove negative data, notify both major credit bureaus mentioned above in writing on the 7th anniversary of a bad debt or a personal bankruptcy filing to clear your record. In only two situations will your full credit history then be revealed: if you apply for an insurance policy over specified limits or if you apply for a job with a salary over specified limits.

Beware of quick fixes. Some companies offer to fix bad credit ratings for a fee. If your report contains accurate information of credit problems, there is no way to remove that information until a certain amount of time has passed.

CRITICISM

Criticize, don't insult. Staging a personal attack to make a critical point negates the effort. Use the phrases "I feel" or "I think" rather than "you should" or "you ought to." "Any fool knows that" or similar put-downs antagonize their victims rather than help clarify what went wrong.

Stay objective. Taking constructive criticism as a personal attack is a recipe for unhappiness. If you receive negative information, try to give it fair consideration. Treat it as useful feedback. Don't let it become a source of anger.

Encourage budding athletes. Studies show that abrasive criticism from school coaches and parents results in a massive dropout rate among youngsters in organized sports, as well as reduced confidence overall.

Nag lovingly; it's good for your spouse. Well-meaning, constructive nagging over a spouse's health or behavior is good medicine, studies show. A spouse who is encouraged—albeit frequently—is healthier and lives longer.

CRUISES

Queasy traveling. If you are prone to seasickness, choose a larger ship and select a cabin in the middle deck area. Avoid routes that cross rough, open sea.

All-inclusive cruises do not cover tips, which may run as much as $10 a day for two. Drinks and shore excursions are also extra. Include these expenses when you calculate your costs.

For a good cabin, study the deck plan before you choose. You may not want a location next to a restaurant or disco.

Inside cabins are usually equal in size to outside ones and offer considerable savings. You won't get natural light in your room, but you aren't likely to spend many daylight hours there anyway.

Theme cruises that focus on history, literature, music, or theater attract compatible travel companions. This means you will likely be cruising with passengers who share your interests.

CRYING

Rhythmic motion can be soothing to a fussy baby. Try rocking the baby in a rocking chair, swaying cradle, or windup swing. Dance to different kinds of music. Give the baby a ride in her carriage.

HOW TO SAVE MONEY ON A CRUISE

▶ *Book your holiday through a travel agency that specializes in cruises. These agencies buy up space on certain cruises in bulk at deep discounts and pass the savings on to customers.*

▶ *Compare rates from two or three cruise specialists to be sure that one is not recommending a line because it gives them the best commission. Nevertheless, if you like the ships a certain specialist has available and the dates are appropriate for you, you will have made a good deal.*

▶ *Book early or late. Cruise lines give the biggest discounts to those who book well in advance and to last-minute travelers who help fill empty cabins. If you book early, buy trip-cancellation insurance in case your plans change.*

▶ *Use airfare packages offered by cruise lines. If a connecting flight is delayed or canceled, the cruise line is responsible for getting you to your ship, even if it means flying you to the ship's first port of call. Packages also usually include transfers from the airport to the ship.*

OLD SAW **Check the obvious.** If the baby is fussy, make sure she isn't hungry, doesn't need to burp or a diaper change, or isn't too cool or too warm. (Feel her head, face, and feet.)

Play soothing sounds. Noise that mimics the experience before birth is often settling to a baby: a droning vacuum cleaner, a whirring dishwasher, or the white noise of a ceiling fan or an off-air radio station.

Help your infant to suck. Babies often need sucking for its own sake rather than simply for nourishment. Let the baby suck the top third of your little finger. (Trim your nail down so it won't poke the roof of the baby's mouth.)

Give yourself a breather. If nothing else works, hand the baby over to someone else for a while.

If no one is available, put the dry, full, and burped baby in the crib, close the door, and do something relaxing for 10 or 15 minutes.

CRYSTAL & GLASSWARE

Sparkling vases. To easily clean a glass vase, fill it with water and drop in one extra-strength denture cleaner tablet. Let the vase soak for a few hours and then rinse it out with water.

No more chips. Before handwashing fine crystal or glassware, lay a heavy towel on the bottom of the sink to help prevent the glass from chipping or breaking against the hard enamel or stainless steel.

To repair a small chip in the rim of an inexpensive glass, rub the rim gently with a piece of fine sandpaper. Rub with equal pressure around the entire rim to create a smooth edge.

CURFEWS

Consult the child. Work out a curfew time that seems fair to both of you. This shows that you take your child seriously.

Remain flexible. Try setting a general curfew time for nonspecific activities. For example, a curfew of 9:30 on school nights and midnight on weekends may be reasonable for a teenager. Allow for later times for special events.

Set consequences. Use a 30-minute leeway for lateness. If a teen is later than 30 minutes, she must come in an hour early the next nonschool night. If she is late two nights in a row, she is grounded the next nonschool night.

Ask to be awakened. If your child wants to stay out beyond the time you want to go to bed, ask him to awaken you upon returning home so that you can establish the time of arrival.

CURRENCY EXCHANGE

Prepay your trip. Consider prepaying a trip in dollars before you leave the country, so that you won't have to bother with exchanging currencies. Plus, depending upon the exchange rates, you may well save money. A travel agent can help you prepay on a credit card for everything from meals to museum tickets.

Get money in advance. Order $50 to $100 in the currency of your destination from your bank a few weeks before you leave. With the correct currency in hand, you won't have to worry about finding a bank or coping with long lines at the currency exchange immediately upon arrival.

Exchange rates. When in a foreign country, look for automated teller machines where you can withdraw foreign currency from your own bank account at the usual ATM rate. Local banks, American Express, or Thomas Cook Ltd. usually give the next best exchange rates. But read the fine print. A local bank may also be charging an extra 3 to 5 percent—on top of conversion expenses—to exchange dollars.

Quick study. Familiarize yourself with the bills and coins of a new country as soon as you can so that you can handle money transactions smoothly. Use coins instead of always breaking a large bill, or you will end up with pockets bulging with change that most Canadian banks won't convert.

CURTAINS & DRAPERIES

Tiebacks. Make quick and handsome curtain tiebacks with ready-made braided tassels. You can find them in upholstery fabric shops, antiques shops, and even at flea markets. Heavy ribbon can also make attractive tiebacks.

Slick trick. When hanging curtains, slip a sewing thimble over the unfinished end of the rod before you try to slide it through the rod pocket. The curtains will slip right on without snagging.

Iron-on magic. Apply a cheery border to the bottom of plain curtains by attaching a length of gingham ribbon or other trim with iron-on interface tape. Or run a series of iron-on transfers along the edges of each curtain.

Body-building protein. To give stiffness to limp curtains, add two tablespoons of powdered milk to the rinse water the next time you wash them. The added body will also help the curtains resist dust and dirt, keeping them cleaner for a longer time.

A NO-NONSENSE CURRENCY CONVERTER

Once you key the dollar exchange rate for a country's currency into this pocket-size converter, you can enter any price and get the dollar equivalent at the touch of a button. Hang the converter around your neck on shopping excursions in foreign countries to make it easy to calculate prices.

CUTS & SCRAPES

Skinned knees and minor cuts are an inevitable part of childhood. Still, small children are often frightened and upset when they get a cut or scrape. Amuse them by covering their minor wounds with bandages in bright or glow-in-the-dark colors or ones that are decorated with their favorite cartoon characters.

Stop the bleeding. Minor wounds should stop bleeding quickly even if blood is oozing from a large area. If bleeding continues, raise the injured area above the heart and apply pressure to the wound with a clean cloth or bandage for a few minutes.

 Get help immediately if the bleeding is profuse or if the wound is deep and extensive.

Flush the cut or scrape with cool water and a saline solution. Don't apply antiseptic directly to the wound; it will cause irritation. Use sterile gauze to clean out any debris in the wound.

Clean the surrounding skin using antiseptic wipes or a gauze pad with soap and water. Work outward to prevent infection. Try not to wipe the wound once it has started clotting; you might restart the bleeding.

D

DANCING TO DYEING CLOTH

DANCING

Choose a dancing school that offers inexpensive beginner classes. Join for just a brief period for the first round to make sure that the school and its instructors are right for you.

Practice, practice, practice—in front of a mirror if possible—any new steps that you've learned. Also review the steps in your mind's eye when you have a free moment. Having the steps down pat makes you a more confident and responsive dancer.

Dance to lift your spirits. Kicking up your heels, besides being great exercise, allows for physical self-expression and old-fashioned fun—a combination that can fend off the blues almost indefinitely.

Marriage booster. Take ballroom dancing lessons with your spouse. It's great exercise, loads of fun, and a delightful new way for the two of you to communicate with each other.

Meet new friends. Dancing is a good way to overcome shyness, and since dancers already share a common interest, there's always something to talk about.

DATING

Ground rules. It may seem antiquated, but it's considered bad form to call any later than Wednesday or Thursday for a weekend date. Even if you have just met someone special and want to see her again as soon as possible, show good manners.

Use common interests in deciding what to do, whether it's eating Chinese food, going to a movie, or visiting a museum. Don't take a first date to a party your friends are throwing; that puts her or him at a disadvantage.

Who pays? Whoever asks pays on the first date, but it's a good idea to alternate payments on subsequent dates. Be considerate: go to places that fall within both of your budgets.

Reading the signals. If someone is attracted to you, he or she will telegraph it by leaning forward, touching you lightly on the arm, or mirroring your behavior. If your date sits with legs and arms crossed and avoids eye contact, don't count on a second date.

DEBT REDUCTION

Track your spending. Keep a journal for a month itemizing every expenditure. Then look for areas to cut costs. Some common ones: eating out (taking your lunch to work can save $25 to $50 a week), subscribing to premium cable TV services, and making long-distance phone calls.

Pay cash or write a check when you buy new things instead of using credit cards. Your total debt will shrink rapidly when you're paying off back bills and not running up new ones.

Be wary of debt consolidation. Taking out one loan to cover all your debts can seem like a good idea—you pay only one loan in low monthly installments. But this works only if you stop creating new debt with your credit cards.

DECISION MAKING

Ask questions. Improve the odds of making wise decisions by making informed decisions. Gather pertinent information. Ask thoughtful questions of people who know and understand the problem you are facing.

Anger, alcohol, and fatigue don't produce the best results. Be calm, sober, and rested when you make up your mind.

Outline the options. Clarify your decision-making process by writing down the pros and cons of all your options. Brainstorm to generate new solutions. The answer may become obvious to you as you study the points you have written down.

DECKS

Pretty private. Use a trellis around the sides of your deck that face the neighbors. You can plant a flowering vine like clematis or morning glory against the trellis for added privacy and decoration.

Tree dilemma. If a large tree stands in the way of a planned deck, consider building around it. Not only will it look attractive, but it will provide shade during the summer months, when you most want to be outside.

Stain a deck rather than paint it. Stain penetrates the wood to create a soft patina that enhances the natural grain, and requires far less maintenance than paint. A painted surface blisters and peels and must be scraped and primed, then repainted frequently, perhaps as often as once a year.

To clean a wood deck with a power washer, choose a wide, 40-degree tip, which washes a 30 cm (12 in.) path. (Using a narrow tip and too much pressure can cut a hole in the wood.) Move the washer lengthwise up and down the boards to avoid making cuts across the grain.

To clean mildew from wood decking, use a solution of 250 mL (1 cup) trisodium phosphate (TSP) and 3.7 L (0.8 gal) each of liquid oxygen-type bleach, and water. Apply with a garden sprayer and scrub with a long-handled brush. Hose the solution off after 10 minutes.

A PLAN FOR GETTING OUT OF DEBT

A spending plan can help you get your finances back on track. First you must set goals, such as reducing debt by $200 a month while also saving $50 a month. To be successful, follow the guidelines below.

▶ *Come up with a realistic figure to put aside each month to pay debts. The old adage of "paying yourself first" applies here: don't set your monthly debt-reduction figure too high or you may get stuck at the end of the pay cycle with little or no spending money.*

▶ *Be flexible. Try making an across-the-board 5 percent cut in your discretionary expenses. Then bargain with yourself. Make sacrifices—such as giving up dining out—so that you can continue to enjoy your favorite amusements, such as a subscription to the symphony.*

▶ *Allow for rewards. Your new spending plan should have enough slack that you can give yourself occasional rewards for sticking to it.*

▶ *When you meet your goals, rework rather than abandon your spending plan. Make a lifelong effort to keep your finances in order.*

DECORATING WITH ANTIQUES

China and porcelain. Keep an eye out for one-of-a-kind pieces at tag sales and junk stores. Often priced very low, old plates and bowls can be mixed beautifully on the dining table or displayed on a kitchen wall. As display items, their occasional chips and cracks become part of their history and character.

Tools for your hobby. Antique tools from a trade you love—cooking, sewing, woodworking, or printing—can make a fascinating display, as well as help you better understand and appreciate fore-runners in your craft.

Use your imagination. Many old household, farm, and even indus-trial items make attractive and interesting decorative accents. Hang an old wagon wheel as a wall sculpture, use a milk can or butter churn as a lamp base, or top the cast-iron base of an old woodstove with a slab of slate to make an indestructible coffee table for a playroom.

Antique rugs, too fragile for the floor but too beautiful to put away, can be used as table cover-ings or wall hangings.

DECORATING WITH COLOR

To understand the impact that color has on a room, study the three bedroom pictures below. What makes the three views look very different is simply the choice of wall paint color, an easy and inexpensive element to change.

BLUE

Blue walls have a calm-ing effect on a room, helping to make it a soothing haven at the end of a hectic day.

RED

Deep red walls make a strong statement and can be quite dramatic while still maintaining a room's intimate feeling.

YELLOW

Sunny yellow walls help you greet the morning on a cheerful note; yellow helps reflect additional light.

DECORATING WITH COLOR

Color temperatures. "Cool" col-ors—greens, blues, and violets—cool down a room that has a sunny southern or western expo-sure. "Warm" colors—reds, oranges, and yellows—occupy the opposite half of the color spec-trum and raise the visual tempera-ture of northern rooms.

Color and space. Cool colors as well as pale tints of warm colors tend to recede visually. Walls painted in cool or pale colors seem farther away. To maximize the illusion of space in a room, use light tints of cool colors on the walls and ceiling. By contrast, use warmer, darker colors to turn a cavernous room into a cozier, more attractively scaled space.

Color associations. Certain color combinations stimulate cultural and historical associations. Bright pinks, yellows, and lime greens, for example, evoke the Caribbean. Dark greens, ocher, mauve, and brown recall the Victorian era. Muted primary colors (created with early American milk paint) and classic combinations such as indigo blue and white suggest Colonial times. Pure primaries evoke the simple pleasures of childhood.

DECORATING WITH FABRIC

Color scheme. Use a favorite pat-terned fabric as a guide in creating a room's color scheme. If a creamy beige is the principal color in the fabric, use that for your walls or floor covering. If blue and terra-cotta come second, let them play supporting roles in upholstery fabrics or in the architectural trim. Pick up the fabric's accent colors in decorative pillows, picture frames, and other accessories. Use the patterned fabric itself to cover a chair or two and create the window treatment.

For adjoining rooms, use coordi-nated patterns in wallpaper, bor-ders, and fabric to achieve a unified look. Mix and match the papers and fabrics differently in each room, so that each room will have a character of its own yet the entire space will maintain a strong family resemblance.

To preview the visual impact of a wallpaper or fabric, tack a large sample up on a wall opposite a large mirror. Stand well back from the mirror and consider the wallpaper as it is reflected. You will get a sense of how strong the pattern will be at twice the distance.

Light test. View samples of patterns that you like in the room for which they are being considered and at the time of day when the room is most in use. Judging colors in the artificial light of a store can be deceiving.

DECORATING WITH FLOWERS

Enhance the color of light-toned flowers simply by adding a dash of food coloring to warm water in a vase and placing freshly cut

stems in it. Within minutes the flowers should begin to take on the new hue.

Unusual flower holders. A colored antique medicine bottle or an art deco perfume dispenser, for example, makes a charming vase. Look for such containers at flea markets or antiques stores.

Adapting flowers to a vase. To lengthen a stem that is too short, give it a lift by slipping the end

into a section of plastic drinking straw. To arrange flowers in a vase that is a little too deep, fill the bottom with marbles, pebbles, or coarse sand.

Clean silk flowers in a plastic bag with 30 mL (2 tbsp) of salt or 250 mL (1 cup) of cornmeal. Shake the bag gently for several minutes; discard the dusty salt or meal. Or blow the dust off silk flowers with a hair dryer set on warm.

DECORATING WITH PATTERNS

Pattern and color. To mix patterns successfully, combine ones that have coordinating colors. For example, juxtapose a blue and green striped wallpaper with a blue and green paisley border and blue and green India print curtains and pillows. The various patterns will be unified by the colors.

Instead of using fabric and wallpaper, introduce pattern into a room through highly veined marble or wood, in textured carpeting, in decorative paint glazes, or in a pattern of tiles. To show off such subtle patterns, however, you need a quiet background that won't overwhelm them.

A pattern with a large repeat may not make a good pillow or seat cover because only a part of the complete pattern will show. Use fabrics and wallpapers with large repeats on long draperies or on large walls, where the full design can be appreciated.

Even a relatively small repeat design may need to be centered on chair seats, sofa cushions, or on a wall. When buying fabric or wallpaper with a repeat pattern, be sure to purchase enough extra to accommodate the centering.

Patterns with tiny repeats can provide the illusion of a single, overall color, albeit one with tremendous richness and texture.

FRESH USES FOR FABRICS

Fabrics bring texture to a room and can be used for more than curtains and upholstery. Many fabrics take well to adhesives and can be used to custom-cover ordinary objects to give unity to a disparate group of items. The ideas below for using fabric are just to start you thinking.

- *Custom-cover lampshades.*
- *Laminate roll-up window shades.*
- *Make an indoor tent to bring a high ceiling into scale or to cover damaged plaster.*
- *Pad and cover an unattractive headboard on a bed.*
- *Use in place of wallpaper to add texture to walls.*
- *Make a decorative border for a sisal rug or doormat.*
- *Make a mat for a picture in a frame.*
- *Make a covering for a bulletin board.*

DEER

D

Shocking simplicity. A single electrical wire stretched 60 cm (2 ft) above the ground will keep deer out of the garden if you smear the wire with peanut butter first. Because deer love peanut butter, they will be attracted to the treat and get a shock on the nose that will usually scare them away permanently.

What deer eat varies from region to region; plants touted as "deer-proof" in one place may be "deer bait" in another. Some plants, however, are popular with deer everywhere, including balsam fir, Norway maple, eastern redbud, winged euonymus, English ivy, apple, cherry, and plum trees, rhododendron, azalea, yew, and American arborvitae.

An ounce of prevention. Deer feed along the same paths and develop strong preferences for certain plants. Any fence or repellent you use to exclude them will be most effective if erected or applied before the deer have developed the habit of browsing in your garden.

Aromatic and deer-resistant. Deer rarely browse on strong-tasting aromatic herbs and flowers, such as sage and lavender. They also tend to avoid any plants that smell like lemon or mint. Add one or more of these herbs and flowers to your border plantings.

EASY DOES IT

STEPS TO A PRETTIER SMILE

Modern dentists offer much more than just dental hygiene. Ask about these new techniques in cosmetic dentistry.

▶ *Stain Removal. Bleaching with a peroxide solution held in a molded plastic tray or laser bleaching can whiten many stained teeth.*

▶ *Composite Fillings. Tooth-colored fillings don't show and often don't require as much drilling.*

▶ *Bonding. A puttylike composite sculpted by the dentist on the tooth is used to cover discolored teeth and reshape chipped ones. Bright light hardens the composite.*

▶ *Porcelain Laminates. These ceramic veneers can correct crooked or chipped teeth, gaps between teeth, and stains that don't respond to bleaching.*

Commercial repellent. Significantly reduce deer damage to your plants with a commercial deer repellent, which gives plants an odor or flavor that the deer avoid. Keep repellents effective longer by mixing them with an antitranspirant, such as Wilt-Pruf or Pro-Tec. Both products are available at garden centers.

DENTAL CARE

Floss your teeth thoroughly once a day. Flossing, even more than brushing, is your best defense against the buildup of plaque, which harbors the bacteria that cause cavities and gum disease.

Give children fluoride drops if the local water doesn't have fluoride added. Fluoride that's taken internally is absorbed into teeth that are being formed, making them stronger and more resistant to decay. Ask your dentist or pediatrician for the correct dose.

Clean toddlers' teeth with a moist gauze pad or washcloth. If your baby or toddler goes to bed with a bottle, fill it with water rather than juice or milk, which stays in the mouth all night and can cause tooth decay.

 Brush your teeth twice a day for at least two minutes using a toothbrush with soft, rounded bristles. Replace your toothbrush as soon as it becomes frayed or once every three months.

Use a fluoride toothpaste or a mouth rinse with fluoride. Topical fluoride inhibits the growth of bacteria in the mouth and keeps plaque from sticking to teeth.

If your teeth ache when they are touched by hot, cold, or acidic foods, try a desensitizing toothpaste. If cold is the particular problem, try a fluoride mouthwash, which desensitizes cold-sensitive roots. Or, ask your dentist about protective sealants, which provide protection at the sensitive gumline.

Use an electric toothbrush if you have arthritis or another disability that makes it hard for you to brush your teeth effectively.

DENTISTS

Have dental phobia? If so, schedule an appointment for a day when you aren't under pressure. Take a friend with you for support, and ask the dentist to explain everything he will be doing. You can even break up one long visit into several short sessions. For severe anxiety, look for a practitioner of "sleep dentistry," who uses a range of calming agents, from nitrous oxide to sedatives to total anesthesia, to relax the patient.

Inform your dentist about your medical history before you have any work done on your teeth. People with artificial hip or knee joints, heart valve problems, or a history of rheumatic fever should take antibiotics before a session in the dentist's chair. Pregnant women should avoid X-rays.

Take children to the dentist for the first time around the age of two; don't wait until the child has a toothache. If children identify dentists with pain, they are more likely to resist future visits.

DESK ORGANIZATION

Plan your space. Place all essential items where you can get at them quickly without having to jump up out of your chair. The basics may include computer, phone, appointment book, pens, pencils, stapler, and paper clips.

Clear clutter. Don't let things on your desk pile up. Clean your desk and "In" basket frequently. Open the mail next to a wastebasket and throw away any unwanted solicitations on the spot.

Keep files up-to-date, not only in drawers but in your computer. Computer clutter can be as insidious as desk clutter and can slow down your system. Delete outdated files once a week.

Hang it up. Install bulletin boards to post important general information. And, don't let your bulletin boards become crammed with outdated information.

DESSERTS

Let fresh fruit or fruit salad substitute for a high-fat dessert.

Chop and mix two or more fresh fruits together in a bowl. Sprinkle with fruit juice, cider, or a couple of tablespoons of liqueur.

For a summer dessert, scoop a fruit sorbet into a parfait or wine glass, add whipped topping, and garnish with berries or a cherry.

Reward a sweet tooth. Don't always deny yourself the rich desserts you love; just indulge infrequently and judiciously. To help in that restraint, resist the so-so treats—indulge only in your favorites. Then it's a real reward.

DIETARY FIBER

Eat raw fruits and vegetables. Both have more useful fiber when they're unpeeled and uncooked. Eat cooked vegetables, such as potatoes, skins and all.

Eat whole grains, such as whole wheat, bran, and oat cereals and breads, to get the recommended daily 20 to 35 grams of fiber.

Full of beans. Beans are among the richest sources of fiber. Substitute beans for meat, snack on bean dip and chips, or toss canned beans into soups or salads. When cooking with canned beans, don't discard the broth; it's full of fiber.

Increase fiber gradually to let your digestive tract adjust. Too many fiber-rich foods at once can result in gas and diarrhea.

RIGHT STUFF

DESK ORGANIZATION

Banish desk clutter with magazine organizers. These samples from Hold Everything are decorative as well as practical, ranging in style from clear acrylic to homey wicker to minimalist metal. Magazine organizers are perfect storage bins for business reports, letters, and notebooks. Look for them in office-supply stores.

D

DINING ROOMS

On a limited budget, furnish a dining room with handsome table settings, good linens, pretty china, and good candlesticks before buying fine furniture. At a party your table and chairs will hardly show. All eyes will be on the food and the table appointments.

Low lighting adds drama. Put the chandelier and wall sconces on dimmer switches. You can keep the lights low during candle-lit meals and create a convivial atmosphere.

Improvise a dining room, if you don't have one, by setting up a collapsible round table in the living room in front of some of the living room chairs. Fill out the seating with folding chairs dressed up in linen slipcovers that match a floor-length tablecloth.

Locate a sideboard or serving table near the head of the table. The extra surface, particularly if it's equipped with an electric hot tray, makes serving easier. It also keeps the table from becoming cluttered with too many dishes.

DINNER PARTIES

A no-fuss main course: a roast. Whether it's pork, ham, beef, lamb, or veal, all you need do is rub the meat with the spices or seasonings that complement the cut, place it in the oven, and cook until done. A meat thermometer makes your work that much easier.

No time to experiment. You're asking for trouble if you decide to cook a new dish for a special dinner party. If you haven't made a recipe before, you won't be able to anticipate what can go wrong or the preparation time.

A QUICK, NO-WORK DINNER PARTY

Having guests over at the last minute? Don't be too proud to order take-out food—served on pretty platters and given a special garnish or two, take-out puts on the dog.

▶ *Best bets: stir-fries, casseroles, or any hearty ethnic fare. Prepare a big tossed salad to serve with finger foods like fried chicken, barbecued ribs, or chilled cooked shrimp. Buy a large batch of your favorite bolognese sauce from an Italian restaurant and cook the pasta to serve with it.*

▶ *Remove the food from its containers and transfer to ovenproof dishes with lids (or use aluminum foil). Put the food in an oven set at 105°C (225°F), the best temperature for keeping food warm without cooking it.*

▶ *Serve the food buffet-style and provide the dishes. Attractive paper plates will lessen your chores even more.*

▶ *Arrange the food on serving dishes. Garnish with fresh herbs, such as chopped parsley, dill, or chives. Put condiments in small bowls.*

▶ *Sit back and let your guests praise the food before admitting you didn't lift a finger to cook it.*

Plus, a recipe may sound good on paper but in practice be a big disappointment. Stick with the tried-and-true.

Make it intimate. Set up several small tables, from card tables to little café tables, instead of one big table. This creates a cozier, less formal atmosphere, and encourages great conversations.

Make a list of friends who don't mind a last-minute dinner invitation. Then, if a cancellation causes you to be a lady or a gentleman short at your table, simply consult your list and call one of those very understanding friends.

One-pot meal. In a big Dutch oven or ceramic pot, make a hearty soup or stew such as *boeuf Bourguignonne* or *coq au vin* for your large dinner party and serve it from a hot plate. Not only are these timeless dishes easy to serve, but they can be made

ahead of time. In fact, many soups and stews often taste better after two or three days.

DISABILITY INSURANCE

Safeguard your income—and your family's well-being—with additional disability insurance if your employer's benefits will be too little and too short-lived. Be aware that the chances of being disabled during your working years are far greater than those of dying.

Shop around for the best rates. Also ask what type of occupations the insurer most often covers. A company that routinely insures people with dangerous jobs may have high premiums.

Get a noncancelable policy that lets you renew as long as the insurance is in effect, and keep the same premiums and benefits. Also make sure that the policy covers both accidents and illness.

Review the policy's waiting period, the amount of time from a person's becoming disabled to the start of benefits. As a rule, the longer the waiting period, the lower the premium. Therefore, opt for the lengthiest waiting period, usually about six months.

Check your policy to see if it allows you to earn income while you are collecting a disability payment. Check that the disability benefit is paid for your inability to work in your chosen field only.

DISCIPLINING CHILDREN

Vary your negatives. Saying "no" and "don't" to a toddler too often lessens the impact of these words—and leaves a stubborn child no choice but to resist. Instead, try other, slightly less adamant expressions, such as "Uh-oh!" or "Wait!" or "Oops!" to get your point across with more humor and gentle distraction.

Draw up house rules. Rules are the best way to deal with issues that keep recurring. It's easier to say "that's the rule" than to say "no." As your children get older, include them in tailoring rules that seem reasonable to everyone.

Show appreciation. Whenever your kids take responsibility, notice it and voice your grati-

tude—especially when a child does something without being asked. If a child cleans up her room, for example, be sure to thank her for taking responsibility and compliment her on her work.

Set reasonable consequences. The most effective way to discipline an adolescent is to suspend or restrict privileges. But not for extended periods—a youngster's sense of time is slower than yours, and he can feel overwhelmed or defeated if the punishment lasts too long.

DISHWASHERS

Conserve energy by running the dishwasher at night, when many power companies offer lower rates. And don't use the dishwasher until it is full. Skip the drying cycle by stopping the machine after its last rinse or setting the controls to do so automatically. Open the door for air drying.

Position light cups and other objects that are easily upturned toward the back on the upper rack—the place where the spray is least powerful.

Put utensils with handles down in the dishwasher's baskets for

most effective cleaning. To save time putting them back in the drawer, separate knives, forks, and spoons in the baskets.

Check the drain if dishes and glasses are spotted with bits of leftover food. A clogged strainer, located at the bottom of the machine, can easily be cleaned.

Place large items like cookie sheets or platters at the sides in the rear of your dishwasher's bottom rack. This ensures that the water spray will reach them and distribute the detergent.

DIVORCE

Maintain routines. Keeping to your own daily routine and to your children's established times for meals, homework, playtime, and bedtime can help lessen the impact of marital separation on the youngsters—and on you.

Credit check. If you are divorcing, ask creditors in writing to close any joint accounts and give you written confirmation. Try to convert or reopen these as individual accounts. Your credit record will suffer if a former spouse handles a jointly held account irresponsibly.

 Shield your children from any disagreements between you and your former spouse, and don't badmouth the other parent. Such negative behavior is often more damaging to a child than the breakup itself.

Consider mediation. If you and your spouse can't agree on complicated matters like custody, try mediation. Trained, neutral mediators can help you arrive at a workable, creative solution. To find a mediator, look in your Yellow Pages under "Mediation Services."

DOCTORS

Keep a medical journal. Over time it's easy to forget details of past illnesses. Take a few minutes to jot down when you were sick, what medications you took, and if you had an allergic reaction. This information may prove invaluable in your medical history.

Make a list of your concerns before you visit a doctor so that you don't forget to ask important questions. Cover what's most important to you first so it won't get overlooked. When scheduling an appointment, tell the receptionist you have several questions for the doctor to answer.

 Get a second opinion. Before making any decisions about a course of treatment, study all the options. Get a second opinion if your doctor fails to listen to your questions or concerns.

To find a new doctor, ask for a referral from a friend or someone in the health-care field. They're usually knowledgeable about doctors in the area.

Be honest. Tell your doctor everything that may influence your diagnosis, including information on your emotional health. Don't let embarrassment keep you from getting proper treatment.

DOG GROOMING

Begin grooming your dog when it's a puppy. Keep to a regular routine of short sessions accompanied by praise and affection. Your dog will soon look forward to being groomed.

Clipping nails. Unless your dog runs on hard surfaces, its nails will need clipping. Nails on dewclaws especially need to be clipped. Use dog nail clippers, available at pet shops, and be careful not to cut to the quick. If you accidentally do, use a styptic pencil to stop the bleeding, then apply antiseptic. File rough edges smooth.

Bathe a dog no more than once a month and not before it is six months old. Too many baths rob the skin of necessary oils. Put a nonslip mat in the bathtub or sink to make the dog feel more secure. Use a dog shampoo (no-tangle varieties are available) and cream rinse. Pay special attention to the underneath areas, checking the skin for pests and irritations.

Before the bath, walk and brush your dog. Brushing reduces matting in the bath. After the bath, dry off your pet thoroughly before you let it back outside.

Keeping teeth clean. Give your dog at least some hard food (biscuits) and rawhide to chew every day. Try to brush teeth and gums at least once a week with special dog toothpaste. Tooth scrapers will also remove excess tartar.

DOG TRAINING

Take charge. A dog's pack instincts prepare it to either lead or follow. If you are firm, clear, and consistent, your dog will identify you as the leader.

Just the right tone. Dogs understand tones of voice. Use an authoritative tone for commands, a higher pitch for praise, and a low, gruff voice for corrections.

RETRACTABLE LEASHES

A retractable leash gives your dog the freedom to roam yet allows you to take control when necessary. Leashes come in different strengths and extensions for different-size dogs and attach to the dog's collar with a safety clip. Apply the brake button and locking lever to stop your dog or to keep it a fixed distance from you as you walk.

Some of the most popular breeds of dogs for family pets are listed below. All are known for their good nature, especially with children. To help make your selection easier, this chart provides some pros and cons. Beyond that, the choice is yours.

BREED	EASILY TRAINED	SHEDDING	COMMENTS
Basset Hound	Moderately easy	Low shedder	Very mild-mannered
Cocker Spaniel	Yes	Medium shedder	Can be hard to housebreak; some bark if left alone
English Springer Spaniel	Yes	Medium shedder	Can bark and become destructive if left alone too much
Golden Retriever	Yes	Medium shedder	Ideal family dog; requires exercise
Labrador Retriever	Yes, but strong on a leash	Medium shedder	Ideal family dog; requires exercise
Poodle	Yes	Low shedder	Toy poodles can be high-strung
Schnauzer	Yes	Low shedder	Friendly, playful; can be yappy

Obedience school. Consider taking your dog to classes. They are usually inexpensive and fun, a good social experience for both you and the dog. Start when your puppy is six months old; a younger dog's attention span is too short.

DOGS

RX: Dog. Owning a dog can do wonders for your health. Not only do dogs make loyal, affectionate, and nonjudgmental friends but petting a dog can actually lower blood pressure. Studies have also shown that caring for a dog can lengthen the lives of people who have had heart attacks.

Walking the dog. The distance a dog needs to walk every day depends on its size and breed. Miniatures like Chihuahuas need no more than a short stroll, but hunting dogs like retrievers can happily cover 13 km (8 mi) or more (you can break this up into two walks). Give these breeds a regular routine by making them your jog-ging companions—and you'll get a workout in the bargain.

"Fed" or "Not Fed". If more than one person in your home feeds the dog, place the dog's dish on a mat color-coded by placing red tape on one side and blue tape on the flip side. Before the dog has been fed, keep the blue side up; after the dog is fed, flip the mat red side up.

DOLLS

Store dolls with inset eyes facedown in the box. The mechanism that makes their eyes "blink" is held in place with plaster; face up, the eyes are drawn away from the doll's head by the weight of the mechanism.

Sun protection. Keep old or antique dolls out of direct sunlight. The sun's ultraviolet rays will fade the doll's clothing and may eventually discolor and rot the material the doll is made of.

Do not disturb. If you buy a doll as a collectible, leave it in the original packaging. It will gain more in resale value if the tags and inserts remain intact.

Display your dolls. Unpack beloved dolls from your childhood toy chest. Wash their clothes, comb their hair, and gently wipe off any smudges with mild soap and water. Arrange your cleaned-up dolls inside a glassed cupboard or on a shelf. These relics of childhood days can make charming displays.

DOOR & WINDOW HARDWARE

Hardware upgrade. Just changing the handles, latches, and cranks on an inexpensive casement window can turn it into a lovely accessory. Using brass gives the window a classic formality; choosing wrought-iron hardware can create a rustic feel.

Safety hardware. To secure double-hung windows, install a lock with a metal bolt that goes through the inner sash as well as halfway through the outer sash where the two overlap. If you never open the window, just drive a long nail through both sashes instead and save the cost of the lock.

When painting windows and doors, remove all the hardware before you start. It's faster and easier than trying to mask complicated handles and hinges, and the results will be more professional. You can soak the hardware clean while you paint.

DOORS

To clean a sliding-door track, spray household cleaner on a rag, wrap the rag around the tip of a screwdriver, and move it along the track. Lubricate the track with powdered graphite or silicone spray. Don't use oil; it attracts dirt.

Latch-side fix. If a door binds, or sticks, on the latch side, first tighten the hinge screws. If you can't tighten them, replace all the hinge screws with longer or larger wood screws.

Hinge-side fix. If a door binds on the hinge side, the hinges may have been set into the frame too deeply. Shim them by unscrewing the hinge leaves and placing strips of cardboard behind them, then reattaching the leaves.

If a door binds all around, it has probably swelled due to the weather. If it binds only at the top, the house has probably settled. In either situation, remove the door and plane it.

To straighten a sagging wooden storm or screen door, use wire cable linked to a turnbuckle. Stretch the wire cable diagonally across the door from the top corner on the hinge side to the lower outside corner, then simply tighten the turnbuckle.

Fix a binding door by rubbing a bar of soap or the stub of a candle on the sticking areas. If that doesn't work, sand the protruding spots. To find the problem spot, rub chalk down the door's edge, then close the door; the chalk will leave marks on the frame.

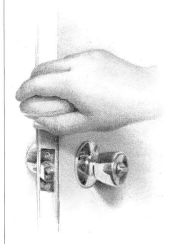

To quiet a squeaky door, remove the pin from the offending hinge, squirt household oil or silicone spray into the pin's shaft, and then reinsert it. Work the lubricant in by moving the door back and forth.

DRAINS

To keep a drain sweet, once a week, add a handful of baking soda or 250 mL (1 cup) of vinegar, let it stand for 30 minutes, then flush with very hot water.

Clog-free kitchen drains. Never put cooking grease or coffee grounds down the kitchen drains —unless you have a garbage disposer. Collect grease in a used coffee can and put it in the rubbish. Toss coffee grounds onto your compost pile.

When unclogging a sink drain with a plunger, rub the plunger's rim with petroleum jelly to get a

---

HANDLES WITH A PAST

Imagination and craft went into the design of doorknobs in eras past, as can be seen in these brass and ceramic examples. Such lovely knobs, which often can be picked up for a song at flea markets and renovation resale companies, give a door—and even a room— extra personality and pizzazz.

better seal. Fill the sink with 7.5 cm (3 in.) of water and close off adjacent drains before you start pumping.

DRAWERS

First things first. What goes into your most convenient drawers depends on what you use most often. Place high-priority items in the most accessible locations.

Use drawer dividers to separate small items sharing a drawer—underwear, socks, and hosiery, for example. Dividers are sold in hardware or home maintenance stores.

Old bookcases can be turned into handy drawers. Hang a curtain over the bookcase or attach a door purchased at an unpainted-furniture store.

Recycle old dresser drawers by using them to store items under a bed. Attach casters to the bottom to make for easy access.

DRESSING SMART

Buy the basics. Save money and time by investing in basics that can be the foundation of many outfits. For example, buy good quality slacks, skirt, and jacket in a basic color (navy blue, black, or tan.) Then select sweaters, blouses, jackets, and accessories to work with the basics.

Invest in quality. Clothes that are well made last longer, drape better, and retain their shape after numerous cleanings. Accessories such as shoes and handbags should also be of good quality. Keep in mind that high quality need not mean high priced; don't pay for a label.

Between sizes? If you find that the item you are considering is slightly tight, go for the next size larger. No matter how much you may want to be a size 8, you'll look slimmer wearing the size 10.

We all have issues with our body shapes—and that includes men as well as women. Here is a list of the more common figure problems and some easy solutions.

▶ *Protruding Tummy. Wear longer jackets, overblouses, tunic sweaters, or drop-waist blousons.*

▶ *Heavy Hips or Bottom. Wear roomy tops and jackets that cover your backside; add shoulder pads or full sleeves to put your shape into better proportion.*

▶ *Large Bust. Wear cinched-waist dresses and unstructured jackets and sweaters; avoid clingy tops.*

▶ *Long Arms. Hold out for dress shirts with the correct sleeve length. Roll up sports shirt sleeves for a casual look.*

▶ *Long Neck. Wear high collars, ruffles, chokers, wide ties, scarves, or turtlenecks to hide a long neck and enhance a pretty one.*

White pants, one pair in cotton or silk for summer, one pair in wool for winter, are a staple for women. White pants can go from casual to dressy with a quick change of shirt, sweater, or jacket.

DRESSING WITH COLOR

The colors for you. To figure out the most flattering colors for you, visit a color specialist, listed in the Yellow Pages under "Color Consultants." The money you will save on clothing mistakes will be worth the expense.

Optical illusion. Colors on the warm end of the spectrum, such as red, orange, and yellow, can make you look heavier, while colors on the cool end of the spectrum, like green, blue, and purple, can have a slimming effect, as do black and dark navy blue.

Lift your spirits. Wear bright colors such as poppy red and buttercup yellow to project an air of energy, daring, and joy. Wear pale blue or pale green to feel calm and serene.

Blue power. Wear a dark blue suit to appear trustworthy and sincere. Dark blue is also an appropriate color to wear for formal or somber occasions. To add authority, add a crisp white shirt or a silky white blouse; to soften the look add pearls or a scarf.

DRIP IRRIGATION

A water saver. Drip irrigation systems are more efficient than sprinkler systems. They slowly and steadily deliver water directly to the soil around plants—either by emitters or through a soaker-type hose—and lose no moisture to evaporation or runoff.

For shrubs, use a separate drip irrigation hose. Shrubs need less frequent watering than vegetable or flower gardens. Snake the hose between individual plants—either on top of the soil or buried beneath the mulch. Turn the spigot on only a quarter turn.

Flush drip irrigation lines monthly to prevent the emitters from clogging. In addition, frequently check the individual emitters; use a toothpick to clean out the heads.

DRIVEWAYS

Prune for an clear view. Lush landscaping may make your driveway look inviting, but it can be a hazard if it interferes with your view of traffic. Ideally, you should have an unobstructed view of the roadway for 152 m (500 ft) in either direction.

Driveway width. The growing popularity of trucks and sports utility vehicles means that older driveways may need to be redesigned. The bigger vehicles need a wider apron to turn smoothly into the driveway.

Fix up a concrete driveway with premixed patching concrete, following the manufacturer's directions. Store leftover concrete in a plastic bag in a plastic garbage can with an airtight lid to keep it dry for future use. The sooner you patch holes and cracks, the smaller and easier the repair is.

Driftless driveway. Make it easier to keep your driveway passable in winter by using natural windbreaks to prevent snowdrifts. Most effective are banks of medium-dense, low trees or shrubs, such as pussywillows, lilacs, or pines, set parallel to the driveway on both sides. (Make sure the trees and shrubs are low enough so that they do not obstruct your view.) Don't put up a fence or wall; either one will promote drifting.

Asphalt potholes. "Cold patch"—premixed asphalt and gravel sold by the bag at building supply centers—makes a serviceable filler for large holes in an asphalt driveway. Mound the material into the potholes to about a half inch above the level of the surrounding asphalt; pack the cold patch in with a shovel, then drive the car back and forth across it to finish. Patching asphalt is most easily done on a warm, sunny day.

Repair a gravel driveway in late spring when the roadway is still damp and workable. Spread and level new gravel over the eroded areas. To correct potholes and ruts, hire an experienced bulldozer operator.

Sealing for longer life. Apply a coat of asphalt sealant, available at hardware or home stores, every 2 to 3 years to prolong the life of an asphalt driveway. Sealants are easiest to spread on cool, dry autumn or spring days.

DRIVING AT NIGHT

When an oncoming car approaches on a two-lane highway, look down at the fog line (the painted stripe on the right edge of the road) for guidance. This will prevent you from becoming blinded by the oncoming headlights.

 Dealing with brights. If an oncoming car has the headlights on the high-beam setting, close your left eye to protect your night vision until the car passes. Blinking your own brights should alert the driver to dim his headlights.

Keep the dash lights dimmed when you drive at night; they diminish your night vision. When you buy a new car, look for red dashboard lights, like the lights used on submarines, which don't affect night vision.

DRIVING IN RAIN OR FOG

Don't use the brakes. In heavy rain, cars going faster than 55 km/h (35 mph) can start to hydroplane, and the wheels ride on a cushion of water above the road. The loss of traction makes it

NEGOTIATING A SKID

Tricks for safe driving on slippery roads, whether they are icy from snow or wet from a summer rain, are the same. The moment you start to skid:

▶ *Take your foot off the accelerator. To slow the car down, lightly pump traditional brakes; apply firm and steady pressure onto antilock brakes. Don't slam on either kind of brake.*

▶ *Shift into neutral gear. In a skid, whether you are driving a front- or rear-wheel-drive car, first disengage the clutch or shift to neutral if possible.*

▶ *On rear-wheel-drive cars, steer into the skid. This will allow the car to straighten out and stop skidding. Just before coming out of the skid, countersteer (turn the wheel the other way) slightly until you are going in the direction you want to go.*

▶ *On front-wheel-drive cars, steer in the direction the car is going until you feel the wheels begin to grip. Then use the brakes to regain control of speed before you steer in another direction.*

impossible for you to steer. If this happens, take your foot off the accelerator to slow the car and keep the steering wheel straight until you feel some traction.

Fog strategy. Use fog lights if you have them on your car; otherwise, use your low beams. Drive very slowly so that you can stop within the range of visibility.

Beware of deep puddles. Proceed slowly through accumulated water on the road. A puddle may be deeper than it appears, or a pothole may be hidden by the water. Water can also splash on your ignition wires, causing the car to stall, or on your brakes, causing them to lose their grip.

Keep your headlights on even in the middle of the day when you drive through rain or fog. (It's the law in many states.) Lights let you see better and also make it easier for other drivers to see you.

DRIVING IN SNOW & ICE

If you get stuck in snow, gently accelerate, then release. Don't rev your engine or spin your wheels, which will only dig your car in further. Don't rock the car more than once or twice; you may damage the automatic transmission.

Getting traction. Carry a small bag of sand or cat litter in your trunk during the winter months. If you get stuck, apply the sand or litter under the wheels.

When you stop or turn in snow, signal, then brake slowly so that you don't skid and the cars behind yours can respond.

DRIVING LONG DISTANCES

Service your car at least two weeks before taking a long trip. If something needs work or a part

requires replacement, you will still have time to have it fixed by your own mechanic.

Bring along books-on-tape to keep you company, especially if you are driving by yourself. Listening to a story can both keep you awake and shorten the long, lonely hours of driving.

Chill out. Keep the car's interior as cold as you can stand it. Heat encourages sleepiness. Every so often, lower the windows and circulate some fresh air.

Take frequent breaks, at least once every two to three hours. Have a light snack, do calisthenics, stretch your legs. If nothing seems to wake you up, take a nap.

In a small cooler, keep a damp washcloth handy in a plastic bag for a quick, wake-up face wash. Keep nutritious snacks such as fruit, raw vegetables, crackers, and bottled water or soda on hand.

Wear glasses, even if you don't need them to correct your vision. Your eyes can dry out as a result of the car's ventilation draft. Dry eyes are uncomfortable and fatiguing. Wear prescription or nonprescription lenses or sunglasses for protection.

Relieve lower-back stress by placing a pillow or rolled towel behind the small of your back. Move the seat so that your knees are slightly bent to reduce stress on back muscles.

Drying Hydrangeas

Dried hydrangeas make gorgeous floral arrangements that look as though they took hours of work to create. The fact is, hydrangeas are simple to dry and take less than an hour to arrange in a basket

1 Pick blooms in a variety of sizes, making sure each has at least a 30 cm (12 in.) stem. Remove all the green leaves, including the small ones at the base of the flower.

2 Using a piece of string or a spring clothespin, hang each stem upside down in a cool, dark, dry area for about 7 days, or until they are completely dry.

3 Select a basket that is relatively deep. Create a stabilizing bed of broken flower heads, then arrange larger blooms around the rim. Fill in with the remaining flowers.

DRY CLEANING

Let 'em know. Tell your dry cleaner if anything was spilled on your garment—even if you can't see a stain. If not treated properly, the spill might react to the dry-cleaning chemicals and form a permanent mark.

Separation anxiety? Have matching clothes—a suit jacket and pants, for example—cleaned at the same time. Otherwise, color discrepancies may result.

Label differences. If a garment says "dry-clean only," take it to a dry cleaner. However, if the label just says "dry-clean," you can hand-wash it, but test the fabric first by dabbing water in an inconspicuous place. If the color runs, have it professionally cleaned.

Women beware! Before patronizing a dry cleaner, check the rates. This is important because many areas prohibit dry cleaners from charging women more than men for the same type of garment—shirts, jackets, and pants.

DRY SKIN

Made in the shade. Stay out of direct sunlight, which robs the skin of precious moisture, as much as possible. For added protection, apply a strong sunscreen—with a sun protection factor (SPF) of at least 15—every day.

Shower smarts. Hot water tends to dry your skin, so opt for warm showers and baths. Leisurely soaks in the tub are luxurious, but long baths can strip moisture from dry skin—especially in the winter. When it's cold out, take showers.

The wetter, the better. After you've finished showering or bathing, slather on a moisturizer while your skin is still wet. The cream locks in the water, keeping your skin smooth and soft.

Start small. Before you invest in a moisturizer that you've never used, ask a saleperson at a cos-

metics counter for a free sample. This will allow you to test for any unfavorable reactions before you make a costly purchase.

Clean with cream. Use a nondrying moisturizing cleanser on your face, and remove it with tissue. If you have really dry skin, don't use cleanser at all; just rinse with warm water.

Work inside out. Moisturize your skin by drinking 8 to 10 glasses of water each day—a practice that's good for your general health too.

DRYING FLOWERS

Timing is everything. When selecting blooms, choose those at the peak of their beauty; don't wait until they start to droop. Cut the flowers in midmorning, after the dew has dried and the blooms begin to open in the sun.

In a rush? To dry flowers quickly, place them in an airtight container and cover them with silica gel, which is available at florist shops and hardware stores. Use

attractively. The only secret is to pick faded flowers in the autumn after the air turns cool but before the first frost.

4 *When you achieve the arrangement you wish, protect the basket with aluminum foil or newspaper, then spray the flowers with lavender or mauve floral paint.*

In less than an hour, you will have created a dramatic and beautiful floral arrangement that will last for years.

this method, too, when you are drying very moist or extremely brittle flowers.

Telephone-book press. Place single blooms in sheets of tissue paper, then insert them in the pages of an old telephone book. Stack a heavy object on top to press the plants, which take about a month or so to dry completely.

DUSTING

Hard to reach? Hardly. Simply tie a soft cloth to the end of a yardstick. Employ this makeshift duster when you're cleaning trouble spots such as the space behind a desk, the corner behind a bed, or the top shelf of a cabinet.

Drop the cloth. Instead of dusting lampshades with a rag, let your vacuum do the work if it has a brush or nozzle attachment.

The dryer did it. Clean your dusty drapes and curtains by simply tossing them in the dryer. Turn the machine to the Air only cycle, then run it for about 20 minutes.

Hit the showers. Clean your houseplants when they become cloaked in dust by toting them off to the bathroom for a brief but refreshing shower. Let them drip-dry before putting them back.

No more diabolical dustpans. To stop dust, soot, and light crumbs from constantly spilling out of your dustpan, wipe the pan with a wet paper towel before you start.

DYEING CLOTH

One for all. To ensure consistent color, dye all matching items in one container at the same time. Even the smallest difference in the amount of dye, the temperature of the water, or the length of soaking time can result in different hues.

For a smooth, even color, be sure that the dye you're using is thoroughly mixed into the water and that the container can handily accommodate all of the submerged garments.

Go natural. Stick with natural fabrics for dyeing. Synthetic fabrics prove to be fairly impenetrable, and blended articles turn out streaked because the different types of fiber absorb varying levels of dye.

Matching thread for sewing. Wrap an adequate supply of white cotton thread around the handle of a wooden spoon, then stir it in the dye while the other items are soaking.

EAR CARE

Remove wax the safe way. First of all, never probe the inside of your ear with anything small, narrow, or pointed. Instead, use an eyedropper to gently flush your ears with a 50-50 mixture of warm water and hydrogen peroxide. Repeat this application twice a day until the wax softens and washes out.

Ear-popping air travel. To ease the discomfort flying causes to your ears, chew gum or continually yawn as the plane ascends to its cruising altitude.

Muffle the hubbub. Prevent hearing loss by wearing earplugs—they're inexpensive yet highly effective—whenever you're exposed to noises like a loud lawn mower or leaf blower.

What's that buzzing sound? If an insect becomes trapped in your ear canal, try to float it out with water. If this doesn't do the trick, rinse your ear with drops of vegetable or mineral oil to kill the bug, then have your doctor remove it from your ear.

Temporarily relieve an earache by holding a hot compress against your ear. Leave it in place until cool; repeat as often as needed.

EARLY RETIREMENT

Look before you leap. Before you jump at an early retirement offer from your employer, be sure to have the details of the package evaluated. Consult a good financial adviser and an attorney to help you analyze your costs, options, and insurance coverages.

The one-step-ahead strategy. When planning for your retirement, save as if you were going to stop working two or more years before the actual date. Any extra time on the job will be icing on the cake, and you'll also be in a good position to opt for an early retirement.

Life preserver? Plan ahead to be involved in activities that help you maintain a sense of usefulness, creativity, and community. Be aware of the fact that retiring with vague plans can be a recipe for depression and loneliness.

 Frugal today, free tomorrow. To afford the leisure of an early retirement, resolve to live below your means while you are still on the job. Also do your best to trim all those expenses that aren't absolutely necessary—dinners out, for example, or elaborate gifts.

EARRINGS

Paired off. To keep matched sets of pierced earrings together, use a button. Just slip the posts through the thread holes, secure them with their backs, and voilà—no more searching for a lost mate.

An ounce of prevention. Wipe a dab of an over-the-counter antibiotic cream on the posts of your pierced earrings. They'll slip easily through your earlobes, and you'll be guarding against the possibility of infection.

A little off balance? To prevent large or heavy earrings from flopping forward, use an earring guard. Cut a small circle out of plastic—the rectangular tabs used to seal bread bags work well—and poke a pinhole through the center. Place the guard between your ear and the earring back.

Hey, it works! In a pinch, use a pencil eraser as a stand-in for a lost earring back. With a pair of scissors, snip off the eraser and slide it over the post.

NO MORE PINCHED EARS

Available at jewelry stores and pharmacies, these small pads—practically invisible when you wear them—save your earlobes from the redness and irritation caused by a hard-pressing clip. One type of pad has a peel-off adhesive; the second, with its small nib, fits snugly into the hole at the end of an earring's clip.

Lost one? Don't discard a stud-type earring if you've misplaced its matching partner; instead, wear the single earring as a one-of-a-kind lapel pin.

EASTER

Make it stick. Before you dye an Easter egg, clean it with a mild detergent to wash away its oily coat. As a result, the dye will color the shell more vividly.

Eggs you can eat. Use only edible dyes when making Easter eggs. Safe ones include food coloring and natural dyes. Avoid fabric dyes, powdered-egg dyes, and coloring drawn from crepe or tissue paper soaked in hot water—all of which are harmful.

Homemade egg dyes. Use supermarket fruits and vegetables—blueberries, raspberries, spinach, raw beets, yellow onions, and red cabbage. In a pot, place the eggs and 500 mL (2 cups) of the vegetable of your choice. Cover with water and add 15 mL (1 tbsp) of vinegar. Simmer for 15 minutes, then let stand for an hour.

Put a shine on it. Give dyed eggs an attractive sheen by coating them with a layer of olive or vegetable oil. Chill the eggs in the refrigerator to further bring out their luster.

Patterns for your eggs. Create dazzling designs—checkerboards, plaids, or diamonds, for instance—by attaching rubberbands or thin strips of tape to the eggs before you dye them. For leafy designs,

TWISTS ON TRADITIONAL BASKETS

Easter baskets are among the most festive holiday symbols, filled with colorful treats and the promise of spring. Surprise the kids with novel, creative alternatives to the standard straw baskets. Here are some ideas.

▶ *Easter Buckets. Use a small, brightly colored bucket or pail. Tie ribbons or yarn to its handle and fill with Easter grass and goodies.*

▶ *Mini-baskets. Fill miniature straw baskets with candy and toys. Stage a scavenger hunt: in each little basket, leave a note or a map giving directions to another small bundle of treats.*

▶ *Big Straw Hats. Turn Easter bonnets into Easter baskets by filling a sombrero, a straw bowler, or a wide-brimmed gardening hat with holiday goodies.*

▶ *Flowerpots. Fill clay flowerpots with some paper grass, colored Easter eggs, and candies. Nothing could be more natural for spring.*

place leaves on the eggs and hold fast with pantyhose before dropping them into the dye pot.

Avoid the Christmas rush. Instead of the Christmas holiday, make Easter your special time to connect with friends and loved ones. Send Happy Spring cards and host an Easter dinner, complete with spring lamb and seasonal vegetables. Have an Easter-egg treasure hunt for grown-ups and children alike.

Apartment hunting. If you live in a small space such as an apartment, forgo hunting for dyed eggs, which are too easy to find. Instead, have the kids search for less conspicuous treats, such as jelly beans and little chocolate eggs wrapped in foil.

Are all the eggs in one basket? When children of different ages search the backyard for Easter eggs, set a limit on the number of discoveries each child is allowed to make. By keeping the older kids

from gathering up all the hidden treasures, the younger ones are assured a good time.

Candle-wax creations. Don't spend hours etching patterns into dyed eggs. Instead, drip candle wax onto hard-boiled eggs, then place the eggs in a cold-water dye. Peel away the wax to expose your creation.

An easy, elegant centerpiece. Place several pots of Easter lilies on your holiday table and surround them with white candles in a variety of sizes and shapes.

EATING OUT

Don't go on an empty stomach. Treat yourself to a light snack, such as an apple or a few crackers, before heading out for a meal. This lowers the chances that you'll overeat—and that you'll run up a large tab.

Health-conscious ordering. Try not to indulge in foods described as au gratin, buttery, sautéed, fried, or creamed. Instead, select dishes that are broiled, grilled, steamed, roasted, or poached.

Out to lunch. If you dine out frequently, make lunch, not dinner, your heartiest meal. During the day the prices are less expensive and the portions are about the same size or just slightly smaller.

Let one entree serve two. If the restaurant serves heaping helpings, go ahead and share an entree with your partner; you may only have to pay an extra-plate charge. Or skip the main course and order an appetizer, salad, and soup.

If you are dieting. Take control of your calories, even when you are eating out. Order meat, poultry, or fish that is grilled, broiled, or steamed and served without gravy or sauce; ask for your salad dressing to be served on the side; request that your vegetables be steamed, then seasoned with lemon juice or herbs; and order a plain baked potato or rice. Above all, avoid butter.

Order first. This helps you keep to your diet because you avoid the temptation of following the lead of dining companions who select calorie-rich foods.

EGGS

For perfect poached eggs, add a tablespoon of vinegar to the water to help set the whites.

Play spin the egg. To determine whether or not an egg is cooked, rotate it on your countertop. Hard-boiled eggs spin smoothly; uncooked ones tend to wobble.

Egg "cookies" for kids. As you pour beaten eggs into a heated skillet, collect them into a metal cookie cutter, cook, then serve.

The better to cook with. Buy "large" eggs for all recipes unless instructed otherwise. Both "medium" and "extra-large" eggs can adversely affect how a recipe turns out.

Store eggs in their cartons, not on the refrigerator egg shelf. This helps to preserve moisture and prevent the eggs from absorbing the flavor of other foods.

Freeze leftover egg whites in small, airtight containers or bags. Mark the container with the amount and date. Better yet, store exactly the amount you need to bake your favorite cake.

Save money with white eggs. Brown eggs, which often cost more than white, offer nothing extra in the way of quality.

 Hard-boiled happiness? Before boiling an egg, prick a hole in the large end with a pin to prevent the shell from cracking and to ease the job of peeling.

Whipping up egg whites. For lofty, well-formed peaks, use a bowl made of copper, stainless steel, or glass. Make sure that the bowl is clean and dry.

ELDER CARE

Recruit a network of helpers. Make a list, complete with addresses and telephone numbers, of the people who are important to your elderly relative or friend. Include friends and neighbors as well as doctors, lawyers, and other professionals.

PLANNING AHEAD FOR SENIORS

If you are a senior, it's wise to make plans to ensure that your affairs are attended to as you wish. The following documents make this task easier for you and your family.

▶ *Will. Keep this indispensable document up-to-date.*

▶ *Power of Attorney. Allows you to name someone to act on your behalf if you are incapacitated.*

▶ *Health-Care Proxy. Gives someone the legal right to make decisions regarding your health care.*

▶ *Living Will. Describes your wishes regarding medical care and what others should do if you are terminally ill.*

▶ *Funeral Arrangements. Documents your wishes concerning your funeral. You can also prepay funeral fees.*

RIGHT STUFF

SPLURGE ON A SURGE PROTECTOR

Protect your electronic devices by plugging them into a surge protector rather than a simple outlet strip. Although many of the latter have built-in fuses that protect against strong currents, the true surge protector also stops voltage spikes. Before you buy one, review the detailed specifications on its packaging; the faster its response time, the better.

Taking medication. If your older friend or relative finds it difficult to swallow large pills, consult with a doctor or pharmacist to see if the medication can be crushed and added to a soft food.

Bathroom safety. Obtain a pair of shower slippers or water shoes that have nonskid soles. They can be easily slipped on in the shower, and will help avoid slips on other potentially slippery surfaces.

Just wait for the doorbell. Take advantage of cost-free delivery services offered by supermarkets and pharmacies. Also contact Meals-on-Wheels, a charitable organization that delivers hot, healthful meals.

Teamwork. When you are helping a weakened senior shift body position, describe beforehand exactly what you are going to do. She will then expect the movement and offer as little resistance as possible.

No more bank lines. Have the Government deposit old age pension benefits directly into your older relative's bank account. The number to call is 1-800-277-9914.

ELECTRIC CORDS

No pets allowed. To deter your pet from gnawing on an electrical cord, wipe some strongly scented laundry soap along its length.

Untangle a knotty cord. Pull outward on the edges to loosen and enlarge the convoluted mass. In the process some twists will untangle by themselves. Then you'll be able to pass a free end through the remaining knots.

Don't run cords alongside heated pipes and heating systems; the warmth of the heat source weakens the cord and causes its insulation to crack.

If a cord shows wear, wrap it tightly in insulating tape. But, be sure to replace the cord with a new one as soon as possible.

Hedge your hedger. To protect the cord of your electric hedge clipper from being gnarled by the cutting blades, put a length of garden hose—wrapped snugly with electrical tape—over the segment nearest to the blades. The teeth of the blades don't separate far enough to damage the piece of hose.

ELECTRIC OUTLETS & PLUGS

Be kind to your plug. Take the time to pull the plug, not the wire, when you're unplugging a device from a wall socket.

Finding the right switch. If you don't want to keep running back and forth from an outlet to the breaker box to make sure the power is off, plug a radio into the outlet and turn its volume on high. When the music stops, you know you've found the appropriate circuit breaker.

Wired down. Wrap wires clockwise around the terminal screw shaft of an outlet. When you tighten the screw, the wire will stay in place and not come unhooked.

Child safety. If you're visiting friends with your toddler in tow and your hosts don't have electric socket guards, improvise your own in a pinch. Place a thick square of cardboard over the outlet, then attach it to the wall with regular or insulating tape.

Easy fix. To replace the plug on a flat cord, make a trip to the hardware store to buy either a clapstyle or a snap-on replacement plug. Cut off the faulty plug and install the new one in seconds—using the directions on the package to guide you.

Insulate your screwdriver. Before you use a metal-handled screwdriver to make an electrical repair, be on the safe side. Wrap some electrical tape around the handle and upper shaft.

RIGHT STUFF

A SIGN OF THE CHANGING TIMES

Some watches do more than just tell the time. This model from Timex and Microsoft, the Data Link, stores phone numbers, appointments, anniversaries, and lists. Most amazing, the watch, which "reads" bands of flashing light off your computer monitor, lets you transfer information from your computer directly onto your wrist. The software that makes this possible comes packaged with the watch.

ELECTRONIC ORGANIZERS

Tiny keys, big fingers. Before you buy an electronic organizer, make sure you're able to press one key without bumping into other keys. Also notice whether the keys respond well to your touch.

Is it too complicated? Select an electronic organizer that's relatively simple to use. Try each model out at the store and see, for example, if you can easily figure out how to update an address, change a phone number, or add someone's birthday to the calendar. Remember, with some models the procedures for such tasks are far more involved than with others. For starters, pass up any electronic organizer that makes the simplest of tasks difficult—things can only get worse.

Keep a backup. The information stored on an electronic organizer can possibly be erased. This has been known to occur if the organizer comes in contact with water, is dropped on the floor, or the batteries fail. Protect yourself by having a backup copy of information you can't bear to lose.

ELECTRONIC SHOPPING

Safe shopping. Never give your credit card number over the telephone unless you're ordering from a company that you know well and trust. If you shop via computer, input your account number only if you're buying from a reliable company or the merchant is protected by an on-line credit card security system, such as Secured Electronic Transactions (SET). You will be notified on-screen whether the company you are buying from is safeguarded by SET or not.

Not comfortable giving your credit card number over the telephone or on-line? Fax your order and pay by check or money order.

Thanks but no thanks. When a telemarketer tries to sell you something over the telephone, ask for his name and telephone number or have him mail you more information. If he refuses, don't do business with him.

The "900" no-no. Never dial a "900" number to get additional facts about a sales offer. Charges for these calls are pricey, and scam artists will do whatever they can to keep you on the line for as long as possible. Make sure your children are aware of this too.

Keep records of everything you purchase by telephone or computer. Note the date, the items you ordered, how much you paid, as well as the company's name, address, and telephone number. Or, make a copy of the advertisement, catalog page, or order form. The information will come in handy if troubles arise.

Before you order from TV shopping channels or over the Internet, compare prices of similar items in the stores. Often the "original" prices quoted are inflated to exaggerate the savings, and "deals" are wildly overpriced.

ELEVATOR & ESCALATOR SAFETY

Pick up your feet. When getting on or off an escalator or elevator, lower the risk of injury by lifting your feet up as you step forward.

Hold hands. When accompanying a child on an escalator or elevator, take his hand, especially as you get on and off. Never allow a child to sit or play on an escalator; his fingers and toes can easily get caught in the moving stairs, leading to serious injury. Never take a child in a stroller on an escalator.

Where's the elevator, please?

Avoid the unsafe practice of rolling bicycles, strollers, and other wheeled objects onto escalators. If you're carrying heavy or bulky items, you'll again want to forgo the escalator. Instead, locate the building's elevator.

 Don't even think about it! During a fire, stay off the elevator and head for the stairs. Elevators often stop working during fires, and the shafts sometimes fill with potentially deadly smoke. Even if elevators are functioning, they might go straight to where the fire is raging because intense heat can trigger the call button.

Don't come unglued. If an elevator gets stuck, never try to crawl out through the ceiling or to force the doors open. Use the intercom to call for help or ring the alarm bell (it usually has a red button).

Crime prevention. If you see someone on an elevator who looks suspicious, wait for the next car. Check the security mirror before boarding to be sure that nobody is hiding. When you're on the elevator, stand near the control panel. If you feel threatened, you'll be able to press the alarm bell and push the button for the nearest floor to try to find help.

No gridlock. Avoid "people" jams at elevator doors by allowing the last people who get on to be the first ones to get off.

E-MAIL

Go off-line for savings. Many electronic mail (e-mail) services allow you to read and compose messages off-line; that is, without being connected to the Internet. Working off-line holds down your expenses and allows you read and write without worrying about your connection being "timed out" by your Internet service provider.

Get free e-mail. If you're enrolled in or affiliated with a college, see whether or not you are entitled to a free e-mail account on the campus system. As an alternative, try a commercial service that provides free e-mail. There's only one drawback: the advertisements that litter your computer screen.

Electronic address books. Most e-mail services provide handy "address books" in which you can store e-mail listings. Once you input an address, you'll never have to type it out again. Many of these address books also let you send a single message to several people at the same time.

A family newsletter. Keep in touch with far-flung family members with an e-mail newsletter. Rotate the reporting chores. Many photo shops will convert your personal photographs to computer files on disk, which allows you to attach them to the newsletter. You can even make and send sound files with your computer's microphone!

Speak up. Most elected officials as well as most major magazines and newspapers have e-mail addresses. To express an opinion quickly and conveniently, transmit your messages by way of electronic mail.

Stay up-to-date. Internet mailing lists, such as "Listservs", provide ongoing streams of messages and discussion among people interested in specific subjects, such as gardening, home improvement, or pets. Electronic newsletters are also good sources of current information. Ask your service provider or a computer-savvy librarian how to access electronic mailing lists and newsletters.

GAINING ACCESS TO E-MAIL

The first thing you'll need to gain access to electronic mail (e-mail) is a computer with a modem, a device that uses telephone lines to make contact with the computer networks that together create the Internet. Many computer models come with a built-in modem. Your next move is to decide what type of provider you would like to use. There are several types; among them are:

▸ *Commercial On-line Services. These include America Online, CompuServe, and Simpatico. Using these on-line services is often the easiest way to go when you're just starting out.*

▸ *Internet Service Providers (ISP's). These range from nationwide providers like NetCom and EarthLink to smaller local firms; many list their numbers in your area's Yellow Pages. They offer basic service, including full access to the Internet. To use e-mail with such providers, you'll have to buy or download software, which fortunately is usually not difficult to obtain and install.*

EMERGENCY PREPARATION

Get the best information on how to cope with potential disasters in your area by contacting your local chapter of the Canadian Red Cross or Saint John Ambulance.

Coach the whole family. Show reasonably mature family members how to turn off the gas and electricity. Also teach them how to use the fire extinguishers.

Check your emergency kit periodically to replenish used items and replace expired medications. So you don't forget, make the inspection on the same day that you adjust your clocks for daylight savings time.

Check your insurance to see if the coverage is adequate for the disasters that threaten your area.

Make sure that your policy provides for replacement costs as well as building code upgrades, which many communities demand in the wake of a disaster.

 Post emergency phone numbers and teach children how and when to call 911. Also choose an out-of-province friend to be a family contact, because local phone service is often unreliable after an emergency.

EMPLOYEE BENEFITS

Make the most of it. Take the time to review your employee handbook—you're liable to be pleasantly surprised. Though they might not advertise the fact, many companies offer fine opportunities, including tuition reimbursement, leaves of absence, fitness programs, counseling services, child care, van pools, and matching donations to charities.

Every little bit helps. Participate in your employer's financial offerings, even if you can afford only a small amount. If you start early and consistently contribute to pretax set-asides, retirement funds, and stock discounts, you'll build a comfortable nest egg.

Boost your credit. Ask your employer if the company recognizes military service, Peace Corps service, or periods of part-time employment as credit toward pension benefits. Such credit can boost your retirement nest egg.

ENERGY CONSERVATION

Use one high-watt bulb instead of several low-watt ones. A single 100-watt incandescent bulb, for example, shines brighter but uses 20 watts less electricity than three 40-watt bulbs.

Install dimmers on your light switches. They save energy and money by cutting down on light levels and wattage.

Let there be light. For maximum efficiency, place lamps in the corners of your rooms so that the light reflects off both the walls and the ceiling.

Don't forget to dust. Wipe the dirt from your bulbs as you do your normal housework. A dust-free bulb shines up to 50 percent brighter than a dirty one.

Green landscaping. Plant a stand of evergreens to create a winter windbreak, several shade trees on the south and west sides of the house to block summer heat, and climbing plants and vines against the house to help insulate the house walls year-round.

 THE WELL-STOCKED EMERGENCY KIT

Relief agencies strongly recommend that you maintain emergency kits, one in your home and another in your car. To simplify storage, use large carryalls or heavy-duty plastic bags. The list below details the items that you'll need.

▶ *Food and Water. A three-day supply of nonperishable packaged or canned food; manual can opener; mess kits or paper plates and plastic utensils; a three-day supply of water (each person needs at least 3.7 L [0.8 gal] a day) stored in sealed, unbreakable containers.*

▶ *Clothing and Bedding. One complete set of clothes for each person. Include thermal underwear, hat, gloves, rain gear, and sturdy shoes. Blankets or sleeping bags.*

▶ *Supplies and Tools. First-aid kit; battery-operated radio and flashlight; extra batteries; fire extinguisher; cash; tarpaulin; duct tape; waterproof matches; aluminum foil; plastic containers; signal flare; pencil and paper; sewing kit; pliers; crowbar; wrench.*

▶ *Personal objects. Special items for babies and the elderly; prescription drugs; extra eyeglasses and contact lenses; games and books.*

Did you remember to lower the thermostat before you left for work? If you install a programmable one, you'll never have to worry about leaving the heat or air conditioning on again. Just select the temperature settings you desire for different times of the day, and the thermostat does the rest, monitoring both your heating and cooling systems. With such precision, these little wonders can trim the cost of your energy bill dramatically.

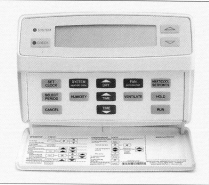

Buy compact fluorescent bulbs in place of regular lightbulbs. They fit into standard sockets, use one-fourth the wattage, and last 10 times longer. Yet the bulbs provide you with the same amount of soft light.

Double up your oven dishes. Cook more than one food in the oven at the same time. If temperatures for each dish vary slightly, pick an average temperature and monitor the cooking time.

ERGONOMICS

The right chair. If you sit for more than an hour a day, choose a chair that can be adjusted. Have the backrest cradle the inside slope of your back, and make sure your arms and legs are well supported. When your weight is evenly distributed over the surface of the seat, your feet should rest flat on the floor.

Invest in a headset. If you're on the telephone frequently, use a headset so that your neck and shoulder don't become strained, and so that your hands remain free to let you type, take notes, or even prepare a meal.

Front and center. Whatever you look at most frequently during the day, whether it's a monitor, paperwork, or a television, place the object directly in front of you. Also as much as possible, try to avoid twisting your neck, especially when you're typing.

ERRANDS

Child labor. Teens, especially those who have learned to drive, can take the car to be washed, pick up dry cleaning, shop for groceries, or take the dog to the vet.

Be a good neighbor. When heading out on errands, ask a sick or aging neighbor or friend if you can take care of any chore for him at the same time. The good feelings you'll generate will more than compensate for the extra work.

Share the tasks. Make arrangements with other parents, friends, and neighbors to share certain errands, like picking the kids up from school or football practice.

Have it delivered. If your dry cleaner, grocer, florist, or any other business you use offers delivery service, accept it. Even if you're charged a small fee, the time and energy you will save will be worth the cost.

Make a list. Take the time to write down what you have to do. With a list you won't forget an item and waste time and energy backtracking to the store.

Buy in bulk and you'll rarely run out of nonperishable items like toilet tissue, soap, and dog food. Watch for sales of the household staples you use to save time, money, and trips to the store.

Shop when crowds are smallest. To save time, shop for groceries in the morning, not in the late-afternoon or early-evening rush hour; shop for clothing on weekday evenings instead of Saturdays.

119

EXERCISE CLOTHING

Light and dry. Some of the modern fabrics used for sportswear are featherlight, breathable, and capable of wicking away moisture, so that you remain relatively dry no matter how hard you sweat. Look for polypropylene, a thin insulator, and Gore-Tex, a waterproof shell.

Self-conscious about your body? For a slimming look, wear dark-colored matching sweats or matching leotard and tights.

Be comfortable. Working out is not an exercise in fashion, so if you're more comfortable in sweat pants and an oversize T-shirt, go for it! One caveat: if you use multigym weight machines, don't wear anything too baggy—you don't want your clothing to snag in the equipment.

Fits like a glove. If you lift free weights or work out on a multigym machine as part of your fitness routine, wear a pair of leather sports gloves. Not only do they provide a better grip, but they prevent unsightly calluses.

Layer it. Keep warm outside in cold weather by wearing several thin layers of clothing. Air trapped between each layer acts as insulation. If you get too warm, simply shed layers one at a time.

EXERCISE EQUIPMENT

Give it a try. Sample equipment before you buy it. Many sporting-goods shops let you take out and test rackets, golf clubs, and bicycles when you leave a credit card number. Try out treadmills and exercise bikes in the store.

Shop around. In many cases, you get what you pay for. Last year's model may be priced to move, but be wary of drastically reduced equipment. On the other hand, if you're just starting an exercise regimen, don't think you have to buy everything. Do your homework: talk to established exercisers and read up on the latest gear.

Stay away from gimmicks and products promising benefits that seem too good to be true. Common examples include claims of immediate results, machines that

PROS & CONS OF EXERCISE EQUIPMENT

Use the chart below to help you decide what type of exercise machine best suits your ability and needs.

TYPE OF EQUIPMENT	PROS	CONS
Cross-Country Ski Machines	Excellent aerobic benefits; great way to tone the lower body, build coordination	Tricky to use; take up space
Free Weights	Shape and strengthen the major muscles; wider range of body movement than with multigym exercisers; easily stored; relatively inexpensive	Higher risk of accidents; weights can be hard to handle; best to work out with a partner
Multigym Machines	Excellent strength conditioning, full-body workout; safer and easier than free weights	Require plenty of space; expensive
Rowing Machines	Low impact; good for strength conditioning, especially for the chest, legs, arms, and abdomen	Fairly uncomfortable; difficult for beginners
Stair Climbers	Low impact; excellent for leg and buttock muscles; excellent aerobic benefits	Difficult for beginners; generally, only the lower body is benefited
Stationary Bicycles	Low impact; high aerobic benefits; easy to use	Most exercise only the lower body; seats can cause discomfort
Treadmills	High aerobic benefits; can be used for walking, jogging, or running; fairly easy to use	Possibility of accidents; impact from running and jogging can cause foot and leg pain; require plenty of space

"do all the work," and gear worn during exercising to increase weight loss—most likely, the result of excessive perspiration.

The feedback advantage. Look for machines that give feedback, such as the number of calories you're burning and your pulse rate. Such equipment lets you monitor your performance and keeps you motivated to increase exercise time and repetitions.

EXERCISE SHOES

The big switcheroo. If you exercise every day, invest in a second pair of athletic shoes—but not the same kind. Alternate the different pairs from one day to the next. The shoes will have a chance to air out and the stress placed on your feet and legs will be slightly altered due to the different fit of each pair. Over time, this slight change can prevent injuries.

Say "no" to slipping and sliding. When fitting yourself for exercise shoes, make sure that your heel feels gently cupped and that it doesn't slide from side to side.

No more squeezing. The toe box—the area that encases your toes—needs to be roomy enough so that you can wiggle your toes.

Be kind to your feet. Replace your exercise shoes as soon as they become worn. When the cushioning becomes compressed, the shoes lose their ability to absorb shock—leaving you exposed to injury.

EXERCISING

Stay motivated. Keep your exercise clothing handy, make friends with people who like to work out, schedule exercise classes, and chart your progress—whatever keeps you going.

Pain is no gain. Disregard the saying "no pain, no gain." Even a slight ache indicates that something is

10 REASONS TO WORK OUT

It's not particularly easy to start a workout routine after years of sedentary living, but by exercising regularly, you'll find that life itself becomes easier. Therefore, the next time you can't get motivated, remember that exercise:

▶ *Improves your self-image*
▶ *Helps fight depression*
▶ *Is a great way to meet new friends*
▶ *Increases your energy level*
▶ *Combats weight gain*
▶ *Keeps your love life in high gear*
▶ *Helps you sleep at night*
▶ *Reduces your risk of having a heart attack or stroke*
▶ *Improves your body's ability to fight infections*
▶ *Leads to a longer life*

wrong with your body. Further exercise will likely only worsen the condition.

Exercise with others. This is often the best way to motivate yourself to get out of the house. Join a running club, a tennis league, or a yoga group.

Cross-train. Do a combination of exercises to work on different areas of the body. For example, bicycle on Monday, jog on Wednesday, and swim on Friday. Or combine a run with walking or calisthenics. Cross-training routines lessen the chance of injury since no one area is overtaxed by a repeated movement, promote overall fitness, and reduce exercise boredom.

Avoid overexercising; give your body time to recover. Otherwise, you increase the risk of injury and inhibit your body's ability to ward off infections.

Colds and exercise. If your symptoms are limited to the areas above your neck—dripping nose, congestion, mild headache—go ahead and

exercise. However, for symptoms such as muscle aches, stomach pains, and fever, take the day off.

Two for one! Do your chores, and you'll not only have the satisfaction of a job well done but also reap the benefits of having burned calories. So pick up that rake, grab your mop, volunteer to vacuum, and get your heart going.

EXTENSION CORDS

So they don't come unplugged, secure the connection between your power tool cord and the extension cord by tying their ends into a simple knot before you plug them together.

Put it in a pail. Improvise a holder for a long heavy-duty extension cord with the aid of a 19 L (4 gal) pail. Cut a hole in the side of the pail large enough for the cord's pronged ends to fit through, then coil the cord inside the pail. The cord will uncoil easily whenever you need it.

Tube ride. Keep small extension cords organized and untangled by tucking them inside the paper tubes that once held toilet tissue or paper towels. Slide the tube over the looped cord and let the loops fan out of the tube's ends.

Use the right cord. For safety's sake, make sure that your cord can handle the job. Know that an extension cord's rating, or wire gauge, is determined by the amount of current it can safely carry; the smaller the wire gauge number, the greater the current-carrying capacity. Compare this rating with the one indicated on your appliances and tools.

EYE CARE

Easy on the eyes. If you get eyestrain when you work at your computer, place the monitor below eye level and tilt it upward.

More remedies for computer eyestrain: Keep your screen free of dust and blink often as you work to keep your eyes moist. Take frequent breaks and put your hands over your eyes for a few minutes or focus on a far-off site.

Potato patches. To temporarily rid your eyes of bags and dark circles, lie down and put a thin slice of raw potato over each eye. Rest with the potato patches over your eyes for 15 minutes, then wash away any filmy residue. Use cooled slices of cucumber in the same manner to soothe red, swollen eyes.

Soothe itchy, scratchy eyes with chamomile tea. Brew a pot of weak tea and allow it to cool slightly. Then, gently rinse your eyes directly with the tea, or soak a clean cloth with the tea, and hold this compress to your eyes for 10 to 15 minutes.

Beware of the rebound effect with decongestant eyedrops that promise to "get the red out." They contain vasoconstrictors, which shrink tiny blood vessels; overuse causes a rebound effect in which the vessels dilate and the eyes become chronically red. Opt instead for prescription drops or over-the-counter drops labeled as preservative-free "lubricants" or "artificial tears."

 Puffy morning eyes? Cool used teabags in a plastic bag in the refrigerator, then place the teabags on your eyes in the morning for about 10 minutes as a quick de-puffer.

THERE'S SOMETHING IN MY EYE!

Sand, pollen, pesky little insects—all of these can lodge in your eye and cause discomfort. When you attempt to remove an object by yourself, follow the steps below so that you won't further harm your eye.

▶ *Avoid rubbing. The offending object may scratch your eyeball or lid.*

▶ *Take out contact lenses. Perhaps the culprit is stuck on your lens.*

▶ *Using a mirror, examine your eye. Pull down the lower lid and pull up the top lid. If you see the object, pull your eyelid over it until your eye starts to water—the tears may wash the culprit away.*

▶ *Rinse it. Carefully wash your eye under cool running tap water. The pressure may flush out the object.*

▶ *Lift it out. Dab at the object with the corner of a very clean, slightly damp cloth.*

▶ *See a doctor if you aren't able to dislodge the object; you can't locate the object; your vision is now blurry; the object is deeply imbedded, not sitting on the surface of your eye; or you have removed the object but the pain persists for a day or more.*

Eyeglass chains have been around for years—but only recently has modern technology gotten into the act. Now the simplest bead chains compete with sporty models made of wetsuit material and suction tips guaranteed to hold your glasses snugly in place even in a hurricane. These durable active-wear retainers can be made to grip your head as tightly as you please and are invaluable for active sports, from tennis to skiing.

EYE MAKEUP

Curl your eyelashes before you apply mascara; coated lashes are more brittle, so curling afterward may cause lashes to break off.

Beautiful brows. Bring unwieldy eyebrow hairs to a shapely standstill: apply a dollop of hair-styling gel and brush upward.

 Nobody's perfect. Use these tricks of the trade to get the look you want. Make prominent eyes look smaller by using a dark eye shadow over the lid. If your eyes are small or close-set, apply a light shadow from your brow to your lashes.

A great eye-shadow base: cream foundation makeup. Apply a light coating over the lid, blending with your little finger, then brush on your eye shadow. The powdery shadow will bind to the base.

Two's a crowd. Never share eye makeup, since infections can easily be passed from one person to another that way.

Prevent irritated, infected eyes. Stop using scented eye makeup and throw out mascara every six months—before bacteria

have a chance to grow. Don't pump your mascara brush in its tube; it introduces airborne contaminants.

Shaping your brows. Hold a pencil vertically and align it with the inside edge of your eye. Then take the pencil and slant it from the tip of your nose to the outside corner of your eye. If any brow hairs are growing outside the area between the two marks, pluck them with tweezers or have it done professionally.

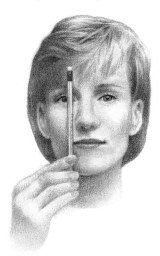

EYEGLASSES

A perfect match. Select the shape of the frame to complement the shape of your face. If you have a round face, choose a

frame with angles. If you have an angular face, opt for a softer, more rounded frame. If your face is oval, you're lucky—you can wear almost any shape frame.

Finding the right fit. A frame is too large if it overpowers the face, if the sides of the frame extend beyond your eyes, or if you can see your eyebrows through the lens. A frame is too small if your eyes aren't centered in the frame or if the edges of the frame fall within the eye area. Make sure that the bridge of the frame fits securely; it should neither slide off nor pinch your nose.

Accident-prone? If you have a tendency to drop your glasses, choose plastic, not glass, lenses. Plastic is lighter and much harder to break. On the negative side, plastic scratches more easily and costs more.

No more streaks. For spotless lenses every time, use a dash or two of rubbing alcohol or vinegar when you clean them.

You don't need a prescription for reading glasses—the inexpensive ones found in drugstores work fine at a fraction of the cost. Make sure to get a thorough eye exam first, however, to determine the proper level of magnification and to rule out other problems.

FACIALS TO FUSES

FACIALS

Quickie home facial. Start by placing a towel over your head and holding your face over a bowl of steaming hot water for about 10 minutes. You can then apply a scrub or mask to tone your skin or simply splash yourself with witch hazel, a natural astringent, before ending with a moisturizer.

Make your own mask to nourish, moisten, or tighten your skin. A mixture of mashed cucumber (no peel) and egg white will soothe sensitive skin; uncooked oatmeal mixed with a tablespoon each of honey, apple cider vinegar, and ground almonds is a good cleanser; the whites of two eggs beaten with a bit of lemon juice will temporarily tighten sagging skin; dry skin is nourished with a coating of buttermilk or a mask made of mashed bananas, strawberries, and avocados.

Pamper yourself with an occasional professional facial. It won't turn the clock back, but it will feel terrific. Be sure to advise the facialist on possible allergens or scents you dislike. A facial also makes a great birthday present for a friend.

Fall cleaning. Get your facial in the autumn. Summer sun can harden the face's outer skin, making it more susceptible to breakouts and clogged pores.

WHERE TO HOLD A FAMILY REUNION

You've decided to gather the clan, but your house is barely big enough to accommodate your own family. So where should you hold the reunion? Here are a few ideas to jog your thinking.

▶ *Locate a site that has sentimental meaning for the family. Does some relative still live on the farm where Grandpa grew up? Were your ancestors seafarers, making a beach or sailing party appealing?*

▶ *Find a place that does the work for you. Resorts or large hotels offer large rooms for parties, where the work of cooking, serving, and cleaning up is done by staff members. Try striking a deal with a resort during the off-season. Or have the reunion catered. Choose from fancy buffet to down-home barbecue.*

▶ *Consider expense. Try to select a place that won't be prohibitively expensive for some members.*

Don't go it alone. Both parents should be involved in explaining how the body works. Single parents should ask a respected friend to be there for support and advice. And don't stick to the stereotype of having Dad answer the boys' questions and Mom talk to the girls. Children may assume that one gender's interests don't concern the other.

Start early. Don't wait until your child is a teenager to start a dialogue about the facts of life. This should be an ongoing conversation with your growing child. A youngster who trusts that her questions will get fair consideration will likely evolve into a teen who feels comfortable discussing sex with her parents—at a time when not communicating can have serious consequences.

Let the children lead you. One way to break the ice is to ask kids how much they know about subjects you surmise are of concern to them. If their knowledge is limited, be honest, but don't overexplain and give your children more information than they can comprehend. Leave the door open for future discussions.

FAMILY REUNIONS

Choose a special date. Suggest a significant date in your family's history on which to hold the reunion. It might be the date your ancestors arrived in Canada or the birthday of a grandparent.

Compile a family cookbook.
Ask each family to send a favorite recipe ahead of time, along with any relevant information or amusing anecdotes about it. Make photocopies of the collection—you may even want to bind them with pretty ribbon—and distribute them at the reunion.

Have T-shirts made up with the family name, a group photo, or a portrait of the grandparents or great-grandparents who started it all. Or have the kids design their own T-shirts using special crayons called dyeing pastels (available at crafts stores), which yield permanent, washable colors.

FAMILY TREE

Plant roots early. Draw a family tree on shelf paper or paint one on a wall in your child's room and paste on photos of relatives.

Create an oral history. Interview all older relatives in the family on videotape. Ask about their childhood, school years, parents, and vintage family stories. Have a videotape store splice the tape together, and premiere it at a family get-together.

 Sharing history. Every generation seems to have at least one member who becomes keeper of the family history. Encourage him to keep digging and to share the findings with the rest of the family.

Cyber-search. Several on-line services feature genealogy forums where readers share information about family histories and often post messages about names of family members they are researching. Numerous free geneology programs are also available on the Internet; one of the best-known is "Brother's Keeper."

Someone has said that family history is the basis of all history. Certainly a study of your own ancestry can offer a greater understanding of the chain of human events that have shaped you and your family. In addition to many books on the subject of practical genealogy, there are several software programs that will make it easy for you to trace your own unique slice of history.

Beware of unsolicited offers that come in the mail, promising a personalized family history for a fee. You are guaranteed little more than general information that may include a history of your family name or a list of famous people with your surname. If you wish to consult a reputable genealogist, contact the Canadian Federation of Genealogical and Family History Societies (227 Parkville Bay, Winnipeg, Man. R2M 2J6, 1-204-256-6176).

FANS

Clean dirty blades with a dry cloth, vacuum cleaner, or even a hair dryer. Blades thick with dust and grime, especially on kitchen fans, can put the internal mechanism out of balance.

Fans vs. smoke detectors. Don't let a fan blow toward a smoke detector. The device might not sound the alarm in time if fumes are blown away from its sensors.

Save on cooling costs. Let fans do some of the work of distributing cool air around the house; that way, the air conditioners can run on a lower setting.

After the flood. If a burst pipe has drenched a room, dry it out in a hurry. After cleaning up any standing water, place two fans—one blowing air in, the other set to exhaust it—in windows in different walls of the room.

Shopping for ceiling fans. Ceiling fans do a great job of keeping a room cool and aerated during hot spells. When buying a fan, study the store models. An annoying hum or rattle may indicate a cheap motor or unbalanced blades. Check the noise level at each setting, from slow to fast.

Fans are not just for cooling. Kitchen range hoods with fans draw up smoke, heat, and grease generated by the stove and oven and keep them from filling the house. A vented fan that exhausts to the outside is best, but even an unvented hood fan will filter out the grease before sending the air back into the kitchen.

A bewildering array of fasteners is available at hardware stores and home centers; all come in many sizes and designs to handle a variety of jobs. The basics about fasteners are spelled out below.

TYPE	VARIATIONS	USE
Nails	Common	Have flat heads and are used for joints where pull-apart pressure is low.
	Finishing	Have insignificant heads and are countersunk, so that they don't show in fine woodwork.
	Specialized	Each is designed for a particular job, such as roofing, drywall, or masonry.
Screws	Wood	Have more holding power than a nail and create a stronger joint between two pieces of wood. Come with slotted or Phillips heads.
	Metal	Used for joining two pieces of metal; easier to remove than a nail. Comes in slotted, Phillips, star, or Robertson (square) heads
Nuts and Bolts	Carriage	Join two wood pieces in stronger bond than screws; joint can be disassembled without damage.
	Machine	Join two metal pieces in stronger bond than screws; joint can be disassembled without damage.
Hollow Wall	Anchors and plugs	Fit in holes just large enough to accommodate fasteners; inserting a screw makes them expand and grip.
	Molly and toggle bolts	Have wings that open inside the wall, bracing against it to hold the fastener securely.

FASTENERS

Rules of thumb. A nail should be about three times as long as the thickness of the wood you're driving it through and should go through the thinner piece of wood into the thicker piece. For a stronger union, use a screw that will reach two-thirds of the way into the second piece of wood.

 Make fastening easier by rubbing nail and screw shanks with oil, soap, candle wax, or beeswax. (Beeswax is best because it leaves no stain.)

To drive a brad or small nail without mashing your finger, push it through a piece of stiff paper, which will hold the brad in place while you drive it. Then tear the paper away. Another alternative: secure the brad between a comb's teeth, drive the brad part way, remove the comb, then finish.

Stop splits when nailing wood by staggering the nails along the grain of a board. Never drive two nails into the same grain line. Blunting a nail's point, by taping it lightly with a hammer before using it, will also lessen the chance of the nail splitting the wood as you nail.

Chopstick trick. If a screw hole has enlarged so that the screw has lost its grip, coat a wooden chopstick with glue and use it to plug the hole. When the glue dries, trim the chopstick flush with the surface and refasten the screw. (You can do the same with a wooden matchstick to plug a smaller hole.)

Lubricate a hard-to-remove nut or bolt with a few drops of penetrating oil or vinegar. Let the lubricant sink in before trying to remove the bolt or nut.

FATIGUE

Beware of boredom. The cause of fatigue is not necessarily physical. Nothing makes you feel more weary than having nothing to look forward to. Join a western dancing group; volunteer in a local hospital or library; learn to bowl. Turn off the TV, get out of the house, and find activities to enjoy with other people.

Fight fatigue with exercise. Physical activity may tire you, but even in the short run it makes you feel better and banishes mental fatigue. If you drive everywhere you go and watch TV more than two hours a day, you're probably not getting enough exercise. Regular aerobic workouts are ideal, but even a 20-minute walk three times a week can do wonders.

Working too hard? Schedule some quiet time into your work week. Take a hot bath or a nap, listen to music, get a rubdown, go fishing, read a book, see a movie, turn off the telephone. People who have regular breaks in their lives tire less easily.

FATS

Remember the rule. Most unsaturated fats—the healthier kind—are liquid at room temperature; saturated fats—the more dangerous type—are solid. Exceptions include palm, coconut, and palm kernel oils, which are all high in saturated fat.

Fat-free cooking. You can fry, stir-fry, or sauté foods without fat if you use nonstick cookware or nonstick sprays.

Fat but not fatal. Avocados are high in fat (Florida avocados have less fat than those from California), but the fat is mostly unsaturated, the healthier kind. And like all vegetables, avocados contain no cholesterol.

To reduce animal fat in your diet, choose "choice" cuts of beef instead of "prime," which is marbled and fattier as well as more expensive. Trim off visible fat on all meat and poultry before cooking, and remove the skin from chicken and turkey.

FEARS & PHOBIAS

Learn relaxation techniques, such as those involving deep breathing and biofeedback. Practice these techniques when you are imagining frightening situations or encountering the real thing.

Find a support group. Many organizations, such as churches and mental health clinics, sponsor groups that help people overcome their fears.

Consult a therapist if you think your problem is not responding to self-treatment. A therapist may employ a variety of approaches, from traditional psychotherapy to meditation.

FEEDING A CROWD

Hostess motto: Be Prepared. When planning a menu for a large party, choose dishes that can be prepared a week, a day, or, at the very least, a few hours in advance. Select dishes that freeze well or that taste better the day after they are cooked. Don't spoil the party for yourself by spending it in the kitchen.

Spice alert. Casseroles and stews multiply well to feed throngs of people. Simply double, triple, or quadruple the main ingredients. Adjust seasonings carefully, though. Hot spices, such as cayenne pepper, should not be increased in direct proportion, while proportionate amounts of mild spices and herbs may need to be increased.

AN EASY-TO-PREPARE CROWD PLEASER

This menu, with basic, easy-to-prepare, make-ahead dishes, will feed 24 guests. Make the menu unique by adding an ethnic or family specialty.

▶ *Roasts or casseroles. One 6.5 to 7.5 kg (14–16 lb) turkey and one boneless 3.5 kg (8 lb), no-cook ham. Substitute a meat casserole for either, if you prefer.*

▶ *Assorted breads. Serve 2 or 3 large loaves of good bread, sliced for making sandwiches. Provide mustards, mayonnaise, and fresh butter.*

▶ *Steamed vegetables. Prepare about 1.5 kg (3 lb) of firm, colorful vegetables such as carrots, broccoli, or green beans. Use a single vegetable, or combine them.*

▶ *Cold pasta or potato salad. To save time and energy, buy 2.5 to 3.5 kg (6–8 lb) of prepared salad at a good delicatessen.*

▶ *One large, green salad. Use 3 heads of a firm lettuce, such as romaine, tossed together with scallions and herbs with an olive oil and lemon dressing.*

▶ *Dessert. Serve strawberries, raspberries, blueberries, or a combination; for 24, you'll need 3 L (6 pints). Add two small bar cookies per guest or 48 cookies in all.*

RIGHT STUFF

Anyone who has tackled the tedious job of painting a picket fence will appreciate the virtues of polyvinyl residential fencing. It looks almost like wood but doesn't fade, rot, crack, or peel. Installed with posts like wooden fencing, it costs a little more but carries a guarantee of 20 years or longer.

FENCES

Save a lot of sawing by designing a fence to take advantage of standard lumber sizes. For example, two pickets for a 1.2 m (4 ft) tall fence can be made by cutting one 2.5 m (8 ft) long board in half. Premade fencing comes in 1.8 or 2.5 m (6 or 8 ft) sections, so plan your fence in those multiples.

Can you dig it? Call the electric and water companies and your community's sewer department to find out where utility lines on your property run before you dig or drill postholes.

Coddle your fence posts by cutting the tops at a 30-degree angle and covering them with post caps—small, overhanging roofs available at lumberyards. By keeping rain and snowmelt from seeping into the posts' ends, caps can prolong the soundness of a fence post for years.

Reinforce, don't replace. Usually the posts fail first in a wooden fence—they tend to decay where they come in contact with the ground. But don't try to replace them; it's more work to dig them out than it is to plant a new post halfway between each pair of old ones.

Nothing beats a hole digger for digging fence postholes. You can dig the holes with a shovel, but as with so many other jobs, using the right tool makes it a whole lot easier. Rent or borrow a posthole digger for a day if you don't think you need to buy one.

Do yourself a favor: buy pressure-treated wood for your fence posts. Ask for "CCA" wood at your local lumberyard. This wood has been treated with preservatives that will protect it almost indefinitely from the rot and decay that plague wood exposed to the weather or sunk in the ground.

FERTILIZING

Which fertilizer? Selecting a fertilizer can be confusing because there are so many different formulas: 5-10-5, 20-20-20, 8-16-10, and so on. Which is best for your particular need? Actually, any formula is adequate, as long as the label specifies that the fertilizer is "complete" and "balanced" and you apply it at the rate recommended by the manufacturer.

Are you a "night fusspot"? Whatever your nocturnal temperament, you can use the phrase as a mnemonic device to help you remember what all those numbers on the fertilizer bag stand for. They represent the percentage in the fertilizer of each of the three major plant nutrients: nitrogen-phosphate-potassium.

Use a proportioner to make sure your garden gets the nutrients it needs. A simple and inexpensive brass fixture that fits between faucet and hose, the proportioner has an intake tube that you dip into a bucket of concentrated liquid fertilizer; as you spray, it feeds the right proportion of fertilizer into the hose so that you water and feed the garden all at once.

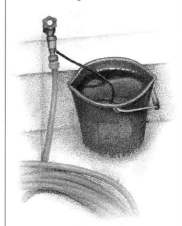

Green manure? After clearing your garden in the fall, sow hairy vetch or winter rye. Often called "green manures," these plants flourish in cool weather and will keep weeds out of the bed. In early spring, dig the green manure right into the soil, where it will nourish the earth and fertilize the flowers or vegetables to come.

FILING

Be fierce in weeding out old, inactive files that you haven't looked at for three or four years. Either move them to well-labeled storage boxes or, better still, throw them away. (But hang on to your tax files for six years, even longer for certain tax records.)

 File, don't pile. Never let a huge pile build up in your "To File" box. Easier said than done—but it will help if you make a regular monthly date with yourself to tackle the file box and write it on your calendar.

Invest in a good filing cabinet. It may not be cheap, but a sturdy cabinet with roomy, well-balanced drawers will make retrieving files much easier, and will make filing seem like less of a chore so you will be more likely to do it.

Buy a box of file folders so that you'll always have one at hand when you need to start a new file. Nothing reduces the paper piles on your desk faster than having the right folders—clearly marked—to put them in.

For easy retrieval, limit folders in your active household files to no more than 20 categories, such as "Taxes," "Health," "School," "Warranties," and "House Repairs." Keep them up-to-date, filing only receipts and records relevant to the current year. Keep old receipts that you need for tax purposes with tax files for the respective year, not with your active files.

FINANCIAL PLANNING

Get professional help in planning a financial course if you don't feel confident about doing it yourself. The important thing is to have a plan, and paying someone you trust to advise you in the process can relieve you of a load of confusion and anxiety.

Pick a planner carefully. Like any other field, financial planning has its share of bad apples. Get references and follow up on them. And be wary of advisers who receive commissions for selling investments and insurance products—they'll have a stake in what they tell you to buy.

Take your time. If you're unfamiliar with some of the recommendations your planner makes, choose just one or two to see how they turn out. When you're confident about the planner's judgment, you can invest a larger portion of your money.

Figuring for the future. Several years before you retire is a good time to find out what's coming to you in your pension. For Canada pension benefits, call 1-800-277-9914; for Quebec pension benefits, call 1-800-463-5533. They will give you an approximation of the amount you may receive when you retire and explain your options for getting them.

Review your debts. If you have a mortgage, consider refinancing before retiring. You may find banks less willing to refinance your mortgage after retirement, when your income will be lower.

Ready for retirement? Gather all the information you can about your Social Security payments, pension plan, other retirement accounts, assets, and investments. If the income from those sources can produce from 60 to 80 percent of your preretirement income, you should be pretty well set for retirement.

FINDING A MATE

Join a club. Singles book clubs, food and wine clubs, travel clubs, bike clubs, film clubs, ski clubs—any kind of club can be a great forum to meet people who share your interests and lifestyle.

Getting personal. Putting a personal ad in a local paper or magazine has become a proven way to meet a mate. When composing an ad, be honest about yourself and specific about what you want in a mate. Have some fun; the most attractive ads are playful and self-effacing. And play it safe: don't give out your home phone number at first, and if you decide to meet, choose a public place.

Take the high-tech approach. If you are cyber-literate, try on-line dating services, which are generally free of charge. Look for groups whose interests you share with their own on-line "bulletin boards" of personal ads.

 Get out of the house. To find like minds, go where your own interests lead you, whether to sports events, church, museums, lectures, wine tastings, or pet shows.

Beware of telephone personals, which can be pricey. Find out how much each call-in response to your ad will cost you. Responding to phone personals can be costly, too; most are 900 numbers.

FINDING INFORMATION

Back to school. If you need more materials than your local library provides, try the nearest college or university library. Many of them offer access to the general public.

Use the technology. Many library resources are maintained on CD-ROM's, electronic data-bases, microfiche, and other non-print media. If you need assistance navigating these materials, ask your librarian for a quick lesson.

Rubber-stamp it. Libraries often require request forms in order to access resources. Save time by bringing a one-piece name and address stamp, available from most office-supply stores. Every time you have to fill in a form, just give it a quick stamp.

Gotta dime? Most libraries provide photocopying machines to help you collect research. If you expect to photocopy many pages from your sources, come prepared with change.

The phone book? Your local White and Yellow Pages are surprisingly good information sources about your region. Spend an hour reading the introductory pages in the telephone book.

Tracking a number. Most businesses and organizations have toll-free numbers. To find the number of a particular company or organization, call the toll-free directory at 1-800-555-1212.

EASY DOES IT

FINDING INFORMATION ON-LINE

The Internet is an almost infinite source of information. Here are some tips for using it effectively.

▶ *For commercial on-line services and information retrieval companies, check out your local public library. Some libraries provide limited access to on-line services from their computer terminals.*

▶ *Crank up the "search engines." Powerful databases such as AltaVista, Lycos, Webcrawler, and InfoSeek are readily available on the World Wide Web, and provide self-help instructions on how to focus searches. Learn to use these techniques to improve your research effectiveness.*

▶ *Federal and most state agencies maintain an enormous Internet presence. You can obtain a vast amount of government information by logging on to the various departmental home pages.*

▶ *Commercial on-line databases such as Lexis-Nexis and Dialog provide powerful research tools for a fee. These services are not inexpensive, but if your need is urgent and your budget is adequate, they can save time and provide valuable information.*

Start close to home. Before calling a government agency in Ottawa, check if the agency you need has an office in your area. For example, many towns have a local passport office.

Check the Blue Pages. When searching for government-related information, be sure to check the Blue Pages of your local telephone directory, which list most federal, provincial, and local agencies in English and French.

A capital idea. Most provincial capitals operate a library that maintains the province's official archives and offers telephone research services.

FIRE SAFETY

Plan your escape from every room in your house. Review the plan with family members. Specify a meeting place outside so that you can quickly assess who may be missing. Practice your routine with an occasional fire drill.

OLD SAW **Police those butts.** Reduce the risk of smoking-related fires in these ways: Be sure the contents of ashtrays are cold before emptying them. Never flick ashes into wastebaskets. Keep matches and lighters out of the reach of children. Do not smoke in bed.

Be wary of halogen lamps. Halogen bulbs tend to become extremely hot. Therefore, position halogen lamps away from curtains or any other material that might easily catch fire. Also, for safety's sake, avoid putting halogen lamps in children's rooms.

Get out first. Leave a burning building as quickly as you can and then call the fire department from a neighbor's house or a nearby telephone booth.

Fight fire with firefighters. Most local fire departments are happy to help families address fire safety issues. Call your fire department and ask if they'll send a person to walk through your home to identify possible fire hazards.

Make fire safety fun. Many insurance companies and fire departments produce coloring books, toys, and other paraphernalia to help your kids identify fire hazards and learn what to do in case of fire.

FIREPLACES & CHIMNEYS

Hire a chimney sweep to clean the flue of your fireplace once a year—more often if you use it frequently. He will remove the buildup of flammable creosote, which causes fires.

Redecorate your fireplace. If your mantelpiece is undistinguished or the style is incompatible with the rest of your home furnishings, consider replacing it. Many home centers carry standard-size mantelpieces as well as the millwork to make them fit various openings. Also, house-wrecking companies sometimes offer a good selection of authentic older mantelpieces.

Install glass doors on your fireplace to prevent warm air from escaping when the flue is open. Or if your fireplace surround is smooth, simply lay a piece of Plexiglas over the opening; the draft will hold it in place.

Fireback payback. Prop a cast-iron fireback against the rear wall of your fireplace. This panel protects the brick and also reflects heat into the room. Traditional fireplace accoutrements, firebacks are now produced in many old-fashioned designs.

To add spectacular colors to holiday fires, soak dried pinecones in a solution of Epsom salts and water (450 g to 3.7 L [1 lb to 0.8 gal]) for a few hours or overnight. Let the cones dry and then toss one or two on a fire to create a rainbow of colored flames.

Clean soot and smoke from fireplace bricks with a 50-50 solution of bleach and water. Spray the solution onto the bricks, scrub them with a soft brush, and then rinse thoroughly by spraying them with water.

FIREWOOD

Store firewood outside the house and bring it in a day or two before you burn it. This will lessen moisture and insects in the house but still allow enough time for the wood to dry sufficiently.

Stack firewood on wooden pallets (available at home centers) laid flat on the ground. Pallets keep the wood dry by letting air circulate under the pile.

Burn only hardwood, such as oak, maple, or birch, in your fireplace; such woods burn longer and cleaner than soft woods like pine. Never burn treated lumber in the fireplace: the fumes are toxic.

Use artificial logs one at a time. If they are stacked on each other or if they are mixed with natural wood logs, they can cause dangerous explosions or even fires.

RIGHT STUFF

GAS LOGS FOR FIREPLACES

Old-fashioned fireplaces have lost some of their charm in recent years as energy- and pollution-conscious householders have learned that burning wood wastes fuel and pollutes the environment. Installing gas logs in the fireplace can impart the warmth and glow of burning wood to a room without a wood fire's mess or fuss— or guilt.

FIRST AID

Save that tooth! A tooth that is knocked cleanly out of the gum may be revived if it is reinserted promptly. Rinse it off with a saline solution, holding it by the crown. If the victim is an adult and conscious, have him put the tooth in his mouth and, if possible, back in the original socket. (Saliva will keep the tooth alive.) Then get to a dentist immediately.

If a bone is broken, immobilize the limb with a splint, apply ice packs to keep swelling down, and call a doctor. If the bone has broken through the skin, cover the area with a sterile dressing immediately. If you suspect multiple broken bones or a broken bone in the neck, back, or pelvis, don't move the victim at all—call 911 and let medical personnel do it.

Make a leg splint by rolling a blanket into a long, thin, tight sausage. Bend it lengthwise around the broken leg, starting at the groin, going down the inside of the leg, under the instep, and up the outside of the leg to the hip. Make at least four ties around the blanket rolls—dish towels will do—to immobilize the leg.

Take a course in CPR, that is, cardiopulmonary resuscitation. You'll learn how to use artificial respiration and chest compression to revive someone who has stopped breathing and has no pulse. It takes only a few hours and may save someone's life. Contact your local Saint John Ambulance chapter for more information.

Stay near a seizure victim to make sure she doesn't hurt herself by falling or bumping into something. Do not, however, try to restrain her or put anything in her mouth. Call 911 immediately if the seizure follows an injury. Once the seizure victim regains consciousness, stay close and offer reassurance until help arrives.

FIRST-AID KITS

Kits for cars. First-aid items for the car should include a blanket and prepackaged wet cloths in an airtight container.

Emergency numbers belong in the first-aid kit—or pasted on the outside. Include the telephone number of a local ambulance service, as well as the numbers for the doctor, police, and hospital. If your area has a poison control center, list that number, too.

FISH

How much fish in a fish? If you plan to cook a whole fish—head, bones, skin, and all—figure on one serving for every 340 to 450 g (¾–1 lb) of whole fish.

Check fish for freshness. The eyes should bulge and be bright and clear, the scales should look shiny, the gills should appear pink-

---

A BASIC FIRST-AID KIT

The jumble of drugstore items that tend to pile up in medicine cabinets won't help much in an emergency. It is wise to buy or assemble a first-aid kit to have ready when you need to do some doctoring in a hurry. A basic home kit should include these items.

▶ *Aspirin, acetaminophen, or ibuprofen for headaches and other types of pain or fever*

▶ *Antibiotic ointment for cuts, abrasions, and burns*

▶ *Ipecac syrup and activated charcoal in case of poisoning (use only if advised to by a poison control center)*

▶ *Elastic roll bandages for sprained knees, ankles, wrists, and elbows; a triangular bandage for making a sling*

▶ *Scissors and safety pins; tweezers for removing splinters and ticks*

▶ *Adhesive tape, rolls of gauze and gauze squares, and adhesive bandages of various sizes*

▶ *Skin closures to close gaping wounds*

▶ *Rubber gloves to reduce the risk of infection when treating wounds*

▶ *Instant-activating ice bags to reduce swelling and bring down a fever*

▶ *A first-aid manual*

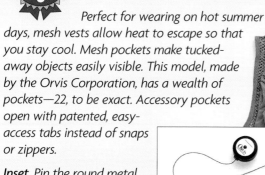

Perfect for wearing on hot summer days, mesh vests allow heat to escape so that you stay cool. Mesh pockets make tucked-away objects easily visible. This model, made by the Orvis Corporation, has a wealth of pockets—22, to be exact. Accessory pockets open with patented, easy-access tabs instead of snaps or zippers.

Inset. *Pin the round metal object, called a zinger, onto your vest. A retractable cord inside attaches to any small object, like this fishhook remover, for quick and easy access.*

ish, and the skin should feel firm and springy to the touch. Finally, fish should smell fresh and never have a suspicious, "fishy" odor.

Hate fishing for bones? Stick to saltwater species, such as snapper, salmon, tuna, and flounder, which have fewer, more easily identifiable bones than freshwater fish.

Leftovers for lunch. Leftover fish makes a tasty lunch. Refrigerate leftover fillets or steaks—tightly wrapped. Serve the next day, cold, on salad greens with a vinaigrette or mayonnaise dressing, or warmed in a simple fish chowder or as the base for your favorite fishcake recipe.

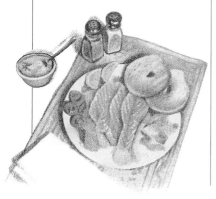

To avoid spoiling, it is safer to thaw frozen fish in the refrigerator. Speed things up by setting the unwrapped fish in a bowl of cold water. Never refreeze thawed fish.

Use the same dish to cook and serve fish. Most fish are too fragile to move from one dish to another without breaking the flesh. A shallow, ovenproof porcelain container makes an excellent oven-to-table fish server.

Something's fishy. To rid a pan of a fishy smell, fill it with a 50/50 solution of vinegar and water, bring it to a boil, let it simmer for 3 minutes, then wash normally. To rid your hands of the odor of fish, rub them with a fresh lemon.

FISHING

Plastic and fiberglass are the best materials for tackle boxes. Models made of steel tend to rust, and aluminum boxes are easily dented.

Keep tabs on your barbs. They can break off easily, so check your hooks often. Also make sure barbs are sharp; dull or rusty ones won't

snag a fish. Either buy new hooks regularly or sharpen old ones; you can get a nifty sharpening tool at most tackle stores.

OLD SAW **Clean your gear** at the end of the day to prevent corrosion and keep everything working. If you fish in salt water, don't fail to rinse your tackle with fresh water.

Mask odors. Fish have a keen sense of smell, and traces of gas, oil, tobacco, sweat, insect repellent, or even soap on gear can repel them. Some expert fishermen use the all-purpose lubricant WD-40 to mask odors.

Change your fishing line after eight hours of use. Worn line doesn't perform well and may break at the moment you are about to reel in your catch. The stretching and twisting it is subjected to when used with a spinning reel take their toll. Throw it away, or, better yet, ask your supplier to recycle it—many do.

FITNESS FOR SENIORS

Get a physical first. If you are over 40, it is prudent to see a doctor before beginning a new exercise regimen, to make sure you have no condition that would rule out exercise.

Twenty magic minutes. For maximum health benefits from aerobic exercise, keep your heart rate up for at least 20 to 30 minutes three to four days a week.

Warm up, cool down. Aging muscles require a good warmup before strenuous exercise. Walk, move about, and stretch. Just as important is the after-exercise cool-down. Dropping into a chair after a vigorous workout can be a shock to your heart. Instead, let your heart rate down slowly by moving around for at least five minutes after your routine.

 A little more each day. Don't overdo your exercising at first. Make a point of stepping it up gradually. "Slow but sure" is the safe and effective way to elevate your fitness level.

Take a warm shower or bath after vigorous exercise. This helps prevent aching, stiffening muscles and encourages a quicker recovery. Then ice down any sore spots.

Weight lifting works to keep aging bones strong. But if you have no weights around, lift 850 mL (28 oz) cans of food instead; they work just fine.

FLASHLIGHTS

Pocket light. Thin penlights that clip into a pocket or fit in a purse make great presents. Some people find them indispensable, such as for reading programs at plays.

OLDER BUT STILL GOING STRONG

An agile mind is as essential to your health and well-being as a physically fit body, so flex your gray matter and leave the mental couch-potato gang behind.

▶ *Get clubby. Join a book club, garden club, investment club, or dinner club for an infusion of fresh ideas.*

▶ *Volunteer. Tutor young students; teach crafts or skills; help out at nursing homes, hospitals, and local libraries.*

▶ *Take a class. Continuing-education classes are booming at universities, colleges, and technical schools. Courses run the gamut, from antiquing furniture to zoology.*

▶ *Be a tourist in your own backyard. Visit those places you were always too busy to see. Tour local museums and historic homes; go on walking tours.*

▶ *Become an activist. Civic-minded seniors make up a powerful political entity. Become involved locally; attend town council meetings; develop your political voice.*

▶ *Compete. Nothing gets the juices flowing quicker than old-fashioned competition. Enter seniors tennis tournaments; sign up for chess or bridge meets.*

▶ *Go to work. Many retired seniors thrive on being back in the workforce, whether full- or part-time.*

Make sure it stays off. When carrying a flashlight in a suitcase or your car's glove compartment, place a strip of tape over the switch so it doesn't get turned on accidentally. For longer storage, reverse one of the batteries.

Try a flexible flashlight that can be coiled to stand on its own or wrapped around a pipe—or even your neck—to leave hands free.

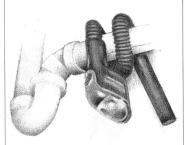

Keep it bright. If the beam is dim or blinking, rub the battery contacts with sandpaper or a clean pencil eraser. Also bend out the spring extending from the switch (inside the case) so that it makes a tighter contact with the bulb mount; clean its surface too.

Save on batteries by getting a flashlight that provides a short, wide beam. Long beams use up batteries more quickly.

FLATWARE

Sign of quality. The best stainless steel used for flatware has "18/8" (or rarely, "18/10") etched into the metal. This indicates that the alloy contains 18 parts chrome and 8 (or 10) parts nickel, and will be highly resistant to discoloring and bending.

Tarnished tines? To clean the hard-to-reach spaces between silver fork tines, coat a string with polish, loop the two ends around one tine, cross the ends, and slide them up and down the tine.

Danger in the dishwasher. Flatware with handles made of non-metal materials, such as wood, stoneware, bone, or bamboo, should not go in the dishwasher. Exposure to super-hot water may soften the glue holding the handles to the metal.

Test stainless quality by holding a magnet to a piece of flatware (but not the blade of a knife, which is made of a different metal mixture). If the magnet attracts the piece, it is made of an inferior grade of stainless steel.

F

FLEA MARKETS

First in get first pick of the wares at flea markets. Follow the strategy used by antiques dealers, who come hoping for bargains: they arrive when the vendors are setting up their booths.

It's no bargain if it will cost a lot to repair. Worn-out wicker chairs, for example, require expensive professional work. And the smell of mildew never goes away.

Chat with vendors when you are looking for something special. Many are collectors themselves and keep tabs on what other vendors have to offer. Many also have shops or more items at home that they will be happy to bring to the market the next week.

 Look around before you buy. Many of the sellers at big flea markets have similar merchandise. Be sure you find the best deal.

Be ready to bargain. Many vendors put on high price tags deliberately so that they can come down and make buyers feel they are getting a better deal. At the least, most dealers will come down 10 percent if you ask.

Come back at day's end if the market is conveniently located. The choicest items may be gone, but anything left unsold at the day's end can usually be picked up for considerable savings.

FLEAS

Birth control for fleas? A recent development in flea control is a medication that interrupts the insect's reproductive cycle. Program, one such product (produced by Ciba-Geigy Corp.), is given to dogs and cats. When an adult female flea bites an animal on Program, the eggs it lays do not develop into mature fleas.

Sunny side. Fleas apparently like shade as well as grassy areas, so keep to sidewalks and sunny spots when walking the dogs—they'll be exposed to fewer fleas.

Keep fleas out of the house by vacuuming carpets and furniture often and discarding the vacuum bag outdoors. Also wash your pet's bedding every week.

RIGHT STUFF

STAINLESS VS. STERLING

Even if you or someone in your family is lucky enough to have sterling silver flatware, chances are, it doesn't get used much—partly because silver needs to be cleaned so often and partly because stainless steel flatware, always cheaper and easier to care for, has become so attractive. There are designs to fit any dining style, from a casual breakfast-for-one to elegant dinner parties for a dozen. And if you buy the best grade of stainless steel, it will always look good.

FLOOR CLEANING

When you wash any floor, wring out the mop until it's almost dry. Using too much water can dissolve protective coatings and raise the grain on wood. It can also loosen the seams of sheet flooring or tiles. Use a second mop for rinsing, since it is hard to get all of the cleaning solution out of the scrubbing mop.

MATERIAL	CLEANING METHOD	SPECIAL PROBLEMS
Ceramic tile	Damp-mop with a general cleaner.	Clean grout between tiles with steel wool dipped in a solution of 250 mL (1 cup) of white vinegar and 9.5 L (2 gal) of water.
Quarry tile	Damp-mop with a general cleaner.	Clean stains from quarry tile with a solution of trisodium phosphate and water.
Resilient flooring (vinyl tile or sheet linoleum)	Spot-clean spills. Wet-mop when needed. Wax to protect linoleum.	Reglue loosened tiles or curling seams in sheet flooring. Worn tiles can be replaced, but sheeting does not patch well.
Wood	Dry-mop or vacuum. Wet-mop only occasionally if needed.	Remove dirt and stains from a urethaned wood floor with a mix of 250 mL (1 cup) of white vinegar and 9.5 L (2 gal) of water. (For really stubborn stains, use 500 mL [2 cups] of vinegar.) Badly worn wood floors require sanding and refinishing.

FLOOR CARE

To hide scratches in a wood floor, use a type of touch-up stain that matches the floor color—or is a shade darker—and apply it according to directions. Touch-up stains are available at most hardware stores and home centers.

Stop a squeak in a wood floor by shaking talcum powder or graphite into the cracks around the squeaky area. If that doesn't work, have someone walk on the floor while you track the squeak from the basement. Squirt caulk between the squeaky spot and the floor joist.

Remove a damaged vinyl tile by first softening the adhesive that holds it to the floor with heat. Use a hair dryer or an iron on a medium setting.

Keep dirt out of the house and off the floors by flanking each entry door with two mats—one on the outside and one on the inside. The longer the mats are, the cleaner the floors will stay.

A two-for-one cleanup. Use your kitchen trash container as a mop bucket. You will automatically clean the bucket while you wash the floor.

Socks appeal. When you move a piece of heavy furniture, protect the floor from being scuffed or scratched by slipping an athletic sock up over the base of each leg.

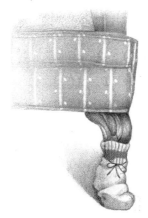

FLOOR COVERINGS

For an instant room makeover, lay sheet vinyl over any clean, flat, structurally sound floor. Sheet vinyl is resilient, water resistant, and inexpensive. It comes in many patterns and colors, in 1.8 and 3.6 m (6 and 12 ft) widths. You normally won't need an adhesive; just move the furniture, unroll the vinyl, and trim it to fit.

Paint to the rescue. If floors are too scarred to be revived by sanding and staining, paint them instead. Latex or acrylic floor or deck paint covers a multitude of defects and can make a colorful statement. It's amenable to decorative techniques as well.

Stencils make striking designs on a painted floor. You can buy stencil patterns in an art supply store, then use acrylic or deck paint to apply the designs. This effect can be especially appealing in a child's room or your front hall.

Protect the concrete floor in your basement by applying a coat of liquid concrete sealer, which can be applied quickly and easily with a paint roller. This invisible covering will make it easier to keep the floor clean.

Get a terrific effect on a country floor by glazing it. Coat the floor with red casein paint, allow it to dry thoroughly, and top off with a coat of khaki-colored glazing paint. While it is still wet, blot off the khaki paint with a rag or sponge to let the base coat show through here and there. Allow the glazing paint to dry, then wax the floor. Natural wear and tear will actually improve the look.

FLOUR

Shake it out. Keep a large shaker filled with flour within easy reach when you bake. If a recipe calls for a dusting of flour to coat a pan, it will be ready to use.

 If you buy only one flour, choose the all-purpose type, bleached or unbleached. It can be used in any recipe, although some recipes, specifically those for cakes and bread, may work better with specially designated flour.

Out of flour? For thickening sauces and gravies, substitute cornstarch for flour, but use only half as much because cornstarch has twice the thickening power.

Flour power. Add fiber, extra protein, and vitamins to your baked goods by substituting whole-wheat flour for half of the white flour called for. If the dark color and nutty flavor of whole wheat are undesirable, try white whole-wheat flour, a milder variety.

Dust mites—the same ones that live in carpets and upholstery—may infest flour and could cause allergic reactions, even if you are not normally allergic to the food itself. They thrive in warm, moist areas. Storing flour in sealed containers in a cool, dry place can help keep them away.

Whole-grain flours turn rancid rapidly (because of the oil in the germ of the grain), so even if you use rye or whole-wheat flour regularly, store it in the refrigerator or freezer in an airtight container.

Freeze flour that you won't be using for a while. Seal the flour in a freezer bag or airtight plastic container before freezing.

FLOWER ARRANGING

Scale your arrangements to the size of their containers. As a general rule, the tallest flowers in an arrangement should be no more than three times the container height. Fine-textured flowers can be somewhat taller. Cut large, bold flowers shorter—about 1½ times the height of the container.

Remove all lower foliage below the water line to discourage the growth of bacteria. Also get rid of excess foliage on flower stems above the water line because it diverts water from the blossoms.

To keep cut flowers fresh, pay special attention to the water in their vase. Fill a vase with warm water because it moves more easily up the stems. Add flower food, sugar, or lemonade, and a few drops of bleach to prevent bacterial growth. Finally, be sure to change the water often.

Make flowers last longer by cutting the stem ends under water to keep air from traveling up the stems and blocking water flow. Cut the ends at an angle to expose more stem area to the water and prevent the stems from sealing to the bottom of the container. Recut stems when you change the water to prolong the blossoms' freshness.

Florist's oasis, the block foam that anchors cut flowers, holds water long after the water in a vase is dry. Soak the oasis in water for a few minutes before placing it in the flower vase.

Improvise an anchor. If you don't have oasis handy, place a ball of loosely crumpled chicken wire or a net bag full of marbles in the bottom of your container.

 ONE-MINUTE FLOWER ARRANGEMENTS

▸ *Exotic. Float three perfect gardenia blossoms in three bowls, or float several camellias in one bowl.*

▸ *Romantic. Place one or two tall roses in a bud vase.*

▸ *Oriental. Arrange three lilies with their stems cut to different lengths—long, medium, and short—in a Chinese porcelain vase together with one or two bare branches.*

▸ *Nostalgic. Bunch an armful of long-stemmed field flowers, such as Queen Anne's lace, tansy, and goldenrod, cut to different lengths, in an old kitchen pitcher.*

FLOWER BULBS

Buy big. Larger bulbs—often called top size, jumbo, or double-nosed—bear bigger flowers and are more likely to sprout new bulbs and thus enlarge your plantings. Big bulbs cost a little more but take no longer to plant.

Leave the leaves alone. To keep bulbs performing as true perennials, resist the impulse to cut off the foliage after the bulbs have finished blooming. Let the leaves wither naturally so that the bulb has lots of time to manufacture nutrients and fatten up for the next year's blossoming.

A pinch of prevention. If chipmunks or field mice are dining on your newly planted bulbs, discourage the critters by sprinkling a pinch of moth crystals over each bulb as you plant it. The crystals last long enough to deter hungry rodents and then evaporate, disposing of themselves. By winter the soil will have compacted around the bulbs, so rodents won't dig for them.

Gopher alert. Gophers are a serious threat to bulbs in the western states. The good news is that they will not eat daffodils (*Narcissus*), squills (*Scilla*), glory-of-the-snow (*Chionodoxa*), or snowdrops (*Galanthus*).

FLOWERS

No need to dig a new flower bed. Instead of stripping away the turf, lay newspaper down over the lawn in a layer 10 sheets thick. Add 5 cm (2 in.) of organic mulch such as shredded leaves, and keep the area moist. Surprise—worms will dig for you. Four weeks later you can plant seedlings right through the mulch and paper, cutting holes with a sharp spade.

Fill your yard with color and reduce its upkeep by converting part of your lawn into a wildflower meadow. Such a planting requires no fertilization and needs mowing just once every fall. Write

BULBS FOR NATURALIZING

The easiest way to grow bulbs is to "naturalize" them—plant species so well adapted to the spot that they rebloom year after year and even multiply and spread. The chart below suggests bulbs that will naturalize in a variety of habitats throughout the temperate zones of the United States.

	BULB	PREFERRED HABITAT	HEIGHT OF PLANT	FLOWER COLOR
Early spring bloom	Daffodil 'February Gold' (*Narcissus cyclamineus*)	Meadow	15–20 cm (6"–8")	Yellow
	English bluebell (*Hyacinthoides non-scripta*)	Woodland or rock garden	45 cm (18")	Violet, pink, or white
	Glory-of-the-snow (*Chionodoxa luciliae*)	Wildflower garden	25 cm (10")	Blue and white
	Siberian squill (*Scilla siberica*)	Woodland or rock garden	10–15 cm (4"–6")	Blue
	Snow crocus (*Crocus chrysanthus*)	Lawn	10 cm (4")	Yellow, purple, or white
Late spring, summer bloom	Canada lily (*Lilium canadense*)	Meadow	15 cm (6")	Yellow or orange
	Nodding wild onion (*Allium cernuum*)	Woodland edge or rock garden	20–45 cm (8"–18")	Pink
Fall bloom	Autumn crocus (*Colchicum autumnale*)	Rock garden or lawn	10–30 cm (4"–12")	Pink, lilac, or white

the Canadian Wildflower Society (4981 Highway 7, Markham, Ont. L3R 1N1) for information on wildflowers in your region.

The versatility of shrubs. Flowering shrubs make beautiful hedges while thorny shrubs offer protection against intruders. Shrubs that are both colorful and thorny include scarlet firethorn (*Pyracantha coccinea*) and rugosa rose (*Rosa rugosa*), which are hardy in cold climates; and flowering quince (*Chaenomeles speciosa*) and trifoliate orange (*Poncirus trifoliata*), which thrive in both warm and cold climates.

Winter-blooming shrubs are a treat for northern gardeners. Chinese witch hazel (*Hamamelis mollis*), fragrant wintersweet (*Chimonanthus praecox*), and winter hazel (*Corylopsis glabrescens*) flower during winter thaws, bearing perfumed yellow blossoms in a wide variety of hues, forms, sizes, and fragrances.

FOOD MIXERS

Test a handheld mixer in the store before you buy. The handle should be easy for you to grip and designed so that you can work the controls while holding the mixer. Perhaps the most important concern: the mixer should be light enough for you to hold without tiring your wrist.

Small but powerful, a mini-processor fits easily into the smallest kitchen and can handle a vast number of food-processing jobs. It offers fewer options than its full-sized cousins, but for anyone who doesn't need to process large quantities of food, this little appliance is ideal— and is reasonably priced as well. It makes a batch of pesto or salsa as easily as it dices carrots or purees peaches.

Get enough power. Handheld mixers have always excelled at beating eggs and whipping cream. But the powerful new models on the market can handle more ambitious tasks, such as mixing cookie dough and mashing potatoes, once reserved for heavy-duty pedestal models.

Keep the mixing bowl from slipping on a countertop when using a handheld mixer by putting a rubberized mat or a damp towel under it.

Beaters stuck? If you have trouble removing your beaters from the mixer, put a drop of cooking oil into the slots where they slide into the machine. Check, too, to make sure the beaters are in their proper slots.

FOOD PROCESSORS

Use brief pulses—two seconds at most—when you start using a food processor, which you'll discover does a lot of work in a hurry. Short bursts help you get used to the machine and ensure

that you gradually bring mixtures to the desired texture without making a mush of them.

Chill soft or gummy foods, such as fruits and most cheeses, in the freezer briefly before processing. The cold firms up the texture of the food and makes a neater job of shredding or slicing.

Get perfect slices every time by first using a knife to cut the end cleanly off whatever food you are slicing, then inserting the cut end into the processor's feeding tube.

Bored with the cleanup? Place a sheet of plastic wrap over the top of your processor's bowl before you put on the lid. After processing, you'll be pleased to discover that the usually splatter-splashed lid has stayed spotless.

Avoid accidents. Never leave a processor's sharp blades lurking dangerously in a sink or even a bowl of soapy water. Also don't tuck blades between dishes in the dishwasher or store them loosely in drawers.

FOOD SAFETY

How cold is cool? To inhibit the growth of most types of bacteria, keep the temperature inside a refrigerator no higher than 5°C (41°F). Check the temperature now and then with a thermometer instead of relying on the refrigerator's internal settings.

When in doubt, toss it out. If the look, age, or smell of food is suspect, always opt for safety: get rid of it. Don't taste-test doubtful food; it's not worth the risk of food poisoning.

Stay cool. Don't leave foods that need refrigeration out for more than two hours. Keep picnics cold with an insulated cooler. For lunch boxes, include a frozen juice pack that will be thawed by lunchtime.

Keep a liquid soap dispenser filled with antibacterial hand soap at the ready on the kitchen sink. Always use it before touching food and also after handling certain foods—such as raw meat, poultry, fish, or uncooked eggs—that are sources of salmonella bacteria and other germs.

FOOD STORAGE

It's OK to store most canned foods in the refrigerator in their original containers for up to two days. This is not a good idea, however, for acidic foods such as tomatoes, which can take on the metallic taste of the can. Store them instead in glass or plastic containers.

To remove lingering smells and coloration from a plastic container for food, rub or spray prewash laundry cleaner into the container, let it sit for a while, then wash and rinse thoroughly.

Solve the problem of trying to hold a limp plastic bag open with one hand while scraping leftovers into it with the other. Simply open the bag and spread it out inside a bowl or glass; fold the top edge of the bag over the rim of the bowl to hold it in place, and carefully scrape in the leftovers.

If a bad odor remains in a container after food has been stored in it, fill the container with crumpled newspaper, cover, and leave it for several hours before washing and rinsing.

Freeze liquids in heavy-duty leakproof containers, leaving an inch or two of air in the container to allow for expansion. Liquids such as chicken or fish stock can also be frozen in ice cube trays and then popped out and stored in freezer bags.

Unstick that plastic wrap. Plastic wrap won't stick to itself and will be easier to use if you keep it stored in the refrigerator.

Before freezing a casserole, line the dish with aluminum foil. Pour in the food and fold the foil tightly around it. Once the food is frozen, remove the foil package and put the dish to other uses.

Avoid staining containers, especially with tomato-based foods, by lining them with plastic wrap before you pour in the food.

STOP THE MOLD!

You can't resist buying several trays of just-picked strawberries, then realize when you get home that you can't possibly eat all this produce before it goes bad. The solution? Store your berries in Evert-fresh or PEAKfresh bags, and they will stay fresh and edible for as long as three weeks. Sold in supermarket produce sections, these bags have a lining that absorbs ethylene gas and moisture—two enemies of produce that advance decay. Washable and reusable, these bags triple the time produce stays fresh in the refrigerator.

FOOD SUBSTITUTIONS

Choosing foods that are lower in calories (which usually means lower in fats, cholesterol, and sugar and higher in fiber) doesn't have to mean eliminating flavor from your daily diet. Try a few of these simple substitutions.

	INSTEAD OF	TRY
Breads and grains	Croissant	Bagel
	White rice	Brown or wild rice
Oils and seasonings	Mayonnaise	Low-fat yogurt
	Butter	Butter-flavored flakes
	Cooking oil	Nonstick cooking spray
	Salad dressing	Oil and vinegar
	Salt	Herbs, spices, lemon juice
Dairy products	Cheddar cheese	Reduced-fat or nonfat cheese
	Cream cheese	Reduced-fat or nonfat cream cheese
	Half-and-half	Nondairy creamer or evaporated skim milk
	Milk, whole or 2%	1% or skim milk
	Sour cream	Nonfat or low-fat yogurt or reduced-fat sour cream
Eggs, fish, and meat	Bacon	Turkey bacon or Canadian bacon
	Skinless roast duck	Skinless roast chicken
	A whole egg	2 egg whites or 60 mL (¼ cup) egg substitute
	Ground chuck beef	Ground round or ground turkey
	Tuna in oil	Tuna in water
Snacks and sweets	Corn chips	Air-popped popcorn
	Ice cream	Ice milk, fat-free frozen yogurt
	Oil-roasted peanuts	Roasted chestnuts; seeds
	Potato chips	Pretzels, bread sticks
	Pound cake	Angel food cake
	Sandwich cookies	Fig-bar cookies

FOOD SUBSTITUTES

One step at a time. If you are trying to stop using regular milk (with 4 percent milkfat) on your cereal but find the watery taste of skim milk unappetizing, get used to 2 percent milk first and then 1 percent. You'll come to like skim faster than you think.

Trade-offs. Don't like bacon substitutes? Go ahead and eat bacon now and then. Just cut down on other high-fat foods on days you indulge in bacon.

FOOT CARE

Keep your feet fit with an exercise that improves flexibility and strength and that you can do anytime you're standing up. Simply rise up on tiptoes 20 to 30 times in succession.

Concrete punishes feet more than any other normal walking surface, and a thin sole is no match for it. Rubber soles are best for protecting your feet from the shock of walking on city streets, but thick leather will also do.

Do the golf-ball roll. For people with heel pain, rolling a golf ball under the foot for a few minutes each day can provide dramatic relief. Prevent heel pain by wearing well-cushioned shoes, but if you do suffer, try over-the-counter shoe inserts or consider investing in orthotic shoes.

Get relief from achy soles after a long jog or tennis session by spending 15 minutes with your feet resting on ice packs.

Soften your feet by soaking them for 20 minutes in a bowl of hot water and 250 mL (1 cup) of warm olive oil and the juice of a lemon. Then dry your feet and rub in some moisturizing cream.

FORMAL ATTIRE

What is "black tie"? Formal wear are now less rigid, but if an invitation specifies "black tie," the basics remain the classiest way to go. For men this means a black tuxedo, a white tuxedo shirt, with black bow tie and cummerbund, or a fancy vest with a matching colored or black bow tie. For women either a long gown or a short cocktail dress works fine.

Why not rent a gown for that special once-a-year formal occasion? Businesses that rent one-of-a-kind designer gowns have cropped up in many cities. Look under "Gown Rental and Sales" in the Yellow Pages.

Find the best buys after Christmas, when formal wear goes on sale. To expand your options, look for separates to pair with pieces you already have.

No longer taboo. It's okay for women to wear black to an evening wedding—or, for that matter, scarlet red. What used to be considered in bad taste is now perfectly acceptable attire for a dressy nuptials. If you want to wear white, however, ask the bride for her approval first.

FREE-STYLE FIRST

Canada Day cake. Celebrate our national holiday in style by making a maple leaf cake. Bake a simple 22 x 33 cm (9 x 13 in.) sheet cake and ice it with plain white butter icing. Whip up some more icing and add some red food coloring to make the red borders. Create the maple leaf using summer strawberries.

Fly the flag. Whether you join a parade or relax on your porch, unfurl a Canadian flag for the day.

Wear a maple leaf. Instead of knocking yourself out to decorate, ask your guests to provide the ambience by wearing traditional red and white, maple leaves, or anything else emblematic of our national holiday.

Patriotic ice. Put raspberries (or maraschino cherries) into empty ice-cube trays, fill with water, and freeze. You will have red ice cubes to put in drinks on Canada Day.

 Why we celebrate. Here's a way to help everyone remember the true meaning of Canada Day: gather the family and your guests and have each person sing, in sequence, the lines of "O Canada," our national anthem.

Sparkler safety. Pretty sparklers are synonymous with Canada Day celebrations, but unsupervised use can be dangerous. Light them one at a time at arm's length and out of the reach of small children. Put a bucket of water by your side to douse each sparkler as it goes out.

FREEZERS

Freezers are most efficient when they are full, so keep yours well stocked—but leave room (about 2.5 cm [1 in.] if possible) between each item so that the chilled air can circulate.

After defrosting, spray a light coating of cooking oil on the freezer's interior walls. This won't stop frost from re-forming, but the ice will cling less tenaciously the next time you defrost.

On vacation? Keep tabs on your freezer while you are away. Before you go, put a bowl of loose ice cubes in the freezer; if when you return the ice has melted and re-frozen into a solid chunk, you'll know that the freezer temporarily malfunctioned or lost power and that some of the food stored there might be spoiled.

Beating bad smells. You've heard about putting baking soda in the refrigerator to absorb odors? Try putting an open container of used coffee grounds in the freezer to suck up any unpleasant or overly strong smells.

FREEZING FOOD

Cooking for the freezer? If you know you will be freezing a dish you are preparing, season it lightly or not at all before freezing, then add more flavor when you thaw and reheat it. Freezing alters the flavor of many spices; for example, it makes pepper, cloves, and garlic strong and bitter, and it subdues the flavor of curry.

Double wrap. Use heavy foil or double layers of regular foil along with plastic to wrap food for the freezer. If the food is something you plan to reheat in the oven, wrap it first with aluminum foil, then plastic: just peel off the plastic and put the item into the oven still in its foil wrap. If you plan to take off the wrappings all at once, then make plastic the first layer—it is easier to detach from frozen food.

 To preserve freshness and inhibit frost buildup on food in the freezer, squeeze all the air from the plastic bags in which you put food to be frozen, then tightly secure the bags.

Organize your freezer by using cardboard containers such as cereal or rice boxes to give shape to nonsolid foods that would otherwise freeze in odd, hard-to-arrange lumps. Wrap the foods well before putting them in the boxes (cardboard is a poor storage material); after they have frozen, remove the items from the boxes.

Mark it up. It may be a nuisance to label and date each item you freeze, but it will make life a lot easier weeks later when you are planning a menu and your freezer is full of look-alike packages.

For quick thawing. Special thawing trays are sold in stores, but here is a home-grown option: Heat a heavy aluminum pan (a good heat conductor) with hot water, then dump out the water and put the frozen food in the pan. Reheat the pan when it cools and turn the frozen food over when you put it back in the pan, so that it thaws evenly.

FREQUENT-FLYER PROGRAMS

Sign on for several frequent-flyer programs, even if you fly infrequently. All are free and you'll get notice of special sales and

EASY DOES IT

FINDING OLD FRIENDS

Wistful for a long-lost pal? Pining to see a face from the good old days? Many avenues are now open for those hunting for a long-ago friend, and finding your past may be as easy as pressing a computer key.

▶ *The Internet. Think of it as a giant computerized phonebook. Simply log on to one of the popular directories on the Internet. Type in the name of your old pal, and in minutes you may be rewarded with a street address, phone number—even an e-mail address. Web sites to check: Switchboard (http://www.switchboard.com), WhoWhere (http://www.whowhere.com), or Bigfoot (http://www.bigfoot.com).*

▶ *CD-ROM telephone directories. Public libraries let you use these for no fee. Keep in mind that any information you can supply, such as a last-known address or an old phone number, can narrow—and speed up—the search.*

▶ *Hire a professional. A small but growing cottage industry has grown up in North America around finding old friends. Check the "Detectives" section in the Yellow Pages of your local telephone directory.*

▶ *Subscribe to your old hometown newspaper. It may not mention your old friend, but news bites and social bits about his family members may lead you to him.*

---

bonuses you would not hear about otherwise.

How many miles? A good way to judge frequent-flyer plans is to compare the minimum number of miles awarded per leg of each flight. Some airlines give 500; others, 750. The more miles awarded, the quicker you can earn free tickets. Look as well for programs that require fewer accumulated miles to earn round-trip tickets.

Program partners are a good measure of comparison among airline frequent-flyer programs. Hotels and car rental agencies give miles as a bonus to flyers on their partner airlines. Choose airlines affiliated with the services you prefer, and your miles will accumulate faster.

Expiration dates can rob you of earned miles. Choose airlines that do not require miles to be used by a certain date. On other airlines, be sure to use credits before you lose them.

Earn miles on the ground when you shop with airline affinity credit cards that bestow a mile for each dollar spent. Be sure to check the card's interest rate and annual fee, though, so that you don't end up paying more than you save.

Dial for miles by using a long-distance service that awards miles on your favorite airline for every dollar on your telephone bill.

The long and short of it. Longer trips aren't always the best use of frequent-flyer awards because air-

---

lines often compete with special fares on popular long routes like New York to Los Angeles. You may make better use of awards for trips to smaller cities where specials are less frequent.

FRIENDSHIP

One up, the other down. It takes an effort from both parties to keep a relationship sweet when one person enjoys a run of success while the other's life remains stagnant. Focus on the areas where you still can meet as equals—sports, music, or hobbies, for instance. That is where the friendship can keep on flourishing.

Encourage your kids to develop friendships. Make their friends feel welcome in your home. Studies show that children who do not learn how to form relationships early can carry this problem over into adulthood and be saddled with chronic anger, unhappiness, and low self-esteem.

Birds of a feather. A great place to find friends is wherever you do things you like to do: Attending church; exercising; participating in community activities; or joining a club, from a chess or bridge club to a fraternal organization.

Remember special days. Birthdays and wedding anniversaries are good times to call or send cards. Letting your friends know that you are thinking about them is a gratifying way to honor old friendships and cement new ones.

FROSTBITE

Redness, tingling, and pain are signs that frostbite—the freezing of the body's tissue—is imminent unless the affected area is warmed. If your toes hurt or your fingers look red, come in out of the cold. Have a hot, sugary drink to help warm up.

Numbness and white, hard skin are signs that you've got frostbite. If an extremity is frostbitten, put it against a warm part of your body. For example, put your fingers under your arm. Avoid letting the injury refreeze, and get medical attention as quickly as possible.

Don't sit near a fire or stove if you have frostbite. The frozen area is numb and can burn before enough feeling returns to signal that damage is being done.

If you can't get to a doctor right away, soak frostbitten skin in warm water with a temperature of about 40°C (104°F). Keep it there until feeling returns to the area. This will be very painful. Don't rub frostbitten skin, which damages tissue further. And if the skin blisters, don't break the blisters or put ointment on them. Do get to a doctor as soon as you can.

FROZEN PIPES

Heat a frozen pipe slowly, using a handheld hair dryer, a heat lamp, or rags that have been soaked in hot water. Do not use boiling water, propane torches, or other open flames. Pipes that are heated too quickly can explode.

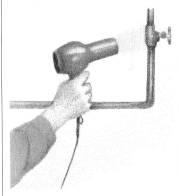

Let your faucets drip a little during cold snaps if you fear pipes might freeze. The slow movement of the water inhibits freezing, and the slightly open faucet may save

---

EXOTIC FRUITS

Few taste treats match that of a perfectly ripened piece of fruit, and the range of varieties available to the average shopper grows all the time. Stores offer more and more fruits that may be standard fare in other parts of the world but are exotic delicacies to North American taste. Try them—they can add new zest to your cooking, baking, and snacking.

FRUIT	BASIC INFORMATION	WAYS TO USE IT
Star fruit (carambola)	When cut crosswise, five-point slices resemble stars; ready to eat when golden.	Eat flesh as is or in fruit salads; sauté to pair with meat, seafood.
Guava	Ready when slightly soft; cut and scoop to eat. use also in fruit salads, jelly, preserves.	When firm, bake; when ripe, eat flesh as is.
Kiwifruit	Ready when soft; cut and scoop to eat; contains enzyme that tenderizes meat and aids digestion, but also sours the taste of dairy products.	Peel with a knife or peeler and slice for salads, drinks, and garnishes; liquefy for dessert sauces.
Mango	Ready when it smells sweet and yields to touch. Beware: Oil in rind can irritate skin.	Use green in chutneys and relishes; when ripe, eat flesh as is and in salads, stir-fries, salsas, or drinks.
Papaya	Ready when yellow and soft to the touch; con tains natural enzyme that aids digestion and ten derizes meat.	Eat flesh as is; add to salads at last minute, as it can make other ingredients mushy; use peppery seeds in marinades, salad dressings.
Passion fruit (granadilla)	Egg-shaped, with thick reddish rind; orange, seedy pulp; ripe when rind is wrinkled.	Use pulp in fruit salads, salad dressings, sauces, cakes, frozen desserts, drinks.
Persimmon	Bright, orange skin. Most varieties, originally from the Orient, now grow in the southern U.S.	Eat flesh as is when very soft; puree in pies, cakes, custards; tastes bitter if heated.
Pomegranate	Hard, red rind; inside, many sacs filled with juicy pulp; lots of seeds.	Eat flesh as is; pureed and strained, pulp can be used for drinks, dressings, soups, sauces; seeds make edible garnishes.

the pipe from bursting if the temperature becomes low enough to freeze the water in it.

Before thawing a frozen pipe, turn the water off at the main valve in case the pipe is cracked. Open the nearest faucet to reduce pressure and allow water to run out as the ice melts.

Guard against freeze-ups by wrapping metal pipes with thermostat-controlled heat tape (or cable for outdoor pipes). When the temperature falls to freezing, the tape turns on and warms the pipes enough to keep them from freezing. (But if a power failure accompanies the cold weather, the heat tape won't work.)

FRUIT

Look for bargains on frozen fruit when its fresh counterpart is in season. When fresh peaches line the grocer's shelves, the demand for frozen peaches drops, and you can often take advantage of the lower price to stock up for the winter months.

Sizing up fruit. If you are planning to eat fruit raw, buy the smallest pieces you can find. With this tactic, you'll be able to buy more pieces of fruit per kilogram or pound. (Don't forget that an average serving of fruit is usually about 250 mL [1 cup].) But if you are planning to cook with the fruit, buy larger—and fewer—pieces so you will have less fruit to wash, peel, core, pit, and chop.

Faux sorbet. For a quick and easy dessert, freeze your favorite canned fruit, preferably one packed in heavy syrup. (Remove the fruit from the can and place it in a plastic container before freezing.) Just before serving, empty the fruit into a blender or food processor and blend for a few seconds. For added flavor, add 30 mL (2 tbsp) of rum or liqueur just before processing.

THE CASE FOR CAST IRON

Hundreds of new products dazzle the modern cook, but one time-tested item is still a must for any well-equipped kitchen: the cast-iron frying pan. True, it is heavy and harder to maintain than more modern pans. But its virtues are many: it is much cheaper than fancier pans; it heats uniformly, so that food cooks evenly; when properly seasoned, it is almost nonstick; and it is virtually indestructible and will provide a lifetime of well-cooked meals.

FRYING FOOD

Contrasts in frying. Foods with high moisture content, such as zucchini, need to be fried slowly at low temperature. This prevents a crust from forming too rapidly, which locks steam inside and makes the food soggy. Fry low-moisture foods, such as potatoes, quickly at a high temperature; otherwise, what moisture there is will evaporate and be replaced by oil, making the food greasy.

 The "pop" test. Cooking oil is at the right temperature for frying if a popcorn kernel pops quickly after being dropped in the pan or a crust of bread browns rapidly.

Don't fill the pan too full. If a frying pan is jammed with food, the cooking oil seeps into the food, making it greasy. Cook the food in batches or use two pans.

Clean up frying oil to use again by pouring it through a sieve lined with a coffee filter (the sieve will be easier to clean). Do this only with oil used for frying vegetables—not fish, meat, or poultry.

FUMES

Smell a strong gas odor? Get out of your house immediately! Don't turn on lights or appliances, and don't strike a match; don't even switch on a flashlight—any spark could ignite the gas. After leaving the house, call your local utility's emergency number from a nearby telephone.

Bug off. Because pesticides sprayed inside a structure can linger in the air for as long as half a day, be sure to open the windows and let the room air out for at least 24 hours after it is sprayed—and before you return.

Oven cleaners work well, but most of them give off caustic fumes; keep your head away from the oven as much as you can when using them. Or look for a cleaner that has no toxic warning on its label; it is safer and cleans almost as well.

FUNERALS

Keep a master list of family and friends who should be notified when a close relative dies. The mourning period is no time to be sorting through the deceased's address book or relying on memory. With an up-to-date list, few will be left out or forgotten.

Get an itemized accounting of expenses from the funeral home director before signing off on any funeral arrangements.

Order one limousine to transport the immediate family to the cemetery. You will want to be together—but you are under no obligation to provide transportation for others at the funeral. They will use their own cars.

In the death notice, name the charity friends should contribute to instead of sending flowers if that is what the family wants.

Use the guest book signed by those who attended the funeral and the cards from flowers or donations to guide you in writing thank-you notes. Ask the funeral director for the book and cards if she does not deliver them to you after the service.

Choose only what you want when making arrangements with a funeral home. Funeral providers are required by law to disclose the cost of everything they offer and cannot require you to buy all-or-nothing "packages" that may include items or services you don't need.

Plan ahead. Make it easier on your survivors by writing down your preferences for your own funeral. You should indicate whether you want to be cremated or buried, and your directions could extend to the kind of service you want, the music, your burial clothes—even to the inscription on your tombstone.

FURNACES

Clean the blades on your furnace's blower fan regularly; grimy blades push air over the heat exchanger less efficiently. Some fans can be cleaned in place, but most require removal.

Choose a furnace filter for its "dust spot efficiency," a measure of how well it removes fine particles from your heating system. A high efficiency filter removes up to 95 percent of these particles.

 Have your furnace checked and cleaned annually by a professional. The cost of the cleaning will be more than met by the improved efficiency.

Reflect heat from radiators into a room by sliding a sheet of foil-faced rigid insulation behind each radiator. Or tape aluminum foil to a piece of fiberboard.

FURNITURE

To create extra storage space without building closets, buy a generous-size armoire. Such pieces come with a number of optional arrangements that include space for hanging full-length garments, movable shelves, and drawers of various sizes. You can find a relatively cheap armoire where unpainted furniture is sold.

Exhibition furniture. Have a glass top made for a coffee table, desk, or chest and mount a display of mementos—photographs, awards, and the like—safely but visibly under cover.

FUNERAL ETIQUETTE

No hard and fast rules apply for friends attending a funeral, but here are a few suggestions to guide your behavior.

▶ *Deliver food you've made for the family early in the day to the site where the meal will be served after the funeral. Never carry it with you to the funeral.*

▶ *If you are asked to speak at a funeral, keep in mind that personal reminiscences are both memorable and cherished. If the deceased had a favorite poet or writer, consider reading a short piece as your conclusion.*

▶ *Black is not required these days. Even family members do not have to wear traditional mourning clothes; they may want to wear something with more personal significance.*

Quick Fix for a Furniture Scratch

It can spoil your day to find that someone has dragged an object across a favorite tabletop and left a shallow but very visible scratch. Luckily, there is an easy way to disguise the nasty scar. Buy a wax pencil made for that purpose at a hardware store or home center. If possible, choose a color a little darker than the table.

1 *Trace along the scratch with the wax stick, working from top to bottom and making sure that the wax fills the scratch completely. While the wax sets, cover a small wood block (a child's block is ideal) with a soft rag.*

2 *Using the edge of the block, rub across the filled scratch with the wood grain to remove the excess wax and flatten the filling.*

3 *Polish with a soft rag. The scratch will be barely noticeable.*

Furniture to go. If you are likely to move often in the next few years, you may want to choose neutral furniture and furnishings that are suitable to many different room shapes and home styles. Furniture that disassembles easily and is rugged enough to withstand cross-country tours also makes good sense.

FUSES & CIRCUIT BREAKERS

Map out your circuits and save time in an electrical emergency. First, turn the lights on all over the house, including the attic and basement. Then turn off a circuit by removing its fuse or tripping its breaker; have a partner walk around telling you which lights have gone off and which wall plugs don't work. Those are on the circuit you turned off. Write that information next to the fuse or circuit breaker, turn it on again, and go on to the next one.

Short fuse. If your air conditioner blows a fuse when you turn it on, install a time-delay fuse. This device will handle the short-term power surge caused by an appliance start, but the fuse will blow normally if the surge lasts for more than a few seconds.

Keep a flashlight near the fuse box or circuit breaker panel so you'll be able to change fuses or reset breakers if the lights go out.

Look in the window of a fuse to find out why it has blown. If it is clear but the metal strip inside is broken, the cause was probably an overload, and you should unplug something from the circuit. If the window is clouded or smudged, you probably have a short circuit, which means a faulty appliance needs repair or replacement.

Replace standard fuses with type S fuses with screw-in adapters that accept only fuses of the correct amperage. This will prevent someone from installing a fuse with too large a capacity, thus creating a fire hazard.

G

GAMES TO GUTTERS

GAMES

Games to entertain kids. Small children stuck in airports, waiting rooms, or cars become restless fast. Turn tedious situations into fun ones. For example, count how many people you can spot who are wearing red. Give a quarter to the first child who sees twins. Tell a story by committee—having each child take a turn in making up a new part.

Level the playing field. If one child constantly wins at a particular activity, the other young players will lose interest fast. Switch to games based on luck, so that everyone has a chance to win.

Old games are good games. You don't need every new board or video game to have fun. Oldies like Hangman and Twenty Questions—even spotting out-of-state license plates from the car—can occupy a group for a long time.

GARAGE DOORS

Before going on a trip, disconnect your automatic garage door opener. While you are away, no one can open it with an opener that has the same frequency.

Check the safety reverse on your garage door opener at least once a year by putting a roll of paper towels on the threshold of the garage and then shutting the door. The door should stop and reverse as soon as it touches the roll. If it doesn't, disconnect the opener until you can have it fixed.

Snow or gravel can build up on the threshold of your garage door and bounce the door up before it rides all the way down. Keep the area swept clean.

Troubleshoot for problems with an automatic door by watching and listening every once in a while when the door is moving. In particular, make sure that the rollers are rolling and not skidding in the tracks. Grease or oil the tracks regularly to keep the door moving smoothly. Then oil the hinges and cables to prevent rust.

GARAGES

The right place. Hang a tennis ball with a string from the garage ceiling to mark exactly where the car should stop when it comes into the garage. Hang the ball so that when it just touches the middle of the windshield, the car is exactly where it should be.

Headlight check. After your car has been inspected and your headlights are properly adjusted, mark where the brightest part of each beam hits the back wall of the garage when the car is standing at a line taped to the floor. You will always be able to tell if the lights are out of alignment.

Install a smoke alarm and a fire extinguisher in your garage. It is just as vulnerable to fire as the rooms in your house—more so if you keep gasoline or other combustibles in the garage.

A better sweep. Before taking a broom to a concrete garage floor, sprinkle the floor with slightly damp coffee grounds. The grounds will keep the dust down while you sweep.

Two-step cleanup. Clean oil and grease left by the car on a cement garage floor by covering the spots

A SCRABBLE CRIB SHEET

Give yourself an advantage at Scrabble by memorizing words with either high-scoring letters or odd combinations to help you use up your tiles. All the words listed here are real—though they may not be in your pocket dictionary. (If you want to know what they mean, look 'em up.)

aa	epopeia	mozo	xylem
aecia	haj	pix	xylyl
ai	iynx	qaid	zax
bezique	izar	revehent	zeugma
crwth	juba	tzar	zoeae
cwm	mojo	xebec	zori

with cat litter. Leave it for a while to absorb the oil, then sweep it up. Sprinkle the remaining stains with dishwashing detergent, let it stand for a few minutes, and scrub it off with boiling water.

GARBAGE CANS

Double duty. A good way to clean a garbage can is to use a toilet brush; the long handle makes it easier to reach the bottom of the can. Then you can pour some bleach into the toilet's bowl and clean the brush and the toilet at the same time.

Stake out. To keep raccoons and neighborhood dogs from knocking over your garbage can, drive a stake into the ground so that it stands about 30 cm (1 ft) higher than the can, then slip one handle of the can over the stake. Secure the lid by attaching a shock, or bungee, cord to the handles.

Sprinkle cat litter over the bottom of your garbage cans to reduce odors. Change the litter when you empty the can.

GARBAGE DISPOSERS

Grind half a lemon, orange, or other citrus fruit in your disposer to remove bad smells. A cup of vinegar also does the job.

TROUBLE-SAVING HOSE ATTACHMENT

This inexpensive mechanical timer, which attaches easily to most faucets, will simplify watering chores. Hook up the sprinkler or soaker hose to the timer, then set the color-coded dial for any length of time you want water to flow (up to three hours). When the time is up, the device will turn off the water flow automatically. This—as well as more elaborate models—is available at most hardware stores.

Mix soft garbage in with harder scraps, such as small bones or chunks of gristle, when feeding your sink disposer. The machine grinds up the mixed garbage more efficiently than if it gets the bones by themselves; there's also less strain on the mechanism.

Keep the blades sharp the easy way: toss several ice cubes into your garbage disposer, then process as usual.

Keep out! Here are some things you should never put in your disposer: banana peels, artichoke leaves, corn husks, seafood shells, large bones, metal objects such as bottle caps and aluminum foil —and, of course, your favorite cooking tools and flatware.

GARDEN HOSES

Hoses are rated by the amount of water pressure required to burst them, and a garden hose's pressure rating is a good clue to the quality of a hose. A hose rated at 3,450 kN/m² (500 psi) is the best quality and, because it lasts longest, is also the best buy.

Protect your plants from being flattened by the hose as you drag it around the garden. Drive 30 cm (1 ft) lengths of rebar (concrete reinforcing bar) into the ground at strategic corners. Then cover the protruding bars with short lengths of PVC pipe to create rotating hose guides.

Better than a hose. New plantings need a slow, gradual soak, but leaving your hose on at a dribble can tie it up for an hour or more. Instead, punch a few small holes in the bottom of an inexpensive plastic bucket and set it next to the thirsty plant. Fill the bucket with water and let it take over the job of watering drop by drop.

A small difference in diameter of a garden hose makes a big difference in the rate at which the hose delivers water. A 12 mm (½ in.) hose delivers one-third as much as a 19 mm (¾ in.) hose. But there is also a large difference in the weight: 15 m (50 ft) of 12 mm (½ in.) hose weighs 4 kg (9 lb) when it is full of water, while 19 mm (¾ in.) hose weighs almost five times as much when full.

GARDEN PESTS

Take a tip from the farmers. Rotate your flower plantings, just as farmers rotate crops. Each type of pest usually favors a particular type of plant. Put plants in the same spot every year, and its pests become entrenched, overwintering in the soil to resume their attack in the spring. Move the plants to a new spot every year, and leave the pests behind.

Clean up your act. Insects harmful to plants can hide and breed in weeds, old leaves, and other plant debris. Rake out or compost these materials from your garden promptly, and you'll dramatically reduce the need to spray.

Bug vs. bug. Make your garden attractive to predaceous insects—those that eat other insects—and they will take care of plant-eating insects for you. Dot your garden with sweet alyssum, asters, daisies, marigolds, sunflowers, yarrow, and herbs like parsley, fennel, and dill. These plants supplement the diet of predaceous insects such as wasps and certain flies.

Solarize your soil to kill off soil-dwelling pests and diseases. Wait until the weather is hot, then clear the bed of vegetation, water it thoroughly, and cover it with a sheet of clear plastic, tucking the edges into the soil around the outside of the bed. Leave the plastic in place six weeks—heat from the sun will sanitize the bed.

EASY DOES IT — DECLARING WAR ON SLUGS

Slugs can reduce a plant's leaves to skeletons overnight or at the least leave them pocked with holes. The purists' way to deal with slugs is to pick them off by hand—but this usually means working by flashlight at night. Here are some less daunting ways to deal with them.

▶ *Scatter so-called slug pellets, which deter the pests, on the soil around vulnerable plants.*
▶ *Lay a broad ring of crushed eggshells, seashells, wood ashes, or diatomaceous earth around the plants.*
▶ *Set small containers filled with beer into the garden soil; the slugs crawl in to drink, drown, and then the alcohol destroys the slugs' body tissue.*
▶ *Some gardeners swear that a strip of copper foil laid around a bed will keep the slugs away because it gives them an electric shock as they slither over it.*

GARDEN PLANT SELECTION

Let nature guide you. Before selecting species of plants to put in your landscape, pay a visit to the local nature center or botanical garden to determine what kind of vegetation is native to your area. Mimicking the natural vegetation ensures that your plantings will thrive with less care.

Fit the plant to the spot. Before buying any plant, especially a tree, check its "mature" size—the height and width it will attain when it reaches its fullest growth—and how long it will take to reach full size. If a plant outgrows the spot you plant it in, you will be forced to remove and replace it. In the case of a tree, replacement can be problematic and expensive.

Beat the drought. Gardeners in regions of chronic drought can save themselves a lot of work by landscaping with drought-tolerant plants that draw adequate moisture from rainfall and flourish without constant irrigation. Usually the local water company or municipal water board can supply a list of such plants and will often help you, free of charge, to plan an irrigation-free garden.

 Know your hardiness zone. Canada is divided into nine hardiness zones based on average minimum temperatures. When choosing plants, check the hardiness zone on the label or in the catalog. Selecting only plants listed as hardy in your zone will prevent many expensive wintertime casualties.

GARDENING TOOLS

Rules for buying tools. Always go for the best quality when shopping for tools. A well-made tool lasts longer and makes any task easier. The handle is usually a good clue to overall quality. Fiberglass handles are light and strong and generally indicate a premium-quality tool. Wooden handles should be unpainted and made of straight-grained ash or hickory.

Easy sharpening. Use a file or sharpening stone to put a fine edge on tools. Remove nicks from a hoe or mower blade by fixing a coarse aluminum oxide grinding disc in your electric drill, and rubbing the disc across the dulled blades. You'll have the blades smoothed out in minutes.

 Take care of your tools, and they'll take care of you. Naturally, you want your gardening tools to be handy when you need them—but always put them away, out of the weather, when you're not using them. Rusty shovels, hoes, and trowels will work for a while, but eventually they'll let you down.

Blister-proofing. Wooden tool handles dry and roughen with age—and that can mean blisters and splinters. Smooth the handles with medium-coarse sandpaper, then douse them with boiled linseed oil. Leave the tool out in the sun for two days, then oil it again.

Make sure the fit is good. The best-made tool may be a bad tool for you if it is too big or too small. Such a mismatch makes garden tasks harder than they have to be. When shopping for any tool, take it in your hands and go through the actual motions of using it in the garden. Other shoppers may stare, but you'll save yourself unnecessary discomfort and work.

It makes sense to rent power tools, such as tillers, leaf blowers, and wood chippers, that you use only occasionally. You can afford to rent efficient, industrial-quality machines that you couldn't afford to buy—and you don't have to worry about repair and storage.

GARLIC

Fresh is best. Whole garlic heads are available year-round in grocery stores and will last for two months or more stored in a cool, dark place. Fresh garlic is more trouble to use than garlic powders, extracts, and minced preparations, but it is cheaper and is incomparable in terms of flavor.

Sauté garlic quickly over low heat in butter or oil until it turns golden; don't let it burn or brown or it will taste bitter. Long-cooked garlic, whether gently sautéed or simmered in liquid, becomes mellow and sweet.

Onions first. If you are going to sauté onions and garlic together for a recipe, start with the onions and wait until they're almost done before adding minced or chopped garlic. This will prevent the garlic from burning.

Chef's trick. The technique most favored by the pros to remove the skin of a garlic clove is simply to crush one or more cloves with the flat side of a big kitchen knife. The skins will then slip off easily.

Remove the skins quickly and easily by dropping the garlic cloves into boiling water for about a minute, or heating them in the microwave for about 30 seconds. Let the cloves cool, then peel off their papery skins with your fingers.

Festoon your kitchen. If you love to cook with garlic, hang braided strands of garlic bulbs around your kitchen. These make a lovely decorative touch, and provide an ample garlic supply.

Garlic spread. Roast whole, unpeeled bulbs wrapped in foil for an hour in a 200°C (400°F) oven. Cool, then cut across the top (not stem end) and squeeze out the roasted cloves. Spread the creamy pulp on crusty bread.

No more garlic breath. If you love garlic but hate the aftertaste, try chewing on parsely sprigs or fennel seeds, or drinking lemon or lime juice.

A BACK-SAVING, PLANT-SAVING HOE

A scudder hoe is a classic tool for cultivating and weeding—and saving your back. The hoe goes into the ground like a long-handled trowel. You can move it back and forth underground to loosen the soil and dislodge weeds without disturbing the roots of plants growing close by.

EASY DOES IT

GETTING MORE MILES TO THE GALLON

Your first decision about gas mileage comes when you buy a car—the difference in fuel efficiency between two vehicles of the same general size can be great (manual transmissions, for example, are more gas efficient than automatics). Once you start driving, the fuel efficiency hints listed here will save you money and clean up the air we all breathe.

▶ *Check your tire pressure. Underinflated tires can lead you down the road to poor fuel efficiency.*

▶ *Air conditioning used in city stop-start driving can be costly to your gas mileage. On the highway, however, air conditioning isn't a factor in gas efficiency.*

▶ *Radial tires give better gas mileage than bias-ply tires.*

▶ *Older cars need frequent tune-ups to stay fuel efficient; proper ignition timing can improve gas mileage as much as one-fifth. Using synthetic oil in any car saves on gas.*

▶ *Poor tire alignment can run up your gas bills while ruining your tires. Have your alignment checked regularly.*

▶ *Don't carry cargo you don't have to; hauling extra weight eats up gasoline.*

GASOLINE

A full tank of gas helps save wear and tear on your fuel pump, which is located in the gas tank and depends on the gas for lubrication. When the tank is less than a quarter full, you risk burning out the pump. Buy gasoline at the first sign of low gas level.

Gas additives that contain detergent can be beneficial for your car. Remember, however, that not all gasolines contain enough detergent to keep your engine clean.

Seasonal changes. Gasoline is blended for either winter or summer driving. When the seasons change, some vehicles develop temporary performance problems that disappear as soon as the old fuel is used up and the more weather-appropriate gasoline blend is reaching the engine.

Hot-weather waste. Don't top off your gas tank when you buy gasoline in the early morning during a summer heat wave. The fuel expands in hot weather, which causes the pressure in the tank to increase, forcing the excess gas to overflow and be wasted.

Low marks for high octane. Unless your owner's manual calls for high-octane gas, don't waste your money buying high-octane fuel. Contrary to the advertising hype, higher octane fuels do not provide more power or keep engines running cleaner. In fact, using a higher octane gas than is needed may reduce mileage and leave harmful engine deposits.

GATES

Squeeze a sagging gate back into shape by running a cable between eye bolts installed at opposite corners of the frame and tightening it with a turnbuckle. If there is no wooden brace, the cable should go from the bottom of the hinge side to the top of the latch side. If the gate already has a diagonal wooden brace, run the cable on the other diagonal, as shown below.

Gate posts need more support than regular fence posts because the swinging gate puts more strain on them. Set gate posts in concrete and be sure they are big enough—if your fence posts are 2x4's, use 4x4's for the gate posts.

Self-closing gates help keep children and pets from getting out of the yard. Bolt or screw a stiff gate spring (found in various sizes at hardware stores) to the hinge side of the gate frame and the gate post next to it. Unlike a screen-door spring, this one "winds up," or compresses, when the gate opens, then springs back to push it closed.

GENERICS

Save on prescriptions. Drugs sold under their generic names contain the same active ingredients and dosage as brand-name drugs, but inactive ingredients may differ and thus alter an individual's reaction to the drug. It's worth asking your doctor whether a generic version of your prescription is the right choice for you—generics are often half the cost of brand-name drugs.

Over-the-counter generics such as ibuprofen can, like prescription generics, be much cheaper than their nationally advertised brand-name counterparts. If the labels list the same ingredients in the same amounts, you can buy safely.

Who gets the savings? Ask the druggist if you are getting a generic version of your prescription drug. If the doctor has not specified a name, some states let pharmacies substitute a cheaper generic. Be sure you benefit from the switch, not the pharmacy.

GIFT WRAPPING

Let your kids create their own hands-on wrapping paper with finger paints. Spread a sheet of plain white or brown butcher paper on the floor (with a protective layer of newspaper under it) and have your children plant their handprints in differerent colors all over the paper.

Outdoor adornments. Tie or glue seasonal greenery, plants, fruits, nuts, or vegetables to your wrapped presents to create unique packages. Try feathers, sprays of fern, ornamental grasses, dried flowers, ears of colorful corn, walnuts, baby vegetables, or autumn leaves.

Out of name cards? Simply cut a small rectangle out of the same paper you've used to wrap your present; fold it in half and tape it to the package. Then write your "to" and "from" inside.

G

Making a Bow

Have you ever thought of making those beautiful bows that are so expensive when bought ready-made? It is much easier than it looks. Here's how.

1 Wrap a piece of ribbon around the box and tie a knot. Allow 15–20 cm (6"–8") of extra ribbon on each end, which you will use to attach the bow.

2 Make a loop the size of the bow-to-be and tape the end of the ribbon to itself to secure the loop. Then wrap four or five more loops neatly around the first one; snip.

3 With thumb and index finger, pinch the circle of loops together. This is where it will be tied to the box, but first you need to make it narrower.

4 Fold the circle back on itself, and trim a triangular wedge from each side of the ribbon where it is folded, leaving about half its width intact.

5 Tie down the loops with the ends of the box's ribbon. Remove the tape and gently separate the loops on each side of the knot. Presto!

G

GLASSWARE

Two stacked glasses stuck? Fill the top glass with cold water and set the bottom glass in warm water. They will separate easily.

Rub out shallow scratches on glasses by polishing them with toothpaste. Tackle slightly deeper blemishes with brass polish or jeweler's polishing powder.

Glasses as cookie cutters. Dust the rims of various-size glasses with flour and use them to cut out circles of pastry dough for cookies, doughnuts, or tarts.

Wipe out streaks and grease on crystal by rinsing with a solution of 80 mL (⅓ cup) vinegar and 160 mL (⅔ cup) water. (The smell disappears as the glass dries.)

Save your special glasses when throwing a big party by laying in a supply of inexpensive all-purpose wineglasses from a restaurant-supply store. You can rent or buy, but buying is best if you entertain a lot—and if you have room to store the glasses.

GLOVES & MITTENS

Place small baskets—wicker, plastic, or metal—near the back door or on a shelf in the coat closet to serve as a handy mitten storage spot.

Nothing beats mittens when it's cold. Mittens create a pocket that captures the natural heat from your fingers and hands, while gloves isolate the fingers, making them more vulnerable to cold.

Wear rubber gloves under your gardening or work gloves when outside on chilly, wet days. They'll keep your hands dry and warm.

Clip children's mittens to their coats with miniature suspenders, available at most notions counters. Or, sew one end of a ribbon or crocheted string to each mitten and thread the string through the coat sleeves. Either tactic keeps mittens easily accessible.

GLUING

A dab of petroleum jelly on the threads of caps and lids will keep tubes or bottles of glue easy to open and close.

DIFFERENT JOBS NEED DIFFERENT GLUES

JOBS AND MATERIALS	GLUE TYPE SAMPLE BRANDS	SETTING AND CURING	APPLICATION, PROPERTIES, AND CLEANUP
Instant bonding of nonporous items: plastics, metal, rubber	SUPER GLUE (cyanoacrylate) Krazy Glue, Hot Stuff, Superglue	Sets in 10–30 sec.; cures in ½ –12 hr.	Apply a drop or two to one surface. Press together for 30 sec. Wear gloves. Strong, water resistant, rigid. Clean up with acetone.
Strongest bonding of most materials: glass, metal, wood, and plastic, indoors and outdoors	EPOXY Devcon 2-Ton Epoxy, Miracle Fast Set Epoxy	Sets in 5 min. to 10 hr.; cures in 3–48 hr.	Mix two ingredients; apply immediately. Use disposable applicator. Wear gloves. Very strong, waterproof, rigid. Clean up while wet with acetone.
General indoor use with wood, ceramics, and paper	POLYVINYL ACETATE Elmer's Glue-All, Dupont White Glue	Sets in 8 hr.; cures in 24 hr.	Apply thin coat to both surfaces. Clamp for at least 4 hr. Water soluble, strong, rigid. Clean up with soap and water.
Outdoor-indoor use with wood (patio furniture, boats, etc.)	RESORCINAL Elmer's Waterproof Glue, Weldwood Resorcinal	Sets and cures in about 10 hr. at 22°C (72°F); faster if warmer.	Mix liquid and powder just before using. Apply to both surfaces. Clamp within 1 hr. for 16 hr. Waterproof, rigid, strong. Clean up while wet with water.
Light mending of glass, china, and some plastics	CELLULOSE Duco Cement, Testor's Model Cement	Sets to 60% strength within 2 hr. Cures to 90% within 2 days.	Apply two coats to each surface for extra strength. Water resistant, some-what flexible. Clean up with acetone.
Wood veneers and plastic laminates to cabinets and counters	CONTACT CEMENT Elmer's Contact Cement, Barge Cement, Seal-All	Sets almost instantly; cures in minutes.	Apply glue to two surfaces and plastic laminates; allow to dry. Bring surfaces together. Press with roller or block.

Soften hardened glues with warm distilled white vinegar. Apply it directly to furniture joints with an eyedropper. Vinegar will also loosen glue stains on fabric.

For easy pouring and squeezing, store glue tubes and bottles upside down. Double a piece of duct tape over the end of each tube, leaving a protuding tab; punch a hole in the tab and hang the tube from a wall hook. Store squeeze bottles upside down on shelves by sticking their spouts in drilled holes.

No glue clamps? Hold freshly glued small pieces in place with elastic bands, paper clips, mouse traps, modeling clay, clothes hangers, or tape. To hold larger pieces together without clamps, use bungee cords padded with rags.

GOALS

Spell it out. Make your goals seem more real—and realizable—by writing them down. Be specific when you evaluate them. Develop sensible timetables, and add incentives by spelling out the benefits that will come from reaching each goal.

Break it down. Even If your goal is a long-term one, focus on a series of smaller goals that will lead up to the major one.

Set a specific time for finishing an unpleasant chore before you start. Then make a game out of it: try to beat the clock or perfect a technique. It will keep you focused on the job.

RIGHT STUFF

TOOLS FOR THE LINKS

The compact, multi-use golf tools shown here may not lower your score, but they'll keep you busy on the course. You can clean out the grooves in your clubs, mark your balls, repair divots on the greens, brush off your woods and irons, and count your strokes per hole—so long as you don't take more than 10.

Gentle reminders. Keep your goals in mind by posting them on a bulletin board, by the bathroom mirror, or on a card you carry in your pocket or purse.

Learn your limits. While it is important to keep reaching for higher goals, you can easily be frustrated if you're not realistic about what you will be able to achieve. Don't take on jobs or objectives that you can't finish.

GOLF

Limber up before teeing off. Your swing places uncommon demands on your spine, back, and legs. So stretch these areas for about 15 minutes on your way to the first tee to help prevent injury.

Envision your swing as a single fluid motion. If you place too much emphasis on any one particular segment, such as the follow-through, the rest of the swing tends to go awry.

Putt in the dark. Line up the shot, then close your eyes when you practice putts. Concentrate on the contact point between the club and ball to develop a keenly sensitive touch.

Golf ball storage. To keep your golf balls from rolling around, use empty egg cartons or the cardboard cores of toilet-paper rolls as homemade holders.

GOSSIP

Trade tidbits. If you can't resist divulging a personal secret to someone, note carefully whether or not your confidante is known to be discrete, and, indeed if she is sharing her secrets with you. You don't want your private business to be fodder for gossips.

 Keep your lips sealed. If you want to listen to gossipmongers, that's your business, but if you confide anything personal to them, it will soon become everyone else's business.

Defend yourself against a gossip-monger who is spreading un-truths about you by making a joke of it. Or, ignore the problem and let the truth speak for itself. If the issue is serious, ask an authority figure to publicly discount the rumors.

MAKING EVERY VISIT COUNT

For grandparents who don't live near their grandchildren, back-and-forth visits are very important in establishing a genuine relationship with the youngsters. The visits will go more smoothly with some advance planning. Here are some ideas that may help.

▶ *Try to arrive on Thursday, with the weekend just ahead, instead of on the more hectic Monday.*

▶ *Research the town you're visiting to find out what activities, sites, and festivals might be fun to share with your grandchildren. Write ahead for tickets to popular events.*

▶ *Plan activities to do on your own so that the grown-ups get a break from you and time alone with their kids.*

▶ *Stay four to five days, not six or seven.*

▶ *Work out special rules for when the grandchildren visit you. You may be more lenient with the kids than their parents are, so ask your children to consider maintaining two sets of standards. They can allow children to stay up later when visiting you, for example, but adhere to their regular bedtimes at home.*

GRADUATION

Plan a party for the day after graduation so that your child's friends can attend. Everyone is busy with their own families on graduation day, but a next-day party gets the crowd back together and helps everyone cool out.

 Money always talks to new graduates, both high school and college, and is, in fact, often the very thing they most need.

Party favors. Order pens, key chains, or some other small gift item to give to your child's friends as graduation mementos. Have your supplier customize the presents with the name of the students' high school or college and the year.

Gift of memories. Gather 12 photos of your favorite graduate and have them made into a calendar to commemorate the special year of his graduation.

Baby bonds. Give a newborn baby a Canada Savings Bond, to mature just in time for college graduation, or give a new graduate a share or two of blue-chip stock.

GRAINS

When cooking grains, substitute chicken or vegetable broth—or even beer or wine—for some or all of the water to achieve a richer flavor. You don't need a highly concentrated liquid to boost the flavor of most grains; for example, the liquid saved from boiling or steaming vegetables is ideal.

Freezer friendly. Plain, cooked grains, if well wrapped, stay fresh almost indefinitely in the freezer, (except for oats which last two to three months), and can be quickly and easily defrosted by placing them in a strainer and dousing them with boiling water.

The word on oats. Old-fashioned oats take about 15 minutes to cook while quick-cooking oats take only about five minutes. Both styles can be used interchangeably in most recipes.

Couscous, a pasta-like grain, can be served as a main or side dish, as a breakfast cereal, or for dessert. It makes a delicious substitute for rice in many dishes, and takes only five minutes to prepare.

Serve all grains in a warmed serving dish since they cool especially quickly after they have been set out on the table.

GRANDPARENTING

Play favorites. Make each grandchild a favorite by spending some special time alone with her once in a while.

A gift to build on. One of the most appreciated gifts for any age is a compact disc player. You can continue to give CD's for it, and your grandchild will always associate you with the pleasure the player gives.

Send your voice to a grandchild by recording a tape of you reading a book, telling a story, or singing a song. It's a special way to keep close to your grandchild.

Encourage communication. If your grandchild goes away to camp or on vacation, make up a bunch of stamped postcards addressed to you. That makes it easy for the child to drop you a line and keep you updated. If the child is too young to write, ask him to draw a picture.

GRASSES

Minimal maintenance. The only care required by most ornamental grasses is an annual butch haircut; cut them back hard in early spring with a pair of hedge clippers to remove shabby old growth. At the same time, to promote vigorous new growth, sprinkle a couple of handfuls of ordinary turf fertilizer around each clump.

A fast-growing screen. Ornamental grasses—taller, huskier relations of the turf grasses in your lawn—are ideal for making an informal screen. Maiden grass (*Miscanthus sinensis*), for example, forms a dense clump of foliage up to 1.8 m (6 ft) tall within a year of planting. (Set young grass plants as far apart as their expected height—maiden grass at 1.8 m [6 ft] intervals, for example.)

Drought dodgers. Ornamental grasses not only are fast-growing but are also remarkably drought-proof. Many types—notably prairie grasses such as big bluestem (*Andropogon gerardii*) and switchgrass (*Panicum virgatum*)—will need almost no watering after a year in your garden.

Canned plants. Bamboos (actually just giant grasses) make fast-growing and exotically beautiful plantings. Many types are aggressive spreaders, though, and will send up shoots all over the garden if left to themselves. To keep a bamboo in check, bury a bottom-less plastic garbage can in the garden, leaving 5 cm (2 in.) of rim above the soil, and plant a clump of roots and shoots in that.

Easy multiplication. To increase your store of ornamental grasses, dig up mature clumps in early spring, cut back the top growth, and wash the soil from the roots. Then, with an ax, chop up the clumps—each piece should have three to five growing points. Replant them immediately into the garden or large pots.

GRAVIES & SAUCES

Perk up bland gravy. To boost the color and flavor of gravy, add 15 mL (1 tbsp) of soy sauce, a pinch of crushed paprika, or 5–10 mL (1–2 tsp) of instant espresso coffee or cocoa powder.

Make no-lump gravy by adding the dry ingredients (flour or cornstarch) to the wet ingredients (meat fat or butter combined with broth or water). Combine the ingredients in a jar and shake until smooth. Or, using a whisk, briskly stir the thickeners into the liquid until the sauce reaches the consistency you desire.

Saucy designs. Fill plastic mustard or ketchup squeeze bottles with just-made sauce and squeeze it out in fancy or whimsical designs to jazz up individual plates or a serving platter.

Cook sauces over low, steady heat. High heat causes them to break down. If this happens, whisk the sauce to cool it down and restore it to its blended state.

Simple sauces. Puree leftover vegetables, stews, or casseroles to create almost-instant sauces.

RIGHT STUFF

LOW-FAT GRAVIES AND SAUCES

If you are trying to reduce fat from your diet, you can still enjoy gravies and sauces, but virtually without the dreaded fat. Instead of ladling off fat or waiting for juices to chill so that you can skim the fat off, use a fat separator. Pour the meat juice into the measured cup; wait a few moments for the fat to rise, then pour the almost-fat-free juice into a pan and continue to make your gravy or sauce as usual.

GREASE

To get the grime off greasy hands when no sink is available, use shaving cream. Keep a can in your car, garage, workshop, or any other place where you might end up with greasy hands but don't have running water.

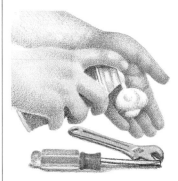

For simple grease spots on work clothes, dissolve salt in water, sponge the solution liberally onto the stain, and then rinse with cool water. (Avoid hot water; it might set the stain.) Add ammonia or vinegar to the solution if the spot persists.

Remove grease from suede by rubbing cornmeal into the spot. Work the meal in gently with a circular motion and give it time to soak up the grease. Then brush off the excess.

Wear rubber gloves whenever you must work with greasy tools. Even professional mechanics have discovered that strong, durable rubber gloves keep their hands clean and still give them flexibility.

GREENHOUSES

Stay cool. Cut the cost of heating a greenhouse up to 50 percent by allowing the inside temperature to drop to 4°C (40°F) at night and heating only to 15°C (60°F) during the day. Such a greenhouse won't serve tropical plants, but it is ideal for overwintering many potted plants, forcing bulbs, raising winter lettuce, and starting seedlings.

Trapping solar heat. Paint ordinary 200 L (45 gal) drums black, fill them with water, and have them do double duty by serving as sturdy legs for the plant tables. During the day, the water in the drums absorbs sunlight (solar energy), then gradually releases it during the night, creating natural warmth. To achieve an even greater warming effect, line up several drums along the sunniest wall of the greenhouse..

Step up plant growth in a window greenhouse unit by setting two or three shallow dishes filled with water on each of the greenhouse shelves. Add a tablespoon of baker's yeast and a pinch of sugar to each dish of water. As the yeast ferments, it will release carbon dioxide gas, which will encourage more vigorous plant growth. Refill the dishes when the contents stop bubbling.

Quarantine new plants. Before adding a plant to your greenhouse, quarantine it for at least a week outdoors or elsewhere in your house. Watch for any sign of insect infestation, and don't let the plant into the greenhouse until you are sure it is pest-free.

Natural pest control. Predatory insects, which prey on plant pests, are desirable visitors to your greenhouse, just as they are to the outside garden. In a greenhouse, though, you can keep them where you want them by covering all outside vents with screens. You can also augment their number by buying them from a mail-order organic-gardening supply house.

USES FOR PETROLEUM JELLY

We usually associate grease with stains, black spots, and messy cleanups. On the other hand, petroleum jelly (or petrolatum), though closely related to grease, is clean—and cleansing—and has many practical uses that you may never have considered.

▶ *Clean leather. Using a soft cloth, simply apply jelly sparingly, then rub it into shoes, handbags, or gloves. Petroleum jelly works especially well on patent leather.*

▶ *Keep soap out of a dog's eyes when administering a bath. Apply a thin layer of jelly around Rover's eyes, then bathe as usual. This also works for babies.*

▶ *Protect metal from corrosion and rust. Put jelly on battery terminals, ax blades, bow saws, or any other metal object that is subject to moisture and rusting.*

▶ *Lubricate locks. Smear jelly on the lock's key and insert the key into the lock.*

▶ *Catch a fish when you're out of bait. Some fishermen claim that a fish will bite a hook with a blob of jelly on the barb.*

▶ *Remove a lipstick or ballpoint pen stain by applying jelly generously and washing it off with detergent.*

GREETING CARDS

Create cards on your computer. Create a personalized message, then jazz it up with graphics available on many software programs, such as textured backgrounds, famous paintings, or vintage photographs. Print it out, fold it up, and send it off.

Use elegant calligraphy to personalize your own greeting cards. Inexpensive, easy-to-use kits that teach you the rudiments of this beautiful handwriting technique are available for under $10.

Send postcards instead of greeting cards, which are getting more expensive all the time. Museums, historic sites, even famous hotels and restaurants produce beautiful postcards that are perfect for quick notes. Postage for postcards is less expensive too.

GRIEF & MOURNING

Don't deny your feelings. The people who cope best with grief are the ones who are best able to get in touch with and openly express their feelings. Don't mask your true emotions under a veneer of stoicism.

Lean on others. Studies show that people with a strong support system are much better able to cope with bereavement than those who try to go it alone. Don't be afraid to ask for help from friends and family.

RIGHT STUFF

Grilling is one of the best things about summer, and topping the barbecue with a grill tray allows you to cook almost anything—small items such as sliced vegetables, or delicate food such as fish—without having to wrap them or worry about dropping them through the barbecue rack.

Get professional help if you feel incapable of coping. Anger, guilt, depression—even chronic physical discomforts—are common responses to the death of a loved one. If any of these problems hinders your ability to function effectively, reach out to a counselor or psychotherapist to help you deal with them.

Don't judge others by the way they express their grief, even if you don't agree with it. Understand that there is no one "correct" way of mourning.

Expect bumps in the road. Grief runs in cycles and has no set timetable. A certain song or place or food can flood you with memories both good and bad. Acknowledge these feelings, embrace them even, but try not to dwell too much on them.

GRILLING & BARBECUING

A pyramid-shaped pile of charcoal in the grill lets air circulate, so that coals heat evenly. Preheat coals about 45 minutes; the fire is ready for cooking when the flames die down and the coals turn gray-white.

No-burn grilling. To grill foods so that they cook through but don't burn, place them on the outer edge of the grill and cook with the lid on. More charcoal will be needed to make the fire last.

Flavor meat, chicken, and fish by adding herbs to the fire or placing them on the grill so that the smoke wafts over the food. Try sage, thyme, or rosemary; citrus rinds work well too.

On the terrace, be sure to place the grill at least 3 m (10 ft) from the entrance to a room, and keep a fire extinguisher handy.

Open or shut? Grilling with the cover on slows the cooking time and is best for roasts, whole chickens, and thicker cuts of meat. Open grilling, or cooking foods directly over the coals without a cover, is recommended for burgers, steaks, or other foods that require quick, intense grilling.

Easy cleaning. Here's a no-fuss way to clean your charcoal grill. After barbecuing, place a sheet of aluminum foil on the hot grill. The next time you barbecue, peel the foil from the grill, crinkle it into a ball, and use it to scrape away any remaining burned food.

Save at least 15 percent on your grocery bill by selecting store-brand foods and supplies rather than commercial brands. Store brands cost less because manufacturers pass along the cost of advertising to consumers.

Scan the scanner. Electronic scanners do make mistakes. Watch as your items go through. Take particular note of items on special to be sure the scanner gives you the advertised savings.

Don't be fooled by supermarket displays featuring sale items. Stores often stock sale products together with related high-profit goods that are not on sale. Just because the soft drinks are a bargain, for example, doesn't mean that the potato chips on the shelf underneath are a good buy.

Stick to food shopping in grocery stores. Batteries, film, and other nonfood items can usually be found cheaper elsewhere.

GROUND COVERS

When you plant determines how quickly your ground cover will spread to fill its area. In cold-winter regions, plant in spring so that the ground cover has a whole growing season to root before its first winter. In regions with hot, dry summers and mild winters, plant in fall; the new ground cover will benefit from winter rains.

Preparing for success. Careful soil preparation before planting helps ensure ground-cover suc-

GROUND COVERS TO SUIT ANY SITE

A ground cover can provide attractive, hardy, and virtually maintenance-free coverage for your landscape, but only if you select the right plant for each situation. Below is a basic list of reliable ground-cover plants.

PLANT	DESCRIPTION	SOIL	EXPOSURE
Aaron's beard (*Hypericum calycinum*)	Small, glossy leaves, evergreen where winters are mild; bright yellow flowers in summer; up to 30 cm (12") high	Tolerates poor and dry soils	Full sun or partial shade
English ivy (*Hedera helix*)	Evergreen vine with glossy lobed leaves, green flowers, and black berries; 16–45 cm (6"–18") high	Rich and humusy	Full sun to full shade
Hosta (*Hosta* spp.)	Broad green, bluish, gold, or white, often multi-colored deciduous leaves; spikes of white or lavender flowers in summer; 30–75 cm (1'–2 ½') high	Humusy, moist	Sun to full shade
Leadwort (*Ceratostigma plumbaginoides*)	Evergreen in mild climates; glossy green leaves, clusters of blue flowers in late summer; 15–30 cm (6"–12") high	Well-drained, humusy	Sun or partial shade
Pachysandra (*Pachysandra terminalis*)	Glossy, evergreen leaves in whorls; white flowers in summer; 15–20 cm (6"–8")	Ordinary, even dry soils	Partial sun to dense shade
Spotted deadnettle (*Lamium maculatum*)	Perennial crinkled dark green leaves striped with silver; pink or purplish flowers in summer; 15 cm (6" high)	Tolerates dry soils	Partial to full shade
Sweet woodruff (*Galium odoratum*)	Perennial with whorls of green leaves; white flowers in summer; 15 cm (6" high)	Moist, acid soil	Partial to full shade
Winter creeper (*Euonymus fortunei*)	Evergreen vine with green or silver-edged, oval leaves; to 90 cm (3') high	Any well-drained soil	Full sun to dense shade

cess. Dig the area to be planted, removing rocks and weeds; add organic matter and fertilizer as called for by a soil test. Water the area and wait a couple of weeks. The moisture will encourage weed seeds to germinate, and these can be hoed out more easily before the ground cover is planted than after.

Restrained ivies. English ivy is a handsome and versatile evergreen ground cover. But in small yards it can be too vigorous, rapidly over-running nearby flowers, shrubs, and paths. To get the benefits of ivy without endless pruning, plant cultivated strains, such as 'Buttercup' and 'Glacier,' which are hardy and shade tolerant but not as aggressive as generic ivy.

For fast coverage, set ground-cover plants one-third closer together than the distance suggested by the nursery. You'll have to buy more plants, but you'll have a full carpet of green—and fewer weeds—sooner.

GUARANTEES & WARRANTIES

Pay for backup. Spend the money for a slightly more expensive product that has a good warranty backed by a reliable manufacturer or dealer. A cheaper product with a limited or bad warranty can leave you empty-handed if something goes wrong.

Compare guarantees. Insist on seeing the warranties before you make your decision about which product to buy. You are legally entitled to see the warranty on any personal or home product that sells for more than $15. Note if the warranty is full or limited, how long it lasts, what parts of the product are covered, and who pays the costs of getting the product to the shop.

Card guard. Buy major home purchases—refrigerators, washers,

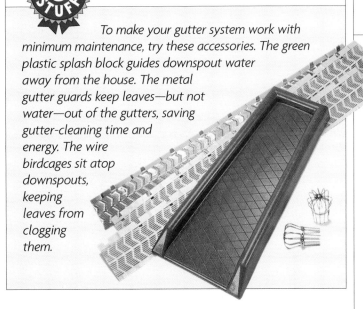

To make your gutter system work with minimum maintenance, try these accessories. The green plastic splash block guides downspout water away from the house. The metal gutter guards keep leaves—but not water—out of the gutters, saving gutter-cleaning time and energy. The wire birdcages sit atop downspouts, keeping leaves from clogging them.

furniture, sound systems, and computers—with a credit card that gives special warranty protection. Several cards, including Visa, Mastercard, and American Express, have programs that double the warranties on products purchased with the card.

 Get it in writing. When a salesperson makes verbal promises about repair or replacement, ask that these guarantees be written on the receipt and signed by the manager. If your request is refused, don't buy.

Gift protection. When you buy a present for someone, put that person's name on the sales contract or the receipt to ensure that the warranty will cover her or him. Some warranties are limited to covering the original purchaser.

Smart filing. Staple a product's sales receipt to the warranty and file them together. Certain warranties aren't honored without the purchase documentation.

GUTTERS & DOWNSPOUTS

To clean out gutters, start at the downspout end and work up. Wear heavy gloves to protect hands from sharp edges. Use a trowel to dig out matted leaves and debris. Then flush the gutter using a garden hose to be sure that the downspout is draining.

Unclog a downspout from the ground up. Start with a stick and a garden hose. If the stoppage won't break up, use a plumber's snake or drain auger.

Dismantle an elbow in the downspout and remove debris with a stick. On soldered systems, which can't be taken apart, use the hose or a plumber's snake.

Check a gutter's slope with water from a garden hose. Wherever water pools, the gutter is sagging. You'll need to hike up or replace hangers in those spots to improve water flow.

Install leaf guards over your gutter system. By keeping debris out of the gutters, leaf guards will prevent most drainage problems.

HABITS

The right time. Habits are often a nervous response to stress. If you decide to quit a bad habit, do so when the pressure is off.

Wean yourself from a habit. If, for example, you want to quit smoking, buy one last pack of cigarettes. Empty the pack and separate the cigarettes into seven small plastic bags for the next seven days and reduce your intake by one or two cigarettes each day. Label each bag with the day of the week, so that on Sunday you'll smoke your last smoke.

Over and over. Good habits can be cultivated only by conscious repetition. Make yourself write a thank-you note immediately after returning from an evening out; it will become second nature. Force yourself to jog or walk the dog every morning as soon as you get up; it will quickly become routine.

Couch-potato school. Can't tear yourself away from the TV set? Turn it into a tool for higher learning. If you have a VCR, check out videocassettes for free from the library on subjects ranging from aerobics to xylophone lessons.

Safety as a habit. Teach your kids home safety habits so they will be able to handle emergencies by rote if they ever need to. Show kids how—don't take safety shortcuts yourself.

HAIR CARE

Don't brush wet hair. To avoid hair breakage, use a wide-tooth comb instead. For the same reason, never tie up wet hair with an elastic band.

A good haircut is the key to a reliable hairstyle. After a good cut, your hair should hold its shape for three or four weeks or more. After a bad cut, your hair quickly becomes hard to manage.

Pool savvy. Prevent chlorine damage by putting conditioner on your hair before you go into the water. Rinse your hair every time you get out of the pool. If your hair turns green from the pool

---

CHOOSING THE RIGHT STYLING TOOLS

The range of hairstyling products on the market today is mind-boggling, but this guide can help you figure out which styling products work best with your hair type. Keep in mind that too much of a good thing can be bad—the liberal use of styling lotions, for instance, can cause a dulling buildup in your hair. Combat that with a clarifying shampoo.

IF HAIR IS	STYLE WITH	A GOOD BRUSH
Fine, limp	Mousse or thickening sprays at the roots for volume. Use gels and creams sparingly, and don't over-condition. Avoid hot rollers and curling irons.	Volume brush with soft, flexible, widely spaced boar bristles.
Curly	A light gel or mousse to help define natural curls. Dry hair by squeezing curls with your hands. Wash with a moisturizing shampoo.	Brush with firm, closely spaced nylon bristles. Straighten with a round boar-bristle brush; the larger the brush diameter, the bigger the curl.
Frizzy	Firm-holding gel, cream, or leave-in conditioner. Use frizz-control products with silicone. If you must blow-dry, use a diffuser—an attachment that controls flyaway ends. Use a deep conditioner once a week.	An all-nylon brush with closely spaced bristles. Untangle hair with fingers.
Coarse, straight	Gels or pomades for hold. Use hot-oil treatment once a week for control and softness.	Nylon vent brush to shape, or a paddle brush for smoothing long, straight hair.
Permed or colored	Light-control gels, lotions, or mousses. Use shampoos specially formulated for processed hair and a deep conditioner—worked into clean, towel-dried hair and left on for at least 15 minutes—once a week.	To prevent frizz, avoid brushing; dry by squeezing curls with your hands. Use a wide-tooth comb or a brush with widely spaced bristles to untangle wet hair.

chemicals, mix the juice of one lemon in a pint of water. Apply to your hair and rinse.

Brushing 100 strokes a day is too much and can damage your hair. Just 10 to 20 gentle strokes is enough for shiny locks. Be sure to clean your brush once a month.

Use hot rollers only on dry hair. Prevent frizziness by putting a dab of setting lotion or gel in your hair before you roll it. Curl hair under on the roller, no matter which way you plan to flip the ends.

To straighten wavy hair, direct the air flow of your blow dryer down the hair shaft. Before doing the ends, add a light coating of gel. Then pull hair taut with a large brush and dry the ends.

Long hair bonus. If you cut off very long hair, you can comb it out and save it to use later as a natually matching hairpiece.

HAIR CLEANING & CONDITIONING

No squeaks. Forget the old wives' tale about washing your hair until it's squeaky clean. Shampooing your hair until it squeaks strips the hair shafts of necessary oils. Instead, apply shampoo to the roots only and work it gently into the rest of the hair. Lather only once, rinse thoroughly, and apply conditioner—unless the conditioner is already in the shampoo.

HOMEMADE HAIR-CARE PRODUCTS

A number of inexpensive and time-tested hair-care aids can be found right in your kitchen pantry. Try these.

▶ *Cornstarch. For a fast, dry shampoo, spread cornstarch into your hair; leave in for 5 minutes, then brush out.*

▶ *Lemon juice. Use as a rinse after shampooing to lighten and brighten blonde hair. Squeeze the juice of one lemon into 250 mL (1 cup) of water, work into hair, then rinse.*

▶ *Vinegar. To make brunette hair shine, mix 15 mL (1 tbsp) of vinegar in 250 mL (1 cup) of water; apply and rinse.*

▶ *Mayonnaise. To condition hair so that it's smooth and shiny, coat hair with mayonnaise, pin it up, and wrap it in plastic wrap. Leave for 30 minutes, then shampoo.*

Dilute your shampoo by half with water—it's highly concentrated. Your hair will get just as clean and you'll save money.

Alternate shampoos to prevent shampoo buildup, which causes hair to look lifeless. Switch between two or more products.

Hard water can make hair dull and flyaway. For soft, shiny hair in hard-water areas, use a clarifying shampoo, designed to strip hair of the minerals that build up from washing in hard water.

Prepare your hair. Several days before you get a permanent, treat your hair with a deep conditioner, available at drugstores. This will lessen the drying effect of the perm process on your hair.

HAIR COLOR

Test first. Before you use any commercial hair dye, try it out. Pull your hair up in back and gather a few strands from the nape area. Apply the dye along these strands according to the package directions to get a sense of how the color affects your hair and to test for allergic or sensitive reactions on your skin to the chemicals in the dye.

One step at a time. If you're uneasy about going all out with a new color, take it slowly. Buy colored mousse or spray and apply it straight from the can. If the color is not for you, it will shampoo right out. Or try color-enhancing shampoo—the more you shampoo with it, the more the new color will show. If you don't like the effect, you can get the color out in about six washes.

Highlights. Painting strips of permanent color onto random strands perks up hair color with less trouble than full coloring. The highlighting shade should be no more than two or three tones lighter than your natural color. Highlights need to be retouched only every three to four months, while full coloring requires attention in three or four weeks.

When covering gray, go a shade lighter than your natural color. Then any new gray growing in will look like highlights.

Double whammy. Getting a permanent and having your hair colored at the same time will damage hair. Allow at least a week after having your hair permed before using color.

HAIR DRYERS

Safety first. Unplug and store your hair dryer after each use. Even with the switch turned off, a plugged-in dryer, especially an older model, can cause severe electrical shock if it comes into contact with water.

For best drying results, hold your blow dryer about 22 cm (9 in.) away from your hair and keep it in motion. Leave your hair slightly damp. Allowing it to finish drying on its own leaves it healthier and more lively looking.

Maintenance. Use an old toothbrush to remove dust, lint, and hair from the air-intake filter at the back of the dryer. Unplug the dryer first. This cleaning can prolong the life of the motor.

HAIR LOSS

Miracle drug? Minoxidil, the topical lotion that stimulates some hair to grow, is now sold over the counter as Rogaine. The most likely beneficiaries are men and women in the early stages of hereditary hair loss. The drug is best at filling in minor bald patches with a fuzz of hair and retarding future hair loss. Using minoxidil is a lifetime commitment; when you stop applying it, the regrown hair falls out.

Consider a hairpiece to cover a bald spot that bothers you. The art of making toupees and hair weaves has advanced and can produce a natural look. Ask your barber for sources.

HAIR DRYERS TO THE RESCUE

Versatility has become a hallmark of the hair dryer. Here are several ways that the appliance can come in handy.

▶ *If your car refuses to start when the weather turns frigid, use a hair dryer to blow hot air on the carburetor.*

▶ *Dry water-clogged ears with a hair dryer. Use a low setting or hold the dryer 15 cm (6 in.) away from your head.*

▶ *Blast sticky adhesive paper with warm air to make it easier to peel off your kitchen shelves.*

▶ *Dry your gloves, mittens, and boots with a hair dryer.*

▶ *Clear a steamed mirror with a swish of warm air.*

▶ *Blow air on delicate objects to dust them.*

▶ *Before you remove an adhesive bandage, warm it with a hair dryer. Pulling it off will be painless.*

Excessive hair shedding may be stress related or caused by an illness (such as hypothyroidism), a vitamin deficiency, or in women, the hormonal changes of pregnancy or menopause. This type of hair loss is usually temporary. Ask your doctor about the best course of treatment.

HAIR REMOVAL

Spot-test a patch of skin before using a depilatory to remove hair. Depilatories can cause an allergic reaction in some people.

Waxing removes hair for up to a month. Because the proper technique is tricky and can cause burns, waxing is best done by an experienced beautician.

Electrolysis, the only permanent hair-removal process, kills individual hair roots with an electric current. Because hair grows in phases, the process takes a series of visits. Find a licensed operator through friends or a trusted salon; a careless operator can cause scarring.

Shape eyebrows painlessly. First numb the area with an ice cube, then use tweezers to pull out hairs in the direction they grow.

HALLOWEEN

Protect your child. Don't buy costumes, masks, or wigs that aren't labeled as flame retardant or flame resistant. Put reflective tape on the fronts and backs of kids' costumes before they go out trick-or-treating.

Fitting costumes. Make sure your child's costume fits loosely enough to allow freedom of movement and—to prevent tripping—be sure that the hemline doesn't fall below the ankle.

Stuffing trick. If a costume requires extra padding, have your youngster put on large pantyhose under the outfit. Fill the pantyhose with rags or pillows.

Alternatives to masks for toddlers, who may not like wearing them, are face painting and handheld masks. For face painting, use hypoallergenic makeup or paints made to be used on skin. You can create a handheld mask by attaching a paper plate to an ice-cream stick. Cut out eyes and paint or glue on decorations.

HAMMERS

To hammer into hardwood, first make pilot holes with a drill. Use a drill bit the same size as the nails. For even easier nailing, lubricate the nails beforehand with beeswax.

Protect your fingers by holding a small nail straight with needle-nose pliers or tweezers before you hammer it in.

Use a hammer in the garden to dig out dandelions and other stubborn weeds. The hammer's claw, designed to remove nails, will neatly take out a weed, roots and all, if you swing it into the ground deep enough.

Fix a loose wooden handle by soaking it in linseed oil for an hour or so. The wood will swell with the oil and fit more tightly into the hammer head.

Glittering Pumpkin Luminaria

This is as easy as pumpkin carving gets. What's more, the look of these glowing, lacy lanterns makes an elegant change from the traditional grinning Halloween jack-o'-lantern.

1 Scrub the pumpkin clean; then cut off the top, preserving the stem, which gives you a handle for the top.

2 Scoop out the seeds and scrape the walls of the pumpkin thoroughly.

3 Use a nonpermanent marker to draw designs on the skin with dots—geometric figures, swirls, or stars.

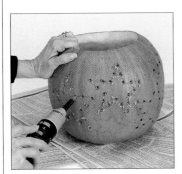

4 With a power screwdriver or drill, make holes at the dots. Place a candle inside the pumpkin; secure with hot wax.

5 Here are the easy-does-it luminaria, a welcoming Halloween window display.

HAMMOCKS

Can't stay balanced? If you're unsteady when the hammock is level, try raising the end where your head rests a few inches.

Keep the pillow in place. If your hammock is made out of rope, attach an adhesive Velcro strip to the underside of your pillow. This stops it from slipping.

Seasonal storage. Don't just pack your hammock away when winter comes—keep it in use. Tie it up in your basement or garage to hold lightweight objects such as the cushions for outdoor furniture.

All-purpose tarpaulin. Collect raked-up leaves in an old hammock. Also use it to hold down loads that are transported on roof racks or in truck beds.

HAMSTERS, GERBILS & GUINEA PIGS

Fitness food. Hang some enticing fresh food—a leaf of lettuce or a sliver of celery—high in the cage. It's good exercise for your pet to stand on its hind legs and stretch for the morsel.

Home sweet home. Keep these furry rodents in roomy, sturdy cages—preferably easy-to-clean ones with hinged roofs and removable bottoms. Or you can use an aquarium. Line cages with an absorbent material such as newspaper or wood shavings and clean them out weekly.

Romper rooms. Hamsters, gerbils, and guinea pigs crave lots of exercise. Make sure that their cages are not only large but also interesting. To this end, build an indoor playground equipped with wheels, ladders, and toys.

Let them chew! Prevent your pet's teeth from becoming overgrown. Let your gerbils chew on hollow cardboard tubes, such as the ones found in paper-towel and toilet-paper rolls. Give hamsters and guinea pigs clean blocks of balsa wood to gnaw on.

Come back here! Here's what to do if your hamster escapes from its cage. In a dark corner, incline a ramp up to a bucket with some food in it. Your pet will be tempted into the bucket—and won't be able to get out again.

Great pets for kids. Because small rodents like hamsters and gerbils are easy to care for, they offer an ideal way for even young children to learn the responsibilities of owning a pet.

EASY DOES IT

A NUTRITIOUS BUFFET FOR YOUR PETS

Feed your hamsters, gerbils, and guinea pigs breed-specific food mixes, and make sure water is always available. For a truly healthful diet, though, all of these animals require fresh fruits, vegetables, and greens at least once a day. So when you're making your own meals, prepare a little extra for your pets. Here are some ideas.

▶ *Raw vegetables. Cucumbers, celery, green beans, peas, potatoes, turnips, and corn.*

▶ *Fresh fruit. Apples, pears, melons, bananas, and grapes. For gerbils and hamsters, chop fruit into large pieces and leave skins and seeds. For guinea pigs, chop smaller pieces.*

▶ *Greens. All your usual salad leaves. In addition, you can gather wild grasses, dandelions, and clover from the lawn.*

HAND CARE

Choose creams. Creams are superior to lotions in moisturizing skin because lotions contain a high amount of water and preservatives; creams do not.

Read the label. A cream is particularly effective if it contains one or more of the following extras among the top three or four ingredients: a silicone additive like dimethicone, which prevents dehydration and smooths the skin; a humectant such as alpha-hydroxy acid, which attracts water to the skin; and an antioxidant.

Never heard of an ingredient? Cosmetic companies regularly change the names of ingredients. Contact the Canadian Cosmetic, Toiletry, and Fragrance Association, which publishes a Cosmetic Dictionary, to find out about the ingredient (CCTFA, 5090 Explorer Drive, Suite 510, Mississauga, Ont. L4W 4T9, 1-905-629-0111).

Cracked, dry winter skin? Avoid harsh, drying soaps and reach for the grease. Slather your skin with petroleum jelly, baby or olive oil, even shortening. Or try the beauty secret that farmers and fishermen—and cows—have enjoyed for years: Bag Balm, a highly concentrated lanolin-petrolatum ointment used to soothe and soften cow udders. Look for it in feed-and-seed stores.

Gloves: the best protection. Hand cream isn't enough in cold weather—only warm gloves can properly protect your hands from the elements outdoors. Indoors, wear rubber gloves for washing dishes or cleaning the bathroom.

Instant manicure. After a bath or shower, prick a vitamin E capsule and apply its syrupy liquid to your cuticles. The gel sets in and gives cuticles a manicured look.

HAND WASHABLES

Get the smell out. Deodorize musty-smelling hand washables by presoaking them in a mixture of 60 mL (4 tbsp) of baking soda and 950 mL (1 qt) of cool water for about one hour.

Use dish-washing liquid for cleaning delicate garments. It's made to be gentle enough for your hands, so it works for fine fabrics too and costs less than specialized detergents and soaps.

Shake 'em up. To loosen dirt from small items such as undergarments, presoak for up to an hour in cool, soapy water. Then place in a large jar with some suds and shake. Rinse thoroughly.

On a roll. Dry hand washables by first rolling them in a towel to soak up excess moisture. Remove the towel and lay heavy knit garments flat to dry on plastic sheets (dry cleaner's bags, slit open, will do). If fabrics can be hung up to dry, use wooden or plastic hangers to prevent rust stains.

Machine rinse your hand washables. Put the items you've just washed, soapy and dripping wet, into your washing machine. Set the washing machine's dial to final rinse. The machine not only will save you the trouble of rinsing, but will rinse your hand washables more thoroughly as well as spin them dry.

HANDBAGS

A weighty problem. Toting an overloaded handbag on one shoulder is a surefire recipe for aches and pains. Never carry around more than 10 percent of your body weight.

Crossover. Wear a shoulder bag with the strap across the chest. This distributes its weight to the mid-pelvis, the body's center of gravity. In this position the bag is easy to reach into, leaves both arms free, and is harder to steal.

Quality pays off in longer wear. Look for a bag with magnetic snaps instead of spring snaps; purse handles attached with rivets, not stitching; sturdy vinyl or leather linings; and an inside zippered compartment.

Thieves look for purses hanging on the bars of baby strollers, sitting loose at your feet in a restaurant, or resting on a store counter. In the restaurant, keep the strap on your knee; in the store, wrap the strap around your hand.

RIGHT STUFF

TURN HEADS WITH THE NEW TOTE HANDBAGS

Leather handbags are coveted for their elegance, but no matter how stylish, they can be costly, heavy, and vulnerable to sudden cloudbursts. As an alternative, opt for the new generation of sleek, versatile tote bags fashioned from a water-resistant microfiber that's light as a feather yet tough as a suitcase. Sporty models have already inundated the market, but the latest versions, like these from Le Sportsac, are sleek enough to take to a black-tie dinner—and cost but a fraction of what you'd pay for leather.

HANGING PLANTS

Double-potting. Because they hang aloft, where the wind can dry their foliage and the sun can warm the soil around the roots, hanging plants need frequent watering in summertime. Reduce their thirst by double-potting: set the plant's container into a larger glazed or plastic pot and pack the space between the two with sphagnum moss. When you water, wet the moss as well; it will help to keep the plant moist and cool.

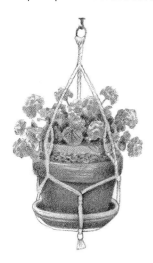

A plain pot is fine. When selecting a container for a hanging plant, don't worry about a decorative appearance. If all goes well, the hanging foliage will soon hide the pot from view.

Soak your plants. The easiest and most effective way to water hanging plants is to keep a large tub of water outdoors. Set the plant—pot and all—into the water and let it soak for half an hour before hanging it up again. The alternative for apartment dwellers: Soak plants in a sink or bathtub.

Frost-free. Because cold air settles to the ground, hanging plants often escape the effects of an early frost. This makes a hanging basket an especially good refuge for frost-sensitive plants such as fuchsias or begonias.

A haven for herbs. If your soil is poorly drained, try cultivating fresh herbs in hanging baskets. Most herbs don't like wet soil.

HANGOVERS

Water trick. Make an effort to quaff a tall glass of water after every alcoholic beverage you drink. A glass of water between cocktails will help slow down and dilute your overall alcohol consumption and also prevent dehydration. And don't forget, before you tuck in for the night, drink a big glass of water.

Head off trouble. After your last drink, take two acetaminophen tablets. Don't take acetaminophen and then drink to excess; the combination in that order can result in liver damage.

Ease your mind. Recent studies have shown that people who experience hangovers after occasional drinking sprees are less likely to become problem drinkers than those who can drink with few aftereffects.

HOW TO TREAT A HANGOVER

It is never pleasant to wake up the morning after a lovely party and discover that your mouth is full of cotton, your stomach is shaky at best, and your head is throbbing. Here are some antidotes—though the best cure may be time.

▶ *Water. Alcohol is a diuretic, so you become dehydrated if you drink too much of it. Drinking lots of water before you fall asleep will replenish the lost fluids in your body.*

▶ *Fresh air. Twenty minutes of deep-breathing oxygen can do wonders. That's why some people find aerobic exercise provides hangover relief.*

▶ *Coffee. Caffeine constricts the arteries dilated by alcohol and may relieve your headache.*

▶ *Vitamin C supplements or a couple of spoonfuls of honey. Either can help your body eliminate the alcohol more quickly.*

HATS

Reshape a felt hat by holding it over a pot of steaming water. Using your fingers, form the brim to the size and shape you prefer.

Try earmuffs. Ears are highly susceptible to cold weather. However, if you don't want to ruin your hairdo by wearing a hat in on cold winter days, use pretty earmuffs instead.

 Store hats upside down in a hatbox or plastic bag. Fill with crumpled tissue paper or newspaper so they will hold their shape.

Don't throw out vintage hats; recycle them in decorative displays. For example, arrange a row of cowboy hats, 1940's fedoras, or Edwardian bonnets along a hallway; line up vintage baseball caps as decoration in a child's room; fill an old straw hat with dried flowers and use it as a centerpiece.

AN ELECTRONIC AIR CLEANER

For pollen relief, many people are helped by electronic air cleaners, which use a process called electronic precipitation to filter out dust, pollen, bacteria, spores, mite pellets, and animal dander. An electronic cleaner with a good HEPA (high-efficiency particulate arresting) rating installed in the return-air duct of a warm-air heating or central air-conditioning system will treat the whole house. Room-size models are are particularly useful for bedrooms.

A raincheck. Protect your hairdo when pulling on sweaters and turtlenecks. Put on a plastic rain hat first, and you'll emerge with hairdo intact and static-free.

Hats off. The rules of etiquette are relaxed these days, but some rules still apply. Modern etiquette suggests that while men should remove hats in indoor settings such as movie theaters, women can leave on their hats if they don't block anyone's view.

HAY FEVER

Keep the windows closed during pollen season. If the weather is warm, use an air conditioner and clean the filter often.

Stay indoors on days when the pollen count is high, particularly in the morning. Pollen clings to you, so if you do go out, shower afterward and put the clothes you wore in a covered hamper.

Use a clothes dryer. Drying your sheets and towels in the sunshine is a nice idea, but if you suffer from hay fever, dry them in a clothes dryer. Pollen collects on items hung to dry outdoors.

Hold down household dust to ease hayfever symptoms. Vacuum instead of sweep with a broom, and use disposable vacuum bags. Dust daily with a damp cloth and clean curtains monthly. Use throw rugs instead of carpeting.

Consult an allergist. Over-the-counter antihistamines will help relieve mild symptoms, but if yours are severe, see an allergist. Prescription antihistamines that don't make you sleepy and cortisone nasal sprays can offer some relief. Finally, consider allergy shots. Taken weekly for one or two years, they can desensitize your system to allergens.

HEADACHES

Keep a food diary if you have headaches regularly. Certain foods or additives can trigger bad headaches, most commonly caffeine, red wine, nitrites, chocolate, aged cheese, monosodium glutamate (MSG), and artificial sweeteners. Try avoiding these foods and note the results.

If caffeine is the problem, cut back gradually on caffeinated beverages, including coffee and carbonated drinks that contain caffeine. Stopping them suddenly can kick off a headache.

Regulate your life. Chronic headaches are often directly related to your lifestyle. Changes in mealtimes and sleep patterns can spawn headaches. Be sure to get enough sleep and regular exercise and eat small meals all day so that you never have an empty stomach. Such precautions may prevent migraines.

Try feverfew capsules if you suffer from migraines. There is some evidence that this herbal medicine reduces the frequency and intensity of migraines when it is taken every day. Anyone who is pregnant should check with her doctor before trying this remedy.

Ice a headache away. At the first sign of a headache, put an ice pack on the area that hurts. Keep reusable gel packs in the freezer just for this purpose.

Massage your temples, the back of your neck, your scalp, and face when you have a tension headache. This relaxes tensed muscles, which will relieve the headache.

Limit the use of pain relievers. Aspirin, ibuprofen, and acetaminophen can relieve headaches, but taking them for too long will actually cause "rebound" headaches. If your headaches persist, consult a doctor.

HEADLIGHTS

In bad weather, pull over and clean the headlights often. Removing accumulated snow, grit, or mud will make a big difference in how well you see the road.

Be prepared. Always carry spare bulbs for your headlights in your car. Be sure to buy ones to fit your car's particular headlights, which differ from one manufacturer and car model to another, and keep them on hand so that you won't be caught short when you need to replace one. You might also keep extra fuses for the electrical system in the car.

Buy brighter bulbs for country driving where there are no streetlights. High-visibility halogen bulbs give you significantly more light than conventional types. You'll see farther and wider in the dark. Just remember to dim the lights as soon as you see another car coming.

HEALTH CLUBS

Find a good fit. Look for a health club that matches your needs. If, for example, you just want a place to lift weights, don't be talked into joining an expensive club that offers saunas and treadmill machines that you'll never use.

Try before you buy. Before you make a long-term commitment,

sign up for a trial or short-term membership. And don't sign a contract before you learn the club's refund policy.

Beware "last-day-only" rates, which may actually be the club's regular rates. Resist high-pressure sales pitches to sign quickly during special promotions.

Visit the health club at the time of day you plan to exercise. Take note of how crowded it is and whether the equipment you want to use is accessible.

HEALTH INSURANCE

Before you buy a policy, verify that the insurer is in good financial standing. To do so, contact the Canadian Life & Health Insurance Association (1-800-268-8099).

Protect yourself from being denied a claim. Follow your health plan's rules, including written pre-approval before a surgical procedure; obtain second opinions, which most insurers cover; maintain a file with all your bills; and

make sure your doctor is on your side should a dispute arise.

 Promptly submit all claims. Most insurers set a time limit, about three months, after which they will not pay, forcing you to foot the bill yourself.

Save time by filling out general information—name, address, telephone numbers, for example—on claim forms ahead of time. Make photocopies of the form, then simply add any new information each time you submit a claim.

A two-policy family. If both you and your spouse have group health insurance plans with different insurance companies, it may be beneficial to keep both plans. Not only are some plans more generous in certain areas of their coverage, such as orthodontistry or extended health care, but you may have complete coverage for illnesses or injuried (after the

HEALTH CLUB ESSENTIALS

The good health club should offer the following amenities.

▶ *Instructors and trainers certified by a reputable agency like the National Fitness Leadership Advisory Committee*

▶ *An orientation session for each new member*

▶ *Staff members monitoring each exercise area*

▶ *Classes, such as aerobics, that are tailored to several levels of individual fitness*

▶ *Updated equipment, with machines kept clean and in excellent shape*

▶ *Neat, ventilated locker rooms that are cleaned and disinfected daily*

▶ *Water fountains or coolers in convenient spots*

▶ *Safety and club rules prominently posted*

deductible has been paid). If a wife's policy covers 80 percent of a medical bill, her husband's policy can pay the other 20 percent.

If you visit the dentist twice a year, make sure that both visits fall within the same calendar year. That way you have satisfied your deductible on your first claim, and you will be fully covered for the second visit.

Going abroad. Some health insurance policies provide health coverage within Canada only. If you are going abroad, find out from your insurer whether you need to purchase additional insurance to cover any medical expenses abroad.

HEALTH TIPS FOR TRAVELERS

Head off trouble by making up a travel first-aid kit; drugstores may not be readily available. Include an antiseptic, antibiotic cream, adhesive bandages, antihistamine pills, cortisone cream for rashes or bites, eyedrops, a headache remedy, an antacid, medicine to control diarrhea, scissors, tweezers, and thermometer.

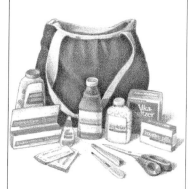

Pamper your feet. Take along your most comfortable walking shoes, and break in new shoes before your trip. If you develop a blister, put a bandage on the blister and moleskin on the problematic part of the shoe.

Beat the sun. You can get sunburned even on city streets. Choose a sunblock with an SPF of 15 or higher and wear a hat, sunglasses with 100 percent UV protection to guard your eyes, and lip balm with sunscreen to prevent dry, cracked lips.

Put emergency medical data in your wallet when you travel. Include your blood type, medications, and the name and phone number of a family member to contact. Carry any prescriptions on your person. Wear a medical ID bracelet if you have asthma, diabetes, or allergies.

Get a physical before you depart, especially if you plan to be away for an extended period of time or are traveling abroad. Visit the dentist, too, to help prevent a dental emergency from ruining your trip.

An extra pair of glasses or contact lenses is a must. You may also want to take along your eyeglasses prescription.

Get your rest. Travelers who don't want to miss a single sight sometimes schedule everything except rest periods. You'll enjoy the trip more if you take rest or exercise breaks during the day and get a good night's sleep.

HEARING AIDS

Insist on a trial period before you buy. Hearing aids are expensive, and you'll want to make sure yours works for you before you invest. Try it out in several settings. Practice changing the battery and working the controls.

Can't afford a hearing aid? Many community organizations like the Kiwanis Club and United Way offer assistance. The Canadian Hearing Society offers a bank of new, used, and revamped hearing aids; for information, call (416) 964-9595. Local hearing-aid dealers can also suggest agencies that offer financial assistance.

Find certified practitioners. Your audiologist should have the letters CCC-A in her title, which means she is certified by the American Speech-Language-Hearing Association. Your hearing-aid dealer should have the letters BC-HIS in his title, certification by the National Board for Certification of Hearing Instrument Sciences.

Carry extra batteries. Many hearing aid models, particularly the new digital aids, use a significant amount of energy, and their batteries need frequent replacement. Hearing-aid dealers often sell batteries in bulk at low prices. Always carry a couple of batteries in your purse or wallet.

 See your doctor if you think you need a hearing aid. Often hearing loss is simply a matter of wax buildup in the ears or another minor medical problem. However, such problems should be treated by a physician, not a hearing-aid dealer. If your doctor suspects a serious hearing problem, he will recommend a qualified audiologist or hearing aid dealer.

HEART RATE

Beginners beware. If you're just starting to exercise, don't shoot for the upper limit of your target heart rate. Instead, take it easy and aim to reach a pulse rate just a bit above the 60 percent range (see box at right).

Don't be fooled. When taking your carotid pulse—the one on either side of your neck just below the chin—be careful not to press too hard. Pressure sensors in the arteries may cause a sudden downturn in your heart rate.

Equipment checkup. Don't rely solely on an exercise machine's monitor to measure your pulse. Test the accuracy of the device by occasionally calculating your heart rate the old-fashioned way.

HEARTBURN & INDIGESTION

The banana cure. Eat a banana at the first sign of gastric distress. The fruit contains natural antacids, which can provide fast relief for people with sensitive stomachs who suffer from heartburn pain.

If you're prone to heartburn, possible food irritants include chocolate, alcohol, citrus fruits, tomatoes, and caffeine. Whatever you eat, don't overdo it. Keep your weight under control.

EASY DOES IT

TARGET HEART RATE AND EXERCISE

Make sure you're getting aerobic benefits from exercise by measuring your target heart rate. When you exercise aerobically, your heart rate should speed up to its target zone, figured as 60 to 85 percent of your maximum heart rate. Use the formula below to determine your range.

▶ *Subtract your age from 220, then multiply by .60 and .85 for the lower and upper limits. (Example for a person 40 years old: 220 - 40 = 180, then 180 x .60 = 108 beats per minute and 180 x .85 = 153 beats per minute.)*

▶ *When you're exercising, the best and easiest way to get an accurate heart rate is to count your pulse before it has a chance to slow down. So as soon as you stop exercising:*

▶ *Count your pulse in your neck or wrist for 6 seconds, then multiply by 10 for the number of beats per minute.*

Chew sugarless gum after eating. This increases the production of saliva, which dilutes stomach acid and reduces heartburn symptoms. It freshens breath too.

Prime position. Don't lie or bend down for one to two hours after a meal. If you eat dinner late, try lying on your left side. In this position the esophagus is above the stomach, so that gravity keeps stomach acid down.

Raise the head of your bed. For people with severe cases, placing phone books or blocks 15 cm (6 in.) or higher under the bed's legs can also provide relief.

If severe heartburn persists, see your doctor. Heartburn pain often mimics more serious heart ailments, even attacks, so make sure a physician rules out dangerous heart problems.

HEAT RELIEF

Ways to cool off. No air conditioning? Visit public places that have it—public libraries, movie theaters, or malls, for instance. At home, take a cool shower to beat the heat.

Dietary measures. Drink plenty of water on hot days, even if you're not thirsty. Also avoid hearty meals, which cause your metabolism to speed up. Instead, eat light dishes such as salads.

Prickly heat or heat rash results when pores become blocked and perspiration cannot be released. Infants and children are prone to heat rash, but adults can be affected, too. To ease itching, try adding 250 to 500 mL (1–2 cups) of thyme tea to bathwater.

Grab an earlobe if your fingers can't take the heat of, say, a lightbulb, a hot pot handle, or a piece of toast. The lobe is an excellent heat conductor—its many blood vessels lie close to the surface—and it draws the heat from your fingers immediately.

HEATERS

Judging a heater. Look for a sturdy, well-balanced heater—one that won't easily be knocked down, say, by a curious child or a rambunctious pet. Some models even shut down automatically when tipped over.

No crowding. Give your space heater plenty of room. Keep curtains, clothes, upholstered furniture, and other potentially flammable objects away from your heater.

Save on heating costs. Lower the thermostat setting on your central heating system and use an electric heater to warm the room where you spend the most time. Area heating is most practical in late spring and early fall, when the weather is just a bit chilly.

Fire safety. When your electric heater is in operation, never leave its cord, which becomes warm with normal use, coiled and don't run it beneath a carpet.

Cord smarts. Don't use an ordinary extension cord—the kind commonly used with lamps, for example—with your electric heater. Look for cords marked heavy-duty—they are designed to handle the heater's high-energy demands without overheating and causing a fire.

HEATING PADS

Check your pad's inside cover before each use. If this protective layer is worn or crumbling, discard the pad. Otherwise it is liable to cause burns or emit shocks.

Do not fold or spindle. Damage to a heating pad most commonly occurs when it is sharply folded. Also, never poke pins or other pointed objects into a pad.

For safety's sake, always position the heating pad atop, not beneath, the portion of your body that needs to be warmed.

Pleasant dreams. Use a heating pad to take the chill off cold sheets in a baby's crib. However, be sure to remove the heating pad before tucking the child in; a hot pad could burn the child while he is sleeping.

HEDGES

Carefree dwarfs. For a compact evergreen hedge that requires no trimming, plant dwarf Chinese holly, dwarf yaupon, or the Pittosporum tobira 'Wheeler's Dwarf'. These naturally compact plants make a dense hedge, 60 cm to 1.5 m (2–5 ft) tall.

A movable hedge. Give flexibility to the design of a terrace or balcony landscape by planting a hedge of compact shrubs in tubs or wooden planting boxes. They can be moved from one area to another to block shifting winds or to shield one part of the landscape from another.

Early training. To create a fast-growing hedge of deciduous shrubs, choose privet, forsythia, or winged euonymous. Cut the saplings back to within 5 cm (2 in.) above the soil at planting time. Branching will begin low on the trunks, which greatly reduces the amount of pruning the hedge needs as it matures.

A hedge with a harvest. For a tall, informal, relatively carefree hedge, plant filbert bushes. The plants provide an annual harvest of tasty nuts, and require only periodic pruning.

RIGHT STUFF

HOT AND COLD PACKS MADE EASY

These simple, inexpensive packs have an incredible variety of everyday uses. Heat the hot pack in a microwave for a few minutes, then use it instead of a heating pad, or to pack in a portable case to keep hot foods warm. Make room in the freezer for the cold pack, and you'll always have a cold compress on hand for pulled muscles or headaches, or to pack in a cooler to keep chilled foods cold.

HEIRLOOM PLANTS

What are they? Heirloom plants are traditional varieties of flowers, fruits, and vegetables that date back at least 50 years. For plant breeders they represent an important gene pool for propagating hearty plant strains. To the average gardener such plants offer a charming link to the past.

How to find them. To obtain heirloom seeds, check garden centers, contact seed exchange societies, or order plant catalogs. You can even search the Internet.

Fragrant roses. Fill your garden with lovely scents by planting heirloom roses, which are more aromatic than modern varieties. In northern climates, grow the compact gallica rosebushes. In warmer areas, plant vintage tea roses; they will flower profusely in both spring and fall.

Bold and beautiful. To treat your family to beans that come in a remarkable palette of colors, plant antique varieties. Try scarlet runners (black and purple) and Jacob's cattle (red and white). Like other heirloom vegetables, the older beans ripen slowly over a long season, but they keep well and are robustly flavored.

Tired of supermarket melons? For superior sweetness, flavor, and freshness, add vintage melons to your garden. Try Jenny Lind or Nutmeg muskmelons or Kleckley

A TABLE TO SHOW OFF HEIRLOOMS

This glass-topped table was designed to hold a special collection. What better way to display— and protect from dust and curious fingers— objects that have special meaning and history for your family? The table at right holds a cherished collection of antique evening bags.

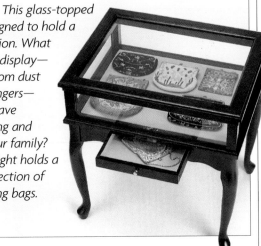

Sweets or Ice Cream watermelons —even their names evoke a bygone time.

HEIRLOOMS

If there's a will, there's a way. Provide in your will for any heirlooms that you own. Jewelry, china, and silver, in particular, grow in monetary as well as sentimental value with each passing generation. Be clear about who you want to inherit each piece.

The right time. Save heirloom toys—china dolls and papier-mâché soldiers, for example— until your children are old enough to appreciate their rarity. If you pass along these items too soon, they may be carelessly damaged and never really enjoyed.

 Teaching tools. Use heirlooms to teach your children about their family history. When youngsters see tangible mementos, they can better understand the past and make connections with relatives whom they never had the opportunity to know.

Show and tell. Display attractive heirlooms in frames or shadow boxes. Behind glass, the fragile tokens from the past are protected from dirt and fingerprints but are still on view for family and friends to admire. A pretty fan, handmade lace, or a collection of cameos or delicate baby clothes takes well to framing.

HERB GARDENS

Hold the fertilizer and water. For the most flavorful herbs, feed plants only with compost and water them as little as possible. This encourages compact growth and intensifies the rich oils that give the herbs their characteristic fragrance and flavor.

An automotive herb dryer. To dry herbs for later use, cut sprigs early in the morning, when the fragrances are strongest. Place the cuttings in large paper bags, using a separate bag for each kind of herb. Fold over the tops of the bags loosely, then put them in a car parked in a sunny spot with the windows closed. The herbs will dry fully within a day or two. They can then be transferred to airtight containers and stored in a cool spot.

A solution for dry sites. Plant culinary herbs, which tend to thrive in hot, dry conditions and in poor soils where nothing else seems to flourish, in exposed, sunny spots. Any of the following are appropriate: sage, oregano, thyme, rosemary, lavender, tarragon, and basil.

Multiplying your herbs. To increase your stock of woody herbs such as lavender, rosemary, and thyme, heap 7.5 to 12.5 cm (3–5 in.) of compost over the bases of the plants in springtime. After several weeks the lowest branches will take root. After this happens, brush away the compost, clip the rooted branches from the parent plants, and plant the clippings immediately.

A winter garden. To preserve herbs for winter use, dig the plants in August and pot them. Place them on a sunny windowsill in fall. For best results, select vigorous but compact plants and use 15 cm (6 in.) clay pots.

HERBAL REMEDIES

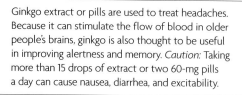

NAME	USE
Aloe	Aloe cream or gel is very effective in healing burns, minor cuts, and skin irritations. Pure aloe works better than "reconstituted aloe" or "aloe extract."
Chamomile	Chamomile tea soothes upset stomachs and aids digestion. It also helps to prevent insomnia.
Echinacea	In capsule form or as an extract, echinacea boosts the immune system to fight off infections, and eases the symptoms of colds and flu.
Garlic	An uncooked clove of garlic a day or an "odorless" garlic pill helps lower blood pressure and cholesterol. Garlic also fights off colds, flu, and bacterial infection.
Ginger	As a capsule, in candied form, or added to tea, ginger prevents motion sickness. It's also recommended for gas, colds, and flu. *Caution:* Taking more than 4 grams of ginger a day can depress the central nervous system.
Ginkgo	Ginkgo extract or pills are used to treat headaches. Because it can stimulate the flow of blood in older people's brains, ginkgo is also thought to be useful in improving alertness and memory. *Caution:* Taking more than 15 drops of extract or two 60-mg pills a day can cause nausea, diarrhea, and excitability.
Ginseng	As an extract or capsule, ginseng is reputed to stimulate the immune system, lessen depression, and reduce stress. Claims that it can increase sexual potency have never been proven. *Caution:* Ginseng may cause diarrhea, insomnia, and skin rashes.
Horseradish	Horseradish root, dried or made into a juice, is used to treat respiratory problems. *Caution:* People with kidney disorders or ulcers should avoid this herb.
Peppermint	Peppermint tea or essential oil is a digestive aid. Putting a little peppermint ointment under the nose can relieve a sore throat and chest congestion.
White willow bark	Tablets of white willow bark contain the active ingredient in aspirin, which reduces fever and inflammation and relieves pain. *Caution:* White willow bark can upset the stomach. Pregnant and nursing women, children, and others who shouldn't take aspirin must also avoid this herb.

Scented mulch. Trim your herb plants frequently to produce lots of tender, flavorful new growth. The sprigs you don't use in the kitchen can be strewn along garden paths as an aromatic mulch.

HERBAL REMEDIES

Consult an herbalist or another reliable source for proper dosages before you try an herbal remedy. Take only the recommended amount, because some herbs can be dangerous in large quantities.

Tell your doctor or pharmacist about any herbs you're taking to prevent possible interaction with prescribed medications.

Do I know you? Buy herbal remedies only from reputable, well-established dealers to get safe products; the growing, gathering, and preparation of herbs are not regulated by any federal agency.

HERBS IN THE KITCHEN

Add fresh herbs to the pot only during the last 30 minutes or so of cooking, since they lose flavor if heated for too long. Do the opposite for uncooked dishes such as salad dressings or marinades: add herbs early to get the most from their flavors.

More flavor. Most dried herbs, if not too old, are more strongly flavored than fresh ones. When substituting dried herbs for fresh in a recipe, use only one-third to one-half of the indicated amounts.

Herbal bouquets. Place fresh herbs in a glass or vase of water and put them in the refrigerator. Cover the leaves loosely with a plastic bag. Change the water regularly, and your fresh herbs will last from a week to 10 days.

Freezing herbs. Wash herbs well, lay them on paper towels, then pat dry. Place the herbs in an airtight plastic bag and freeze. When you are ready to cook with them, don't bother to thaw; simply transfer them from the freezer bag to the simmering pot.

Quick-dried herbs. If you are using an electric oven, place the herbs on a baking sheet and warm them in a 38°C (100°F) oven until dry. If you have a gas stove, preheat it to 93°C (200°F), turn it off, then set the herbs inside until dry.

HICCUPS

A spoonfull of sugar can help the hiccups go away. Quickly swallow 5 mL (1 tsp) of granulated white sugar for quick relief.

Slow down. When you eat too fast, you may be asking for hic-

Homemade Culinary Herb Blends

Ever wonder what to do with an abundance of fresh herbs? Here's an easy solution: create simple herbal blends for cooking or to give away. Below is a classic French blend, but you can create others using herbs at hand. When packaged in an attractive container, they make a welcome gift.

1 Pick fresh herbs, bunch them together with string, then hang them in a cool, dry place until they have dried.

2 Using a mortar and pestle, a blender, or food processor, crush the herb leaves to the consistency you desire.

3 In a clear measuring cup, combine equal parts of the herbs. Shown here are oregano, thyme, and rosemary.

4 Store your blends in attractive airtight containers, available at cookware and home-supply stores.

cups. Excessive eating, drinking, and smoking, as well as rapid temperature changes and too much nervous excitement can also trigger hiccups.

A bartender's cure. Swallow a teaspoonful of bartenders' bitters, followed by the juice of a fresh lemon wedge. Your hiccups should be gone.

Hold it! Take a breath for as long as you comfortably can, then exhale very slowly. Repeat this exercise several times.

HIKING

Children on the trail. Avoid taking young kids on arduous hikes. Children might be good walkers, but their balance is still developing, making downhill and uphill treks intimidating and dangerous.

Blister buffers. If your boots are not yet perfectly broken in, take along some moleskin, cut into patches. At the first sign of irritation, stop and put a patch on the sore spot to prevent blistering.

Don't be caught high and dry. When you go on a hike, especially if the area is arid, carry several medium-size containers of water, not just a single large one. A sole container could be lost or spring a leak, leaving you short on your most essential supply.

HIRING HELP

Personal ads. When searching for household help such as cleaners, babysitters, or clerical workers, first ask neighbors or friends for a referral. Then post eye-catching notices at colleges, libraries, churches, supermarkets, laundries, and other public places. Place an ad in the local newspaper.

Use a temp agency. To find full-time help quickly, call on a temporary employment agency. If the temp turns out to be wonderful, make a permanent offer for the position. Even if the agency charges a fee, it will be worth it.

The letter of the law. If you're in doubt about your legal rights and obligations when hiring household help, contact Revenue Canada and your provincial department of labor.

Put it in writing. Cement your dealings with a letter of agreement or a contract, even if the job is only for part-time cleaning or clerical work. Ask a lawyer to review the document if you have any questions.

 Get references. Ask for referrals from former employers, clients, church leaders, and friends. Check the references carefully.

Employing a contractor? Even if you find a contractor you like, you should seek price estimates from at least two others to be certain that the fee proposed by the first contractor is fair.

Licensed contractors. Make sure that the contractor you hire is properly licensed. To find out which services require certification in your state, contact a local building inspector.

HOME EQUITY LOANS

Insist on a cap. Look for lenders that offer caps that limit the amount the interest rate can rise during the life of the loan. Shop carefully: you may be able to find lifetime caps as low as five points.

High credit lines. Avoid taking out a larger home equity credit line than you need. You'll pay closing costs on the entire amount, even though you may use only a fraction of the money, and the full amount also shows up on your credit report as an outstanding loan. More of your home's value will be at risk too.

The life of the loan. When borrowing against home equity, keep the term of the loan as short as possible. If you agree to a long term, you may end up paying more interest than if you had taken out a short-term, higher-rate, personal loan.

HIRING A CATERER

When hiring a caterer, make your agreement specific and crystal clear so that you are not surprised on the day of your special event. Keep in mind the following:

▶ *Book early. For a special event, reserve catering services as early as possible. For a wedding, you may want to reserve as much as a year in advance. Call several times before the event to confirm the date and services.*

▶ *Know the basic fees. Caterers usually charge on a "price per person" basis. Be sure you understand that you may have to pay for extras, such as wine, and that you will probably be required to pay for no-show guests.*

▶ *Ask questions to clarify the details. Are bartenders and waiters included in the fee? Will the caterer supply tableware, serving dishes, table linens, and flowers? Who is in charge of cleaning up? Will timing be a problem?*

▶ *Get a written contract. In it, outline in detail all of your arrangements. Include costs and the terms of dissolution, in case either of you wants to break the contract.*

Expand the benefits of your computer by making it your communications center—allowing you to do more, appear to have a bigger business, and operate smarter. These software packages can "teach" your computer to answer your telephone, offer callers a touch-tone menu, serve as a speaker phone, automatically send faxes, page your beeper, transfer electronic files, and handle e-mail. They can create an address list that includes e-mail, fax, and phone listings, and have automated broadcast commands that allow you to send information to groups of recipients with a single keystroke. With so much information centrally located, your home office will run far more efficiently.

HOME NURSING

A room with a view. If the patient is confined to bed, provide an interesting vista. Put the bed near a window or make up a bed on the couch so that the patient can feel a part of household activities.

 It takes two. Don't lift an invalid adult by yourself; you may injure your back. Instead, help the patient into a sitting position, then with a helper, grab each other's wrists under the patient's thighs and lock hands behind the person's back.

Use a portable intercom, the kind designed for monitoring babies. With this device, the ailing person can use it to call you when you're out of earshot.

Keep boredom at bay. Provide books on audiotape, a television set complete with remote control and VCR, or a radio/cassette player. Provide the patient with a selection of favorite tapes.

HOME OFFICES

Set it apart. Create an environment conducive to sustained concentration by setting your office apart from the rest of the house. Consider soundproofing your office to block distractions.

Install an extra phone line. Telecommunication services like faxing, e-mail, file transfers, on-line services, and the World Wide Web have become so important to most home offices that a second phone line is almost essential. Keep in mind that being available to your clients is a key to success.

Where to go for advice. Write the Business Development Bank of Canada at 5 Place Ville-Marie, Suite 400, Montreal, Que., H3B 5E7, or call (514) 283-5904. They can provide a wealth of information that can help you set up a thriving, successful home office. The Internet also has many excellent Web sites on home offices.

Write it off. Many home-office expenses are tax-deductible. Ask your accountant to help you make the most of what is allowed. Also call your local Revenue Canada office about publications and workshops on tax obligations and tax returns for entrepreneurs.

Dress the part. Feel more motivated and professional in your home office by dressing as if you were in a regular office. Furnish the office nicely, especially if you receive clients at home.

HOME SECURITY

Don't be an easy mark. Never make it obvious that you're not home. Stop mail and newspaper deliveries before leaving or make sure a friend or neighbor picks them up. In winter, arrange to have snow removed from your porch and walkway. During warm weather, have someone mow the lawn and keep the yard tidy.

The buddy system. Get to know your neighbors and agree to keep an eye out for suspicious activities at one another's homes. Join a block-watch group or organize a neighborhood-watch program.

Use timers to automatically operate lights, radios, and televisions. Set them to run during the day if your house sits empty, while you're out for the evening, or when you're on vacation.

Clear hiding places where burglars could conceal themselves; cut trees and shrubs back from windows. Or make sure the shrubs by your windows are the thorny kind—holly and barberry do well.

Take a survey. Many local police and sheriff's departments offer a free home-security survey to help identify vulnerable areas around your home and provide tips to reduce the chance of a break-in.

Key-chain savvy. Never put your name or address on a key ring. If it is lost or stolen, thieves will know exactly where to go.

HOMEOWNERS INSURANCE

What kind is best? Insure your home and belongings with a replacement-cost policy.

Although the alternative cash-value policy is less expensive, it usually will not completely finance the rebuilding of your house, and will cover objects such as carpets and couches only at garage-sale prices.

Now you know. Be aware that most homeowners insurance policies do not cover in-home businesses. Also, if your home office or workshop causes damage to the rest of the house, your policy may not cover your losses. Remedy any gaps in your coverage by adding a rider or obtaining an additional policy.

Get a better deal. If you install a burglar alarm, check with your home insurance agent to see whether you qualify for a deduction in your premium.

Consolidate all your policies— your homeowner coverage chief among them—with one agent or broker. This can result in discounts and less paperwork .

HOMEWORK

Set the ground rules for homework before the school year begins so that your children know what is expected of them. Most important, be sure to set up a specific at-home study time,

which, experts say, should never be just before bedtime.

Be attentive but not overly involved in your child's studies. Refrain from doing the homework yourself. But be interested, available, and always ready with encouragement.

Seek real-life applications for lessons. Let kids learning math, for example, try to guess the total of a grocery bill. Treat assignments as challenges and don't forget to praise a job well done.

 One of life's lessons. Be sure to stress the importance of homework; it has an impact that reaches far beyond the lesson at hand. It can help children learn to establish schedules and handle responsibility.

Break down big assignments. Ease a child's mind by dividing large, seemingly unwieldy assignments into manageable parts.

Hire a tutor if you sense your child is having trouble. Before you do, confirm your suspicions with the teacher. But don't wait until problems are overwhelming.

YOUR CHILD'S FIRST OFFICE

Help to ensure that your child does her homework effectively by establishing a distinct work area—her very own office—complete with the following amenities.

▶ *Peace and quiet, with as few distractions as possible*

▶ *Ample, direct lighting*

▶ *A sturdy, comfortable chair*

▶ *An uncluttered work surface that is the right height*

▶ *Nearby storage for supplies, including pencils, paper, and dictionary, plus any equipment needed for specific classes*

HOOKS & HANGERS

Convenient and quaint. Line a narrow entryway with strips of simple Shaker-style pegs to serve as a coat closet. Make sure these wooden pegs have rounded edges so that nothing gets snagged.

Training hooks. Put coat hooks in the hall closet level with the doorknob. Children can then hang up their own coats easily.

Use plastic hangers to hang up drip-dry shirts and dresses. Plastic, unlike wire, won't rust, and it's thick enough not to make ridges in the shoulders of the garments.

Traveling hangers. When deflated, blow-up plastic hangers take up very little space in your suitcase. Filled with air, the hangers will shape fine washables as they dry—something hotel hangers generally don't do very well.

No more slipping. If light garments slide off your hangers, wrap some old yarn or scraps of fabric around the upper angled bars.

HOSPITAL BILLS

Keep a daily log. In private clinics and some hospitals, billing mistakes can crop up. Document all your medications, procedures, tests, and services, then compare your log to the bill. (If the bill is not itemized, ask for one that is.) Discuss any discrepancies with the billing office.

Bring your own. If the clinic or hospital allows, bring your cellular phone and avoid unnecessary telephone charges. Long-distance calling charges can be steep.

Delicious. If you are allowed to eat a normal diet and require no special meals, save money—and perhaps your taste buds—by providing your own food. However, make your intentions clear before you are admitted—the hospital may not allow you any savings.

Avoid weekend admissions. In many clinics and hospitals, specialized medical care may be unavailable. If possible, wait until Monday.

HOSPITAL STAYS

A touch of home. If there's room, take photographs of loved ones with you to the hospital. Their familiar faces will be a comfort.

Child hospitalization. If your youngster has to go to the hospital for an overnight stay, try to ease his anxieties beforehand. If your child wants to, visit the facility in advance. Find out if the hospital offers a preadmission program for children in which a staff member takes the child on a guided tour.

Stay involved. Ask questions when you're not sure about a medication, procedure, or diagnostic test. If you don't feel alert enough to do this, have a friend or family member be your advocate.

Do your homework. For complex procedures, choose a hospital whose medical staff frequently performs them. You're less likely to suffer complications if the staff is highly experienced.

Be as active as possible. Try not to lie in bed for long periods of time; it causes your muscles to lose strength. As soon as your doctor gives you the green light, walk around the halls and hospital grounds and do some stretching.

This bed's just right. If you or someone you know has decreased mobility, request a low hospital bed instead of the traditional high one. Getting into and out of bed will be more convenient.

VISITING SOMEONE IN THE HOSPITAL

To make a hospital visit as easy on the patient as possible, follow the guidelines below.

▶ *Call before you go. Sometimes only family members and close friends are allowed to visit hospital patients, particularly if the patient is critically ill. Stay away if you have a cold or virus.*

▶ *Keep it short. You don't want to tire the patient, and you should allow time for other friends of the patient to visit. Coordinate with others the times you will be there so that visits will be staggered.*

▶ *Bring a small gift. Before you go, ask whether the patient is allowed flowers, food, or candy. Bring fun, uncomplicated gifts. Magazines are always welcome.*

DOOR JAM FOR HOTEL SAFETY

Feel secure and get a good night's sleep by attaching this metal door jam over the lock in your hotel room. Even if people on the outside have keys, they won't be able to enter—the jam keeps the bolt in the lock. Easy to install, this device weighs less than a pound and fits neatly into your luggage.

Return to mender, not sender. When you mail get-well cards to hospitalized friends, write their home address as the return address. Even if they've gone home, the card will reach them.

HOT TUBS & SPAS

Tub style. Keep a particular bathing suit to wear only in your hot tub or spa. Otherwise, you may introduce pollutants picked up from other bathing areas.

 A healing soak. If your muscles ache or you are recovering from an injury, seek relief in heated, swirling waters. When you are submerged, the warmth of the water relaxes the tension in your muscles while its buoyancy helps to support much of your body weight.

Cleaning your hot tub. Wipe down the sides with a mild liquid detergent and vacuum the vents of the tub's motor occasionally. Each month, add 250 mL (1 cup) of bleach mixed with 30 mL (⅛ cup) of dishwashing liquid to the water and run the jets for five minutes.

A well-oiled machine. After your hot tub or spa has been idle for a period of time, spray the motor and impeller with pump lubricant, which is available from whirlpool and spa dealers.

HOTELS

Don't always use 800 numbers to reserve hotel rooms. You may save a little on phone calls but miss out on big discounts. Nationwide reservations services aren't always aware of special deals at individual hotels.

The corporate comedown. Get corporate room rates—usually 20 percent less than standard rates—simply by asking. Even people working for small businesses and the self-employed can qualify. If a hotel wants identification, your business card should be enough.

Try discount hotel brokers, who often get better discounts—sometimes as much as 50 percent—than corporations. To locate one, contact the tourist office in the city you're visiting.

Ask for a better rate. An empty hotel room means zero profits. Many inns may be willing to offer you a better deal, if they have a number of vacancies. Just ask.

Make yourself at home. Go ahead and rearrange the items in your hotel room to make yourself more comfortable—or, better yet, ask a porter or maid to help you. Don't hesitate to move the telephone, lamp, or clock; position the television set closer to the bed. Also, if you don't like the pillow or need an extra blanket, call the desk and ask for another.

Who's there? If a stranger knocks on your door and claims to be a hotel employee, do not open the door. Call the front desk to verify the person's name.

Telephone tips. Cut down on inflated telephone charges by connecting to your own long-distance carrier before you make any long-distance calls. For local calls, use the lobby pay phone to avoid extra fees.

A creature of habit. Always leave the key to your room on the nightstand so that you won't have to waste time searching for it in an unfamiliar environment.

Guarantee your room with a credit card number even if you expect to get in early. Plane or road delays could cause you to lose your reservation if you arrive after 6:00 P.M. Ask for—and take note of—your confirmation number as extra insurance that your room is booked.

H

QUICK FIXES TO SELL YOUR HOUSE

Sprucing up your home before you put it on the market pays off in two ways. It adds "curb appeal" to the house for prospective buyers, and it may reduce your taxes. (The cost of repairs done to your home—whether you are selling it or not—can be deducted on your income tax returns.) Here's a list of some proven fix-ups that can help you sell your home and save you money at tax time.

▶ *Paint the front door and its immediate surroundings.*

▶ *Mow the lawn and edge the walkway with new flowers.*

▶ *Trim hedges and replace any lifeless shrubbery.*

▶ *Paint the front entryway a light, neutral color such as cream, off-white, or light beige.*

▶ *Repair any leaking faucets or toilets.*

▶ *Scrub down or repaint the kitchen.*

▶ *Recarpet hallways in neutral low-pile carpeting.*

HOUSE BUYING

Consider rent-to-own. If you want to live in an area for a year or two before making a permanent move, renting with an option to buy can make more sense than outright ownership. Have a real-estate lawyer review any rent-to-own contract before you sign.

 Know the market. Before making an offer on a home, have a real-estate broker prepare a comparative market analysis. This will show you recent sales prices of similar homes in the area. Use these figures to determine if the asking price is fair.

Real-estate auction sales can offer great buys, but they can be extremely risky for buyers. Specifically: you may not be allowed to inspect the property before you bid; you may get stuck with liens and major property defects; you

may have to pay the full price in cash within a week or 10 days; and it may take months or years to complete the transaction.

Home Buyer's Plan. If you are a prospective home buyer, you may withdraw up to $20,000 from your RRSP tax-free for the purchase of a house. You can do this one time only over the life of your RRSP, but you have up to 15 years to pay back the withdrawal without being taxed. For more information, you can order the "Home Buyer's Plan" form from your local tax office.

HOUSE SELLING

Negotiate commissions. If you own a relatively expensive home for your area, ask for a one-point discount off the agent's normal 6 percent sales commission. But if your home is in a tough market, consider offering the agent a 1 percent bonus commission as an extra incentive.

Arrange for prompt payment. Settlement attorneys often hold

on to buyers' cheques until the necessary legal documents have been recorded. Make sure your attorney has discussed with the settlement attorney or agent exactly when you will receive your cheques, and have the dates written into the sales contract.

Invest in a professional sign. If you sell your house yourself, splurge on a large wooden sign—it's more attention-grabbing than the standard metal kind. If you want to cut down on the number of calls from buyers outside your price range, include the asking price on your sign.

Savory scents in your home. Real-estate agents have long advised home sellers to have a loaf of homemade bread baking in the oven so the house smells great when buyers show up. To get a similar homey effect, add vanilla to a pot of boiling water.

Keep good records so that you have documentation for any tax deductions you may claim—which can includes not only repair costs prior to the sale of your old house but also moving costs to your new one.

HOUSE SWAPPING

Why do it? If you swap houses or apartments with vacationers in other states or countries, you'll keep your lodging costs to a minimum and have all the comforts of home. For books on home-exchange clubs, check your library or bookstore. Once you pay a club a membership fee, your name appears on its list of potential swap partners from around the world. Start early—good homes are in demand.

Play up your assets when you compose a house-swap listing. In addition to the special features of your house, include references to local historic sights or amusement parks and readily-available leisure time facilities such as tennis courts, pools, beaches, or parks.

Make it official. Since you need a written agreement, use one of the contracts available from home-swap networks. It should include a guarantee that swappers will pay replacement value for any damaged item.

Protect valuables. Most home swappers are honorable, but don't take chances. Leave jewelry in a bank vault or with friends. Disconnect the computer keyboard and store it. Stash important possessions and papers in a locked closet or cabinet.

Leave a list of emergency numbers. Include the plumber and the electrician. Note your home's quirks: "Jiggle the door key if it sticks," for example, or "The air conditioner works best on low."

Let your neighbors know that visitors will be staying in your home. That way, when the out-of-towners appear, your neighbors will have no cause for concern.

HOUSEGUESTS

Sleep in your own guest room once in a while to see how accommodating it is. Then you'll know, for example, if it's time for a new mattress or a softer pillow.

Now, that's hospitality! Before your guest retires, place a glass of water, a napkin, some fruit, and a chocolate on the bedside table.

Clarify the time. Suggest an arrival and a departure time, as in "Come for dinner on Friday and stay through Sunday brunch." Everyone will be more comfortable knowing what is expected.

Wake-up call. Furnish the guest room with a small alarm clock, which is far easier to operate than an unfamiliar clock radio.

Part of the family. Ask guests to help out with some small chore. It makes them feel included in the routine of family life.

Towel tricks. Offer guests a set of dramatically different colored towels so they don't have to worry about whether they are using the right ones.

Pamper them. Determine beforehand what your guests like to eat and drink and lay in a supply. In the bathroom, fill a welcome basket with toiletry essentials. Include soap, shampoo, and toothpaste.

Don't overschedule. Too many activities can be more work than fun. Always ask whether or not your guests are interested before you plan an activity.

HOUSEGUEST ETIQUETTE

Being a houseguest is not exactly stress-free. Following proper houseguest protocol, however, can greatly ease anxiety—for both guest and host.

DO'S

Bring a gift. It doesn't have to be expensive or elaborate; a bottle of wine, some homemade cookies, or a pair of coffee mugs will do.

Amuse yourself. Don't hang around waiting to be entertained. If your hosts are occupied, read a book, take a walk, offer your services.

Pitch in! If your hosts cook for you, help: chop vegetables, go to the grocery store, make the salad. When the meal is finished, insist on cleaning up.

Make your bed each morning. On the day you are leaving, strip the sheets from the bed unless your hosts ask you not to. Arrange the bedspread neatly on the bed.

Send a thank-you note within a week—it's a way to acknowledge a hospitable stay.

DON'TS

Ask to bring additional guests. If you have been invited for a weekend to someone's home, don't ask to bring your boyfriend, child, or best friend unless your relationship with the hosts is very close. Never bring a pet.

Ask for special treatment or favors, such as car rides hither and yon; your hosts do not run a chauffeur service.

Pick a fight. Sidestep controversies by avoiding issues that you know are sore subjects with your hosts.

Quarrel with your spouse or children. Everyone will be uncomfortable.

Monopolize the telephone or make long-distance calls.

Smoke in the house. Do your smoking in the backyard or on the terrace.

Monopolize the bathroom.

HOUSEHOLD BUDGETS

Set goals. Establish one or two objectives and resolve to put money aside for them every month. Keeping focused on such goals, which might range from next summer's vacation fund to the down payment on a house, provides a strong motivation for sticking to your monthly budget.

 Pay yourself first. Savings are a crucial element of every household budget. Each month, before you pay anything else, put some amount into savings. It's not just for your future security but also for the emergencies that can happen anytime.

Start small. Make your start-up budget a six-month plan so you can see how it works and where it needs changing. A whole year is too long a period to project ahead if you are just setting out to learn where your money goes.

Add a reserve fund. Make sure your budget provides for an emergency fund equal to at least three months' living expenses (more if you are self-employed). You will need it if you are laid off or if you have emergency home repairs or unexpected medical bills.

Give allowances. A successful budget includes a personal allowance for all family members—old and young—to spend any way they want.

HOUSEHOLD INVENTORIES

Keep equipment data in a folder or notebook so that you can always lay your hands on the instructions for all your household appliances. Maybe you can't fix the furnace, but you ought to be able to change the bulb in your microwave oven—if you can find the instructions.

Videotape your belongings for insurance purposes. Walking from room to room with a camcorder, film your valuables as you describe them in a voice-over and estimate their worth. Open closets and drawers and film what's inside. Back up the tape with a file of receipts for large purchases.

What color is the bedroom? The painter is long gone, but the bedroom needs a touch-up. How do you know what paint to get? You look in the household inventory folder, where you have recorded the colors and brands of paint used throughout the house. The folder should also list the

---

AN EASY WAY TO PROTECT YOUR VALUABLES

A fire can be devastating, but picking up the pieces afterward will be easier if you still have the household inventory that lists everything that may have been damaged or destroyed. One way to make sure the list survives a fire is to keep it, as well as many other compact valuables such as passports, wills, deeds, insurance policies, and jewelry, in a sturdy, fireproof container like the one shown here, made by First Alert. This mini-vault comes complete with lock and key and does double duty as a safe. Unlike a bank's safe-deposit box, it lives at home, so its contents are available when you need them—and secure when you don't.

dimensions of screens and specifications on other items that may need replacing someday.

HOUSEHUSBANDS

Role reversal—when the wife is the breadwinner and the husband takes care of household—can open up uncharted areas of responsibility. Who makes breakfast and who maintains the cars are easy decisions; who buys new lampshades or who takes your daughter to ballet class may be complicated. Couples must work out a specific division of labor.

Keep to your bargain. Once you've taken on the job of househusband, follow through right down to the vacuuming and dusting. You may find that you're better at it than your wife is.

Real men wear aprons when in the kitchen. Cooking can be messy work, and aprons are not just for show—they keep clothes clean and also give you some-

place, besides your jeans, to wipe your hands. And don't forget: blacksmiths wear aprons too.

You're not alone. Stop worrying about what others may be thinking if you are a househusband. One out of every five preschool children in North America is being taken care of by his father during the day.

HOUSEKEEPING

A family message center is a vital link in the housekeeping chain of command. Set aside

counter space for a telephone answering machine and baskets for incoming and outgoing mail, a notepad, and a pen. Hang a calendar and a bulletin board nearby and reserve a place on the board for each person's messages.

Delegate, delegate, delegate. Resist the temptation to do everything yourself just to get it done. Get everyone who lives in the house involved in keeping it right—and, within reason, let others do their chores their own way. When a job gets done well, be generous with your compliments.

Tackle big jobs with a team of family members and set time limits. If it is time to clear out the garage, for instance, give everyone a part of the job to do, and schedule a deadline to get it done.

Don't do everything at once. Instead of cleaning the house in one session, dust and vacuum one or two rooms or a floor at a time. Wash sheets and towels one day and clothing another.

HOUSEPAINTING

Before painting your house, remove dirt and mildew from the outside walls with a mixture of 1 L (4 cups) of bleach and 112 g (4 oz) of trisodium phosphate stirred into 7.5 L (1.6 gal) of water.

Fight moisture with latex. For areas that always seem damp, use latex paint or stain. Latex contains no vegetable oils to attract mildew, and it dries with a more porous film than oil-based paint, so it can let moisture escape.

In summer, try to paint in the shade. Paint applied in direct sunlight during hot weather will dry too quickly, and it won't adhere firmly or weather well.

Freeze a brush instead of cleaning it every day. Store it in a plastic bag in the freezer; allow a half hour for it to thaw before reusing.

LIGHT AND YOUR HOUSEPLANTS

Some houseplants need more light than others, and since light varies in different parts of the house, it is critical to find the right spot for each plant. Your camera's built-in light meter can be a big help. Set the film speed to ASA 400 and the shutter speed to 1/125th of a second, then focus on the spot where you plan to set a plant. If the camera calls for a lens opening of *f*4, the spot is good only for plants that can survive in low light; a reading of *f*5.6 indicates a spot suitable for medium-light plants; an *f*8 to *f*11 spot will support plants that need a lot of light. The chart below lists some familiar houseplants—and some not so familiar—according to their light requirements.

LOW-LIGHT PLANTS	MEDIUM-LIGHT PLANTS	HIGH-LIGHT PLANTS
Aglaonema (*Aglaonema* spp.)	Asparagus fern (*Asparagus densiflorus* 'Sprengeri')	Aloe (*Aloe variegata*)
Bamboo palm (*Chamaedorea erumpens*)	Boston fern (*Nephrolepis exaltata* 'Bostoniensis')	Begonias (*Begonia* spp.)
Cast-iron plant (*Aspidistra elatior*)	Dracaena (*Dracaena deremensis*)	Burro's tail (*Sedum morganianum*)
Common philodendron (*Philodendron scandens*)	Dumb cane (*Dieffenbachia* 'Exotica')	Calamondin (*X Citrofortunella mitis*)
Corn plant (*Dracaena fragrans* 'Massangeana')	Dwarf date palm (*Phoenix roebelenii*)	Crassula (*Crassula* spp.)
Emerald ripple (*Peperomia caperata*)	English ivy (*Hedera helix*)	European fan palm (*Chamaerops humilis*)
Kentia palm (*Howea fosterana*)	Ficus (*Ficus* spp.)	Kangaroo vine (*Cissus antarctica*)
Neanthe bella palm (*Chamaedorea elegans*)	Grape ivy (*Cissus rhombifolia*)	Mock orange (*Pittosporum tobira*)
Snake plant (*Sansevieria* spp.)	Hybrid philodendrons (*Philodendron* spp.)	Wandering Jew (*Tradescantia* spp.)
	Japanese aralia (*Fatsia japonica*)	
	Lady palm (*Rhapis excelsa*)	
	Living vase plant (*Aechmea fasciata*)	
	Prayer plant (*Maranta leuconeura*)	
	Schefflera (*Brassaia actinophylla*)	
	White flag (*Spathiphyllum* 'Mauna Loa')	

HOUSEPLANTS

Make more light for your houseplants wherever daylight doesn't measure up by using fluorescent lights as a supplement. Two 1.2 m (4 ft) tubes, one cool white and one warm white, provide an inexpensive and effective substitute for sunlight.

Vacation watering. To keep plants from drying out while you're gone for a week, set the pots on folded bath towels in a tub, then pour in 10 cm (4 in.) of water to soak the towels.

Use an ordinary humidifier to improve the health of your houseplants in wintertime. Humidity in the average home can fall to 20 percent during the heating season; with the exception of cacti and succulents (which thrive in a desertlike atmosphere), houseplants generally prefer a humidity of 40 to 60 percent—which happens to be optimal for human health as well.

Plastic pots or clay? If you have to move your houseplants around, plastic pots offer the advantage of being lightweight. They also come in many sizes and colors and are cheaper than clay pots. The latter, however, are more stable for tall plants and, being porous, are less likely to let plants become waterlogged. And many gardeners prefer their earthy look.

Good air circulation increases the health and vigor of seedlings in a greenhouse, a cold frame, or on a windowsill. Train a small electric fan on a windowsill full of seedlings and let it blow all day long. On cold nights a fan also keeps chilly air from settling around the plants that are nearest the window.

HOUSEWARMING

Celebrate your arrival in a new home by having an informal party before you have fully unpacked. It's a casual way to break the ice with your neighbors. Moving crates and boxes can provide extra seating and serving tables.

Hold the party in shifts if your new digs can't accommodate all your friends and neighbors at the same time. When you invite guests, stagger their arrival and departure times during the course of an afternoon or evening so that you have a steady stream of people coming by and a continuously festive atmosphere.

Send a basket of fruit or flowers ahead of time to a housewarming. Fruit helps the host feed a crowd; flowers will decorate the house.

Go to the garden when you want to find a special housewarming present. A cutting from a plant, a dozen bulbs, or a clump of daylilies makes an excellent, easy-to-plant gift for someone with a new yard to landscape.

HUMIDIFIERS & DEHUMIDIFIERS

Room-temperature water belongs in a humidifier's container. Hot water wrecks the machine, and cold water produces less mist.

For best results, place your humidifier—its spray nozzle aimed toward an open space—as near to the center of a room as possible.

Position ultrasonic humidifiers with care—they form a fine white dust that can damage electronic appliances such as computers, TVs, and VCRs.

A muggy workshop could use a dehumidifier. Tools will stop rusting, lumber won't swell, and glue, paint, and other finishes will dry more quickly. A plus: you'll cool off in the bargain.

Stop emptying drip pans. If your basement has no floor drain to handle a dehumidifier's liquid, drain the machine into a big plastic trash barrel fitted with an automatic sump pump; lead the pump's hose outside the house.

ICE CREAM

Read the label. Frozen desserts with reduced fat often have more sugar added to compensate—and with it, more calories. Check the grams of sugar per serving, keeping in mind that 4 grams of sugar equal a teaspoonful.

Stop the drip from the bottom of your cone by dropping a mini-marshmallow into the cone before the ice cream goes on top.

Baked jimmies. Crush your favorite cookies—gingersnaps or chocolate chip cookies work well. Roll scooped balls of ice cream in the cookie coating, or sprinkle the cookie crumbs over ice cream served in a bowl. This sweet trick works just as well with chocolate chips or candy pieces.

Soft shoulders. Soften a large tub of hard-as-a-rock ice cream by heating it in its container in the microwave oven on LOW for about 30 seconds.

ICE CUBES

Make pretty cubes for drinks by adding rose petals, violets, blueberries, cherries, or lemon slices to the water in ice-cube trays.

Unstick ice trays by occasionally spraying the tray compartment with nonstick cooking spray.

Hate leftover tomato paste? Open a can of paste, spoon it into an ice-cube tray, and freeze. Then pop the cubes out of the tray and store in freezer bags; use as needed.

Make party ice a few days ahead of time. Empty frozen ice-cube trays into paper bags in the freezer—the cubes won't stick together. Refill and repeat the process until the freezer is full.

Extra punch. Freeze lemonade, punch, or iced tea in ice-cube trays. When served in its respective drink, the ice will melt but the drink will not be diluted.

RIGHT STUFF — TWO SCOOPS, PLEASE

Either of these scoops is a must for ice cream addicts. The tapered cutting edge and weighted handle of the Tupperware tool (with white grip) give good leverage for scooping. Oxo's model has a soft, ridged handle for a firm grip and a squared-off edge that digs through any frozen dessert.

ICE SKATING

Be careful where you skate. If a rink is not available, find a flooded field or a shallow pond that is solidly frozen over. Never skate on ice formed over moving water—such as a river or tidal inlet—or on a lake, unless the ice is clear and at least 10 cm (4 in.) thick.

 The right fit. Of all childhood's pains, few are more excruciating than that of feet stuffed into ice skates that are too small. Before sending the kids off for the winter's first day on the ice, be sure their ice skates fit.

Fear of falling. Learn how to take a spill the right way: raise your hands as soon as you start to slip, bend your knees, and sit down. Don't use your hands to break a fall; you may injure your wrists.

Introduce small children to ice skating by putting 5 cm (2 in.) of water into an inflatable or plastic pool and leaving it out overnight to freeze. The kids can get their first try at ice skating on their own small-but-private rink.

Avoid the whirlies. If you're good enough to practice spins on the ice, bend your knees after a spin to help you slow down gracefully and avoid dizziness.

Get better faster by taking ice-skating lessons at the nearest rink with a good school. If you are serious about becoming a figure skater, start an exercise program that includes dance classes.

EASY DOES IT — DEALING WITH YOUR CHILDREN-IN-LAW

Comics love making jokes about mothers-in-law, but parents have to put up with children-in-law too. Here are ideas for keeping a potentially difficult relationship sweet.

▶ *Look for things in your child's spouse (and family) that you can compliment. Keep your criticisms to yourself.*

▶ *Resolve sticky issues in advance: What will your child-in-law call you? Which parent-in-law goes to help when a grandchild is born? Whom might that baby be named for?*

▶ *Never make your child choose between pleasing you and pleasing his spouse. Even if you win, the resentments that develop will make you the eventual loser.*

▶ *Don't try to mediate disagreements between your child and her in-laws. They must work things out themselves.*

IN-LAWS

Plan for holidays. If both sets of parents are equally eager for their married children to spend the holidays with them, the matter should be resolved well in advance. And all concerned must be prepared to take turns from year to year.

Discourage competition. Don't let grandparents vie with one another to gain an advantage with your kids. If each set of parents repeatedly tries to "top" the other in gifts to their grandchildren, for example, put a damper on the problem by calling a temporary halt to all gift-giving.

Joining your in-laws' business may not be a great idea; it can put stress on your marriage. Find others who are in-laws in a family business and ask about problems they've encountered. Try to determine whether your in-laws will treat you the same way at work as they treat blood relatives.

Stay in touch. If a death or divorce makes you custodial parent of your kids, try to maintain contact with your former in-laws. Children deserve the benefit of knowing both sides of their family, even if you are not on the best of terms with their grandparents.

IN-LINE SKATING

Skates that are too big provide poor ankle support and are hard to control. When buying in-line skates, slide your foot forward until your toes touch the front. If there is any space behind your heel, the skates don't fit.

Know the rules of the road. Keep to the right, pass on the left; avoid traffic; let others know your intentions by signaling or speaking; always yield to pedestrians.

Stay focused. Keep your mind on your skating—don't let your attention be diverted with distractions such as giving the dog a run, listening to headphones, or holding hands with your honey.

Double-duty helmets. There's no need to buy a helmet for skating if you already have one for biking. Helmets differ only in style, not in the kind of protection they provide should you fall.

False security. Wrist guards will protect you from abrasions, but they will not prevent a fracture or even lessen the severity of the fracture if you stick out your hands in trying to break a fall. Learn to fall on your side instead.

INCOME TAX

Compare tax returns. Before you sign and mail your tax return, compare it to the previous year's return line by line, and note any differences between the two. If you can't explain a difference, it may be that an error was made in the preparation. Regardless, Revenue Canada will hold you responsible for any mistakes, whether you prepared the return or hired someone else to do it.

Your last resort. If you have tried and failed several times to correct a problem with Revenue Canada, turn to the Problem Resolution Program. PRP officers are trained to come to the rescue of taxpayers who are getting the runaround from the tax bureaucracy. For the number of the nearest PRP office, call 1-800-236-4888.

PROTECTION FOR IN-LINE SKATERS

Even the best in-line skaters get into accidents. Always protect yourself by wearing a helmet and pads on your knees, hands, wrists, and elbows. Check gear for a sticker of approval from the Canadian Standards Association or the Snell Memorial Foundation.

Can I get an extension? An extension on the April 30 deadline to file your federal tax return is only granted in special circumstances, such as a natural disaster. Otherwise, you will face a penalty of 5 percent of the balance owing plus 1 percent for every full month up to 12 months. To see if you are eligible to have these penalties waived, send a letter with your return explaining why you cannot pay. Read Information Circular IC922 or call the general number of your local taxation office.

Keep abreast of changes. Changes to the tax laws from one year to the next may mean that some deductions you take for granted may no longer be tax free. Instead of waiting until tax time, check with your payroll office in January to see that you are being taxed at the proper rate to avoid a nasty surprise come April.

Give yourself RRSP options. Open an RRSP account at a financial institution that offers a variety of investment products, such as a discount broker or mutual fund company, instead of a bank that offers fewer investment opportunities.

Make your contribution early. You realize a substantial increase in the return on your RRSP if you make your deposit at the beginning of the tax year rather than at tax time the following April. Your contribution will accumulate tax-free earnings for up to 15 months longer than it would if you make your deposit at the last minute.

 Avoid tax-free investments. Even though you are allowed to put your RRSP contributions into municipal bonds or other tax-exempt vehicles, it makes no sense to do so. Use the RRSP to shelter investments that would otherwise be taxable.

Learn a lesson. If you always fail to pay into your RRSP regularly, beginning early in the year, and then come up short of your tax-exempt contribution at tax time, consider setting up a monthly payment plan with the institution that manages your RRSP account. The plan will guarantee that you make the maximum contribution every year.

Test for radon. It is estimated that 6 percent of all North American homes have high levels of this colorless, odorless—and dangerous—gas. An inexpensive DIY test kit is sold in hardware stores, or call Occupational Health and Safety at 1-800-263-8466.

Detection. Install detectors for both smoke and carbon monoxide. These can be lifesavers.

Call the gas company immediately if the blue flame in your oven pilot light changes to yellow or orange, which signals an excess of carbon monoxide in the air. Open windows all over the house.

HOW CLEAN IS THE AIR IN YOUR HOUSE?

Indoor air pollution can transform your house from a refuge into a health hazard. Tobacco smoke and leaky gas stoves are obvious hazards; others, such as invisible dust mites and radon (a colorless, odorless, and dangerous gas) are more subtle. This diagram pinpoints sources of potential danger and suggests some preventive measures you can take.

1 Air conditioners. Clean fans, air conditioners, humidifiers, and dehumidifiers regularly.

2 Woodstove and fireplace. Burn hardwood instead of softwood, and no plastics or treated wood. Check all flues and chimneys annually.

3 Ventilators. In the attic, basement, and bathroom, adequate ventilation is the key to keeping dampness, mildew, and dry rot at bay. Opened windows and exhaust fans and vents help.

4 Dust mites. Bed linens, carpets, and rugs harbor tiny mites that can cause allergies. Change linens and vacuum rugs often.

5 Bacteria. Close the toilet lid before flushing; airborne bacteria can spread.

6 Carbon monoxide. Install carbon monoxide detectors (battery-operated ones are best) throughout the house, especially in bedrooms.

7 Sawdust. Do your major cutting or sanding jobs outside; sawdust can cause allergic reactions.

8 Houseplants. Many plants are natural air purifiers.

9 Formaldehyde. Used in carpet backing, upholstery glue, pressed-wood products, and some insulation, it emits noxious fumes, especially in moist conditions.

10 Tobacco. Smoking or inhaling someones else's smoke is unhealthy.

11 Kitchen fumes. Vent the fumes from gas and heating appliances outside.

12 Radon. Test for dangerous levels of this radioactive gas.

13 Chemicals. Normal household chemicals, when mixed, can give off noxious gases (example: chlorine bleach and ammonia cleaner). Read and follow safety labels.

INSECT BITES & STINGS

Keep those bugs from biting. Rub baby oil or imitation vanilla extract on your skin when outdoors in mosquito country. This is a non-toxic way to repel mosquitoes and other biting insects.

To ward off ticks during walks in the woods, wear long-sleeved shirts and long pants; tuck the cuffs into your socks and spray insect repellent on your clothes.

Clean up a picnic quickly to keep wasps and bees away. They are particularly attracted to meat as well as to fruit, soft drinks, and other foods that contain sugar.

Don't impersonate a flower. Since bees are drawn to anything that is brightly colored or has a sweet scent, you should be careful about wearing perfume, aftershave lotion, or bright clothing when bees are around.

Don't use tweezers to remove the stinger if you get stung—they can squeeze more venom into you. Remove the stinger by scraping the skin with a fingernail or a credit card.

Get emergency medical help as fast as possible if a sting causes nausea, itching, hives, a rapid pulse, or difficulty breathing. These symptoms usually indicate a very dangerous allergy to bee or wasp stings; you may need an immediate shot of epinephrine to keep your airways open so you will be able to breathe.

INSULATION

Wrap up the warmth in your water heater and hot water pipes to save energy and money. You can buy and easily install an insulating kit to enclose the heater, as well as tubular insulation designed specifically to cover bare pipes that transport the hot water around the house.

Stop heat seepage. Electrical outlets or receptacles on the outside walls in your house let surprising amounts of heat leak away. Your hardware store probably carries precut foam mats that fit inside the face plate of the receptacles to cut down this heat loss. All you need is a screwdriver to put them in place.

Blue jeans and T-shirts? Cotton insulation, made from polyester fibers mixed with ground-up leftovers from blue-jean and T-shirt factories, does as good a job as standard fiberglass, but it doesn't itch and you don't need protective clothing to install it.

When insulating a floor, use batts that are the same thickness as the depth of the floor joists. They cost a bit more, but there's less chance for compression or gaps, so the insulation will pay for itself over time.

 The vital "R" factor. All commercial insulation is rated by its "R" value—or resistance to heat flow. What you need to know, whether you are dealing with mounds of attic insulation or thin liners on your draperies, is that the higher the R, the better the insulation will perform.

INSURANCE AGENTS & BROKERS

Know who's who. Strictly defined, an agent, though usually employed as an independent, is a representative of a specific insurance company. A broker is your representative, who may buy policies for you from many insurers.

Be choosy. Shop around, ask acquaintances if they have any recommendations, and interview several agents and brokers before you choose one.

Be tough when interviewing. Don't let your questions be shrugged off, try not to fall for hard-sell tactics, and don't feel guilty about taking up the broker's or agent's time. Finally, if you do buy a policy, always make your check out to the insurance company, not the agent.

INSURANCE CLAIMS

Do your homework. Before you file a claim, determine your exact coverage by thoroughly reviewing your policy. Be sure to fill out the claim form according to instructions and include all information, noting why your claim is justified.

Provide proof of damages. Take lots of photographs. Keep receipts and make copies of all bills. Also take into account less tangible items, such as mental suffering and quality-of-life issues.

Be assertive. If your claim is treated unfairly, by all means contest it. In most cases those who dispute a denied claim prove victorious—or at least manage to increase the value of the settlement they receive.

Hire an expert. For a flat fee or a percentage of damages, an independent adjuster can detail your claim and will often get better results—that is, higher payments from the insurance company—than you can get on your own.

INTERIOR DESIGNERS

Have a plan. When hiring a designer, be sure you have settled on exactly what the services will be and what they will cost. Design fees vary widely, and even small jobs should be confirmed in writing before any work begins.

Timing. Agree on a timetable and on a process that stipulates when during that schedule you can still change your mind about details.

Take Polaroid photographs of your furniture and write down its dimensions as well as the dimensions of the rooms you are working on. Carry these, along with your color board, when shopping for other selections.

A color board is an interior designer's tool that makes shopping for fabrics, carpeting, paints, and other elements of your redecorating scheme much easier. As you shop, collect samples of the actual materials you have chosen for the project. Take the samples home and mount them on a sheet of stiff cardboard. This color board helps you coordinate your choices as you are buying them. Keep the board updated with the new selections you make.

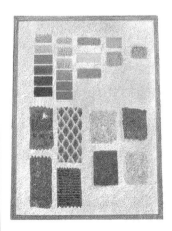

Part-time help. If you are confident of your own tastes and think you need professional advice only

to solve technical problems or to find sources for particular furniture items or carpentry services, try hiring a design consultant, who typically charges by the hour.

INTERNET

Flat fee or by the hour? If you don't spend much time on the Internet, your most economical route to cyberspace may be an on-line service that charges by the hour. But if more than one person in your house surfs the Internet, costs can build up fast; you're better off paying a flat monthly fee.

Net talk. You can talk via the Internet to friends across the country or overseas if your computers are equipped with sound input, microphones, and the proper software. The sound quality is not always dependable, but the savings in long-distance charges can be significant.

Vacation planner. New travel sites on the Internet offer more than travel itineraries and lists of

interesting sights. Now you can find schedules and reservations facilities for hundreds of airlines and booking information on thousands of lodgings worldwide.

Information sorters. The most efficient way to search for information on the Internet is to use a search service such as Yahoo!, Alta Vista, InfoSeek, WebCrawler, or LookSmart. Type in a few key words describing what you are after, and these services will display a list of potential sites, thus leading you to the information.

INTERRUPTIONS

Get a reputation. Let others know that you are a stickler about keeping appointments and making deadlines and that you and your schedule are both upset by unscheduled interruptions.

Send a clear signal. Close your door about halfway when you don't want to be disturbed, and pass the word to your family or coworkers that this means you should be interrupted only if the matter is urgent.

Plan your escape. Have a handy phrase to help you cut short an interruption. Try, for example, "I'm sorry, I can't talk right now because I'm expecting an important phone call" or "I'm facing a deadline; can I get back to you?"

Avoid interrupting yourself by keeping your desk well organized. You can waste as much time fumbling through the piles on a messy desk as you would if someone stopped in to chat.

INTRODUCTIONS

Introductions are easy if you remember S-R-S (Seniority-Rank-Sex). Present younger people to seniors; lower-ranking persons to higher-ranking ones (such as the mayor or your minister), and men to women.

Can't put a name to a familiar face? Assume that the other person has forgotten too, and reintroduce yourself. Then the person will tell you his or her name.

Be informative when you make introductions. You might say, for example, "Susie, this is George, our family lawyer," or "George, I want you to meet Sarah. She and I went to college together." This provides a point of interest and helps the two strangers find a quick and easy topic to discuss.

Practice introductions with your children to get them comfortable with what you expect of them when they meet a stranger.

Make a game plan with your date or spouse before plunging into a crowded party: if you do not introduce him, it's a sign that you've forgotten the name of the person you are speaking to. His mission is to introduce himself, thus forcing the other person to respond in kind.

 To remember a name, make a mental association the first time you meet someone that will help you recall the name later. Tell yourself, for example, that Jane Pettit is short—in French that's *petite*—or that Charles Greene is an avid gardener.

Use prompt cards if you have to make a formal introduction. Writing down exactly what you want to say in advance helps cement the words in your memory—and rescues you should you suddenly freeze in front of a large group.

INVESTING

Invest regularly. Improve the odds of doing well in the stock market with a technique known as dollar-cost averaging. Make regular investments (say, $50 per month in a mutual fund), and you will acquire more shares when prices are low and fewer when they are high.

Go for the DRIP. A dividend reinvestment program (DRIP) lets you buy more shares of a stock you already own without paying a commission. To find the names of firms that offer this program, point your Internet browser at http://aries.phys.yorku.ca/~rothery/stocks.drips.html.

Stock prices tend to rise during the week; in general, it pays to buy stocks late on a Monday or early Tuesday and to sell on a Friday.

When buying a security, drop the confirmation slip into a "Holdings" folder. When you sell, you'll be able to find out what you paid.

JOINING AN INVESTMENT CLUB

If you want to learn about the stock market without risking a lot of money, consider starting an investment club.

▶ *Find a group of friends—10 or 12 people seems to be a good size—who want to learn about investing and are willing to put time into research and a certain amount of money, such as $50 a month, into an investment pool.*

▶ *Invest the pool in stocks that members have researched and chosen. Carefully track each stock's performance and try to apply what you learn from it to your next purchase.*

▶ *For a free packet of information on how to start a club, write the Investors Association of Canada, 26 Soho St., Suite 380, Toronto, Ont., M5T 1Z7, (416) 340-1722.*

INVITATIONS

What to include. Make sure your invitations contain the names of the honorees and the party hosts as well as the date, time, appropriate dress, and place of the event. When the occasion calls for it, include RSVP—the initials for the French phrase that means "please reply"—or, if appropriate, a note stating "no gifts, please".

 OLD SAW **Include the day of the week** next to the date so that people don't automatically assume that your event is on the weekend.

Allow extra time if you want printed invitations. You'll need to tack an extra three weeks or more to your party-planning time for a print job to be completed. Ask a friend to help you proof the draft of the invitation carefully to avoid the expense of a bulk print run of invitations with errors.

Why ask for a reply? A request for a reply to an invitation should be made for parties that require a specific head count—intimate dinners, say, or sit-down buffets.

Ironing a Man's Cotton Shirt

Ironing a tailored cotton shirt is not difficult, but it can be time-consuming. Knowing how to do it right is guaranteed to make your life easier. You can produce a perfect finish if you take a moment to iron the undersides of the collar, cuffs, and plackets as smoothly as the parts that "show."

1 The yolk. Fit the shoulder of the shirt, inside out, over the board. Iron from sleeve to center back; do the same on the opposite side. Repeat with the right side up.

2 The cuffs. Spread a cuff open, with the inside up. Press, using the point of the iron on buttons and seams. Press the placket, inside and out. Flip and iron the right side.

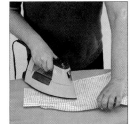

3 The sleeve. Spread the sleeve flat; smooth the material from the underseam upward. Iron, making a crease along the top. Flip the sleeve over and do the other side.

4 The front. Iron the underside of the placket and pocket. Turn the shirt right side up; iron the top side of the placket, then iron the front.

5 The back. Spread the shirt over the board so that the back of the shirt faces up. Fold the center pleat and press it, then iron the entire shirt back.

6 The collar. With the underside up, press wrinkles away from seams with the iron's point. Flip, iron the right side, then fold the collar down.

7 Place the shirt on a hanger, button the top button, and hang it on a rod. Let the shirt dry completely before you either wear it or put it in your closet.

Some invitations include a request that responses be made by a certain date. Use "regrets only" for larger parties where a head count is less important.

How early? For large events, mail invitations four to five weeks in advance. For small parties or dinners, two weeks is plenty of time.

Include a map or written directions to your house in your invitations to out-of-town guests. Describe the house and nearby landmarks. Keep a set of ready-to-go directions in your computer for easy printout when called for.

Postcards as invitations are fun and cost less to mail than invitations in envelopes. Find one that matches the theme of your party. Look for a postage stamp that also relates to your party theme.

IRON

Have a citrus fruit or tomato when you eat iron-rich vegetables. Foods high in vitamin C help your body absorb more iron from vegetable sources.

Pass up coffee and tea with meals. Both contain tannins, which bind with the iron in food and make it much harder to absorb. Give yourself at least an hour between eating meals and drinking coffee or tea.

Try iron-fortified cereals, flour, bread, and baking mixes. A serving of some iron-enriched cereals can provide up to 50 percent of your daily requirement for iron.

Red meat gets bad press, but it is still one of the best sources of dietary iron. A serving or two a week provides most of the iron your body needs. If you don't eat meat, you should consult a nutritionist; your body may not easily absorb enough iron from vegetable sources and vitamin pills.

Cook with a cast-iron pot, especially when you're whipping up tomato-based soups or sauces. The acid will draw out some of the iron from the pot and make it available for your body to absorb.

IRONING

Delicate situation. To iron delicate fabrics such as silk without leaving a mark, cut off the bottom of a brown paper grocery bag, tear open one side, flatten it out, and place it on the garment. Iron directly on the bag two notches hotter than the fabric requires.

Get steamed up. To remove wrinkles without making iron marks on the fabric, set your iron to the steam notch. Then proceed as if ironing normally—except that you hold the iron slightly above the fabric without making contact.

Oversized items. To iron a curtain, a tablecloth, a long dress, or other large, unwieldy cloth, prop the ironing board near your dining room table. Iron normally, allowing the ironed cloth to slide gently and neatly across the table as you proceed.

Starch it. The easiest way to starch linens is to use spray starch. You may want to use a coated iron cover to press, as starch may leave a residue on your iron, and then on other clothes.

The charm of linen. Don't be discouraged if some linen garments are not perfectly smooth after ironing. Part of the charm of some linen garments is their wrinkliness.

New irons. If you've just bought a new iron, be sure to test it first on scraps of different fabrics, since standard settings vary. Find out whether your iron needs a heavy hand or a light touch; how the steamer works; how it behaves with different fabrics.

Easy does it. To avoid twisting the warp of delicate fabrics, press the iron up and down the garment instead of sliding it across. The garment's own seams and hems help to keep the fabric in shape, so a minimum of heat, pressure, and moisture is required to get rid of wrinkles.

ISOMETRICS

Before you start, consult a physician if you plan to try isometric exercises; they tend to elevate blood-pressure levels, thereby posing a threat to people with hypertension, heart disease, and other medical problems.

No equipment required. Isometrics are exercises in which muscles are strengthened through resistance—such as when you press your hands together for a few seconds. You can do these simple workouts just about anywhere—during a train ride, at the office, in front of the TV.

Grab a partner and perform isometric exercises. You'll enjoy the company while providing resistance to each other's movements.

JARS & BOTTLES

Workshop storage. Jars with metal or plastic screw tops make first-class containers for bits and pieces of hardware in the shop or garage. Nail the tops onto the bottom of a shelf or into a wooden or Peg-Board wall panel (the bottles can be vertical or horizontal), then screw the jars back onto their tops.

No bottle brush? A brush is the best tool for cleaning the inside of a narrow-necked bottle, but you can also get good results by shaking coffee grounds with water and a little soap in the bottle. The abrasive grounds scour the glass without scratching it.

Recycle pretty bottles from wine, olive oil, or jams. Turn them into flower vases or window displays or reuse them as gift bottles. Refill with colorful edibles— flavored vinegars, jellybeans, spiced nuts—or decorations such as dried flowers or seashells.

To open jar lids that won't budge, hold the lid end firmly in one hand and slap the jar bottom with the heel of your other hand. This gesture should break the air bubble that is sealing the lid.

JEALOUSY

Talk it out. Jealousy generally stems from personal insecurity and fear of loss. If you find yourself irrationally jealous in a personal relationship, talk it over with your partner. Even if your fears are unfounded, your partner may be unintentionally contributing to your insecurity through a certain pattern of behavior. Getting your feelings out in the open can erase your fears and change your partner's behavior.

Block bad thoughts! Stop jealousy before it becomes an obsession by consciously replacing a negative thought with a positive one. The second a jealous thought pops into your head, conjure up a fond memory or a favorite image to replace it.

Start fresh. Don't let the past influence the present. Just because you felt betrayed in a past relationship doesn't mean you should be suspicious in a new one.

JEANS

Choose your hues. While jeans come in many colors, you can wear any hue you like by dyeing white or natural denims. Choose from dozens of fabric dye colors and follow the package directions. After dyeing, wash the jeans once before you wear them.

All dressed up. Jeans-style pants made of velvet, silk, or silky synthetic blends are perfectly appropriate to wear on dressier occasions. Combine with a satiny blouse, a tuxedo-style jacket, or a cascade of pearls.

Pants to skirt. It's easy to turn jeans into a short or long skirt. First cut the jeans to the desired length, with 5 cm (2 in.) to spare. Take the inseams apart, sew together skirt-style, and hem.

Lint-free living. To clean corduroy jeans that collect lint, use a lint brush. Remove by stroking

THE LATEST IN JAR OPENERS

The standard rubber jar opener (right) is a trusty friend when jar tops won't budge, but now it comes in an array of shapes and sizes. Progressive's ridged, conical opener (far right) fits snugly in your hand—and over small lids. Oxo's easy-grip jar opener (near right) has stainless steel serrated teeth that grab a top and don't let go. All are available in most home-supply or kitchenwares stores.

with the grain of the fabric. If you don't have a lint brush, improvise with masking tape.

Neat stuff. To keep the bottoms of jeans from unraveling after they've been washed, affix a wide strip of iron-on mending material (normally used for patching) to the inside of the bottom hem.

Denim jackets can be worn plain to create a classically casual look, or they can be decorated with sequins, fake jewels, or elaborate embroidery to make a unique and amusing garment.

JELLIES & JAMS

Beginners should start out preserving jams before they tackle jellies. Jams are basically just purees of fruit, while jellies involve a more complicated two-step cooking process.

For a more healthful jelly, look for recipes that do not require pectin. Pectin requires added sugar to make the fruit juices jell, so jellies with pectin are always higher in calories. Instead, make jellies using fruits with naturally high-pectin levels, such as apples, plums, or cranberries.

Substitute honey for sugar in jelly and jam recipes. Use it to replace up to half the sugar called for in a recipe. Depending on the kind used, honey can result in a more flavorful, complex taste.

Artificial sweeteners can be used to make jams and jellies, although the flavor and texture of the jam will change. Follow the directions very carefully when using a sugar substitute.

Check for mold on jars of home-made jams and jellies. Although mold was once considered harmless, experts now advise that jars containing mold be discarded.

Foam-free. When making jams or jellies, add 5 mL (1 tsp) of butter to the pot in which the fruit is cooking. The added butter helps prevent a rather unsightly foam from forming.

JET LAG

Start adjusting days before the departure by getting up a half hour to an hour earlier or going to bed later, depending on the time zone you are traveling to.

HOW TO FIGHT JET LAG

You ask a lot of your body clock when you zip through time zones at jet speeds. These suggestions will help ease you through the transition.

▶ *Drink plenty of fluids on the plane; dehydration can intensify the problems of jet lag. Avoid caffeine and alcohol; both are diuretics that further dehydrate the body.*

▶ *Exercise counters the fatigue brought on by jet lag. Take a long walk outdoors to refresh you when you arrive.*

▶ *Sunshine particularly affects the body's daily rhythm. Travelers who have flown east should bask a bit in the morning sun to help their bodies adjust to the new time schedule; those recovering from a westbound flight will find that afternoon outings help their bodies adjust.*

▶ *Set your watch to the time at your destination when you board the plane; start adapting as soon as you land. A morning nap may only throw your body clock further off.*

Readjustment time. Allow one day of recuperation for each hour of time change. For example, if you are traveling to a city that is five hours different from your home town, you will need five days to feel fully adjusted to the new time zone.

Eat light the day before, the day of, and the day after a long flight. Digestive problems are common at the beginning of a trip, and a light diet is easier on the system.

 Late-day arrivals ease jet lag on longer trips. Flights that arrive in late afternoon or early evening allow you time for a light dinner and a good night's sleep.

Postpone big decisions until at least a day after landing; you won't be at your sharpest until your body has had time to adjust. This is especially important if you are traveling for business.

J

EASY DOES IT — SHOPPING FOR A DIAMOND

Diamonds are beautiful, durable, rare, valuable—and hardly inexpensive. These properties are used to evaluate a stone; keep them in mind when you shop for a diamond.

▶ *Weight. The carat is the unit of weight for diamonds. There are 142 carats per 28 g (1 oz), and 100 points to a carat. So a 45-point diamond weighs about half a carat.*

▶ *Color. Most diamonds are a shade of white, but they also come in canary, red, green, and blue. To see the true color of a diamond, place it on a white surface.*

▶ *Clarity. A diamond's clarity is determined by the lack of "inclusions," or external surface irregularities, and is ranked on a scale from "imperfect" to "flawless."*

▶ *Cut. Diamonds are cut in facets, or flat planes, to show off a stone's sparkle. The light reflected by these facets is called the brilliance of a diamond. The cut of a diamond also refers to its shape, such as round, pear, or emerald.*

JEWELRY

Go fishing. Make your own jewelry box by heading for the sporting-goods store. A fishing tackle box makes a colorful, whimsical container. Give it a soft touch by lining the inside compartments with colored felt and decorating the outside with gold paint.

What's it worth? Have important pieces of jewelry appraised by a trustworthy jeweler. Take photos of each item next to a ruler to show scale. Store photos with matching appraisal certificates in a secure place that is separate from the jewelry itself.

Pearly white. Natural and cultured pearls scratch easily and require special care. Protect pearls from household chemicals, cosmetics, and hair sprays, which cause scars in the delicate surface, by storing them in a soft chamois sack in your jewelry box.

Shop right. Before you buy an expensive piece of jewelry, make sure that the retailers where you are shopping are reputable. Compare services such as cleaning and repairs, as well as guarantees and return policies.

Insure it. Protect the value of expensive jewelry by insuring it. Most home insurance policies offer coverage for jewelry, but you should ask your insurance agent about additional coverage if your jewelry is rare or worth an extraordinary amount.

No green skin. If your old costume jewelry is leaving green marks on your skin, clean the jewelry thoroughly. Then apply a coat of clear nail polish to the part of the jewelry that touches your skin.

Save aspirin tins. They make great individual storage bins for those dainty chains or bracelets that tend to become tangled when stored together in one place.

JEWELRY CLEANING

Nonprecious metals. To shine costume jewelry made of brass, pewter, copper, chrome, or stainless steel, use a liquid brass cleaner. Apply with a soft cloth, let dry, then polish with the cloth. Rinse under cool water to remove residue; dry immediately.

Tender turquoise. This blue stone is particularly susceptible to damage from oils such as skin creams or suntan lotion, which can turn it a dirty green. Shine turquoise with a chamois cloth and finish with a dry toothbrush.

Make gold sparkle by mixing 250 mL (1 cup) of warm water with 125 mL (½ cup) ammonia and soaking your jewelry in it for 10 minutes. Scrub it with a soft toothbrush, then rinse and dry.

Toothbrush tool. An essential item for cleaning jewelry at home is an old toothbrush. Use it with the appropriate cleaning solutions to scrub gently along the inside of rings and under mounted stones or along the crevices on pins or around the holes of pendants.

Silver two-step. To clean your silver jewelry, first wash it in a mild detergent to remove dirt, grease, and oils, then remove the coat of tarnish with tarnish remover. Or save time by using a silver-cleaning foam (for gold, too) that performs both functions at once.

Clean costume jewelry by laying it on a paper towel and covering it with a thin layer of baking powder. Gently brush off the powder with a soft toothbrush.

Travel ease. To keep jewelry sparkling during trips without fuss, buy a polishing cloth at any jeweler for about $5. Its built-in cleaners buff up jewels in a jiffy. To pack the cloth for your trip, enclose it in a small plastic bag and store it with your jewelry.

JEWELRY MAKING

Instant heirlooms. Make jewelry using family trinkets: a baby ring, grandmother's earrings, foreign coins from your travels, charms from a child's bracelet, or an antique locket. Have a jeweler attach the trinkets onto a simple gold chain to wear as a necklace or bracelet.

 Stringing beads into jewelry is a wonderful, creative hobby for kids—but not for the very young. Make sure toddlers are safely out of the way so that beads don't end up in a little one's mouth, nose, or ear.

Bead savvy. Select a threading material sturdy enough to hold the beads you choose and thin enough to pass through the bores (holes) in the beads on a threaded needle. No string for beading? Use waxed dental floss, nylon fishing line, or yarn coated with beeswax.

Make a pinecone brooch. Gently flatten a miniature pinecone on one side. Spray it lightly with green or gold glitter paint. Glue the flattened side to a brooch pin, found in crafts or jewelry stores.

JEWELRY REPAIR

To repair chips on gold- or silver-plated costume jewelry, buy a fine-pointed paintbrush and a can of gold or silver spray paint. Spray a small puddle onto a piece of cardboard, dip in the brush, and touch up your jewelry.

Tangled mess. To untangle knotted chains, lay your necklace on a piece of wax paper. Put a drop or two of baby oil or salad oil directly on the knot. Use a pair of needles to gently untangle the knot, then blot the oil with tissue.

Watch it! If the crystal face of your wristwatch becomes scratched or breaks, have it replaced immediately. Even a hairline crack can let dust or moisture into the finely tuned watch mechanism, threatening its accuracy.

A broken post on your pierced earring can be fixed in a jiffy. With a nail file, smooth off excess glue on the earring back, then apply super-strength glue, and mount a new post.

JIGSAW PUZZLES

Prevent puzzler's pain. Avoid hunching over your puzzle for too long at a time. Every 15 minutes or so, stand up, walk around, and gaze at a distant point to give your eyes a chance to refocus.

Work puzzles on plain tabletops, not multicolored or patterned ones, so that you can see the pieces more clearly. Tape solid-colored wrapping paper, butcher paper, or a piece of cardboard over the tabletop to give it a neutral finish.

Preserve your finished puzzle with a fixative spray, available in crafts stores. Depending on its size and shape, a puzzle can be used as a wall hanging, or glued to a serving tray or tabletop.

Quiet little table in the corner. A jigsaw puzzle can take days to complete, so don't start it on a surface that sees constant, daily, use, such as the kitchen table. Set up a card table that can be moved aside when you are not working on the puzzle.

RIGHT STUFF — JEWELRY REPAIR TOOLS

Instead of allowing your jewelry box to fill up with neglected necklaces with tiny broken clasps and much-loved earrings with bent posts, invest a few dollars in these incredibly useful jewelers' tools and fix your costume jewelry yourself. The cutters will help you clip worn out wires and the pliers (that come in various shapes) will help you grip and tighten without leaving a mark on your treasures.

JOB APPLICATIONS

Just the facts, ma'am. Be objective in describing your work experience. Employers can judge for themselves whether or not your previous responsibilities were considered "important" or "big." State the facts instead of supplying subjective descriptions or exaggerations.

Tell the truth. A job application may remain on file permanently. Embellishing your achievements or qualifications may cost you your job or even your career.

Sleep on it. Ask if you can fill in the job application form at home. If so, take as much time as you need to be sure the information is accurate and the spelling correct.

JOB HUNTING

Network, network. Experts suggest that less than a quarter of all job openings are advertised in the classified sections of newspapers. Most jobs are found through networking. Let friends, family, religious leaders, and neighbors know you're looking for work. Stay in touch with former coworkers and mentors. Scan industry journals for new sources or growing firms.

Temp your way to a job. Temporary employment agency referrals often lead to full-time jobs. Temping is also a great way to expose yourself to a variety of work environments and to aquaint yourself with life in the workforce.

The business of job hunting. Make your search for employment a full-time job. Toward your ultimate goal of landing a job, set short-term goals to drive your search forward. For example, plan to spend a precise number of hours each day researching prospects; making a minimum number of networking calls; or taking a refresher course.

JOB INTERVIEWS

Give examples. Don't just provide a laundry list of accomplishments to prospective employers —give examples of how you were able to achieve them.

Bring solutions. Employers hire people who meet their organizational needs and goals. Ask how

---

UNDERSTANDING JOB-HUNT JARGON

One key to job-hunting success is being able to interpret what a potential employer is communicating to you. It's also knowing how to follow up on a job lead without being a pest and learning to decipher a prospective employer's responses to your inquiries. The chart below was adapted from Ilise Benun's *The Art of Self-Promotion*.

WHAT THEY SAY	WHAT YOU HEAR	WHAT THEY MEAN	WHAT TO DO
"I have an opening coming up and expect to be hiring soon. Could you send me your résumé?"	They're interested in hiring me.	They're gathering a list of candidates.	Send your résumé and follow up a week later.
"I know your résumé arrived, but I haven't had time to review it yet."	They're not interested in me.	Other issues have occupied their attention; the job for the moment is a low priority.	Ask when would be a good time to call back.
"I've reviewed your résumé and it looks good, but we haven't yet decided what direction we're going to take. We'll be in touch."	I'm out of the running for this job.	They're still in the decision-making process.	Ask when they expect to make a decision.
"The position is on indefinite hold. We'll call you if we decide to reactivate the hiring process."	Someone else got the job.	The company is not hiring at this time because of financial cuts or restrictions, or the job is under review.	Check in every three months or so.
Nothing. No letters, faxes, or call-backs.	Someone else has the job.	They're very busy, or perhaps they did hire someone else.	Be optimistic. Check in every few weeks.

your prospective position contributes to the department. Emphasize how you can help achieve company goals rather than how the job will help you.

Accentuate the positive. Don't talk about difficulties in a previous job, which may create a negative impression. If you are asked why you left a job, describe your thirst for new challenges and environments, not your anger at your old boss.

Body talk. Be attuned to signals your body is sending out. Don't fidget or glance at your watch. Maintain eye contact. Don't glance at paper on your interviewer's desk. Let the interviewer finish a question before you answer, then answer clearly.

Follow up the next day with a personal note thanking the interviewer for meeting with you. Briefly restate your interest in the position and ways you can be an asset to the company.

 Do your homework. Make a good impression by researching your potential employer's business. Check the Chamber of Commerce, press clippings, business registers, and databases. Study the annual report. The more you know, the more prepared and relaxed you'll be.

JOB LOSS

Don't be blindsided. Anticipate potential job loss by being sensitive to clues and signals in the workplace. For example, a drop in company profits or major shakeups in procedures often foretell layoffs.

For a rainy day. While you are employed, build a contingency fund to help cover your expenses

GET THE FACTS

If you lose your job, you'll need to get answers to the following important questions from your employer.

▶ *Will I get severance pay?*

▶ *How much will I receive, and for how long?*

▶ *How long will my health and life insurance policies be covered, and what are the rules and costs for continuing them on my own?*

▶ *What will happen to any money I have set aside in pension plans, stock options, and profit sharing?*

▶ *Will I get credit for unused vacation time or sick days?*

▶ *Will the company pay for an outplacement service to help me look for a new job?*

for three to six months in case you do lose your job.

Don't burn bridges by acting out your anger if you are laid off. Be polite—it may help you get hired back or snag a positive recommendation for a job elsewhere.

Reach out for support. Let family members and friends help you if job worries become too much to handle alone. Their support can alleviate stress and give you the energy to resume the search.

JOBS FOR TEENS

Learn before you earn. Don't let the allure of a part-time paycheck lure you away from your first priority: school. If you put earning before learning, you risk short-circuiting your long-term college and career prospects. Work reasonable hours so that you can keep up with your schoolwork.

Look to the future. Look for jobs—even lowly ones—in businesses related to your interests and potentially to your life's work. If you are interested in publishing, get a job as a clerk in a book shop; if you think you want to be a doctor, ask to help out at your local

hospital. These connections can pay off in college recommendations and future job referrals.

Look for internships or apprentice programs, which can provide excellent learning opportunities. Even if the internship does not pay well, it may lead to a solid job after graduation. Ask your guidance counselor or your local Allied Trades Council for suggestions; or check the Internet.

JUGGLING

Learn in slow motion. Start by juggling scarves—made out of nylon or some other lightweight material—instead of balls. Scarves travel much more slowly through the air and are easier to catch.

Cardinal rule 1: Never look at your hands; look at the top of the arch that the objects make in the air as you pitch them up. Also, don't think too much; just try to get a feel for the body's rhythm as you pitch and catch.

Cardinal rule 2: Practice is the essential, unavoidable—and tedious—key to good juggling. One guide, for example, suggests that you practice throwing a ball from one hand up to eye level and catching it with the other hand (without looking at your hands) a minimum of 200 times before moving on to another juggling step.

The right backdrop. If you have trouble seeing the objects you are juggling, face a plain wall or curtain and stand a few yards away from it.

Huggy juggle. Have fun juggling with a friend. Facing the same way and standing side by side, put your inside arms around each other and use only your outside arms to juggle.

JUICES & JUICING

Vegetable juice is a winner as a filling thirst quencher or snack. Juices from carrots, tomatoes, celery, and beets provide a wallop of vitamins, minerals, and potassium without a lot of calories.

Spice up a veggie cocktail by mixing in fruit juices. Carrot juice marries well with pineapple or orange juice, and tomato juice is enhanced by a hint of orange juice. Keep in mind, though, that fruits are more caloric than vegetables, so go light on the fruit juices if you are watching calories or if you are diabetic.

Cut calories in fruit juice by mixing it with sparkling water or seltzer. Citrus juices work particularly well in this combination. Add more sparkle with a sprig of mint or a lemon or lime twist.

Don't pitch the pulp. For heartier, healthier fruit juices, return some of the pulp to the liquid after processing. Pulp not only results a heartier drink, but it provides natural fiber. Fruit pulp also adds extra flavor and fiber to muffins, cakes, roasts, stews, and meat loaf.

Keep a juicer in top shape by cleaning it often, paying particular attention to its blades and internal crevices. Pulp residue not only impedes the blade's cutting action and strains the motor, if left in the machine, fruit pulp will also decay, ultimately imparting an off taste to your next batches of juice.

A tool with teeth. The perfect tool for cleaning any kind of juicer is a toothbrush. Its small head and thin bristles will quickly and easily clean fibrous strands from hard-to-reach areas.

EASY DOES IT

CHOOSING A JUICER

Electric juicers are a great addition to the kitchen, as they are both easier and faster to use than hand juicers. But not all juicers are equal. Here are some questions to ask yourself as you shop for a serious juicer.

▸ *Is it simple to use? A complicated appliance gets used less and less with time. Insist on a full demonstration, and if the juicer doesn't look easy to use, don't buy it.*

▸ *Do I have room for it? A juicer that is too bulky to leave on a counter or too heavy to take out and put away without a hassle won't be used.*

▸ *Can I keep it clean? All juicers demand a fair amount of cleanup time in order to perform well and serve up fresh flavor. But the less, the better: look for a simple juicer with few parts that are easily and quickly disassembled, cleaned, and reassembled.*

▸ *Is it quiet? Juicers tend to be noisy, but some are quieter than others, a point to consider if you plan to make juice first thing every morning.*

▸ *Do I have to cut everything into little chunks first? In other words, how much work will the juicer do for me?*

RIGHT STUFF

WORK WONDERS WITH WEIGHTED HANDLES

If you want to develop shapely shoulders and sinewy arms, take your workout an extra step by using a jump rope that has weighted handles. The high-tech approach to an old idea shown here, by ALL-PRO, has handles that weigh 450 g (1 lb) each and grips that will help you high-step your way to fitness and form.

JUMPING ROPE

Not just for kids. Jumping rope can be as much fun for adults as it is for children. With its rhythmic motion, it is an ideal exercise—easily building leg and arm muscles and functioning as an easy aerobic workout.

 Figure the right length of rope by standing with the midpoint of the jump rope under your feet. When extended, the rope's ends should reach the level of your armpits on both sides.

Don't jump too high. Jumping only an inch or two off the ground will give you a decent workout and reduce the chance of hurting yourself by landing wrong or losing your balance.

Be kind to your legs by wearing aerobic-dance shoes or well-made tennis shoes, which provide the necessary support and cushioning for your ankles and knees. It's also better not to jump rope on cement floors or other hard, no-give surfaces.

Give it a rest. Don't try to set world endurance records: take a break when you're tired. Jump rope for a minute, then take 30 seconds or so to catch your breath before resuming.

JUNK MAIL

Get off mailing lists by writing to the Canadian Direct Marketing Association, One Concorde Gate #607, North York, Ont., M3C 3N6, or call (416) 391-2362. Ask them to take your name off the mailing lists of their 3,500 member companies. This won't eliminate all unwanted junk mail, but it should cut down the flow considerably.

Tell charities and mail-order companies that you patronize to keep your name to themselves. Most mail-order companies provide a phone or mailing address to contact if you want your name withheld from lists they sell to other companies.

Don't return warranty cards, because mailing lists are compiled from the information asked for on these cards. Almost all warranties are valid as long as you keep the receipt; but if you are more comfortable returning the card, give no information beyond your name and address.

Send your own notices if you have moved to a new address.

Believe it or not, the information from Canada Post change-of-address cards is available to direct marketers, who use it to update their mailing lists.

JURY DUTY

Reply promptly in writing if you want your summons for jury duty to be postponed or excused. Explain your reasons and include copies of documents that support them. Some provinces are making it harder to get out of jury duty, but you may be able to postpone service once or twice if you have a crunch time at work, are suffering from poor health, are self-employed, or are in certain professions.

Be prepared to wait when you serve. You may spend most of your time sitting around, so go armed with snacks, magazines or books, portable music (don't forget the headphones), or writing paper to help you pass the time. Some courts allow you to check in for jury duty in the morning and then stand by at home or work to be called if you are needed.

You can keep it private. You will be asked "voir dire" questions by the judge or attorneys when the jury is being selected. If your answer to any question is especially sensitive or painful for you, you can say that the matter is personal and that you'd like to respond to the judge in private.

KENNELS TO KNOTS

KENNELS

A familiar token. Leave something that smells of you—perhaps an old T-shirt or a bedroom slipper—or a favorite toy with your dog when you leave it at the kennel. The token will comfort the animal in your absence.

Always visit a kennel before you board your pet there. Look for clean, dry, and roomy cages with raised beds to keep the animals off the cement. The kennel should be odor-free or smell of disinfectant. The kennel also should have exercise runs. Most of all, you should like the way the handlers relate to their charges.

Home care may be better than a kennel, especially for older animals that are less tolerant of change. A dog, which needs more attention than a cat, may require a professional pet sitter, who costs about the same as a kennel. The sitter will visit your home to feed, walk, and play with your pet twice a day. A neighborhood youngster can feed and pet a cat once a day for a modest fee.

A vaccination certificate showing that your dog's immunizations are up-to-date will speed his

acceptance at any kennel. Check with your veterinarian.

Flea trap. Be sure your dog is flea- and tick-free before you take it to the kennel. Otherwise, the kennel will take steps on its own to get rid of the pests and charge you for it.

KEYS

Loosen a sticking lock by putting a little graphite on the key. Insert the key in the lock and turn it a few times to loosen it.

Leave only the ignition key of your car at a parking garage or parking lot. Detach it from your key ring or keep it on a separate ring by itself. You don't want unscrupulous attendants making a copy of your home keys (and finding your address in the glove compartment).

Keep an extra house key with a trusted neighbor rather than under a stone, in a fake thermometer, or in a magnetic holder

under the mailbox. Thieves scan the catalogs that sell those clever gimmicks too.

KISSING

Resist kissing friends and family if you're coming down with a cold or the flu. If a kiss is expected, simply announce, "I can't kiss you because I think I'm getting sick."

When in Rome. While Americans kiss on one cheek or in some cases resist casual kissing completely, be prepared to kiss—and be kissed—on both cheeks when in Europe.

Be sensitive to the fact that some people, especially children, don't want to kiss or be kissed as a greeting. You need not be offended; just smile and shake hands instead.

Surprise your spouse. If you normally avoid kissing in public, surprise your partner with a light kiss on the cheek the next time you meet in a public place. An outward, public acknowledgment of affection is a nice way to express love.

KITCHEN CABINETS

Inside a cabinet door is a convenient place to keep pan lids, wax paper and foil, or a small garbage can. Special holders for

---

RIGHT STUFF

KEY CLAPPER

Misplaced your keys again? With four claps of your hands, this battery-powered key ring will beep and let you know where they are hiding. A computer chip keeps the key clapper from beeping at just any noise, so it truly is your personal key tracker.

these items, easily installed with a few screws, are available at any hardware store.

No silver lining. Shelves can be maintained spotlessly without the fuss and expense of shelf paper. Use the brush attachment on your vacuum cleaner to pick up dust and food crumbs. Wash occasionally with soap and water to take care of grease and odors. If your shelves are wood, be sure dishes are dry when you put them away to prevent water stains.

Low-down storage. The unused space under most floor cabinets can be used for storing baking pans, placemats, and other shallow items.

Putting new knobs on the doors of kitchen cabinets can give the whole room a lift. Look for interesting knobs in renovation catalogs, at antiques shows, and at your local home center.

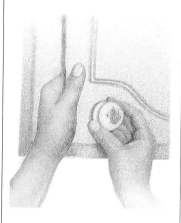

Reasonable redo. You can change the whole style of your kitchen at minimum expense and bother by refacing your cabinets, rather than replacing them. The old doors are removed, the framework is sanded and refinished, and new doors are installed for a totally new look.

Dish protection. No cabinet can protect dishes from a kitchen's

FINDING MORE COUNTER SPACE

Few kitchens have enough counter space; here are some quick and easy ways to stretch the space you already have.

▶ *To create an extra working counter in a hurry, pull open a drawer, place a cutting board on top, and shut the drawer until the board fits snugly.*

▶ *Buy metal trays that fit over range burners to provide short-term storage when the burners are not in use.*

▶ *Design a cutting board to fit across the kitchen sink for peeling and slicing vegetables and fruits. Simply scrape the peels into the sink or garbage disposer to speed cleanup.*

▶ *Install a collapsible counter behind a kitchen door that can be pulled up when you need it, but normally hangs down, out of the way.*

▶ *Invest in a rolling cart with a butcher-block top that can be easily moved around the kitchen. Such carts often have shelves drawers for extra storage.*

▶ *If you have the room, add a center island to your kitchen. Its top expands your work space, while the storage space underneath holds extra cooking gear. With stools, the island becomes a convenient breakfast counter.*

grease and dirt. But if you keep your best china in quilted dish caddies, you won't have to wash it before each use.

Old kitchen cabinets, taken out during a kitchen renovation, can have a useful second life around the house. Scrubbed down, sanded, and painted, they will handsomely hold tools and paint supplies in the basement, toys in a child's room, or extra stationery in a home office.

KITCHEN COUNTERS

The right height. Standard countertops are not a comfortable working height for everyone, but you can make adjustments without redoing your kitchen. To raise a counter that's too low, add a 5 cm (2 in.) thick piece of butcher-block or other counter material to the area you use the most.

Install a tilting storage trough in the panel just below the front edge of your sink to hold cleaning supplies like sponges and scrubbers. Kits for these counter savers are available at home centers.

Butcher-block counters, made of hard maple, make a kitchen look warm and inviting. They will serve you longer, however, if you don't do your chopping on them. Clean them frequently with soap and water and periodically rub them down with mineral oil.

Under-counter storage. Use any extra knee space under an eating counter to create a shallow pantry to store canned goods.

Rust buster. Clean rust off your stainless steel counter with non-gel toothpaste. Rub the toothpaste into the stain with a rag, then rinse and dry.

KITCHEN EFFICIENCY

Guest list. For early-rising guests or for babysitters who have to feed the kids, make a short list detailing where kitchen essentials are kept. Post the list in a convenient place, and you'll be spared a long recitation—and the guest or babysitter will feel more at home in your kitchen.

Telephone saver. Keep a plastic bag by the phone in the kitchen. When you get a call while preparing food, slip your hand in the bag and pick up the receiver, keeping it clean while you talk.

More telephone savvy. Install a speaker phone in the kitchen; then you can keep both hands free for cooking while you carry on a conversation.

Clear your counters by making use of the space beneath wall-mounted cabinets. You can buy under-the-cabinet coffeemakers and toaster ovens, among other appliances, and home centers carry under-the-counter racks for stemmed glassware, napkins, and paper plates.

Keep your cookbook clean by slipping it, open to your recipe, into a plastic bag. A bonus is that you won't lose your place.

Look up for extra storage. Pot racks, wire baskets, and string bags can be hung from the ceiling to hold cookware, utensils, and pro-

A USER-FRIENDLY KITCHEN

Modern American kitchens, for all their electronic and mechanical conveniences, can present a challenge for many people who aren't as spry as they used to be nor as dexterous with their fingers. Below are some easy fixes.

◗ *Buy a pole grabber (found in restaurant supply stores and some home centers) to reach items in high cupboards.*

◗ *Replace knobs on kitchen drawers and doors with pulls and levers, which are easier for people with arthritis to grasp and manipulate.*

◗ *Change to a single-lever sink faucet, which is easier to manipulate than separate faucet knobs.*

◗ *Replace a bottom-hinged oven door with a side-hinged door to make lifting out heavy pots less difficult.*

◗ *Install a pull-out shelf underneath the oven on which to rest heavy items being moved to and from the oven.*

◗ *Exchange a cooktop with knobs in front of the range for one with knobs on top of the range.*

◗ *Replace gas or electric burners with a cooktop. The level surface makes maneuvering pots and pans off and on burners smoother and cleaning up a snap.*

duce that doesn't need refrigeration, like potatoes and onions.

KITCHEN GARDENS

A cook's delight. If you have sun and a patch of dirt in your yard, you can cultivate a kitchen garden—your own private stock of fresh herbs and salad greens, baby string beans, and ripe tomatoes. Home-grown produce will make your meals healthful, delicious, and economical.

Mulch magic. Mulching your garden with 5 to 10 cm (2–4 in.) of straw or shredded leaves will keep down weeds and preserve moisture. Timing is important, though. Mulch cool-loving crops like lettuce and spinach early in the season to keep the soil cool as long as possible. For heat-loving crops such as tomatoes, wait until the plants set fruit before mulching.

To avoid tilling, confine your garden to one or two beds no more than 1.2 m (4 ft) wide. This way, you can plant, fertilize, and harvest crops without standing on the soil. If you don't compress the soil by stepping on it, you won't have to turn it the next spring. Instead of digging, just push back the mulch and start planting.

For high yields in a small garden, sow warm-weather crops where the early-spring spinach and peas have already been harvested. Interplant fast-growing radishes with slow-growing tomatoes; the radishes will be gone before the tomatoes start to shade them.

Save room in a small kitchen garden with dwarf varieties of lettuce, cucumbers, squashes, and other vegetables. Seeds are available at garden centers or through garden catalogs.

KITCHEN SAFETY

Range fire watch. Wear short sleeves while working at the stove, or use rubber bands to bind up long, loose sleeves. If you have long hair, tie it back before leaning over a saucepot. Hang pot holders, mitts, and kitchen towels away from burners. Be sure that window curtains can't blow within sparking distance of the range.

Don't use a tablecloth when a crawling infant is around. He may try to pull himself up on it, bringing down the table setting, and injuring himself at the same time.

Steam heat. Open covered pots with care; bursts of hot steam can cause painful burns. Lift the far side of the cover first, letting built-up steam rise safely away from your face and hand.

Close cabinets and drawers as soon as you replace or remove what you want. You'll prevent many bumped heads and scraped shinbones.

For safe footing, don't wax the kitchen floor. Clean up spills promptly, using a degreaser on fats or oils. Don't use scatter rugs in the kitchen, just nonskid mats by the sink for comfort or by the door to keep dirt from being tracked into the kitchen.

KITCHEN UTENSILS

Use a sewing thimble on your first finger while you grate, chop, and slice. Then all you have to watch out for will be your thumb.

Keep your busiest utensils in open holders—pewter mugs or ceramic vases—on the counter, where they are in easy reach.

Money-saving improvisations. Some kitchen utensils can be used in more than one way, saving you the cost of more specialized tools. An inexpensive strainer, for example, can sift flour and dust powdered sugar over a cake as well as strain soups and sauces. Hook it over a bowl to drain freshly washed berries. Look around for other double-duty kitchen tools.

Wooden spoons make the best stirrers and scrapers in the modern kitchen. They don't get hot, and they won't scratch nonstick coatings. Soak new ones in cider vinegar overnight to prevent them from absorbing food smells.

KITES

In a good breeze, you don't have to run to launch a kite. With your back to the wind, simply hold the kite up above your head and watch it fly right out of your hand.

Use a fishing rod and reel for easy kite flying. Tie the kite to the end of the fishing line. Then twirl the kite over your head and reel the line out slowly until the breeze lifts the kite away.

Tree launch. A good place to launch a kite is from beneath a tall tree with no low branches, where the wind is often strong. Place the kite upright against the trunk, facing the breeze. Walk about 15 m (50 ft) away, letting out the string as you go. Snap the string upward, pump it to get the kite aloft, and move away from the tree, allowing the kite to clear the branches.

The best kite string is strong thread, such as carpet thread or nylon fishing line. A 28-pound-test fishing line is a good weight for a medium-size kite. Don't use fuzzy brown wrapping twine, thick white twine, or wire.

FOLDING STEP STOOL

Reaching high shelves, replacing lightbulbs in ceiling fixtures, watering hanging plants, and cleaning upper wall areas are made much easier with this inexpensive step stool. Constructed of sturdy steel, it has anti-skid step surfaces and rubber-tipped legs for safety. It folds neatly for handy storage behind a door or in a closet.

A LOW-MAINTENANCE LITTER BOX

You'll have no need for expensive litter-box liners that convert to disposable bags if you follow the litter-box basics below for easy cleanup.

▶ *Use a basic litter liner that is large enough to drape over the edges of the litter box.*

▶ *Secure the liner with a piece of elastic or rubber-bands looped together to form a chain. Stretch it around the box right under the rim.*

▶ *To change the litter, remove the elastic, pull the edges of the liner together, and lift it out of the box.*

▶ *Place the full liner in an ordinary garbage bag and add to the bag any paper towels used in the cleanup.*

▶ *About once a month, scrub the empty litter box with borax or a mild cleanser. Rinse and let dry thoroughly before refilling.*

KITTENS

Orientation. To help a new kitten adapt, limit it to one room initially—with food on one side and the litter box on another. Then over several days, expand its world to other rooms. When the kitten is comfortable everywhere, move the food and litter box to their permanent settings and give your pet the run of the house.

Breaking in. Kittens do housebreak themselves, but it helps to have a litter box ready when you bring home a kitten. Show the box to the kitten and gently push its paws into the litter. Leave it alone with the box for a half hour or so.

Training aid. Clap your hands or slap a folded newspaper down beside a kitten to register your displeasure at offensive behavior. Cats dislike loud noises and will avoid provoking them.

Groom a kitten often and clip its claws regularly. It will become accustomed to this kind of handling when it is still young and will grow to expect it.

KNEES

Knee pain can be caused by any number of problems, from arthritis to tendinitis to residual discomfort from an old injury. If you exercise regularly and your pain is chronic, see a sports doctor to find ways to minimize what is likely exercise-related pain.

High-impact activities like jogging, jumping rope, and some aerobic dancing can be hard on knees. To avoid problems, wear the right shoes for your activity. Buy running shoes that give you proper support and cushioning, and replace them every six months or 800 km (500 mi). Work out on soft surfaces like dirt, grass, or an all-weather track rather than on concrete, blacktop, or wood.

To save your knees, strengthen your leg muscles. Swimming, rowing, and biking are good low-impact exercises for leg muscles and won't threaten your knees. Find exercises specially tailored to strengthen the quadricep muscles, which support the knees.

KNITTING & CROCHETING

Too much yarn is better than too little. Always buy a little more yarn of the same dye lot than you need to complete a knitted or crocheted article. Otherwise, you might have to finish off with yarn of a slightly different color. Some stores will allow you to return unused skeins within a reasonable length of time.

No more baggy sweaters. Check a yarn's recovery before you buy. Stretch out a 15 cm (6 in.) section. If it doesn't return to its original length after you release it, you can assume that a garment knitted with it won't hold its shape.

For stitch and row markers, use the plastic tabs or wire ties taken from loaves of bread.

Start a new ball of yarn at the beginning of a row whenever there are only 38 or 50 cm (15 or 20 in.) of your old yarn left. Knot the old and new ends together. When the piece is finished, untie the knots and darn in the ends.

Don't lose your place when you're trying to follow a knitting chart. To keep track of the rows you've finished, highlight them with a yellow marking pen.

Handy holder. Your yarn ball won't unroll while you're working if you put it in an oatmeal container. Poke a hole in the top to thread the yarn through.

KNIVES

A sharp investment. When buying knives, invest in a high-quality, high-carbon stainless steel or forged carbon steel chef's knife. You can use a chef's knife for most kitchen chopping and slicing tasks, and if you buy a good knife and keep it sharp, you will find that the tedious chopping chores will be faster and easier.

If the knife fits. Hold a knife you want to buy in your hand to test its feel. The handle should be comfortable and secure in your grip. The weight of the blade and the handle should balance comfortably in your hand.

Carving and slicing require a fine tapered, extra-sharp knife edge, but not power. A good carving knife need not be expensive; just make sure it is made of an alloy that you can keep sharp easily. For the best cutting edge, hone the blade on a sharpening steel every time you use it.

 Dull blades are more dangerous than sharp ones; a dull blade can easily slip. Keep your knife blades sharp with a whetstone or an electric sharpener.

Use a wooden cutting board. Hard plastic and stone are hard on knife blades. Try to do most of your chopping and slicing on a wood counter or board.

Store good knives in a wood block or on a magnetic strip, tips up. Avoid storing knives in a drawer with other cooking utensils where they can get nicked or otherwise damaged.

KNOTS

To undo unyielding knots, sprinkle cornstarch on them. Detangling often proves easier if the cord has been "lubricated" with this slippery pantry powder.

Wiggle knots loose. Use a thin, blunt object—a sturdy chopstick, for example—to work a knot free. Maneuver one end into the knot, then with a leverlike motion, steadily loosen the taut rope.

Tighten your knots with special care when using synthetic rope. Knots that hold securely in clothesline or manilla rope can lose their grip on slippery modern nylon or polyethylene rope unless they are snugged down hard.

THE "CUTTING EDGE" LIST OF KNIVES

With the right knife, properly sharpened, you can slice onions, chop nuts, or carve a turkey just like a professional chef—quickly, cleanly, and easily. Good knives can make food preparation a pleasure. The chart below suggests a set of knives that will cover the needs of almost any home kitchen.

TYPE	USE
Chef's or cook's knife	For chopping vegetables, fruits, nuts, herbs; also for slicing and cutting. The most useful knife, it has a heavy blade that curves toward the point and a bolster, a thick end near the handle, that protects the hand from the blade edge. Blade: 18–33 cm (7"–13"); most common, 20 and 25 cm (8" and 10")
Carving or slicing knife	For carving meats; also for slicing large fruits and vegetables. Long, thin, straight (or slightly curved) blade. Blade: 18–20 cm (7"–8")
Serrated or bread knife	For slicing bread, cakes, fruits, and vegetables; also for shredding. Long knives with serrated edges are good for cutting food with a hard outside but soft inside. Blade: 18–20 cm (7"–8")
Paring or utility knife	For executing decorative cuts; also for peeling and trimming. Small and light, for control over both the blade end and tip. Available with rounded and straight edges. Blade: 10–12.5 cm (4"–5")
Boning knife	For boning fish, fowl, meats. Strong, thin-bladed, with sharp point. Blade: 12.5–15 cm (5"–6")

L

LABELING TO LUMBER

LABELING

Tag sale tags. An easy way to label objects for a tag sale is to cut off pieces of masking tape, stick them onto the objects, and write on the tape with a ballpoint pen or felt-tip marker.

Save time paying bills by using a rubber stamp with your name and address to fill in return-address blanks. Rubber stamps can be ordered in most stationery stores.

Label boxes of screws, nuts, and bolts by hot-gluing samples to the box ends. You'll never again need to open the boxes just to see what's inside.

Organize CD's and tapes by using little colored press-on dots, making each category—country

music or musical comedies, for example—a different color.

Ward off refrigerator raiders by putting red press-on dots on food you don't want touched. Put a note under a refrigerator magnet on the door explaining that a red dot means "Please don't eat!"

Make leftovers work for you. For quick solo dinners, pack leftovers in individual containers and label them with the contents, the date, and cooking instructions.

LACE

Fancy trim. Dress up a blouse by removing a plain collar and cuffs and replacing them with lace ones. You'll find good choices at your local trimmings store.

Wrinkle-free. Instead of folding a lace tablecloth for storage, roll it. First, fold it lengthwise over acid-free tissue to prevent a middle crease. Then roll it around a cardboard tube covered with acid-free

tissue paper. Rolling protects the lace from damaging creases and helps keep its shape.

Black tissue trick. Wrap lace gloves, tablecloths, or other items in acid-free black tissue paper for storing. The tissue, available from jewelers and cutlery shops, protects the lace from light, which can cause yellowing.

Lay flat. Keep lace gloves and lingerie flat in your drawer to protect the lace from breaking. Linen and cotton lace, in particular, may become brittle over time.

Careful cleaning. Lace should be washed or dry-cleaned frequently to remove built-up dirt and dust. If hand washing is recommended, use a mild detergent. If machine

---

DO-IT-YOURSELF ELECTRONIC LABELS

Making labels can actually be fun when you're using computer software like Labels Unlimited or My Label Designer. You can make your own return-address labels and mailing labels, of course. But you can also custom design labels for your homemade cookies and favorite family videotapes. Some software programs even include templates for making raffle tickets, name tags, and business cards.

EASY DOES IT

Many people who are intolerant to lactose—the natural sugar in milk—can, with some help, eat moderate amounts of milk products with few or no problems. Since most milk products are good sources of calcium, vitamins A and D, and protein—and taste delicious—it is worth taking some measures to tolerate them.

▶ *Drink milk during meals. Food slows the passage of lactose through the small intestine, giving the enzyme lactase more time to digest it.*

▶ *Drink whole milk. The fat in whole milk—and ice cream—makes it easier for your digestive tract to tolerate these foods.*

▶ *Add chocolate to milk. The chocolate improves lactose digestion.*

▶ *Eat firm, naturally aged cheeses, such as Swiss, cheddar, and Parmesan. All are good sources of calcium and contain next to no lactose.*

▶ *Try yogurt, buttermilk, and sweet acidophilus milk. The words "live and active cultures" on a yogurt carton means the yogurt contains bacteria that make lactose more digestible.*

▶ *Look for lactose-reduced milk at the grocery store. It contains 70 percent less lactose than regular milk.*

▶ *Chew a lactase enzyme tablet whenever you eat dairy products, or add Lactaid to your milk. These helpful supplements are available without a prescription.*

---

washing is suggested, put the lace in a pillowcase to protect it.

Low-budget lace. Enjoy the look of fine lace without paying the price for linen or silk by choosing synthetics. Machine-made polyester or nylon lace lingerie, tablecloths, and clothing cost less, launder easily, and still look great.

LACTOSE INTOLERANCE

Symptoms of lactose intolerance include abdominal pain, gas, bloating, and diarrhea after drinking milk or eating other products that contain lactose. If you suspect you are lactose intolerant—that is, unable to digest milk and milk products easily—cut milk products from your diet for a few days and see if your symptoms disappear. If you have never been lactose intolerant but suddenly show symptoms, see your doctor.

You are not alone. An estimated 70 percent of people worldwide—primarily those of Asian, African, Mediterranean, and American Indian descent— are lactose intolerant.

Don't expect to outgrow it. Lactose intolerance usually develops in early childhood and, if anything, gets worse with age.

LADDERS

Grounding advice. On uneven ground put a firm, flat block under the ladder's lower foot; on soft ground, put a board under both of the ladder's feet. Increase stability even more by anchoring the ladder with sandbags or tying its base to a stake driven into the ground.

Shock warning. To protect yourself from electrical shock, never use an aluminum ladder or a wet wooden ladder to make electrical repairs. Use fiberglass instead.

Don't go all the way. An extension ladder's maximum length is 90 cm to 1.2 m (3–4 ft) longer than its safe working length. A ladder's two sections must overlap by at least 90 cm (3 ft). That gives a 6 m (20 ft) extension ladder a maximum working length of 5 m (17 ft).

To test a stepladder, stand on the lowest tread and shake it from side to side. If it feels shaky, tighten the nuts on the reinforcing rods under each tread.

Use a standoff—a brace that steadies the ladder firmly against the house but at a distance—especially when cleaning windows or gutters. The standoff not only stabilizes the ladder, it protects the windows or gutters, which could easily be damaged by the weight of the ladder.

LAMP REPAIR

If a lamp won't light, unplug it, tighten any loose connections, and check the cord for frays. If the lamp is not damaged, you probably need a new switch.

Fluorescent bulbs can explode if they are broken. Wear gloves and goggles when replacing one. Wrap a burned-out bulb in newspaper and break it so it won't explode.

A flickering fluorescent tube may simply need rotating to seat it properly in the sockets. If that doesn't fix it, turn off the switch and remove the tube. Discolored ends and bent or broken pins are signs that you need a new tube.

LAMPS & LAMPSHADES

To create lamps for a traditional room, look for bases that can be electrified. Crocks, biscuit tins, old kerosene and gas lamps, jugs, and candlesticks are good candidates.

Hire an electrician to wire it properly; or if you are handy, do it yourself, finishing with an appropriate harp and shade.

Static control. To prevent the buildup of static electricity in lampshades, dust them with fabric softener sheets. This will also reduce the amount of dust attracted to the shade.

Customize a lamp by adding collage materials to a plain shade. For a girl's dressing-table lamp, for

Replacing a Lamp Cord

Rewiring a lamp with a frayed or damaged cord is an easy fix that saves you the trouble and expense of taking the lamp to an electical repair shop. Buy a new cord at a hardware store.

1 Unplug lamp and remove bulb. Unscrew finial, if any, and lift off shade. Slide up harp sleeves to expose clips at end of harp holder; squeeze harp arms to release harp.

2 Depress outer shell of socket where it is marked Press. Pull off socket shell and insulating sleeve to expose socket.

3 Free old cord from socket by loosening terminal screws. Untie underwriters knot and unscrew socket cap.

4 Remove felt from base. Cut off plug. Untie any knot in the cord. Splice the nonplug end of the new cord to the old one (inset) and secure with tape. Pull old cord up tube until tape emerges.

5 Remove old cord. Split top 7.5 cm (3 in.) of new cord; strip 2 cm (¾ in.) of insulation from ends. Replace harp holder and socket cap; then tie an Underwriters knot, as shown.

6 Connect the cord's ridged (neutral) wire to the silver terminal; connect the smooth (hot) wire to the brass terminal. Reassemble the rest of the lamp.

example, try lace cutouts. Brush a thin coat of PVA adhesive over a piece of fabric with embroidered or lace flowers and let it dry. Then cut out the flowers with a craft knife and apply them, using a little extra adhesive, to the shade.

LANDLORDS

Choose your tenants carefully, which is your right as long as you honor the laws that prohibit discrimination and invasion of privacy. Ask prospective tenants to sign a form entitling you to get their credit reports and job information. Contact a credit-rating agency to find out if they pay their bills. Also call a job reference and former landlord.

Lead protection. If you are a landlord, you must give your tenants a disclosure form stating whether or not lead paint is present in property built before 1978, along with a booklet about lead paint hazards. For more information on lead protection, call Occupational Health and Safety at 1-800-263-8466.

LANDSCAPING

Simplify plant care by collecting plants with the same needs into islands. Plant acid-loving evergreens—rhododendrons, azaleas, and mountain laurels—together, and feed the whole bed with a quick sprinkling of an acid fertilizer. Put drought-tolerant shrubs

As a renter, you probably know that your rental property must comply with local health, housing, fire, and safety codes. You are also entitled to other specific rights.

▶ *You have the right to enjoy your rental property without unreasonable interference by the landlord.*

▶ *Except for emergency repairs, the landlord must give you 24 hours notice before entering your apartment.*

▶ *You can complain to your landlord about neglecting her responsibilities without reprisals.*

▶ *You can join with other tenants to bargain the terms of the rental agreement.*

▶ *The landlord may not take your personal possessions for the purpose of recovering overdue rent.*

▶ *As long as you hold up your end of the rental agreement, you have the right of exclusive possession of the property until the lease expires.*

together, and you create an area that will seldom need irrigation.

Group high-care plants, your lushest and most colorful ones, in the areas of the yard you use most, such as the patio. Use low-maintenance, less spectacular plants in parts of the yard where you spend less time.

For easy mowing, draw the final outlines of your planting beds with your lawn mower. This ensures that you can quickly and easily cut the grass around each bed every time you mow.

LAPTOP COMPUTERS

Security savvy. Laptop, or portable, computers are among the most frequently stolen items in the field of consumer electronics. To let authorities find you if your stolen laptop is recovered, use an engraving tool to write your name, phone number, and the laptop's serial number on the case. Also use a security program with a password on your laptop to keep thieves from getting into the hard drive.

Fax yourself for hard copy. If you need a hard copy while you are traveling and don't have access to a printer, use your laptop's built-in fax modem to send the document directly to your hotel's fax machine.

Use two battery packs for laptop efficiency. While one is recharging, you can use the other one freely, knowing that a fresh pack will be ready when you need it.

LAUNDRY

Dirt-free. Blast mud out of gritty jeans and gardening overalls with a garden hose before laundering. You'll avoid washing dirt into other clothes.

Lint-free. Reduce the lint that can stick to dark-colored garments in the dryer by adding 250 mL (1 cup) of vinegar to each laundry load during the final rinse.

Wrinkle-free. When clothes are wrinkled from sitting in the dryer too long, put in a damp towel and run the load for five more minutes. The wrinkles will disappear.

Delicate protection. Small, fragile items can be placed in pillowcases before they are machinewashed. Close the cases with thick rubber bands.

Speed up drying time for a lightweight garment that you must wear immediately by hanging it on a plastic hanger and gently blowing it dry with a hair dryer.

Communal sock sorting. Hand out individual zippered mesh bags to use just for dirty socks and hosiery (write names on the zipper tapes with an indelible marker). Wash and dry the bags.

Then family members can sort their own socks.

Less handling. Put a laundry basket in each family member's bedroom closet. Take the laundry to and from the washer and dryer in these baskets. Launder only one or two baskets at a time to reduce sorting. Return the baskets containing folded items for each person to put away.

Drying washable knits in the dryer tends to shrink them. Instead, hang garments such as your favorite T-shirt and leisure pants on plastic hangers to dry.

Don't overmeasure detergent. Use only the amount indicated on the package. Excess detergent isn't always washed away completely in the rinse cycle and can leave a film on fabrics that attracts dirt, causing garments to look dingy.

LAWN MAINTENANCE

Don't overfeed. Lawns that are pushed to grow develop more diseases. Northern lawns need only one feeding per year, applied in late summer or early fall. In the South, apply only half of the lawn's annual fertilizer dosage late in the spring and the other half late in the summer.

Pest-proofing. To give your lawn a natural resistance to pests such as chinch bugs, billbugs, webworms, and armyworms, sow seed that has been inoculated with endophytic fungi (available at most garden centers). Inoculated grasses are also more resistant to disease and drought.

If your lawn is mossy, consider encouraging the invader rather than trying to curb it; a moss lawn has a special velvety green beauty and requires no mowing. To promote moss, treat your lawn with sulfur dust or aluminum sulfate (available at garden centers). Rake out the grass as it dies, then tamp down the soil and keep its surface moist. Sprinkle the bare patches with crumbled clumps of moss.

LAWN MOWING

Cut a wider swath. Rotary mowers are not created equal—the wider the swath, the fewer passes needed to cover your lawn. For example, switching from a 45 cm (18 in.) mower to a 60 cm (24 in.) model can slash your mower-pushing distance on 0.1 ha (¼ acre) of lawn by nearly 1.6 km (1 mi).

Wear ear protectors when using a gasoline-powered mower; the noise from such a machine can cause measurable hearing loss if you are exposed to it for more than 30 minutes at a time.

RIGHT STUFF

WEEDING MADE EASY

No more backbreaking afternoons weeding your lawn or garden with The Weed Hound (produced by Hound Dog Products). Just center the tool over a weed, gently push the handle down, and the weeder grabs the offender; pull the handle up, and the weeder removes the culprit, roots and all. These dogged tools are available at most garden centers.

WATERING THE LAWN

Watering your lawn is a chore—and in some areas, a waste of precious water. Here are ways to cut down on watering.

▶ *Let grass go dormant during very dry summers. It will green up during fall rains and suffer fewer pest and disease problems than grass that is constantly irrigated.*

▶ *2.5 cm (1 in.) of water a week from rain or irrigation is sufficient during the growing season. To measure rainfall, set an open peanut butter jar in a corner of your lawn. Once a week, measure the rainwater in it and adjust your watering schedule to make up the difference.*

▶ *Water early in the day, before it is hot. You will reduce incidental evaporation and double the amount of water that reaches the lawn. Also, there will be time for the moisture to dry out before nightfall, when wet grass is most likely to develop fungal diseases.*

▶ *Compacted soil dries quickly because water cannot soak into it. Run an aerator over your lawn; it punches tiny holes into the soil that allow water, along with air and fertilizer, to reach the grass roots.*

Go wild. Meadow plantings of wildflowers mixed with tall grasses have become a popular alternative to lawns because of their informal, countrified charm and low maintenance. Just mow them once a year (usually in late winter or very early spring) and forget the fertilizers.

Southern plantings. In warm climates the best time to seed a lawn is in spring or early summer because southern grasses thrive in hot weather as long as irrigation is adequate. Most southern weeds germinate in the fall, so they will give the new grass little competition for moisture and nutrients.

Northern plantings. Gardeners think of spring as seed-planting time, but in northern climates late August or early September is the best time to sow grass seed. For northern grasses, the cool weather will encourage strong germination and healthy seedling growth. Competition from annual weeds is also minimized because in the North most weeds germinate in the spring.

For safety's sake, watch out for those whirling mower blades. When mowing, always wear long pants and sturdy shoes, preferably ones with steel-reinforced toes. And never mow up and down a slope—if you slip, you might slide under the mower's whirling blade. Instead, mow across a slope.

OLD SAW **Cut your lawn higher** in summer—an extra 12 mm (½ in.) will do. The added height helps shade the roots of the grass and protect them against drought, reducing the need for watering.

Mow high and mow less. It seems that cutting grass short should reduce the number of times you mow in a given summer, but in fact the opposite is true. Tall grass grows more slowly, so cutting high means that you actually cut less often. In general, cut most lawns at least 5 cm (2 in.) high. In hot climates, cut them 2.5 to 5 cm (1–2 in.) high.

A mulching mower can save you time and money. You don't rake up grass clippings after you cut the lawn with it; instead the mower shreds clippings so finely that they sift down into the grass and out of sight. (The clippings also provide 30 percent of your lawn's fertilizer needs and keep grass roots moist and cool.)

LAWNS

In clover. Clover stays green in dry weather and provides your lawn with a natural fertilizer as well. Add the seed of white Dutch or strawberry clover to your grass seed (1 part clover to 3 parts grass). You can also patch any bare spots in your lawn with a handful of clover seed.

Go wild legally. Before converting your lawn to a wildflower meadow or prairie, check for any local antiweed ordinance prohibiting unmown growth. If such an ordinance does exist, discuss your project with town officials before proceeding; when consulted, they may be supportive about such plans.

LAWSUITS

Identify the other party. You will need the exact name and address of the party you want to sue. If it's a company, get the name of the owner and the legal business name from the Chamber of Commerce or from a local consumer affairs or business-licensing agency. For an individual, a listing of the exact name and most recent address can be found on a copy of the driver's license or car registration at the provincial department of motor vehicles.

Make a diary. Keep a written chronology of every event involved in your problem. Note the date of each event, who was involved, what happened, who witnessed it, and what documents, photographs, or other items can verify it. This chronology will establish your cause of action, showing how you have been harmed by someone else and what damages you have suffered. If you speak to a lawyer, take the chronology with you.

Look for assets. Before you go to the trouble of suing—even in small claims court—find out if the other party has any money. Courts don't collect judgments. If you win, but the other party is unemployed, bankrupt, conceals assets, or is not insured for this problem, you may end up with an empty victory.

LAWYERS

Scout for advice. If you want to know if you should handle a legal problem on your own, find a sympathetic lawyer to consult with you. For the fee of an hour or two, the lawyer can review your case and tell you what you might gain by legal action.

When to hire one. If a problem is emotionally difficult, get a lawyer to offer neutral advice and pursue rational solutions. Other cases when a lawyer is essential: if there is a pending criminal charge, if large amounts of money or property are at stake, or if an opposing party lives in another province.

Picking your counsel. Select a lawyer with care at the outset because changing lawyers can be costly and complicated. Interview lawyer prospects as you would shop for a major purchase. Ask about experience, fees, and their approach to cases. Ask about their strategy for your problem, any obstacles they see, and any extra expenses involved. Seek alternative ways to approach the problem. Find out how and when they will communicate with you.

LEAD POISONING

Danger! Take steps to safeguard yourself and your family from mental and physical damage caused by overexposure to lead. Get accurate information about identifying hazards, testing, and finding certified removal contractors from Occupational Health and Safety (1-800-263-8466).

Have a professional inspection if you live in or plan to move into

---

HOW TO LOWER YOUR LEGAL EXPENSES

Hiring a lawyer can be expensive. But sometimes you simply must have good legal help to protect yourself or your family. Here are ways to minimize your legal fees.

▶ *Ask your lawyer to consider a lower fee; she may negotiate. Or ask about a contingency fee—a percentage of the money you win (and only her expenses if you lose).*

▶ *Invite your lawyer to assign you tasks that will reduce your bill: photocopying, typing, or getting documents.*

▶ *Volunteer to undertake specific library research, such as searching for experts, a patent history, or the track record of a consumer product.*

▶ *Consider nonlawyer services. Some paralegals can help you prepare documents for a bankruptcy filing or uncontested divorce. In property tax cases a less expensive specialist might help direct an appeal for your case.*

▶ *Contact local law schools about free legal clinics; they often handle such subjects as juvenile or consumer cases. Experienced lawyers supervise the students, who usually are quite dedicated. But ask to meet the person who will take over if your student lawyer graduates.*

BIODEGRADABLE LEAF BAGS

Biodegradable leaf bags may look like oversized brown paper sacks, but they are especially made for disposing of fallen leaves and are safer for the environment than plastic. Tough enough to be filled up, even with wet, heavy leaves, they obligingly disintegrate along with the leaves and serve as mulch. Find them at hardware, grocery, and garden stores.

a house or apartment painted before 1980, two years after lead paint was banned (some paint may have stayed on store shelves that long). Hire a certified professional if you find that removal of lead-based paint is required.

Check paint. About 75 percent of paints sold before 1980 contain lead-based ingredients. Paint in good condition is no hazard, but flakes and paint dust are harmful. Keep paint in good repair. Damp-mop floors, window frames, and walls regularly to remove dust. If you rent, report flaking paint to the landlord without delay.

Protect small children. Wash their hands often, especially before meals and at bedtime. Wash bottles and pacifiers thoroughly, as well as toys and stuffed animals that attract dust. Keep children from chewing painted surfaces.

Flush the pipes. Before drinking, run water for 30 to 60 seconds, or until it gets noticeably colder. This is especially important if you have not used a tap for several hours. (You can collect the water and use it for your plants.) Cook with water from the cold faucet; hot water can leach lead from pipes.

LEAF REMOVAL

The big blow. A homeowner's leaf blower is rarely adequate to remove a season's leaves, especially if the lawn is large. Instead, after all the leaves have fallen, rent a heavy-duty professional machine—a push-around model with a 5- to 8-hp engine. It will move even wet leaves and clear a large yard in a couple of hours.

Let gravity help. In a sloping yard, always rake leaves in a downhill direction. Use gravity to help pull the leaves into a pile; you'll find this easier, even when it takes extra steps to haul the pile away.

Mow the leaves. Instead of raking, chop and blow leaves with your gas-powered mower. Start on one edge of the lawn with the mower's discharge chute facing toward the lawn's center. Push the mower to the end of the lawn, then pull it going back. Repeat,

working across the lawn with the discharge chute always pointing in the same direction. Eventually you'll have a window of organic mulch along an edge of the lawn.

Free mulch. With an inexpensive electric leaf shredder—the kind with a string trimmer attached to the bottom of a cone—turn the piles of leaves that you heap up by the curb into a season's supply of organic mulch.

LEAKS & DRIPS

Pin down the source. Interior water damage can be caused by leaks in radiators or plumbing pipes as well as in a roof. Since water can travel a circuitous route, the damage site may not be where the leak is. Trace all possibilities and make repairs before restoring cosmetic damage.

To find a roof leak, check your attic rafters on a rainy day with a flashlight. Mark all damp spots so you can trace them to the outside problem points in better weather.

To kill mold, mildew, or fungus on damp wood, spray it with a mixture of half bleach, half water combined in a plastic spray bottle.

Plaster fix. Wash water-damaged plaster with a mix of 1 L (1 pt) of vinegar to 3.7 L (0.8 gal) of water. (If the plaster doesn't harden as it dries, it needs to be replastered.)

LEATHER & SUEDE

Give it to the experts. Removing stains from leather and suede is tricky; unless a spot on a garment or piece of furniture is minor, you should have it cleaned by a professional leather-cleaning firm.

Waterproof a new leather garment with a spray that also helps to protect the leather from superficial stains. Silicone-based sprays work for boots and dark colors but are hard to spray evenly on soft leathers. Instead, apply a temporary fluorocarbon spray such as 3M Scotchgard every few weeks.

Darken tan belts and shoes by wiping them with a cloth dipped in ammonia. Apply the ammonia as evenly as possible to avoid leaving streaks on the leather.

Cold cream cleans and softens leather just as well as more expensive leather-conditioning compounds. Rub it in with your fingers and wipe away excess with a cloth or paper towel.

No plastic bags. Leather clothes stored in plastic can dry out and become discolored. To keep dust off hanging leather clothes, cover them with cloth.

LEFT-HANDEDNESS

Go for the gold. Being a lefty presents its problems, but if you want to do well at sports, get involved in those in which left-handers tend to excel, such as baseball, tennis, racquetball, boxing, and bowling.

Left-handers, unite. Hook up with one of the national associations that exist to promote the care and comfort of left-handed people. Ask at your local library for an encyclopedia of national associations and look in the index under "left-handed."

Teach left-handed kids to tie knots or bows—or to copy any action of a right-handed person—by facing them and acting as a mirror instead of having them mimic your behavior at your side. They'll learn manual skills the way that's natural for them.

Teaching lefties to write takes understanding and sometimes patience, but here's a tip that will make the learning a lot easier: a southpaw should turn the writing paper clockwise so that it slants toward 1 o'clock instead of turning it toward 11 o'clock, as most right-handed people do.

Seat left-handed guests at a left-hand corner of the dinner table to give them room to drink, cut their food, and eat without banging elbows with a right-handed neighbor.

LEFTOVERS

Refrigerate leftovers quickly. Allowing hot foods to cool down before storing invites spoilage. The sooner you find room in the refrigerator for leftovers, the safer they will be to eat the next day.

RIGHT STUFF — MAKING LIFE EASIER FOR LEFTIES

To ease the inconvenience of being left-handed in a right-handed world, a growing industry is now supplying a variety of everyday tools and devices specially designed for lefties. The sampling below includes (clockwise from left) pruning shears, baseball glove, LEFTHANDER magazine, notebook, spiral-bound binder, scissors, and can opener. Order from THE LEFT HAND (1-800-462-5338). Subscribe to LEFTHANDER magazine by calling Lefthanders International (1-913-234-2177).

A car owner's worst nightmare: You discover that you have bought a lemon. You complain to your dealer, but he refuses to help. What do you do? Unlike the United States, Canada does not have "lemon laws," but consumer protection legislation exists to protect Canadians against lemons. These laws vary from province to province; check with your local department of motor vehicles. Before taking legal action, first try writing a letter to either the dealer or manufacturer.

Go to the top. Send your letter to the top person at the car dealership or manufacturer—the president or chief executive officer.

List repairs in detail. Attach copies of all repair orders for your car as well as invoices for any other related expenses you have incurred, such as car rental (if not provided for under your warranty) to strengthen your case.

Ask for a resolution. State exactly what you want to happen: your expenses paid and the car replaced, or some other solution in accordance with CAMVAP arbitration rules.

Debra Simon
311 St. Mary Ave.
Winnipeg, Man. R3C 3Z5

November 4, 1997

Arthur Barton, Chief Executive Officer
Oxbow Motors
1215 Auto Lane
Winnipeg, Man. R3K 0X3

Dear Mr. Barton:

I bought a United Motors Chariot (ID C7DE9334SW219983) seven months ago, on April 1, 1997, from Oxbow Motors; the odometer has 10,379 kilometers on it. Since the purchase, the car has required repeated repairs due to faulty cylinders that cause the engine to stop.

As documented on the enclosed work orders, the dealer has made the following attempts to repair the vehicle:

1. April 20, 1997, at 725 kilometers; engine stopping; loss of compression; cylinder head damaged; repairs. Car in shop 4 days.
2. June 27, 1997, at 5,133 kilometers; engine stopping; defective cylinder head; repairs. Car in shop 10 days.
3. September 18, 1997, at 8,070 kilometers; engine stopping; cracked cylinder head; repairs. Car in shop 12 days.
4. October 8, 1997, at 9,446 kilometers; engine stopping; cylinder replaced. Car in shop 9 days.

Under the Canadian Motor Vehicle Arbitration Plan, I believe I am entitled to redress. Specifically, the car has required repair more than three times for the same problem within a year of purchase; it has spent over 30 days in the shop in less than a year; and the car has been driven less than 19,000 kilometers. In addition, all requirements under the warranty have been met.

I ask that Oxbow Motors either replace this car or refund the purchase price. Please contact me with your response within the next two weeks. Unless I hear from you within that time, I will be forced to pursue other remedies under the law.

Sincerely,

Debra Simon

Give details. List the car's make and model with the serial number; the date of purchase; the name and address of the dealership, and the number of kilometers the car has been driven.

Legal reference. Explain how your complaint qualifies under CAMVAP arbitration rules or your province's consumer protection laws.

Set a deadline for a response within a reasonable—but specific—time period. Proceed with legal steps if no action is taken.

Recycle leftover bread into crumbs and croutons. For crumbs, dry out bread in a 150°C (300°F) oven for about 10 minutes, then grind it up in a food processor. For croutons, cut bread into cubes and sauté lightly in olive oil or safflower oil. Stored in airtight jars, crumbs and croutons will keep for about 10 days—or they can be frozen in airtight bags.

Stuff it. Chop or grind leftover meat, chicken, or vegetables, season the mixture, then pack it into bell peppers, large mushroom caps, or giant pasta shells. Bake with a sauce for a creative dish that may surprise your family.

LEMON AID

Go for the dealer. If you're sold a lemon, you can sue either your dealer or the manufacturer, or both. You will have a much better case of compensation, however, by suing a local dealer who has a lot more to lose than a huge car manufacturer.

An alternative remedy to court is the Canadian Motor Vehicle Arbitration Plan (CAMVAP), available through every province's department of motor vehicles except Quebec. The plan is a voluntary arbitration program which resolves disputes between automobile manufacturers, dealers, and their customers in a fair, inexpensive and fast manner. To qualify for CAMVAP arbitration, you must have purchased your vehicle from an authorized dealer and it must be this year's model or a model from within the last four years.

What you can ask for. Under CAMVAP arbitration rules, you can ask for one or more of the following rewards: (1) that your vehicle be repaired; (2) that the manufacturer buy back your vehicle; (3) that you be reimbursed the costs of repairing your vehicle; or (4) replacement of your vehicle.

LEMONS

Need only a few drops? Don't bother to slice open the lemon; just jab it with a toothpick and squeeze out several drops. Stick the toothpick back into the hole and put the lemon away; it'll be ready the next time you need one.

Lemon savvy. For the freshest taste and most juice, shop for heavy, thin-skinned, evenly yellow lemons with no tint of green.

How much juice? An average lemon produces about 45 mL (3 tbsp) of juice and 30 mL (2 tbsp) of grated peel, or zest. You will need five or six lemons to obtain 250 mL (1 cup) of juice.

Zesty sugar. Lemon sugar is a delicate and delicious way to fla-vor teas, fruit salads, even cus-tards. To prepare it, mix 15 to 30 mL (1–2 tbsp) of grated lemon zest into 250 mL (1 cup) of sugar. Let the flavor develop for a week before using.

Lemonize your pots. Don't throw away an old, scruffy-look-ing lemon. Instead, cut it in half, put some coarse-grain salt on the surface, and apply it—with a little elbow grease—to your copper pots. They'll shine like new.

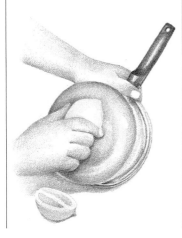

Use lemon water on apples, pears, and other fruits that brown easily when cut. Add 5 mL (1 tsp) of lemon juice to water in a small bowl and sprinkle it on fruit that has to stand for a while.

Heat and roll. You can nearly double the amount of juice you get from a lemon by warming it—either in the microwave or in hot water—and then rolling it on the counter before squeezing.

Zesty save. After juicing lemons, wash the rinds thoroughly, place them in a plastic bag and freeze them. When you need lemon zest, for cooking, baking, or even a cup of tea, grate the still-frozen rind quickly and easily with a hand grater or zester.

LIABILITY INSURANCE

Above and beyond. Your home-owners policy covers you for a certain amount of liability in case of injuries to others that are judged to be your fault, but it goes only so far. The best way to avoid having to pay a lot of your own money for a claim is to have an umbrella policy providing addi-tional liability coverage after your homeowners policy pays its limit.

Who pays the lawyers? Before you buy umbrella liability insur-ance, make certain that it covers the cost of legal fees; they can snowball into substantial amounts in many liability cases.

Give fair warning of all hazards on your property that you can't fix. Put a fence around the swim-ming pool (required by law in some areas) and boldly mark a steep step or a wide glass door that someone might walk into. These warnings will convince your insurer that you've acted reason-ably and will improve your chances of success in a lawsuit.

Renting a car? Collision and lia-bility insurance may be offered to you by the rental company, but you may well be covered for both by either your own car insurance or the credit card you're charging the rental on. If you are, turn down the offer and save money.

EASY DOES IT — HOW MUCH LIFE INSURANCE?

As a rule of thumb, the dollar amount of life insurance you should carry is five to seven times your gross annual salary. Factors that could increase or decrease that amount might include the following.

▶ *How many years will your potential survivors need benefits? For example, when will your youngest child become a self-sustaining adult?*

▶ *Do you need to establish college funds for children?*

▶ *How much debt have you incurred, including your home mortgage and car loan?*

▶ *Do your potential survivors work? Could they work?*

▶ *Can you count on additional life insurance from your employer or from some other source?*

▶ *Will potential survivors draw on other resources such as savings, investments, and pension benefits?*

LIFE INSURANCE

Tell the truth when filling out life insurance applications. Insurers will check the accuracy and completeness of statements, and may obtain access to information that may have resulted in you being turned down for coverage with another insurance company. Any misrepresentation can cause cancellation of or drastic reduction in the value of your policy.

The whole picture. For full medical records from either a hospital or your physician, insurance companies in Canada still have to obtain your consent.

Go with term life insurance if you think you'll need coverage for only 10 to 15 years. Cash-value policies, such as whole life, universal life, and variable life, need that length of time before they produce returns as an investment, and they are a lot more expensive. Therefore, you'd pay higher premiums without getting any reward.

Rule no. 1. Good health means better rates. Refrain from smoking, strive to keep a normal weight, exercise regularly, and practice good eating habits. Those who follow these guidelines are generally classified as "preferred" and are entitled to the best prices offered by an insurance company.

LIGHTING

Glare-free illumination can be created by bouncing light from recessed fixtures or broad-beam track lighting off walls, ceilings, and background areas. Bulbs placed behind valances also add effective indirect light.

Accent lighting draws attention to proud possessions or dramatic areas. Provide it with narrow-beam track lights, spotlights, or art lights.

Task lighting focuses on specific activities. Spotlights, desk lamps, bathroom mirror lights, and reading lamps all provide task lighting.

Never use ceiling lights to illuminate a desk or counter space; as you bend over, you will cast a shadow on your work. Instead, place lighting under a cabinet or shelf in front of you, or to the side and slightly above your work.

LIGHTNING PROTECTION

If you are indoors during a violent thunderstorm, stay away from electrical appliances and telephones. Don't take baths or wash dishes, since metal pipes and water both conduct electricity.

If you are outdoors during a storm, avoid metal; fishing rods, golf clubs, guns, tennis rackets, and radio antennas all act as natural lightning rods. Also remove jewelry and hearing aids.

Stay in the car if you're driving—it's one of the safest places to be in a thunderstorm. Just park away from trees, power lines, or other structures that could fall on the car. Close the windows and don't touch any metal parts inside.

If you're boating, try to reach land or take shelter under a bridge. If you're swimming, get out of the water immediately and move quickly to a shelter.

In the woods, stay clear of a single tall tree. Go to a low clump of trees or to the lowest ground around. Hug your knees to you, tucking your head between them.

Call for help immediately if someone is struck by lightning—the shock can make the victim's heart stop. If you are trained, administer CPR or other first aid until medical help arrives.

RIGHT STUFF

A LIGHT FOR WHEN THE LIGHTS GO OUT

Power failure lights (manufactured by Honeywell, Intermatic, and others) go on automatically when power fails, giving light for about 45 minutes—as well as a warm sense of safety and security. They plug directly into an average wall outlet, contain rechargeable batteries, and can easily be used as flashlights. These indispensible little tools are available at most lighting stores.

LIPSTICK

Glossy lipstick makes thin lips look fuller. Adding gloss or petroleum jelly to the center of the lower lip over matte lipstick creates a plumper look.

Removing lipstick stains can be tricky, but you'll have better luck if you pretreat the stains. Try rubbing the stains with cold cream or petroleum jelly and rinsing with club soda. Soak white garments in lemon juice.

Repair a broken lipstick by applying a candle flame delicately to each side of the break. Push the softened edges together gently, then smooth the outer edges with the side of a toothpick. Put the lipstick in the refrigerator for a while to firm it up.

Use a thin lipstick pencil to trace the lip shape you want, then fill in the center with color. Make the outline one shade darker than the color in the center.

LISTENING

Body language. Become an active "whole body" listener by using both verbal and nonverbal signals to show you're listening. Nod your head, and offer short exclamations or verbal cues to encourage the person speaking.

Close your eyes to help you focus on an important speech or

something you're listening to on tape. This can work well in a big crowd or when you're alone, but obviously you don't want to try it with one person or just a small group—they'll doubtless think you're either bored or asleep.

To get others to listen to you, speak in a pleasant voice but use enough volume and dynamic emphasis to hold their attention. Minimize your movements to help your listeners stay focused on what you are saying.

LIVING ALONE

Commit yourself in advance to events that will get you out: Buy season tickets to plays, concerts, or ball games; sign up for a course; join a book group or an exercise class. Invite a friend to join you—the obligation will help you follow through. When living alone, it is essential to plan time to be with others.

Recently bereaved? It is important to keep up your social life, so ask good friends over for a potluck supper or coffee after a movie. Be as casual as you can, but if you do feel weepy, these are the people who will understand and try to comfort you.

A woman alone? Depending on how secure your neighborhood is, you may want to take steps to keep your solitary status under wraps. List only your initials in the telephone book and don't give away your single status on the telephone answering machine or your building's roster.

Set up a singles' support group, in which members accept package deliveries for one another and keep an eye on each other's houses or apartments. Each individual should leave housekeys with several others in case of an accidental lockout. Neighbors who have keys can also let a repairman into the home or go in themselves if there is an emergency.

Tired of frozen dinners but uninspired to cook for yourself? Invite friends for dinner and cook more than you need. Freeze the leftovers in single portions to enjoy when you're eating alone.

LIVING ROOMS

In a large living room, group the furniture into several conversation or activity areas. Avoid the temptation to spread out furniture to fill the space; it may look well proportioned, but you and your guests can end up shouting at each other across the room.

Install floor outlets when you build or renovate. You will be able to set lamps near furniture placed in the middle of the room—and you will eliminate the need for unsightly and possibly hazardous extension chords.

Ceiling fans are a bright idea for living rooms. By circulating the air, they enhance your heating and cooling systems; and since some include light fixtures, they can help illuminate the room.

Screen out an ugly view while keeping a source of natural light in the room by hanging a framed panel of stained glass over the window. If only the lower part of the view is offensive, put shutters over the bottom of the window.

LIVING WILLS

Carry a card in your purse or wallet that indicates where your living will is filed and the name of the person who is to be notified in an emergency. Select a depository for your living will which can

be accessed quickly. Give copies to your doctor, lawyer, and any family members or friends who will be caring for you.

If you move to another province, redo your living will. Doctors may not be able to honor a living will that doesn't conform to local law.

Check your living will annually and revise it if necessary. If it is in order, initial it with the current date. In an emergency, doctors will want to know that the document is the latest expression of your wishes regarding treatment.

A LIVING WILL

To ease your mind and the minds of your loved ones, prepare a living will (also called an advance care directive). A living will states the extraordinary health care measures you wish to have taken (or withheld) if you become incapacitated or terminally ill. Forms are available through your doctor or your local hospital. Ask your doctor to check your living will to ensure that your wishes are medically feasible. Since the specific wording for living wills varies by province, ask your lawyer to look over your living will to make sure than it abides by your local laws.

Specifications. Spell out all procedures you want—or don't want—such as cardiopulmonary resuscitation, chest compression, defibrillation, or assisted ventilation.

Rights. Reiterate your right to refuse treatment and ask those involved to honor your wishes.

Distribution. Sign and date the living will according to your state's witnessing requirements. The witnesses should not be heirs to your estate, relatives, or medical personnel. Distribute copies to your proxy, family members, your doctors, and your lawyer.

LIVING WILL DECLARATION
To My Family, Doctors, and All Those Concerned with My Care

I, _____, being of sound mind, direct that my life shall not be artificially prolonged under the circumstances set forth below.

If at any time I should have an incurable injury, disease, or illness judged to be a terminal condition by my attending physician who has personally examined me and has determined that my death is imminent except for death delaying procedures, then I direct that such procedures which would only prolong the dying process be withheld or withdrawn, and that I be permitted to die naturally with only the administration of medication, sustenance, or the performance of any medical procedure deemed necessary by my attending physician to provide me with comfort care.

I especially do not want: _____
_____
_____

Other instructions/comments: _____
_____
_____

These directions express my legal right to refuse treatment. Therefore I expect my family, doctors, and everyone concerned with my care to regard themselves as legally and morally bound to act in accord with my wishes and in so doing to be free of any legal liability for having followed my directions.

Proxy Designations Clause: I appoint _____ to be my health care agent for all matters relating to my health care, including, without limitation, full power to give or refuse consent to all medical, surgical, hospital, and related health care. This power of attorney is effective on my inability to make or communicate health care decisions.

If the person I have named above is unable to act on my behalf, I authorize the following person to do so:

Signed: _____ Date: _____
Witness: _____ Witness: _____
Address: _____ Address: _____

Purpose. Make a general statement outlining your wishes with regard to your health care should you become severely incapacitated, comatose, or terminally ill.

Palliative care. Even if you refuse artificial life support systems, you may want to ask for pain medication and nursing care to ease your death.

Proxy. Name someone to speak for you if you are dying and cannot make decisions yourself. (For more encompassing protection, draw up a medical power of attorney, naming a health-care agent who has authority to make decisions about your treatment should you become totally incapacitated.)

LOANS

Improve your chances of getting a loan by being well prepared for your meeting with the loan officer. For most loans you'll be asked to present in writing a list of all your assets, liabilities, and debts. You will also be required to fill out a credit application form, which gives the financial institution the right to verify your credit.

Borrow from yourself. Most RRSP plans offer borrowing privileges—as much as 50 percent of the balance, to a maximum of $50,000. Interest rates are usually lower than for conventional loans, but you'll probably have to repay the loan within five years. (If you leave your job, you might have to repay the loan immediately.)

Avoid credit card loans. Interest on credit card cash advances is often higher by several percentage points than the normal interest rate on your credit card. Furthermore, most cards allow no grace period for cash advances; interest charges start the minute you take out the advance.

Be a prudent lender. When lending someone money, make the deal as businesslike as you can, even (or perhaps especially) if the loan is to a friend. Write a simple "promissory note" stating the amount loaned, the interest charged, and the schedule for repayment. Both of you should sign it and keep copies.

LOBSTERS

Buy live—and lively—lobsters to be sure they're fresh. A lobster should move when touched, and its tail should roll back onto its body when you pick it up. (Make certain that its large claws are bound before you grab it, though.)

To keep lobsters fresh until mealtime, store them in the refrig-

How to Eat a Boiled Lobster

Dealing with a lobster is very much a hands-on exercise—and the more napkins, the better.

1 *Twist off the claws and the legs from the body. Break each delicate leg at the joint, then suck out the meat through the breaks.*

2 *Break apart the pincers of the claws; crack the shells with a nutcracker and use a small fork to extract the meat.*

3 *Holding the body in one hand and the tail in the other, twist off the tail. Pull the flippers off the tail's end and suck out their meat.*

4 *Insert a fork into the small tail opening and push the meat out through the larger end; cut it into bite-size chunks.*

5 *Crack open the shell of the body and pick out the small nuggets of meat inside.*

DIFFERENT KINDS OF LOCKS

This chart lists the major types of locks available for residential use. Locksmiths suggest both a principal and an auxiliary lock on entry doors. New privacy locks for bathrooms have safety devices that allow you to open the door from the outside if a child gets locked in.

TYPE	CHARACTERISTICS	USES
Cylindrical lock	A key-in-knob lock with an interior latch button or thumb turn.	Exterior door: principal lock
Dead bolt	A sturdy lock with a bolt that extends 2.5 cm (1 in.) through the strike plate.	Exterior door: auxiliary
Interconnected lockset	A strong lock with two bolts or a bolt and a latch, operated with one key.	Exterior door: principal lock
Mortise lock	A lock with a bolt and a latch recessed into a door's edge (mainly found in older houses); often needs a reinforcing plate because its installation weakens the door.	Exterior and interior doors: principal lock
Privacy lock	Latch button or thumb turn inside to lock door so it can't be opened from the outside. A hole in the outside knob allows release in emergencies.	Bedroom or bathroom doors
Rim lock	Mounted inside the door, near the edge, to allow vertical bolts to drop through the eyes of a strike plate attached to the door jamb.	Exterior door: auxiliary

erator, in an open container, covered with layers of damp newspaper. Don't put them on ice or in water, as either may kill them. You should cook and eat lobsters within hours of buying them.

The easiest way to cook a live lobster is to boil it. Carefully place it headfirst into a pot of boiling, salted water deep enough to cover it completely. Put a lid on the pot immediately. After the water comes to a boil again, cook a 450 g (1 lb) lobster for about eight minutes; for larger lobsters, add three minutes for each additional 450 g (1 lb).

Make it easier for your guests when you are serving lobster by cracking the shells and the large claws with a nutcracker or mallet in the kitchen, the way professional chefs do.

Contrary to popular belief, meat from big lobsters is as tender and sweet as meat from little ones. So if you're planning lobster salad, you'll save yourself a lot of trouble and mess by getting a 1.3 kg (3 lb) lobster instead of four 450 g (1 lb) lobsters.

LOCKS

Keep a door from locking accidently (if it has no bolt to leave out) by twisting a rubber band into an X, pressing it against the latch, and looping its ends around the knobs on each side of the door. The rubber band must be snug enough to hold the latch down without slipping off.

Thaw a frozen lock by heating the key with a match or cigarette lighter and then pressing it into the lock. If the key won't slide in

completely, keep warming the protruding portion. Wear gloves to protect your hands when heating the key.

Another way to thaw a lock is to warm it with your breath. Blow on it, using a cardboard tube, a drinking straw, or a rolled-up scrap of paper to channel the air.

LOFTS

Add space by putting in a loft. You could put your bed or your office or sleeping space for guests on the loft platform, depending on which would involve the least climbing up and down.

The ceiling's the limit. To accommodate a loft, the ceiling in your house or apartment should be at least 3.6 m (12 ft) high. This allows for no less than 2 m (6 ½ ft) of standing room below the loft and 1.4 m (4 ½ ft) above (enough to sit up in bed or sit in a chair at a desk), plus 30 cm (1 ft) for the platform of the loft.

Control clutter in a kid's room by building in a loft bed. Elevating the bed frees up floor space below it, which can be used for a snug, private niche and storage for clothes and toys.

Plan for ventilation before you begin to build a loft. Warm air rises, so the space close to the ceiling may get stuffy.

LONELINESS

Alone, not lonely. For an antidote to feelings of loneliness, learn to enjoy being alone more. Meditate, exercise, learn a new language or skill, plunge into a hobby, read a good book, take a long walk, go to a museum, and just enjoy your own good company—it can be the best.

Pet companions are invaluable for making you feel less lonely. They are there through thick and thin, they are good listeners when you want to blow off steam, and you don't have to argue with them about which programs you should watch on television.

New on the block. Overcome isolation in a new city by getting yourself involved as quickly as possible in community activities, from book clubs to sports teams. Volunteer for a local church, a charity, a community group, or a school committee.

Move kids with care. Your children can suffer major developmental setbacks from the loneliness that results from relocating. Include them in moving plans and house hunting. Let them decorate their own rooms. Above all, help them seek out activities that can help them make friends.

Nature nurtures. Ward off loneliness by immersing yourself in nature. Walk on a beach or in the woods, do some gardening, ride

EASY DOES IT — WHEN THE GIVING GETS GOOD

The best remedy to loneliness is giving to others. There are so many people in need, near and far, that your options for volunteering abound. Do whatever moves you most.

▶ *Feed the hungry. Prepare holiday meals for hungry families through local relief organizations. Or help out at an international hunger-relief charity.*

▶ *Tutor school children. Become a volunteer to help kids of all ages through local schools or public libraries.*

▶ *Help the disabled. Find a local organization that helps the elderly or housebound with shopping and errands. Or just visit with those you know for a few hours a week.*

▶ *Movers and shakers. If you're athletically inclined, become a Little League team coach.*

▶ *Not for profit. Get involved in a local or national non-profit organization. Become a museum guide or a big brother or big sister; join local environmental groups.*

▶ *Be a friend. Invite someone whom you suspect is lonely for coffee, a meal, or a movie.*

your bike on a quiet open road, relax by a lake or under a tree, or just smell the flowers.

LOTTERIES

You won? Be safe. Secure your winning ticket by signing the back, which seals your right to the proceeds. Make photocopies of the front and back to protect yourself in case the original is lost by the lottery bureaucracy. Keep copies in a safe-deposit box until you have your prize in hand.

Seek financial guidance. Get professional advice immediately about what portion of your money you need to set aside for the future, as well as how the money will change your entire financial situation—whether you should consider investing in tax-free securities, for example.

Live it up—a little. Few people are accustomed to dealing with large sums of money, so give yourself time to adjust to the new wealth. Indulge yourself by spending 10 percent of your first cheque on anything you want. Put the remainder of your winnings away for at least three months (in something safe, like a money-market mutual fund or 90-day CD) while you research ways to allocate your new money.

Avoid foreign lotteries. Lotteries in some foreign countries such as Hong Kong and Australia have been known to solicit customers in other countries through the mail. But buying lottery tickets through the mail in Canada violates federal law, so it's best to stick to the 6/49.

LOW-FAT COOKING

Cut the oil in cooked or prepared dishes by one-third to one-half. For example, when a recipe for hummus calls for 125 to 225 mL

(½ – ¾ cup) of olive oil, start with 60 mL (¼ cup) and add only enough to achieve the desired texture and taste. If it needs to be thinned, add yogurt, broth, or lemon juice. Except for the butter used in baking, the amount of fat you cook with is more a matter of taste than a requirement.

Skin it. Cut the fat content of chicken in half by removing the skin before cooking. Removing skin after cooking saves less fat, but it is still enough to be beneficial.

More beans, less meat. To lower your fat intake, replace some meat meals with bean meals. Like meat, beans are high in protein, but unlike meat, they are low in fat. As a bonus, beans provide lots of fiber. Eat beans with bread or a grain such as rice or corn to enable your body to use bean protein most efficiently.

Rack it. Cook roasts on a rack so the fat drips away. Avoid adding extra butter, fat, or oil to meat while it is roasting.

For low-fat vegetables, blanch, steam or roast them, then dress them with plain lemon juice or balsamic vinegar. If you crave oil, use a small amount of olive oil.

Spot low-fat cuts of meat. They have little or no marbling, and all the visible fat is in places where it can be trimmed off. For example, loins, round cuts, and chops are leaner than rib roasts and steaks.

LUGGAGE

Choose two small bags rather than one big one that, when full, is hard to handle in a busy terminal. A carry-on case with wheels plus a garment bag with a shoulder strap makes a practical combination that can be taken on board with you, avoiding the problem of lost luggage. Garment bags with wheels are also available.

Quality pays off. Luggage with reinforced corners and strong zippers is more expensive, but it pays off because it is less likely to come apart in the middle of a trip. Look for Cordura or other strong fabrics that resist rips.

Backpacks that convert into suitcases can be smart buys. Carry the conventional suitcase when necessary, but ease your load by turning it into a backpack.

Big wheels. A bag with two large wheels is easier to steer—and less likely to tip over—than a bag with four small wheels, which can be hard to keep balanced.

Reduce the hassle of lost luggage when traveling with friends and family by mixing people's clothing in each bag. If one gets lost, everyone will still have something to wear until it is found.

LUMBER

Light choice. When picking trim boards from a lumber pile, choose those that weigh the least. They're drier and will be the most stable.

Store boards up high, hung from a garage or basement ceiling holder or laid on a shelf. They will stay warmer and drier, and they won't be underfoot for you to trip over. Make sure you have room at the end to pull long planks out.

Pressure-treated lumber, used commonly for decking, has a naturally high moisture content when new. Butt the boards together as tightly as possible as you build with them; otherwise, as the wood dries out and shrinks, wide cracks are bound to develop where the edges meet.

A PACKABLE EXTRA BAG

It seldom fails—when returning from a trip, you discover that you need another piece of luggage. Here's the ideal solution. Outbound, these almost-weightless bags virtually disappear in the bottom of your suitcase; on the way home they easily handle the extra load. Made of durable, synthetic fabric, these bags are inexpensive, colorful, and incredibly useful. Available at luggage stores.

M

M A I L B O X E S   T O   M U T U A L   F U N D S

MAILBOXES

Think big when you buy a mailbox. Get one that can handle all the mail you normally receive, including newspapers and magazines. Otherwise, the letter carrier will have to overstuff the box, so that the top stands open, or leave mail outside the box. Either way, your mail could get wet.

For nonpostal deliveries, provide a separate box. Commercial carriers aren't allowed to leave anything in a postal mailbox.

When building a house in a rural area where standing mailboxes are required, find out early on if your box will be on your side of the road. If you will need to cross a busy highway to get to your mailbox, ask the local postmaster if the route can be altered to deliver on your side. It may take a while to arrange, but sometimes delivery routes can be revised.

The post for a rural-route mailbox should be made of pressure-treated wood or a naturally decay-resistant wood such as cedar or redwood. Add a waterproof coating every two years to ensure a long life.

MAILING & SHIPPING

Avoid long lines. Statistics show that post offices are least crowded on Thursday afternoons. Try mailing your packages and registering letters on that day whenever you can.

Protect mailing labels on packages by covering them with trans-

parent tape. They will stay unsmudged and in place until the package reaches its destination.

 To return merchandise, use registered mail so that you will have proof that it was received, or insure the package so that you will be paid the value of the merchandise if it is lost.

Damaged packages that arrive in the mail should be refused and returned to the sender. If you discover damage after the package is opened, hold the merchant responsible for paying the return postage. Call the company for instructions on how to send the package collect.

Compare rates when you are shipping heavy packages. Sometimes overnight air delivery services are cheaper than mail—and they offer home pickup.

To wrap packages for mailing, use brown paper grocery bags. Just cut off the bottom, slit one edge, and turn the printed side in. For smaller packages, cut open a manila envelope. Use wide mailing tape to secure your wrap.

Protect outgoing mail from rain by putting it in two plastic bags. Take off the wet outer bag when you get to the mailbox, but leave your letters in the dry inner bag to protect the addresses from other wet envelopes in the box.

Paste labels lengthwise on large mailing envelopes. Post office machines do not process big envelopes vertically, and the need for special handling will delay your mail.

MAIL-ORDER SHOPPING

Don't pay for postal insurance. Mail-order companies are legally responsible for making sure that

---

CUSTOMIZED MAILERS

Special mailers, designed to protect different kinds of items, make sending packages easier. Padded book mailers protect the corners of books and small boxes. Mailers specially designed for computer disks prevent them from being damaged in transit. All are available at stationery stores and the post office.

HOW TO MAKE THE MOST OF YOUR FACE

Makeup can do more than give you a fresh face; with proper application, it can compensate for small imperfections and help you feel better when you look in the mirror. Some of the best makeup tricks are listed below.

▶ *Hide undereye circles with a warm-toned concealer stick. Use a color one shade lighter than your regular makeup. Pat on with a fingertip, then set with a dusting of powder.*

▶ *Create bigger eyes. Apply coffee-colored eye shadow along the crease of the eyelid to emphasize the eye's shape. Use a smoky liner along the upper lash line and a rosy beige shadow on the brow bone. Finish off with a coat of black mascara on your lashes, applying it from the inner corner of the lid outward. Repeat on the lower lashes.*

▶ *Warm the color of sallow skin with a bronzing powder. Dust it onto the cheeks, nose, chin, temples, and sides of the neck for a healthy year-round glow. Be sure to blend the edges well to avoid spotty-looking color.*

▶ *Avoid hard lines when emphasizing eyebrows. Instead of heavy, dark eyebrow pencil, try using eye shadow one shade darker than your brow. Apply it with a brow brush.*

the merchandise they send arrives safely at your door.

Unordered merchandise that comes in the mail is legally considered a gift. You don't have to donate it to a charity or respond to a bill. Bills may constitute fraud, however, and should be reported to Canada Post.

Check the calendar. By law, a mail order company must ship an order within 30 days. If a shipping date cannot be met, the customer must be notified and given the option of waiting for the merchandise or cancelling his order for a full refund.

MAKEUP

To choose the right makeup for your skin type, be aware that brands labeled hypoallergenic are less likely to irritate sensitive skin. Those labelled noncomedogenic may prove helpful to oily skin by preventing pores from clogging.

Double duty. Save money by buying products with more than one purpose—if you need them both. Try foundation or moisturizer that contains sunblock, for example, or a compact with a combination cream-and-powder foundation. Use a sunscreen with built-in bug repellent or lipstick that contains an extra moisturizer.

For a becoming glow, choose a foundation color as close as possible to the natural tone of your face. To test the color, apply it to your chin and lower cheek, not the skin of your hand or wrist, which is much paler.

Keep loose face powder in a clean saltshaker. Dispense as much as you need into the palm of your hand or a small dish; then use a makeup brush to apply it.

Revive a hardened compact by rubbing fine sandpaper or an emery board across the top to loosen the powder. To prevent caking, store the powder puff upside down so that makeup and oil from your skin don't get absorbed into the powder.

MAKEUP APPLICATION

Moisturize first. Makeup can be applied more easily to smooth skin. Use a moisturizer before you apply foundation.

Always blend makeup carefully to avoid unnatural lines. Key spots for attention are the edges of your foundation at the hairline and jawline, the eye shadow in the crease above your eyelid and along your brow bone, and the blush along your cheekbones.

Use natural light for putting on your makeup to avoid an over-done, theatrical look. Colors that seem attractive at a bathroom mirror can look artificial when checked next to a window.

Use a lighter blush when you reapply makeup at midday. As the day goes on, oils from the skin may absorb and intensify color.

Makeup lasts longer if you apply a finishing coat of loose or pressed powder, then dab with a lightly dampened sponge to set it.

MANICURES

Never cut cuticles. Instead, moisturize them daily with a rich lotion and push them back with a cotton-wrapped cuticle stick. To heal damaged cuticles, apply petroleum jelly at night and soak them weekly in warm baby oil.

To make a manicure last, apply a colorless top coat every day. Protect your hands by wearing rubber gloves when you wash dishes or do other household and gardening chores.

Experiment with brands. People react differently to various nail polish formulas. Test several polishes to find out which one wears longest on your nails.

For short fingernails, choose a clear or light-colored polish. Using darker colors will only emphasize the shortness of your nails.

To cover a damaged nail, use an acetate press-on nail, which is easily removed. More permanent artificial nails can cause infections and, for some people, severe allergic reactions.

Summer savvy. Sand, salt, and chlorine can cause nails to split and chip. Wear a coat of clear polish on your nails for hot-weather protection. After each swim, use a small spray bottle to rinse your nails with fresh water, then massage sunscreen into them to restore moisture.

MARINATING

Flavor versus texture. Many culinary experts believe that marinades don't really tenderize meat; instead they soften the surface of the meat slightly and enhance the flavor. Tenderizing occurs when meat is pulverized or when it is marinated in juices containing certain protein-dissolving enzymes, such as papaya juice.

Marinade basics. A marinade is made of an acid (such as vinegar,

An Easy Home Manicure

A home manicure is easy to perform, even when using professional techniques. Although it's a small exercise, it can help to make you feel that you are well-groomed in every detail.

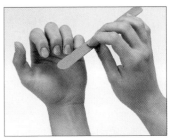

1 Remove any old polish or natural oils using a cotton ball saturated with a non-acetone nail polish remover.

2 File dry nails with an emery board, shaping them into ovals by filing from the outer edges to the centers.

3 Soak your fingers for a few minutes in warm, sudsy water. Rinse and dry your hands. Put cuticle remover on the bases of your nails.

4 Gently push back your cuticles with your fingers or with an orange stick. Buff your nails (unless they are thin and tend to break easily).

5 Apply a clear base, then two coats of polish. Use three strokes from nail base to tip, starting in the center. Let each coat dry for 3–5 minutes.

6 Allow your nails to dry for 20 minutes so that the polish hardens before you use your hands in any activity.

wine, lemon or other citrus juice); an oil (such as olive, peanut, or vegetable oil); and an appropriate combination of herbs, salt, and pepper. You can also add such ingredients as mustard, horseradish, or minced vegetables to enhance the flavor.

Poke holes in a thick cut of meat so that it can absorb as much flavor as possible from a marinade.

Where to marinate. Keep most meats in the refrigerator while they are marinating; it is unsafe to leave them at room temperature for longer than an hour.

A big plastic bag, zippered or closed tight with a rubber band, is an ideal container for marinating meat. It takes up less space in the refrigerator than a bowl or pan, and it's easy to pick up and shake or turn over every half hour. It also saves cleanup time.

MARRIAGE

Accentuate the positive. Most couples express their feelings only when they're angry or upset—not when they're happy. Tell your spouse at least once a week about something that he or she does that you love. When you notice—and comment on—your spouse's strengths, you won't take that person for granted.

 Never go to bed angry. Always come to some resolution—even agreeing to disagree—before you turn out the light.

Allow for time off. Everyone needs personal time and space. Make sure you and your spouse respect each other's need to read, take a solitary walk, and pursue special interests and hobbies.

Discuss your expectations about the way your life should be

The strength of a marriage often hangs on how a couple resolves differences. Some suggestions from the experts:

▶ *Learn to fight fair. Avoid attack phrases that put your spouse on the defensive. Use positive statements, such as "I like it when the room looks neat and your clothes are off the floor." It's easier to listen when what's being said does not sound like a criticism.*

▶ *Change your viewpoint to resolve ongoing arguments. Your spouse may enrage you by always making plans at the last minute. If you stop and realize that some of those plans have been fun and that life with her or him is never boring, you may still get frustrated but not quite so angry.*

▶ *Offer suggestions. When you criticize, be sure to provide some possible answers as well. For example, if you believe your spouse is favoring one child over another, suggest actions or activities that might redress the balance.*

▶ *Try marriage counseling when you're stuck. Instead of living with misunderstandings and constant irritation, let a trained third party help you both gain perspective.*

lived. For example, talk about what it would be like to have another child, say, or to vacation at a certain resort. If you have differing views, you can perhaps negotiate a satisfactory resolution before irrevocable actions have been taken by either of you.

Danger signs for a marriage: not making up after fights; being sure you're correct and your mate is always wrong; tabling arguments and emotions because you've lost the ability (or desire) to negotiate.

Stay close physically. Make affectionate gestures a habitual part of your relationship. Exchange hugs, hold hands, and enjoy the way these small things help to draw you together.

Switch routines. Take turns being in charge of various aspects of your lives, such as driving the kids, taking the car for repairs, making dinner, paying bills, and

planning vacations. Your marriage will be less predictable, and you will learn more about each other.

Take a second honeymoon. To add spice to your marriage, revisit the place where you went on your honeymoon. While there, take the time to recall happy memories of your wedding, your original honeymoon, and your years together.

MASONRY

Repointing trick. Make repointing brick easier by applying the mortar with a grout bag. Load the bag with mortar, place its nozzle in the joint line, and squeeze it as you pull it along. You can press the mortar farther into the joint with a pointing tool.

Clean brick walls and walks with a power washer on a low-power setting. To kill mold and mildew, add 250 mL (1 cup) of bleach to each 3.7 L (0.83 gal) of water. Rinse well with plain water.

Quick walls. To create a low wall (up to 1.2 m [4 ft]) around a terrace or garden plot, try using segmented retaining wall units, or SRWs. They look like mortared stone, but are much easier to put together, since the modular concrete blocks are held together with interlocking pins or tongue-and-groove joints rather than mortar. They cost half as much.

Drill twice, save time. When you have to drill a hole in stonework or brick, drill a hole smaller than the one you need, then do it again with the right-sized bit. This is both easier and faster than starting out with the larger bit.

MASSAGE

Ease neck tension by pressing firmly on the muscles at the base of the neck on either side of the spine. Using the fingertips of both hands, make circular movements, working up the neck to the base of the head, then back down.

Tension headache relief. Place the tips of both middle fingers in the center of your forehead, pointing toward each other. Gently stroke outward to the temples. Then place your thumbs where the temple meets the hairline and place the fingertips back on the forehead. Make firm, slow circles with your thumb and fingers for 30 to 60 seconds.

Shoulder self-help. To reach aching shoulder muscles, stand against a wall and press a hard rubber ball or an orange against the sore spot. Roll it gently.

Relieve stress with a hand rub. Hands respond quickly to massage. Use the thumb of one hand to gently massage the palm and the fleshy area under the thumb of the other hand. Use your fingers for massaging the back of the hand. Work on each finger individually, pulling the joint slightly.

MATTRESSES

Turn your mattress frequently to equalize the support. Switch it end to end as well as turning it over. Some manufacturers recommend turning every two weeks for the first three months, then turning every two months. To keep track, put a bit of masking tape with the date last changed at the top of the mattress.

Count coils. The number of coils determines the quality of an innerspring mattress. Full-size mattresses should have at least 300 coils inside; queen size at least 375. For king-size beds, the minimum should be 450 coils.

Think thick. When the coil count is the same, thicker-gauge steel is the winner. It is stiffer and provides more support. The lower the number, the thicker the wire —10 gauge is stronger than 12.

Tests for two. Bedmates should test a new mattress together. Move around—a healthy sleeper moves 40 to 60 times a night. When you move, the mattress

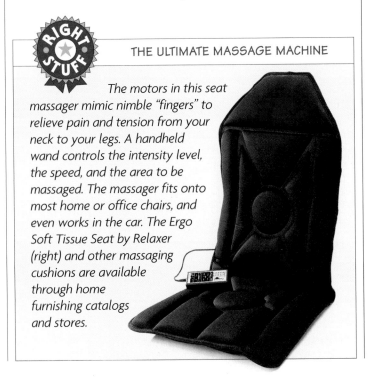

THE ULTIMATE MASSAGE MACHINE

The motors in this seat massager mimic nimble "fingers" to relieve pain and tension from your neck to your legs. A handheld wand controls the intensity level, the speed, and the area to be massaged. The massager fits onto most home or office chairs, and even works in the car. The Ergo Soft Tissue Seat by Relaxer (right) and other massaging cushions are available through home furnishing catalogs and stores.

should not creak, crunch, or wobble. If you bump your partner when you roll over, consider buying a bigger bed.

The bounce test is the first way to judge quality. Sit down on the edge of the mattress and bounce up and down. If you can feel the foundation, the mattress is not thick enough. Mattresses should be at least 18 cm (7 in.) thick.

Lie down. Labels like "firm" and "extra-firm" mean little. The best mattress for you is the one that feels most comfortable, and the only way to find out is to lie down on several mattresses in the store.

Keep your old mattress until the new one is delivered, or you may be sleeping on the floor. Failure to deliver when promised is a frequent consumer complaint.

MEASUREMENTS

To measure accurately, mark wood stock in the place where it will be used instead of transferring measurements with a tape or ruler. For example, when casing a door, lay the side casings in place, mark their top edges, and cut them. Then set the top piece in place, mark it, and cut.

To improve accuracy, align the end of a board with a tape measure's 1 cm (or 1 in.) mark rather than the end of the tape. Then subtract 1 cm (or 1 in.) from the final measurement.

Mismatched measurements. Try to use the same measuring device during a project. Although manu-

facturers aim for precision, tapes and rulers can differ slightly. Switching them risks throwing your measurements off.

Mark wood stock for cutting with a sharp pencil to draw the finest line possible. This is especially important when you install moldings or other trim elements that must make a tight fit.

Tack a long ruler to your workbench for quick, easy measurements. Gluing a ruler to your toolbox is another convenience you'll appreciate.

MEDICAL BILLS

Going to the dentist? If you pay for your annual checkup or other dental work by credit card, schedule your appointments just after your billing date. This way, if you are filing an insurance claim, your

refund will be processed and mailed to you before you are actually billed for the checkup, and you will incur no interest.

Choose generics. Unless you are completely covered by a health insurance plan, it is best to choose generic versions of the drugs your doctor has prescribed for you if available. They are far less expensive than brand-name drugs and have the same effectiveness when taken properly.

Ask for a break. If your doctor or dentist bills you for more than the standard fee paid by your insurance company for a certain procedure, discuss the extra charge with her. The doctor may accept the standard fee and waive the difference, especially if you have incurred large bills under her care. If not, consider switching health insurance plans.

MEASURING WITHOUT A RULER

A "rule of thumb" literally means using your thumb as a ruler. It dates back to a time before measurements were standardized, when parts of one's body were used as units of measure. Such measurements are still useful, but only as averages, because they vary from person to person. That is why these definitions indicate averages for the foot and the fathom—two names now used for the modern, standardized measurements of 12" (30 cm) and 6' (1.8 m) respectively.

Finger		The distance from the joint of the thumb to its end, about 2.5 cm (1").
Great span		The distance from the thumb to the little finger with fingers fanned out, about 23 cm (9").
Little span		The distance from the thumb tip to the index finger with fingers fanned out, about 15 cm (6").
Handbreadth		The palm's width, about 9 cm (3 ½ ").
Cubit		The distance from the elbow to the tip of the middle finger, about 45 cm (18").
Foot		The foot's length, between 25–30 cm (10" –12").
Pace		The length of a stride, about 81 cm (32").
Fathom		The distance from the tip of one middle finger to the other when the arms are outstretched on either side, about 1.8 m (6').
Reach		The distance from ground to fingertips when the arm is extended overhead, about 1.8 m (6').

RIGHT STUFF

MEDITATION MADE EASY

Meditation exercises, presented by professionals in the fields of medicine, religion, and psychology on audio tape and CD, provide an easy way to achieve physical, mental, and emotional well-being. A wide range of such tapes are available through book and record shops.

and turn off the television and radio. Whenever possible, change into loose clothing.

Try mini-meditation as a form of relaxation. Just be aware of something for a few minutes at a time. Watch clouds or people or focus on an activity such as walking the dog, brushing your teeth, or eating your favorite dessert. Even washing your hands can give you a quiet break.

MELONS

The sniff test. Your nose knows when to buy any melon (except watermelon). Honeydews, cantaloupes, and Crenshaws all smell sweet when they ripen.

A smooth scar at the stem end shows that a melon was not picked—it was allowed to ripen until it fell off the vine naturally. Melons that ripen fully on the vine always taste sweeter.

To peel a melon slice, place it on a cutting board and anchor it with your left hand (if you cut right-handed). Run a sharp knife along the rind, but only to the center of the slice, sparing the fingers of your left hand. Turn the melon end around and repeat the cutting process from the other tip. Cut it into chunks if desired.

MEDICINE CABINETS

Not in the bathroom. Most medications deteriorate in a bathroom's warm, moist environment. They keep much better in a cool, dry place, such as a linen closet. Put them on a shelf that's out of reach of children.

Discard old drugs—prescriptions and over-the-counter medications alike—after the expiration date (look on the label); they lose their effectiveness. Take them with you on your next visit to the doctor and ask that they be discarded as hazardous medical waste.

OLD SAW **Lock up medicine,** whether prescription or over-the-counter, if there are any children or pets around. And don't forget vitamins. A handful of certain vitamins can make a child seriously ill.

Keep a plastic spoon in the medicine cabinet. If you need to get up during the night to take medicine, you won't have to make a trip to the kitchen.

MEDITATION

Meditate to reduce stress and lower your heart rate, blood pressure, and blood glucose levels as well. Choose a mantra—a simple word or phrase such as "relax" or "one." Sit comfortably with your eyes closed, breathing naturally. Focus on your breathing, saying your mantra silently each time you exhale. Work up to doing this for 20 minutes twice a day. You'll feel refreshed and better able to cope with life's problems.

Relax from head to toe. For another meditation technique, lie down and, starting at your head, tense and then relax one set of muscles at a time. Continue down your body, breathing naturally. By the time you reach your feet, you'll feel calmer.

Avoid food before meditation. The digestive system often slows down during meditation, so meditate before or at least an hour after eating to avoid indigestion.

Choose a quiet place to meditate if you can. Close your office door or ask family members not to interrupt. Unplug the phone

Wash melons thoroughly before cutting into the fruit. Washing protects the flesh from insecticides and bacteria that may have accumulated on the rind.

Melon magic. Dissolve a 15 mL (1 tsp) of sugar in 250 mL (1 cup) of balsamic vinegar and sprinkle this sauce over the flesh of honeydew, casaba, or another favorite melon.

MEMORY AIDS

Special occasions. To keep track of special events in your calendar, color-code the entries—blue for birthdays and red for anniversaries, for example. You'll be able to see at a glance the kind of card you will need to buy.

Photographic memory. Write two columns of 10 words each. Stare at the lists for five seconds, then write down as many words as you can recall on a blank paper. Practice with simple words before applying this technique to words you need to use for work or study.

Name tag. If you think you'll forget the name of a person you've just met, start repeating it in your head as soon as you hear it. Imagine the person's face as you repeat the name to yourself. Make an effort to address the person by name during your conversation.

Brain regimen. Aerobic exercise sustains blood flow to the brain, maintaining a wide range of cognitive functions—including memory. To stimulate your mind, get on your stationary bicycle, take a walk, go for a swim, or walk the dog, and do it on a regular basis.

Secret codes. To easily remember your personal identification number (PIN) for banking or other accounts, choose a childhood phone number or address or a number that's equally familiar—but not currently in your wallet.

If it goes in your mouth, put it on a different shelf from other products. That will keep you from reaching for mouthwash and grabbing nail polish remover instead.

MENOPAUSE

Hormone replacement therapy (HRT) is strongly recommended for most menopausal women. Estrogen and progesterone in one combination or another can relieve the symptoms of menopause and protect against heart disease and osteoporosis. Studies indicate that HRT may increase the risk for breast cancer in a few women, but for most women the benefits far outweigh the risks. Discuss with your doctor how HRT might benefit you.

Eat foods high in vitamin E. Doctors recommend 200 to 400 mg of vitamin E a day to reduce night sweats and hot flashes. You can take the vitamin as a supplement or eat foods high in vitamin E including nuts, whole-grain cereals, and leafy green vegetables.

Hot flash defense. Dress in layers that can be taken off or put on as needed to reduce the discomfort of hot flashes. Keep your rooms cool, especially your bedroom. Keep consumption of caffeine, alcohol, and spicy food to a minimum.

A regular sex life raises the level of sex hormones and helps prevent vaginal dryness after menopause. Vaginal lubricants made for postmenopausal women also alleviate the dryness.

Weight-bearing exercises, such as jogging or walking, help to stave off the threat of osteoporosis as you age.

REMEMBER THE RAINBOW

For a simple way to remember things better, especially large blocks of information, associate the unfamiliar with the familiar. Try these time-tested devices.

▶ *Create an acronym for a group of words you must memorize. To remember the colors of the rainbow, for example, think of ROYGBIV. Each letter represents a color—red, orange, yellow, green, blue, indigo, and violet.*

▶ *To memorize a speech, use your house or office as an imaginary model. Create visual associations between each room and a part of your speech. Then mentally move through the building as you speak. For instance, if your first point is that women are using the Internet more, imagine the front hall lined with women at computers.*

▶ *Remind yourself of tasks you keep forgetting to do by leaving something in an unaccustomed spot. When you see it, you'll associate it with the task that needs doing. For example, tie a scarf to the door handle of the refrigerator to remind yourself to clean it.*

MENTORS & MENTORING

Go for it. Seek out mentors to help guide your career. Identify experienced professionals you admire and respect, then ask for an opportunity to meet—the worst that can happen is that the person says no. Even a short session with an expert in your business can be rewarding.

Advice for recent graduates. Call your alumni association to find out if your college has a mentoring program. Many schools will match new graduates with older alumni who are accomplished in their fields.

All in the company. If your firm offers a formal mentoring program, by all means take advantage of it. A senior adviser in the company can help you navigate departmental politics and gain a better perspective on workplace issues as you talk over your personal career strategies.

Share your experience. Take the time to serve as a mentor yourself to young people in your field. By doing so, you'll demonstrate your commitment to the future, and you will be rewarded with a satisfying sense of pride in their accomplishments.

MICROWAVE OVENS

When reheating a hot drink such as coffee in the microwave, use a moderate power setting; the highest level tends to destroy the flavor of the drink.

Dispel offensive odors from your microwave by placing a thick slice of lemon on a paper towel and microwaving it on *High* for about a minute and a half. Leave the lemon wedge in the oven overnight.

Freshen soggy snack foods, such as crackers or potato chips, by microwaving them on *High* for 30 to 60 seconds. Let them stand for 2 minutes, then serve.

Soften tough vegetables—raw acorn squash, for example—in the microwave briefly to make them easier to cut. Pierce the vegetable's skin with a fork or a knife point to vent it, then cook it on *High* for 1 to 2 minutes.

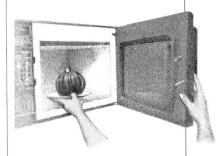

Steam-clean. Boil a bowl of water in your microwave before cleaning the interior. The steam softens grease, so that you can easily wipe the oven clean.

Spill cleanup. Cover cooked-on spills with a wet paper towel and run the oven on *High* for 10 seconds. The mess will wipe right up.

MILK

Out of the can. Use evaporated milk as a convenient substitute for fresh milk. Regular, low-fat, or skim, it has a long shelf life. Once reconstituted—add an equal measure of water—the milk works well in sauces, gravies, and baked dishes. (Condensed milk is a sweetened version—use only when called for in a recipe.)

Hidden helper. For a richer texture without extra fat, add 15 or 30 mL (1 or 2 tbsp) of nonfat dry milk to skim milk, cream soups, omelets, or puddings. The pow-

THE MICROWAVE CHEF

Wonders of convenience, microwave ovens work even better if you follow these tips.

▶ *Position food in the center of the oven with the thicker, denser parts—the meaty ends of drumsticks, for example—nearest the sides of the oven.*

▶ *Decrease seasonings by about 50 percent when microwaving; the process strengthens their flavors.*

▶ *For tastier results, buy leaner cuts of meats. Carve the meat into thin strips, slicing against the grain.*

▶ *Give meat a browned appearance by brushing it with a mixture of soy sauce and water before cooking.*

▶ *Use round, shallow dishes, and cover them with plastic wrap, wax paper, or a lid so that food heats more evenly. (Never let plastic wrap touch food while it cooks—the plastic can leach harmful chemicals as it heats.)*

▶ *Prevent overflows by making sure that cookware is tall enough to contain boiling foods such as soups and sauces.*

▶ *Look for cookware that can go straight from freezer to microwave—it's a real time-saver.*

RIGHT STUFF

When you're on the road, you'll never have to crane—or strain—your neck again with this titan of a mirror. It gives a broad view of the traffic that's behind you, making your life on the road safer and less stressful. This model, called the Rally/Wink Fullview Safety Mirror, is made of light-absorbing glass that also lessens headlight glare.

dered dry milk also provides extra calcium and protein.

Buttermilk substitute. If you need buttermilk or sour milk for a recipe, but have none on hand, try this alternative. Put 15 mL (1 tbsp) of lemon juice or vinegar into a measuring cup: add enough milk to equal 250 mL (1 cup); set aside for five minutes, and it will turn sour enough to use in your recipe.

Freeze it. You won't run out of milk if you freeze it in small zip-seal freezer bags, labeling each one with the amount. The bags store flat in the freezer and can be thawed quickly in the refrigerator.

When you buy milk, pick a carton or bottle with the latest sell date. But keep in mind that the date does not indicate exactly when the milk will go bad. If properly chilled, milk should last for at least a few days past the sell date.

Slim milkshake. Skip the ice cream and make easy and healthful milkshakes. For a single serving, use about 500 mL (2 cups) of milk (skim is the least fattening, and it whips up well). Freeze the milk for about 1 ½ hours until slushy. Put the partly frozen milk in a blender,

add the fruits and flavors you like, then whip. In seconds it's ready!

Minimize lumps. When you add milk to a mixture that contains flour or some other starchy ingredient, heat the milk before blending. Then remove the flour mixture from the heat briefly while you are whisking in the milk.

Low-fat chocolate milk. Don't fret too much if a family member will drink only chocolate milk, but do choose brands made with skim or 1 percent milk for adults (children need whole milk). The levels of calcium and other nutrients are about the same as in regular milk, but the sugar in the chocolate does raise the calorie intake.

MIRRORS

Mirror, mirror, on the wall. Hang a large mirror in a strategic location to give added length or width to a room. You'll get a similar effect with mirrored tiles (they are also less costly per square meter/square foot). You can even cover an entire wall with them.

Reflected light. To amplify the light from a deep-set window, line the sides of the window recess with mirrors.

Mirrored wall. Create a different kind of mirrored wall by grouping framed mirrors of various shapes and sizes on a wall, much as you

would arrange a group of framed pictures. If you can assemble a collection of attractive antique frames and have mirrors cut to fit them, so much the better.

Worn backing. Tape shiny aluminum foil over spots where your mirror's backing is in bad shape.

Framing ideas. Recycle an ornate antique picture frame by putting a mirror in it. Hang it above a bedroom dresser or in a small bath. For a larger-scale mirror, seek out an old wooden window frame to use as a rustic holder.

Magic window. Hang a mirror on the wall directly opposite a window. The reflected outdoor view will give the illusion of a second window in the room.

MAKING THE MOST OF TIGHT SPACES

Whether you are settled in a mobile home, camping in a recreational vehicle (RV), or cruising the coast on a boat, you need to know how to make the most of small living spaces. Below are some pointers that should help you.

▶ *"A place for everything and everything in its place" should be your cardinal rule. Mount tools and utensils around the kitchen, for example, so that they can easily be pulled down for use and just as easily replaced.*

▶ *Choose dual-purpose tools and equipment. A double boiler, for example, gives you two pots and a lid but takes up the space of only one.*

▶ *Add partitions, bins, containers, and shelves to existing storage areas. This organizes the space to hold more and also keeps things from shifting around and falling over when you are moving in an RV or a boat.*

▶ *Install boxes inside cabinet doors to hold garbage cans and wastebaskets; keep them lined with plastic bags to facilitate dumping when you're on the move.*

▶ *A plastic double hook over the shower rod gives you a place to hang wet things to dry. Hooks can be useful for many other purposes in tight quarters, from holding the laundry bag to suspending clothes that need brushing.*

MOBILE HOMES

Vacation living. Look for mobile homes for rent in resort communities. Such lodgings often prove to be more economical than a vacation house.

 Rent before you buy. Once a mobile home is installed, it can't be easily moved to another location. Before making a long-term commitment for a space in a mobile home park, live there as a renter for a few months.

Safety alert. Before you move in, find out how the mobile home was installed. Check for proper bracing to protect the home from earthquake damage and be sure there are sturdy tie-downs to hold the home in place during high winds. Since there are no federal standards for installing mobile homes and provincial regulations vary widely, you may even want to hire an engineer to evaluate your mobile home's installation.

Buy for pleasure, not for investment. Mobile homes—unlike conventional homes—do not appreciate in value over time. In that respect, they are more like cars than houses.

MODEMS

Hassle-free communications. Simplify your at-home computing by obtaining a second phone line for your modem, the device that connects your computer to the Internet. Otherwise, you may miss important business calls while you have your line tied up with Internet searches.

Insurance may beat a bargain. Before you purchase a modem, make certain that you can return it if you have a problem. This is not always the case, especially when you buy at a discount.

Faster is cheaper. If you're going to pay for Internet access by the hour, opt for a fast modem. Though costlier to buy than a slower one, it saves you money because individual tasks—basic surfing and downloading files, for example—will take less time.

MOLD & MILDEW

Wipe mold off book pages with a soft cloth and put them in the sun to kill the spores. (If the pages are damp, sprinkle them first with talcum powder, baking soda, or cornstarch, then dust it off.)

The basics. Get rid of excess moisture to combat mold and mildew problems. Use dehumidifiers and exhaust fans in a damp basement. Run air conditioners and heaters to reduce moisture upstairs. Keep a lightbulb burning in moist closets to dry out clothing and combat musty odors.

A magical elixir. When you're buying paint for your bathroom or some other humid place, have the paint store employee mix in an antimildew additive.

Dirt or mildew? To determine what's causing a spot on paint, plastic, or tile, wet a cloth with liquid laundry bleach and blot the affected area. If the stain disappears or lightens, it's mildew. If the spot stays the same, it's dirt.

No more scrubbing. Remove mildew from a plastic shower curtain by machine-washing it with detergent. Add one or two towels to the washing load to act as buffers. Hang the curtain on its own rod to dry.

The home remedy. Remove mildew from a painted surface with a mixture of 250 mL (1 cup) of liquid laundry bleach, 1.8 L (2 qt) of water, and 30 mL (2 tbsp) of a cleanser such as Spic'n'Span or Soilax. Wipe it on with a rag and scrub with a brush. Allow the mixture to dry on the painted surface, then rinse it off with water.

MOLDINGS

Installation. Buy or borrow an electronic stud finder. This handheld device finds the framing hidden behind the wall by measuring changes in the wall's density. Press a button and slowly drag the stud finder across the wall. A series of lights will come on to indicate the edge and the center of each stud.

Paint or stain moldings before you install them. Finishing the trim then becomes a simple matter of filling in and touching up the nail holes and the cut lines.

Short for savings. If you're on a budget, shop for short pieces of molding, which usually cost less than longer ones.

A perfect match. If some centrally located part of your home needs replacement molding and you can't find a match at the stores, use the molding from one of your closets or another out-of-the-way place. Buy a closely matching standard molding to replace the strips you remove.

MORTGAGE LOANS

Prequalify. Before you begin to shop for a house, ask a lender to prequalify you for a loan. This gives you an idea of the properties that realistically fit your budget, and real estate agents will look more favorably on you.

 Effective negotiations. Call several lenders to get an idea about the mortgage deals available in your area. Armed with this information, ask for decreases in rates and fees that aren't competitive. Few of the expenses are set in stone; for instance, you can negotiate closing costs, application fees, appraisals, lawyers' wages, and loan points.

Beware of 25-year mortgages. Some lenders now offer 25-year mortgages that require smaller monthly payments than shorter loans. The catch, though, is that you'll usually pay more in interest during those extra years.

Refuse prepayment penalties. Many provinces let lenders impose a penalty when a mortgage is paid off ahead of schedule. If you're handed a loan agreement with a prepayment penalty clause, ask that it be waived. If you are refused, ask about short-term open mortgages.

Refinance if you can obtain an interest rate at least 1.5 percent less than your current mortgage and if the savings from the lowered interest will pay for the closing costs in five years.

RIGHT STUFF

FAUX MOLDINGS

Add the look of antique molding or accent existing molding with a decorative wall covering like this design called Profile Moulding. Easier to apply than wallpaper— and cheaper than wood molding— you simply remove the backing and press the paper to the surface.

PROFILE MOULDING

MOSQUITOES

Take mosquitoes seriously. They are not just pesky insects that raise itchy welts—they can pose a serious health hazard. Spray yourself with repellent if you are likely to be in an area where you will come in contact with mosquitoes.

The natural oils of pennyroyal, eucalyptus, and citronella, available at health-food stores, act as mosquito repellents. Mix about 10 drops of one of these oils with 30 mL (1 oz) of olive oil, sunflower oil, baby oil, or almond oil.

Use amber lightbulbs on porches and patios; the amber color is less attractive to mosquitoes than white light.

 Prevent mosquitoes from breeding in the vicinity of the house by finding and draining all sources of water. After a rain, check the gutters for clogs. Also look for places where water accumulates indoors, including the containing pots and saucers of your houseplants.

Muddled puddles. If water accumulates on a flat roof, spray cooking oil over the area where puddles form. Mosquitoes are less likely to breed in water topped with an oily film.

MOTELS

Anyone for a swim? Swimming pools are nice when the temperature is steamy, but motels with pools sometimes cost more. If you won't have the time to swim or the weather won't let you, stay at a motel without a pool and avoid the extra cost.

Safe inside. Avoid rooms with doors that open directly to an outside parking lot; the most secure rooms are the ones along inside corridors. Ask for a second-floor room for extra safety, and be sure your door has a dead-bolt lock and a security chain.

Wedged shut. To thwart forced entries through a sliding door, ask the management for a barrier rod; never rely on a slider's lock.

Stretch your dollars. When deciding where to stay, look for motel chains that offer extras, like free breakfast and free local phone calls.

Discourage intruders by turning on the lights and the television or radio when you leave your room.

Taking an extended holiday? Rent a house or apartment for your family instead of two or three motel rooms; you get more space for less money. Ask tourist offices about rental services.

MOTION SICKNESS

Snacks for sufferers. To prevent queasiness, eat dry toast or crackers about a half hour before setting out on a trip. Also avoid big meals and alcohol.

Choosing a seat. When you're in a car or bus, sit by a side window—opened a little to let fresh air in—and make sure you can see out the front. On a plane, opt for a window seat over the wings, where the aircraft is most stable.

Steady as she goes. If you go on a cruise, request a cabin close to the ship's center. Stay on deck as much as possible and keep active. On a ferry, remain outside. Look at the horizon or a fixed point directly ahead of your course.

Avoid reading. Your eyes will focus on the words on the page, which will not be moving in conjunction with your body. This can cause dizziness.

Remedies. Try motion-sickness pills; or make gingerroot tea, which will stave off queasiness without making you feel drowsy. Take a half hour before traveling.

When all else fails and motion sickness strikes, find a comfortable place to lie down, close your eyes, and stay as still as possible. To help yourself relax, breathe as deeply as you can.

BAND PREVENTING MOTION SICKNESS

Forestall queasiness from air- or seasickness by wearing these wristbands. The nodules press key points that help you to maintain equilibrium (without the drowsiness common to motion-sickness medications). Look for Sea-Bands or BioBands in drugstores.

EASY DOES IT

Avoid having your possessions damaged during a move by keeping the following in mind.

▶ *Instead of stacking plates, pack them on their sides with crumpled newspapers cushioning and separating them.*

▶ *Rent portable wardrobes or closet cartons to transport hanging suits, jackets, dresses, and coats. You'll make up the rental fee from savings on pressing bills.*

▶ *Move valuable or fragile items such as computers, sound equipment, or bottled wines in your car. Wines, for example, should not be subjected to temperatures much higher or lower than 13°C (55°F), but on summer days the temperature in a moving van can exceed 38°C (100°F).*

▶ *Pack each lampshade in white wrapping paper (not newspapers) and put no more than two or three in a box.*

▶ *Prepare washers and dryers by bracing tubs and securing spring-mounted motors (check the instruction manuals for details). Disconnect hoses and place them in plastic bags in the tubs. Tape the doors shut.*

▶ *To prevent mildew, defrost the freezer and refrigerator two or three days before the move. Wash them inside and out with baking soda and water. Leave doors ajar so that interiors dry. Tape the doors closed just before the move.*

MOVING

Ask friends to recommend movers. Get references from the movers you contact and also check them out with your local chamber of commerce and Better Business Bureau office.

Pare down your possessions. Before you move, rid yourself of junk. Give it away to friends, donate it to charity, or have a yard sale, but don't waste time and money moving it.

Cost comparisons. If you plan to have professionals help you move, get at least two separate bids. Ask them to calculate costs for doing all the packing themselves versus allowing you to pack and for moving everything versus moving only the larger items.

Use old boxes. Collect them weeks ahead of the move from your local liquor store and supermarket and save all your old newspapers. New packing materials are expensive.

Get a floor plan of your new home or make one yourself. Figure out where each piece of furniture is going to be located. Check the widths of every door to be sure that your larger pieces will fit through them.

As packing proceeds, label every box with its contents and the room in your new home where it should be delivered.

Schedule your move for early in the morning, when the moving crew will be fresher and less likely to make any major mistakes.

Ease the transition. If possible, make your new home more livable by moving and unpacking kitchen staples and utensils, pet supplies, kids' toys, and toiletry items before the main move.

MOVING HEAVY OBJECTS

Plan your path before you lift a heavy object to move it. Walk through the path, taking special note of difficult spots—stairways, narrow spaces, loose carpets, low ceilings. Never wait until you've lifted the object to figure out how to get it from here to there.

Mechanical measures. Use a hand truck, dolly, roller, winch, or pulley to move objects too heavy to lift. To find a shop that rents such equipment, look under "Tool Rentals" in the Yellow Pages or try your local hardware store.

Don't do the twist. Point your toes in the direction you plan to move a heavy object. Then twist your body as little as possible as you move the load. A twisted position not only is awkward to maintain as you lift a weight but also exposes you to injury.

Warm up. Before you move heavy items, stretch and limber up your body just as you would for exercising. This reduces your chances of injuries such as pulled muscles.

MUSHROOMS

Buyer's guide. Unless you are cooking them right away, choose mushrooms with intact veils (the membrane on the underside of the cap). After the veils open, the mushrooms dry out quickly.

Save mushroom stems. Chop them up and add them for extra flavor to stock, stuffing, or soup.

Cleaning. Swipe mushrooms with a damp towel or mushroom brush just before preparing them. If you want to wash them, spritz with a sink hose or rinse briefly with water. Never soak mushrooms; it robs them of nutrients and flavor.

Make a little go far. Mix a small amount (about 14 g [½ oz]) of dried specialty mushrooms with a much larger amount (about 450 g [1 lb]) of button mushrooms. The intense flavor of the dried mushrooms will saturate the rest.

 OLD SAW

Paper, not plastic. Keep mushrooms in paper bags in the main section of the refrigerator. Plastic bags and fruit drawers reduce air circulation, leading to slimy, quickly spoiled mushrooms.

Danger in the wild. Choosing wild mushrooms to eat requires an experienced eye. If you are not trained to do it, don't take a chance with your life by picking and eating wild mushrooms.

Slice mushrooms in seconds. Cut off the stem and gently push an egg slicer through the cap.

Cook mushrooms in stainless steel or ceramic pans. An aluminum pan turns mushrooms gray.

MUSIC LESSONS

How old should a person be to start lessons? Some music teachers will work with a child as young as three years; others recommend beginning when a child is four or five. There's no upper age limit.

Carnegie Hall, here I come. The key to learning an instrument is practice, practice, practice. Don't commit to lessons unless you can devote at least 20 minutes almost every day to polishing your skills.

TRY A NEW MUSHROOM

Today's supermarkets and specialty food stores offer several types of mushrooms in addition to button mushrooms, the long-time favorite. Here's a chart to help you sort out the choices and decide which mushrooms you may want to try.

NAME	DESCRIPTION	FLAVOR & TEXTURE	HOW TO COOK & USE
Chanterelle	Trumpet shaped; flower-petal-like cap; golden to orange; dried available	Light, almost fruity	Braise, sauté. Use in pasta dishes, sauces, soups.
Cremini	Similar to button mushroom but with darker cap	Medium, with a dense texture	Sauté, steam, bake. Can be eaten raw.
Enoki	Tiny white cap; long, thin stem; sproutlike; sold in bunches	Mild, almost sweet	Sauté, braise. Use in soups, stir-fries. Can be eaten raw.
Morel	Small brown (also yellow, black) conical cap; hollow inside; short stems; dried available	Intense, earthy, with a tender texture	Sauté, steam, braise. Use in sauces, stuffings.
Oyster	White-brown color; shell-shaped cap	Dense, chewy texture	Grill, sauté, broil, braise. Use in sauces, soups, meat and pasta dishes, and rice.
Porcini/Cèpe	Thick stem; spongy underside; no gills under cap; dried available	Meaty, with nutty overtones	Grill, braise, sauté. Use in pasta and grain dishes.
Portobello	Large, flat, circular cap; thick stem	Rich, meaty	Grill, sauté, broil. Use in appetizers, entrees.
Shiitake	Large, thin, dark brown cap (thin, tough stem inedible unless cooked for long period)	Smoky, meaty	Sauté, braise. Use in soups, stews, pasta dishes, stir-fries.

Have you ever fantasized that you were a brilliant concert pianist playing with a major symphony orchestra or a great jazz saxaphone player jamming with the likes of Ron Carter and Kenny Barron? Compact discs by Music Minus One and Jamey Aebersold allow you to play along with great classical and jazz artists in your own home. A complete score accompanies each of the recordings to give you your cues. These play-along CDs and tapes are available at music stores.

Name that tune. Be sure to devote some of your lesson time to playing the music that you enjoy most. You're bound to progress faster that way.

Foundation building. Wondering what instrument to study? Try the piano. A basic knowledge of its keyboard helps you learn other instruments faster and better.

MUSICAL INSTRUMENTS

Rent to save, particularly if the instrument will be used by a young, growing student who may want a different one later. Visit several dealers and compare rates.

Ask an expert, a knowledgeable teacher or player, to check out an instrument you're thinking of renting or buying. Nothing discourages a novice more than attempting to learn on an inferior instrument.

Try before you buy. Ask the seller to allow you to take an instrument home for a trial. Look for a reputable dealer who guarantees repairs and offers a 100 percent trade-in value for a well-kept used instrument.

Beware of low-cost used guitars, which are often warped so badly that the strings are as much as an inch from the frets, making them nearly impossible to play.

Use it or lose it. To keep a wooden instrument in shape, play it! If unused, these instruments dry out and come unglued.

MUSTACHES & BEARDS

Which style? To decide which style of beard or mustache suits your face, have several copies made of a photo of yourself, then draw on different shapes of facial hair with a marker.

Trim a mustache when it's dry since wet hair lies flatter. For a neat, flat mustache, cut the top layer of hair slightly shorter than the bottom layer.

Groom your beard and mustache with a toothbrush—but not the same one you use on your teeth.

Tame unruly beards and mustaches with hair-styling gel. Work the gel into the hair with your fingers to create a smoother look.

MUTUAL FUNDS

Beware of bank mutual funds. Unlike savings or chequing accounts, or certificates of deposits, mutual funds sold through banks are not federally guaranteed. Before buying a fund, review its performance history.

 Go the distance. Commit yourself to owning a fund for at least five years. Trying to "flip" funds for a quick profit is sure to lose money: what you gain in return, you give away in taxes.

One for your money. If you're just beginning to invest in mutual funds, stick with one management company; however, make sure it offers the flexibility of numerous funds and the opportunity to switch between them at no cost.

NAIL BITING

A snappy reminder. Try wearing a snug rubber or elastic band around your wrist and snapping it every time you catch yourself biting your nails.

Keep nails well-groomed. Children tend not to bite smooth, attractive nails. Buy your youngster a manicure set and teach her how to use an emery board to smooth out those jagged edges.

Don't nag kids. Negative attention may only make the problem worse. Conversely, it seems to help if you give your child a small reward for each day he refrains from nail biting.

Bitter nail polish is often the best way to break the nail-biting habit. Look for commercial polishes blended for this purpose, with names like Nail Biter.

New outlets. Try to find a substitute activity when you feel the urge to bite your nails. Keep your hands busy by kneading an eraser or squeezing a ball. You might even take up needlepoint.

Chronic nail biters should be checked by a doctor or a psychiatrist. In rare instances the habit is associated with disabilities requiring professional attention.

NANNIES & AU PAIRS

Go to the source. Nanny schools are a valuable resource for parents seeking qualified nannies. But the waiting list is long for graduates, so contact a school as long as possible before you require a nannie's services.

Clarify your expectations. Nannies and au pairs normally focus on child care, not on running errands or doing housework. Spell out ahead of time exactly what you require of a nanny regarding household tasks.

Try it out. When you offer the job, emphasize that the first one or two months will be considered a trial period during which either of you can cancel the arrangements. This trial period gives both parties an easy way to back out.

Remember your taxes. Be sure to observe the requirements for reporting and withholding taxes for caregivers who work in your home. For more information, consult a tax adviser or request forms T778 and T1065, which detail tax requirements for child care, from your local taxation office.

NATIONAL PARKS

Reserve campground space. Most national parks accept campers on a first-come, first-served basis. Some national parks will take reservations up to two months in advance. To assure that a campsite at these national parks will be waiting for you, call 1-800-213-PARK.

Surf before you set out. A fully searchable list of Canadian national parks and national heritage sites are online on Parks Canada's website. Check out http://parkscanada.pch.gc.ca/parks/np/np_e.htm.

 Avoid the crowds. Visit major destinations during the off-season or take in one of the lesser-known parks. When you do find yourself at a crowded national park, search your map for nearby provincial parks, which tend to draw fewer sightseers yet offer many natural splendors.

Follow the kids. Most national parks offer nature courses, walks and activities for children; these can be fascinating, and an ideal way of discovering the unique ecosystems preserved in our parks.

NAUSEA

Soak in a warm bath to relieve nausea due to stress. Add four to eight drops of lavender oil or sandalwood scent to the bathwater.

The menthol in mint can help. Sip some peppermint tea or eat peppermint candy to soothe a stomach upset by overeating.

For nausea during pregnancy, eat several small meals throughout the day and avoid heavy or greasy foods. Before going to bed, have something starchy, such as rice pudding or soda crackers.

Drink colas or ginger ale for the nausea and vomiting caused by the flu. They not only ease stomach upset but help to replenish the fluids that your body has lost.

After nausea subsides, stick to bland fat-free foods until you feel better. Good choices include dry toast, bananas, applesauce, rice, clear soups, and soda crackers. Drink lots of water and fruit juices.

If you have recurring problems with nausea, do not delay in seeking medical attention. Nausea can be a symptom of a number of serious illnesses and injuries; many of them can have serious consequences if they do not receive expert care.

NECKTIES

Hang with care. Drape ties over a curtain rod attached to the inside of your closet. This not only keeps ties well sorted and visible but also protects them from creasing.

Bow-tie candidates. If you have a heavyset face or a short neck or wear your hair very short, a bow tie may not be flattering. Unless you're attending a black-tie-only affair, opt for a traditional tie.

Colors make the match. To wear intricate ties with striped or patterned shirts, pick a tie that has colors similar or complementary to the shirt's color. Patterns that seem to clash can blend this way.

How to Tie a Bow Tie

Tying a bow tie isn't much different from tying a shoelace. Knowing the moves will come in handy if you have to go to a formal event, or if your mate is all thumbs and can't help you out.

1 Put the tie around your neck, fold the collar down over it, and tie a simple overhand knot in the tie. Snug it up to your neck. One end should be about 2.5 cm (1 in.) longer than the other.

2 Make the first loop of the bow by folding the shorter end up under the longer one (which in turn will go down, around, and back up behind the first loop).

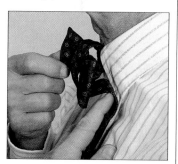

3 Take the longer end around and up behind the first bow. Now the new loop (at the left fingertip) has to go through the hole and out the other side to make the second bow, so reverse your hands here to get the loop through.

4 After poking the second bow through the hole behind the first bow, pull it out—holding the first bow with the other hand—until the two bows are the same length.

5 Tighten the knot by pulling the bows in opposite directions at the same time. Adjust the bows with finger and thumb on each side until the knot is tight and centered.

6 Fiddle with the bows until they are horizontal and lie flat.

NEEDLEWORK

Take it with you. Needlepoint and embroidery projects travel well. Put them in your purse or in a backpack and take them out at the doctor's office, in an airport waiting area, or wherever you find you have time on your hands.

Feeling bored and uncreative? Consider taking up needlepoint or embroidery as a hobby. You can learn the basics by buying a kit at your local craft store and then graduate to your own designs.

Make television time count by working on a needlework project while you are watching a program or a sports event.

Start a child off on needlepoint with a kit designed for kids. The canvases have very large holes so that they can be completed rapidly, and the large plastic needles are safe and easy to use.

If you have a computer, look into the various needlework programs that allow you to design your own patterns on-screen and transfer them to cloth.

NEGOTIATING

Go to the top. Spend your negotiating time with the most senior person you can find. Ask if the person you are talking to actually has the power to make a decision. If not, find out who does. Your negotiation efforts can be wasted if a higher-up later nixes an agreement you thought was complete.

Be prepared. You can speed up any kind of negotiation—whether it is a simple buy-and-sell deal or a serious contractual disagreement—by knowing all the facts about the transaction or dispute in advance. Gather documents, photographs, and evidence supporting your position.

Calculate your bottom line. If you have something to sell, decide upon the lowest offer you are willing to accept before entering serious negotiations, and stick to it. Negotiation is the art of compromise, but it's no good if you give up too much.

 Start high. At the outset of negotiations, always ask for more than you expect to get. A back-and-forth of offers and counteroffers is part of the process.

Have a cheque in hand. When you are the buyer, go to a negotiation meeting with a cheque or money order already filled out for the amount of your offer. A cheque on the table can be very tempting, even if it is for less than the amount anticipated.

Be likable. Always maintain a friendly attitude while sticking to your bottom line. Negotiation is all about psychology, and psychologists tell us agreeable people are more likely to get positive results than disagreeable people.

Consider alternatives. Open yourself to creative solutions that meet your underlying interests. For example, consider payment with services instead of cash.

PICK A QUICK NEEDLEPOINT KIT

Needlepoint is rewarding, creative, and fun, but it can be very time-consuming. If you are a beginner, start with a project that you can finish in two or three weeks. Find a canvas with a mesh count of between 7 and 10 (the lower the count, the faster you'll progress). Also, look for a canvas with a pattern printed on it showing where each of the colored yarns is to be used. Many needlepoint kits are available through shops and catalogs, such as these produced by Deluxe Designs and Erica Wilson Needleworks.

KEEPING NEW YEAR'S EVE SAFE

Here ares some tips for hosting a fun but safe party.

▶ *Start the party late, around 9:00 or 10:00 P.M., so that it lasts only four hours instead of six or seven.*

▶ *Offer door prizes to guests who agree to forgo alcoholic beverages in order to be designated drivers.*

▶ *Slow down—or stop—alcohol consumption shortly after midnight. Offer a selection of enticing hot beverages such as coffee, tea, hot cocoa, and warm nonalcoholic punch.*

▶ *Cap off the evening with a hearty breakfast of scrambled eggs, bacon, sausages, and sweet rolls.*

▶ *Contrary to popular myth, caffeinated beverages do not sober people up, but having coffee with the breakfast will put some time between the last drink and the drive home.*

▶ *Hire taxicabs or a minibus, or appoint designated drivers to take the guests home.*

▶ *If all else fails and you judge a friend unable to drive home, take those car keys away and arrange for a ride.*

NEIGHBORS

If your view is blocked, you must prove malicious intent to have any legal recourse, or you must prove that your neighbor's new structure or plantings violate local laws.

Draw the line. If you and your neighbor aren't sure of your properties' boundaries and one of you wants to build on questionable terrain, hire a licensed surveyor to determine the exact dimensions and location of your properties.

Tree trimming. If a neighbor's tree overhanging your property is diseased or hazardous, ask the owner to trim or destroy it. If he doesn't, he may be liable for damages. Check local ordinances.

Lend a hand. When a neighbor complains that fruits and nuts from your trees are falling into her yard, offer to help clean up.

Noisy neighbors. Ask occasionally noisy neighbors to be quieter and negotiate hours when, for instance, their teens won't have band practice. If serious noise problems persist, call the police.

For neighborly disputes, try compromise first. If that fails, check the phone book under "Mediation" or ask your local bar association about dispute resolution services. Some are free.

NETWORKING

Mingle at seminars. Professional conferences, workshops, and seminars are golden opportunities to network. During coffee breaks, lunch hours, and while exploring exhibits, introduce yourself to others in your field, enjoy a friendly chat, and exchange business cards.

Show appreciation. Take time to thank people who give you valuable information, advice, or referrals. Send a note or gift, and return favors when you can.

Write yourself note whenever you say you'll so something for someone. Review your notes daily and follow-up promptly. If you can't respond promptly, let that person know why. You'll soon establish a reputation for delivering on your promises.

Be a good listener. Build business contacts by making notes about conversations, and later impressing a client or customer by recalling an incident or fact that indicates your interest.

NEW YEAR'S EVE

Add a dash of spice. Go to the best or most interesting ethnic restaurant in town and ask them to prepare a typical New Year's dinner for you and your party.

Ask for help. After the Christmas rush, you're likely to be worn out. Ask your guests to bring food or wine for a potluck. The important thing is that you'll all be together.

Plan a "black-tie" affair by asking all your guests to wear a black tie—with their favorite dress-down, comfortable clothes.

To stretch caviar, make it part of a spectacular dish such as blini (the small Russian pancakes served with sour cream) or use it as an elegant garnish on a tray of less-fancy appetizers.

To save money on champagne, buy only enough to fill glasses for a first toast. Then switch to a less expensive sparkling wine.

NEWBORN BABIES

Keep baby's nails trimmed. Tiny hands with little control can do a lot of scratching, especially of baby's own face. Always use special baby nail scissors, which have rounded tips—if your baby wiggles at the wrong moment, no one will be jabbed or scraped with a sharp point.

No-slip gloves. Bathing a squirming, slippery infant can unnerve first-time parents, so pull on a pair of white cotton gloves for the task. The gloves will give you a slip-proof hold on him.

Make your own baby powder. Keep a powder puff and a covered margarine tub filled with cornstarch with your baby's bath items. By using cornstarch, you avoid the possibility of your baby breathing in any irritating substances in commercial talc.

Smile, please. From the earliest months of life, a baby's smile and then her laugh are forms of communication. To encourage your baby's good humor, talk to her, sing to her, and rock her gently. Around the second month, spend time trading cheerful looks and making funny faces at each other. Use a mirror so your baby can see both of you at once.

NEWSPAPERS

Make wrapping paper by printing or stenciling designs in strong colors on newspapers. Carve a potato to turn it into a printing block, or make a cardboard stencil, or cut sponges into interesting shapes. Dip the block you've made in fast-drying acrylic artist's paint, then press it all over the black and white paper.

When you vacation abroad, carry home foreign-language newspapers and use their pages to wrap the presents you bring back.

Dry newly washed windows with newspaper instead of paper towels; the chemicals in newsprint make glass shine.

If you are caught in the cold without warm clothing, stuff newspapers underneath your shirt or between your shirt and sweater. You'll be surprised by how much warmer you'll feel.

NOISE POLLUTION

Too loud? Prolonged noise can cause permanent hearing loss. You know the volume of your headphones is too high if you can't understand someone speaking from less than 90 cm (3 ft) away, if a person standing near you can hear the sound from your headset, or if you have to shout above the background noise when you try to talk to someone next to you.

Too long? Don't listen to a rock concert for more than three hours if the sound level is over 100 decibels (about as loud as a car horn).

Cut clatter by placing rubber mats beneath noisy washing machines and dryers, dishwashers, computer printers, or typewriters. Put gaskets around window air conditioners to deter vibration.

Make a quiet house. Arrange television sets and stereo speakers so that they do not touch the walls. Furnish your house with carpets and heavy drapes. If noise from overhead is a problem, consider installing suspended ceilings. If your plumbing or heating system makes noise, talk it over with a repairman.

Create a shield of neutral sound to drown out noise by running an air conditioner or electric fan, or a tape of soothing sounds such as running water or pounding surf.

PAINT WINDOW SASHES FASTER

Use newspaper instead of masking tape when painting several window sashes with panes all the same size.

▶ *Make a cardboard template that fits over one of the windowpanes. Don't fit it too snugly; the paint must touch the glass (barely) in order to seal the wood thoroughly.*

▶ *Count the windowpanes in the windows you are going to paint. With a utility knife and the template, cut out enough pieces of newspaper to cover each pane.*

▶ *Dip one of the precut pieces of newspaper in a dish of water, blotting off excess moisture on a folded newspaper.*

▶ *Pat the piece onto the pane you want to protect. It will stick to the glass. Then paint the sashes around the pane.*

▶ *When the piece of newspaper dries, it will easily peel off the glass, leaving the pane free of paint.*

(You can find recordings of natural sounds at your record store.)

Keep it down. Don't turn up the car radio to drown out traffic noise or turn up the TV volume while you vacuum. Unlike a neutral noise, these extra decibels only add to the din and risk further damage to your eardrums.

NOSEBLEEDS

To stop a nosebleed, have the person sit up and lean forward a little so he doesn't swallow blood. Gently pinch his nostrils together and hold them together for five minutes. If the bleeding continues, keep holding his nostrils together for as long as it takes to stop the blood flow.

Chill a nosebleed. While the person holds a tissue to her nose, apply crushed ice in a towel to her nose and cheeks. Or crush a little ice and hold it under her upper lip until the bleeding stops.

Sleep with a humidifier in your bedroom in the winter or whenever the air in your house is dry. It helps you keep nasal membranes from cracking and bleeding.

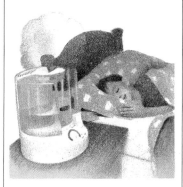

Sneeze with your mouth open. Sneezing through your nose alone may rupture nasal membranes and cause a nosebleed.

Call the doctor when blood from a nosebleed goes down the back of the throat rather than out

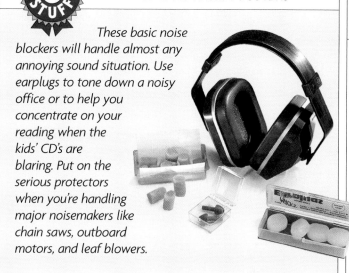

CLASSIC RACKET BUSTERS

These basic noise blockers will handle almost any annoying sound situation. Use earplugs to tone down a noisy office or to help you concentrate on your reading when the kids' CD's are blaring. Put on the serious protectors when you're handling major noisemakers like chain saws, outboard motors, and leaf blowers.

the nostrils. This type of nosebleed is more common when the bones of the face or nose have been injured. When you suspect such a skull injury, don't try to stop the nosebleed; pressure could make the injury worse.

After the bleeding ceases, refrain from blowing your nose for several hours. Try not to lean over or lift anything heavy, and don't exert yourself any more than is absolutely necessary.

In dry air or at high elevations, prevent the nosebleeds caused by low humidity by rubbing a little petroleum jelly inside both of your nostrils. Since cold winter air can also be drying, use petroleum jelly under these conditions, too.

NUISANCE CALLS

Slow down telemarketers when they call by asking them to remove your name from their list. If the same company persists in calling you, report the company to the Canadian Direct Marketing Association.

Help to prevent calls by letting telemarketers around the country know that you are not phone-

friendly. Send a postcard to the Canadian Direct Marketing Association, One Concorde Gate Suite 607, North York, Ont., M3C 3N6, or call (416) 932-2262. Ask that your name be removed from all members' telemarketing lists. (Your request is good for a period of five years.)

 Don't even say goodbye. The great thing about telephones is that you control the connection. When someone annoys you with phone calls, your first line of defense is simply to hang up.

Control unwanted calls by using the latest new technology. Check with your telephone company about blocking certain calls from the central office. Also, screen calls through voice mail, a caller-identification system, or an answering machine.

Report repeaters. Keep a pen and pad by the telephone and note when you get annoying calls. Report them to the telephone company or to the police.

NURSING HOME VISITS

Bring photos of family events such as school plays, Little League games, and Christmas; they will help keep the patient feeling she's part of the family.

Favorite foods are always welcome. Be sure to bring enough so that treats can be shared with roommates, nursing home staff, and friends in nearby rooms.

Special guests. An occasional visit from a grandchild, a new baby in the family, or an old friend is sure to bring cheer. Don't make the visit a big suprise, however; give the resident time to prepare.

Outings. As long as the resident is able, a walk in the neighborhood, a meal at a restaurant, a holiday visit, or even a ride in the car can break the daily routine.

Joint project. Puzzles, games, and crafts projects that you can work on together will make visits brighter. Reading a new chapter of a book aloud on each visit is another welcome diversion.

NURSING HOMES

Check options. Nursing homes are not the only alternative when care for a disabled person is required. In some cases adult day care centers, assisted living facilities, or in-home care may be more appropriate. For help in determining what's available in your area, check for senior's counselling services or nursing homes in your Yellow Pages.

Ask for provincial evaluation. Many provinces inspect nursing homes to ensure that they meet health codes and care standards. Copies of reports and current licenses should be available to any interested party on request.

Helpful extras. Life is pleasanter in facilities with room telephones, in-house beauty parlors, crafts classes, and recreational options.

 Good signs. Cleanliness, a cheerful atmosphere, and a warm, friendly staff are the crucial indicators of a well-run nursing home.

Ease the adjustment. Move in familiar books and tapes, family photos, favorite quilts, and pillows to help to make the room cozier and more familiar.

NUTRITION LABELS

Be wary. Terms like "low fat" and "high fiber" can appear on labels only if they meet strict government standards; other terms, such as "lite", are not standardized. Check the label to be sure the product actually contains fewer calories than similar foods.

Health claims indicating that a food helps reduce the risk of osteoporosis, cancer, coronary heart disease, or high blood pressure, require government regulation. For example, a food that is supposed to help prevent osteoporosis must provide at least 200 mg of calcium per serving.

Watch for signs or handouts at the produce department at your market; many grocers' associations have begun to post nutritional facts on fruits and vegetables displayed in the produce section.

NUTS

It's nutty not to eat 'em. Yes, nuts and seeds are high in calories and fat—but most are also high in unsaturated fat, the kind that helps lower cholesterol. Nuts and seeds are also loaded with protein and vitamin E, and seeds provide some fiber.

SELECTING A NURSING HOME

Seek recommendations from family, friends, and professionals such as doctors, social workers, or clergy. Visit prospective homes often and at different times of the day to evaluate how well they are run.

▶ *Talk to residents and ask to visit their rooms.*

▶ *Visit lounges and recreation areas; look for a friendly, relaxed atmosphere and activities residents seem to enjoy.*

▶ *Eat a meal in the dining room; note whether the food is nutritious and tasty and if the staff is respectful.*

▶ *Ask the management if a doctor is always on call and if the home is affiliated with an accredited hospital.*

▶ *Find out if residents receive transportation to doctors' appointments, nearby shops, and plenty of outside events.*

Nutrition Facts labels are required on some processed foods by the federal government. The label lists those nutrients of greatest concern to consumers, and gives a quick reference to all the nutritional information you need in order to select the healthiest foods. The label below is from a 300 g box of cereal.

Calories per serving are noted; calories from fat are also highlighted so you can quickly see the relative amount of fat in the food and choose low-fat items.

Vitamins and minerals are listed in normal (not bold-faced) type so that if a product contains many vitamins and minerals, the listing does not overwhelm the more important basic list. Calcium, iron, and vitamins A, C, and D are listed on many products, whether or not they are contained in the food.

Percent daily values for each nutrient are based on a 2,000-calorie diet, an average caloric intake for most Canadians. These values will be different if your caloric need is higher or lower.

Nutrition Facts

Serving Size 30g (1⅔ cup) + 125 mL (½ cup) milk
Servings Per Container: 12

Amount per serving
Calories 175 (740 kJ)

	% Daily Value*
Total Fat 2.6g	less than 1%
Total Carbohydrate 32g	10%
Dietary Fiber 0.8g	3%
Starch 23g	-
Sugars 8.5g	-
Sodium 355mg	15%
Potassium 230mg	-
Protein 6.4g	-

Vitamin A 7%	•	Calcium 14%
Vitamin D 23%	•	Iron 29%
Vitamin B1 50%	•	Niacin 13%
Vitamin B2 63%	•	Phosphorus 12%
Vitamin B12 25%	•	Zinc 6%

* Percent Daily Values are based on a 2,000-calorie diet. Your daily values may be higher or lower depending on your calorie needs.

Calories		2,000	2,500
Total Carbohydrate		300g	375g
Total Fat	Less than	65g	80g
Dietary Fiber		25g	30g
Sodium	Less than	2,400mg	2,400mg

Serving sizes are standardized for each food (in everyday terms and metric measurements) to reflect the amount that most people consume. The number of servings per container is also included.

Important basic nutrients. Fat, cholesterol, sodium, carbohydrates (including dietary fiber and sugars), and protein are the nutrients of greatest concern to consumers. Listed with each nutrient are the number of grams and the percentage of the recommended daily requirement in 1 serving.

General nutrition chart. This listing gives the amount, in grams, of each of the most important nutrients required for a healthy diet.

For longer-lasting nuts, look for unshelled, unsalted ones. Plan to use them within a month or two, though, because they can turn rancid if stored longer.

Buy nuts in bulk. Health-food stores display them in bins and barrels and pass the savings along to customers who don't mind the lack of packaging.

Add freshly ground nuts into soups, stews, and ground meat dishes for a pleasant surprise in both flavor and texture. Some nuts, like peanuts or walnuts, can even be added whole.

Store nuts in airtight jars and cans in the refrigerator; freeze if you are storing them for more than a few months. Almonds and cashews last longer than other kinds of nuts. Walnuts, pecans, Brazil nuts, hazelnuts, and peanuts are especially perishable.

If you are allergic to peanuts (as thousands of people are), be sure to read labels on processed foods carefully. Peanuts are sometimes used as a substitute for walnuts or almonds in processed foods—the peanut flavor is replaced with another one. So look for peanuts in the fine print of the ingredients list.

If you use a food processor to grind nuts, be careful not to overprocess them. Pulverized nuts release their oils, which bind the bits together and create a paste or puree very quickly. Grind nuts 250 mL (1 cup) at a time, pulsing for only a few seconds at a time. If the recipe calls for sugar, add a little of it to the nuts to help prevent binding. Grind toasted nuts only after they have cooled.

 Toast nuts and seeds to intensify their flavor. Spread them in a shallow pan, then place in a 175°C (350°F) oven (or toaster oven) for about 10 minutes, or until they darken. You'll smell the sweetness of natural sugars and oils coming to the surface.

OFFICES

Reduce distractions by positioning your desk so that your back is turned to the entrance of your workspace. You'll be less often sidetracked by daily office traffic.

Cubicle cacophony. If the audible conversations of your coworkers make your cubicle too noisy for you to concentrate, use earplugs or even headphones to muffle the sound.

Keep personal business to a minimum. Feeling at home in your office doesn't mean nonstop phone conversations and visits from family and friends. Decorate your office or cubicle with favorite photographs—and leave your home life at home.

Professional decorations. To present an image of professionalism in your office or cubicle, have successful work projects framed and hung, along with any awards or certificates you have earned.

Beat the cold by keeping a sweater or jacket on a hanger in back of your door. Office air-conditioning can be chilly enough to make you sick.

OILY SKIN

See a doctor. If your oily skin is associated with pimples, a dermatologist can best help you break the cycle of clogged pores and infections—whatever your age. Oily skin and pimples are not a problem limited to teens. A topical antibiotic may be prescribed.

Use special products to keep your skin free of excess oils—oil-free sunscreen, water-based foundation, and oil-blotting powder. Avoid astringents, however, because they are harsh and can irritate the skin.

Cleansing technique. Oily skin, like dry skin, needs gentle cleaning. Wash with a mild unscented soap or cleanser, such as Dove, Basis, or Cetaphil. Lather up with

your hands rather than a washrag, and rinse well. Don't wash your face more than twice a day.

Oatmeal mask for oily skin. For a soothing, moisturizing pick-me-up, make a paste of oatmeal and warm water. Apply to your face—avoiding the area around the eyes—and leave on for 10 minutes. Rinse away with warm water.

Causes. Oily skin is hereditary, not the result of bad diet. To keep from aggravating it, avoid too much stress, not chocolate.

ONIONS

No more teary eyes. Put onions in the freezer for up to 30 minutes before cutting them. This reduces the onion spray that's released into the air, keeping tears at bay.

 Fight odors. Rub lemon juice over your hands after peeling onions to take away the smell. Then wash your hands in soap and water.

Easy peel. To peel a batch of onions, blanch them first in boiling water for 10 seconds, then quickly immerse them in cold water. This will loosen the skins and make them easier to peel.

FOOTREST FOR THE OFFICE

Sitting for long hours can cause discomforting pressure on your back and lower legs. To relieve stress and stay comfortable, get up and stretch periodically and put your feet on a footrest. The model on the right rocks to boost blood circulation. The footrest on the left has tilt and height adjustments to accommodate the length of your legs, and a textured surface to massage your tired feet. Footrests are available through many catalogs and at housewares stores.

Just a slice. If you need only a small portion of an onion, leave the peel on and cut a slice from the middle. Fit the remaining halves back together, wrap in plastic, and refrigerate.

Cooking onions. For an intense taste, cook onions until they are translucent. For a mellower flavor, sauté them until they turn golden. Cook onions slowly for a long time for a rich, sweet flavor and brown color. Cooking onions over high heat produces a bitter flavor.

A parting of ways. Although onions and potatoes taste terrific when cooked together, they should be stored separately when raw. Potatoes emit moisture and a ripening gas; both cause onions to decay faster.

A ready supply. Freeze uncooked chopped onions in an airtight plastic bag, pressing out all the air. Use them for cooked dishes within three months; there is no need to thaw them first.

ORGANIC GARDENING

Good neighbors. Planting two synergistic plants near each other can increase crop harvest, discourage pests, or improve the soil. Snap beans planted near sweet

Although there is no cure for osteoporosis, you can work to stave it off and lessen its effects with a daily health routine. The younger you start, the better.

▶ *Take in from 1,000 to 1,500 mg of calcium a day, the amount recommended for women to protect them from osteoporosis. This means eating three to four servings of low-fat dairy products and other sources of calcium, in addition to taking a calcium supplement.*

▶ *Get enough vitamin D in your diet. Vitamin D allows the body to absorb calcium and stimulates the growth of bone cells. You can get it from drinking fortified milk, eating fish, or being in the sun for about 30 minutes a few times each week.*

▶ *Exercise for healthy bones. If you participate in weight-bearing exercise, such as brisk walking, jogging, tennis, aerobics, and weight lifting, your body builds more bone tissue, delaying the onset of osteoporotic conditions.*

peas, for example, benefit from the pollinating insects attracted by the peas. Setting French marigolds in the vegetable garden repels nematodes. Planted together, peanuts and squash both increase in productivity.

Water saver. Boost the organic content of your soil by digging in plenty of compost or peat moss at planting time. Such enrichment early in the season can multiply by a factor of six or more the amount of water the soil can absorb. You won't need to water as often.

Fight fungal diseases by setting plants far enough apart to provide good air circulation. Since fungal diseases attack damp foliage, water fungus-prone plants in the morning, when leaves dry quickly.

OSTEOPOROSIS

Not just dairy products. Help prevent osteoporosis, a disorder in which bones become more brittle as you age, by eating dairy

products and other calcium-rich foods, such as arugula, canned salmon, and sardines. People who suffer from lactose intolerance can take calcium supplements in place of dairy foods.

Get calcium from antacids. If your diet is low in calcium, take sodium-free antacid pills, which consist mainly of calcium carbonate. These tablets are effective and less expensive than traditional calcium supplements.

Consider estrogen. If you've reached menopause, hormone (estrogen) replacement therapy combined with 1,500 mg of calcium a day helps to prevent osteoporosis. Even if you already have osteoporosis, estrogen helps to prevent dangerous fractures.

If you suspect osteoporosis, consult your doctor, who can recommend a bone-density test. This painless X-ray procedure tells you if you have the disease or if you are at risk for it. Keep in mind that it can be inherited.

OUTDOOR FURNITURE

Treat the feet. Each spring, flip your wooden lawn furniture upside down and brush some shellac on the feet. This prevents rot at its starting point—where the wood touches the ground.

The cream of the crop. Choose teak for your outdoor furniture; it not only resists decay but also weathers naturally to a handsome silver. Redwood is also highly resistant to rot, but unless treated annually with a sealer, it cracks and turns a splotchy gray.

Weatherproof with wax. Coat the metal parts of your outdoor furniture with automobile wax. Applied once a year, the wax weatherproofs the metal, adding years of life to your furniture.

OUTDOOR LIGHTING

An automatic timer. To come home to a well-lit house, set the timer to turn on garage and porch lights at sunset. Then set the lights to go off later in the evening, and you'll never have to worry about leaving lights on overnight.

No wiring required. If you need only one or two lights—to illuminate an outdoor flight of stairs, for example—and there is no electrical outlet nearby, consider solar-powered fixtures. Though relatively expensive—a single light may cost from $60 to $120—they install without wiring and have built-in switches that turn the lights on at nightfall.

MOVEMENT-SENSITIVE LIGHTS

Mounted over your garage door or front steps, motion-sensitive floodlights turn on as you steer your car into the driveway or walk toward the door. Such lights also alert you when an unexpected visitor shows up, and the shock of having the lights turn on can deter prowlers. Motion sensitive lights are available at lighting and hardware stores.

Keep your light to yourself. To avoid conflict with the neighbors, make sure that any outdoor lighting you install doesn't illuminate surrounding yards or homes.

OUTLET SHOPPING

Brand-name game. Don't think that buying clothes with a top designer's name on the label is always a bargain; some firms manufacture lower-quality merchandise expressly for outlet stores.

Do a double check. Visit regular retailers first so that you have a basis of comparison with the prices found at outlet stores.

Irregulars are irresistible when you know that flaws won't show. Prices for socks, underwear, shirts, and T-shirts from major manufacturers are often reduced by half if they have a slight snag or a poorly sewn label. Some outlets offer catalogs that let you do your discount shopping at home; ask to be put on the mailing list.

Before you buy a garment in an outlet store, examine it for flaws. If the item is damaged, but you are still willing to buy it, ask the manager for an even greater reduction in the price.

Whose name? Discounters often advertise "famous maker" but cut the names from labels and tags. However, federal law requires labels to carry a specific number assigned to each manufacturer, and these numbers can be found in a manufacturers directory, available in large libraries. Consumers can look up the numbers of their favorite designers and then match them to the numbers on the tags.

Go for the biggest bargains, which are usually found on holiday weekends like Easter weekend and Labor Day.

OVENS

Oven racks. When scrubbing your oven racks, place one directly atop the other and scour both racks at the same time.

Cooking in a crowded oven. Ensure even heating by letting the air in the oven circulate as freely as possible. Keep dishes as close to the oven's center as you can, but stagger the arrangement so one item is not directly above another.

The aluminum safety net. Avoid messy overflows by putting a baking sheet lined with aluminum foil or just a sheet of foil beneath foods that tend to bubble over as they cook.

Salting the spills. As soon as you notice a mess in the oven, drizzle a layer of salt on it. For hard-to-reach spills, use a spoon—the longer its handle, the better. Pouring salt on food spills reduces odors and smoke. And when the oven cools down, the spill will be easier to clean.

Self-cleaning smarts. Turn on your oven's self-cleaner immediately after you have finished cooking. Doing so is an energy-efficient way to clean because your oven doesn't have to be heated a second time.

OVER-THE-COUNTER MEDICATIONS

Inspect packaging, making sure that there are no signs of tampering. Check to see if the safety seals are in place, and don't buy a package that has any cuts or tears. When you open medicine, make sure the pills match each other.

Read the label when you buy a new package of medication, even if it's something you've taken in the past. Sometimes manufacturers change the strength of a medication or add new warnings.

Look for the active ingredient in the drug, then buy the cheapest brand. A generic or store brand of a drug is often less expensive than a brand name.

Avoid drug interactions by telling your doctor about any over-the-counter medications you use. Consult your doctor before using any nonprescription medication for a long period. Some, such as nasals sprays, eye drops, and laxatives, can be used safely for only a few days at a time.

Is bigger better? Buying the large economy size of an over-the-counter drug isn't a good deal if its expiration date comes before you use it up. Buy only as much medication as you'll use in a year.

OYSTERS

Are they fresh? Choose oysters with sealed shells or those that close their shells when tapped. Shucked oysters should give off a scent reminiscent of the sea.

Open sesame. Soak oysters for five minutes in carbonated water. This relaxes the muscle, making the shell a snap to open.

Grilled oysters. Place unshucked oysters on your grill, 8 cm (3 in.) from a hot fire and roast for 5 minutes. Serve the oysters in their shells straight from the grill. Provide forks and cocktail sauce or hot butter for dipping.

COMPARING PAIN RELIEVERS

Taken in the proper dose, over-the-counter pain relievers are all effective for fever and aches. However, each of the medications has an up side and a down side; ensure your health by knowing these pros and cons.

TYPE	ADVANTAGES	DISADVANTAGES
Aspirin	Low doses can help prevent a heart attack.	Can cause gastrointestinal upset; long-term high doses may lead to hearing loss or tinnitus; prevents blood clotting; should not be taken by children or teenagers, or those with certain ailments, such as ulcers, asthma, liver and kidney diseases, and bleeding disorders.
Aceta-minophen	Most gentle on the stomach; safe for relieving fever in children and teenagers.	Not for people with liver or kidney troubles; chronic use of heavy doses can damage kidneys; may lead to liver disease and even liver failure in heavy drinkers.
Ibuprofen	Recommended for muscular aches and pains.	May interfere with diuretics and other hypertension drugs; can cause liver damage and gastric bleeding in heavy drinkers; people who can't take aspirin also should avoid this medication.
Naprosyn sodium	Long-lasting relief (up to 12 hours).	Can cause liver or gastric bleeding in heavy drinkers; should not be used by people with ulcers, asthma, or kidney disease or by pregnant or breast-feeding women.

PACKING

Make a list to avoid leaving things behind. Keep the list after you've packed, in case your luggage goes astray and you need to account for the contents.

Sizing up. To save space, pack mini-bottles of shampoo and lotions. Don't fill them to the top, as pressure may cause the contents to expand and leak. To be safe, put them in a plastic bag.

Packing by colors. When packing, select clothes that work together by sticking to one or two basic color themes—brown, black, navy, and gray are the most practical. You will need fewer accessories, especially those prime luggage space hogs—shoes, boots, and handbags.

The perfect fit. Avoid overpacking your bags, which can lead to damaged hinges, zippers, and seams. Underpacking is almost as bad because it leaves luggage vulnerable to rips and dents.

Leave heirlooms at home. Try never to pack valuable items of clothing or jewelry, especially those things that are irreplaceable. Even the best-watched bag can sometimes get lost.

PAINT

A little dab will do. When choosing a color, have the store mix a modest batch for you. At home, paint a good-sized section of the actual wall to see how the color will look before you buy enough for the whole room.

Marine paints. When painting an item or room that will be exposed to excessive moisture, buy durable, mildew-resistant deck paint, usually found at boating-supply as well as paint stores.

Stir it up. To make mixing paint easier, use a paint stirrer with holes in it. Perforated metal ones are sold at hardware stores.

Punch drainage holes in the groove at the top of a paint can. Excess paint left after you pour it will drip back into the can instead of settling in the groove and then overflowing when you put the top back on. (Make the holes wide enough so the thick paint will drip through them.)

Lumps in your paint? Strain them out by stretching and securing either cheesecloth or pantyhose across the top of an empty can. Pour the paint from its original can through the makeshift strainer to catch the lumps.

Alcohol test. Before you repaint an area, find out if the existing coat of paint is oil or latex. Dip a cloth in alcohol and wipe a small area of the surface. If the paint rubs off, it's most likely latex.

Oil for oil. Use vegetable oil to clean oil-based (alkyd) paint from your hands; it doesn't dry the skin as paint thinner does, and is especially good for children's skin.

Keep your hands clean when handling paint by wearing latex gloves—the thin, tight-fitting ones like those surgeons use.

Shoe guard. Pull an old pair of throwaway socks over your shoes to protect them from being spat-

SAVE SPACE AND PREVENT WRINKLES

Use these packing techniques to ensure that clothes will come out of your bag looking as presentable as possible.

▶ *Pack garments in plastic dry-cleaner bags or put layers of tissue paper between them.*

▶ *Lay long items such as slacks and dresses across the bag with the ends hanging over the sides. Place shorter pieces like shirts and blouses in the center, then fold the ends of the longer garments back over them.*

▶ *Fill in corners with underwear, socks, leggings, and shoes. Roll up garments such as pajamas and sweaters so that they fit along the sides.*

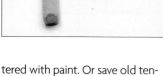

TELESCOPIC HANDLE

This extension roller has a telescoping arm, which allows you to paint ceiling or walls without changing handles—a boon when you're busy painting. The spatter shield on the roller minimizes the mess.

tered with paint. Or save old tennis or running shoes to wear when doing messy jobs like painting.

PAINT REMOVERS

What works best. Use liquid paint removers on horizontal surfaces, and paste removers on irregular or vertical surfaces. Don't cover too large an area at a time, since you must be able to scrape off the remover before it dries.

Catching drips. When stripping a piece of furniture, stand its legs in cans. The cans will catch the paint remover as it runs down.

Keep it moist. To get the most action out of a paint stripper, slow down evaporation by covering the remover with aluminum foil while it is working.

Remove shellac with denatured alcohol and fine steel wool. You can tell that a finish is shellac if the alcohol dissolves it.

PAINTBRUSHES & ROLLERS

Unexpected visitor? If you're interrupted while working with latex paint, slip your paintbrush or roller into a plastic bag, then seal it with a big plastic tie or several turns of a string. It will stay moist until you can resume painting.

Don't drown the bristles. The proper way to load a brush is to dip only one-third of the bristles

in the paint. If there's room in the can, gently tap the brush on its interior sides rather than the rim.

So smooth and soft. If the bristles of your paintbrush have stiffened slightly, lather them with a hair conditioner, then rinse well.

Roller-pan plan. Before you pour in the paint, line your roller pan with a large plastic bag or aluminum foil. When you have finished, throw away the lining. There's no mess to clean up!

Recycle worn brushes. If your brush is too frayed to paint effectively, clip off the tips of its bristles and use the brush for dusting delicate objects. Use stiffer ones for applying liquid detergent to tough stains on clothes.

That's no brush! To touch up scratches and other small spots where paint has been scraped off, improvise a "brush" to fit the task. Everyday items can do the trick— a toothpick, a drink stirrer, or the nonsulfurous end of a match. When you finish painting, simply throw away your brush substitute.

PAINTING AS A HOBBY

Simply stunning. For brilliant, lively colors, mix no more than two or three colors together at a time. If you combine too many different paint colors, you'll frequently end up with dense, muddy results.

For ease of use and fine detail, reach for acrylics in tubes. They are relatively new, versatile paints that are much simpler to mix and apply than watercolors or oils. Acrylics dry to a hard, impervious finish, so you can isolate areas with a border of masking tape or a film of rubber cement (remove the cement with an art gum eraser after the paint dries).

Eliminate dents when you're stretching a canvas by lightly rubbing the back of the dent with a damp rag or sponge. As the canvas dries and shrinks, the dent will disappear.

Roll away. To roll a painted canvas for storage, make the cylinder as large as possible to help keep the paint from cracking. Roll the canvas so that the painted surface faces outward so any cracks that do form will close up when the canvas is unrolled.

PAINTING CEILINGS & WALLS

Some basics. Paint a ceiling across its width rather than its length. Starting in a corner, work in 90 cm (3 ft) patches; doing it this way requires fewer tiring arm swings than painting larger swaths.

Hand guard. When painting overhead, prevent drips on your hands by putting the handle of the brush through a small paper plate.

Paint the edges of the ceiling with a brush, which creates a sharper, cleaner line next to the wall than a roller does. Make this brushed edge around the ceiling at least 5 cm (2 in.) wide.

Minimize the mess. Clean up spills with a damp rag as you go along. Moisten the cloth with water for latex paints and with paint thinner for alkyds.

Drip catcher for your paint can. Prevent rings caused by paint spilled over the edge of the container by gluing or taping a heavy-duty paper plate or a plastic plate to its bottom.

Keep paint out of your hair. Wearing an inexpensive shower cap protects your hair when you're painting above your head.

Protection for odd shapes. Before you paint behind a toilet or radiator, cover the object with plastic food wrap.

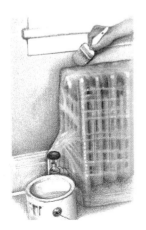

EASY GLAZING TECHNIQUES FOR WALLS

Create interesting finishes for your walls by glazing, a technique in which a thin coat of paint (the glaze) is applied over a completely dry base coat. Below are the techniques.

▶ *Stippling. Apply the glaze with a roller. While the glaze is still tacky, jab a stiff brush into it to create an overall pattern. Stippling is easy when two people work together—one applying glaze and the other following with the stippling tool. Be sure to use alkyd (oil-based) paints— they dry more slowly than latex (water-based) paints.*

▶ *Sponging. You will need a generous supply of clean natural sponges. Dab on a coat of glaze with a sponge over a 90 cm (3 ft) square area. Taking a new sponge, apply glaze in a similar dabbing pattern over the next 90 cm (3 ft) square area. Continue until the room is done.*

▶ *Rag rolling. Apply a glaze of alkyd paint over a dry alkyd base. While the base is still sticky, use strips of cotton cloth—folded, rolled, or crumpled—to blot off part of the glaze in a pattern. Have a partner prepare clean rags to replace the ones you are using as they fill up with glaze.*

A hidden record. When you paint a room, note the paint manufacturer's name and the color name or number on the back of a light-switch plate. You'll be able to find the right color if you need to do some touch-up work later.

It's curtains. Save your old shower curtains to use as drop cloths; they are more durable than run-of-the-mill plastic ones.

Before you spackle any large crack in a plaster wall, dampen the deformed area with water to keep the plaster from absorbing all the moisture in the spackling compound.

PAINTING METAL

A tough task made bearable. Use a wire brush attachment on an electric drill to strip and remove the rust from wrought-iron railings and furniture.

To paint the heads of screws before installing them, poke them into a piece of cardboard or Styrofoam so that they are held firmly in place.

Beat rust problems on painted metal with a rust converter such as those made by Rustoleum or Duro. It transforms rust into a hard, paintable surface.

Spray-paint metal porch furniture with a rust-retardant enamel for speedy, even coverage. Work in a well-ventilated space over newspapers or a drop cloth. The painting takes a very short time, and the cleanup is minimal.

Before you paint a radiator, mask the wall behind it with plastic and use a spray paint for hard-to-reach areas. Make sure the radiator is slightly warm, because the heat strengthens the bond between paint and metal.

PAINTING STAIRS & TRIM

Slippery cellar stairs. If the stairway that leads to your basement is made of concrete that's always slippery, apply a coat of paint with some sand mixed in with it.

Going up. To paint stairs and still be able to use them, paint every other step; when those are completely dry, then paint the others.

Beautiful railings. Use a plush painting mitt (available at most paint stores) to paint the curvy balustrades that hold up the handrail of your stairway.

A new use for skateboards. Spare your knees: sit on your teenager's skateboard and just roll along as you paint baseboards and other low-lying areas. (Better yet, ask your teen to do the painting!)

Stain cover-up. Before painting over a stain in a wood floor or counter, cover it with a white shellac stain killer. You can also use the stain killer to cover knots in new woodwork before painting it. If the stains or knots show through the first coat of stain killer, apply another coat.

Vinegar bath. Before you paint something that is made of galvanized metal—a mailbox, for example—wash it with vinegar. This helps the paint bond better with the galvanized surface.

PANTS

Too tight. Don't wear tight-waisted pants; not only are they uncomfortable, but they can impede digestion and aggravate heartburn. Measure your waist before you buy new pants.

Try again. If the first pair of pants you try on don't fit, find another in the same size. Despite same-size labels, the waist measurements of pants may vary by more than 2.5 cm (1 in.).

Even Steven. When hemming pants, complete one leg, then hold the inseams together and pull both legs taut. Use the length of the completed hem to mark the unhemmed leg.

Save the material you cut off when you shorten a pair of pants, and use it later to repair holes. Extra fabric comes in especially handy for repairing children's wear.

Handle with care. Lay velvet, satin, and silk pants, folded only once or twice, in a drawer for storage. These delicate fabrics can be badly marred by hanger marks.

Vinegar smooths the way. To get rid of deep creases in your trousers, sponge white vinegar on the fold. Press the creased area gently with a warm iron until the vinegar dries.

Hang smart. The best way to hang a pair of pants is to place the bottom of the legs in the vise of a pants hanger with the inseams together. This avoids the crease at the knee caused by folding pants over a hanger or in a drawer.

Tour with trousers. Seasoned travelers recommend including a pair of wool trousers and a pair of black jeans or khakis in your bag. Male or female, old or young, wearing one or the other style together with various jackets or sweaters, you can go any place.

Hem lock. Hem your pants to at least 2.5 cm (1 in.) above the sole of your shoes to prevent the hem from touching the ground.

RIGHT STUFF

THE PANTS THAT GO WITH EVERYTHING

Leggings are not just for exercise anymore; worn under a tunic or a long sweater, they're a useful part of a woman's wardrobe. These pants go well with both casual and dressy outfits, and come in a wide variety of styles and colors too, from velvety red to soft burgundy to faux animal prints. Best of all, they are made of stretch fabric and are very comfortable.

PANTYHOSE

Size it up. Pantyhose sizing varies, so before you buy, check the chart on the back of a package to see where your height and weight fall. A size "B" of one brand may be a size "C" in another.

Long life. To prolong the life of pantyhose, wet them when they're new, wring out the excess water, then put them in a plastic bag and freeze them for a few hours. Thaw them out in the bathtub and hang them up to dry.

Color coordinated. To give an elongated look to your figure, match your pantyhose to the color of your shoes. Hose that doesn't blend with your shoes will stand out, visually shortening your body line.

Thicker, stronger. Opt for opaque pantyhose or tights, which will outlast sheer ones. The types of hose that contain spandex not only provide extra support, they are also extra durable.

PARKING LOTS

Seek the light. Always park under a streetlight or in a well-lit area, even if it's farther from your destination. Thieves and muggers prefer to operate in the dark.

 Choosing a lot. Whenever possible, leave your car in an attended parking lot. Statistics show that a car is five times more likely to be stolen from an unattended lot than from the street or an attended lot.

Tight as a drum. Before you leave your car, check for windows that are slightly open; they are an easy means of unlawful entry.

Replace the cigarette lighter. A missing lighter tips off a professional car thief that you may have a valuable car phone hidden away in your automobile.

Van alert. Never park next to a van—the shield of choice for many wrongdoers. From the other side of a van, no one can see you or your car.

PARTY ETIQUETTE

Set the tone. If you must be free for last-minute tasks in the kitchen or at the table, be sure to station someone—your spouse, your co-host, or an early arrival—near the door to greet guests and help them put away coats.

Tag lines. Use name tags to smooth introductions among your guests—but don't stop there. Ask your guests to add any pertinent information about themselves—their favorite sports team, for example, or a funny nickname.

Mingle among your guests. Talk to each person attending your party at least once. It doesn't have to be a long conversation, but at least ask each person how he is and tell him you're glad he came. At your party's end, stand by the door when guests leave so that you can say goodnight to each guest and thank him for coming.

Hostess gift. Bring a small token whenever you are a guest at a party—even if it is an inexpensive bouquet of flowers. Enclose a card so that your hostess will know who brought the gift, especially if she is too busy to acknowledge it when you arrive.

PANTYHOSE AREN'T JUST FOR LEGS

Don't throw away that pair of ripped pantyhose. Here are some ways it might come in handy.

▶ *Soft stuffing. Cut up old pairs of pantyhose, then use them to create soft, washable stuffing for homemade toys, dolls, pillows, or seat cushions.*

▶ *String. Use pantyhose to tie up boxes and stacks of newspapers and magazines.*

▶ *Ties. Fasten tomato plants to stakes and cages.*

▶ *Scouring sponge. Place a regular sponge inside a section of pantyhose—its coarse texture scrubs things clean.*

▶ *Lint-free rag. Use old pantyhose for dusting and other cleaning chores. They're also great for applying finishes to unstained wood.*

▶ *Deer repellent. Stuff pantyhose with clippings of human or dog hair and hang them in your garden to ward off antlered grazers.*

Decorating for a holiday party is fun and creative, but some of us need a little help getting started. The suggestions below are meant to inspire you when you're ready to start creating the decor for your next party.

THEME	COLORS	TABLE TRIMMINGS	AROUND THE HOUSE
Christmas	Red and green; gold or silver accents	Glass bowls filled with shiny balls; a gingerbread house; lots of candles and silver	Lighted tree; evergreen boughs and wreaths with plaid ribbons; holly branches, velvet swags, and silver-paper snowflakes
Chanukah	Blue and white; silver accents	Blue runner spread with dreidels and small gifts wrapped in blue (for favors)	Chanukah menorah and ornaments; blue and silver ribbon streamers; bouquets of white flowers
Easter	Pastel colors of spring	Baskets of colored eggs; bouquets of tulips and irises in crystal vases	Easter baskets; stuffed bunnies and ducks; candles; oversized decorated eggs; crystal bowls of multicolored jelly beans
Valentine's Day	Red, pink, white	Single red rose at each place; lace and red-ribbon runner	Strings of cut-out hearts; silver or glass vases filled with red flowers and baby's breath
Halloween	Orange, black	Jack-o'-lantern centerpiece	Cobwebs, scary stuffed figures, sheet ghosts
Thanksgiving	Yellow, brown, tan, and gold	Colored leaves, cornucopia, brass or rustic pottery vases	Indian corn, gourds, and pumpkins; shocks of cornstalks; wreaths of dried flowers

If you spill something, tell the hostess right away. Offer but don't insist on cleaning the mess yourself. Let her do it her way.

PARTY GAMES

Line dance party. Before the event, make a tape of music suitable for doing line dances, both old and new. Do the macarena as well as the mambo, the samba, or even the bunny hop.

Pin the tail on the celebrity. Choose a famous figure you've all heard too much about. Cut a photograph out of a magazine and have a blow-up made at your local photography store. Let your guests pin something amusing on it, such as a crown on Lady Diana.

Kid stuff. Play blindman's bluff, pass the orange, or any other silly kids' game at your next adult party. Such games are easy to organize and pleasantly nostalgic.

The life of the party. Spice up every guest list with one special person—even a downright eccentric—who will charm your other guests. The unusual person will keep conversation fascinating.

PARTY PLANNING

Inventive invitations. For your next party, put together a collage of old photographs or interesting pictures from magazines and newspapers. Arrange your own type over them and make photocopies of your creation to send out as unique invitations.

On schedule. Do major preparations—shopping, cleaning, decorating—ahead of time. On the day of the party, post a list of all your last-minute chores, right down to chilling the wine and taking the butter out of the refrigerator.

Draw up two lists to help plan your party—one for food and the other for linens, serving platters, dishes, glasses, and utensils. When the party's over, hold on to the lists for future parties.

Wear something spectacular to your party to create a festive mood. Think of your outfit as part of the decorations.

To keep people circulating, hold your party in a room that will be crowded when guests arrive. Parties tend to feel sedate and unexciting when guests are spread too far apart.

Mix hot and cold courses. Plan no more hot dishes than your oven and stove can handle. Use space in a neighbor's refrigerator for cold things.

PASSPORTS

Apply early in the year (January is the slowest month) to avoid long lines at passport offices. Take proof of citizenship (a birth certificate or certificate of naturalization), proof of identity (a driver's license), and two identical 5 cm (2 in.) square photographs.

Renew by mail, which is allowed if you meet these criteria: you have had a previous passport, you were at least 18 years old when you obtained your last passport, you received it less than 5 years

ago, and your name has not been changed since.

Allow time for mail renewal— three to four weeks, up to six weeks in summer. Renewal forms and applications can be obtained from any Canada post offices or from a travel agent.

Speed up mail-in renewals by specifying an upcoming travel date on your application. For extra speed, use Express Mail or one-day air courier service to send your application; enclose a pre-paid air bill to cover the return.

Travel backups. When you travel abroad, take copies of the major pages of your passport and a set of extra photos; they will speed the replacement of your passport in case of loss or theft. As an extra precaution, also leave copies at home with a friend or family member whom you can reach in case of an emergency.

PASTA

The right beginning. Use a large, deep pot. Once the water reaches a rolling boil, add the pasta in batches so that the water stays

No-Cook Mexican-Style Sauce for Pasta

This sauce takes less than 15 minutes to make and tastes delicious. While you're preparing the sauce, cook and drain 280 g (10 oz) of short pasta, like fusilli, or bow ties. The recipe serves three to four.

1 Trim, halve, seed, and finely chop 1 or 2 jalapeño peppers. (Be sure to wear thin rubber gloves when cutting the peppers.)

2 Thinly slice 4 green onions (tops and bottoms). Coarsely chop enough fresh cilantro to make 125 mL (½ cup).

3 In a large bowl, combine peppers, onions, cilantro, a 450 mL (16 oz) jar medium (or mild) salsa, 5 mL (1 tsp) ground cumin, a pinch of salt, and 30 mL (2 tbsp) olive oil.

4 Cut 225 g (8 oz) of Monterey Jack cheese into 1 cm (½ in.) cubes. Add the cheese to the sauce mixture and toss.

5 Add the pasta, and you have a spicy dish, perfect for a summer supper.

PATIENTS' RESPONSIBILITIES

Now that patients' rights are well established, you can get the best care by being a savvy patient. Here are pointers.

▶ *Keep your own medical history. List details of chronic and acute conditions, treatments, any medications you take, hospitalization dates, and a family medical history.*

▶ *When undergoing medical care, list the names of the personnel involved and make notes of any conversations.*

▶ *Check for inflated costs; review itemized hospital bills.*

▶ *Check your medical records. Ask your clinic, physician, or hospital. You must look at your medical records with supervision in most cases. If you find errors in your records, submit corrections to the clinic, physician, or hospital.*

Child's play. To young children who keep asking "why," respond clearly and sincerely. Their questions may prove tiresome, but your patient response teaches them that their desire to learn matters to you.

Take action. To alleviate anxiety when waiting for an important event or information, keep busy with productive activities. Focus on actions, not expectations.

PATIENTS' RIGHTS

Suddenly sick. Under Medicare, all Canadians are entitled, by law, to emergency care in a hospital until the urgent medical condition is stabilized.

Get comfy. If you are to be hospitalized, pack personal items for the stay. You can wear your nightclothes, use personal toiletries, and enjoy gadgets such as your computer or radio, as long as they don't interfere with your medical care or the care and comfort of other patients.

hot, but take no longer than one minute to put in all the pasta. Stir the water two or three times as the pasta cooks to keep it from clumping together.

How much? For a pasta side dish, you need about 56 g (2 oz) of dried pasta per serving; for a main dish, prepare 112 g (4 oz) of pasta per portion.

It's done when? The only way to know when pasta is done is to taste it, often several times as you cook (use a wooden spoon so you won't burn your mouth). When there is no taste of flour but still a slight bite of texture, remove the pot from the heat and drain.

PATHS & WALKWAYS

Shovel-proof paving. Pave paths with materials that are easy to clear snow from. Flagstone, brick, concrete, or asphalt can be cleaned off easily in winter, but gravel and wood chips get shoveled up with the snow.

People-friendly paths. Instead of forcing others to follow paths you create, let the paths follow people. Tracks worn through grass

and other plantings mark common routes; place stepping stones along these trails to provide footing and to protect plantings.

Weed-proofing. Cover the sand bed you prepare for flagstones, bricks, or precast pavement with several sheets of newspaper. This keeps the finished path free of weeds for years.

PATIENCE

Wait for love. Give personal relationships time to grow. Allow others to become intimate at their own pace, without pressure or guilt. Treat others' shyness or fear of intimacy with respect.

 Deep breathing. If you find yourself growing restless or edgy over a situation, take 10 deep breaths before proceeding. You'll manage the moment better.

Practice patience. Use a relaxation method—meditation, yoga, long walks—in your daily life to help maintain a state of calm.

You are in charge of your own health care. Before you agree to undergo medical treatment of any kind, you are entitled to complete information about costs, potential dangers, and alternatives. You are also free to get a second—or even a third—opinion. A doctor can proceed with a procedure only when you or someone you designate consents in writing.

PATIOS

When a deck is better. Where the ground is damp or uneven, a wooden deck may provide a more practical and economical outdoor living space than a paved patio. Because wood reflects less heat than masonry, a deck is also more comfortable in hot, sunny regions.

Patio trees. Compact flowering trees planted alongside a patio provide color and shade without heaving up the pavement as a large tree would. To avoid creating a maintenance problem for yourself, select trees that won't drop messy fruits or seed pods. Bradford pears, flowering or kousa dogwoods, and sweet bay magnolias are all good choices.

Quick fix. To set a speed record patching cracks in your brick or flagstone patio, mix equal parts of sand and cement. Scatter the mix over the patio, sweep it into the cracks, and sprinkle it with water.

Wind buffer. The fence encircling your patio will block the wind far more effectively if you mount a baffle on top. Build it from a 30 cm (12 in.) wide board so that it juts up and out at a 45-degree angle.

Make a hot patio cooler by setting up "misters" (a type of sprinkler head available at most garden centers) to throw water over hanging baskets of plants or adjacent shrubs. One of these spray heads emits about 11.3 L (2.4 gal) of continuously evaporating water

READ YOUR JOB CONTRACT CAREFULLY

If you are asked to sign a contract as part of a pay increase or promotion package, ask for time to review the details.

▶ *If your contract ties compensation to a division's performance or to some other marker, carefully research past performance and current trends before you sign.*

▶ *If your pay is tied to commissions or incentive rewards, be sure that you're not signing on with a sinking ship.*

▶ *Find out if incentive pay is limited; some contracts actually stifle high achievers by establishing pay ceilings.*

▶ *Read warily any clauses demanding that you be able to travel on a moment's notice or work longer hours. Such conditions will require discussions with your family.*

▶ *Before accepting a higher pay package entailing new responsibilities, compare your offer to industry standards.*

▶ *Consider having your attorney review the contract. Be prepared to negotiate questionable items.*

an hour and cools the surrounding area by several degrees.

PAY RAISES

Ask. There's nothing wrong with expressing interest in getting a salary increase. Your silence may be misinterpreted as satisfaction.

Less is more. When you make your case for a pay raise, give a simple, clear presentation. Provide your boss a short list of specific points and then let her have the floor. Too much talking on your part may weaken your argument.

Emphasize mutual benefits. Don't focus on your need for a raise or the fact that you deserve it. Instead, emphasize how you're contributing and helping your firm become more competitive, efficient, and cost-effective.

Quantify your achievements. The value of your performance can be presented in a more compelling way when it is bolstered by hard numbers.

Time your request to coincide with the completion of a big deal or a major project you helped develop. Hold off from asking for a raise during a downturn or right after a business loss.

Survey the market to find out what other employers are paying for the type of work you do. Trade journals and professional associations often publish annual salary and wage surveys. Knowing industry rates helps prepare you to present your case.

PEDICURES

Cut carefully. To avoid ingrown toenails, take care not to cut toenails too short or to cut into the corners. Smooth off sharp nail edges with the coarse side of an emery board.

Foot steps. Prepare your feet for a perfect pedicure. Soak them for 10 minutes in warm water with mild soap, bubble bath, or Epsom salts. Dry, then use a pumice stone to gently rub off rough or hardened skin from the heels, sides, and soles. Rub in cuticle cream and push back the cuticles with the cotton-wrapped blunt end of an orange stick. Use a nail brush to scrub the nails clear of dead skin and cuticle cells.

Clean sweep. Before applying polish, sweep over the nails with a cotton-coated orange stick dipped in polish remover to remove any leftover cuticle oil.

Hold the color. Paint your toe-nails, not your toes, by cutting a sponge into triangle shapes and using them to keep your toes separated while you apply polish.

Reapply clear polish daily to prolong the life of your pedicure. Remove all polish and repeat the pedicure once a week.

PEER PRESSURE

Negotiate, negotiate. Give your preteen practice in the art of give-and-take by negotiating with him about everything from TV privi-

leges to household chores. Make him formulate and express his point of view clearly. He'll be able to use these skills during his teens, when his views will be challenged.

Start young. Arrange opportunities for your preschooler to play with peers so that she can learn how to get along with others.

So what? If you're a young person feeling pressured by a group to do something you don't want to do, act disinterested. Tell your peers

that you think it's boring or that you've tried it and didn't think much of it.

Just walk away. Teens and pre-teens often react impulsively to situations with anger when among peers. Show them how to calm themselves or walk away from a stressful situation. Ask them to visualize a peaceful place or thought, to count to 10, or even bite their tongue.

PENCILS & PENS

More mileage for the buck. The best value in writing instruments is still the reliable wooden lead pencil. A typical pencil can draw a line longer than 48 km (30 mi); the average ballpoint pen runs out of ink after only 1.6 to 3.2 km (1–2 mi).

Avoid airborne leaks. Fill fountain pen reservoirs completely or empty them completely before taking them on a plane. Air inside partially filled reservoirs can expand in flight and cause a leak.

 Try a mechanical pencil if you don't like sharpening wooden pencils. Always sharp, they're particularly good for people who do a lot of writing while they are traveling.

Cover up your roller ball. Roller-ball pens use liquid ink, just as fountain pens do, but they have durable points similar to ballpoints. Their ink lasts only a few weeks and dries out fast too. After using yours, remember to replace the top to keep it rolling.

Clean your fountain pen periodically with cold water to keep it from gumming up with ink pigment. Never use hot water to wash a fountain pen; it can cause some pigments to harden.

RIGHT STUFF

EASY WRITERS

The ballpoint pens below, manufactured by Sensa (top and bottom) and Pilot (middle), are ergonomically designed to reduce finger fatigue and cramping. With contoured, soft-plastic grips that cushion the fingers, these pens are particularly valuable for people suffering from arthritis or carpal tunnel syndrome. In addition, the pressurized Fisher cartridge in both Sensa pens allows them to write underwater and upside down.

PENNY PINCHING AT HOME

Use cloth napkins. Wash them whenever you do the laundry, and they'll be ready for the next meal (they don't need ironing if you buy the wrinkle-free kind). They'll pay for themselves quickly in paper-napkin savings.

Buy air conditioners in winter when they are least expensive. Install the air conditioner in the most frequently used room, and, come the hot days, close off the rest of the house.

Always take seconds. Purchase irregular bathroom towels, shower curtains, and rugs: the flaws are usually not noticeable, and good quality seconds cost less than lower quality regulars. Ask in household furnishing or department stores about seconds sales.

Buy used exercise equipment. Scan the want ads and mention your need to friends. You may pick up a good, slightly used rowing machine for a song.

Go to yard or tag sales when you need something specific for your house—you'll find what you're looking for surprisingly often, and it will cost a fraction of a new item. If you bargain, you're likely to pay even less.

 Buy high quality home furnishings, especially items that are used long and hard such as sofas or mattresses. You'll pay more up front, but the items will last far longer.

Good to the last drop. Upend old bottles of dish soap, shampoo, conditioner, vegetable oil—whatever—in a funnel stuck into the new bottle and leave it for a while. You'll find there's usually a lot left in an empty bottle.

Even a true penny pincher can have fun while traveling. Here are suggestions for seeing the world without breaking the bank.

▶ *Free information. Write to local tourist offices or ask your librarian for good guidebooks and photocopy pages relevant to your trip. Throw away the photocopies as you go from place to place.*

▶ *Travel free. Form a group for a tour operator, and your trip could be on the house. Just recruit a group of friends who share special interests, and the tour operator will do the rest.*

▶ *Be a courier. Fly to faraway places for half the cost by delivering packages for businesses. The only catch—you can take only carry-on luggage. Look in the Yellow Pages for courier brokers.*

▶ *Alternative lodging. College dormitories, lighthouses, hostels, and religious retreats are among the offbeat lodging choices that can cut way down on hotel bills. Check the tourist office at your destination for local possibilities.*

▶ *Off-season savings. Travel off-season to reap big savings. Caribbean beaches are still cooler than Canadian cities in summer, and winter ski resorts like Aspen are equally beautiful and far less costly in the summer.*

Rebid insurance for your house and car every year or two. You can save hundreds of dollars by switching insurers or by getting a lower competing bid and asking your current insurer to match it.

PENNY PINCHING AT LEISURE

Buy a series. Subscriptions to plays and concerts or season tickets to sports events are cheaper than individual tickets. If you can't attend all the events, share the series cost with a friend or use some of the tickets as gifts.

Wait for movies until they come out in video, and you'll see them for less than half the price. If your video store has a two-night rental policy, you can split the cost with a neighbor and save even more.

Use your local library for more than books. These days libraries offer CD's, videotapes, and even posters and art works on loan.

Go out for lunch instead of dinner when you feel like splurging. Even the priciest gourmet restaurants have far more reasonable luncheon menus.

Free fun. Check for admission-free days at museums. Watch for no-charge rehearsals at concert halls, theaters, or churches, and open recitals at music schools.

PENNY PINCHING AT THE BANK

Negotiate lower interest rates on major credit cards—and never pay an annual fee. The institution that holds your credit card will usually waive the annual fee and may even offer you a lower interest rate if they know you are thinking of taking your business elsewhere. If they won't, find an institution that will.

Beware ATM charges. Some banks now charge customers for every exchange over a minimum number per month. Other banks sock you with high fees when you use another bank's ATM.

PENNY PINCHING AT THE MALL

Buy two identical pairs of gloves at the same time. If you lose one glove (as everyone does sometime), you'll have a spare.

Have your winter coat relined when it starts to look shabby, and you'll get an extra season or two out of it; wear your ski parka while doing errands in town and you'll get even more.

Shop at end-of-season sales. Clothing sales usually start long before the season is actually over, as stores add new stock.

Haunt thrift shops and garage sales for children's clothes. Often, more expensive items, such as winter coats, snowsuits, and dressy clothes, have not been worn much and are great buys.

PENNY PINCHING AT THE SUPERMARKET

Fruit yogurt. Buy plain yogurt in large containers and add fresh fruit or jam; it's cheaper than the pre-mixed small containers.

Buy day-old bread and save up to 50 percent. If the wrapper is intact, the bread shouldn't taste noticeably different from fresh. If the bread is dry, toast it.

Frozen shrimp taste just as good as fresh when used in recipes where they are cooked, and cost about half as much.

Do the math. Not all family and jumbo sizes of products are cheaper in bulk than in smaller amounts. If you have a pocket calculator, use it as you cruise the aisles.

Buy frozen concentrate juices, which are almost half the price of juices sold in cartons—and just as nutritious.

Pay attention to unit pricing by reading labels carefully. Many "new and improved" products actually contain less in the package than before, yet you will still be charged the full price for a "downsized" product.

Buy a small spray bottle, put whatever vegetable oil you use in it, and never buy an expensive can of spray oil again.

Ask for large plastic bags when shopping at the mall, then use them as trash bags instead of buying expensive, brand name bags.

A PENNY SAVED

If you save your loose change for a year, you may collect enough money to take a family outing or buy a luxury item such as a camera. Use a traditional piggy bank or save time (and aggravation) by putting coins in a convenient change sorter. These devices, which sort and wrap coins so they are ready for bank deposit, are available through home furnishings stores and catalogs.

PEPPERS

Enjoy restaurant-style peppers at home by roasting them yourself. Halve or quarter peppers, remove the seeds and ribs, and broil, cut-side down, until charred. After they cool, pull off their skins. To preserve the cooked peppers, cover and refrigerate. The peppers should keep for up to two weeks.

Protect your skin from the irritating oil in hot peppers by coating your hands with vegetable oil before chopping the peppers. It works as well as rubber gloves.

Preserve peppers by freezing them. Peppers are among the few vegetables requiring no blanching beforehand. Simply dice or chop them and pack into plastic bags.

PERENNIALS

Save mowing time. Replace the grass in hard-to-trim areas under fences and along foundations with low-maintenance perennials like daylilies, hostas, or astilbes.

 When you buy perennials in pots, pick plants with few or no open flowers. These will take root in your garden faster than plants already in full bloom. Later you'll enjoy even more flowers than you might have brought home on the plants.

The best perennial buys are found in catalogs offering bare-root plants. Dug up while they're dormant, these plants are shipped without soil around their roots. If they are planted immediately, their survival rate is very good.

Reduce garden maintenance by avoiding tall perennials, such as large delphiniums, that require stakes. If you must have these plants, select compact varieties—Connecticut Yankee delphiniums, for example—which are more likely to stand up by themselves.

PERFECTIONISTS

Everything in moderation. Instead of placing unreasonably high demands on yourself and failing to meet them, reduce your expectations a bit. Set new, more realistic goals.

A PECK OF PEPPERS

No matter what tastes you prefer—mild and sweet or pungent and searing—peppers can accent any dish with bold flavor and color. Here's a pepper primer to help you tell what's hot from what's not. Note that when cooking with hot peppers, use just a small amount at first. You can always add more heat, but you can't make a recipe milder if it's too hot.

KIND	HEAT	DESCRIPTION
Bell (also mango pepper)	Mild	Comes in six different colors: green, red, yellow, orange, purple, and brown. Green peppers are the most familiar type, but as they mature they turn red and become sweeter. Used in salads, sautés, and casseroles.
Pimiento	Mild	Similar to red bells, but with a more orange cast and a pointy base. Usually sold in jars, roasted and peeled. Good in salads and sandwiches.
Cubanelle	Mild	Longer, thinner, and richer in flavor than bell peppers; usually light green or mottled green-red in color. Can be eaten raw; are best when sautéed or fried.
Banana	Mild to Mildly hot	Shaped like a banana; resembles a large, mild pepper called Hungarian wax. Banana peppers start out green and turn yellow (Hungarian wax peppers start out yellow and evolve to red). Available fresh or pickled. Taste before preparing to be sure you have the sweet one. Used as a pickled condiment or in chili.
Anaheim (also New Mexican)	Mild to mildly hot	Slim, tapered, often used fresh for Mexican stuffed-pepper dish called *chiles rellenos*. When dried, it is used to make long strings known as *ristras*.
Jalapeño	Medium hot	Small, about 5 cm (2 in.) long; often eaten at the green stage. Used in salsas and sauces, on nachos, and often mixed into sausage or cheese.
Serrano	Very hot	Small; shaped like slender, miniature lightbulbs. Sold mostly at the green stage. Commonly used fresh, in salsas.
Habañero	Super hot	Round, pocked, most often a yellow-orange color. Some pepper experts claim it is the hottest chile in the world. Used for salsas and barbecue sauces.

Accept failure. Failure can be a great teacher and a source of much personal growth. Rather than condemning yourself for not succeeding, learn from the experience. Start working on new strategies to achieve future success by persistent, steady effort.

Building blocks. Break down a large or complex project into a series of small tasks. Organize them sequentially in ascending order of difficulty if you can.

Means are an end. Focus on the process and not just the final result. Evaluate your success not only in terms of what you achieve but by how much you enjoy—and learn from—doing the task.

Look back. Use what you've been able to accomplish in the past to help set realistic goals. Take advantage of skills you've developed and lessons you've learned.

Ban black-and-white thinking. Change your all-or-nothing attitude that equates imperfect accomplishments with failure. Differentiate between high- and low-priority tasks. Try to do your best in both, but let some of the less important things go.

PERFUME

Layer it on. You needn't over-apply perfume to make its scent linger. Instead, layer different forms of the same scent—dab on a cologne over a lotion, then use a spray. For best results, apply perfume after a shower or bath while your skin is still moist.

Apply gently. Don't rub in perfume, as friction can take away some of the delicacy of a fragrance. Pat scent on wrists and throat, where blood is close to the surface, to help the scent circulate freely.

Solids travel best. Scents in stick form are good choices for travel because you don't have to worry

about spills. A waxy base also gives solid perfumes a longer life than liquids, which tend to evaporate over time.

Prevent evaporation by storing expensive perfumes—stoppered tightly—in the refrigerator, away from heat and light. Never leave perfume sitting in direct sunlight.

PERSONAL ADS

Learn the code. To avoid possible misunderstandings, familiarize yourself with all of the abbrevia-

tions when you write or respond to a personal ad. Ask the newspaper or magazine what each abbreviation stands for.

Headline news. Come up with a catchy headline for your ad, to grab the reader's attention and make her want to respond. Try to be original, but also be honest.

Electronic ads. Instead of a print ad, try a voice ad or a video ad. While these ads are more expensive, they can be more effective in helping you to select a date and to reveal your own personality.

Cover the following points in a personal ad: marital status, age, height, weight or size, smoking status, profession, personal interests, and the type of relationship you are seeking.

Public space. If you are meeting someone you have found through a personal ad face-to-face for the first time, get together in a neutral, public place for a limited period of time, such as for cup of coffee at a coffee shop.

PERSONAL CORRESPONDENCE

Schedule it in. Set aside a special time for letter writing. You will soon look forward to this "date" with yourself to communicate with absent friends and family members.

Global village. Help your kids locate and join an international pen-pal club. You can research options at your local library, or if your computer has Internet access, find pen pals electronically.

The computer age. E-mail is a great way to keep in touch. It's quick and easy to type and send a note—you don't have to worry about ink, paper, envelopes, stamps, or mailboxes. Best of all, your messages will be received the same or the next day. And if you want to send party invitations or spread news, you can contact many people at the same time.

Fun cards. Enlist your younger kids to help you make cards for holidays or other special occasions. In your local bookstore or library, look for card-making ideas under "Crafts." Help your kids personalize their own stationery—use photocopies or drawings of their favorite movies, for example, or a favorite cartoon character.

Keep copies. For any letter you write for nonsocial purposes, such as a consumer complaint or letter to your health insurance company, retain a copy for yourself for at least six months.

PERSONAL TRAINERS

Capable hands. If you're busy—and can afford it—hire a personal trainer to help you to get in shape. She can devise an exercise schedule that tailors workouts to your personal needs, and can keep track of your progress. A good instructor will teach you how to exercise properly, avoid injury, and achieve the best results.

Check credentials. A reliable personal trainer should be certified by a reputable organization, such as the National Fitness Leadership Advisory Committee, and should be trained in CPR by the Canadian Red Cross or St. John Ambulance.

Getting to know you. Before you sign on with a trainer, try to determine whether you'll be compatible. Seek out referrals, then sit down for a one-to-one talk. Find out his fitness "philosophy." Also note if the trainer seems enthusiastic, patient, and reliable. Plan one workout together before you agree to a long-term program.

Good trainers motivate you and actually make exercise fun. They are there to push you when necessary, perhaps giving you the extra boost needed to encourage you through those last five repetitions—or even to exercise at all.

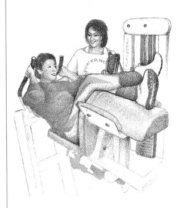

PERSPIRATION

Stubborn perspiration odors that remain in clothing after laundering can often be removed by sponging the area with a mix of 5 mL (1 tsp) of white vinegar with 250 mL (1 cup) of water. Rinse thoroughly with clear water after you apply the mixture.

EMBOSSED STATIONERY

Give plain stationery the look of expensive embossing by using a personal hand embosser. With just a quick squeeze, your name and address (or logo, if you wish) appear in raised letters on the flap of any sized envelope or on sheets of personal or business stationery. Much less expensive than buying engraved paper, an embosser is an economical way to create beautiful stationery. Hand embossers can be ordered through home furnishings catalogs or at your local stationer.

There are many alternatives to pesticides that are environmentally safe and often very effective if you use them correctly. Consider these easy solutions:

▶ *Biological controls. Introduce predaceous insects such as ladybugs and praying mantises, to eat plant pests; or various bacteria and diseases, such as Bacillus thuringiensis, which controls cabbage worms. Because biological controls injure only the pests, they are not only more environmentally friendly than chemical pesticides, they are often more effective too. Available from garden centers.*

▶ *Do-it-Yourself Traps. Many kinds of insect pests locate plants by homing in on the yellow light reflected from the foliage. Japanese beetles, for example, can be easily fooled by squares of yellow poster board enclosed in clear plastic freezer bags coated with petroleum jelly. Simply hang the trap out; when it becomes covered with bugs, replace the plastic bag.*

▶ *Horticultural oils. Effective in controlling many kinds of insect pests that can infest trees and ornamental shrubs, horticultural oils are harmless to most other wildlife. Spray "dormant" oil on plants before the buds open in spring to smother overwintering insects and eggs. Spray "summer" or "superior" oils after plants have leafed to kill active pests.*

Allergic to deodorants? Mix equal parts vinegar and water (the vinegar smell will disappear) and apply to underarm area. Talcum powder, baby powder, and witch hazel are other good options.

 If you perspire heavily after exercise on hot days, avoid dehydration by drinking lots of water, juices, and other caffeine-free liquids to replace lost fluids.

Launder promptly. Wash perspiration-soaked clothing as soon as possible. The salt in sweat has a tendency to weaken fabrics, and the moisture can leave permanent, unsightly stains.

Sweatproof? Although there are stringent federal standards for such terms as "perspiration-resistant," add sunscreen at frequent intervals when working out to be sure you are protected.

PEST CONTROL

Prevent flies from breeding in your garbage cans by hosing the cans out during warm weather. Let them dry in the sun, then pour a little powdered laundry detergent in the bottom.

Dog off. To keep dogs away from your garbage cans, sprinkle undiluted ammonia over the garbage bags and in the cans.

Slow down a flying insect long enough to give it a good swat by spraying it first with hair spray.

Before storing woolen clothing for the summer, put cloves in the pockets. They deter moths just as well as mothballs, but they smell much better.

Repel ants inside the house the nontoxic way by putting spearmint, broken eggshells, pennyroyal, camphor, or clove oil in a dish in closets and on shelves.

PESTICIDES

When mixing pesticide concentrate with water, make only small amounts. If you make too little to finish the job, you can always mix a bit more, but storing an excess is unsafe, and disposing of it by pouring it on the ground is environmentally irresponsible.

Check the expiration date. Many modern pesticides are designed to quickly break down to inert ingredients after application so they won't persist in the environment. Because their shelf life is limited, always check the expiration date when buying pesticides; buy only as much as you will use before that date.

To eliminate a plant pest, collect samples of the pest together with the damaged plants and take them to your provincial department of agriculture office. (The number is located in the government listings in your telephone book.) The specialists there will tell you (without charge) what pesticide will be the best remedy for your problem.

CHARACTERISTICS OF PET BIRDS

Birds are popular pets in the North America. Wide variations occur within each species, but the characteristics noted below apply generally to each kind of bird.

BIRD	FOOD	LIFE SPAN	HOUSING	SIZE	VOICE & PERSONALITY
Budgerigar (small Australian parrot) and parakeet	Prepared budgie mix	7 years	Hardy, but house inside in cold climates	18 cm (7")	Good mimics; males best talkers; social with owners; most popular pet bird; great color variation.
Canary	Canary seed and variety of other foods	10 years	Hardy; cage or aviary	10–15 cm (4"–6")	Males sing; never tamed; mostly yellow.
Cockatiel	Cereal and fruit	6–20 years	Some hardy; need aviary	12–45 cm (5"–18")	Not very tame; can be antisocial and aggressive.
Parrot, macaw, cockatoo, and lovebird	Parrot mix; fruit; greens	20–50 years	Some hardy, some not; cage or aviary	Lovebird: 15 cm (6"); parrot: 30–38 cm (12"–15")	Parrot very tame; social with owner. Cockatoo can be aggressive. All tend to be noisy.
Softbill (toucan and mynah)	Fruit and berries; prepared birdseed; some require live insects	7–10 years	Most not hardy; cage or aviary	35–45 cm (14"–18")	Some, such as mynah, are excellent mimics; others have appealing songs.

PET BIRDS

Start small. Before investing in a large bird, buy a small one that is easy to care for. Once you have gained experience, you'll know if you want to move on to a larger, more exotic bird.

Buy from a reputable breeder or a specialty bird store. Birds sold in pet stores are often unhealthy.

Remove your bird from your house for 24 to 48 hours when you use insecticides. As miners have always known, birds are especially vulnerable to airborne pollutants.

Feeding a feisty bird. If your bird bites at your hand when you try to feed it and give it water, use a baster to replenish water and a funnel to refill the seed dish.

Buy a birdcage that is big enough for your bird to fly easily from one perch to another. Also, make sure dishes can hold at least a day's food supply.

PET COLLARS

Collar tags. A dog is required by law to wear a tag that shows it has been vaccinated for rabies. You should also attach a second tag to the collar, listing your name, address, and telephone number and the dog's name.

When traveling, add a temporary tag to the standard address and vaccination tags on your dog's collar to indicate where you can be reached during your trip.

Skip fancy flea collars. Electronic, ultrasonic, and other gadgety flea collars don't do a good job and are expensive. Some also emit sounds that may annoy your pet as well as the fleas.

Air out a flea collar for two to three days before putting it on your pet, to reduce the chance of contact dermatitis.

PET EMERGENCY

If an animal is poisoned, get it to a veterinarian immediately, along with a sample of the poisson. If this is not available, take a sample of the vomit. Or call the nearest Poison Control Center. If there is an antidote on the bottle, administer it without delay.

When an animal is in shock, wrap it in a towel or blanket and transport it quickly to a vet. Signs of shock are initially rapid, then weakening heart and respiratory rates, accompanied by shivering.

To stop bleeding, apply a pressure bandage or use your hand to apply direct pressure. A chest wound with bubbling blood and the sound of releasing air requires immediate veterinary attention.

Traumatic injury. Stay with an animal that has been hit by a car or has suffered other serious injury; it may try to move or flee. Ask someone else to call for help.

Snakebite is a hazard for curious animals. If your pet shows signs of swelling around the face, has trouble breathing, or has a slowed blink response, obtain prompt medical attention for him.

PET HAIR

No show. Pet hair is less noticeable on upholstery fabric that is neither light nor dark and has some texture or pattern.

After laundering a pet's blanket, wipe out the washer and dryer with a damp cloth and clean the filters on both machines.

Protect the spot. Cover your pet's favorite sleeping area with a towel or blanket rather than trying to train it to stay off furniture. Don't wash it too often; its smell is what attracts your pet.

Pickup. Before vacuuming, dampen a broom and sweep over the area with it. Use a damp cloth to remove pet hair from baseboards and under cabinets.

PET SELECTION

 A breeder is the best source for a purebred dog or cat. Animals from pet stores and puppy mills are generally not as well-bred, healthy, or socialized.

Don't count on a pedigree as a guarantee of good health or tem-

Like people, animals become frightened when they are injured. Follow these tips in order to safely transport a pet to a veterinarian.

▶ *An injured dog. Talk to it reassuringly. Temporarily muzzle it with a bandage (never tape) if you are concerned about biting, but not if it is having trouble breathing. Gently slide the dog onto a blanket. When carrying it, support the head, back, and pelvis. Use two or more people to move a large dog.*

▶ *An injured cat. To restrain it, hold the cat by the scruff of the neck. Wrap a towel around it and swaddle it; then hand-hold or place the cat in a carrier. Never raise an injured cat's head higher than its body, as this can interfere with breathing. If a cat is loose and resisting assistance, throw a towel or blanket over it and firmly pick it up.*

▶ *An injured bird. Scoop it up gently in both your hands and place it in a dark, warm box. Capture a loose bird by covering it gently with a light cloth. Never use a heavy blanket, which could break its fragile bones.*

perament. Large, national dog clubs seldom see the animals they register, and many high-volume puppy mills have reputations for producing inbred dogs.

To mutt or not? Although buying a mixed-breed dog can be risky, mutts are often healthier and have a better temperament than purebred dogs. Many purebreds have emotional and physical problems from inbreeding.

Check out the parents. The physical and emotional condition of the mother and father are good indicators of the offspring's future health. Also, the way a puppy or kitten plays and interacts with other animals is also a good indication of temperament.

Best ages. To avoid behavior problems, adopt puppies at 6 to 10 weeks and kittens at 8 to 9 weeks. Or select a pet earlier, then leave it with its mother and visit often so it begins to know you.

When adopting a cat, ask about its past. Kittens that are not socialized to humans early on may be standoffish, aggressive, or afraid of strangers.

Tummy test. Roll a puppy on its back and hold it down. The puppy that struggles briefly and then acquiesces will be relatively easy to train.

PHARMACISTS

Use one pharmacy for all your prescriptions. Pharmacists keep a record of their customers' medications (usually on a computer), so they can warn you when a new drug might interact dangerously with one you are currently taking.

Question your pharmacist about a new prescription from your doctor. What is the drug and how is it supposed to help you? When and how should you take it? What are possible side effects?

For minor complaints such as colds, upset stomachs, or sore muscles, ask your pharmacist for advice. She can probably recommend effective over-the-counter treatments for such problems.

PHONOGRAPH RECORDS

Hidden treasure? Think twice before you discard old records—78's, 45's, or 33 ⅓ LP's—which might be valuable collector's items. Your local library may have a book that indicates their value.

To straighten a warped record, place it on a flat, warm surface—the top of a TV or stereo, for example—and pile on three or four books. Give the process a couple of days to work.

 Store old records upright and away from direct sunlight and radiators.

Dust-free storage is beneficial for an old record. If you still have the paper dustcover, put it on the record, then slip the disk into its cardboard jacket with the dust-cover opening at the top.

PHOTO STORAGE

Digital storage. If you have a computer, look into the various systems now on the market for storing photographs digitally. Photofinishing stores can send out your favorite pictures to be scanned onto CD's for a reasonable fee, or you can use a home scanner. Either way will allow you

to view, manipulate, and print out the images however and whenever you please.

Date-stamp your prints and slides as soon as you receive them from the photofinisher; also date-stamp the envelopes of negatives. Doing so makes locating photographs and negatives a snap.

Keep photos in a cool, dry place where the temperature remains relatively constant between 15°C (60°F) and 21°C (70°F). Hot attics and damp basements won't work; heat causes fading, and moisture encourages mold.

For the record, take black-and-white as well as color photographs of your family and of special occasions. The dyes in black-and-white prints are more stable than those in color prints, making black-and-white prints likely to last much longer.

To show off favorite photos, arrange them in albums with acid-free paper or PVC-free plastic sleeves. (PVC plastic emits gases harmful to photographs.) Don't

---

Four Tips for Taking Great Family Photos

With today's fast films and automatic cameras, taking really good family snapshots is easier than it has ever been. Instead of worrying about the right exposure settings and properly focusing on your

Keep it simple. *People look better when you photograph them against an uncluttered background. Check for branches growing out of heads and distracting reflections and highlights.*

Get close. *To capture his mood, move in on your subject so that his face fills almost half of your viewfinder's area. Put the sun behind him to reduce squinting and harsh shadows.*

STORAGE BOXES FOR PHOTOS

Convenient and attractive storage for family snapshots is provided by special photo boxes with acid-free linings, obtainable in most camera shops. Store prints upright in the boxes along with their negatives. Label the boxes by year or occasion and use the subdividers to further categorize pictures.

use so-called magnetic albums, which grip photos on sticky adhesive covered by plastic, because acid in the paper may cause yellow staining over time.

PHOTOGRAPHY

To take a good scenic shot, work early in the morning or late in the afternoon—times when the sun casts dramatic shadows and the light is soft and warm. Put your camera on a tripod so that you can use a lower shutter speed and a higher f-stop for greater depth of field. Check to see if framing a distant view with objects in the foreground or middle ground might add interest and drama to your picture.

For great nature photos in your own backyard, use a time-lapse technique. Try documenting the seasonal story of an apple branch from the moment it begins to bud out until the last apple has fallen. Or take pictures of one of your flower beds from the same vantage point through the seasons.

Vary your format. Many people stick to horizontal pictures just because that's the way the camera viewfinder is oriented. Try taking your pictures both vertically and horizontally. You'll develop an eye for the shots that demand a vertical orientation.

Take more than one. Whenever you encounter a good photographic opportunity, take a number of pictures from different angles and distances with different focal-length lenses or with different settings of your zoom. Great photographers seldom settle for one shot.

Experiment with black-and-white portraits, which are often more effective and powerful than those done in color.

subject, you can concentrate on what you are seeing in your viewfinder. You'll take better pictures of your family and friends if you keep a few simple rules about composition in mind.

Fill the frame. *Empty space around the edges of a photo can be boring. Don't worry about including every last inch of your subjects. Compose to get the faces as large as you can.*

Tell a story. *When people are busy doing what they like to do, get your camera out, find the best angle, compose the picture in your finder, and wait for the right moment.*

A WHOLE BAND IN ONE SMALL BOX

Though it can't match the feel and rich, full-bodied sound of a real piano, an electronic keyboard can do a pretty good job of imitating one and dozens of other instruments as well. If you love to play the piano but don't have the room or the money for one—or if you want to practice at 2 A.M. without waking people up—an electronic keyboard may be just the ticket.

PIANOS

The right spot. Don't put a piano where the temperature is likely to fluctuate during the day—near a sunny window, a frequently opened outside door, a fireplace, an air-conditioning vent, or a poorly insulated outside wall. Choose an inside wall free of drafts and direct sun.

 Tuning up. Have your piano tuned at least once a year—even if you don't use it much. If you play it frequently, you may want to have it tuned more often.

To move a piano, hire a professional who knows how to avoid damaging the instrument. After the piano arrives at its new location, give it a month to settle in before calling the piano tuner.

Leave repairs to the pros. It's better not to dust the strings or attempt any routine maintenance on a piano's mechanical parts. Wipe the keys with a damp cloth, but don't use chemical cleansers.

To find a good piano tuner, ask a piano teacher. If you refer to the Yellow Pages, look for a member of the Piano Technicians Guild. A list of Canadian tuners associated with the Piano Technicians Guild can be found at the PTG website at http://www.ptg.org/rptlist.htm#canada.

Before you buy a piano, ask a registered piano technician for advice. A piano made more than 20 years ago is likely to have problems. Spinets are usually the least desirable; their sound is inferior, and they are harder to service.

Try to play every day. A piano that isn't played on a regular basis becomes stiff and sluggish.

PICKPOCKETS

Don't display money in public—it draws the attention of pickpockets and muggers. If you get cash at an ATM, put it out of sight immediately. If you make small purchases from street vendors, pay for them from a small "walking-around" supply in your pocket rather than pulling out your wallet or money belt and showing the world your bankroll.

Keep your wallet in a front-pants or inside-coat pocket, not a rear-pants or outer-coat one with easy access for thieves.

Divide and protect. Carry some cash in your wallet and some in a separate pocket. If your pocket does get picked, at least the robber won't get everything.

Public commotion alert. Fights, loud arguments, and people falling down or pushing and shoving in crowded places are often situations created by pickpockets. They may be working in teams to distract you from your valuables.

Ho, ho, ho. Everybody loves the year-end holidays, especially pickpockets. Be alert and watch your valuables. Skilled pickpockets are out in force around shopping malls, department stores, airports, and office buildings during the holiday season.

PICNICS

A large galvanized metal tub makes a fine outdoor ice bucket. Fill it with crushed ice and set it in a shady place. For a large party, use two tubs, filling one with alcoholic beverages, the other with soft drinks.

Picnic ware. Invest in good plastic plates and glassware and inexpensive stainless steel flatware for picnics; they're easier to use than paper plates and plastic utensils. Best of all, they pay for themselves after a few outings.

Use white to decorate the table for an evening picnic. Like a white flower garden, it will look luminous in the ebbing light.

Make location the attraction for a picnic. Drive to a place with a spectacular view and have a tailgate picnic; bike to a favorite woodland site and stop for lunch; or meet on an urban rooftop at dusk and picnic as you watch the city's lights come on.

PICTURE FRAMING

Make your own frame. To set off your favorite vacation photo, buy a simple but oversized frame and glue your trip's receipts, tickets, newspapers, and even small currency all over it.

Cluster framed pictures on one section of a wall instead of spreading them along its entire length. A variety of different types of frames can add interest and impact. Maintain one unifying element, though, such as the color of the frames or the mats.

Frame vintage family photos with dark frames and warm-toned mats. Mat papers should be acid-free so that your priceless mementos won't deteriorate.

Use picture glass rather than window glass in frames; it's thinner and more transparent, so that photos and prints look clearer and brighter. For valuable pictures, request special glass for screening out the ultraviolet rays, which can damage works on paper.

In a child's room, use acrylic instead of glass in picture frames. If a picture falls, the acrylic won't shatter and leave dangerous glass shards on the floor.

Buy appropriate frames. Contemporary art demands simple frames; traditional prints look better in old-fashioned-looking frames. Pictures are enhanced by artistically suitable frames.

PICTURE HANGING

Wall hooks. Weight determines the size picture hook needed to hold a picture (the packages indicate weight limits). Two hooks can give wide or heavy pictures added lateral stability.

Gallery rods, used in many art galleries (and available at frame shops or art supply stores), allow you to change pictures frequently without ruining your walls. A narrow strip of rigid metal, the rod hooks over a picture molding near the ceiling and hangs vertically. Adjustable hooks hold pictures on the rod at any height.

A work of art. As an alternative to hanging a favorite artwork, display it on an artist's easel. The artwork takes on greater importance.

Make Your Own Starstruck Picture Frame

You'll need an unfinished frame, blue and gold acrylic paint, and a few of the embroidered gold stars available in notions stores.

1 Paint the front of the frame with blue acrylic paint. Also paint the inner edges of the frame but not the outer edges.

2 Paint the outer edges of the frame with metallic-gold acrylic paint, being careful to keep the gold off the front.

3 Dab glue lightly on the backs of the embroidered stars and place them on the front of the frame.

4 Add glass and a backing board for a picture-perfect finish. These make great gifts at a fraction of the cost of store-bought frames.

A WORLD OF SAVORY PIES

Instead of fruit or other sweet filling, savory pies come filled with meat, vegetables, and cheese, and make delicious main dishes. Virtually every national cuisine features some sort of savory pie—Italian pizzas, French tarts, Mexican tacos, and American pot pies, to name a few. Here are some tips for making them with ease.

▶ *International pizzas. Although pizza was originally an Italian dish, you can make it to reflect other ethnic cuisines—for example, Mexican (tostadas topped with salsa and jack cheese), Greek (pita topped with ground lamb, spinach and feta), or Provençal (French bread topped with tomato sauce, olives, and goat cheese). Be creative.*

▶ *Quiches. A quiche is an unsweeted custard pie that is generally flavored with some combination of cheese, vegetables (spinach, mushrooms, zucchini), or meat (sausage, bacon). Quiches are easy to prepare and also freeze quite well, making them ideal dishes to prepare ahead.*

▶ *Deep-dish pies. Steak & kidney pie and chicken pot pie are two examples of this hearty type of savory pie. Shepherd's pie, another variation, is the easiest deep dish pie to make because it has no bottom crust and is topped with mashed potatoes.*

soften and reattach to the crumbs, and each slice will come out intact.

A custard pie should come out of the oven when the middle is still slightly wobbly, otherwise it will be tough. The middle will firm up as the pie cools.

When baking ahead, make fruit or nut pies; they keep best. They can also be frozen and simply thawed for a party. Custard and chiffon pies become soggy when prepared in advance. Prevent this by making the filling and crust separately and simply spooning the custard filling into the baked crust at serving time.

Pie à la mode is no accidental mating of ingredients. Adding ice cream is an excellent way to sweeten a naturally tart pie, such as cherry or apple.

PILLOWS

Goose-down pillows are wonderfully comfortable and so durable that they warrant their extra expense. However, people with allergies should avoid them in favor of polyester fill or latex foam pillows.

Use oversized floor cushions instead of chairs in a child's room. Easier to move around than rigid, heavy furniture, they give a greater sense of freedom and flexibility. They also make soft landing pads for a youngster who likes to jump.

PIES & PIE CRUSTS

To put a frozen pie crust into your own pie pan, allow it to thaw until it is pliable. Slip it into your pan and gently flatten it, particularly where the sides meet the bottom. You can then reflute the top for a one-crust pie or wait and crimp the top crust to it. For a 25 cm (10 in.) pie pan, buy deep-dish frozen pie shells.

 Handle pie dough gingerly. Work quickly without kneading or stretching the dough, which makes it heavy and tough.

Fresh pie-crust dough is available in the refrigerator sections of your supermarkets. Since it comes

folded into quarters, it's easy to unfold, fan out, and mold into your pie pans.

When baking an unfilled crust, prick the bottom and sides with a fork, cover with heavy aluminum foil, and top with ceramic pie weights (dry beans also work). This prevents overbrowning and keeps the dough from puffing out of shape as it bakes.

Substitute gingersnaps for graham crackers in your favorite crumb-crust recipe. This crust is especially tasty with a pumpkin or lemon custard filling.

Chilled pies made with crumb crusts can be tricky to serve. If the crumbs stick to the bottom of the pie plate, set the plate on a hot, damp towel for a few minutes. The butter in the crust will

Insert a sachet of lavender, chamomile, tangerine, or rose inside a decorative pillow and

enjoy a luxuriously fragrant bedroom year-round. Refresh the sachet with new potpourri every few months, as needed, or substitute a spiced tea bag.

Pillows as unifiers. Use pillows on sofas, chairs, beds, or the floor to tie together the color and design elements of a room.

PINECONES

Prepare evergreen cones for craft projects by heating them to kill any insect eggs or larval residents. Spread the cones in one layer on a baking sheet and bake them for 25 minutes in a 95°C (200°F) oven. Or put them in a paper bag and microwave them for 8 to 10 minutes at 50 percent power. Cones harvested with their scales closed may require more heating time to open fully.

String a festive cone garland to decorate a mantelpiece or banister. Use large cones substantial enough for holes to be drilled near their bases with a 3 mm (⅛ in.) drill bit. Thread them with florist's wire or carpet thread and a sailmaker's needle, separating each cone from its neighbor with a bead or a knot of ribbon.

Fast pinecone wreath. Cut out a wreath-shaped base from an old corrugated cardboard box (for extra strength and rigidity, cut out two bases and glue them together). Hot-glue the pinecones directly to the cardboard in three concentric rings, placing the largest cones in the center ring and smaller cones on the outside and inside rings. Fill in gaps where the cardboard shows through with smaller cones or nuts.

Give old frames a woodsy look. Hot-glue tiny cones, such as those from larches or hemlocks, to the front of a picture frame so that they completely cover its surface.

PIZZA

Prepared bread dough makes a quick pizza crust. Follow the package directions for handling it, but instead of forming a loaf, roll the dough out in a large circle. Place it on a greased pan or baking sheet, top with your favorite pizza toppings, and bake.

Pizza cheat. Ready-made fresh or frozen pizza dough is available in most supermarkets. Or, use day-old French or Italian bread, pita bread, or English muffins as your bread base.

Before baking pizza, spray the surface of the pan or the baking tiles with vegetable oil, then scatter cornmeal on it. This prevents the pizza from sticking.

Quick finger food. If you need a fast and delectable cocktail party treat, order a pizza and then cut it into elegant, bite-sized pieces.

For low-fat pizza, use a fat-free tomato sauce and stick to vegetable toppings such as broccoli, eggplant, green peppers, mushrooms, onions, spinach, and zucchini. Top with part-skim-milk mozzarella and a little Parmesan.

Kitchen shears slice pizza better than a pizza cutter. They cut all the way through the first time, for a quick, neat job.

Dessert pizza—a flat pie made with a sweet crust and topped with fresh fruit and a dollop of whipped cream—is particularly popular with teenagers.

RIGHT STUFF

BAKING TILES FOR CRISP-CRUST PIZZA

With unglazed terra-cotta tiles, you can create your own brick oven at home—and then make pizza just like a professional. Place the terra cotta tiles in the bottom of your oven; the porous tiles will draw moisture out of the dough's crust, making your pizza delightfully crispy. You can use simple terra cotta tiles, available from builders' supply stores. Or try gourmet tiles, like Hot Bricks, a complete tile kit that fits easily into most ovens.

PLANT PROPAGATION

Rooting cuttings from healthy plants is the most common way to propagate plants. Use a sharp knife to make the cut. Dip the ends in rooting hormone and plant them in covered flats until they form roots. Keep the soil warm and moist. Pot the cuttings as soon as roots emerge; keep the plants out of direct sun until the plants sprout new leaves.

Water rooting. Many houseplants and half-hardy perennials, such as impatiens, will root in water. Cover a glass of water with aluminum foil; stick the cutting through (to keep the leaves dry). Pot the plants when roots appear.

Heirloom and miniature roses are good candidates for propagating by cuttings because they needn't be grafted to other roots as many roses do. When plants have bloomed, pick out healthy new-growth stems with at least four leaflets intact. Cut, dip in hormone powder, and plant. Expect roots in a few weeks.

Propagate narcissus and tulip bulbs by digging them up in the fall, breaking off their tiny offsets, or bulblets, and planting them.

PLANTING

Start small. Extra-big (and extra-expensive) trees and shrubs suffer more root damage during the planting process than do smaller specimens and take longer to resume growing. Commonly, a tree or shrub that is small and vigorous will actually be larger 10 years after replanting than an extra-big specimen.

Guarantee a big success. If you decide to invest in a large tree or shrub, arrange with the nursery to transport and plant it for you. The nursery will charge for this service, but it has the equipment and skilled labor to handle heavy plants. Also, most nurseries will guarantee the plant, replacing it for free if it dies during the first growing season.

Gimme shelter. Give young plants a break in windy locations by setting them first inside small paper bags containing soil. Bury the bags in the garden, leaving 5 to 7.5 cm (2–3 in.) of the tops sticking out of the dirt. The seedlings will be protected and the bags will decay.

Real burlap, often used to hold the ball of dirt around the roots of a shrub or tree being transplanted, can be left in the planting hole to disintegrate. Just remove the ropes that bind it and loosen the top folds. If the burlap is shiny or slippery, however, remove it. It is likely a plastic imitation that will prevent the roots from spreading.

Bare-root plants, dug out of the ground and shipped while dormant, are a bargain when given a good start. Open the package as soon as it arrives and unpack the plants, setting the roots in a bucket of water mixed with soluble houseplant fertilizer (one-quarter of the quantity called for on the fertilizer label). Plant the new arrivals the next morning.

When to plant. In the South, where winters are mild and summers are hot, plant trees, shrubs, and perennials in the fall. The new plants will have several months to send their roots deep into the soil before they face a summer drought. In the North, where summers are temperate and winters severe, plant trees, shrubs, and perennials in early spring. This gives them a lengthy growing time before they must weather a winter.

PLAYGROUNDS

Injuries commonly occur when children play on equipment they are too young to handle. Buy a system that adapts as kids grow, with swings and play platforms that can be raised and more difficult equipment—monkey bars and rings—that can be added later.

Beware of the hard surfaces of older playgrounds (gravel, concrete, or asphalt). Newer playgrounds have cushioning materials (mulch, wood chips, pea gravel, or sand) that make them a safer place to play. To minimize injuries, there should be 23 cm (9 in.) of shock-absorbing material over the play area, extending 1.8 m (6 ft) from its perimeter in all directions.

Set rules for safe behavior. Make sure that your children and their friends understand playground safety rules: no jumping from the highest point, no wrestling on monkey bars, no jumping off a moving swing. Watch out, too, for loose clothing that can get caught in equipment.

PLAYING CARDS

Magical sanding block. Wrap sandpaper around an old deck of cards. As you sand, it will conform to the shape of irregular surfaces, including rounded edges, moldings, and grooves.

Long-lasting plastic. Use plastic-coated playing cards, which hold up much longer than uncoated ones. They are also easy to clean.

Go on-line. Log on to the Internet to play card games—bridge, gin rummy, hearts, spades, and many others—with fellow enthusiasts around the world.

Teaching tools. Use cards to help young children learn numbers and life skills, such as following rules and waiting for a turn. Keep games simple—"go fish" is a good starting point. (Remove the face cards to simplify matters.)

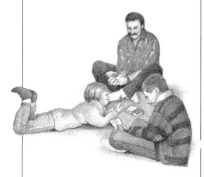

PLAYTIME

A safer sandbox. If your toddler tends to throw sand or put it in her mouth while she's playing in a sandbox, show her alternatives, such as burying a toy or molding sand shapes or castles. Give your child a bucket of sand and another bucket of water, and let her create "mud."

PLAY DATES FOR CHILDREN

Play dates help children learn how to get along with their peers. Your youngster can have a wonderful time with a playmate if you follow the suggestions below.

▶ *Start with short visits, about an hour or less.*

▶ *Invite the parent or caregiver the first time and let that person stay if it seems appropriate.*

▶ *Have a project or two up your sleeve, in case the youngsters have a hard time getting started on something to do.*

▶ *Be prepared to reinforce manners about sharing and being the host; give-and-take isn't learned in a day.*

▶ *Be sure to reciprocate play dates to which your child has been invited; your youngster needs the experience of being both host and guest.*

Make a mess. When children under five years old play, they enjoy getting stuff all over themselves. Find activities such as bubble-blowing, plasticine clay molding, and finger painting with water-soluble paints, which allow them to splash and pound and dribble away to their hearts' content. (Washable clothes are a must for this, of course.)

Try playing no-lose games. If your child is going through a period of being a sore loser, switch to no-lose games for a while. Play badminton and Ping-Pong, striving for the longest volley instead of the highest score. Have a game of catch, or put together a picture puzzle.

Go bowling at home. Empty 2-liter plastic soda bottles can double as bowling pins. Save enough for a set of pins, and use any soft ball as your bowling ball. The bottles can also serve as safe knock-overs for toy bulldozers and trucks.

Animal cracker race. This game is ideal for younger children. Two to four kids move animal crackers around the outside squares of a checkerboard, moving the number of squares indicated on a thrown die. If your animal cracker lands on a "hurdle" (created with a hard candy or marshmallow), you have to go back two squares—but you get to eat the hurdle. The first animal cracker to make the complete circuit of the board wins.

Let young ones help you with cooking or gardening. They can start out by playing with toy dishes or miniature trowels beside you in the kitchen or garden. Gradually show them how to do small tasks—stirring cookie dough, for example, or planting a pot of geraniums. Until they reach school age, don't force them to finish a task if they get restless.

Avoid animal swings. Molded-plastic and aluminum animal swings—which weigh from 14 to 36 kg (30–80 lb)—can cause severe injuries to a child struck by one. If you see one of these swings in a public park or school playground—more than 10,000 were installed between 1951 and 1991—ask the park or school officials to call the manufacturer to have the swing removed.

PLUMBING

Rule no. 1: Make sure that you and all family members know the location of your house's main water shutoff valve and how to work it. If you ever have a burst pipe or a flood, turning off the water right away can prevent damage to your home. Once the valve has been turned off, open the lowest faucet in the house. This will reduce pressure in the pipes while they drain.

To patch a leaking pipe temporarily, first shut off the water supply to it and let it drain. Remove any rust on the leaking area with steel wool, wipe it dry, and wrap a rubber pad or a piece of garden hose around the leak and secure it with clamps.

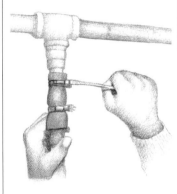

Noisy water. Muffle clanking in your water system by wrapping pipes with fiberglass or foam insulation. You can also install an anti-hammer device, sold at hardware stores, which quiets the water running through the pipes.

A quick fix. For a tiny leak in a lead or plastic pipe, put petroleum jelly into the crack and wrap the pipe with a rag or tape.

To silence a midnight drip, tie a string to the end of the faulty faucet. The drops of water will flow quietly down the string into the sink, allowing you to get some sleep before you have to get up and fix the faucet.

FLEXIBLE FAUCET

This faucet combines the flexibility of a sprayer with the reliability of a traditional spigot. The spray wand, ridged for a good grip, pulls out from the fixture to rinse awkward-size dishes or fill deep pots. With the touch of a button, you can change the water flow from spray to stream.

Getting out of hot water. If there is a problem in the hot-water line of your house, shut off the water supply to the water heater. The main line can be left on so that the house at least has a supply of cold water.

Double problem. If your sink has two bowls and one needs to be unclogged, you will have to stop up the other drain before you can use a plunger on the stopped-up drain. The bowls are connected, and air from the free drain will hamper the power of your plunging in the other one.

Smart timing. Start a plumbing job early in the day. Then if you find you are missing a part and must make a trip to the hardware store, you'll have time to finish the project without waiting until the next day to turn the water back on in the house.

Replacement washers. Buy several spares whenever you pick up washers to fix a faucet. Store them in a place where you will not forget them—near the main water shutoff valve for the house or in your tool kit.

PLYWOOD

Bed too soft? You don't have to spend a fortune on a new mattress and box springs. A plywood sheet, either ½ or ¾ inch thick, makes a fine back support. Slip it between the mattress and box springs of your bed.

When insulating an attic, use a sheet of plywood over the joists as a platform to work from. Move it along as you unroll the batting.

Tote a sheet of plywood with a 5.4 m (18 ft) rope tied into a loop. Slip the loop vertically over the sheet, put your arm over the plywood, and grasp the rope with your hand. Use the other hand to steady the sheet.

 Quick shelves. Have plywood cut into 30 or 35 cm (12–14 in.) widths to build storage units in the attic or basement. Stack bricks at either end of the boards to support the shelves at whatever heights you need.

POISONING

Call a poison control center first and tell them whatever you can about the poison involved. They may advise you to give the victim milk or water to dilute the poison, to take ipecac syrup to induce vomiting, or to go to an emergency room right away.

Use only original containers to store medicine, toxic chemicals, and household cleaners. Never put a potentially poisonous substance into a soda bottle or food container.

For inhaled poisons such as carbon monoxide, get the victim into fresh air as quickly as possible and open all doors and windows. Then call for medical help.

If poison touches skin or eyes, remove any clothing that came into contact with it and flood the area with water. Eyes especially need flooding with lukewarm or cold water for at least 15 minutes. Get immediate medical attention.

Beware poisonous spider bites. If the person bitten by a spider experiences pain, swelling, sweating, or nausea, put something cold on the bite mark. Seek emergency medical attention without delay.

POISONOUS PLANTS

A big problem? Although some 700 species of toxic plants inhabit North America, actual reported incidents of poisonings are few and far between. In fact, there are twice as many cases of poisonings from household cleaners as from toxic plants reported in the average year.

Kill poison ivy, oak, or sumac with the herbicides 2,4-D and triclopyr used together. When sprayed on the leaves, these systemic chemicals go to the plants' roots. A natural, if not necessarily practical, remedy to poison ivy is a pet goat. Goats eat poison ivy with relish and with no ill effects.

If hiking near toxic plants, keep your skin covered by wearing long pants tucked into your socks, laced-up shoes, a long-sleeved shirt, and gloves. If you touch a poisonous plant, be careful not to rub your eyes. Also, wash your clothes through two full cycles when you get home.

Small children are especially at risk, and parents should teach their youngsters never to eat any plant or plant parts before checking with parents or caregivers.

Protect pets by training them never to eat any plants in the house or around the yard. Because cats love to chew leaves, you should keep plants that are harmful to them, such as ivies and philodendrons, out of the house. If your dog has been exposed to poison ivy or oak, put on a pair of rubber gloves and give it a bath.

POISONOUS PLANTS

Of all the toxic plants that surround us, the greatest threat comes not from wild species in the woods but from plants commonly used in home landscaping and indoor decorating. Listed below are the most common poisonous plants, the parts that are dangerous, and their effects.

PLANT NAME	POISONOUS PARTS; SYMPTOMS
Amaryllis *Hippeastrum* spp.	Bulb is potentially fatal if eaten.
Azalea *Rhododendron* spp.	Whole plant can cause nausea, paralysis, and convulsions if eaten.
Crown-of-thorns *Euphorbia milii*	Milky sap may cause skin or eye irritation; severe irritation of mouth, throat, and stomach result if swallowed.
Dumbcane *Dieffenbachia* spp.	Leaves and stems cause irritation and numbing of mouth and throat if eaten.
English ivy *Hedera helix*	Leaves and fruits cause difficulty in breathing, possibly coma if eaten.
Hydrangea *Hydrangea macrophylla*	Leaves and buds can cause nausea, vomiting, abdominal pain, difficulty breathing, dizziness, and convulsions if eaten.
Lily-of-the-valley *Convallaria majalis*	All parts highly poisonous; can cause cardiac disturbance, nausea if eaten.
Lantana *Lantana* spp.	All parts; causes vomiting, diarrhea, visual disturbance, and weakness if eaten.
Oleander *Nerium oleander*	All parts; a single leaf or flower may be fatal if eaten; even smoke is toxic.
Philodendron *Philodendron* spp.	Leaves and stems cause irritation of mouth and throat if eaten.
Pothos *Epipremnum aureum*	Leaves and stems cause irritation to mouth and throat if eaten; juice may irritate skin.
Yew *Taxus* spp.	Seeds and leaves may cause gastroenteritis and cardiac disturbance if eaten.

PORCELAIN

Dishwasher safe? Plain porcelain dishware can be safely cleaned in a dishwasher. However, if the dishes are embellished with gold leaf, platinum, or hand-painting, wash them by hand.

When buying a porcelain set produced in the 19th or 20th century, examine the pieces together under bright light; if the colors don't match, pieces from different sets may have been mixed. Porcelain sets from the 18th century have slight color variations due to less precise kiln-firing techniques.

Remove dust from porcelain with a hair dryer on the low-heat or cool setting. Soak intricate pieces in warm water with a bit of mild detergent. Clean crevices with a soft-bristled brush.

Heat and serve. Many newer lines of porcelain are microwave safe; look on the back of a plate or cup for the notation.

To repair valuable porcelain, contact a local art museum. Curators of porcelain collections can suggest a good craftsperson.

PORK

Streamlined pigs make today's pork a low-fat meat. Modern pork tenderloin and loin chops have 4.1 and 6.4 g of fat respectively, barely more than a chicken breast's 3 g, and far less than a chicken thigh's 13 g of fat.

Read canned-ham labels. Some require refrigeration in the can; others can be kept unopened on a cupboard shelf. Once opened, both kinds must be refrigerated.

 Perfect bacon. Start cooking bacon in a cold skillet or broiler or microwave oven. There's no need to add fat to this already fatty cut. Cook it slowly to minimize shrinkage, and watch it carefully—bacon burns quickly.

Drippings. Collect pork and bacon drippings in a used coffee can. (Don't pour them down the drain because they will clog it.) When the fat hardens, discard the fat, can and all, in the garbage can.

POSITIVE THINKING

Look for silver linings. Try to extract some good from most of life's experiences, including those that are painful or disappointing.

Live in the here-and-now. We can't know what the future holds, and dwelling on the past only keeps us chained to events or persons that may no longer affect us.

Let go of life's little annoyances—not because they aren't annoying or because others should behave better than they sometimes do, but because they are not worth getting upset about.

Count your blessings every day. It's trite but true that taking a few minutes to think about the good occurrences and people in your life helps to diminish the power that bad events have over you.

Pick an object—a cheery postcard, framed motto, small pillow, or some witty object—to remind

 HOW TO LOOK ON THE SUNNY SIDE

It takes practice to develop a sunnier viewpoint. Here are some ideas for honing your positive-thinking skills.

▶ *Choose positive phrasing. Instead of saying you'll try to do something, say you will do it. Replace excuses like "It wasn't my fault because . . ." with "I'm sorry—it's my responsibility and I'll take care of it."*

▶ *Put on a happy face. Even if you're feeling upset, act happy. Put a smile on your face, pretend cheerfulness, and simulate friendliness. Actions actually trigger emotions.*

▶ *Be friendly. Sociability is crucial to a healthy mental attitude. When you feel anxious or depressed, push yourself to reach out to friends or join a new interest group.*

▶ *Make plans. If you face problems, avoid comparing your life now with your life in the past. Focus instead on devising solutions to problems.*

▶ *Move your body. Physical exercise not only helps you stay fit but also can engender an optimistic attitude.*

Now you can easily transport food to potlucks (and picnics) with insulated carriers such as Tupperware Rock 'N Serve (left) and Pyrex Portables (right). These carriers help to ensure that your salad will arrive at the party crisp and chilled and your lasagna will smell and taste as if it just came out of the oven. The containers that come inside the carriers can make life easier for stay-at-home meals as well; they are versatile enough to go from the freezer to the microwave to the table without a pause.

you of your intention to think positively. Put it in a place where you will see it every day and be reminded of your goal.

POTATOES

Cook twice as many potatoes as you think you will need. The leftovers can later be quickly reheated, mashed, or used in soups and salads. And if you are boiling potatoes, save the cooking water. It makes a nutritious, tasty stock for soups and breads.

To avoid poisoning, toss out any potatoes with sprouts. Pare away any greenish skin to a depth of 3 mm (⅛ in.) But don't be concerned about the black ring that sometimes shows up inside potatoes; it is harmless.

Top baked potatoes with low-fat yogurt and chives or parsley instead of butter or sour cream. For even fewer calories, use non-fat sour cream or yogurt.

Microwave speed. You can cook up to three baking potatoes in 10 minutes or less in a microwave oven. (It takes longer to cook more potatoes.) For a crisp skin, put the potatoes in a hot (220°C/425°F) conventional oven for 10 additional minutes.

The right potato for the job. For baking, deep-frying, or mashing, use mealy-textured russet or Idaho potatoes. For boiling, steaming, or roasting, select thin-skinned varieties, including new potatoes; these have a waxy flesh that holds their shape, even when served cold in salads.

For variety, bake sweet potatoes or yams, which are low in calories, fat-free, and rich in flavor. To create a tasty variation on mashed potatoes, boil white and sweet potatoes together.

For quick baked potatoes, use a potato baking rack. The metal tine on which the potato is skewered helps to heat it internally, thereby reducing the cooking time.

POTLUCK SUPPERS

If you are the host, arrange for someone—a noncook perhaps—to bring the centerpiece as well as extra napkins, plates, silverware, and glasses. Supplying these items is often unfairly left to the host.

 Dish ID. Write your name, address, and telephone number on masking tape and stick it on the bottom of all serving dishes you take to a potluck dinner.

To create a balanced menu, draw lots to decide who brings what. List food categories, such as main dishes, salads, breads, desserts, and beverages, on slips of paper. Fill out enough slips so that each guest is assigned one thing to prepare. If every person provides a dish that will feed at least six, there will be plenty of food. Guests should be free to trade categories with each other.

Casserole carriers. Save bakery boxes to reuse when carrying a cooked dish to a potluck dinner. Line a box with crumpled newspaper to both brace and insulate the dish.

POTPOURRI

When the fragrance diminishes, you can resuscitate potpourri by crushing and crumbling it to release scent still stored in the leaves. Placing it in the humid air of a bathroom will also coax out the last remaining aroma.

Make quick holiday sachets with small handkerchiefs or the little muslin bags available in stores that sell dried flowers and herbs. Fill these with a potpourri mixture and embellish the package by tying it closed with a red ribbon and a sprig of holly.

Fragrance in a bag. To create a spicy garden potpourri, start with 1 L (4 cups) of dried flower petals in a brown paper bag. Add 15 mL (1 tbsp) each of orange peels, ground cloves, allspice, cinnamon, rosemary, and crushed bay leaves. Add 45 mL (3 tbsp) of powdered orrisroot and 10 drops of rose, jasmine, or lilac oil or a combination of oils. Tie up the bag and shake it every few days for three weeks.

POTS & PANS

Prevent oxidation from attacking rust-prone cookware (like cast-iron frying pans and steel woks) by drying them well, then lining them with absorbent paper towels before you put them away.

Stain chaser. Cream of tartar, best known as a stabilizer of delicate foods, is also a powerful cleaning agent to use on alu-minum pots. Fill a stained pot with water, add 15–30 mL (1–2 tbsp) of cream of tartar, and boil for 20 minutes. Then buff the pot with steel wool to give it a shiny finish.

 Hang 'em high. A pot rack screwed or bolted into the kitchen ceiling or along a pantry wall is a neat way to keep your pots and pans handy. It also allows you to free up counter and cabinet space. Pot-hanging racks, sold in houseware and department stores, are decorative as well. They look especially attractive holding copper pots and pans.

POTTERY

When buying handmade pottery, ask if metals were used in making the glazes or decorations. If they were, avoid using them as serving pieces for such acidic foods as vinegar-based dressings, fruit juice, tomatoes, or wine. Acid can leach out toxic metals such as cadmium and lead.

A pottery-painting party is a novel way to entertain. Many pottery studios provide materials and space, even cake and balloons, for such parties. The guests turn unglazed ceramic pieces into personalized works of art with an array of paints and glazes. After the pieces are fired in a kiln, guests receive their handmade art.

Microwave warning: Use an oven mitt or pot holder the first time you take a pottery cup or bowl out of the microwave, unless you know it is microwave safe. If the clay or glaze contains traces of metal, it will absorb heat and make the piece too hot to handle.

POWER OF ATTORNEY

Doing business while away. Use a power of attorney to appoint someone else to sign your name, if you are going to be absent for the signing of an important contract, such as at the closing of a house sale. The person whom you appoint need not be a licensed attorney, but simply someone you trust to represent your best interests on this occasion.

ONE TOP—LOTS OF POTS

A universal pot cover is designed to top all of those pots in your kitchen that have either lost their lids or never had one. This model, manufactured by Cook's Club, is made of heavy-gauge stainless steel with specially-styled ridges to fit snugly on top of most pans and skillets. It also has heat-resistant handles. A tool no kitchen should be without, universal pot lids are available at most housewares and gourmet stores.

With a "Special Power of Attorney" (also called a "Limited Power of Attorney"), you authorize someone you trust to act on your behalf in a special situation, such as when you are traveling or incapacitated. This is a typical example.

Name the province.
Exact terminology may vary by province, so be sure to comply with provincial laws.

Specify the situation in which authorization may be required while you are unavailable, making sure to include emergency medical treatment. If it involves other people (such as children), include their full names.

Trusted person.
The person you authorize need not be a lawyer, but is called an "attorney-in-fact" because the word "attorney" refers to someone who acts on another person's behalf.

Special Power of Attorney

I, Alice Cunningham, of (street address, city, county, province), do appoint Betty Johnson, of (street address, city, county, province), as my lawful attorney-in-fact, for the specific purposes of:

authorizing ordinary or emergency medical care, school trips, release or participation from school, activities, lessons, after-school care, or other acts relative to custodial care and supervision for my two children, Kenny Cunningham and Ginger Cunningham, and for any costs attendant to such activities, care, or treatment.

I also give my lawful attorney-in-fact permission to function in any and every way that I might if I were personally present. My attorney-in-fact is empowered to undertake any acts necessary and proper to the exercise of these duties.

This power of attorney takes effect on (beginning date) and terminates on (ending date), and shall not be affected by my disability, incapacity, or incompetency.

Executed on (date signed) at (city where signed.)

_____
(Signature)
Alice Cunningham

I, Betty Johnson, accept appointment as attorney-in-fact for the above-named prinicpal and for the purposes described.

_____
(Signature)
Betty Johnson, Attorney-in-Fact

Province of (name)
County of (name)

Appearing before me personally Alice Cunningham and Betty Johnson were duly sworn and voluntarily signed the above document as their free act on this (date signed).

_____
(Signature)
Sally Stern, Notary Public
My commisssion expires on 1/1/98

Your lawyer should advise you about when you might need a special power of attorney, and exactly what it should cover.

Limit authority to the time that you will be unavailable by naming the exact start and end dates.

Signatures. Both you and the designated caretaker are required to sign in front of a Notary Public.

Limit the power you give. In a written power of attorney, specify exactly what the person you designate as your "attorney-in-fact" may do on your behalf: manage your property, withdraw money from the bank, sign a settlement document, or consent to a child's field trip. Without such limits, you would be liable for anything your designee signs in your name.

You can designate two people in your power of attorney to sign jointly for your affairs. This is an extra protection against having one person take advantage of you—for example, by writing a lot of cheques on your account.

Take back your power. You can revoke a power of attorney any-time—if there is only one copy, just tear it up. But you must inform interested parties that it is no longer valid. If the document has been presented to a bank, for example, make sure it knows of the revocation.

No power of attorney you sign is effective after you die. Only your will can designate control over your assets once you're deceased.

PRAYER

Social spirituality. If you feel alone in your spiritual life, try practicing your faith in a setting that offers fresh perspectives from other people. There are many venues for communal prayer besides church—weekend retreats, Internet-based groups, and telephone prayer hotlines.

Teach your children your beliefs about prayer by setting an example at home with blessings over meals and nighttime prayer. Help them understand the words and the purpose of their prayers.

Prayer as action. Instead of thinking of prayer only as preparation for taking action, think of praying also as an action in itself— a potent spiritual weapon against life's difficulties.

PREGNANCY

Walk. A half-hour stroll a day increases blood circulation in the legs, which helps prevent the varicose veins that sometimes appear with pregnancy. It also stimulates a sluggish intestine and strengthens the abdominal muscles.

Take a nap at lunchtime during the first trimester, when you may feel overwhelmingly sleepy. Eat small, frequent meals to help keep your energy from fading.

A home pregnancy test gives you the news as early as possible. You can stop drinking and smoking and start on a healthy diet even before you see a doctor.

Baby your hair during pregnancy and in the three months after delivery, when excessive hair loss may occur. Use a mild shampoo and let hair dry naturally. Avoid permanents and coloring.

PREMENSTRUAL SYNDROME (PMS)

Cut caffeine and alcohol from your diet for two weeks before menstruation begins, and limit sugar, salt, and dietary fat. These foods can promote water retention, mood swings, and other unpleasant symptoms of PMS.

EASY DOES IT   TO REST YOUR ACHING BACK

During pregnancy, your bulging abdomen pulls your spine into an arch, which can cause lower or middle back pain. Try the following back relievers.

▶ *Lie on your back and raise your knees (with feet flat on the floor) until your back is completely flat. Hold for several minutes.*

▶ *Sit cross-legged. Roll your head forward and lower it toward the floor as far as you can. Hold there for 30 seconds, then repeat three or four times.*

▶ *Stand with your back against a wall and with your heels about 20 cm (8 in.) away from it. Tilt your pelvis slightly forward and press your lower back into the wall. Hold the pose for 2 to 3 minutes.*

Keep a diary. The "black moods" of PMS may indicate a more serious condition. By keeping a diary, you can document how often symptoms of depression occur. If you find yourself feeling blue or angry more than 50 percent of the month, seek help from a doctor or therapist to rule out a deeper, psychological problem.

Eat often—at least every three hours. Fruits, vegetables, complex carbohydrates, and low-fat dairy products are good food choices.

Take acetaminophen or aspirin to prevent or at least relieve cramps, backaches, headaches, and pains in your joints.

Evening primrose oil, sold in health-food stores, is thought by many to relieve breast soreness and other PMS symptoms. Take the herb three days before you expect symptoms to start and continue until your period begins.

Get regular exercise, especially during the two weeks before your period begins. Aerobic exercise releases into the bloodstream pain-relieving endorphins, which can also pick up your spirits and promote relaxation.

PRENUPTIAL AGREEMENTS

Do you really need one? Prenuptial agreements are important for only 10 to 20 percent of married couples, so think carefully about proposing one. Many lawyers have noted that the process of drawing up an agreement often raises damaging issues of trust between the partners, which can jeopardize the relationship.

 Two lawyers. You and your prospective spouse will each need your own attorney to review a prenuptial agreement. Homegrown agreements or ones involving only one attorney are frequently rejected later.

Telling all. Disclose all of your assets to your prospective spouse before signing a prenuptial agreement. The agreement will not be valid later unless both parties have full knowledge of each other's finances. Most lawyers include a list of assets right in the prenuptial agreement itself.

Provide for your children from a prior marriage with a prenuptial agreement stipulating that they will inherit your money. A spouse ordinarily inherits a portion of the wife's or husband's estate, but spousal inheritance rights can be waived by a prenuptial agreement. Together with a will, this document will ensure that your entire estate goes to your children.

Tape the signing. Have a videographer attend your prenuptial signing as well as the marriage festivities, and videotape the exchanges of vows. If consent to the agreement is challenged later, the videotape will clearly show both parties saying "I do" at the signing of the prenuptial agreement and at the wedding, and will prove that both parties agreed to it with full knowledge of its content and meaning.

Plan ahead. For a solid prenuptial agreement, plan it in detail well in advance of your marriage. A rushed agreement can be considered coerced and tossed out if it is later contended.

PRESCRIPTION MEDICATIONS

"Brown bag" it. Put all your prescription and nonprescription medications (including vitamins) into a brown paper bag and take them to your doctor. She will weed out the drugs that you no longer need and warn you about potential adverse interactions among the remaining medications.

Stop choking. If a pill—prescription or non-prescription—gets stuck in your throat, chew a bite of a banana thoroughly, then swallow it. The banana should dislodge the pill.

Ask your doctor before substituting a generic drug for the prescription you are taking. With certain medications, such as those used to treat epilepsy, the brand-name drugs are better.

Use a mail-order pharmacy to buy drugs taken for chronic conditions such as high blood pressure. It not only will save you trips to the drugstore but is often cheaper.

Can you take fewer pills? If you take a medication several times a day, ask your doctor if there's a newer version of the drug that you can take less often.

PRESSURE COOKERS

A new breed of pressure cooker relieves some of the anxiety caused by the old-fashioned jiggle-top type. Now pressure cookers feature spring-valve pressure gauges and backup safety features that will keep dinner off the ceiling and help you get it to the table in no time.

Bigger is better. You fill a pressure cooker only one-half to two-thirds full for most recipes, so you may need a bigger one than you'd expect. An 8 L (8 qt) cooker is a good size for most families.

The best bottom for a pressure cooker is one made of a stainless steel and aluminum blend. The bimetal base distributes heat more evenly and prevents scorching better than all-stainless-steel or all-aluminum bottoms.

Use a timer. Pressure cookery requires precision because foods are easily overcooked. Start timing most foods when high pressure is reached; vegetables, however, turn out better if you begin timing from the start of cooking.

Keep the steam vent of your pressure cooker unclogged by running a pipe cleaner through it every so often.

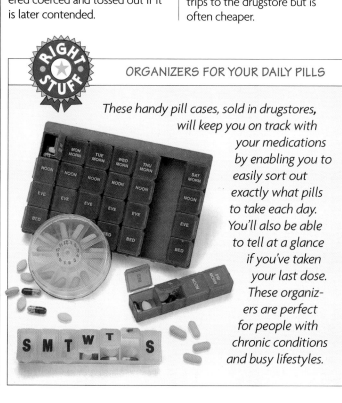

RIGHT STUFF

ORGANIZERS FOR YOUR DAILY PILLS

These handy pill cases, sold in drugstores, will keep you on track with your medications by enabling you to easily sort out exactly what pills to take each day. You'll also be able to tell at a glance if you've taken your last dose. These organizers are perfect for people with chronic conditions and busy lifestyles.

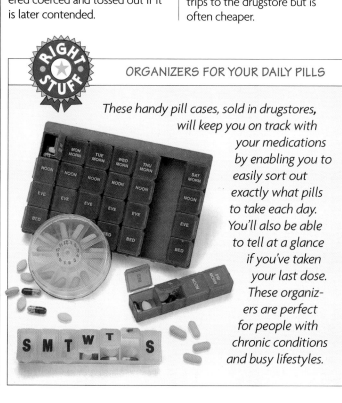

PRIVACY

Not for your eyes. Parents need to keep an eye on their children, of course, and may have to poke into bedrooms and closets occasionally, but one place a kid should have complete privacy is in a diary. Resist the urge to pry into this most private venue.

Do you go to a therapist? If so, ask him if your sessions are confidential. Private psychotherapists can protect most of your confidences, but in some cases mental health counselors working for your employer may be required to report on your personal problems and your need for therapy. All therapists may be legally obligated to answer a subpoena or report child abuse and life-threatening behavior.

Mail privacy. Take immediate action if you suspect that someone has stolen letters or opened packages left in your mailbox. Call the Canada Post, Customer Service, listed in the Blue Pages of your telephone book. Once alerted, the inspectors conduct investigations and press criminal charges when appropriate.

Because more and more patient information is being computerized, give your doctor a statement that you do not want your medical records entered into any computer database accessible by a third party without your express, written consent.

PRIVATE INVESTIGATORS

Look for experience. Hire a private investigative agency that specializes in the kind of work you need, whether it be searches for documents, missing persons, or assets; process serving; personal background and reference checks; integrity testing; questioning of employees; or private security.

Gather the facts. Since most investigators charge by the hour, you can save money by collecting facts before the the clock starts running. Provide names, addresses, telephone numbers, records, and any pertinent details on the matter to be investigated.

 Get a written contract with the agency that states the nature of the investigation, the fee, a cap on costs and expenses, the type of report you'll get, and when you can expect to receive it.

Stick to the law. Work only with an investigative agency that uses lawful means and walk away from any private investigator who suggests otherwise. You could be liable if you knowingly hire an investigator who engages in illegal activities, such as wiretapping a telephone, invading personal privacy, or failing to follow the strict laws covering debt collection.

Insist on meeting the agent assigned to your case. Look for prior investigative experience, "street smarts," and a personality that fits your situation.

PROBATE

Make a will! A valid will that designates your heirs is "proved up"—or probated—after you die, and your wishes turn into inheritances for those you name. But if

---

RIGHT STUFF

DO YOU NEED A LIVING TRUST?

Computer programs such as Living Trust Maker by Nolo Press or The Personal Estate Preservation Plan by The Estate Plan explain the revocable living trust—a way to manage your assets while you are alive and protect your heirs from probate hassles after you die. Both programs are available through software stores.

you die without a valid will or other advance planning that avoids probate altogether, the state decides under its intestacy laws who should inherit your wealth in a probate proceeding.

Skip probate. Family members may be able to distribute the assets of a relative without going through formal probate proceedings if the deceased owned very little—say, the furniture in an apartment and some personal belongings. Ask a lawyer about tax liability and other complications. If any beneficiary objects, for instance, probate proceedings will be necessary.

Pursue alternative probate. Because of simplified probate procedures in some provinces, surviving spouses can probate a will with little hassle, even without a lawyer. To qualify, the entire estate must be left to the spouse. Other streamlined alternative probate procedures are available in some states when the assets are relatively small—$25,000, for example. Call the clerk of courts to find out your province's rules.

Negotiate the fee when you engage a probate lawyer. Some base their fee on a percentage of the value of the estate, and you can ask for a lower percentage. If a lawyer charges by the hour for work undertaken in identifying property, collecting debts, paying taxes, and preparing an accounting, you can propose a lower hourly rate. Whatever you agree to, get it in writing.

PROCRASTINATION

Cold turkey. When you're at your computer, do you too often feel an irresistible urge to call up the solitaire file and then spend the next half hour playing games? If so, one way to get rid of the temptation altogether is by erasing the file from your hard drive. Take a deep breath and just do it.

EASY DOES IT

When you have to accomplish a task, keep the following in mind to help you finish on time.

▶ *Divide and conquer. Separate the job into smaller chunks and take them one by one.*

▶ *Choose a sensible time slot. For example, don't plan on balancing your checkbook when your favorite television show is on. The temptation to watch will be too great.*

▶ *Reward yourself. When you do accomplish what you set out to do, give yourself a little treat: dinner out perhaps or a midafternoon sitcom.*

▶ *One for dear old Dad. A good way to motivate yourself is to keep someone in mind who will be pleased that the job is done or proud of you for finishing it.*

The lesser evil technique. Tackle another chore that seems less distasteful than the one you're avoiding. At least something on your to-do list will get finished—and you'll get to that other chore tomorrow.

Lower your sights a little. If you can't make the final push needed to complete a task, perhaps you're worried about not achieving perfection. Judge yourself and the job's requirements less severely; usually getting a job done is more important than doing it perfectly.

Put yourself on notice. Let others know that you must complete a project by a certain time. Knowing that other people will be aware of your failure if you don't make the deadline may be just the motivation you need to get going.

PRODUCT RECALLS

Catch recalls. Unsafe products may be recalled by the Product Safety Bureau or by the manufacturer. Buyers are entitled to a refund or a free repair, but often it is up to the buyer to find out about the recall. Look for *Consumer Reports,* which publishes a list of recalls every month, or call your regional Product Safety Bureau with questions about specific products.

Toy stores are required to maintain a recall notice board. Keep up with new postings on toys that may be dangerous.

Report hazardous products. Complaints alert government agencies about unsafe products. Call the Product Safety Bureau in your province. Check the blue pages of your phone book.

P

PRODUCTIVITY

Turn off the television, and you may be amazed at how much more productive you'll be. Now there will be time for gardening, painting, reading, playing the piano, going fishing with the kids—not to mention changing lightbulbs or folding the laundry or filing the papers on your desk. Shuck the couch-potato habit by setting firm limits on TV-watching time for yourself and your family.

Focus on a major project when you're fresh and most productive—in the morning for most people. Dig right in on important issues and save the miscellaneous odds and ends for later in the afternoon. You may find that you're finishing big tasks sooner than you expected.

 Share the load. Learning that you can't take on every detail yourself is a key to becoming more productive. The feeling that "if I don't do it myself, it won't be right" is a recipe for burnout. Be a good team leader: delegate and allow others to do their jobs so that you can focus on your main priorities.

EASY DOES IT

EATING FOR PRODUCTIVITY

What you eat affects not only how you feel but also how productive you are. These nutrition hints, endorsed by the American Dietetic Association, can help you ward off brain drain on the job.

▶ *Breakfast: Don't leave home without it.*

▶ *Pass on the doughnuts, except as a special treat. Try bagels and fresh fruit for a breakfast on the run.*

▶ *Snack on low-fat foods—crackers, pretzels, or fresh fruit—when there's no time for lunch. Keep a cache of sensible snacks handy in your desk and briefcase.*

▶ *Drink lots of water. You can contribute to your daily water needs—minimum 2 L (8 cups)—by drinking herbal teas or hot water with a twist of lemon.*

▶ *Limit coffee drinking if you suffer from gastritis, indigestion, insomnia, or anxiety. Caffeine is a diuretic that causes the body to lose the fluids it needs to function efficiently.*

▶ *Keep power lunches light. Overeating at midday can make you drowsy and ineffective for the rest of the day.*

▶ *Take five. A five-minute walk or stretching break is a much better way to ease stress than eating.*

PROFANITY

Reality check. It's easy to slip into the habit of swearing, almost without realizing it. But your spouse or friends notice. Ask them about it, and you'll probably get revealing, helpful answers.

Give yourself a reason to give up swearing. Draw up a list of forbidden words and then make a vow that you'll forfeit a dime—or a dollar—every time you use a word on the list in public.

Don't get angry when your young child uses profanity in front of you for the first time. Explain calmly what "bad" words are and why they shouldn't be used.

Teen talk. Encourage your teenagers not to swear—at least in your presence—by setting up a reward system: this privilege or that sum of money for a week free of foul language.

PROPERTY TAXES

Check for discounts. Many tax districts allow discounts for early payment of property taxes. Ask your local assessor or tax collector if your district offers them.

Claim your exemptions. Every province grants tax-relief exemptions to certain qualified groups, such as veterans, senior citizens, and handicapped persons. Check with your local assessor to determine what tax-relief exemptions are available in your province.

Review your assessment. Examine public records at your local tax assessor's office to make sure that your property is correctly described. Also look to see if similar homes in your neighborhood are assessed less than yours. If you think your assessment is unfair, you can ask your local tax assessment board for a review.

PRUNING

The right saw speeds up pruning work and improves the results. For pruning trees, get a saw that cuts "on the pull," or as you pull the tool toward you. Your weight helps to draw such a saw. Fine-toothed saws work better on hardwood trees, while coarse teeth are more efficient for softwood conifers, such as pines.

Don't wait until a tree or shrub is fully grown to trim off inconvenient or unsightly growth; by that time, pruning will be heavy work. Instead, visualize the type of growth you want while the plant

is still young. Removing the excess then is just a matter of a few snips with the hand shears.

Expensive pruning shears often turn out to be the best bargain. They work better and are more comfortable than less expensive models, and scissors-type shears that have replaceable blades cut like new year after year.

PUBLIC SPEAKING

Learn the craft just as you would learn any other skill. Take a class or join an organization like Toastmasters. Read books and articles, and practice, practice, practice. Have yourself videotaped so you can see yourself in action.

Rehearse your reading. Always test your words on your own ears before reading to an audience

from a prepared text. To keep a written speech from sounding contrived or pompous, you should reduce the text to short notes that will help you make your important points in an organized sequence but free you to speak spontaneously and maintain eye contact with your audience.

Take a deep breath. Stage fright causes quick, shallow breathing, making your voice sound tinny and disrupting your concentration. Good breathing habits give your voice resonance and your mind added clarity. Force yourself to breathe deeply before—and during—your presentations.

Make body language work for you by developing habits that keep your audience focused. A good starting point is to hold the lower half of your body still and rest your hands calmly on the podium. Speak with your hands only when such movements might arise naturally in the course of talking. Contrived gestures to create dramatic effect often can appear artificial.

Get a critic. Ask someone you respect to attend your presentation and give you honest feedback. You need to know which anecdotes won points and which habits or gestures made you look awkward or ill at ease.

A PRUNING CALENDAR

This pruning guide is for areas where winters are cold and summers warm. In regions of the West Coast where the climate is marked more by wet and dry seasons than hot and cold, trees, shrubs, and vines should be pruned as they emerge from dormancy after the dry season.

Winter	In cool and cold climate regions, this is the best season for major pruning of shade trees, evergreens, and deciduous shrubs grown mainly for foliage effect. Prune fruit trees now. Be aware, though, that winter storm damage might do some pruning you hadn't counted on.
Spring	Trim off winter-damaged branches; shear evergreen hedges; prune modern everblooming bush roses. Prune summer and fall-flowering shrubs such as buddleia, tamarix, stewartia, and beautyberry.
Early summer	Prune spring-blooming ornamental trees and shrubs—azaleas, forsythia, flowering cherries—as soon as they finish flowering. Prune spring-blooming species and old-fashioned roses after they finish flowering; prune climbing roses as the first flush of flowers fades.
Late summer	Thin branches of overgrown shade trees. Prune trees, shrubs, and vines whose growth you want to restrict or hedges you want to shape, but avoid drastic cuts now.
Fall	In mild-winter climates, this is the time to shape deciduous and evergreen trees and shrubs and to prune everblooming roses and woody vines such as clematis.

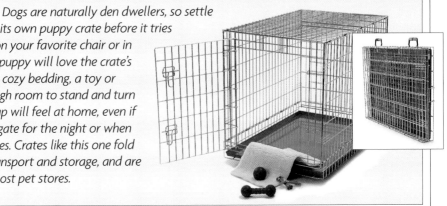

Dogs are naturally den dwellers, so settle your puppy in its own puppy crate before it tries to bed down on your favorite chair or in your bed. The puppy will love the crate's confines. With cozy bedding, a toy or two, and enough room to stand and turn around, the pup will feel at home, even if you close the gate for the night or when company comes. Crates like this one fold up for easy transport and storage, and are available at most pet stores.

PUMPKINS

Carry a pumpkin carefully—by holding it on the bottom. If you grab the stem, it could break off.

Halloween tools. A small pumpkin-cutting knife, much like a small saw, is sold around Halloween at home centers and discount stores. In a pinch, use a small handsaw to remove the top of the pumpkin. For detailed work, use an inexpensive wood-carving kit.

Not just for pie. Pumpkin is delicious in stews, curries, and soups, as a side dish, or served over pasta or rice. Look for firm pumpkins that feel heavy for their size. To cook, carve off the top and scrape out the seeds. Cut the pumpkin vertically into large chunks or bake it whole in a 175°C (350°F) oven for 45 minutes to an hour, until the flesh is tender. Pare off skin before using.

PUNCTUALITY

Rise and shine. Keep your alarm clock out of reach so that in the morning you are forced to get out of bed to turn it off.

Build leeway into your morning schedule by planning one task that doesn't really have to be done then. If you start running late, you can scratch that task, gain an extra 20 minutes, and still be on time for your lunch date.

Punctuality in the workplace. At the scheduled starting time of a meeting, close the door and begin. Make it clear that going back over material for latecomers is a waste of time for everyone else. Those who were tardy will be motivated to be on time for the next meeting.

A head start. The best way to be ready in the morning is to prepare the night before: pick a wardrobe, iron your shirt, shine your shoes, pack a lunch, plot the route, rehearse the speech. You'll wake up ready to go.

Quit making excuses. Few white lies are more transparent than those spouted by the chronically late, such as "Traffic is terrible today" or "The telephone rang just as I was leaving." The truth is, those people who know you well know that you're never on time. Try starting out earlier than you think you should, and you will always be on time.

Selective tardiness. It's usually not rude to be a bit late arriving at someone's home for dinner, but if you're meeting in a restaurant, be on time so that your dinner companion doesn't have to sit alone waiting for you.

PUPPIES

Don't give a puppy an old shoe or a worn-out purse to chew. A puppy doesn't know the difference between old leather and new, and may decide that it is OK to chew up your new shoes.

Protect your house. Confine your puppy to its own space or crate until it is housebroken. Very young puppies can't control their bladders or bowels, so if yours roams the house, some accidents will be unavoidable.

Give a puppy its own bed from the moment you bring it home. Five pounds of puppy sleeping with you in your bed is adorable, but 18 kg (40 lb) of grown dog will feel quite different.

QUARRELING

Get to the point at the beginning of a quarrel and come out in the open with what it is that's really troubling you. If you beat around the bush or hide behind a smokescreen, you can't expect the other person to figure out what your complaint is.

Schedule family meetings to discuss issues that cause quarrels. Keep them short, especially if young children participate, and let everyone have a say. Above all else, settle on a course of action that you can try, even if only temporarily. If it doesn't work, meet again to work out another solution. It is important for children to learn how problems get resolved.

Eliminate shouting at family meetings by passing around a two- or three-minute timer. Have a firm rule that whoever holds the timer has the floor and cannot be interrupted—but that he or she must stop speaking when the timer goes off.

Defer arguments that start at a bad time—late at night or when you don't feel well or have a deadline to meet. Try to deflect a quarrel, but make a firm date to sit down and discuss the problem.

EASY DOES IT

FIGHTING FAIR

All married couples have fights, but not all couples know how to fight fair. Here are some hints on how to quarrel and still keep the relationship intact.

▶ *Don't change the subject. Starting an offensive from another direction may seem like a good defense, but it won't solve the problem at hand.*

▶ *Explain how you feel. This is more important than quibbling over whose facts are right, because what you feel is what's causing the problem.*

▶ *Avoid broad generalizations. "You never . . ." and "You always . . ." are words that only escalate a fight.*

▶ *Never hit below the belt. Never take advantage of the weak spots that only you know about your partner. Even when you argue, be protective of each other.*

▶ *Kiss and make up. When you reach a compromise—or when the quarrel simply fades away—make a point of reaffirming your affection for each other.*

QUILTING

Estimate generously when buying quilt fabric; you might need more—after the store has run out.

Buy a rotary cutter. It's faster and more accurate than scissors, allowing you to measure and cut several layers of fabric at one time and skip the process of marking fabric. (Follow instructions carefully; a rotary cutter is sharp!)

Always wash quilting fabric before you begin to work with it. Washing removes the sizing and shrinks the fabric. It also allows you to to test for colorfastness. During the rinse cycle, throw in a scrap of white fabric to test if the colors have run. If a fabric still runs after several rinsings, don't use it in your quilt.

If you are a beginner, start with a small quilting project (a crib quilt or a pillow, for example) and a simple pieced-quilt pattern consisting only of strips, such as the Fence Rail design. Once you are familiar with basic pieced-quilting techniques, you can graduate to larger projects and more complicated patterns, such as squares, triangles, and diamonds.

White basting thread is best for an appliquéd quilt. Colored threads can leave behind lint, which may show through white or other light-colored tops.

Making a Simple Tied Baby Quilt

You can create this cheery and practical gingham baby quilt in just a few hours. It's reversible and doesn't need hand or machine quilting— ribbons, threaded from one side to the other and tied in bows, hold the batting in place between the outside layers. To make the quilt, you will need two pieces of prewashed cotton gingham fabric and one of medium batting, each cut 94 cm x 110 cm (37" x 43"); and 3.6 m (4 yd) each of 3 mm (⅛") washable satin ribbon in two colors.

1 Lay the two pieces of fabric, right sides facing each other, on top of the batting, smooth out all the layers, and pin around the edges.

2 Stitch all three layers together with a 12 mm (½") seam allowance; leave a 20 cm (8") opening at one edge. Stitch the corners to reinforce them. Trim allowance to 6 mm (¼").

3 Turn the quilt right side out by reaching in and pulling the layers through the opening. Push the corners out and smooth the surface and seams. Sew up the opening by hand.

4 Pin layers together at nine evenly spaced spots. Use a large needle to pull a 40 cm (16") length of ribbon through each spot; tie bows. Use the remaining ribbon for bows in back.

QUILTS

You can machine-wash and dry a well-made new quilt. Put the machine on gentle cycle with cold water. Set your dryer on low heat. Use a mild, bleach-free detergent.

Store quilts by wrapping them in clean sheets. Don't use plastic; it encourages mold by preventing air circulation and retaining moisture.

Beware cedar chests. Wood — especially cedar—is highly acidic and can cause brown spots on fabrics. Always wrap a quilt before storing it near any exposed wood.

Don't wash an antique quilt unless it is very soiled. If you must wash it, press a damp white cloth on the fabrics in the quilt to see if dye comes off. If not, soak the quilt in a bathtub in tepid water for an hour. (If there are spots on the quilt, add 15 mL (½ oz) mild detergent.) Gently agitate the quilt with your hands, then rinse it six times to remove all the detergent. Lay it flat to dry on plastic sheets or dry-cleaning bags.

QUITTING SMOKING

How to quit. Nicotine gum and patches give you small amounts of nicotine to ease you through the process of quitting. But the best way to quit smoking is stopping cold turkey. A recent study showed that 80 percent of all successful reformed smokers had quit in this manner.

Set a date for quitting. This gives you time to work up to the big day. Pick a significant date—a birthday perhaps. It's even more effective if you announce your red-letter date to others.

Don't try to quit and diet at the same time. You may eat more to compensate for not having the cigarettes. If you put on weight as a result, put off dieting until several months after you've completely quit smoking.

RADIATORS TO RUGS

RADIATORS

Dust on a radiator's surface acts like insulation and reduces the heat it gives off. Use a vacuum cleaner's crevice tool to get rid of the dust, or tie a heavy sock onto a straightened-out wire coat hanger. Dampen the sock so that it will pick up more dust.

Metallic paint reduces a radiator's effectiveness, so use regular interior paint. Sand the radiator before painting, and use spray paint for the hard-to-reach spots.

Bleed radiators at the start of the heating season to release air from the system. Open valves with a key, a screwdriver, or a special tool; have a pan ready to catch the water. When a steady stream of water comes out of the valve, all the air has been bled. Work from the top floor down.

RADIOS

Digital precision. Buy a radio that has digital tuning. The extremely well-calibrated dials on such receivers will make zeroing in on stations much easier.

 Crime prevention. Discourage would-be intruders when you go out in the evening by leaving lights on and your radio playing at medium volume.

Antenna stuck? Use petroleum jelly, not a silicone lubricant, to free up a hard-to-extend telescoping antenna on a radio. Silicone is nonconductive and will inhibit reception.

RAILROADS

Comfy riding. Choose a seat midway between the doors for the smoothest train ride. Take a sweater in summer in case the air-conditioning is chilly.

Diverse discounts. Most railroads offer special fares for seniors and families, and vacation packages for all. Many also have discounted weekend fares and seasonal rates.

Window, please. If your trip goes through beautiful scenery, make reservations ahead of time if possible, or go to the station early so that you can get a window seat.

Plan early. The best discount prices are limited. Also, discount rail passes for travel abroad usually must be bought before you leave the country.

Take your own food. You'll eat better and less expensively than if you buy munchies and premade sandwiches from the snack bar.

RADIO RECEPTION

These suggestions can help banish the annoying static and interference that spoil your radio's delivery. Every location has unique reception problems, however, and some devices mentioned below may not help in your particular situation. So before you buy one, make sure it can be returned.

▶ *Switch the mode. Change from stereo to mono to decrease background noise.*

▶ *Move the radio. Nearly every house has "hot spots" where reception is best. Find the ones in your home by walking around with a portable radio.*

▶ *Outdoor antenna. Installation is not easy, but nothing ensures quality reception like this type of antenna, especially if it is a directional model.*

▶ *Indoor antenna. These types have a so-so track record, but recent developments have made them more effective.*

▶ *Antenna amplifier. If you live in a fairly remote area, this device, which boosts the radio signal, might do the trick.*

R

RAINWEAR

Trench coats with zip-out linings are ideal for travelers. They can be used in fair or foul weather, in warm or cool temperatures. The lining can even double as a wrapper in a chilly hotel room.

Business rain gear. For office workers on the go, the essential rainy-day gear includes a plastic rain hat or hat cover, a cloth or canvas raincoat (plastic doesn't breathe, so you would sweat in it), compact rubber overshoes, and, of course, an umbrella.

Keeping kids dry. For camping, sports, or school, make sure that your children have a sturdy rain poncho with an attached hood. Many models can be stowed away in a handy plastic carrying case. Look for high-quality ponchos at military supply stores or sporting goods shops.

Fight the frizzies in humid weather by putting a light coat of gel on your hair before going out. Tuck your hair under a snug-fitting rain hat, so hair stays dry.

RAINY DAYS

Story sack. Fill a bag with pictures cut from old magazines. Take turns with your children picking out images and making up stories about them. Write out or tape-record the tales you create.

PORTABLE RAIN GEAR

Be prepared—even for a surprise shower — with a compact umbrella or a lightweight foldable poncho. Either packs easily into a purse, briefcase, or backpack, and can be purchased inexpensively at most department stores.

Recording star. Give your child a tape recorder on a rainy morning, and she can become a rock musician, a famous actress, a captivating storyteller, a speech-making president—or a weather reporter.

Let the games begin. Turn your living room, garage, or basement into a private Olympics arena and make up your own competitions. Who can unpile, then repile a stack of pillows the fastest? Who can hop on one foot for 60 seconds? Who can walk along a length of string without "falling off"? Have prizes for all players.

Build a dream by starting an indoor construction project that becomes an ongoing rainy-day special event. Save boxes, paper-towel rolls, and other household items that can be transformed in the building of fantasy castles, pyramids, or monuments.

Stir-crazy. Allow the kids to help in the kitchen. Assign fun activities they can tackle with their bare hands, such as kneading bread dough or baking cookies. Decorating a sheet cake or a batch of sugar cookies is another favorite; supply the youngsters with an array of sprinkles, chocolate bits, jelly beans, nuts, or fresh berries and tell them to be creative. Let them eat their masterpieces when they are done.

RAKING

Wear gloves or tape your thumb-to-palm joints the first few times you rake in the spring. Your hands may have softened up over the winter, and it doesn't take long to raise a nasty blister.

Walk in a straight line, raking sideways across your body, throwing debris off to one side; go back, swinging the rake the opposite way. Alternating sides eases the strain on your arm muscles and lets you keep going longer.

Use the wind. Rake downwind when cleaning up the lawn, so that the breeze can give the leaves an added lift every time you swing the rake.

 Rake in rows. Rake leaves into long rows 1.8 to 3 m (6–10 ft) apart, depending on how much material you're moving. Then walk down the rows, raking them into piles ready to be picked up.

Get the right rake. They come in all sizes and materials. Bamboo is probably best for raking lawns; wire is good for gravel and sodden leaves; and iron rakes are right for raking earth and heavy accumulations of gravel. Use a rake that you can manage comfortably.

RANGES

Cooking room. If you are buying a range, be sure the burners are spaced far enough apart to allow two large pots to sit side by side.

Automatic electric ignitions on gas ranges are 30 percent more energy-efficient than gas pilot lights. If there is a power outage, you can always light the burners with an ordinary match.

Save energy with an electric stove by turning off the heat before the food is completely done. The elements take a few minutes to cool down, so food will continue to cook.

Be energy-efficient—fit the pot to the burner. A pot that is smaller than the unit wastes heat; a pot that is larger won't heat properly.

Clean ventilating hoods regularly. The grease that accumulates on the inside of the hood or filter can start a kitchen fire.

Keep it clean. A stove top with a rim and back guard keeps spills from running down the sides of the range; a lift-up top simplifies cleaning under the burners.

RASHES

Chill a heat rash. Soak the itchy area in cool water several times a day, then let it air-dry. Calamine lotion may reduce the itch.

Beat diaper rash by changing diapers frequently. Use water and a washcloth instead of disposable wipes when the baby's skin is irritated. Let the baby's bottom air-dry, then lightly coat the rash with zinc oxide ointment before putting on fresh diapers.

Soothe itchy rashes from poison ivy with a soak made from 1 L (1 qt) of warm water and 250 mL (1 cup) of uncooked oatmeal. Then apply calamine lotion or 1 percent hydrocortisone cream to the rash.

To relieve hives, take an antihistamine. Then rub the affected area with an ice cube or take a cool bath. Apply calamine lotion, witch hazel, or zinc oxide.

RANGE CHOICES

Serious cooks generally prefer gas ranges to electric because of the fine-tuned heat control that a gas flame affords. For baking, cooks often prefer an electric oven because the temperature is more accurate. Both types have advantages, and the newer smooth-top ranges are also a factor in the mix. Some comparisons are listed here.

TYPE	HOW IT WORKS	PROS	CONS
Electric range	Uses electric coils to heat.	Reaches hotter temperatures. Coils burn off most spills, cutting down on cleaning. Plug-in coils are easy to replace.	Burners may be hot even when they do not glow, requiring extra caution. Coils cool and heat slowly, so that cooking requires more constant attention. Pots must be removed as soon as food is done. Foods that fall between coils can be hard to clean up.
Gas range	Uses natural gas or liquid propane (LP) gas supplied in refillable tanks	Can be regulated instantly. Heat level can be seen and controlled directly. Less expensive to operate.	More expensive to buy than electric. LP tanks need to be replaced regularly. Sometimes hard to hold the flame at very low heat. Some danger of gas leaks, especially in older models with pilot lights.
Smooth-top range	Heating elements hidden under ceramic glass surface (only burner areas heat; rest of surface stays cool). May use radiant heat or newer halogen elements.	Attractive. Easy to clean. Heats evenly.	Ceramic surface is scratchable. Requires pots with perfectly flat bottoms. Burner area retains heat after being turned off. Most expensive range option.

READING

Be a reader leader. Stimulate a passion for reading by setting aside certain times when your family reads together. Get each family member to choose a book to read aloud from or pick one book and have everyone read a passage aloud.

So many books, so little time. Catch up on your reading and socialize at the same time by forming a reading group. Meet once a month, and have each member serve as host as well as group discussion leader.

Read while you wait. Make it a habit to carry a book, magazine, or newspaper with you whenever you're out doing errands. Waiting for the doctor, riding the bus, or standing in line at the bank or post office, you can catch up on the reading you never seem to have time for at home.

Switch places. Children often ask questions and make comments as a story is being read to them. When your child reads aloud, take on the role of active listener. When he pauses or turns a page, discuss one of the characters, ask his opinion of the action, or talk about a difficult word.

REALTORS

Go for experience. Meet in person with three Realtors when you are selling your house. Other factors being equal, base your choice on the broker's track record; let a

SPEED READING

It is never too late to improve your reading ability, so instead of cringing at how quickly your "To Read" pile stacks up, follow these hints for getting through it faster.

▶ *Choose carefully. Scan titles, chapter headings, captions, pull quotes, and the first few paragraphs; decide quickly if it is material you really want to read. If the subject isn't relevant or intriguing, skip it for something more appealing or more important.*

▶ *Exercise your eyes. Read two pages every day as quickly as possible. Your speed will increase within the first week. The more you practice, the better you'll get at it.*

▶ *Force your eyes to swing back and forth without stopping. Try it first on short lines, such as those in newspaper columns, then work on longer ones. You will be surprised at how much information you can absorb this way.*

▶ *Keep your place. When reading complicated material, hold an index card, bookmark, or piece of paper above the line you are reading to prevent your eyes from wandering.*

▶ *Keep moving. Don't break the momentum of your reading speed. If you don't understand something right away or come upon something important, mark it lightly with a pencil or a Post-It note and continue reading; return to the marked passage another time.*

new broker cut his teeth working for someone else.

Limit an agent's selling time. When you sign with a broker who has an "exclusive right to sell," limit the agreement to 90 days. Many agents seek a six-month agreement, which will tie you up if the agent's efforts slack off.

Hold your tongue. If you are buying, refrain from telling a broker how much you like a house you have seen, what your top-dollar price is, or much about your personal situation. Regardless of how friendly a broker may be, he represents the seller and is legally bound to help his client.

Look it over. Ask a lawyer to review a broker's agreement with an eye to getting you the best deal possible. Many agreements are negotiable, and a savvy lawyer can suggest alternatives.

Discount fees. If you have the time, hire a discount broker, who lists your property on selling lists or with a multiple listing service, but permits you to show your house to prospective buyers and close the deal yourself. Discount brokers charge half as much as conventional brokers or Realtors.

RECIPES

Read all the way through a recipe before cooking with it, then follow its order of steps carefully. In a well-written recipe the order is logical and often crucial to your success.

Time-tested gift. A wonderful present for a child or grandchild—especially a bride or groom—is an album or recipe box filled with favorite family recipes. You can include anecdotes about the dish, the family legacy of the recipe, or photos of a special occasion when the dish was served.

 Trying to cut down on salt? Add more of the spices and herbs that are called for in the recipe, since one of the main functions of salt is to intensify other flavors. Garlic and onion also make excellent flavor boosters when you are cooking with little or no salt.

Make notes directly on a recipe when you make any changes or shortcuts while using it so that you won't forget them the next time you make the dish.

Organize a complex recipe by doing all the peeling, paring, chopping, dicing, and mincing at one time. Put the ingredients in bowls or plates and line them up in the order you will use them.

RECORD KEEPING

Photocopy important cards that you keep in your wallet—your driver's license, health insurance card, and credit cards, for instance. File the photocopies in a central file in your desk. If your wallet is lost or stolen, it will be easier to get these cards replaced since you will have the numbers close at hand.

Records of improvement. If you own a house or apartment, keep receipts for home improvement expenses. If your home is later sold at a profit, records of these expenditures will cut the tax bill.

Make a master file of important records. Include your will, living will, passport, birth certificate, insurance policies, and any other important documents. Store the file in a fireproof cabinet; store copies in a safe-deposit box.

Compile a master list of the numbers of your bank and investment account, insurance policy, and credit cards. Also write down the names and telephone numbers of your lawyer, accountant, brokers, insurance agents, and the executor of your estate. File the list in a convenient place, and tell family members or close friends where this list is located.

RECIPE SUBSTITUTIONS

Even the most organized cook occasionally runs out of an essential ingredient. If it's too late to shop, try a substitute. Certain substitutions are fairly standard in baking and general cooking. Here is a list of the ones most frequently used.

WHEN YOU ARE OUT OF	YOU CAN USE
Baking powder 5 mL (1 tsp)	2.5 mL (½ tsp) cream of tartar + pinch of baking soda
Butter 250 mL (1 c.)	250 mL (1 c.) margarine or 220 mL (⅞ c.) lard
Buttermilk, 250 mL (1 c.)	250 mL (1 c.) yogurt, or 250 mL minus 15 mL (1 c. minus 1 tbsp) milk plus 15 mL (1 tbsp) lemon juice or distilled white vinegar
Chocolate, unsweetened, 28 g (1 oz)	45 mL (3 tbsp) cocoa + 15 mL (1 tbsp) butter or margarine
Chocolate, semisweet, 28 g (1 oz)	45 mL (3 tbsp) cocoa + 15 mL (1 tbsp) butter or margarine + 45 mL (3 tbsp) sugar
Cornstarch, 15 mL (1 tbsp)	15 mL (1 tbsp) arrowroot or 30 mL (2 tbsp) flour
Flour, white, 15 mL (1 tbsp)	8 mL (1½ tsp) cornstarch, potato starch, or 10 mL (2 tsp) quick-cooking tapioca as thickener
Flour, cake, 250 mL (1 c.)	220 mL (⅞ c.) sifted all-purpose flour
Honey, 250 mL (1 c.) (baked dishes only)	300 mL (1¼ c.) sugar + 60 mL (¼ c.) water or other liquid in recipe (reduce the amount of that liquid by 60 mL [¼ c.])
Milk, whole, 250 mL (1 c.)	250 mL (1 c.) skim milk + 8 mL (1½ tsp) butter
Milk, skim, 250 mL (1 c.)	80 mL (⅓ c.) powdered milk + 190 mL (¾ c.) water
Peppers, dried	2 or 3 drops of Tabasco or other hot sauce
Sugar, 250 mL (1 c.)	190 mL (¾ c.) maple syrup (decrease other liquid slightly)
Tomato puree, 250 mL (1 c.)	250 mL (1 c.) tomato sauce, or 85 mL (3 oz) tomato paste plus 125 mL (½ c.) water

RECREATIONAL VEHICLES

Get the best rental rates on recreational vehicles during the January to March "low" period—and treat the whole family to a trip south for the winter. For rental sources, check the Yellow Pages or the Canadian listings of the Internet's RV resource at http://www.rvamerica.com/data/canadadir.htm.

An RV plus. When you're not traveling, put your idle RV into valuable service as a guest room, play room, or quiet home office.

Write for reservations before setting out on a trip in your RV to be sure you have a space to park at each of the sights or parks you hope to visit. RV travel is becoming more popular every year, so the competition for campsites can be fierce.

Find a truck stop if you can't get into a campground. Truck stops offer showers and safe parking places for recreational vehicles. Avoid roadside rest stops; they can be dangerous after dark and are not recommended for overnight stays.

RECYCLING & DISPOSAL

Sort your trash. Develop a system for keeping your recyclables easily separated and ready to be taken to the recycling center. How you recycle depends on your local regulations, but it's always useful to have separate plastic bins for newspapers and magazines, cans, and bottles.

Choose reusables. Replace as many throwaway items as possible with reusables: Use a string bag instead of plastic or paper bags on every shopping trip; save on kitchen towels and napkins by using cloth instead of paper; buy a permanent coffee filter instead of restocking paper filters; switch to fluorescent instead of incandescent lightbulbs.

Recycle aluminum. Manufacturers use 90 percent more energy to create aluminum from scratch than when they use recycled cans, foil, and other aluminum packaging to create new products.

Aerosol cans, whether or not they are empty, should never be incinerated. Take them to a sanitary landfill, or set them aside for special collection.

Paint poisons. Oil-based paint, paint remover, paintbrush cleaner, paint and varnish stripper, varnish, shellac, and polyurethane are highly flammable and can be poisonous. When discarding such substances, save them for a special collection day or contact your local Health Department.

Water-based latex paint can be disposed by diluting excess paint with water and pouring it down the drain, then wrapping the cans in plastic and throwing them in the household trash.

Reuse glass containers to store flour, rice, oatmeal, and other food staples. They are also handy for neatening stashes of paper clips and push pins on a desk, or screws, nails, and other small fasteners on a workbench.

Precycle. Think about recycling even before you buy. Avoid products that are overpackaged; don't buy disposables; look for refillable containers; buy in bulk to save containers—and money as well.

REFERENCES

Augment your reference file by getting reference letters from internship supervisors, former teachers or academic advisers, and leaders of organizations for whom you have volunteered.

Never surprise someone whose name you wish to supply as a reference by not getting permission before giving out his name. Alert your reference that he may receive a call, and follow up with a note thanking him for the favor.

 Don't leave any job without asking for a letter of reference from your employer. It may come in handy to strengthen a future job application.

Don't list references in your first application to an employer; offer to provide a list of references upon request instead.

If you recommend someone, be honest and relevant. Cite specific accomplishments and anecdotes that relate to the person's performance on the job.

Negative references. If you are asked to provide a reference for someone you cannot recommend highly, stick to the facts regarding his job performance (even if they are negative), but refrain from

Never go jogging, bike riding, or walking in the dark without wearing some sort of reflector. Many reflecting products are available, such as vests, bands, and stick-ons to light up gear you already own. Or buy a cap or jacket with reflective fibers woven into the fabric. These attractive designs look like everyday fabric until a beam is applied and they light up.

saying anything that might be construed as defamatory. (You could be sued.) Remain neutral, and avoid personal opinions. If your response is reserved, your point should be obvious.

REFINISHING FURNITURE

Work from the inside out, from the least conspicuous part of a piece of furniture to the most visible. Your refinishing technique will improve with practice, so you'll want to do your most accomplished work on the areas that show.

An easier way. A refinishing liquid differs from paint remover in that it removes just the top layers of old finishes, thus reducing the need for heavy scraping and sanding. Refinishing liquid does not work well on all finishes, however, so check the label carefully.

Attack a water ring by rubbing it with a rag dipped in turpentine or denatured alcohol. If this doesn't work, try rubbing on toothpaste that contains a light abrasive with a soft cloth. If the ring still remains, sprinkle salt on it and rub it with a rag dipped first in lemon oil, then in vinegar. Restore luster to the wood with furniture wax.

Dismantle larger pieces of furniture you plan to refinish, if at all possible. Working on smaller sections permits you to work on each section at a convenient height.

Remove hardware before you start refinishing. As you take them off, mark handles, hinges, casters, and screws with tape and pencil so you can put them back in their original positions.

Use the cotton-ball test to be certain that a furniture refinisher will work on your project. Press a cotton ball soaked in nail polish remover against the surface of the piece; if it sticks, refinisher will do the job. If the ball doesn't stick,

then you will need to strip the piece down with paint remover.

Test stain colors before you apply them. Rub them in places that aren't going to be seen, such as the bottoms of chair seats and the undersides of tabletops.

REFLECTORS

Store reflectors in your car in case it breaks down on the road after dark. Reflectors attached to metal posts that you can poke in the ground on the road shoulder are sold at auto-supply stores.

Light up your dog with a reflective dog collar or tag. If your pooch wanders into the street after dark, the collar could save its life by giving a startled driver a timely warning.

Supply your boat dock with reflectors, attaching them to the end and sides. They make it easier to locate your dock when coming in from the water at night.

Bicycles and reflectors go together like seat belts and cars. Attach plastic or adhesive reflectors to pedals, handlebars, wheels, and other bike parts. Make your bicycle helmet highly visible by adding bright reflective materials to the front, sides, and back.

REFRIGERATORS

Is it really dark inside? To make sure the light inside your refrigerator goes off when the door closes, locate the push-button switch and press it with the door open. If the light doesn't go off, the switch needs replacing.

The money test. Close the refrigerator door on a five-dollar bill, then pull it out. If you don't feel resistance as it slides, the door's insulating gasket is not doing its job but is allowing cold air to escape. Wash and dry the gasket periodically, as sticky food residue can cause it to wear down and loosen. The gasket may then need replacing—which can be costly.

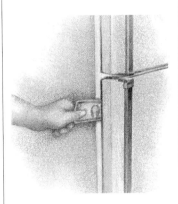

Warm room, cool fridge. Place your refrigerator in a spot where the temperature stays above 15°C (60°F). At lower temperatures (on a back porch, for example), the appliance's compressor won't work properly; below 5°C (40°F) it stops working altogether.

Keep a lid on. Cover liquids tightly before putting them in the refrigerator. Evaporating moisture can increase the interior humidity, making the refrigerator motor work harder than it should.

Clean the condenser coils regularly, as dust noticeably lowers the unit's efficiency. (Pet hairs compound the problem.) To get to the coils at the bottom, behind the

refrigerator's front grill, bind a bulky rag to a yardstick with elastic bands, slide the stick under the front grill, and swish it around.

Cold hard facts. Refrigerators with top freezers are less expensive both to buy and to operate than those with side freezers. However, side freezer compartments are usually larger than top freezer compartments, and can come with convenient extras, such as ice-making machines. The choice depends upon your needs.

Power failure? Food in the refrigerator keeps for at least 24 hours and sometimes as long as 36 hours after the power goes off. Putting dry ice in the freezer and the main compartment will give you a few extra hours before food starts to spoil. Most important: don't open the door any more than is absolutely necessary.

RELAXATION

Don't be laid back about relaxing. Set aside time every day to relax and make it a strict part of your schedule. Listen to music, practice yoga, play cards, read a

TECHNIQUES FOR RELAXING

Not everyone relaxes in the same way. And what works for some people does little for others. Here are a few tried-and-true techniques to help you unwind.

▶ *Look for laughs. Laughter relaxes your muscles and brings more oxygen into your bloodstream. Call a friend who has a good sense of humor or pop a comedy into the VCR. Both will make you feel good.*

▶ *Shut down for five minutes. Lie or sit in a dark, quiet room. Inhale deeply and exhale slowly, relaxing your body as you do. Imagine a place that's calm and inviting and focus on that image for five minutes.*

▶ *Work up a sweat. It may seem a contradiction in terms, but a good physical workout can produce profound relaxation in both mind and body.*

book, take a walk—whatever changes your pace and puts a buffer between you and stress. Just be sure to do it regularly.

Take a few deep breaths every now and then, making sure that your stomach expands at the same time that your chest does. By breathing deeply, you take in and let out more air than usual. This in turn pumps more oxygen into the blood, which can help reduce tension.

Soak your feet. Fill a basin with hot water and stir in a handful of salt. Put your bare feet into the water, close your eyes, and relax.

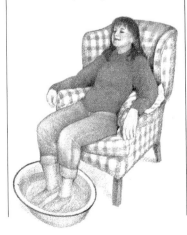

Go limp. You can make yourself feel surprisingly relaxed by simply lying on your back and forcing or willing your muscles to relax. Start with your forehead and work down the body to your toes.

Take a tension check every so often while driving your car. Are you holding your shoulders stiffly without realizing it? Make a conscious effort to drop your shoulders; let your upper arms relax completely for a few seconds.

REMARRIAGE

Remember Social Security. If you are a widow or widower who is collecting benefits based on your late spouse's Social Security account, your benefits will halt if you remarry before age 60. If you are over 60, however, you will be eligible to draw on the account of either your late spouse or your new mate, whichever provides the greater benefit.

No secrets. Before you remarry, make sure there are no hidden financial matters that will lead to trouble between you and your intended. Exchange lists of your assets and liabilities, insurance policies, and real property. Be sure to reveal any costly promises you have made, such as supporting aged relatives.

Expect emotional setbacks. Don't be surprised if your remarriage awakens considerable sadness or remorse about the failure or loss of a first marriage, for both you and your children. Young children especially may hang on to reunification fantasies even after both parents have remarried.

Find a neutral ground, if possible, by moving to a different house. When one spouse moves into the established household of the other, the potential for conflict greatly increases because the "old" children are forced to share existing space with the "new" kids.

REMOTE CONTROLS

Where is the *@%! thing? Keep track of remote controls—as well as anything else that you continually misplace around the house —with an electronic gadget called a finder, that you can buy in electronics stores. Attach the transmitter to the electronic device and the receiver to your remote. When the remote is lost, push a button on the transmitter and track down the elusive "beep."

Keep sticky fingers from gumming up a remote control by sealing it in a plastic zipper bag or wrapping it tightly in plastic wrap. Change the cover every week.

Lay down the law in your house by insisting that the remote controls for your television, VCR, CD player, and other electronic devices stay in one place. Put a small basket or box in an appropriate place, and insist that the remotes be returned to it every time they are used.

RENTAL SERVICES

Rent sickroom equipment of all kinds, from a hospital bed to a bathtub seat, when someone in your house is bedridden for an extended period of time. Hospital-equipment rental companies will deliver whatever you need and set it up in your home. You may be able to charge the cost to your health insurance plan if you can prove necessity—but be sure to check with the insurance carrier first.

OLD SAW **Tuxedo tactic.** If you attend more than three black-tie events each year, you should own your own tuxedo rather than rent one. Select a traditional style, and you'll use it for years.

Rent the glassware, china, and linen when you host a large party. You will avoid putting your good china at risk, and have nicer tableware than the usual paper and plastic alternatives.

Rent-a-tent. If your invitation list is longer than your house is wide, think about renting a tent for your backyard. It can be expensive, but you'll have a festive venue for a fabulous party.

RIGHT STUFF — UNIVERSAL REMOTE CONTROL

Instead of a different control device for every piece of electronic equipment in your home, invest in a universal remote, a gadget that allows you to work your TV, VCR, audio system, computer, and even your lighting, all through one central control. Universal remotes come in various styles; some can control as few as 3 pieces of equipment, others as many as 8 or more.

RENTER'S INSURANCE

Insure yourself. Your landlord's insurance does not cover you if someone sustains an injury in your rented dwelling and sues for damages. Protect yourself with your own liability insurance.

Renter's best bet. If you rent your living space, consider buying a complete tenant's policy. This not only gives you liability coverage for personal injury incurred in the rented space but also covers you for theft and for damage to your possessions there.

Reduce the cost of your premium (as with other types of insurance) by choosing a renter's policy with a high deductible—the more cost you are willing to absorb in case of a loss, the less you have to pay for the insurance.

RENTING YOUR HOME

Custom-design a lease for your specific property by working with a lawyer who specializes in real estate law instead of using a form lease. Such a document allows you to establish rules specially tailored for your property (regarding pets, for example, or access to certain areas) that also are legal.

In a slow sales market, try renting your house with an option to buy instead of leaving it empty after you move. An uncertain buyer may be convinced after settling in for a while. You are still entitled to roll over the money you earn on the sale without paying capital gains tax if you sell the house within two years after buying a new one.

Hire a manager. Pay a retired senior citizen to look after your

rental property if you have to be away a lot. Your manager can keep an eye on the house, fix small problems, and notify you if anything goes wrong that needs your attention. The stipend you pay will produce a major dividend in the peace of mind you'll enjoy.

Who pays the extras? Specify in the lease whether you or the tenant will pay for water, electricity, gas or oil, phone, cable, garbage pickup, yard maintenance, and other expenses. If you are responsible for any of them, remember to notify the utility and other suppliers of your new mailing address. Transfer all other accounts to your tenant's name.

No strangers. When renting, include a clause in the lease that prevents the tenant from subleasing the property. This is your home, and you don't want people living there whom you haven't met or checked out.

RESIGNING FROM YOUR JOB

Don't leak the news that you're resigning to the office rumor mill—tell your boss first. Ask for a meeting, courteously announce your intention, and give your reasons for leaving. This will help in retaining your employer's esteem —and make it easier to obtain good references.

GETTING READY TO RENT

Before your tenants move in, you may need to make improvements to your house to ensure that it conforms to requirements for rental property in your insurance policies and under local city codes.

▶ *If you don't already have them, install smoke alarms and fire extinguishers and consider a security system; if necessary, put child safety guards on windows.*

▶ *Fix up small problems that you overlooked when living on the property—broken rails on stairs, drooping wires, shaky steps, potholes in the driveway.*

▶ *Write out instructions about clearing the sidewalk in winter, cutting the grass in the summer, recycling, and putting out the garbage. These are responsibilities that you as a property owner have to the community, and you may be liable if the tenant fails to assume them.*

▶ *Document the property. Take pictures of the property and its condition before the tenant moves in. Pay particular attention to appliances that are part of the rental. Write down serial numbers, give the tenant copies of all warranties that are in effect, and keep copies for yourself.*

It is wise—and professional— to send a formal letter of resignation to your boss, but only after you and your employer have reached accord on all of the details of your departure. Such a letter is equally important if you have been laid off.

Address. Direct your letter to your boss or the person who will hire your replacement.

Dates. Decide on a departure date that is mutually acceptable to you and your superior, then confirm the date in your letter.

Health insurance. Note any agreement between your employer and yourself concerning drug plans or group health insurance.

Pension. If your company has a pension plan, the company must make arrangements to distribute monies due to you.

Return address. Write the letter from home on personal stationery. You are writing this on your own behalf, not on behalf of your employer.

Intention. Reiterate the fact that you are resigning and state the reason why.

Final pay. Spell out the arrangements you and your boss make concerning your final paycheque, which can include vacation and bonus pay.

Stock options. Your employer must refund any funds deducted from your pay toward purchasing shares in company stock.

Don't burn bridges. Express good feelings about your work experience. A graceful exit can pay off in the future.

Henry Carlos
98 Louisbourg Lane
Dartmouth, N.S. B2W 3A9

February 8, 1997

Mr. John Dana, Vice President
Rio Telecom, Inc.
2354 Tobin Street
Halifax, N.S. B3H 1S3

Dear Mr. Dana:

This letter serves as formal notification that I have resigned my position with Rio Telecom, Inc., and have accepted a new position at Peters Business Systems in Newbury Park, California.

As we agreed yesterday, my last day of employment with Rio Telecom will be March 7, 1997, which will give me time to complete my current assignments. In addition, we agreed to the following points:

• **Final pay.** Rio Telecom will keep me on its payroll at my present salary through March 7, 1997. I will receive my final paycheque on that day, which, in addition to my basic pay, will reflect five unused vacation days and a prorated share of my annual bonus of $2,750.

• **Health insurance.** Under the terms of my health plan, I can continue the policy at the group rate for the next 18 months if I so choose.

• **Stock options.** I have purchased 300 shares of Rio Telecom Class A non-voting stock over the last three years. It is agreed that Rio Telecom will refund the funds deducted from my pay over the last three months towards purchasing of new shares, and that I will request stock certificates for the shares I have already purchased.

• **Pension plan.** I understand that I will receive a lump sum payment of funds due me from Rio Telecom's pension plan within six months.

My decision to move to another company was a difficult one, but it was an opportunity I could not refuse. Working at Rio Telecom has been a rewarding experience, and I am proud to have been a part of this company's team.

Sincerely,

Henry Carlos

Give **two weeks' notice**—more if the job entails major responsibilities. (Some businesses, however, can insist that you leave immediately.) It is both considerate and professional to give your old employer every opportunity to make a smooth transition.

Stay on good terms with co-workers and supervisors when you resign from a job. Leaving your old job on a positive note will preserve relationships that could turn out to be important to you in your new job, or in your future career.

RÉSUMÉS

Put vital information—your name, address, and contact information—at the top of the résumé, ideally in a boldfaced type. If the résumé gets separated from the cover letter, a prospective employer can still contact you.

One page is best. The person screening your résumé may give it only 10 seconds' attention, so keep it short. Highlight important accomplishments. Starting with your most recent position and working backward, use concise, bulleted points to explain your professional history.

A winning look. Get a head start in the job hunt with a crisp, clean-looking résumé. Use a high-quality stock of paper and type no smaller than 10 point. Check your spelling (use a dictionary), your grammar, and your language usage meticulously. Ask someone who writes well to edit and proofread your text.

RETIREMENT ACTIVITIES

Preserve the past. Join a local historic preservation group. Retirees are the mainstay of a nationwide effort to save fine old properties from demolition. You can be involved in fund-raising or have a more hands-on responsibility in restoring a historic or trust-property. Contact your provincial historic preservation society to track down regional historical organizations.

Join a senior center, where you can often work on projects with others. Senior centers organize dances, bridge or quilting clubs, lectures, exercise classes, art exhibitions, games, and day trips.

FROM RETIREE TO VOLUNTEER

Retirees are prized not only in the workplace but by volunteer groups as well. And increasingly, retirees are choosing more adventurous ways to help out—traveling to exotic locales or making long-term volunteer commitments in their own backyards. Here are a few choices for the energetic retiree. For further information, write the Coalition of National Voluntary Organizations, 947 Bronson Ave., Ottawa, Ont., K1S 4G8, or call them at (613) 238-1591.

VOLUNTEER GROUP	EXAMPLES OF VOLUNTEER WORK	WHERE TO CALL
Canadian Red Cross	Helping disaster victims with clothing, food, and shelter; volunteering at races and marathons.	(613) 739-3000
Canadian International Development Agency (CIDA)	CIDA supports many non-governmental organizations—such as CUSO, Oxfam-Québec and Canadian Crossroads International—which send volunteers overseas for a variety of humanitarian missions (a one- or two-year commitment is required in most cases).	1-800-230-6349
Parks Canada (Volunteer Coordinator)	Maintaining trails (retiree volunteers are the "backbone of trail maintenance" in most national parks); archaeological digs.	(819) 994-5127
Special Olympics	Coaching special olympics athletes; serving as greeters or escorts to the games; planning outings and picnics.	(416) 927-9050
Habitat for Humanity	Building low-income homes (Habitat Gypsies are retirees who travel around the country in RV's on house-building blitzes).	(519) 885-4565
Sierra Club	"Service trips" may include helping maintain and run a 1934 snow lodge in the Sierra Nevada; cleaning inner-city neighborhoods; or leading hikes, canoe trips, or bike trips.	(613) 241-4611
Elderhostel Service Programs	Helping to restore parks, build housing, teach, and perform cultural and ecological services.	(613) 530-2222

RETIREMENT & MARRIAGE

 Keep outside interests. Too much togetherness can be stifling, even for the closest of couples. Each of you should have activities that you pursue on your own. At the end of the day, you'll have lots more to talk about.

A new kind of togetherness. After retirement, finding activities to enjoy as a couple is as important as maintaining separate interests. Look for pleasurable things you can do together: Take up golf, travel, go hiking or camping, learn ballroom dancing, join a reading group, go to sports events.

Don't be a dictator around the house. Whether you're the one who's traditionally maintained the house or the one who's new on the scene during the day, remember that nagging and criticism breed resentment

RETIREMENT COMMUNITIES

Well looked after. If you want to live in your own space but be relatively free of responsibilities, consider moving to a retirement community. You can enjoy a range of services—meals, cleaning service, grounds maintenance, laundry, even local transportation. Many communities also offer nursing facilities so that you will not have to worry if your health care requirements change.

Read the fine print before you buy into a retirement community. Research at least three different communities, and study the prospectus of each carefully . Such communities vary greatly not only in terms of the services they offer, but with regard to their financial stability. Make sure you are making a sound investment.

Stay overnight to check out whether or not a potential community is right for you. Is it clean and well maintained? Is the food good? Do you like the activities? Do residents look like people you'd like to befriend?

RETIREMENT JOBS

Add to your skills by tackling new technology. Computer systems are user-friendly these days, and you can find basic courses in many places, from college continuing education departments to technical schools.

Surf the Net. Hundreds of opportunities for retirees can be found on the World Wide Web. Just point your web browser at the Age of Reason home page (http://www.ageofreason.com/canada.htm), or at Seniors Net (http://www.seniorsnet.com/jobbank.htm).

Work part-time. Corporate downsizing has created a demand for part-time workers who don't need much training or supervision. You may just fit the bill. Look for part-time employment at banks, insurance companies, hardware and grocery stores, and nurseries.

Network. Work out an "on-call" arrangement with your company

EASY DOES IT — DON'T RUSH TO RELOCATE

Don't rush to move after retiring. If you decide you want to relocate, get to know the place you are considering well before making the plunge. Here are some ways to do so.

▶ *Visit during different seasons of the year. The town that seems divine in the dead of winter may be stifling in July.*

▶ *Rent before buying to get a feel for living in the area as well as in the neighborhood you think you prefer.*

▶ *Check out the cost of living—rents, utility rates, gasoline prices, groceries, clothing, and household goods.*

▶ *Study tax particulars, from inheritance tax laws to sales and property taxes. Call the local Taxation Office.*

▶ *Consider the lifestyle. Visit the library. Learn about local cultural events. Attend local religious services.*

▶ *Look into the area's medical and dental facilities and find out if any special services are offered to seniors.*

▶ *Subscribe to the local newspaper to study area activities and gauge safety and crime issues.*

to help out on special projects, to substitute, or to work as a consultant. Keep memberships in professional organizations active to retain old ties and form new ones.

RETIREMENT RELOCATION

Become a caretaker. Well-to-do owners of second homes—which are often located in spectacular areas—sometimes hire caretakers to live on the premises. Retirees who are reliable and handy around the house are in particular demand for these positions. Look for opportunities in the want ads of your local newspaper.

Don't downsize too far when you retire. Many retirees find themselves living in uncomfortably close quarters after years of being used to bigger environs. Make sure your new house or apartment accommodates you, your spouse, and potential guests comfortably.

Buck the exurban trend and move to the center of a city instead of to the country when you retire. Suburbs are great for raising children, but they can be isolating for seniors and retirees. In the city you'll find a wealth of culinary and cultural choices. Also, public transportation options may make it easier to live without the responsibility of a car.

Don't bite too fast if you are offered a deeply discounted property. The low price may well indicate that something is wrong with the house itself, or that the town or area is economically depressed. Find out how long a property has been on the market—and why it is being sold at a cut-rate price—before you consider it seriously.

Change your mind? Don't sell right away if you find that you are homesick after relocating. Give yourself time; it takes at least a year to adjust to great change.

RETURNING MERCHANDISE

Charge major purchases. This ensures that you will have a record of the sale date and price, even if you lose your receipt.

 Save sales slips until you are sure the item is satisfactory. It is always easier to make returns if you have the original receipt.

Have a reason ready when you return goods; the sales clerk is required to ask why goods are coming back in order to fill out the store's return form.

Know your rights. Manufacturers' warranties usually provide for repairs at no charge if the item doesn't work.

Check the return policy before you buy, especially when dealing with small stores. You may be better off paying a little more but knowing you can get a refund.

To return mail-order gifts without telling the giver, start by calling the company's customer service department and explaining your problem. Return the gift with a note instructing the company to refund the price to you, not the original purchaser. Ask the company to pay the postage for your return or exchange.

RICE

The long and the short of it. Use short-grain sticky rices with Chinese and Japanese recipes requiring chopsticks, and for making risotto. (Arborio, a short-grain white Italian rice, makes the best risotto.) Use long-grain rices with stews, curries, and pilafs. (Basmati and its American cousin, Texmati, are long-grain aromatic rices, and are the best rices for use in spicy Indian, Middle Eastern, Cajun, and Mexican dishes.)

Try brown rice, a nutty-flavored hulled rice seed that still has its bran layer. Because white rice has been processed to remove the bran, brown rice is more nutritious. The only hitch is that it takes twice as long to cook (40 minutes versus 20 minutes).

Don't rinse rice. It's unnecessary and even harmful. It removes nutrients and some of the starch that makes rice so tasty. Cook rice straight from the box or bag.

Mixing oil and water. Add 10 mL (2 tsp) of vegetable oil to the cooking water to keep it from boiling over. Adding oil (or butter) to the cooking liquid also keeps the rice grains from sticking to one another.

Keep the lid on. When cooking rice in a 2-to-1 proportion, keep the lid on. Cook on low heat in a pan with a tight-fitting lid. Lifting the lid while rice is cooking lengthens the cooking time. Also, if you peek and stir, you'll release too much starch from the rice, resulting in a gummy mixture.

Wild rice isn't rice at all but the seed of another aquatic grass. Cook and serve wild rice the way you would brown rice. Mixed with sautéed onions and mushrooms, for example, it makes a delicious stuffing for poultry or a hearty side dish with game. Cook wild rice together with brown rice for a rich-tasting dish.

RINGS

New looks for old rings. Give new life to an old family ring. Hang it from a chain and wear it as a pendant. If the ring features a nice stone, consider having the gem reset in a modern ring design.

Find another way to wear your engagement ring after a divorce, such as resetting the stones in a cocktail ring or necklace. The new look will allow you to display your stones with fresh meaning.

ANCIENT CHINESE METHOD

For thousands of years the Chinese have cooked their short-grained white rice by this foolproof method.

▶ *Place uncooked rice—any amount you desire—into a saucepan.*

▶ *Put your middle finger into the pot, touching the top layer of rice. Cover the rice with water up to the top of the nail on that finger.*

▶ *Bring water and rice to a boil, turn down the heat, and cover and simmer until all the water has been absorbed—about 20 minutes. Fluff the rice and serve.*

Skin sensitivity. If you're allergic to any metal or alloy, from chrome to sterling silver, coat the bands of your rings with clear, low-gloss fingernail polish to protect your fingers from irritation.

Quick release. When a ring is stuck on your finger, put ice on the knuckle to reduce swelling. Then spread skin lotion on your finger and slide the ring off slowly. Or, try the old standby: Wash your hands with soap and water. While your finger is still soapy, twist and remove the ring.

Mind the storage. Store all of your rings in a soft cloth or jewelry box. This will help to prevent the metal and stone parts from getting scratched, and will also keep fine dust particles from accumulating in the crevices.

ROAD MAPS

Use two maps to plan the most practical routes for your travels. A large regional map is best for plotting the entire trip, but provincial and local maps provide the detail needed for fine-tuning your itinerary over smaller roads.

Measure miles by using a piece of string marked with a pen to equal the kilometer or mile markings on the map's scale. Pin the string along your route on the map to get a good estimate of the total distance for your trip.

Free road maps are available from almost every provincial tourist office; these maps often show helpful street maps of major cities as well. Write or call early, however, because the maps may take several weeks to reach you by mail.

Neat and handy. Fold a map down to the smallest section you need to see, then fasten the map onto a clipboard or slip it into a plastic bag. This will make it easy to zero in on the right panel without any fumbling.

Mark your route on a map with a brightly colored highlighter so that you can see it quickly while driving. Write out complicated directions in detail and clip your notes to the map.

ROAD TRIPS

Auto clubs are a worthwhile investment if you plan to take a long trip by car. These organizations will help you plan your trip, offer excellent maps and travel guides, provide discounts on car rentals and hotels, and guarantee emergency service and towing when you need it. (In fact, one service call more than pays for a year's membership.)

Take binoculars. They'll help you read unfamiliar road signs at a distance, and check out spectacular scenery when you come upon it unexpectedly. A pair of binoculars can also amuse a restless child for hours on a long trip.

Road safety. To avoid trouble, keep car doors locked and windows rolled up in slow traffic and at red lights. Don't stop for a disabled car in a sparsely populated area; instead, go to a phone and report it to the police.

Road smarts. Don't stop if you are bumped by another car or if a person signals that something is wrong with your car. Drive to a populated area or a gas station where you can see several attendants before you get out to check for damage. Report any bumping to the police.

Airport hotels on the edge of town are convenient if you arrive in a strange city after dark and are having trouble finding your way. Resume your journey at first light, when the route is more visible.

Have you ever wanted a flashlight to help you read a map at night—especially when you were navigating a car along an unfamiliar road? Now you can have one. Powered by your car battery through the lighter plug, this bright beam, attached to a bendable cord, allows you to focus on map details easily. This style, the Deluxe Flex-Light by Allison, is available at automotive stores.

OVEN ROASTING BAGS

Making a perfectly moist, beautifully browned chicken or turkey is incredibly easy with these new roasting bags by Reynolds. All you do is slide the bird into the bag and roast it in the oven for the appropriate time—which is less in the bag. You'll be astonished at the ease—and the flavorful results. Available at supermarkets.

ROASTING

Starting temperature. Bring meat to room temperature before roasting to make the cooking time more predictable. Don't do this with poultry, however, because it is more perishable than meat.

Roast meat fat side up. The fat will melt down and tenderize the roast as it cooks. Top the meat with bacon or fatback if it has little fat. Rub the side surfaces with vegetable oil to help keep the meat moist. (A sprinkling of sugar on the meat will form a caramelized layer that also helps to seal in moisture.)

To cut down on cooking time, cook two small roasts instead of one large one. This approach works particularly well when you are cooking for a crowd. You can please many tastes by cooking one roast rarer than the other.

For perfect roast chicken, rotate the bird during cooking. A 2.5 kg (5 lb) chicken, for example, should be cooked for 20 minutes on each side and then for 20 minutes with the breast up. Finish breast side down for 15 minutes. There's no need to baste, but rub the breast with butter or olive oil beforehand to keep it moist. The chicken is done when its juices run clear.

ROCK GARDENS

Turn a liability into an asset. If your yard is punctuated by a boulder or a rocky outcropping, make it the centerpiece for a rock garden. Arrange smaller stones of the same type around the natural rock to create pockets of gritty, well-drained soil. Plant these pockets with rock garden flowers, such as moss phlox, alpine poppies, and basket-of-gold, which thrive in such a setting.

To stabilize an eroding bank, use rock garden plants. Insert flat pieces of stone into the bank in layers like natural ledges, angling them inward and downward so that they catch the water running down the bank's face and drain it back into the soil. Plant the ledges with drought-tolerant rock garden ground covers, such as creeping thyme and lavender.

Build a budget rock garden. Traditional rock gardens require substantial stones, which are expensive to buy and arrange if they don't happen to occur in your garden naturally. You can grow rock garden plants just as successfully in the crevices of an unmortared stone retaining wall. Dig behind it and replace the old dirt with 30 cm (1 ft) of well-draining soil made from one part coarse builder's sand, one part topsoil, and one part compost.

Ideal for chilly sites. If your yard has a north-facing slope, you'll find it a difficult site for most kinds of plants; such a garden is extra cold in winter and cool even in summer. But this is an ideal site for rock garden plants that hate heat but are invulnerable to cold as long as the soil is well drained.

ROCKING CHAIRS

A nursery must. A rocker is the ideal chair for parents with a newborn. As the child grows, the rocker can also foster bedtime reading and quiet conversations.

Smoothing the path. Prevent the rockers on your rocking chair from scratching the finish of a wood floor by running a strip of adhesive tape—the first-aid type—along the bottoms. The tape won't show if you trim it off 5 cm (2 in.) short of the tips of the rockers.

Porch magic. Furnish a screened porch or an open patio with sturdy wooden rockers. Inviting to look at, they create a relaxing atmosphere conducive to good talk and quiet contemplation.

ROMANCE

The little things. If you're dating someone you don't know well, pay attention to the nuances of that person's behavior. Does he interrupt you when you're speaking? Does she never ask about your work or family or friends? Don't let a pretty face or a charming personality blind you to troublesome personal characteristics.

 A touching moment. A quick hug, holding hands for a minute, or walking arm in arm across the street is a natural way to show your affection.

A friendly circle. It should be easy and natural to introduce someone you are dating and like to your friends and family. Beware of a relationship in which you—or your date—don't feel comfortable integrating a new person into the rest of your life.

Listen to your feelings when you're in a relationship. Are you happy being with this person, or do you feel depressed and angry? Does this person make you feel confident or insignificant? If your feelings are not positive most of the time, move on.

Surprise your loved one by remembering a certain wish or need and fulfilling it. Pay attention to little comments: a book he's always wanted, for example, or a food she's always craved. Keep a list if you have to. Then, if your surprise comes months or weeks later, your loved one will be touched that you remembered.

ROOFS

If your roof is leaking, first check the flashing around the chimney and vents. Cracked or loose flashing is most often the culprit behind a roof leak.

Just right. Don't work on an asphalt-shingled roof when it's too cold (lower than 10°C/50°F) or too hot (above 29°C/85°F). Cold shingles are brittle and may break. Warm shingles are soft, easily damaged, and dangerously slippery to walk on. In summer, work on the roof in the early morning before the sun gets too hot.

Glue down a curling or buckling asphalt shingle with roofing cement, available from home stores in a caulking-type tube. Wait for a warm day when the shingles will be pliable. Carefully lift the curled section of shingle and apply a few dabs of roofing cement beneath it. Press the shingle down with a weight, such as a rock or brick, until the cement dries—about 30 minutes.

Clean valleys and gutters of leaves and debris regularly. Leaves can form dams that cause draining water to back up under the shingles and seep into the house.

Look for leaks by spraying the roof with a garden hose on a sunny day. Spray for 15 minutes or so, starting at the bottom of the roof, then go inside and look for wet spots. Work your way up each side of the roof.

 ROMANCE ENHANCERS

Busy people may loose their sense of romance in a fast-paced mix of jobs, running a home, and maybe taking care of children, too. Here are some ways to keep romance alive, even in hectic times.

▶ *Dress for dinner now and then. Use the best china, have flowers on the table, and enjoy an elegant meal together.*

▶ *Set aside one day a month for an adventure with your partner. (Hire a sitter if there are children.) Go somewhere outside of your daily routine—an antiques market, a ball game, or a museum.*

▶ *Get away from it all at a hotel for a weekend—or even one night—every few months. Do use room service but don't use the telephone—except to check on children.*

▶ *At least once a week, offer a special kindness. Give her a neck massage after a long day or pick up the suit he forgot to get from the cleaners.*

ROOM DIVIDERS

A freestanding bookcase can create a wall for dividing a large room into smaller, more private spaces. Fill a row of bookcases ranging from waist height to ceiling height with books or with decorative accessories such as pottery or antique toys.

Use rugs to define discrete areas of a large living room—perhaps a conversation grouping around the fireplace and a listening area near the sound system.

Folding screens are versatile, easily rearranged dividers of living space. They can also hide parts of the house you don't want seen— the working part of the kitchen during dinner, a sofabed where a child is napping, or even a stretch of unsightly architecture. Cover the panels with paint, wallpaper, fabric, or even a display of family photos. Or mount a collection of matchbook covers, travel post-cards, or other memorabilia on the panels of a screen.

A touch of nature. In a large room a massive indoor plant or two can create a natural and attractive room divider. Consider a 1.8 m (6 ft) weeping ficus, a sweet olive, or several huge parlor palms. Put the plant in a large container to give it more visual weight as a divider. The foliage will provide enough screening to

define a space without making it seem too confined.

ROOMMATES

Spread a wide net. When looking for a roommate, tell everyone you know. Contact organizations such as your church, alumni groups, or professional associations whose members have interests and values similar to yours.

Gut response. Interview prospective roommates to see if you are compatible. Be sure to discuss your standards of neatness, the division of household labor, and the way you expect the payment of household bills to be handled. Follow your intuition.

Ask for references before you take into your home a roommate whom you don't personally know. Also ask for the person's permission in writing to run a credit check, especially if you are expecting your roommate to carry half of an expensive rent.

Take the initiative. If you are seeking to room with someone in his home, a tactful gesture is to offer to supply both personal and credit references before you are asked for them.

Draw up a written agreement. Define the costs (rent, utilities, and other joint expenses) as well as when and how they will be paid. If you are the one moving in, ask if your name can be added to the lease or if you can sublet the place if the leaseholder leaves.

Agree to a trial run of one or two months, after which the two of you will sit down to discuss whether you want to continue to live together. This gives you both a way out if either of you finds the relationship incompatible.

Telephone time. Even in a small apartment, each of you should maintain your own phone line. If you don't have separate lines, agree on rules for using the phone and paying the bills for it.

USING A ROOMMATE SERVICE

If you can't find a roommate through word of mouth, try using a roommate service, following these guidelines.

▶ *To find an agency, check the Yellow Pages or newspaper ads or ask friends for a recommendation. If you are referred to more than one agency, comparison shop. Use a service that screens candidates by weeding out undesirables and matching people with similar lifestyles.*

▶ *Make sure that the service is licensed. Ask for references from the firm. Check with the Better Business Bureau or the Department of Consumer Affairs.*

▶ *Visit the offices. Evaluate the service employees and the interview you receive. Read the contract thoroughly.*

▶ *Make certain that your fee is good for at least a year, so that if you or your roommate moves during that time, you can use the service again for no additional cost. Clients who list apartments to share are usually charged less than clients who are looking for a place to live.*

If you like living alone but need someone to share the expenses, look for a roommate who travels frequently on business, who often goes away on weekends, or who works days when you work nights (or vice versa).

ROOT VEGETABLES

In selecting root vegetables—carrots, celery roots, beets, parsnips, parsley roots, potatoes, rutabagas, and turnips—look for firm, uncracked surfaces.

In the dark. Onions and potatoes keep well when stored in a totally dark, cool, dry place. Other root vegetables can be refrigerated.

Roasting root vegetables caramelizes their sugars and intensifies their flavors. Cut them into pieces, drizzle with olive oil and fresh herbs, and roast, covered, for 20 minutes in a 230°C (450°F) oven. Remove the cover and continue roasting for another 20 minutes. Add salt and pepper and serve. Combinations to consider: potatoes, garlic, and rosemary; carrots, onion, parsley, and thyme; sweet potatoes and marjoram.

A good mix. Try adding a turnip, a parsnip, or some celery root when you fix mashed or scalloped potatoes. Complementary root vegetables add an intriguing flavor. Boil the root vegetable with the potatoes before slicing or mashing. Follow your usual recipe.

Baked beets. Baking is the easiest and most nutritious way to cook beets. Wrap each beet in aluminum foil and bake for 1 hour at 175°C (350°F). The skins should slip right off. While they're still slightly warm, chop or slice the beets and season with a vinaigrette dressing.

ROSES

Spray-free roses. The busy gardener's favorite hedge is a row of rugosa roses. Naturally disease- and pest-resistant, these ever-

STEAM CLEANING MADE EASY

Keeping your carpeting clean insures that it will enjoy a long life—and save you money. Finally, there's a convenient and economical tool to help you: The Steam-Vac Jr., manufactured by Hoover. This lightweight, easy-to-maneuver cleaner allows you to tackle accidental spills, keep busy passageways spotless, or steam clean an entire wall-to-wall carpet. You can even use it to shampoo your car's interior. Best of all, it is compact, and takes up minimum storage space.

blooming bushes don't require artificial pesticides or fungicides.

A borer barrier. To protect roses against borers—the maggotlike larvae of various flying insects—carry a tube of white glue at pruning time. After each cut, seal the wound with a dab of glue so that the borers can't gain access. The glue dries clear.

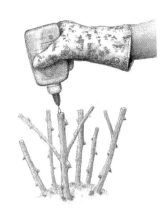

When hips are helpful. "Deadheading"—snipping off fading flowers before they can produce seed-filled hips—encourages your

rosebushes to continue blooming throughout the summer. In climates with frigid winters, however, stop deadheading after September 1; the bushes will develop hips as part of a preparation for winter dormancy that reduces cold-related damage.

RUGS

Not just for floors. Beautiful rugs can be used in a number of decorative ways around the house. As wall hangings, rugs help bring the noise level of a room down and create a striking focal point. They also make handsome table coverings.

Moving savvy. Roll up a rug you plan to move rather than folding it (folding damages the backing). Roll a valuable rug top side out to keep from crushing the pile.

Deep cleaning. Vacuum area rugs once a week and clean up spills as they happen. At least twice a year, vacuum the padding and the floor beneath an area rug. This prolongs the life of both rug and pad.

RUNNING

Downhill running. When you reach a sharp decline in the road as you're running, shorten your step and take a zigzag path to the bottom instead of heading straight down with long strides. This will lessen stress on your muscles and joints, reducing the risk of extra soreness or injuries common to downhill running.

Slick cover-up. During cold-weather runs, cover exposed skin with petroleum jelly. It helps you keep warm by slowing the loss of body heat and also protects your skin against drying and chapping.

Minutes, not miles. Start a running program with time in mind, not distance. Begin by walking 20 minutes nonstop three or more times a week. Add jogging intervals as walking gets easier, with an eventual goal of running for all 20 minutes. For full aerobic benefit, gradually increase your time until you can do a 45-minute run. Then you can start thinking about speed and distance.

Let your body talk. If you feel a minor ache but don't want to stop your running regimen, wait until after you return from a run to take pain medication. If ingested before a run, it mutes your body's pain signals, making you unaware of injuries that may be developing.

ENERGY GELS AND WATER PACKS

Two necessities for running: energy and water. For fast fuel, try energy gels, such as PowerGel, GU, or Squeezy. For hands-free hydration, try a water-carrying system by Camelbak or Solo. Buy energy gels through health food shops; find water carriers at most sporting goods stores.

Keep a log of dates, distance, and times to track your running progress. Note injuries, weather, and road conditions. The distance tally will be a great motivation for keeping at it, and the notes may help you spot injury patterns and set realistic goals for yourself.

Run your own race. Before a race, work out a strategy that suits your capabilities and strengths. Then when the race starts, stay focused on your personal plan; ignore what your competition is doing. Control the adrenaline rush that can push you to run a pace you are not used to. Conserve your energy for the race finale.

RUSH HOUR

To avoid the crush, travel to and from work before or after rush hour if you possibly can. Many companies allow flexible hours for people who want to commute earlier or later.

Go public. Take public transportation or carpool with coworkers to avoid the daily hassle of driving in heavy rush-hour traffic.

In rush-hour traffic, follow the crowd. Drive at the same speed as the cars around you, giving yourself enough space to stop if the car ahead of you brakes suddenly. Stay in one lane; weaving from lane to lane seldom saves time and can cause an accident.

Use rush hour to unwind. If you commute in a car, listen to music or a book-on-tape to take your mind off work and ease into your personal time. On a train or bus, relax with an entertaining book.

Family rush hours. Lessen the morning turmoil of getting the children off to school and yourself off to work by planning ahead. Make lunches and set out clothing and keys the night before. In the evening, assign specific duties so each member of the family helps with dinner preparation and cleanup. Spend 15 minutes before bed preparing for the next day's rush.

Where's my homework? Line up good-size baskets or assign shelves near the front door, one for each member of the family. Ask each person to drop off backpacks, lunch boxes, keys, and books on his own spot, and eliminate frenzied last-minute searches in the morning.

Private time. Get up a little earlier than everyone else to give yourself a period of calm before the day's activities begin. Some people need this time alone—for coffee, meditation, or a quick look at the paper—to start the day off in the right frame of mind.

RUST

Rust stains in the toilet bowl and around sink drains may be a sign of excessive iron in your water supply. Have your water tested for iron content. If the tests are positive, then get an expert to advise you. An ion-exchange water softener may do the trick, or you may need an oxidizing filter.

On siding and roofs, prevent rust stains by using only rustproof aluminum, stainless steel, or galvanized nails and screws. Countersink nails on the house trim and fill the holes with waterproof caulk before you paint.

Erase rust on fixtures in your bathrooms or kitchen with a solution of lemon juice and salt or with a powdered lemon or orange drink mix straight from the pack.

On painted surfaces, remove rust by rubbing the surface with fine sandpaper or using a commercial rust cleaner.

Protect tools by keeping several pieces of chalk in your toolbox; they will help to absorb moisture and deter rust.

If small metal tools begin to rust, brush off as much of the rust as you can and then apply a penetrating oil or a gel-type rust remover as directed.

In the kitchen, remove rust from a metal kitchen utensil by rubbing it with scouring powder. Then coat it with vegetable oil and wipe with a paper towel.

S A F E - D E P O S I T   T O   S Y M P A T H Y

SAFE-DEPOSIT BOXES

Keep keys in a safe place. A safe-deposit box typically comes with two keys. Store each in a separate, safe location that you can easily remember. There's little point in keeping both keys together if there is a chance they could be lost together.

Are you insured? Find out if your homeowner's insurance policy covers the contents of your safe-deposit box. If it doesn't, ask if the bank offers insurance.

SAFETY BELTS

Retighten safety belts often, particularly on long drives; as you ride along, they tend to loosen. To function properly, the belts must have no slack.

 Always wear them. The fact that safety belts save lives has been well documented. They are particularly important in cars with air bags because it is the safety belt that holds the driver or front-seat passenger back far enough to avoid the air-bag danger zone.

Replace safety belts after a serious accident. The force of a high-impact accident can compromise the works of the reel mechanism.

SAFE-DEPOSIT BOX INVENTORY

Items such as these are too valuable to be replaced easily in case of theft or fire. Store them in a safe-deposit box.

- *Certificates of birth, death, marriage, and divorce*
- *Adoption and citizenship papers*
- *Military discharge papers*
- *Diplomas*
- *Stock certificates, savings bonds, certificates of deposit*
- *Titles to real estate or other property*
- *Mortgage records*
- *Valuable or heirloom jewelry that is rarely worn*
- *Rare coins and stamps and valuable silverware*
- *List, with snapshots, of household goods (to facilitate insurance claims if your home is burned or flooded)*

SALAD DRESSINGS

Classic vinaigrette. Use 3 parts oil to 1 part vinegar. Add a pinch of dry mustard, salt, pepper, garlic, and an herb or spice, then mix.

For a lighter dressing, substitute low-fat or nonfat yogurt or sour cream for up to half of the mayonnaise in any creamy salad dressing. It is especially good on coleslaw and potato salad. Also try using a low-fat mayonnaise.

A single note. One strong flavor should dominate a salad dressing; whether it comes from oil, vinegar, or a particular herb. Experiment by adding just a small amount of a flavored oil, flavored vinegar, or herb combination to a classic vinaigrette dressing.

Use pureed tomatoes (fresh or canned) mixed to taste with low-fat or fat-free yogurt to make a diet salad dressing. A little oil will bind the ingredients.

Less oil, more flavor. Cut down on fat—and calories—in a salad dressing by using flavored oils and vinegars instead. Just a teaspoonful or two of hazelnut or walnut oil (half as much as plain vegetable oil) will add an earthy note, while a raspberry or balsamic vinegar will impart a flowery zip.

Good to the last drop. Mix salad dressing in a nearly empty mayonnaise or mustard jar. You will make use of all the jar's contents and create a tastier dressing, too.

Vary the taste of a salad dressing by using orange, lemon or lime juice, apple or pear cider, or wine instead of vinegar.

SALAD GREENS

Iceberg advice. Remove the core from iceberg lettuce to release the leaves and make them easier to separate. Make a deep cut around the core, then pull it out.

Color key to nutrition. The darker the green, the more nutritious it is. Romaine lettuce, for example, has six times more vitamin C and five times more beta carotene than iceberg lettuce. Deep-colored greens such as spinach, watercress, chicory, and arugula pack even more nutrients.

OLD SAW **The drier the greens,** the better the salad. Excess water dilutes the flavor of the salad dressing and makes the greens soggy instead of crisp. Use a salad spinner for best results.

Don't load salads down with high-fat, high-calorie garnishes such as cheese, eggs, bacon bits, nuts, or croutons. Instead choose nutritious, low-calorie bean sprouts, fruits, or fresh vegetables.

Wash salad greens thoroughly. For loose-leaf types, remove the base and float the leaves in a sink or tub full of water, allowing the dirt to sink. Dry the greens as thoroughly as possible in a salad spinner, wrap in a dish towel or

---

SALES CALENDAR

Save by buying as many items as you can during annual sales, which are often geared to holidays or periods when sellers are clearing out seasonal inventory.

MONTH	SALE ITEMS
January	Sheets, towels, bedding (white sales); housewares; winter coats; wool and cashmere sweaters; gloves, hats, and scarves
February	Winter clothing; fine jewelry; winter boots
March	Winter clothing; skis, snowboards, and other winter sports equipment
April	Spring dresses and raincoats
May	Cosmetics and beauty products (after Mother's Day)
May/June	Audio and video equipment (to make room for new models arriving in summer)
July	Bathing suits (after Canada Day)
August	Summer clothing; white sale items; furniture; early back-to-school items (children's clothes and school supplies); cars (dealers need to clear their floors for new models)
September	Back-to-school and fall clothing (Labor Day); summer sports equipment; picnic wares
October	Winter clothing (Thanksgiving); air conditioners and lawn mowers (dealers need to clear the floor for winter items); cosmetics and beauty products
November	Winter coats; pre-Christmas items
December	Cars (business is slow during the holidays); clothing, Christmas cards, ornaments, and gift wrap (after Christmas)

A USER-FRIENDLY SANDER

A small electric sander that fits in the palm of your hand is the perfect sanding tool for the home workshop. It can be maneuvered easily and has a rotating motion that prevents gouges in your work. The orbital palm sanders below, from Porter-Cable (left) and Black & Decker (right), also come with detachable dust catchers.

paper towels, and store in a plastic bag in the fridge. They will keep, crisp and ready to eat, for up to six days.

Easy does it. Packaged mixed salad greens save you time and trouble, but they must be used as soon as possible for the best taste and nutrition. A single package will serve two people; four if you add halved cherry tomatoes, shredded carrot, and sliced bell pepper, cucumber, and red onion.

SALES

Shopping smarts. Before you hit the sale, ask yourself what you really need. A shopping list can help you look for the items you hope to buy and cut down on impractical impulse purchases.

Clothes questions. When you are in the dressing room, stop to quiz yourself about your potential new purchase. How will it fit into your wardrobe? Will the item require a whole set of new accessories? Where will you wear it?

Be savvy about price. Be sure you know what an item is really worth before you decide if the sale price is a bona fide bargain. For instance, a coat that is marked down to $200 might be similar to one you can purchase at another store for $150 at full price.

SALT

Egg tricks. Hard-boiled eggs will peel more easily if you boil them in salted water. Egg whites will whip up faster if you add a pinch of salt when beating them.

To cut down on salt, cover all but two or three holes in your salt shaker with tape. Eventually you may not even miss what doesn't come out.

 Keep salt free-flowing by adding 5 to 10 grains of rice to the salt shaker. You can also keep dampness out by covering the shaker with an inverted glass.

Key words. If you're reducing salt intake, look for "very low-sodium" or "sodium-free" on the labels of processed foods. Beware of "no salt added"; it may appear on products that contain foods naturally high in sodium.

Salt in canned goods such as vegetables or tuna can be lowered by draining off the liquid and rinsing the food under cold water. More than a third of the salt will be washed away.

Rescue too-salty soups and stews by tossing in a cut-up raw potato. The salt will be absorbed by the potato slices, which you can discard when they soften.

SANDING

A sanding sponge is good for smoothing rounded or irregularly shaped pieces of wood. The flexible backing will allow you to sand all the curves uniformly.

Use a sanding block instead of your fingers to hold sandpaper when you work on a flat surface. Your fingers will tend to follow irregularities in the wood and dig welts and waves in the surface.

Fill in first. Sanding the gouges or dents in a wood surface only creates even more noticeable craters. (Try to raise dents first with a steam iron, then treat the same as scratches.) Fill a scratch with wood putty and let it dry before sanding and finishing.

A manicured finish. Sand intricate, hard-to-reach cutouts and the carving on wood furniture or fine architectural details with an emery board.

SANDWICH GENERATION

You're not alone. Because of longer life spans for the elderly and parents having children later in life, a generation of people now finds itself at midlife having to juggle the demands of teenage children with the needs of elderly parents, who are often frail or in financial straits. The size of this group grows larger each year.

 Avoid hasty decisions, particularly at a moment of crisis. If your elderly mother breaks her hip in a fall, you may be tempted to immediately sell her house and have her move in with you. Instead, take the time to let her injury heal, and to research alternative ways to cope. For example, many frail elderly people can remain at home with assistance from home-care services.

Try private-care managers. A geriatric-care manager (usually a nurse or social worker) can find home health workers, recommend nursing homes, pay regular visits, and handle emergencies. Fees will vary depending on location and the complexity of services required. Ask for a referral from your doctor or a hospital's social services office.

Seek help if you work. You can't possibly do it all alone. Caregiving duties may require you to miss work, reducing both your income and your self-esteem. Try to find supplemental help, so that you can continue to work full-time. Or negotiate, if possible, flex-time or part-time work, or try job sharing. If that can't be arranged, consider looking for work that you can do at home while continuing to be a caregiver.

HOW KIDS CAN HELP

Young people, who make up one slice of the bread in the Sandwich Generation, can make a big contribution to relieving family stress by helping their grandparents.

▶ *Run errands and help with household chores.*

▶ *Play card games and chess or read aloud.*

▶ *Mow grass, rake leaves, and do other yard work.*

▶ *Cook for a grandparent—while maybe learning a few techniques and recipes from the older generation.*

▶ *Take a grandparent to a football game or a concert when a member of the family is participating.*

▶ *Go through family pictures with grandparents, writing on the backs names and dates only they would know.*

▶ *Encourage a grandparent to start a family history; interview him by tape recorder or videotape.*

SANDWICHES

Add fruit, nuts, and seeds to sandwiches for a nutritional boost. Combine bananas and peanut butter; add apples, grapes, pineapple, walnuts or almonds to tuna or chicken salad. Make these sandwiches on multi-grain bread.

Use pita bread to make fun "pocket" sandwiches. "Sloppy" fillings such as hummus or ratatouille, which don't work as well between two slices of bread, fit neatly into the pita's pocket.

Dieter's delight. Create the illusion of a hearty sandwich and still save calories by using only thin-sliced bread. (Making your own by cutting frozen bread into very thin slices.) For sandwich spreads, use mustard or low-fat mayonnaise, butter, or cream cheese.

PB& J. Peanut butter and jelly sandwiches remain the most popular, especially among children. Not only do they taste delicious, they are nutritious—especially if served on multi-grain bread.

Themes and variations. Be creative when selecting breads for sandwiches. Instead of just the conventional two slices of ordinary bread, use a croissant, a dinner roll, a hamburger bun, or a pita pocket. Also, a sandwich is just as delicious rolled in a Mexican tortilla, or even a leaf or two of iceburg or Romaine lettuce.

Cook your own sandwich meat instead of buying prepared meats that are not only expensive, but often include unhealthy additives. Roast a small ham, a turkey breast, a chicken, or a cut of beef. Covered with plastic wrap and refrigerated, the meat will keep for several days, allowing you to make sandwiches for up to a week.

SATELLITE DISHES

If you're short on yard space, a direct broadcast satellite (DBS) dish may be for you. These small dishes deliver up to 175 channels of nearly laser-disc-quality video and CD-quality sound. But they don't access overseas programming, and they don't carry local television stations.

For the most channels at the lowest price, large satellite dishes are still the best buy. They provide access to about 350 television channels from all over the world—but not local stations. They have higher start-up costs than the new mini-dishes, but they are cheaper to operate.

Look for "super video input" when shopping for a TV, if you have a DBS dish. Most new television sets with 68 cm (27 in.) screens or bigger have this feature, which provides an ultra-clear picture with the DBS.

The perfect site. Before you buy a satellite dish, make sure that you have a clear line of sight to the southwestern sky, which is where the signals come from. A large dish requires about 23 m (75 ft) of space between it and any buildings or trees; a DBS dish needs less. Check to see that no phone lines or other microwave sources will interfere with your reception.

Keep snow off a dish with a cover. Snow interferes with the signal and can warp the dish. Covers can also camouflage a big dish as a patio umbrella or a boulder.

SAVINGS

Retirement first. If you can contribute to only one savings account, put your money into a tax-deferred retirement plan such as an RRSP or workplace pension plan. Set up a separate college savings account only if you have money to spare since these accounts use after-tax dollars.

Consider savings bonds. If you're looking for low-risk options, the 4 percent interest rate on newly purchased savings bonds may look good when compared with the returns on other low-risk savings choices—money market funds, CD's, and savings accounts.

Time your redemptions. Savings bonds purchased before March 1 and held at least 30 months will increase in value twice a year. The dates on which the value of your bonds increases depend on when you bought them. Try to redeem your bonds shortly after one of the periodic increases.

Look beyond banks. Even after management fees, the average money market mutual fund pays 1 to 1.5 percentage points more than the average bank money market account.

Give at the office. If your employer offers Canada Savings Bonds through payroll deduction, you should take them up on the offer. You won't miss the small weekly withdrawal from your paycheque, and come October, you won't have to cough up big bucks.

Automated savings. If you have trouble saving, sign up for a savings plan at work that deducts money from your pay—you seldom miss money you don't see. Or ask your bank to move money regularly from your checking account to your savings account.

Invest long-term savings. After taxes and inflation, your real return is close to zero for bonds and certificates of deposit. So if you want your money to grow to meet long-term goals such as retirement, consider no-load mutual funds that invest in stocks.

BONDS FOR EDUCATING YOUR KIDS

As an investment for parents who are saving for their children's education, Canada Savings Bonds are reasonable and practically risk-free. They offer minimum interest rates for up to 10 years, so your bonds will keep earning money right up until they mature.

SAWS

A smooth-cutting saw. To help your handsaw glide more easily through wood, run the stub of a wax candle along the sides of its blade. Don't worry about leaving some wax on the blade's teeth; the film will come off as you saw.

Rust prevention. From time to time, oil the blades of your saws to stop rust from forming. Use a rag to rub the oil onto the blades.

Music to the craftman's ears. To determine the quality of a steel saw, give the blade a tap: the clearer and sharper the ring, the higher the quality of the steel.

Don't ruin new blades. If you're cutting through painted wood or drywall—both of which tend to dull saw blades—use an old saw for the job. And don't use your newer blades if you're cutting something that may contain nails.

SAYING NO

The real reason. You can say no without hurting someone's feelings if you're honest, polite, and succinct. For example, when asked to join a bridge game, say, "Thanks anyway, but I don't play bridge."

No, thank you. To keep high-pressure salespeople from pestering you, try old-fashioned good manners. Simply say "No, thank you" calmly and quietly. You'll be surprised how quickly and easily

assertive salespeople can be subdued by this response.

Stick to your guns. If someone tries to persuade you to do something that you don't want to do, remember that your refusal is as valid as another person's insistence. State your no with conviction and move on.

Take a rain check. If you have to say no to a get-together with friends, don't extend regrets without scheduling another date. If you are unable to make firm plans on the spot, be sure to call back within a week; otherwise friends will assume they have been brushed off.

SCAMS & SWINDLES

 No free lunch. Resist the pitch that sounds too good to be true—it usually is. The swindler's mask of sincerity is but a ploy to gain your confidence and separate you from your money.

Bait and switch. If you are lured into a store by a sale, but discover that all sale items are "gone" and you are offered something more expensive, you've probably been

BEWARE OF COMMON SWINDLES

Sadly, our world is full of scam artists and swindlers. Here are a few of the most prevalent ones. Being aware—and wary—of them will save you humiliation and money.

▶ Pyramid schemes. Although legitimate pyramid schemes make money for a few, most participants lose. Be cautious about any pyramid business, including a chain letter that asks you to pass on money or anything else of value.

▶ Run-your-own-business schemes. Be wary of come-on ads for making lots of money in your own home. Be especially cautious if a scheme asks for money up front, the purchase of materials, or lists of potential clients.

▶ Diet rip-offs. Beware of any product that promises that you'll lose weight without cutting calories or exercising, but simply by taking the "magic" liquid, pill, or powder. At best, these don't work; at worst they may be harmful.

▶ Credit card fraud. Never give out a credit card number to a telephone caller requesting verification in order for you to win a prize. This scam is also common on the Internet, where scammers ask you to confirm your enrollment in an on-line service by revealing a password or credit card number. Don't fall for it.

▶ Investment deals and time-share schemes. No matter how attractive the deal, ask for a written proposal or prospectus and suggest that the person talk to your lawyer. A legitimate businessperson will cooperate.

conned. Shop elsewhere in the future and report the store to the Better Business Bureau.

Minor bandits. Tell swindlers who take advantage of minors that you are not honoring the contract. Minors cannot enter into legal contracts without the signature of their parents, and parents need not pay for items contracted for by minors. This includes 900 calls made by an under-18 child or products from book, music or fan clubs. Return all products and notify the seller that the contract is void.

Be smart. If you have any questions about an offer through the mail or over the phone, contact the National Fraud Information Center (1-800-876-7060).

Act promptly. You have the legal right to void purchases for over $25 that you made in your home or at a seminar by sending a cancellation notice to the seller's address within three days of the day of purchase. Be sure to send it by certified or registered mail.

SCARVES

Shawl sense. While shawls or extra-large scarves provide added warmth and style, don't forget to consider the proportions. A large shawl can overwhelm a small woman, while a small scarf can look skimpy on a bulky coat.

Glamour wrap. Buy an oversized scarf made of silk, velvet, or lace, and drape it over a sleeveless or strapless dress. The scarf adds elegance and covers bare skin.

The obliging oblong. Oblong scarves can be more versatile than square ones. Hang an oblong scarf over or under a jacket collar, coil two around your neck for a cowl effect, or wear one in a floppy bow on a shirt or hat.

Fabrication. Buy a yard or two of silk or wool challis fabric, hem the

ROTARY CUTTERS

Instead of old-fashioned scissors, try a simple-to-use rotary cutter like these models from Fiskars and Olfa. The circular blade can slice easily through several layers of craft paper or fabric at a time. The blade creates a razor-sharp, straight edge, or it can be changed to make a pinked edge.

edges by hand or machine, and create a beautiful scarf for less than half the price.

Store right. To prevent scarves from becoming creased or wrinkled when they are stored in a drawer, roll them around the cardboard tubes from aluminum foil or plastic wrap.

SCISSORS

Sharpen with the pros. Poor sharpening can ruin a good pair of scissors. Don't try to sharpen scissors with a stone; have a professional do it. (Ask for referrals at fabric or cutlery stores.) Don't bother to have cheap scissors sharpened—just replace them.

Scissor blades should brush each other lightly at the tips while being opened and closed. If they don't, adjust the pivot screw.

Tighten the riveted pivot on a pair of scissors by placing it on a metal surface, then striking it with the head of a hammer.

SCREENS

Wash window screens by laying them on a smooth, cloth-covered surface. (An old sheet on a table is ideal.) Scrub the screen gently with soap, water, and a brush, then rinse outdoors with a hose.

Simple patches. If a small hole develops, seal the opening by applying coats of clear glue, nail polish, or shellac. If necessary, use tape as a temporary backing, then remove it after the liquid dries.

To mend a big hole, cut a piece of screening 12 mm (½ in.) larger than the hole and unravel its edges to leave points all around. Bend the points at right angles to the patch. Slip the points through the screen, then bend them back flat to hold the patch. Coat the edges of the patch with clear glue.

SCREWDRIVERS

The ABC's. Use a screwdriver tip that fits snugly in the screw head and is the same width as the slot. A screwdriver bigger than the slot can damage the surrounding work; one that's too small can't gain a proper hold and will strip the screw's slot.

Torque, or turning power, drives screws, not pressure, so don't bear down on a screwdriver (although you may have to push a little at first to firmly seat the tip of the screwdriver in the screw head).

Big grips are good. When buying any type of screwdriver, be aware that you can apply more torque with one that has a fat handle.

SEASHELLS

Craft a one-of-a-kind soap dish from a large scallop or clam shell by gluing three small shells to its back for legs. Drill two or three holes between the legs for water to drain through.

Make beautiful buttons by drilling holes in shells and stitching or tying them to sweaters, vests dresses, and jackets.

Create the perfect frame for a beach photo by hot-gluing shells to a plain wooden frame. Collect plenty of similar shells in three or four different sizes. Glue a row of the smallest shells on the inner

RIGHT STUFF

POWER SCREWDRIVERS

Press a button, and you can drive or remove screws all day long— and your hand will never tire. Cordless power screwdrivers, such as the Skil Twist Extra (shown here), come with several sizes of slotted and Phillips-head tips. To recharge, plug into the charging unit. Look for them in hardware stores and home centers.

edge, then a row of shells the next size larger outside the first row. Increase the size of each row until the frame is covered.

Perk up drab shells by bleaching them overnight in a 50-50 mixture of chlorine bleach and water. For hard-to-whiten shells, increase the proportion of bleach. To let shells bleach naturally, set them out in the sun.

Embellish combs and barrettes by gluing tiny shells and bits of coral to them. Before you apply the glue, roughen the plastic surfaces with an emery board.

Make a unique necklace by drilling holes in shells and stringing them together. Use a large shell for the center of the necklace and graduate the size of the shells on either side. For a dramatic look, wear a single shell on a slender black cord.

SECOND HOMES

Look for a local lender. Your bank at home is less likely to lend money on real estate that's out of town. Even if the bank is willing, you might be charged a higher interest rate and extra points, and possibly also have to put more money down.

Check out rental prospects, if you'll need extra income to maintain your second home. However, don't rely on a broker's or owner's projection of rental income; look into the history of the property or properties like it.

One home, one deduction. Unlike the United States, in Canada only one home can be considered a personal residence for deductions on your income tax. All other domiciles you may own, whether you live there or rent them, will be taxed as such.

SEEDS

Spreading small seeds. Tiny, dustlike seeds such as those of flowering tobacco or impatiens are hard to sow evenly—unless you mix them with a handful of clean sand first. This makes even the tiniest seeds easy to handle and distribute.

A sterile start. Newly sprouted seedlings are especially vulnerable to fungal and bacterial diseases. To keep seeds healthy without sprays, sow them into packaged soil-free "seed-starting mix." A blend of sphagnum moss, vermiculite, and peat, such a mix is naturally sterile and disease-free.

Jump-start indoor germination.
Immediately after sowing, set the pots containing seed atop a furnace, water heater, or television. Germination will occur more quickly in the warm soil (24° to 32°C [75°–90°F]).

Saving seeds. To keep unused seeds for use next year, put the packets into a screw-top glass jar or a canning jar. "Feed" seeds by wrapping 125 mL (½ cup) of dry powdered milk in tissue, and adding it to the jar. Seal the jar and refrigerate.

Sandpaper tricks. Some seeds, such as those of morning glories, moonflowers, and New Zealand spinach, have tough coats that make germination slow and uncertain. To help them to sprout faster, rub them gently with a sheet of medium-grit sandpaper before planting.

SELF-DEFENSE

Act confident when walking, especially down darkened streets. You're a mugger's ideal target if you are daydreaming or busy fumbling for your house keys. Walk briskly with your head up, keep your eyes and ears open, and be alert to people around you. Move as if you know where you're going, even if you don't.

Be prepared for the possibility of physical attack by enrolling in a self-defense course. Check the

Yellow Pages under "Self-Defense Instruction," or call your local police precinct for recommendations. Interview instructors and check for endorsements before you sign up.

Auto alert. People getting in and out of their cars—especially on dark streets or in empty lots and garages—are also popular targets for muggers. Select parking spots carefully. Look for those positioned under street lights or near a garage entrance door. When you return to your car, have the key ready for quick access; better yet, invest in an automatic door opener. Leave the space as quickly as possible. If you must take time to check a map or deal with another problem, drive to a more populated area first.

 Use the buddy system to ensure your safety. Check that another colleague is present when you work late at the office. Join up with a friend when walking at night, going to a nightclub, or venturing into any other situation that might be dangerous for someone on his own.

Self-defense devices such as mace, stun guns, and sirens risk making an attacker angry and violent—thereby putting you at even greater risk. If you carry a protective device, be certain that you are trained in its proper use. Also, be sure that the device you carry is legal in your community.

EATING AND COOKING WITH SEEDS

High in protein, seeds make wholesome snacks and enhance the flavor and texture of many other foods. (Seeds are also high in calories, so use them sparingly if you are watching your weight.) Store all seeds in airtight containers. Here are some ways to use popular seeds.

▶ *Pumpkin seeds. Buy prepared seeds or harvest seeds from a fresh pumpkin. (To prepare harvested seeds: Boil seeds in salted water for 10 minutes; drain; then toast them with butter or oil in a 175°C [350°F] oven for 25 minutes.) Eat as a snack, or mix with granola, breads, salads, or in various ethnic dishes.*

▶ *Sunflower seeds. Buy prepared seeds or harvest seeds from sunflowers. Eat as a snack raw or toasted, salted or unsalted; or use in granola, breads, and salads.*

▶ *Sesame seeds. Buy prepared seeds. Use in salads, as a topping for breads, or as a flavoring in stir-fry dishes. Ground into paste, sesame seeds serve as a basic ingredient in many sauces and spreads, such as tahini, as well as the primary ingredient in a candy called halvah.*

▶ *Poppy seeds. Buy prepared seeds. Toast and crush before using to bring out the full flavor. Delicious as a topping on noodle dishes, as well as on baked goods.*

SELF-DISCIPLINE

Post goals. To be more efficient, set one or two small goals each time you engage in an activity—at work, school, sports, or a community organization. Have realistic expectations, but don't quit without making a spirited attempt to meet your goals.

Pace yourself when challenged with a major project. Carefully plan the time and energy you give to it. Avoid intense bursts that can exhaust you and cause burnout.

The big picture. If you feel your intent wavering or your discipline faltering, remind yourself that your future is dependent on the efforts you make today.

Wholesome habits. You can stay the toughest course by maintaining a balanced lifestyle. Get plenty of sleep, eat properly, exercise, and have some fun. You'll be better able to stay focused.

SELF-EMPLOYMENT

Free tax help. If you're starting a small business, give your local Revenue Canada a call for free help on tax obligations and preparation of returns.

Legal eagle. In the early stages of planning, contact the Business Development Bank Of Canada at 5 Place Ville-Marie, Suite 400, Montreal, Que., H3B 5E7, to find out what certificates, licenses, or other credentials are needed for your new business. Their telephone number is (514) 283-5904.

 Speak up. Don't be shy about letting people know that you've started a business. There's a difference between being pushy with your acquaintances and simply telling them the exciting news of your recently launched enterprise. Many of your first and best referrals may come through friends, neighbors, former co-workers, or family members.

A modest start. Don't waste money on expensive new furnishings. Instead, look for bargains at liquidation sales and stores that sell used office furniture. For key business meetings, rent a conference room at a club or hotel to make a good impression.

Take it step-by-step. Wait until your business is earning revenue before you buy equipment that's not absolutely essential. For example, don't spend a bundle on your own copier; use the local photocopy center for a while.

Telephone tips. Your customer's first impression is usually formed over the telephone, so use a professional-quality voice-mail service to pick up calls when you're already on the phone. Have a pleasant voice give the name of your company and a polite invitation for the caller to leave a name and number for you to return the call. Get more than one business line if you also use electronic communication. Never share your family's line with the business.

SELF-ESTEEM

Be fair to yourself. Lack of self-esteem often comes from setting standards for yourself that are too high, even unattainable. Don't harp on one or two slipups; learn from them instead. The most creative people make many, but they use them to their advantage.

Due credit. Nurture healthy self-esteem by giving yourself credit when good things happen. Pat yourself on the back and share your success with another person. Try to compliment yourself for two small successes every day.

BUILDING SELF-ESTEEM IN KIDS

Here's how you can help children build confidence in their abilities, in their sense of worth, in their feelings of being loved, and in their right to be happy.

▶ *Tell kids often that you love them for being themselves. Love and hugs go a long way toward building self-esteem.*

▶ *If shyness inhibits your child from joining social activities he'd like to do, ask questions about his social anxieties and respond to his fears with practical reassurances.*

▶ *Help your child participate in a volunteer program such as a local food drive. Volunteering helps her experience the positive impact she can make on another person's life.*

▶ *Encourage your child to choose a sport or hobby to pursue with dedication. The process of practicing and learning a new skill is a great boost to self-esteem.*

GLOVES FOR SENSITIVE SKIN

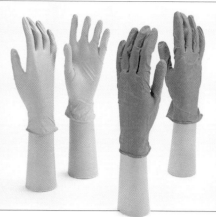

If your hands are very sensitive to cleaning products or if you are allergic to the latex of other household gloves, try these gloves from Interplus. They are made of an industrial-strength polymer material that is more puncture resistant than latex gloves of similar thickness. They're more comfortable, too, because they conform to your hand. Choose from small, medium, or large sizes, with or without a powder coating inside. Visit Interplus on the world wide web at http://abigworld.com.

The gift of friendship. If you're feeling a lack of confidence, contact a good friend or dear relative. Such people can remind you of how much you are valued by the people who love you.

A pitfall. Watch out for what psychologists call false self-esteem. This occurs when you need continual recognition and praise from other people. Real self-esteem comes from within and isn't dependent on the responses of people around you.

Spirit lifter. Performing small, random acts of kindness for people with whom you live and work can help you feel good about yourself. A generous spirit can enhance your own self-esteem.

SENSITIVE SKIN

Be alert to additives. Avoid cosmetics that contain fragrances and preservatives; they can cause adverse skin reactions. Shop for products free of additives.

Be wary of soaps. Some soaps, particularly those with heavy scents, can be very harsh and will dry and irritate sensitive skin. Use gentler brands like Basis or Dove.

Laundry trick. Use washing-machine products labeled "free," such as Tide Free or Cheer Free, to wash your bed and bath linens as well as your clothes.

Shower break. You needn't wash yourself all over every day unless you've been doing hard physical labor or exercise. Showering every other day is kinder to your skin.

No abrasives. Never use beauty grains or other abrasive cleansers if you have sensitive skin or broken capillaries.

What to wear? Opt for clothes made of natural fabrics, such as cotton and wool. If you buy an item made with a synthetic fabric, launder it several times before you wear it. This will remove some potential irritants.

Test new products if you are prone to contact dermatitis or allergic skin reactions. To try a new cosmetic, for example, rub a small amount on your inner arm, then cover the area with a bandage for 24 hours. If no irritation occurs, you can probably use the product safely.

SEPTIC SYSTEMS

Clear the area. Never plant trees or shrubs directly above or around a septic system or in its drain field. Deep roots can clog and damage the pipes. Plant only grass or short-rooted ground covers in these areas.

Keep out! Never put toxic or hazardous chemicals, such as paints, varnishes, thinners, waste oil, photographic chemicals, or pesticides, down the drain or in the toilet. Even in small amounts, these solutions destroy the bacteria that treat waste in the system.

If a substance won't dissolve, don't put it down the drain because it will likely harm your septic system. Grease, eggshells, coffee grounds, paper towels, and tissues all fall under this rule.

Make a map documenting your septic system and its drain field to make maintenance and repairs easier. Keep permits and a log of when it was cleaned out or repaired together with the map.

SERVICE CONTRACTS

Know the facts. Service contracts, or extended warranties, cover repairs on appliances or electronics after the manufacturer's warranty runs out. Expect a strong sales pitch—salespeople are paid extra commissions to sell service contracts because they mean extra profits for the company if no repairs are needed.

Think twice before you buy a service contract. Statistics show that most problems in electronics show up within a few weeks of purchase. Only 12 to 20 percent of those who buy extended warranties ever use them.

 OLD SAW **Depend on quality.** Purchase the finest products that you can afford. It is better to spend a few more dollars on the product itself rather than on an expensive service contract. Good quality is your best insurance against the cost of repairs.

SEWING

Through the needle's eye. Make the task of threading a needle easier by cutting the thread at an angle so that its end tapers to a point and by holding the needle's eye over a white background.

A polished thread. If you're having trouble threading a needle, moisten your finger and twist the end of the thread, then shoot for the eye.

Stop thread from tangling. After threading the needle and

Sewing on a Coat Button

Retrieve and save the lost button. New buttons can be expensive and time-consuming to match. For heavy coats, create a shank by sewing over a toothpick and winding with thread, as shown here.

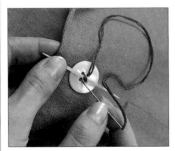

1 *Thread a short needle with 45 cm (18") of buttonhole thread. Knot the end. (To keep thread from tangling, run it over candle wax or beeswax.)*

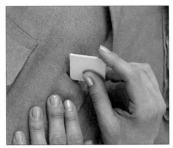

2 *Align the closing. Stick the needle through the round end of the buttonhole. Mark with chalk where the point sticks into the lower coat front.*

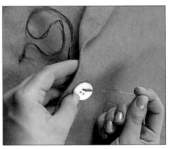

3 *Make a tiny stitch on the chalk mark and pull the knot onto it. Place the button over the mark, and pull the needle up through one hole.*

4 *Place a toothpick over the button, then push the needle down through another hole, making an X or two straight lines to match the stitching on other buttons.*

5 *Sew 8 to 10 stitches, ending under the button. Remove the toothpick, and lift the button. To create the shank, wind the thread 6 times around the stitches. Backstitch twice.*

tying a knot, run the length of thread over a cake of beeswax or slip it through a fabric-softener sheet that you use in the dryer.

Stay out of the spotlight. If you're not particularly accomplished with a needle and thread, use patterned and dark fabrics to minimize sewing mistakes. Errors show up more conspicuously on plain, light-colored fabrics.

Colorful machine stitches. For multicolored fabrics, match the spool's thread to the garment's predominant color; choose the bobbin's thread to coincide with the fabric's secondary color.

Needle news. To sharpen a machine needle, sew rows of stitches through a piece of fine sandpaper. Discard nicked or bent needles, both of which can damage fabric.

Picking up pins. Dropped pins can be dangerous, especially on carpets. Use a magnet to pick up stray pins and needles. To retrieve dropped pins in out-of-the-way places, tape the magnet to the end of a yardstick. Vacuum the carpet thoroughly when you finish sewing for the day.

 Anticipate future growth. If you're working on a garment that may eventually be let out, cut the seam allowances 1 inch wide. For children's clothes, allow for deep hems.

Pins close at hand. Use a wrist pincushion when you're working on a project that requires a lot of pinning. With your pins always close at hand, you will be less likely to drop them.

Use a pair of eyebrow tweezers to pull a reluctant needle through dense or heavy cloth or multiple layers of fabric.

CONTENTS OF A BASIC SEWING KIT

A basic sewing kit should include the following tools and supplies. If you want to make clothing and home furnishings such as curtains, you'll need a sewing machine.

▶ *A box with compartments to keep small things in, such as a tackle box or a store-bought sewing basket*

▶ *Measuring devices: a tape measure, a 12-inch ruler, a seam gauge*

▶ *A thimble that fits your middle finger without falling off*

▶ *Cutting instruments: a pair of 4- or 6-inch scissors and a pair of 6- or 7-inch sewing shears*

▶ *Short, rustproof needles: sharps for general sewing, ball-points for knits, betweens for quilting stitches*

▶ *Rustproof pins: regular straight pins and thinner silk pins (their ball heads are easier to see in fabric)*

▶ *A pincushion*

▶ *Needle threader (optional)*

▶ *Thread in a variety of colors, including black and white, and in a variety of weights for different tasks*

▶ *Tailor's chalk (optional)*

▶ *Assorted snaps, hooks, and basic buttons*

A good steam iron is essential for finishing seams and producing truly professional-looking work. Look for one with a wide temperature range. If you work with delicate fabrics or synthetics, make sure that the iron produces steam at the lower settings.

SEXUAL HARASSMENT

Press disconnect. Be frank with someone who makes uncomfortable advances at work. In a straightforward, nonthreatening manner, say: "I like you, but please understand that I am not interested romantically."

Seek help. Behavior that can be legally construed as sexual harassment can be overt—or it can be subtle and difficult to prove. If you are being subjected to conduct that makes you uncomfortable, contact a lawyer, a women's center, or the Canadian Human Rights Commission in Ottawa by dialing (613) 995-1151 for professional guidance. Don't make a formal complaint before doing your homework.

Keep a chronology. Write down the date, time, place, and other details of sexual harassment as soon as it occurs. This log will provide critical information when you make a formal complaint.

Tell others. Let coworkers and friends know that you've encountered uncomfortable sexually oriented behavior. By expressing discomfort, you protect yourself from harassers who claim you welcomed their behavior.

SHADE PLANTS

Bulbs for shade. Plant bulbs that flower in the early spring (tulips, daffodils, grape hyacinths, or snowdrops, for example) underneath mature deciduous trees. The flowers blossom before the trees are leafy, then go dormant as the foliage emerges. During dormancy, such bulbs even benefit from the shade's cooling effect.

Enliven shady areas. For maximum impact, plant light-colored flowers in areas that receive little sunlight. White flowers stand out best, and a small cluster of them catches the eye far better than a bed of red ones.

Ground covers. Use English ivy, pachysandra, or other spreading plants in shaded soils that are laced with the shallow roots of trees. Don't try to remove the roots; this injures the trees and is only a short-term solution, since the roots regenerate.

Lend a helping hand. If your shade plants are near trees, be sure to give them extra water and fertilizer. Tree roots are greedy eaters and will draw off most of the moisture and nutrients. To cut down on watering, grow drought-tolerant plants in such areas.

When planting shade lovers, keep in mind that most evolved in woodland habitats with organic-rich soils. So mix an extra-large batch of compost or peat moss into the soil at planting time.

SHAVING

To get your beard really soft before you shave, apply a warm washcloth for two minutes. Use plenty of shaving cream or foam to avoid irritating the skin. Raise whiskers by applying the shaving cream against the grain. Leave the lather on for a few minutes.

Reduce irritation. Use sharp blades and shave just once over each part of the beard. Move the razor in the direction the beard grows. Avoid stretching the skin.

Tea to the rescue. If you nick yourself while shaving and there's no styptic pencil around, put an end to the bleeding by wetting a teabag with cold water and then pressing it on the cut.

Exercise first, shave later. Newly shaved skin is more vulnerable to the stinging sensation caused by the salt in perspiration.

Apply sunscreen instead of aftershave. Your skin will be soothed and, of course, shielded from the harmful rays of the sun.

Shave your underarms at night. With your skin given a chance to recover as you sleep, your morning application of deodorant won't cause irritation.

SHEETS

Decorate with sheets. Use the accessories found in sheet sets in creative ways. Consider matching

UNUSUAL USES FOR SHEETS

An inexpensive source of pretty matching fabrics, sheets have hundreds of uses. Some ideas to start with:

▶ *Headboard. Cover a padded headboard with a sheet, using a staple gun to attach the fabric to the back.*

▶ *Duvet cover. Protect a fine comforter by making a washable cover for it out of two flat sheets. Turn the sheets inside out, sew seams on three sides, and insert a zipper on the end. Pipe, trim. or top-stitch the edges if you wish.*

▶ *Curtains or draperies. Cut a twin flat sheet lengthwise into two 84 cm x 244 cm (33 x 96 in.) panels. Sew a narrow hem along the raw edges. Run a curtain rod through the top hem. Hang with tiebacks cut from scraps or ribbon.*

▶ *Shower curtain. Cut and hem a full-size (double) flat sheet bottom to fit the height of the curtain rod. To make holes at the top for hanging, use the button-hole attachment on your sewing machine or a grommet-setting tool (found at sewing centers). Hang a plastic liner on the shower side.*

▶ *Wall covering. Cover a bedroom wall with sheets. Trim the hems and edges to fit. Attach with a staple gun or use glue made for attaching fabric to walls.*

TOOLS FOR SHELLFISH

Using designated tools when preparing fresh shellfish will make your work not only quicker and easier—but safer, too. For clams, a blunt, round-tip knife (left) snaps the shells right open. For oysters, the knife (center) has a sharp blade to get between the shells while the collar prevents you from cutting your hand. For shrimp, the simple tool (right) lets you shell and devein shrimp with one quick and easy motion. All these tools are available through gourmet shops and catalogs.

dust ruffles, pillow shams, and curtains, letting the bed be the center of your room's decorating scheme. Or mix and match sets in attractive combinations—color-coordinated stripes with florals, for example, or plaids with solids.

Bargain hunting. Save big on sheets and other bed accessories by shopping manufacturers' outlets for discontinued patterns, seconds, and irregulars.

Night and day. If a bedroom serves a daytime purpose, choose a fitted spread and a tailored look. Make the bed look like a sofa with solid colors or a neat, geometric print.

Rags to riches. Tear old sheets into rags—they're perfect for light household chores. Use them as well for messy spills, then throw them away when you're done.

SHELLFISH

Stay healthy. Avoid sicknesses caused by tainted shellfish by eating only cooked dishes. If you can't resist the occasional raw delicacy, buy from a reputable fish market, ideally a busy one that has constant turnover of its seafood.

Steaming shells. Don't stop steaming clams and mussels once their shells have opened; continue

to cook for 1 or 2 minutes. This heats the food to a temperature that makes it truly safe to eat.

Save the stock that develops as you cook shellfish. Strain the liquid if necessary, and use in chowders, gumbos, and other soups. Freeze some in ice-cube trays to pop out and use in the future.

 Hurry up. Keep shellfish alive and chilled, and prepare and eat it as soon as possible, preferably right away. Shellfish is highly perishable, and it also tastes best when it's as fresh as can be.

Skip the tomalley, or liver, when you eat lobster or crab. Although considered a delicacy by some, the organ filters toxins, so it may contain unhealthy chemicals.

An economical substitute. Try surimi in place of shellfish. Also labeled "sea legs," surimi is a processed product made with fish. It is an inexpensive substitute for crab and lobster (use it in cooked dishes like fish cakes), and because it is processed, it is also less perishable. A word of warning, though: it has 10 times the salt content of fresh shellfish.

SHELVES

Window dressing. Put a series of glass shelves across a viewless window and fill the spaces with colorful glassware. The changing effects of daylight on the glassware add sparkle to the room.

Upstaging your shelves. To better see what's in the back of a deep shelf, add a step or two, ascending toward the rear. Make the risers from two-by-fours, or find ready-made "stepped" shelving in home centers.

Use racks instead of shelves to unclutter a child's room or hall closet. A sports rack, for example, may hold soccer balls. helmets and tennis rackets. Racks of all kinds can be found at sporting goods or home furnishing stores.

SHIRTS & BLOUSES

The long and short of it. For men or women, cuffs look best either flush with the jacket sleeve or protruding up to half an inch beyond for a dash of color.

 Banish collar stains. To scrub out stains on your collars, mix baking soda and water into a paste. Scrub the paste on the stains with a soft toothbrush before washing the shirts.

Same shirt, new look. To achieve visual variety with a single shirt, buy one that requires cuff links, and change the links frequently. Or use button covers to alter the buttons' appearance.

Flip frayed collars. If your old shirt has a frayed collar, remove it carefully at the seam where it joins to the shirt, turn it over, and reattach it with the unworn side up. Or sew the seam closed and leave the shirt collarless.

SHOES

What size shoelaces? If you're not sure what size shoelaces your child needs, count the pairs of holes in one shoe and multiply by four. For adults, multiply by seven.

Don't be a fall guy. To safeguard yourself or your kids from slipping in new shoes, roughen the soles lightly with coarse sandpaper or an emery board.

Rise and shine. To add shine to leather or patent leather shoes, first polish them as you normally would, then rub lemon juice directly onto the shoes and buff. For the highest shine on patent leather, use petroleum jelly.

Back relief. If you have lower back pain, toss your high-heeled shoes aside and opt for a pair with low heels to relieve the pressure on your spine. Add cushioned shoe pads for extra comfort.

Good fit. Stand on a piece of paper or cardboard, and with a pen or pencil, trace your right foot. Cut out the shape. Slip it into your right shoe. If the shoe is the correct size, it should be as wide as the paper and half an inch longer at the toe.

Canvas care. Clean canvas shoes and bags by dipping a toothbrush in carpet shampoo and scrubbing up a lather. Rinse, then let dry.

SHRUBS

Easy mowing. Plant shrubs in "islands" amid mulch-covered beds. This simplifies mowing by eliminating the need for trimming around each plant.

TROUBLE-FREE SHRUBS

Many shrubs are naturally resistant to pests and diseases, and this makes them easy to care for. As always, though, gardening success also depends on selecting shrubs adapted to the climate and soil found in your region of the country. Here are some suggestions for each region.

REGION	SHRUB
East	Barberry (*Berberis spp.*) Kerria (*Kerria japonica*) Mock orange (*Philadelphus coronarius*) Mountain laurel (*Kalmia latifolia*) Japanese spirea (*Spiraea japonica*) Weigela (*Weigela florida*)
Central	Burford holly (*Ilex cornuta 'Burfordii'*) Carolina laurel cherry (*Prunus caroliniana*) Dwarf yaupon (*Ilex vomitoria 'Nana'*) Japanese pittosporum (*Pittosporum tobira*) Silverberry (*Elaeagnus pungens*) Wax myrtle (*Myrica cerifera*)
Prairies	Barberry (*Berberis spp.*) Common lilac (*Syringa vulgaris*) Japanese spirea (*Spiraea japonica*) Rugosa rose (*Rosa rugosa*) Tatarian dogwood (*Cornus alba*) Weigela (*Weigela florida*)
West	Beauty bush (*Kolkwitzia amabilis*) Cotoneaster (*Cotoneaster spp.*) Heather (*Calluna vulgaris*) Leucothoe (*Leucothoe fontanesiana*) Oregon grape (*Mahonia aquifolium*) St. Johnswort (*Hypericum calycinum*)
West Coast	Acacia (*Acacia spp.*) Bottle-brush (*Callistemon spp.*) Cassia (*Cassia artemisioides*) Texas ranger (*Leucophyllum spp.*) Autumn sage (*Salvia greggii*) Hop bush (*Dodonaea viscosa*) Yucca (*Yucca spp.*)

Avoid salt injury. When landscaping next to a driveway or a roadside where salt will be spread in wintertime, plant seaside shrubs such as rugosa roses, bayberry, or beach plum, which are naturally salt tolerant.

Carefree dwarfs. When creating a foundation planting, you can save yourself lots of trimming in coming years by using dwarf shrubs, such as 'Crimson Pygmy' barberry, the dwarf deutzia 'Nikko,' and dwarf cranberry bush viburnum. These plants will remain compact without pruning.

When renting, you can improve the appearance of your temporary home by landscaping with shrubs that are planted in containers. When you move, it will be easy to take the shrubs with you. (This is especially helpful if you take the time to shape shrubs into topiary.)

SIBLING RIVALRY

Avoid comparisons. Don't compare your children to one another in their presence. Refrain from holding up one as an example to another ("Why don't you mind the way your sister does?")

Forget the 50-50 split. Parents can go a long way in keeping sibling rivalry from escalating by recognizing that each child has different needs and by focusing on each child as an individual. Strive for overall fairness. Respect individual preferences in clothing and activities.

Rotate privileges. Assign each child a special day or days when he may make decisions, select menus, have first dibs.

Foster caring attitudes. Encourage an older child to read to a younger one. See that each remembers the others' birthdays and makes or chooses cards and gifts. Remind your children that they are very special to one another because they are siblings.

EASY DOES IT

WHEN BABY MAKES FOUR

Sibling rivalry can become an issue the minute a new baby comes home to stay. There are ways, however, to keep sibling rivalry at bay and ensure that both the older child and the new baby are happy and content.

▶ *Plan for baby's arrival. Add new activities to your older child's life (a music or gym class or a preschool program) well before a new baby arrives. That way an older sibling won't feel as "pushed out" by the baby and will have a special activity to enjoy.*

▶ *When visiting a new baby, take a small gift to the new big sister or big brother too. It makes the older child feel included in the excitement over the newborn.*

▶ *Prepare your child for any changes. A new "quiet time" may be instituted, for example. Explain the baby's limitations as a playmate and that it takes a baby time to grow up and do the things big kids do.*

▶ *Enlist the older child as a helper. That way, you include her in the process of taking care of the baby. It also shows that you trust her and think she's responsible.*

SILK

Year-round wear. Choose silk to wear in any climate. The fabric keeps you cool in summer—it's breathable and light—and warm in winter, especially when layered with other fabrics.

First aid for stains. To treat new stains on silk clothing, dampen a clean washcloth with club soda or seltzer water, and sandwich the silk between two layers of the cloth. Although the soda helps to dilute a fresh spill and deter staining, the garment should be dry-cleaned as soon after as possible.

Easy on the curls. To keep hairstyles intact, sleep on silk pillowcases. Hair doesn't cling to silk, as it normally does to cotton or flannel pillowcases when your head moves around at night.

Silk around the clock. To get the best look out of silk, choose matte silk for daytime clothes and shiny silk for evening attire. If you want to wear a silk jacket with a silk shirt, choose either a matte or shiny look for both.

Silk hang-ups. Hang silk clothes on plastic or padded hangers. Wood hangers can snag silk, and thin metal hangers frequently leave small creases or imprints in the garments.

SILVER

Beautiful and cheap. Cruise flea markets, secondhand shops, or garage sales for great buys on sterling silverware. Old silver serving pieces, dessert forks, and teaspoons add an elegant touch to your table—even if the patterns don't match—and cost much less than if you bought them new.

Savvy shopping. If a silver piece is heavier than it looks, and if it is marked "weighted sterling," it isn't the good stuff. It has a cement, plaster, or lead base covered by a thin sheet of sterling silver, and it can dent or break if dropped.

Couch-potato polishing. A perfect time to shine your silver is while you're watching television. If you normally loathe the task, keeping up with on-screen action will break the monotony.

Handy polishers. Polish silver wearing silversmith gloves instead of rubber gloves, which can tarnish silver. Silversmith gloves protect your hands while making your task easier. Made of cotton with polish-treated surfaces, they can be found in hardware stores.

Salvaging sterling. There's no need to despair if your heirloom silver is severely tarnished or scratched. Professional silversmiths can restore damaged sterling, no matter how old it is, with polishing machines. Shop around to get the best price.

Do you have a friend or neighbor struggling to bring up children alone, and wonder how you can help? Here are some ideas for taking pressure off the parent and widening the world of the youngsters.

▶ *Share a hobby with one of the children; let her help you walk the dog or let him plant your vegetable garden with you. It's good for children to have other adults in their lives and it gives the parent a respite.*

▶ *Include the whole family at a backyard barbecue with other neighbors. It's important for single parents to feel that they are a part of the neighborhood and that their children belong.*

▶ *Offer to do errands for the family while you're at the shopping center. Having to take the children with them every time they go out makes it hard for single parents to do their shopping efficiently.*

▶ *If you're comfortable with the kids, offer to let them stay with you in emergencies or even just to give the parent a night out. Single parents need a break now and then without worrying about the children.*

Don't wait too long to wash. Silverware that has touched salty or acidic foods and sits unwashed for more than two to three hours may react chemically and stain. If you can't thoroughly wash silverware right away, rinse it quickly, then clean it properly later.

Polishing quick fix. Working with a handful at a time, poke the tines of the forks, bowls of the spoons, and handles of the knives into a paste silver cleaner. Use a damp sponge to spread the cleaner lightly over the utensil. Rinse off the polish, then wash in dish detergent. Rinse again, dry, then buff with a soft cloth.

Appraisal options. To learn the market value of your silver, consult reputable jewelry stores or department stores that carry silver or contact dealers in out-of-stock silver patterns. The appraisal should note the manufacturer and pattern and whether the pieces are sterling silver or plated.

SINGLE PARENTING

Create new traditions. Don't try to replicate holiday traditions from your married days; you and your children will likely be disappointed. Invent new ones: Spend the holidays in a new location. Share holiday activities with friends—a tree-trimming evening, say, or a cookie-decorating party. Invite an elderly friend or neighbor to attend your child's school concert with you. Have a potluck open house for New Year's Day.

Build a support network. Cultivate friendships with other single parents and neighbors, with whom you can barter or trade services such as babysitting, yard work, or cooking.

Be cautious about dating. Wait awhile before getting the children involved with someone you are dating. Once the relationship is serious, allow your child to become a part of it gradually. Be sure to spend plenty of time alone with your child, even if you start to date someone steadily.

Let kids be kids. Avoid using your children as confidantes, but make clear your willingness to listen to their concerns. Find another adult to help you with grown-up problems, but be as available as you can to help your children deal with theirs.

SINKS & FAUCETS

When buying a new faucet, store the manufacturer's instructions in your "equipment data" file. Faucets come in washer, washerless, diaphragm, disc, ball, and cartridge types. Some are real puzzles to take apart and repair, and you'll need the instructions to put things right.

A leak in a washerless faucet means that the working parts need replacing. Hardware stores sometimes carry kits with the parts that you are likely to need.

Clean porcelain sinks easily by soaking paper towels with bleach and spreading the towels over the bottom of the sink. Leave the towels for about 30 minutes, then rinse thoroughly with plain water.

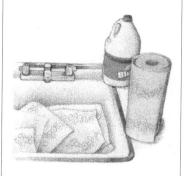

SKIING

Equipment pit stop. Save money when renting ski equipment by picking up what you need before you get to the ski resort. Usually the farther you are from the resort, the better the rental deal.

Before buying a costly multiday lift ticket, think about whether it will pay off. You may want to ski a full day, rest the next morning, then buy a half-day pass for the afternoon. Or you may choose to alternate days of skiing with days off the slopes. And you may want to test the slopes before buying.

The best in boots. Shop sales and outlets for cheaper models of skis, poles, or clothes—but never skimp on ski boots. Shop around, but always buy the ones with the best fit, not the best price.

Prevent cold, wet feet by wearing ski socks made with polypropylene or silk rather than cotton or wool. Synthetic fibers such as polypro wick moisture away from skin. Before putting on fresh socks, sprinkle your feet with cornstarch or baby powder to help keep them dry. Don't put cold feet into ski boots. Take along a change of socks if you plan to ski in the afternoon.

 Safe skiing. If you and a friend are on different levels of competency, compromise. Ski together in the morning on a low-level slope, then after lunch go your own ways. Or start on a trail you can both begin, then split up when you reach a fork for runs of different levels.

Store boots in a warm place. Cold ski boots are stiff and hard to put on, but warm boots conform to your feet, making an injury less likely. If you plan to ski on consecutive days, take out your boot liner to dry each night, or use a hair or boot dryer.

SHAPED SKIS FOR EVERY LEVEL

Gliding effortlessly down steep slopes has never been easy, but with these specially shaped (or parabolic) skis, you will have far greater control over your edging and steering. These skis are extra-lightweight, allowing you to move faster while exerting less energy. Elan's SCX skis (below) were parabolic pioneers, but other companies such as Fischer, Volkl, and Volant produce models to suit skiers at every level of experience.

SKIN CARE

Save on moisturizers. Baby oil or plain mineral oil can be used just as effectively as expensive cosmetic brands to soften skin or remove makeup. Petroleum jelly is a good moisturizer for hands and a gentle eye makeup remover.

 For healthier skin, avoid strong sunlight as much as possible. About 80 percent of wrinkling comes from exposure to the sun's ultraviolet rays. The sun also plays a key role in skin cancer. Wear a wide-brimmed hat in summer, and use protective sunscreen on exposed skin whenever you are outside for any length of time.

For softer-looking skin, try a cream with alpha-hydroxy acids (AHA). These acids stimulate cell renewal by exfoliating the skin.

Don't overuse over-the-counter products containing AHA on the face, however, and never use on the thin skin around the eyes or on extremely dry skin. AHA's can be very drying.

Drink lots of water. Water moisturizes from within, helping prevent dryness and making your skin look and feel healthier and more supple. Drink at least six glasses of water a day; eight is even better.

Bye-bye, blemishes. A paste of baking soda and water applied at bedtime will help dry up and draw out pimples overnight.

Check yourself every month or two for skin cancers. Stand in a well-lighted spot in front of a mirror and use a hand mirror to see inaccessible places such as the middle of your back. Look for changes in the sizes of existing moles or birthmarks and for new moles, scaly spots, and sores that have oozed or bled for more than a week. Report any suspicious findings to your doctor.

MAINTAIN A GLOWING COMPLEXION

Here are the four basic steps to proper care of your facial skin. Repeat the first three twice a day—when you get up and again just before bedtime. Pat your skin instead of rubbing it, to avoid stretching the underlying tissues.

▸ *Cleanse. Use a gentle cleanser designed for your skin type. Apply with your hands, not with a facecloth.*

▸ *Tone. Toning lotion or freshener cools the skin, temporarily causing muscles to contract and pores to look smaller. Avoid products with alcohol if you have dry or sensitive skin.*

▸ *Moisturize. Moisturizers help to hold moisture in, plumping up the cells and making the skin look softer. Choose oil-based products for dry skin, water-based for oily complexions. Don't forget to moisturize your neck.*

▸ *Lubricate. Patting on a night cream before bedtime can help the top layer of the skin rehydrate while you sleep.*

SKYLIGHTS

A skylight on the north side of the house gives clear light without the glare of direct sun that a skylight on the east, south, or west side of the house can have.

Clean glass skylights the same way you clean windows. Acrylic plastic skylights stand up to a weak ammonia solution, but polycarbonate plastics do not and should be washed only with mild soap or detergent solutions. (Never use strong solvents, which can damage plastic surfaces.) Buff plastic skylights with car wax.

Be flexible about installing a skylight. Wait for a day when no rain is forecast. Have all tools and materials on hand. Keep a tarp ready in case you get an unexpected rain shower or something happens to delay completion.

Plastic bubble skylights are easily damaged. To deter scratches, leave the protective paper coating on until the skylight is completely installed. Handle the skylight carefully to prevent small chips or cracks that can cause leaks.

Use moisture-resistant drywall on the sides of a skylight well. It is less likely to be damaged by condensation, which is not uncommon near skylights.

Open and close skylights on high ceilings with electric cranks. These handy devices can even be

If your neighbors are partying late or you are struggling to sleep in a strange hotel, try a sound machine. The Ultra Heart and Sound Soother (left) gives you 10 relaxing sound choices (rain, summer night, etc.), while the Marsona Sound Machine (right) not only provides sound to relax, it wakes you gently, too.

equipped with rain sensors to close skylights automatically in case of rain. Some cranks are available with battery backup.

SLEEP

Maintain a sleep routine. Go to bed and wake up at about the same time every day. Staying up later and sleeping later on weekends disrupts your sleep rhythm in the same way that jet lag does.

To sleep more soundly, exercise aerobically four to six hours before you go to bed. If you exercise right before bedtime, you'll be too energized to sleep.

After-dinner no-no's: caffeine, nicotine, and alcohol. Caffeine and nicotine will keep you awake. Alcohol will make you sleepy initially but may disturb your sleep pattern later in the night.

Wind down before going to sleep. Read or watch television sitting in a comfortable chair, or take a warm bath. Lie down in your bed only after you are feeling sleepy.

Don't sleep too much. Getting more sleep than your body really needs can make you feel tired and can cause headaches and sinus congestion.

Take a nap if your energy flags in the middle of the day. Sleeping for a half hour to an hour in the early afternoon can be refreshing and reenergizing. But don't use a nap as a substitute for nighttime sleep on a regular basis.

SLEEPING BAGS

Cotton-covered sleeping bags are best used indoors or, when camping, in a sturdy tent. They provide comfort and warmth but are not suitable for more rigorous outdoor conditions.

A sleeping pad provides comfort and insulation against the cold, hard ground that a sleeping bag alone can't. The best kind available is an inflatable mattress wrapped in a nylon shell. The puncture-resistant, waterproof pad inflates as it is unrolled and deflates as it is rolled up again.

Sleeping bag sleepovers. Keep two or three inexpensive sleeping bags on hand for when your kids invite friends over for the night, or when nieces, nephews, or grandchildren come to visit. Sleeping bags store easily, and kids love the idea of "camping out" on the living room floor.

Polyester or down? A novice outdoor adventurer should start with a durable polyester-fill bag. A serious hiker or camper should invest in a down bag—it costs more but is lighter, provides better insulation, and lasts longer.

Rainproof a sleeping bag on a trip by stowing it in a taped-seam waterproof stuff sack and securing it in a plastic bag. (To prevent condensation buildup between trips, open the bag.)

Try it on. Before buying a sleeping bag at a store, get into it to size it up. You should have enough room to move your feet, elbows, and knees, but there shouldn't be more than 10 cm (4 in.) of empty space on either side of you when your arms are at your sides.

SLEEPWEAR

Comfort first. To breathe comfortably and enjoy good circulation while you are asleep, choose pajamas with expandable waists. Avoid nightgowns that twist a lot as you toss and turn.

Loungewear to go. Take a silk bathrobe along when you travel. Silk robes are lightweight and roll up tightly for packing.

Maintain flannel fluff. To keep your favorite flannel pajamas or nightgowns from pilling, wash them in a pillowcase or net bag and dry them on plastic hangers.

SLIPCOVERS

Try summer slipcovers for upholstered furniture. Light-colored linens or cottons can go on in spring and come off in fall, changing the room into a brighter, cooler-feeling haven during the hot weather. Six months of slipcovers annually will also prolong the life of your upholstery.

For a quick cover, use a large, inexpensive painter's cotton drop cloth. Drape it over the chair and tuck the fabric into the angles between the seat, arms, and back to anchor it. For a bolder effect, choose a brightly striped or deeply colored solid, but be sure the fabric is wide enough to make the necessary tucks.

Furniture saver. Salvage a soiled but well-designed upholstered chair or sofa by getting a custom-made slipcover, which is cheaper than reupholstering and is easily removed for cleaning.

Dress up folding chairs or director's chairs with inexpensive slipcovers that drape the backs, seats, and legs in one simple design or color. These covers can pull the decor of a room together or provide extra seating for parties.

SMALL CLAIMS COURT

File a claim in small claims court when you have suffered a monetary loss because of someone else's actions. You don't need a lawyer to sue for minor car accidents, consumer rip-offs, lousy repairs or services, unpaid loans, or broken contracts when the amount you seek is less than the small claims limit in your province.

Map your venue. When you sue in small claims court, file in the court located in the county where the person you are suing lives, where the injury took place, or where the business that sold you a faulty product is located.

Visit the court before your hearing to see how the process works. Find out how long you will have to present your case, if you must speak with a mediator first, and when and how you will receive the judge's decision.

Practice presenting your case to a friend before your court appearance. Start with a single sentence that summarizes your claim, for example: "My problem is that the defendant ran over my bicycle and I had to spend $350 to repair it." Briefly outline how the problem arose, the extent of the harm you suffered, and the expenses you incurred.

Back up what you say with documents and evidence. Take to court witnesses or notarized statements from them, along with any original receipts, advertisements, bills, contracts, warranties, checks, or photographs. Prepare three copies of each, so that you can give one to the other party, leave one with the judge, and keep one for yourself.

If you win a judgment, take steps to collect the money from the other party. Write to the person and ask for payment, saying you wish to avoid further legal proceedings. If the party has money but refuses to pay, get a court order to garnishee the person's wages or bank account. Talk to the court clerk or a lawyer about how to proceed.

SMOKE DETECTORS

Know your options before buying a smoke detector. Consider which types best meet your needs. For example, ionization-detecting devices work best to warn of flaming fires and fast-burning smokeless fires, while photoelectric models are more sensitive to slower-burning, smol-

---

SMOKE DETECTOR SPRAY

Millions of installed smoke detectors don't work because of dead batteries, damaged electrical components, blocked vents, or parts failures. Test your detectors monthly with the Smoke Detector Tester from Home Safeguard Industries. Spray it toward the smoke detector for a second or two. If the detector is working, an alarm will sound, which automatically stops in less than a minute. To stop it sooner, fan a newspaper at the detector.

dering fires. Discuss the features you need with the salesperson.

For hearing-impaired people, consider adding a special device to the smoke detector that also activates nearby strobe lights.

 Replace the batteries in your smoke detectors each fall when you change your clocks back to standard time. You will reduce the chance of a tragic fire occurring in your home during the heating season.

Before painting a room, remove the smoke alarm. Paint on the surface may prevent the detector from functioning properly.

Vacuum-clean smoke detectors to keep them in good working order. Use a vacuum attachment to clear dust from the detector surface and its smoke entry holes as part of your regular household vacuuming routine.

"Hush buttons" are available on some smoke detectors for those occasions when smoke from cooking or cigarettes accidentally trips the alarm. Never disconnect a smoke detector to shut off its alarm—you may forget to reconnect it again.

SNACKS

Reach for a piece of fruit. The sugar from an orange, tangerine, or apple can satisfy a sweet tooth, and the resulting "sugar high" lasts longer and declines more slowly than the high from candy.

Give in to snacking. Snacking has an undeserved reputation as a diet destroyer; it can actually wean a dieter from eating large amounts at one time, and make it easier to eat less. Try having several small meals instead of two or three large ones. To reduce the number of calories you consume, go for wholesome snacks such as fruit, low-fat yogurt, or soup.

SNORING

Sleep on your side. Most snorers sleep on their backs. Use strategically placed pillows or foam wedges to keep yourself on your side, or sew a pocket into the back of a T-shirt and put a tennis ball in it. When you roll onto your back, the discomfort will force you to turn back to your side.

Maintain your correct weight. Being overweight is one of the main factors contributing to snoring. By losing even 2.5 to 4.5 kg (5–10 lb), you can dramatically reduce the frequency and intensity of your snoring episodes.

Use a cool-mist humidifier in your bedroom at night. It will keep your nasal passages from drying out and reduce the likelihood that you will snore.

Alcohol and smoking. Alcohol relaxes the muscles of the throat, which increases snoring. Smoking promotes nasal congestion, which also can lead to snoring.

Earplugs, anyone? If you're a snorer, buy your sleeping partner a pair of earplugs. Or wait until he's fast asleep before you retire.

HEALTHY SNACKS

If snacking is a way of life for you and your family, try to make those between-meal noshes healthy. If you follow these suggestions, it won't be as hard as you think.

▶ *Eat a bagel instead of a calorie-laden muffin or croissant. Bagels have almost no fat, and their chewy texture makes them satisfying to eat.*

▶ *Reach for fig bars or graham crackers when you want something sweet. Low in fat and calories, they're a healthier alternative to cookies.*

▶ *Try baked chips or crackers if you can't resist salty snacks. An ounce of baked potato chips has only 1.5 g of fat, versus 10 g for an ounce of fried chips.*

▶ *Choose low-salt packaged pretzels, rice cakes, and un-buttered popcorn when looking for low-fat snack choices.*

▶ *Soft pretzels, sold in the frozen-food section of supermarkets and on the street in some cities, are another healthful snack choice.*

▶ *Don't forget the standby: crisp, raw vegetables. Update them with a dip made from low-fat sour cream or yogurt.*

SNOW & ICE

Heart stopper. Respect snow shoveling as the strenuous labor it is (heart attacks from snow shoveling are a major cause of death after winter storms). Don't shovel snow right after smoking cigarettes, drinking coffee, or taking decongestants—all of which can raise your pulse rate. Take breaks and finish the job in shifts.

 Stock up on shovels, gloves, and deicing materials in the off-season, when prices are generally lower. You'll also avoid the crowds of shoppers at stores after the first snowfall.

Dress in layers when you go out to shovel the walk. As you begin to sweat, peel off outer layers to avoid getting overheated.

Watch your back. Most people know about bending the legs instead of the back when lifting a shovelful of snow. But you should also be careful not to twist your body around when dumping the shovel; instead, turn your feet in the direction you're dumping so that the motion is straight ahead.

Unclog snowblowers carefully. Every year people are maimed trying to clear their snowblower's entry chute. Even if the engine is turned off first (which is a good idea), the blades can still snap back sharply after they're cleared. Use a stick, and keep your hands away from the blades.

Clear your pipes. Never start a car if snow is piled up behind it where it could block the tailpipe; carbon monoxide gas can fill your car if the exhaust is blocked.

SNOWBOARDING

Learn the right way. Take a professional lesson and use proper equipment. A friend who is a hot boarder isn't necessarily a good instructor, and a borrowed board or boots may be wrong for you. Proper training and equipment can help you avoid accidents.

Wear your gear. Boarders tend to fall straight back or straight forward, so the thumbs, wrists, knees, and ankles are the areas most vulnerable to injury. Wrist guards, in a large size to fit over gloves, and knee pads are essential. If you're a beginner, you may want to add "butt padding," to protect your backside in the event of a fall.

Don't get stuck. Study trail maps and talk to people familiar with the course before you set out so that you'll know how to avoid "catwalks"—flat connections between trails that stop snowboarders in their tracks. If you do hit one, take one or both feet off the board before proceeding to the next slope.

Head for the trees. If you are snowboarding on a mountain when a weather change dramatically reduces visibility, stay close to the edge of the trail, near trees, rather than in the center. The trees will provide contrast to the whiteness around you and help you find your way.

Are you in the way? When snowboarding tires you out—and it will—don't plop down wherever exhaustion catches up with you. Park yourself by the side of the trail, in a spot where you can be easily seen.

BEND THE SHOVEL, NOT THE BACK

Shoveling snow may not be fun, but with an ergonomically designed shovel it doesn't have to be a backbreaker. An S-shaped shovel such as the MTD Back Saver (left) cuts down the amount of bending you do, although it will give your arms a good workout. Quickie's Double Bubble Shovel (right) has two loop handles to grab on to, to give you better leverage and reduce strain on your back.

> To be sure that the Canada Pension Plan and/or the Quebec Pension Plan has your correct earnings history, ask for your report on your contributions once a year. Here is how to do it.
>
> ▶ Call the CPP at 1-800-277-9914, the QPP at 1-800-463-5533. You will be asked for your social insurance number.
>
> ▶ If you find an error in your work record, locate supporting documents, such as tax returns, for the period in question. It doesn't matter how long ago it was.
>
> ▶ Find your nearest CPP/QPP office in the phone book and call for an appointment. Say that you want to correct an error on your earnings record and you would like to speak to an administrator in person.
>
> ▶ Take your report and supporting documents to the interview. Copies will be sent to headquarters. If your proof is convincing, the error should be corrected—but ask for another report after four months to make sure of it.

Falling 101. Practice falling before you head downhill the first time so you'll be prepared to do it properly. Falling forward, pull your arms to your chest to reduce impact on the wrists, and fall onto bent knees. Falling backward, land first on your seat, then your back, pulling your chin down so you don't bang your head.

SOAPS

Deodorant soaps are not meant for facial use; they tend to dry the skin. A creamier soap is better. In winter, use creamy soap even for bathing to prevent itchy, dry skin.

Transparent soap is gentle and nonirritating, but it melts easily. To make the soap bar last longer, dry it after each use.

Save soap by collecting remnants in a cotton sock. Tie it off with string and use it as a washing mitt when you bathe. You can also dampen the bag and use it to pretreat stains on clothes.

Sew and soap. Soap slivers make a good substitute for tailor's chalk on washable fabrics. Use them to mark hems or darts; the lines will disappear in the wash.

Soap scraps make inexpensive sachets. Put them in little fabric bags in drawers or luggage to keep the contents smelling fresh.

SOCIAL SECURITY

It's up to you to tap into the system. There are many benefits you may be eligible to receive from the Canada Pension Plan or the Quebec Pension Plan if you retire or become disabled, or that members of your family may obtain if you die. Remember, though, that you or your survivors must apply at the local CPP or QPP office.

Name change. Don't forget to notify your local CPP or QPP office promptly if you change your name so that you will be credited for earnings received under your new name.

Allow enough time. Unless you are already receiving disability benefits, you should file a claim with the CPP or QPP at least six months before you want your retirement benefits to commence. You can apply in person or by telephone.

Extend your work years. Work at least 35 years if possible before retiring. The calculations for your benefits assume a minimum of 35 years of wages. If you retire after 32 years, for example, zero earnings for the remaining 3 years will lower your average, substantially reducing your retirement benefits.

SOCKS

Those darn socks. For a quick fix for socks with holes, use iron-on mending strips or sheets available at fabric stores. Press the strip onto the outside of the sock so it does not rub directly against your skin and create a blister.

Pattern play. Male or female, add interest to your wardrobe with patterned and colored socks. Try matching socks to your jacket or shirt, or wear colors that compliment pants or shoes.

Instant dust cloth. Give worn-out cotton socks a thorough washing, then use them for various housecleaning chores. Since they fit comfortably over your hand, they are ideal for dusting and furniture polishing.

S

SOFAS

The best-made sofas have a hardwood frame, joints secured with dowels or screws, and fitted blocks at the inside corners for added strength. Spring coils, 8 to 12 per seat, offer greater comfort than horizontal steel springs.

Quality stuffing holds its own. Good sofa stuffing ranges from posh goose down to very comfortable urethane foam. Shredded foam will soon lose its shape.

Love that loveseat. Consider a two-seater sofa if you're cramped for space. It is an adaptable piece of furniture that gives the same kind of mass and weight to a room arrangement as a conventional three-seater sofa while taking up less space. A pair of loveseats framing a fireplace offers a cozy seating arrangement.

SOFT DRINKS

Punch up the party punch by adding carbonated drinks to it just before the guests arrive. If you do it too early, the punch will go flat.

Read the label. Some soft drinks are full of sugar, some are high in salt, and many contain caffeine. If you are cutting back on any of these ingredients, pick your potion carefully.

Cut down consumption of soft drinks, especially those filled with sugar or caffeine, by serving them as you would a special cocktail. Fill a wineglass with ice and your soft drink, dress it up with a sprig of mint or a slice of lime—and then sip it slowly.

Create a sophisticated drink by adding a splash of fruit juice—tangy lemon, lime, grapefruit, or cranberry juices work especially well—to plain seltzer or club soda. These easy-to-make homemade flavored waters are tastier and less expensive than premixed store-bought varieties.

EASY DOES IT

SITTERS DOUBLING AS SLEEPERS

Everyone needs to put up an overnight guest occasionally, and a sofa that doubles as a sleeper is a space-saving way to do it. You have several options for these stowaways.

▶ *A sofa bed has a mattress and frame that pull out to become a full-size or queen-size bed. It costs slightly more than an ordinary sofa. Usually you can't tell the difference in appearance, although it can be less comfortable to sit on than a conventional sofa, and less comfortable to sleep on than an ordinary mattress and box springs.*

▶ *A daybed with bolsters can serve as a sofa until you remove the bolsters and make up the bed. It is practical in small quarters but sleeps only one, unless it is the kind with a trundle bed underneath.*

▶ *A futon, an adaptation of a Japanese sleeping mat, is simply a loose, cotton-stuffed mattress on a frame. More casual than a sofa, the futon is a favorite of buyers on a budget. It can be taken off its frame and laid on the floor for sleeping. One model has a frame that slides out at bedtime to form a low, flat platform for the mattress.*

SOIL

Walk the plank. If you have to step into your garden, put down plywood planks first. Walking on planks distributes your weight evenly and reduces compaction of the soil. (Soil compaction is serious because it can rob plant roots of air and moisture.)

Keep things at arm's length. A definitive solution to the problem of walking on (and compacting) your garden soil is to plant in beds no more than 90 cm to 1.2 m (3–4 ft) wide—narrow enough so you can reach into their centers to plant, weed, or harvest while standing or kneeling beside them.

Get your soil tested. A complete soil test—available from many garden centers—can cost less than $20 and is the best investment a gardener can make. The results will provide an exact prescription for treating your soil, allowing you to set up ideal conditions for your plants with no wasted effort.

SORE THROAT

Liquids soothe a scratchy throat and help to wash phlegm away. Try fruit juice, herbal tea with lemon and honey, or warm broth. Make sure the liquid is not too hot; a scalding liquid will further irritate the throat.

Go for gum or lozenges. Honey and eucalyptus lozenges make a sore throat feel better by coating it with a protective film. Chewing sugarless gum will ease throat irritation by stimulating the flow of saliva, which moistens sore tissue.

Silence is golden. If you develop laryngitis—an inflammation of the voice box—try not to talk. If you must speak, talk in your normal voice. Don't whisper; whispering actually puts more stress on the vocal cords than using your normal voice.

Take aspirin, ibuprofen, or acetaminophen to relieve sore throat pain, except don't give aspirin to children under 12. If a sore throat lingers more than four days or if it is accompanied by a high fever, call your doctor.

 Gargle with salt and warm water to sooth a sore throat. Stir a little salt into a cup of warm water and gargle with the solution four or five times a day.

SOUND SYSTEMS

Trying out speakers? Play music at the level you would listen to at home. Some speakers that sound great at top volume are not so impressive at a softer level.

Cover sound systems when they're not in use and vacuum the speaker grilles periodically to keep down dust buildup, which can cause the system to overheat.

Place foam rubber pads under your CD and record player to keep CD's or records from skipping when you walk (or dance) by. Also, put pads between pieces of equipment and under speakers to keep interference to a minimum.

Position speakers at ear level and keep them away from corners, which can force the bass to sound too strong. Speakers work optimally when placed at least 1.8 m (6 ft) apart and at an equal distance from the place where you usually sit to listen.

If you make tapes from CD's, buy the same brand of CD player and cassette deck; it will be easier to use options that make taping more convenient, such as synchronizing the starts.

Clean playback heads on your tape player once a month for optimal sound production. Special cleaners are available from electronics stores.

SOUPS & STEWS

Make a double batch whenever you cook soups or stews, then freeze half. It takes no time to double a recipe, and the payoff is an effortless meal on another, busier day.

Soup front and center. A hearty soup featuring some protein-rich component such as beans, meat, or poultry makes a filling main dish and needs little more than crusty bread and a green salad to complete a satisfying lunch or dinner menu.

Use a leftover rind of Parmesan cheese to flavor vegetable soup. Put it in when you begin cooking, and take it out before serving.

Skip the cream in soup if you're concerned about fat or calories. Create a creamy texture by adding pureed vegetables. If you want to add a dairy product, go for less caloric whole milk or plain yogurt.

ELEGANT SPEAKER STANDS

Speaker stands allow you to place speakers where they will produce the best sound for your listening needs. Speaker stands come in a wide range of designs, from the sturdy Standesign platforms by Melody Audio (left) to the elegant Bell'Oggetti risers, which place components up high, then hide unsightly wires in elegant tubing. Speaker stands are available at electronics stores.

SPICES & SEASONINGS

Date your spice jars—put tape on the bottom—to make sure you don't keep them too long. Spices are best bought in small quantities and used within a year. Don't store spices near a heat source.

Use more of old herbs than a recipe calls for to compensate for their fading flavor. Plus, by using them up faster, you can buy a fresh supply sooner.

Use dried herbs in tomato sauce and other long-cooking dishes; they hold up better than fresh ones. Fresh herbs, on the other hand, are better than dried ones in uncooked dishes like salsas and salads, or as a garnish.

Enclose whole spices, such as peppercorns, cloves, mace, or cardamom, in a mesh tea ball or wrap them in cheesecloth while they cook in a stew or casserole. They'll be easy to remove, and you can take them out as soon as the dish tastes right to you.

Three to one. Dried herbs are considerably stronger than fresh ones, so triple the amount of fresh herbs you use in a recipe that calls for dried ones. A teaspoon of dried equals a tablespoon of fresh.

SPLINTERS

Splinter silhouette. Not sure if you've picked up a splinter? Go into a darkened room and put a flashlight against your finger. You should be able to see the outline of a splinter if it is there.

Soak splinters out. If you can't get a grip on a splinter to pull it out—or if there are a lot of them—soak the affected area in warm water for 10 to 15 minutes. As the

No more need to bother with a mortar and pestle or worry that your bottled seasonings have gone stale. Instead, use a coffee grinder to unleash the flavor of whole spices—peppercorns, cinnamon, or star anise—and dried herbs. These grinders by Braun (left) and Krups (right) are small and inexpensive enough so that you can keep two—one just for spices and one just for coffee.

wood swells, it may push out far enough for you to grab it.

Coat a splinter with glue, the white nontoxic kind. After the glue has dried, peel it off slowly. The splinter may pull out with it.

Leave a splinter alone if there is no sign of infection. Most small splinters will break down or come out on their own over time.

SPONGES

Clean cellulose sponges in the washing machine by enclosing them in a net bag and adding bleach. Let them dry naturally, not in a hot dryer and never in a microwave—they can catch fire.

A natural sponge is the soft skeleton of a sea creature and must be treated tenderly. Apply soap to your skin rather than to the sponge. Rinse and squeeze dry after a bath (wringing it out destroys the tissue). Let it dry where air can circulate around it.

Soften your feet in those areas where they are corn- and callus-

prone by rubbing them after your bath with the abrasive side of a two-sided household sponge made for scouring pots and pans.

STAINS

The mayo miracle. Gently rub a new water stain on a wood table or counter with a mixture of equal parts mayonnaise and fine ashes from the fireplace or an ashtray. You'll be amazed at the results.

Shaving cream removes dirt and fresh stains from upholstery and rugs. Spread it on, brush lightly, then rinse it off with clear water.

Rub stained marble with half a lemon sprinkled with salt. Use a light hand to avoid scratching the surface. If any discoloration remains, brush in a baking-soda paste and leave it on for half an hour. Rinse with warm water.

Remove candle wax from wood by softening it with a hair dryer, then sponging it away with vinegar diluted with water. Rinse with clear water and dry well. Never scrape wax off with a knife.

Treat every spot and spill as soon as possible; the longer you wait, the more difficult the stain will be to remove. When immediate blotting or rinsing doesn't get rid of a stain, you need a well-stocked cache of antistain weapons at hand. Some may already be in your closet or under your kitchen sink. The rest you can find at the supermarket. This armory, together with a book devoted to stain removal, will prepare you to deal with almost any stain attack.

1 Alcohol (rubbing or denatured). Use clear, not colored type; good for grass or dye stains. Caution: FLAMMABLE.

5 Stain-removal book. There are dozens of books devoted specifically to removing stains of all kinds; buy one and keep it on your laundry shelf.

2 Ammonia. Mix 5 mL (1 tsp) with 125 mL (½ cup) water to make an effective antidote for many stains. DO NOT COMBINE WITH CHLORINE BLEACH.

6 White vinegar. A mix of 80 mL (⅓ cup) vinegar and 160 mL (⅔ cup) water is recommended for many food stains; safe for all fibers but can alter some colors.

3 Dry-cleaning solvent or powder (nonflammable). Can be useful for spot cleaning, especially on nonwashable fabrics.

4 Chlorine bleach is a basic weapon in the fight against stains, but follow directions carefully. Do not use chlorine bleach on nonwashables. DO NOT COMBINE WITH AMMONIA.

7 All-fabric bleach (also called oxygen bleach) is safe on most fabrics. It is milder than chlorine bleach and better for some stains, such as red wine.

8 Petroleum jelly. Will help soften hardened paint, tar, and rubber cement on washables. Launder immediately after applying the jelly.

9 Club soda. Prescribed for rinsing many different kinds of stains, not only on clothes but also on carpets, upholstery, and tablecloths.

10 Nail polish remover (nonoily or amyl acetate) works on glue or lacquer stains; keep away from plastics and furniture.

11 Detergent with enzymes. A few liquid and powdered detergents contain enzymes that help get rid of stubborn stains. Not for use on nonwashables such as wool, mohair, or silk.

12 Hydrogen peroxide (3% solution) can be used safely on wool or silk; mixed with a small amount of ammonia, it makes a mild bleach.

13 Tools. Keep on hand an eyedropper, clean cloths, and a clean sponge for applying stain removers.

14 Glycerin, a heavy form of alcohol, helps get rid of ballpoint ink, fruit, and coffee stains.

15 Boosters include sticks, pump sprays, aerosols, liquids, and powders. Generally applied in prewash treatments, they add extra kick to regular laundry soap to fight hard stains such as dirty motor oil.

RIGHT STUFF

STATIC STOPPERS

Keep computers, telephones, and televisions free of electric charges by swiping them with a static repellent such as StatFree or StatClean. They come in moist towels or sprays and are nonflammable and nonstaining. Treat shoes, doorknobs, and rugs as well, to protect yourself from sparks. Antistatic sprays such as Static Guard are formulated to keep clothes cling-free.

STAIRS

Don't despair over a squeaky step—you may be able to stop the noise. A squeak is caused by loose boards rubbing against each other, so you need to look and listen carefully to find which are loose. Glue narrow wedges in cracks between boards, and nail or screw down treads or risers that are loose.

Do your stair repairs after everyone else who uses the stairs has gone to bed. Glue must have time to dry before the stairs are used again.

Clear the way. Keep stairways free of the piles of mail, clothing, and books that tend to collect there—and that someone could trip over. Put a small table, shelf, or basket near the top and bottom of the staircase to hold those bits of flotsam until you get around to putting them away.

STATIC ELECTRICITY

Tame hair that stands on end because of static electricity with a few drops of hair oil. Rub the oil on your hands, then run your fingers gently through your hair to break the static charge. Or try a humectant hair-styling product, which attracts moisture.

Don't use hairpins and metal barrettes; they interrupt the flow of static electricity along the strands of hair, causing the hair to heat up, expand, and become brittle. Tie back your hair with yarn or cloth-covered elastic.

Put fabric softener in the wash, especially in winter. It adds emollients to your clothes that help to control static electricity.

 Slap shot. If you think you're about to get a static electric shock from a metal object—say, a doorknob after you've walked across a wool carpet—give it a slap instead of a touch, and you won't notice the shock.

A temporary fix. Spritz water on your clothes and hair with a spray bottle that creates a fine mist. The mist will tame the static electricity for a short time, until the dry air that is causing the electric charge evaporates the water.

STEAMING FOOD

Just a little water—about 2.5 cm (1 in.)—is needed when steaming most vegetables that cook in 5 to 10 minutes. For large root vegetables like beets, which can take 35 minutes or more, you'll need at least 5 cm (2 in.) of water. Check periodically to see if you need to add more water.

Safe steaming. Don't forget: steam is water at its hottest—far beyond the boiling point. To avoid burns, always lift the lid of a steaming pot so that the steam blows away from you. Use tongs and potholders, preferably the gloved variety, when you remove food from the steamer.

Steaming tools. Start with a collapsible steamer basket—it is inexpensive and will fit into most pans you already own. A pan with a customized steamer insert costs more, but is worth the extra expense if you steam food often.

Add delicate flavor to steamed foods (which can be bland) by seasoning the cooking water with lemon or lime juice, wine, or herbs. The scented steam infuses the food with a subtle taste.

Stenciling Stationery

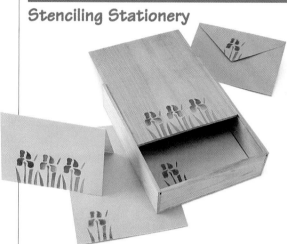

Make your own distinctive stationery by stenciling a decorative motif on high-quality paper. Repeat the design on a stationery box to create a handsome gift package. Start by enlarging the iris pattern (inset) on a photocopier to approximate the dimensions shown; make two stencils and, using fast-drying acrylic paints and stenciling brushes, paint the design onto each sheet of paper and the box lid.

1 Trace the pattern of iris petals and leaves onto tracing paper. Then, using carbon paper and a ballpoint pen, transfer the complete design to two different pieces of stiff stencil paper.

2 With a craft knife, cut out all of the leaves on the first stencil. On the second stencil, cut out the petals and also a bit of the leaf tips to help you align the stencil when you are painting the petals.

3 With the first stencil, paint the green leaves on the edge of a piece of stationery paper and the box top. Let them dry. Then line up the second stencil atop the leaves and paint the petals blue.

STEEL WOOL

A versatile smoothie. Steel wool is good for more than scrubbing pots. Use it to remove paint and dirt from enamel and chrome (on which sandpaper would leave scratches) or to give a silky finish to a final coat of varnish. Look for grades ranging from "4 extra-coarse" to "0000 super-fine."

Clean up carefully after using steel wool on any surface you plan to paint or varnish because it leaves tiny filings that will mar the finished work. Worse, they cause rust stains if the surface gets wet.

Go for the bronze. If you are working in a damp environment such as on a boat, use bronze wool. It is sturdier and longer lasting, it doesn't shed as much, and when it does, the filings don't rust.

STENCILING

Serviceable recycling. You can easily cut a stencil from a discarded manila file folder. It will work fine for a stenciling job that doesn't call for many repeats.

Make transparent stencils from sheets of artist's acetate, available at art supply stores. Choose a

weight that is not so thick and stiff that it will be hard to cut, but not so thin that it will tear.

Brush business. Most stencilers use the blunt, round stencil brushes found at crafts and art supply stores. In a pinch, though, a regular paintbrush will do; cut the bristles off so that the bottom of the brush is flat, not tapered.

Lace or eyelet doilies can be turned into stencils by stiffening them with varnish. The intricate antique designs they make look especially appealing on older pieces of painted furniture.

RIGHT STUFF

UNGLUE THE *GOO*

Forget scraping and soaking when price tags, stickers, and decals won't come off. Tackle the problem with solvents designed for the job, such as Goof Off or Goo Gone. They not only lift off stickers (and the gummy gunk left behind), but they also remove crayon scribbles, dried glue, chewing gum, tape, and tar.

STEPCHILDREN

Give yourself time. Don't force yourself to be emotionally close to your new stepparent; instead, give your affections a chance to grow naturally. Indeed, several years of physical and emotional contact are often required for a relaxed, truly caring relationship to become firmly established.

Sensitive stepsiblings. Agree on this one rule with your stepsiblings: never borrow or use anything without asking first. Whatever it is—clothing, radios, sports equipment, or cars—if you're not certain whether something is privately owned or shared by the whole family, be sure to ask.

Request your own space. If you feel like an outsider when you visit your parent and stepparent, tell them you'd feel less so if you had a special place of your own in their house. It doesn't have to be a whole room—even a private shelf or a desk drawer where you can leave things between visits can give you a sense of belonging.

Compromise at weddings. If you feel close to your father and stepfather and want to include both in your wedding ceremony, you can ask one to escort you down the aisle and the other to give you away.

STEPPARENTING

Develop shared interests. Look for pastimes you and your stepchildren both enjoy. You might connect through a passion for music or cooking, or you might both take part in the same sport.

The house rules. Discuss rules, limitations, and unfamiliar parenting situations with your spouse ahead of time. At first it's best to let the biological parent do most of the disciplining; then gradually share the task. If there are two sets of children, make the rules the same for all of them but enforced by the biological parent for each child.

Discuss your "name." Let all the children participate in deciding what you, as a stepparent, will be called. Some might immediately want to call you Mommy or Daddy; some might not. First names often work well, or you might agree on a nickname.

Make it legal. If your stepchildren are minors, ask your spouse to grant you limited power of attorney over them, to allow you to authorize emergency medical care, obtain school records, and sign important documents.

STICKERS

When you go on a car trip, keep your youngsters happily occupied by giving them stickers that have been specifically designed to be put on (and peeled off) windows.

Heat application. If a sticker clings tenaciously, you can try loosening it with blasts of heat from your hair dryer. It should then be easier to peel off.

Bumper stickers. Rub car wax on the spot where you intend to put a bumper sticker. This makes removal much easier later on.

Kid's stuff. Add appeal to your children's lunches by sealing their sandwich bags and brown paper bags with playful stickers.

Protect doors from sticker-crazed youngsters. Cover the surface of a door with a large sheet of clear plastic, electrostatically charged to adhere. Then let them attach stickers guilt-free. The stickers will come off easily when the "decorative" phase passes, and so will the plastic, leaving the door as good as new.

Use a razor blade as a scraper to remove a sticker or its gummy residue from glass, enamel, glazed ceramic, or hard plastic surfaces. (Don't use it on paint, wood, or soft metal—the blade can scratch the surface.)

STOCKS & BONDS

Look about you to find potential investments. Whether you're busy raising a child, working for a company, or just dropping by the grocery store, make a mental note of any particularly useful product or service. Find out if the company behind it is publicly traded. If so, write for the annual and quarterly financial reports. Study them to see if an investment is warranted.

Keep it simple. Stick with "plain vanilla" stocks and bonds. Other opportunities such as options, commodities, and limited partnerships are complicated and carry a higher degree of risk.

Choosing a stockbroker. Research the background and reputation of any broker you are considering. Call your provincial securities commission or the National Association of Securities Dealers at 1-800-289-9999 to check out the broker's credentials and whether he's had any disciplinary actions taken against him.

Beware of churning. If you invest with a full-service broker, watch out for churning, whereby a broker advises you to make frequent buys and sells so that he can accumulate the commission fees. To determine such activity, compare profits from a sale with the commission fees to see if the sale was worthwhile.

Buy new-issue bonds. When purchasing individual bonds, always buy new issues—offered to the public by government bodies or by corporations. You can depend on new-issue bonds to be sold at an honest market price—no one can manipulate the stated yield. You save money too, because the issuer pays the broker's commission.

STOCKS & BROTHS

Freeze homemade stock in ice-cube trays, muffin tins, or plastic containers of various sizes. When a recipe calls for stock, simply toss the amount you need into the pot—no need to defrost.

Keep canned broths on hand to make sauces and to add flavor to steamed rice or couscous. Keep bouillion cubes in your cupboard as well; they last for years and, when added to water, make a quick, tasty broth. Canned broths and bouillion cubes are usually high in salt, so taste any dish you are making with them before adding more salt.

 Start stocks and broths in cold water; the process of raising water temperature to boiling extracts extra flavor from the foods.

Add aging vegetables, just past their peak but never rotten or slimy, when you make stocks and broths. The taste will be fuller than if you use immature or even ripe vegetables. You'll also be putting to good use those elderly mushrooms, carrots, and other finds from the back of the refrigerator that you'd otherwise have to throw away.

To prevent cloudiness, skim the film that rises to the surface of stocks and broths as they cook, using a skimmer or shallow ladle.

EASY CHICKEN STOCK

Chicken stock is a valuable staple to keep in your freezer or refrigerator, and it is simple to make.

▶ *Save and freeze chicken backs, necks, gizzards, and bones. When you have enough on hand, make a stock.*

▶ *Brown the bones in a large Dutch oven or stock pot. (Browning imparts a richer flavor and color.) Add chopped aromatic vegetables, such as onion, garlic, celery, and carrots; and your favorite herbs.*

▶ *Add cold water to cover by 2.5 cm (1 in.) and turn the heat to medium. Cook for 1½ to 2 hours, adding water as needed; strain.*

▶ *To remove fat from the stock, refrigerate it. Within a few hours the fat will congeal on the surface. Simply lift the fat from the broth and discard it.*

STORAGE COMPANIES

Don't overestimate the space you will need to store household or office goods. Let the storage company compute the right room size for you.

Think twice before you store an old sofa or other worn article. Often you could buy a new one with the money you would pay to store it for years.

Movers available. Ask the storage company if it will transport your items to its facility. This may cost extra but will save you a lot of time and work.

To make stacking easy, use the same size boxes whenever possible. Write a contents list on all four sides so that you will be able to consult the list no matter how a box is stored.

 Least used, first in. Put belongings that you are least likely to need into the storage room first and those that you may need sooner by the door. Leave a walkway to the back, though, in case you change your mind.

Seasonal reviews. Install shelves and a hanging rod in your storage area to make it easier to browse through recreational gear, holiday decorations, and seasonal clothes that you need easy access to.

HELP CUT NEIGHBORHOOD CRIME

One reason crime proliferates is that residents are not involved with their community. Follow these hints and you might help turn your neighborhood around.

▶ *Become better acquainted with your neighbors. Host a neighborhood coffee, potluck, or picnic and exchange phone numbers with everyone. Agree to call one another or the police to report suspicious activities.*

▶ *Attend community board meetings, and introduce yourself to your local political representative. Suggest that every few months, neighbors get together for a block cleanup day. Notify the sanitation department of any abandoned vehicles, burned-out streetlights, or other public sanitation issues.*

▶ *Form a neighborhood crime-watch group with the cooperation of the police department. Notify the police of problems in public parks, schoolyards, or playgrounds. If you fail to get a response, call the local newspaper or TV or radio station. Ask local law enforcement officers to join you in neighborhood social and political events.*

▶ *Get legal help for serious problems. Some issues—excessive noise, property disputes—can be solved through legal channels. Many law firms do a percentage of pro bono work; ask your political representative for information.*

STREET SMARTS

When jogging or walking, leave the headset at home—or at least turn the volume down or leave one ear free. Not being aware of the noises around you is a surefire way to make yourself vulnerable to a mugger.

Before you leave an ATM in a bank or enclosure, count your money and put it away. Don't wait until you're in the parking lot or on the street to stuff it into a pocket or purse; that makes you an easy target for a thief.

No show. Squelch the desire to show off flashy or expensive-looking jewelry in public, especially on the street. Pocket that bracelet, brooch, or necklace until you are indoors.

Read maps discreetly. Standing on the sidewalk staring at a map is a sure sign that you're new in town. Criminals target people who appear unfamiliar with the turf. Try to plot your course before venturing out.

Look out of the booth when talking on a pay phone rather than facing the telephone. You'll be alert to anyone approaching.

STRESS

Create order in little ways to reduce stress: tidy a closet, neaten your desk, or clean out your car's glove compartment, for example. By gaining control of small areas of your life, you'll feel calmer about tackling the big ones.

Prioritize. Make a "To Do" list and rank each item in order of importance. Tackle the most difficult or stressful jobs first. When they are completed, the remaining chores will seem easy.

Delegate. Get rid of stress by entrusting responsibilities to others, whether at home or on the job. Neither shirk your own obligations nor take on others'.

Make your own flash cards, especially for subjects that require memorization, such as foreign languages or mathematics. On index cards, write down phrases, words, equations, dates, or concepts that are important. Writing will help fix the words or concepts in your mind, and the cards will aid you when you need to review at test time.

Don't procrastinate. Instead of putting off a major assignment for some future day when you think you'll have more time, begin a difficult project immediately. Starting it will build confidence and a sense of momentum. Also, working on it in short spurts—instead of in a long siege at the last minute—will make the project seem less overwhelming.

Study with a partner. When preparing for an exam, team up with another student and quiz each other on facts and concepts.

Stretching to Relieve Stress at the Office

Sitting for hours in an office can be stressful. You can obtain quick relief with gentle stretching, and you don't even have to leave your chair. Try these exercises two or three times a day, breathing evenly throughout. The longer you hold each stretch, the better.

Knee Squeeze. Sit on a chair with your back straight and feet flat on the floor. Lift your left knee toward your chest, grasping it with both hands; squeeze the knee to your chest and hold for 5 counts. Release, and return your foot to the floor. Repeat with the right leg, then repeat the sequence 3 times.

Head Roll. Tilt your head to the left until you feel a slight stretch. Slowly roll your head forward, touching your chin to your chest, and over to the right; hold for 5 counts. Reverse. Repeat the cycle 3 times.

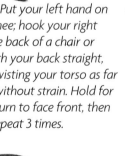

Spine Twist. Put your left hand on your right knee; hook your right arm over the back of a chair or armrest. With your back straight, turn right, twisting your torso as far as you can without strain. Hold for 5 counts, return to face front, then twist left. Repeat 3 times.

Shoulder Rolls. With arms hanging, lift both shoulders, then roll them in a circle, first forward, then backward. Repeat the cycle 3 times.

Spine Stretch. Sit in a chair with your feet flat on the floor. With your arms hanging, lean forward letting your head hang over your knees until you feel a gentle stretch in your back and neck muscles. (If this is difficult, cross your arms on your knees and rest your head on them.) Hold for 10 counts.

EASY DOES IT

HOW TO PICK A SUMMER CAMP

Sending children to summer camp has come back in vogue. In the last 20 years, the number of day camps alone in North America has more than doubled and, counting resident facilities, there are now over 10,00 summer youth camps in all. Here are some tips on finding a good one.

▶ *Do your research. Talk with other parents and their children for feedback. Ask a camp administrator about the average return rate for both campers and staff—a good return rate year after year is the best recommendation.*

▶ *Visit first. If at all possible, visit the camp the summer before you apply. You'll be able to get a feel for the type of staff the director hires, how the day is organized, and whether the children seem happy.*

▶ *Make sure that the program includes activities your child likes—and that you want your child to do.*

▶ *Look for a camp's membership in an organization such as the Canadian Camping Association, which will assure high standards of health care, food service, personnel hiring, and emergency procedures.*

SUGAR & SWEETENERS

Don't bake with substitutes. In baking recipes that call for sugar, it's not a good idea to use artificial sweeteners or sugar substitutes. You can try using a substitute for a small portion of the sugar, but the taste and texture will probably disappoint you. It's better to find recipes specifically designed for substitutes, since some—aspartame, for example—lose sweetness as they cook.

Dark and light brown sugars can be interchanged most of the time, but when a recipe calls for dark brown sugar, a more intense flavor is desired. Also, bear in mind that granulated brown sugar isn't as sweet as regular brown sugar.

Skipping sugar? When you want to lower the sugar in your diet, check the labels on prepared foods for sweeteners that are

different forms of sugar: lactose, maltose, dextrose, fructose, and sucrose. They all affect your body in the same way.

No sugar switching. When baking, don't try to switch granulated sugar for confectioners' or liquid sugar—the weight and volume vary too much. If a recipe calls for granulated sugar, for example, confectioners' sugar or corn syrup usually won't be suitable.

Revive caked brown sugar by sprinkling it with water and setting it in a 95°C (200°F) oven for 10 minutes or in a microwave oven for 20 seconds. Or place caked sugar in a canister, add a slice of apple, and close tightly. The sugar will soften in a few days.

Bury a vanilla bean in a canister of sugar. The sugar will soon be suffused with the scent of vanilla, and you can use it in any recipe that calls for vanilla flavoring.

When honey sugars, forming a white crust, place the lidless jar in boiling water until the original texture is restored. You can also liquefy honey in a microwave.

SUMMER CAMP

Send a care package to allay homesickness soon after your camper waves good-bye. Make sure that the goodies have staff approval, and send enough to be shared with pals. Add small trinkets and stationery with stamped envelopes addressed to yourself.

Provide support. Having a friend or sibling at the same camp reassures a first-time camper. Introducing your child beforehand to someone who has been to the camp before helps too.

A packing list. Paste a list of the contents of your youngster's trunk on the inside of the lid. It will give her a blueprint to follow when she's packing to come home.

Label those clothes! Make sure that nametags are securely sewn onto all of your child's clothes. Many camp-supply and army-navy stores will do this for you.

SUN PROTECTION

Not just at the beach. The damage that ultraviolet radiation causes is cumulative, so it's important to protect your skin anytime you're in the sun. Women should use makeup with an SPF of 15 or higher. Men can use sunscreen instead of aftershave lotion.

Shun the sun at its peak— between 10:00 A.M. and 3:00 P.M. If you must be outside, cover up with a broad-brimmed hat and tightly woven clothing.

 Slather on sunscreen to protect against skin cancer, whatever your skin color. Use a sunscreen that filters out both ultraviolet-A (UVA) and ultraviolet-B (UVB) rays, with an SPF of 15 or higher. Apply it at least 20 minutes before going into the sun, and reapply every two hours or after heavy exercise.

Avoid tanning salons and sun lamps. Tanning lamps emit UVA rays, which will prematurely age skin and make it more susceptible to skin cancer.

Get a tan from a bottle. You can get that healthy-looking glow without damaging your skin. For the best results, clean your skin first with a brush to remove dead skin cells, dry the skin, and apply a self-tanning lotion or spray.

SUNBURN

Take extra care with drugs— some make skin so sensitive to light that you can burn even with very little sun exposure. Check the label on all prescription and over-the-counter medications you take to see if they "photosensitize" your skin; if any of them do, stay out of the sun.

Soothe a sunburn by putting ice wrapped in a towel on the sunburned area several times a day. It will reduce swelling and ease the burning sensation. Damp teabags will also ease the heat.

Pain relievers. Take aspirin, ibuprofen, or acetaminophen to relieve sunburn pain and reduce the inflammation.

Heal the peel. Put aloe vera gel on peeling skin; it can soothe the burn and speed the healing process. To relieve itching, use a water-based moisturizer.

SUNGLASSES

Smart shades. The sun's ultraviolet rays can encourage the formation of cataracts in the eyes, so for maximum protection, look for labels that specify "100 percent UV blockage."

See more clearly. To find out if nonprescription sunglasses are distortion free, hold them at arm's length and look through them at a straight line in the distance, such as a roof's edge or the horizon. If the line becomes crooked as you move the glasses slowly, the lenses have imperfections.

The right squeeze. To make sure that new sunglasses fit well, put them on and look at your feet; if they slip down your nose, they're too loose. At the same time, though, you have to be careful that the earpieces don't pinch your head too tightly.

What color is it? You will see the truest colors with gray- or smoky-toned lenses. Brown and green lenses heighten light and dark contrasts while red, orange, blue, or yellow lenses all make reading traffic lights difficult.

SHADES FOR CHANGING LIGHT

Whether you're driving on a bright day or skiing under overcast skies, you can ease your eyes by wearing photochromic sunglasses, which darken or lighten with changing light intensity while blocking 100 percent of UV rays. Photochromatic sunglasses are available with prescription or non-prescription lenses and come in many styles, including clip-on and lightweight for sports use.

SWIMMING

Ideal exercise. Swimming gives you a great cardiovascular workout, uses almost all major muscle groups, and places virtually no strain on your joints and ligaments. It's great for people of all ages—even those recovering from injuries.

Lane-sharing etiquette. If there are more than two people in your pool lane, swim in a circle pattern. When you enter the pool, pace yourself at least five to ten seconds behind the swimmer in front of you to give her adequate space.

Good form. Slice through the water with greater ease by rotating your hips and trunk from side to side as you do the crawl, staying on each side as long as possible. This narrows your body profile, reducing your drag. The torquing action also propels your body forward more powerfully.

Vary your swim. Have more fun and maximize the health benefits by alternating different strokes—the crawl, for example, with the butterfly or backstroke—when you swim laps. From time to time, use swimming fins and paddles to improve your strength and speed.

Keep a steady stroke when doing laps; you will reach your swimming goal more efficiently than if you start fast, then slow down as you tire. Track your pace by counting the number of strokes it takes to swim a length.

Turn your tyke into a tadpole. Children who learn to swim at an

early age often become confident and skillful swimmers. You can safely begin teaching babies to swim at six months. Many recreation centers offer parent-child swimming classes especially designed for infants and toddlers.

SWIMMING POOLS

For pleasure, not profit. A swimming pool is a boon to family fun, but don't expect it to raise the price of your home when it's time to sell. Real-estate brokers say that a swimming pool usually adds little to a house's value—and sometimes even detracts from it.

Clean feet. Put a small plastic wading pool across the entrance to the swimming pool. Swimmers can step in it to rinse off the dirt, sand, and grass that otherwise ends up in the pool. Cleaning the wading pool—a matter of dumping it and hosing it out—is easier than having to vacuum the pool.

Protect the health of people using your pool by having the water tested at the beginning of the season and testing it yourself once a month during use.

AUTOMATIC POOL CLEANERS

Keeping your pool as clean as possible will add life to your pool—and save you time and money. To make this chore quick and easy, try the Hayward/Arneson NaviGator (left) which cleans in-ground pools without missing a spot, or the E-Z Vac (right) specially designed to skim and scrub above-ground pools.

SYMPATHY & CONDOLENCES

Thoughtful notes. When writing a condolence letter, include some fond memory about that person, perhaps an act of kindness, that his family might not know about and will appreciate.

Suggest help. Rather than asking a grieving friend to think of ways you can help, make a concrete suggestion, such as "I'd like to do this for you," and let him respond.

 OLD SAW

The gift of time. Allow a mourner to grieve at his own pace; it is not for others to judge whether he has grieved too long or too little.

Follow up later. Invite a widowed friend to dinner a few months after her loss, or send a note to a widow on the anniversary of her husband's death. People who are grieving need support long after the rest of us have gone on with our lives.

TABLE MANNERS

To circulate food "properly," pass the potatoes—and everything else—from left to right. Tradition, which favors right-handed people, puts the serving dish on your left so that you can easily help yourself with your right hand. If someone starts passing the wrong way, don't make a fuss—he may be left-handed.

Be a copycat. When faced with any unfamiliar food or dish, take a cue from your hostess. She is supposed to take the first bite; you can then simply follow her lead.

An old salt. When asked to pass the salt, put it down on the table rather than handing it to the next person—many people are superstitious about passing salt from hand to hand. Setting a small shaker on the table also makes handling easier for those with arthritis or other disabilities.

Taste food before adding salt. It's healthier for you and more flattering to the cook to at least determine whether the food has been salted enough for you.

Food on his face? Help your fellow diner. Contrary to popular belief, it isn't kind to ignore this situation. Often just a look and a raised finger to the corresponding spot on your face is enough. If the hint is unheeded, say something to him in an unobtrusive way.

TABLE SETTINGS

Creative alternatives. Use inexpensive bandanas or colorful linen dish towels for napkins. Not only are they less expensive than napkins, they are often larger and launder more easily.

Set a formal table for very little money by shopping flea markets for incomplete, and therefore inexpensive, sets of porcelain, silverware, and crystal. Fill in the missing pieces from one of the many mail-order houses that specialize in old tableware patterns. These suppliers often advertise in home-decorating magazines.

Must everything match? Thanks to today's casual dining, dishes, glasses, and silverware no longer have to come from the same set. In fact, at the most creative tables, they rarely do. Link diverse place-setting elements with a uniform color or design scheme.

Double duty. Look for plastic or laminated placemats that have maps, games, or other learning devices for children. The games grab their interest while the plastic allows for easy cleanup.

Grace notes. For a special meal, substitute inexpensive ribbons for napkin rings. Tuck a sprig of rosemary or a rose under the bow.

TEACHING TABLE MANNERS TO KIDS

Children learn their table manners at family meals, not at charm school. They are far more likely to copy what they see adults do than to follow any verbal instructions.

▶ *Make sure youngsters wash up before dinner and that you and your spouse do too. Clean hands and faces are a part of good table manners.*

▶ *Show children how to place their napkins in their laps and to use their tableware. They may have to struggle at first. Remind them gently, but don't nag.*

▶ *Include children in the dinner conversation. Treat their opinions with respect, and expect the same good manners from them.*

▶ *Teach your child to say, "May I please be excused?" This is the polite way for a restless child to request to leave the table before all the adults are finished.*

TABLECLOTHS

Layer several tablecloths artfully on your table. You won't have to worry about how to make a favorite relative's round tablecloth fit your rectangular dining table and you can camouflage stains on large cloths by covering them with smaller ones.

Improvisation. Top a printed sheet tablecloth with solid-color placemats, or a feminine pastel cloth with lace-trimmed mats. For the Christmas holidays, cover a bright red or green tablecloth with Grandma's old lace cloth; it's both festive and traditional.

An invisible shield. To help keep tablecloths free of stains, lightly coat them with a commercial silicone spray. Apply after every cleaning and well in advance of a party so that no chemical odors interfere with the aroma of food.

An oversized solution. To cover an extra-large table, buy a length of lightweight fabric and make a simple cloth. The woven selvage edges of the fabric need no finishing, and the raw edges can be hemmed with iron-on tape. In a pinch, use any large swath of fabric—a flat sheet, for example—as a tablecloth.

Take wrinkles out of a tablecloth by tossing it in the dryer with a damp towel; set the machine on the *Air* cycle. Take the cloth out as soon as the machine stops, and put it on your table.

Mark the size of clean tablecloths with stick-on labels as you put them into the linen closet. Then you can see at a glance the one you want, no matter how many leaves are in the dining table.

TABLES

Choose a round dining table if you have the space. Guests can more easily see and converse with each other around one. Pedestal-style round tables, in particular, allow you to comfortably seat a large number of guests because there are no table legs to dodge.

 The table for the space. If space is limited in your dining room or apartment, opt for a drop-leaf table. Keep the table pushed to the side unless you are entertaining—then its capacity can more than double.

For ad hoc eating, buy a set of handsome stacking end tables. They take up no extra room but are always ready for guests when you serve buffet-style or for avid television viewers in your family.

Double-duty coffee table. Look for a coffee table with a shelf. You can store your knickknacks and magazines out of the way when hot drinks and snacks are being served on top.

Wrap dining table leaves in old sheets or blankets to protect them from scratches and dirt before you tuck them into the back of a closet or under a bed.

TANTRUMS

Heed early warning signs that your toddler is getting fatigued, hungry, or overwhelmed. Encour-

---

RIGHT STUFF

TABLE EXTENDER

Increase the capacity of a conventional card table to accommodate as many as eight people with a handy table extender. The Porto-Top from Meco (right), creates a 1.2 m (48 in.) circular surface, and is made of hardboard cushioned with a vinyl cover. When your party or card game is over, the Porto-Top folds flat for easy storage under a bed or in a closet. Table extenders are available through housewares stores and catalogs.

age him to nap or eat if he needs to, or get him interested in a restful activity, such as looking at a picture book.

Reward good behavior on the spot so that your child feels it's worth the effort to behave well and to remain calm. The rewarding experience can be very simple: a hug, a pat on the head, or a few words of appreciation.

Give your child a choice. Offer simple alternatives rather than directives that may invite defiance. For example, ask your child if she wants oatmeal or cold cereal for breakfast, or whether she prefers to wear sneakers or sandals. This approach allows her to retain some control and still do what you want.

Time-out. Designate a "time-out" place or chair where, when your child becomes enraged, he must sit for a prescribed period of time to cool off. (One minute for each year of age is a good rule-of-thumb.) Put a timer beside him so that he can anticipate when the time-out will be over.

TAXICABS

Get the name. Memorize or write down the cab driver's name and license number as soon as you are seated. It will help to locate the driver in case you leave something in the cab or you need to make a complaint.

Tipping. Cabdrivers should be tipped 15 percent of the total fare. Increase the tip if you have an excessive amount of luggage or if the driver is overly helpful.

Car service or taxi? Car services, which were once used only by the rich or those on an expense account, have become increasingly affordable, especially in larger cities. To compete with taxis, most car services establish flat rates that are the same as, if not lower than, a local taxi fare.

If you start with fresh, high-quality tea leaves, this tried-and-true method will make a great spot of tea.

▶ *For each cup of tea, pour 175 mL (6 oz) of cold water into a kettle and set the kettle over high heat to boil. (If you are using mugs, add 85 mL (3 oz) extra water per mug.)*

▶ *Rinse out the teapot with hot water to warm it. Put loose tea in the teapot, allowing 1 heaping teaspoon per cup of tea. If you are using an infuser, simply place the same amount into the metal ball.*

▶ *When the water boils, pour it over the tea leaves and swirl the pot gently. Put the lid on the pot, then wrap the pot in a tea towel or a tea cozy to keep the tea warm.*

▶ *Steep the tea 4 to 5 minutes to the strength you prefer.*

▶ *Pour the tea into cups or mugs, using a tea strainer if the tea is loose.*

▶ *Provide lemon slices, milk, and a sweetener such as honey or sugar, and allow each person to serve himself.*

By the numbers. Count your bags each time you get in and out of a cab to be sure that you aren't leaving anything behind.

TEA

Too much caffeine? Drink tea instead of coffee to cut down on caffeine. A cup of tea contains about half the caffeine of a cup of coffee.

Rx: Drink green tea. Green tea (as compared to black or oolong tea) contains important polyphenols or antioxidants, which, some studies suggest, may help to prevent certain cancers.

Control the strength. Instead of using loose tea—which will continue to steep as long as the water is hot—make your tea with an infuser, a small perforated metal container. Fill the infuser with the tea, place it in the pot, pour in boiling water, then remove it after the tea has steeped to the strength you desire.

Ease menstrual cramps. Certain herbal teas, including raspberry leaf, chamomile, and valerian, are often recommended to help relieve menstrual cramps.

Herbal tea trap. While many herbal teas are light, refreshing, caffeine-free drinks, some can cause allergic or toxic reactions. When trying a new kind of herbal tea, brew it weak and watch for reactions. Pregnant women should not drink herbal teas at all.

TEACHERS

Appropriate gifts. If your child wants to give his teacher a gift, suggest that he make something by hand—home-baked goodies, crafted bookmarks, plants grown from cuttings, or a piece of art.

Early and late. Ask to meet your child's teachers early in the school semester. By taking the first step, you show that you care. Then meet again with them later on. Teachers are likely to be more forthright after they have gotten to know your child better.

Prepare for conferences with your child's teacher. Ask your child if there are subjects she wants you to discuss and prepare a list of your own questions and concerns. Be sure to arrive on time.

Teacher problems. If your child is having problems with the teacher, allow him to express his anger. Meet with the teacher to find out if she is aware of your child's unhappiness. If the troubles persist, arrange to transfer your child to another class.

TEACHING TOOLS

TV posture. When you are trying to study a topic using an educational television program or videotape, beware of the "couch-potato syndrome"—a lowering of alertness that occurs when people relax in front of a television set. Keep yourself alert with good lighting and a sturdy, classroom-style chair.

Not just books. To research the latest teaching tools, spend a few hours at your local library. Most libraries have a good supply of up-to-date educational materials for both children and adults, including audiocassettes, educational videos, and on-line research services. Most tools and services can be borrowed for no fee.

The interactive edge. Investigate CD-ROM's to help children learn. There are several interactive encyclopedias and hundreds of creative games that introduce children to many subjects.

Handouts help. When making a presentation, use the most basic teaching tool to get your points across. Even if the material you're presenting seems elementary to you, having something in hand will help others retain the information you are giving them. For a source of ideas, collect handouts from any seminars or workshops that you attend.

TEENAGERS

Behavior modification. Work on one aspect of a teen's behavior at a time, perhaps changing your focus every week. Overlook minor transgressions in one area while attending to another. Save your absolute, no-compromise positions for health and safety issues, and consider everything else somewhat negotiable.

Room to grow. If your child is reluctant to discuss a particular topic, try not to insist that he tell you what's on his mind. Instead, let him attempt to solve things by

---

"TECH" TOOLS FOR TOTS

Even toddlers can learn how to use a computer with these delightful, interactive toys. My First Laptop by Tiger Electronics (left) is ideal for children under age 4, offering exercises with numbers, letters, and colors; hooked up to a multimedia PC, it provides even more activities. Fisher-Price's Wonder Tools Cruiser (right) plugs into a multimedia PC, and teaches computer skills as the child "drives" through animated venues.

himself—a sure sign of growing independence—but always be available should he seek advice.

Respect privacy. Show the same respect for your adolescent's privacy that you would show for any adult in your family. Never read her mail, and allow her phone conversations to be private.

Teens and telephones. If your child constantly talks on the telephone, tell her that she can talk for 15 minutes, but then she must stay off the phone for at least an equal amount of time. This not only frees up your telephone line so that other family members can receive calls, but teaches your teen moderation and discipline.

Bite your tongue. Most teenagers are hypersensitive about their appearance. Although highly critical of others' clothes, they are unable to handle much criticism of their own. Self-image is very important to them, so keep a cool head about the fashions they choose to wear. Look for ways to support and reinforce any positive comments they make about themselves.

TEETHING

Avoid frozen "gnaw-ons." Avoid giving babies ice cubes or other frozen foods when they are teething. Small pieces can break off and choke them. Instead, offer

cool, soothing foods such as chilled applesauce. Some infants like to bite on a damp washcloth, which combines a nubby texture with the coolness they crave.

A risky remedy. Forget that old wives' tale about dabbing brandy or whiskey on a baby's gums to alleviate teething pain. Even a very small amount of alcohol can be toxic to a baby.

Keep those new teeth clean. Preventing decay is critical, even for baby teeth. To clean them, wipe at night with a moist washcloth or a clean piece of gauze, then give your baby a sip of water.

 Rx for drool rash. Teething often stimulates drooling, which in turn leads to skin rash or chapping around the mouth and chin. To help prevent this, gently wipe the saliva periodically during the daytime, and place a towel under the crib sheet to absorb the excess while your baby sleeps.

TALKING TO TEENAGERS

You can form trusting relationships and good communication with teens if you follow these guidelines.

▶ *Leave room for negotiation. Discuss "scenarios" that may come up. Ask, "What would you do if . . . ?"*

▶ *Cultivate listening skills. Try not to correct your teenager while he's speaking. Avoid trying to make him change his feelings and perceptions.*

▶ *Make a point of talking with your child for 15 minutes each day just to find out what's on her mind. Schedule your talks for different times so that this doesn't seem like a job or duty. Don't try to accomplish anything specific— just keep the lines of communication open.*

▶ *Avoid put-downs, even those meant to be humorous; teens will not find them funny.*

TELECOMMUTING

Don't be a total stranger. Make periodic visits to your employer's office. Face-to-face contact lends a human touch to the usual disembodied communications. It works both ways—your face will be better remembered at the office and your colleagues will be identifiable people to you.

Keep in touch. Reply promptly to telephone messages, faxes, and e-mail messages from your office and from clients. This lets everyone know that you're on the job.

Internet info. The World Wide Web offers a wealth of data for employers, managers, and workers regarding telecommuting. Start at the Telecommuting Advisory Council; their Web site is http://www.telecommute.org.

Build good relationships. Get friendly with your technical support team and the main recipient of computer files you send via modem or the Internet. Make sure that the person receiving your files knows how to process and distribute your work promptly.

TELEPHONE BOOKS

Leave your mark. After locating a number in your phone book that you'll probably use more than once, mark it with a bright-colored pen or highlighter. You'll be able to find it much more easily the next time.

Still the best solution. When youngsters are too big for high chairs but too small to reach the table comfortably, telephone books can come to the rescue. Cover one or two old ones with a tea towel or a piece of fabric to make a booster seat.

Save steps and more. Use the Yellow Pages to check that a merchant has what you want before you leave the house, and to compare prices without traveling from store to store. Sometimes you'll find money-saving coupons, too.

TELEPHONE CALLING CARDS

No change needed. Convenient calling cards allow you to make local or long-distance phone calls away from home and charge the calls to your home telephone or a credit card. You may pay a bit more, however, because a service charge is added for each call made with certain cards.

Protect against fraud. When you use a public phone, guard your calling card number. Snoops may be watching and listening, and if one manages to steal your number, you can wind up with a big bill. When possible, punch in the number rather than saying it to an operator. The safest pay phones are those that read the magnetic stripe on your card.

To avoid service charges, use prepaid phone cards. You can buy a card worth $5 to $50 or more from most telephone companies. To make calls, you punch in a personal identification number and then the number you want. After you complete your call, an automated voice tells how much credit you have left.

Which card? Calling cards are issued by both local and long-distance companies. When making out-of-town calls, use a long-distance carrier, which usually gives lower rates than the local company.

Calling home from abroad. Many countries subscribe to Canada Direct, a long-distance service that allows you to call home from overseas at Canadian rates instead of the local rates.

Information is available at your local passport office.

TELEPHONE ETIQUETTE

Send a message. Make the message on your answering machine short and clear. While some find it cute to record a three-year-old telling a story or an extended jazz riff, most callers don't want to spend the time to listen—especially after they've heard it once.

Call-waiting courtesy. If you get a second call while you're already on the phone, just take a call-back number and get back to your original conversation right away. If your second call is urgent, take a moment to sign off on your original call and promise to get back to that person later.

Sorry, wrong number. If you dial a wrong phone number, apologize to the person who answers. Tell her the number you're trying to reach instead of asking what number you dialed.

Thanks, but no thanks. If you get an unwelcome telephone solicitation, tell the caller politely but firmly that you're not inter-

ENDING A TELEPHONE CONVERSATION

Try these gentle persuasions to help end the conversation without hurt feelings.

▶ *As soon as there's a pause in the conversation, quickly say, "I'll let you go now, but we'll talk again soon."*

▶ *Say "This is fascinating and I want to hear more about it." Then, suggest a time and place where you can meet to talk longer face to face.*

▶ *Or say, "I'm sorry to put a stop to this but I'm pressed for time today." Then explain that you have a deadline or an appointment to make and promise to call back.*

▶ *Excuse yourself by saying that you have to get off the phone because you're expecting an important call.*

ested and then hang up. You'll avoid wasting his time and yours.

The polite host. If you have a guest in your home, keep your conversations on incoming phone calls short and sweet.

Teach your children how to answer the telephone properly and take clear messages. Keep a pen and paper nearby so they can write down names and numbers.

TELEPHONE SERVICES

Better than unlisted. If you want to keep your phone number private without paying extra for having an unlisted number, have the phone company list it under your pet's name, your middle name, or a nickname.

Call-answering service. If you run a business from your home, consider replacing your answering machine with call answering. For a monthly fee, the phone company answers your calls and lets callers leave a message even when you're on the phone with someone else.

Call waiting, the phone company service that beeps you during telephone conversations to announce other incoming calls, may be a necessity for businesses and some busy individuals, but it can irritate customers and friends who are left dangling. A prompt return the first time is only slightly annoying; frequent interruptions are enraging.

Caller-ID service. Before you answer the phone, this telephone service shows you the phone number and, in some areas, the name of the person calling on a screen either built into the telephone or on a special monitor. A

TELEPHONE-CORD DETANGLER

Is your telephone cord always in knots? This ingenious cord detangler, which attaches to your receiver, ends those twists—and potential damaged cords—forever. It swivels with every movement, keeping the cord aligned even as you move around with the receiver. Find these devices in most phone centers.

fee for the service is added to your monthly bill.

Name the number. An alternative to looking up and punching in frequently used phone numbers is voice dialing. This service allows you to program up to 50 phone numbers into your telephone. To make a call, you just lift the receiver, say the name of the person you're calling, and the phone does the dialing for you.

TELEPHONES

Clean telephones with rubbing alcohol or cleaning liquid on a cloth, but keep moisture from getting into the holes in the mouthpiece. If you can unscrew the mouthpiece, wash it in dishwashing soap and warm water, then rinse and dry carefully.

Speed dialing is fast. Phones that have speed dialing let you store a whole list of phone numbers in memory. You simply press a single key to dial each number.

Phone safety. To prevent shocks, don't use the telephone when you're in a swimming pool or bathtub. Steer clear of telephones

during lightning storms; lightning can travel through phone lines.

A keypad of a different color. Keypads are available that address an assortment of special needs. Phones with light-up keys let you make a call in the dark. Phones with large-size keys make it easier for children, the elderly, and people with poor vision to dial.

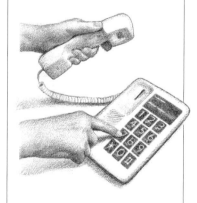

Stay connected—always. Have at least one "corded" phone at your home for emergencies. Cordless phones won't work if the power goes out, since they run on household current.

TELEVISION VIEWING

No passive viewing. You don't have to be a couch potato to watch TV. Use your viewing time to finish some busy work, such as ironing, sewing, cleaning out a drawer, or doing your nails.

Limit children's TV time by emphasizing other activities. Children who are engaged in sports, playing with siblings and friends, doing homework, pursuing hobbies, or helping around the house won't have time for TV viewing.

Watch what your kids watch or at least be close enough to hear the television. When a show finishes, remark on what you liked and didn't like (taking note of commercials, too), and ask for their opinions. You will be teaching your kids to be discerning viewers, not merely passive ones.

Dieters beware. Cut down on viewing time when you are trying to lose weight. TV and snacking often go hand in hand.

TELEVISIONS

Shopping for a TV? If sound quality is important to you, buy a bigger set—63 cm (25 in.) or larger. In general, the larger the set, the better the sound. If you want extra features, such as picture-in-picture, shop for a screen that's at least 68 cm (27 in.).

In the dark. For the best picture, watch a big-screen TV in an unlighted room. The screen of a jumbo set would reflect ambient light back into the room and give the picture a washed-out look.

Breathing room. Leave space between your TV set and the wall or furniture. Air must circulate around the vents at the back to keep the set from overheating.

Cleaning your TV. For safety's sake, pull the plug and wait until the television has cooled down before cleaning the screen. Spray window cleaner on a cloth or paper towel and wipe the screen. Never attempt to clean the screen of a projection television; ask for professional help.

Are you too close? To reduce eyestrain, try to sit at a distance of at least 2 ½ times the screen's diagonal dimension. That's about 1.5 m (5 ft) for a 63 cm (25 in.) screen.

Snooze shutoff. If you regularly fall asleep in front of the television, look for one with an automatic shutoff timer. Just set the TV for a predetermined time, and it will turn off automatically.

TEMPORARY EMPLOYMENT

In season. Employment opportunities increase during specific times of the year. For instance, look for hotel and restaurant jobs during the summer tourist season. Department stores hire more people during the holidays. Farmers need help at harvest time.

Learn new skills. To maximize your earning potential, ask the employment agencies that you deal with if they offer courses or other training opportunities.

Earn extra dollars. Ask about incentive programs offered by your temp agency. For example,

TEMPORARY EMPLOYMENT

Temporary work provides a viable employment option for those who find themselves in any of these situations:

▶ *Entrepreneurs starting small businesses who need an income flow to get the business started.*

▶ *Parents who want to generate income while remaining home with their families the majority of their time.*

▶ *Unemployed workers who are in the midst of a search for a full-time position.*

▶ *Students who want to work around their class schedules or during summer vacations.*

▶ *Full-time employees who want to earn some extra income for expenses such as home improvement.*

▶ *People returning to work after a period of nonemployment who want to test the waters in different environments before committing to a permanent employer.*

some companies pay bonuses to employees who refer other workers to the agency.

Be dependable. If you are punctual, eager, and capable, you will develop a reputation for being just the kind of worker companies need. You'll be first in line for offers of permanent positions.

When you interview, ask for the names of a temp agency's major clients and its areas of specialization, to be sure that your background and skills are suitable for businesses served by that agency.

Seek out the extras. Some companies that employ freelancers and temporary employees offer benefits such as paid vacation time and health insurance; ask under what circumstances you might become eligible for them.

TENNIS

Release the tension in your arm and fingers by frequently relaxing your grip. Use the lulls between points to shift the racket to your free hand and uncurl the fingers of your playing hand.

Choose your surface. Hard (asphalt) courts are fast and give you less time to reach the ball. Soft courts, like clay or composition, are slower; the ball bounces higher, giving you more time to get to it.

Stay focused on the baseline by thinking of the following three words: hit, bounce, hit. This sequence will remind you to watch the ball when your opponent swings, to follow the ball as it bounces into your court, and to keep your eyes fixed on that round target as you make a shot.

Match strategy. If you're out to win, scrutinize your opponent's game and adapt to it. If he has trouble with high backhands, that's where you want to aim the ball. If he isn't in the best shape,

GET A BETTER HANDLE ON TENNIS

Improve your tennis game by taking advantage of these products. Whatagrip, a cushioned overgrip tube and Prince's DuraZorb overgrip help you fit your racket snugly in your hand. Liquids such as PrinceGrip (spray) and PrinceGrip Plus (lotion) prevent sweat on your hands from interfering with your swing. Shock Off (inset) reduces hitting vibrations, easing pressure on your elbow and wrist. All are available at sporting goods shops.

make him run. If he hates coming to the net, play drop shots.

Get a good grip. To properly evaluate the grip on your racket, take the handle of your racket in your playing hand as you normally do for a shot. Put the index finger of your other hand in the space between the fingertips and the heel of the hand holding the racket. Your index finger should just fit in that space. If it does not, find a racket with a bigger—or smaller—grip.

Restring your racket as many times annually as you play in a week. For example, if you play three times a week, restring your racket at least three times a year.

Spare your strings by storing your racket indoors. Never leave it in the car in summer or winter. Cold air makes synthetic strings so brittle that they can snap, and extreme heat stretches them out.

TEST TAKING

Get a good night's sleep. Fatigue reduces your energy and your confidence. If you haven't learned the subject by the night before the exam, you won't learn it by cramming at the last minute.

Scan earlier exams to evaluate how well you know a subject and to get an idea of likely questions.

Skim through the exam before you start to answer questions so you'll be able to grasp the scope of the test and to plan how to budget your time.

THANK-YOU NOTES

Show off. To thank someone for a household or personal gift, have a picture taken of you using or wearing the item; send the photo along with a note of gratitude.

Make a list. To thank a large number of people from a wedding or other major occasion, keep a typed or computerized list of your guests. When you receive a present, mark down what it was next to the person's name who gave it, and as you send out each thank-you note, keep track by writing the date next to the name.

Considerate kids. To encourage children to write thank-you notes after major holidays, have them invite their friends to a party dedicated to making thank-you notes. Supply the kids with paper, pens, and paint, as well as refreshments.

Personal touch. To thank those who gave you wedding, engagement, or shower presents, write handwritten notes for each giver. Preprinted cards are inappropriate.

Be courteous. Even if you dislike the gift that someone has given, thank him graciously. Say you have nothing else like it and how nice he was to think of you.

THANKSGIVING

Honor the tradition. Ask a family member, even a child, to prepare a presentation—a poem or a picture, for example—that illustrates the meaning of Thanksgiving. Say grace in a specific and personal way before dinner.

 Familiar fare. Try one or two new dishes, but don't revamp your entire Thanksgiving menu. This is a traditional holiday, and many celebrants look forward to enjoying the family favorites.

Plan tasks for all who may want to help with the Thanksgiving meal. Many hands not only make light work, but give guests a chance to talk with one another easily. If possible, assign people to prepare their specialties. For example, ask your mother to make her special salad dressing or your nephew, the Eagle Scout, to build a fire in the fireplace.

Special guests. Each year, ask one or two additional, non-family guests, such as new neighbors, your daughter's college roommate, or your mother's bridge group. New people keep the conversation lively and gratifying.

Collect extra food containers before Thanksgiving to save time when storing the leftovers and for sending food home with guests.

THEME PARTIES

Cultural exchange. Have a good time—and learn a thing or two—by celebrating the national holidays of other countries. Some to consider are France's Bastille Day on July 14, England's Guy Fawkes Day on November 5, and Chinese New Year in late January or early February. Serve native dishes and

Carving a Thanksgiving Turkey The Easy Way

As much as we idealize the notion of carving the Thanksgiving turkey at a festive table, the easiest way to serve a large bird is to carve it (with a sharply honed knife) in the kitchen first, then serve the meat, sliced and elegantly arranged, on a platter. So roast your turkey and let it rest for 15–20 min.

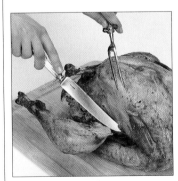

1 Steady the bird with a fork. With the knife tip, find the joint where thigh meets body and cut through the joint. Remove wings the same way.

2 Separate the drumstick from the thigh at the joint. If the turkey is not too large and ungainly, you can serve the legs whole.

3 If the legs are large, cut slices from both drumstick and thigh, holding the bone at an angle to the board and cutting parallel to the bone.

research customs of the holiday so that you can duplicate them at your celebration.

Hero worship. Celebrate the life of your favorite president, author, musician, athlete, or other famous person you admire—by giving a party in his honor. Ask guests to wear appropriate costumes and to to give relevant toasts.

A day to be bad. Choose a notorious character from history, and plan a party around the anniversary of his birth or demise. Or, simply have a "Bad Guys" party, and ask guests to come as their favorite villain.

Mad-hatters' party. Invite your friends to a costume party at which the only requirement is to wear an old, silly, or wildly inventive hat. Ask each guest to come prepared to explain his headgear.

Make it a tradition. Host an unusual theme party each year—a Greek Mythology party one year, a Dog Days of Summer party the next. Have all facets of the party reflect the theme—from the invitations to the costumes to the food. Both you and your guests will look forward to it.

THERMOMETERS

Differences in degrees. Allow for variations in temperature readings depending on the kind of thermometer you use. Rectal readings are normally one degree higher than oral temperatures, while armpit readings are one degree lower than oral ones.

To avoid false readings, don't take someone's temperature if she has just had a bath, drunk a hot or cold beverage, or eaten a meal. The reading may also be skewed if she has been even moderately active just before it is taken.

Under the arm. Taking a child's temperature is easiest if you seat the child, place the thermometer tip in the center of the armpit, and then have him cross his arms. Allow 3 minutes for a digital thermometer; 5 minutes for a glass thermometer.

If your thermometer breaks, use an eyedropper to collect the elusive mercury, which can be harmful to children and pets. Be sure to clean the eyedropper thoroughly when you are finished.

If you have an infant, invest in the kind of thermometer that comes in the form of a pacifier or a quick-acting thermometer used in the ear. One of these can be worth the extra expense when you are worried about your unhappy, squirming baby.

Show off your perfectly roasted bird to the gathered throng, then return to the kitchen, place it on a cutting board, and follow these simple, professional chef's steps.

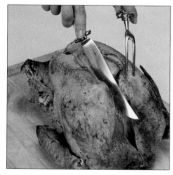

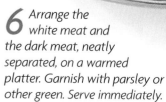

4 *Slice along the breast-bone, close to the rib section. Cut all the way to the wing and lift off the breast. Repeat on the other side.*

5 *Carve the breast meat diagonally against the grain, in 6–12 mm (¼"–½") slices. Each slice should include a sliver of golden skin.*

6 *Arrange the white meat and the dark meat, neatly separated, on a warmed platter. Garnish with parsley or other green. Serve immediately.*

TICKS

If you find a tick, remove it promptly, although ticks generally must be attached for at least 24 hours to transmit disease. Grab the tick close to the victim's skin. Use tweezers or cover your fingers with rubber gloves or a paper towel. Pull gently but do not squeeze. Flush the tick down the toilet or put it into a jar of alcohol and have your doctor identify it.

Cover up and spray. In tick-infested areas, wear light-colored clothes so ticks will be easier to see. Cover bare skin with a long-sleeved shirt and long pants, and tuck the pants into your socks. Spray your clothes (not your skin) with a tick repellent containing permethrin, which is sold at garden and hardware stores. Insect repellents containing deet can be used on the skin—but read the directions before applying and ask your doctor before using it on a child's skin.

Watch for Lyme disease. Symptoms include a painless bull's-eye rash that appears at the site of the bite within a few days or weeks, and sometimes flulike symptoms —low fever, chills, and achiness. If you have these symptoms, see your doctor immediately.

Beware of tick fever. Some ticks carry Rocky Mountain spotted fever and other diseases. Among the symptoms are chills, muscle pain, and a high temperature. See a doctor if these occur.

A spot check. After walking in an infested area, shower to wash away any ticks that haven't bitten. Then check your children and your pets carefully all over. Look closely at hairy areas where ticks may be hard to notice. Ask someone else to check the areas on your own body that you can't see.

TILES

Tiles must be symmetrical and even to be effective. If you are laying tiles yourself, design the layout on graph paper before you start. On a wall, mark a plumb line in the center and then draw reference lines every 60 cm (2 ft) or so from that line. On a floor, start the pattern in the middle of the room and work out to the edges.

Hide a room's shortcomings with a well-planned tile pattern. A border can make a large room appear cozier; vertical lines make a low ceiling appear higher; a tiled wall can add pizzazz to a kitchen.

Update a vinyl tile floor by removing only some of the tiles and replacing them with accent tiles in a contrasting color or pattern. Use the accent tiles to create a new border or a new design.

Create a dramatic stairway. Decorate the risers of a staircase or a single step leading to another level with colorful tiles.

Wall or floor? Smoothly glazed ceramic tiles are ideal for walls, especially in kitchens and baths, where they are washed often. For floors, textured vinyl or unglazed quarry tiles are less slippery.

Replace a ceramic tile by drilling a starting hole with a masonry bit, then, using a hammer and chisel, scoring an X in the tile from corner to corner. Chip away pieces from the center to the edges.

If a replacement wall tile slips down while the mastic (the ceramic adhesive) is drying, put wooden wedges or spacers made out of matchsticks in the space below it until the mastic dries.

TIME MANAGEMENT

Make the best of it. If you have to take a day off from work to receive a delivery at home, for

---

RIGHT STUFF

A NEW TOOL FOR TILES

The grease, mold, and scum that builds up on tiles and grout is difficult to clean. But the battery-powered ScumBuster by Black & Decker (the same people who brought you the DustBuster) helps you to clean bathroom and kitchen tiles until they sparkle with very little elbow grease. Small and lightweight, the scrubber is easy to handle. Two special brush attachments help get into deep crevices and tight corners.

example, schedule the appointment with the refrigerator repairman that you've been putting off.

Just say no. Politely decline requests for your time if they interfere with precious family time or a work project you must finish.

Eat either earlier or later than the usual noon-hour lunchtime so that you can get work done when the office is least crowded.

Review your calendar at the end of the month. Note when you fell behind schedule and what days went smoothly. Then decide how many activities, meetings, and appointments you realistically are able to manage.

Self-awareness. Determine when you are at your best and brightest. Schedule those times for your most difficult tasks.

TIME-SHARES

Resist promises of free gifts and "today only" bargains for signing on the spot. Never agree hurriedly to something requiring payments stretching over 20 or 30 years.

Disregard claims of high returns. Time-shares seldom appreciate much. If you want financial returns, you can do better investing in more conventional ways that earn interest.

If your club assigns points, you can maximize your holiday time by analyzing the point system and taking advantage of special offers.

Buy from someone reselling a share instead of a developer. Search resort-area newspapers or place an ad in one. Because they are often eager to unload them, resellers can offer discounts of 30 to 70 percent off the same product that developers offer.

You can cancel time-share agreements in some provinces if you act quickly—within three to five days after signing the con-

tract. Contact your attorney general to find out about your rights.

TIPPING

Don't forget the paperboy. Your paperboy is probably getting up very early to make sure you have your newspaper with your morning coffee. Remember him with 10 or 20 dollars during the holiday season. He will appreciate the remembrance.

TRAVELER'S TIPPING GUIDE

Knowing whom to tip and how much makes a traveler's life easier. Tips are often included in the bill when you are abroad (ask if you are unsure), but in Canada you usually must calculate your own. Here is a sampling of rates.

SERVICE	AMOUNT OF TIP
Bartender	10%–20% of the bill
Bellhop, porter, skycap carrying luggage	$1 per bag
Concierge	For special services beyond ordinary travel arrangements or dinner reservations, $5–$10.
Doorman hailing a taxi	$1
Hairstylist, masseuse	15%
Hotel housekeeper or maid	$1–$2 per day (leave it on the dresser)
Parking valet	$1–$2
Restaurant waiter	15%–20% of the pretax bill, depending on the level of service.
Room-service waiter	Check the bill; a service charge is usually included. If not, add 10%–15%.
Taxicab driver	15% of the fare
Tour guides	Optional, but $1 for a day tour and $5–$10 for a week of touring is usual.

If you live in an apartment building or other communal situation, ask neighbors how much they tip the doormen and other service personnel. It helps residents to standardize the tipping; but be generous—it is equally useful to have happy helpers.

Use a pocket calculator to figure quickly the amount you should leave for a tip. Base the tip on the before-tax total of your bill.

Tipping beauty operators. Hairdressers and cosmetologists expect a 10 to 15 percent tip. You are not required to tip the owner of a salon, but if you are a frequent customer, give her a small token at holiday time or bring flowers or cookies for the staff.

The size of the tip you leave should be based on the quality of the service. If you feel you've been shortchanged on service, you can shortchange the server.

DIGITAL PRESSURE GAUGE

Pressure gauges at gas station air pumps are notoriously inaccurate, and old-fashioned individual gauges can be hard to read. With a digital pressure gauge, such as the Schrader 100, you can easily keep your car tires at the correct pressure, saving wear and tear on the tires while improving your gas mileage. Digital gauges are sold at auto supply stores.

TIRES

Watch the weather. Choose your tires to match the environment you normally drive in. In wet areas, choose a rain tire or one with water channels to prevent hydroplaning problems. In hot, dry areas, pick a tire specially made to withstand heat. If your winters are severe, opt for a tire that is rated for mud and snow.

Tire ratings are not uniform among brands. Use ratings only when you are comparing one model of tire to another made by the same manufacturer.

When selling your car, don't buy new tires as part of the fix up; they don't increase the value of the car enough to warrant the added expense.

Steering wheel vibrating? Ask a mechanic to check the weights on your wheels. Some of the weights on the rims, which are usually adjusted when the tires are balanced, may be missing.

Changing tips. Always loosen the lugs on a wheel before you crank up the jack (you may have to stand on the wrench to start the lugs). Then jack the car up, change wheels, and turn the lugs hand-tight. Lower the jack and tighten all lugs with the wrench, working on opposite pairs in succession.

Tire mileage. Don't buy tires expected to last for 80,000 km (50,000 mi.) if you only drive 8,000 km (5,000 mi.) a year. The tires will become unsafe before they wear out. Most tires are too old to be safe after five years, even "high mileage" tires.

TOASTERS

Small slices won't get lost if you run wooden toothpicks through the top of the bread so that they lie crosswise over the toaster slots. The bread will then hang from the toothpicks instead of dropping to the bottom when you push the handle down.

Unplug your toaster before you try to retrieve broken-off pieces of bread. And never stick a metal tool into a toaster; you'll risk getting an electric shock or damaging the toaster. Instead, turn the unplugged toaster upside down and shake it gently to remove dried crumbs.

Look for wide slots. If you plan to toast bagels, English muffins, or other thick breads, make sure the toaster's slots are wide enough to accommodate them without sticking or jamming.

Fire fighters. To avoid the danger of fire, never try to stuff oversized food into the toaster. Buttered bread or frosted pastries can also cause a blaze.

Toaster ovens are ideal for broiling or baking small items. Besides toasting well, they use less energy and generate less heat than conventional ovens.

TOILET TRAINING

OLD SAW

When to begin. Whether or not your child has expressed interest in toilet training, you should introduce him to the potty at around 18 to 24 months. Let him know what the toilet is used for, but don't force him to use it.

Praise your child for using the potty, but don't act disappointed or angry when she doesn't. And don't tease her—even in fun—about the fact that she is still wearing diapers. This is especially true if she has older siblings, who may take up your cue and make the little one an object of ridicule.

Leave diapers on at bedtime. Keep diapers on your child at nap time and at night until he regularly wakes up dry. Most children become potty trained during the day before they learn to control their bladders at night. It often takes six months or longer after after a child has begun to wear underpants during the day before he can go through the night without a diaper.

TOILETS

Leaky toilets waste water—as much as 300,000 L (66,000 gal.) a year in an average home. Most of this water is lost through leaky flush and refill valves. To check for a leaky flush valve, turn off the water supply and make a mark on the inside of the tank at the high water level. Periodically check the mark to see if the water level has dropped; if it has, you have a leak.

If a toilet runs after the tank refills, water may be draining into the overflow tube before the toilet gets a chance to shut off. Try flushing the toilet and gently bending the float rod down slightly toward the bottom of the tank. This should shut off the flow before the level gets too high.

Avoid in-tank cleaners. These are expensive, do not clean a bowl that is already soiled, and at best will only slow the accumulation of residue. The best way to clean a toilet bowl is with ordinary household cleanser. For stubborn stains, add bleach to the bowl, let it soak for an hour, wipe gently with a brush, then flush.

Flush a cup of baking soda down the toilet every week or so. The baking soda will help to prevent the build up of bacteria in the tank as well as guard against clogging or backing up in the tank and drain field.

GROWING TOMATOES

Everyone loves homegrown tomatoes. Here are some simple rules for growing your own tomatoes successfully:

❱ *Start tomato seeds indoors eight weeks before the last frost date in your area. Or buy plants from a nursery after frost seems unlikely. Pick small, bushy plants that have no flowers or fruit; they will transplant best.*

❱ *Pick a sunny bed and work plenty of organic material into it. Some gardeners put a banana peel in the bottom of each hole; others, a dead fish.*

❱ *Plant every 60 cm (2 ft) in rows 90 cm (3 ft) apart.*

❱ *Install 1.8 m (6 ft) stakes or wire tomato cages to support the seedlings as they grow. Tie the vine to the support loosely with strips of soft cloth.*

❱ *Keep the plants watered and feed them weekly with a liquid fertilizer. When the ground warms up, apply 5 to 7.5 cm (2–3 in.) of organic mulch to retain water.*

❱ *Put a collar of aluminum foil, shiny side up, around the base of each plant to discourage aphids and speed the ripening of the fruit.*

❱ *Pick tomatoes when they have a good, red color and feel firm but not hard.*

TOMATOES

To peel tomatoes easily, cut a shallow X in the bottom end of each tomato and put them in boiling water for 20 to 30 seconds. Remove them with a slotted spoon. When they're cool enough to handle, strip away the skins with the edge of a knife.

Ripen tomatoes at room temperature in a bowl with other fruit or in a closed brown paper bag. Tomatoes turn mushy if you try to ripen them in the sun. Also, tomatoes will not ripen in the refrigerator; in fact, they turn pulpy and lose flavor in cold temperatures.

Add a pinch of sugar or baking soda to a tomato sauce or tomato soup that tastes a bit too acidic. Or, if you have the time, simply simmer the sauce or soup a few minutes longer, and usually the natural sweetness of the tomatoes will emerge.

When making tomato sauce, include some tomato paste or puree. Both help thicken a sauce, and each contains more vitamin C and beta carotene than an equal volume of whole tomatoes.

Cold tomato. At season's end, use the last of your homegrown tomatoes to make—and freeze—tomato sauce or tomato soup. You can also freeze ripe tomatoes, cut up or whole, in plastic freezer bags. Remember, however, that after tomatoes have been frozen, they will be suitable only for cooking in soups and sauces.

TOOLS

Wax the blade of a handsaw with an old candle to help it cut more smoothly through wood, especially green wood.

 Buy the best. Good-quality hand tools are a solid investment. They make any job go smoother, and if you take care of them, most will last a lifetime. Inexpensive tools cost you more in the end because they never last as long or work as well.

A Phillips screwdriver that is well made will have a flat tip. Avoid one that ends in a thin, sharp point; it won't fit tightly into the screw head.

Torque power. When buying any type of screwdriver, be aware that you can apply more torque if it has a large handle. If you use a screwdriver frequently, invest in a power screwdriver.

Rent power tools that you use only occasionally, such as power drills or large garden implements. You'll be spared not only the initial cost of the tool, but the expense of upkeep and storage.

TOURS

Get credentials. Use only tour operators that are members of the National Tour Association. This ensures that the company has operated for more than three years and has posted a $1 million surety to guarantee claim coverage. Visit them on the Internet at http://www.ntaonline.com.

Check the reputation of a prospective tour operator by asking friends and acquaintances who have recently traveled abroad. A good travel agent also can tell you if any complaints have been filed against the tour companies you are considering.

Special needs. Tours are the ideal way to travel if you are traveling alone (you automatically meet people); are a senior citizen (all your baggage is taken care of); or are not a seasoned traveler.

Tour benefits. A well-run tour can save you money (group rates for airfares, hotels, ground transportation, and meals are usually less expensive) and the hassle of booking rooms, finding transportation, and securing tickets to sights you want to see.

A tour for every interest. You can find specialized tours to fulfill any of your passions—bicycling, riding horseback, hiking, gardening, art history, or literature. See your travel agent, check out travel magazines and newspapers, or search travel sites on the Internet. Many organizations, such as alumni and museum members' groups, also sponsor tours.

Nights count when comparing tour costs. The number of days indicated for a tour is often not a safe guide for the overall length—and overall cost. Tours may start at noon or dinnertime and end with breakfast. With some foreign tours, two of the days may be taken up just with air travel, not actual sightseeing.

Exotic tours. Package tours are an ideal solution if you want to visit faraway parts of the world but still feel intimidated about negotiating such adventures on your own, especially when the local language may pose a problem. Whether you want to travel down the Nile, up the Andes, across Siberia, into the African bush, or through China or South-

---

A BUCKET TOOLBOX

What could be more perfect for keeping tools organized than this bright canvas toolholder? It fits snugly over any large bucket to create a handy carryall and keeps your tools at your fingertips while you are working. Lightweight and inexpensive, these toolholders are available at hardware and housewares stores and through catalogs.

east Asia—tours are an easy and safe way to go.

Learning tours for seniors. Inexpensive study-travel packages organized by Elderhostel sponsor tours to over 50 countries. Most programs are open to those over 55 (spouses and companions may be younger). For a free catalog send a postcard with your name and address to Elderhostel Canada, 308 Wellington St., Kingston, Ont., K7K 7A7, or see the home page on the Internet at http://www.elderhostel.org/.

TOWEL RACKS

A towel rack near the back door is handy for hanging wet scarves, gloves, and umbrellas.

Hang scarves or neckties from a towel rack (or a series of them, one above another) inside your

closet. Install a few cup hooks next to the rack and you'll have a place to hang belts too.

Use hooks or pegs for towels if you don't have room in your bathroom for towel racks. Eliminate confusion about which towel is whose by putting a name tag above each hook.

SAFE SUBSTITUTES

Many harsh household chemicals can be replaced with gentler products. Here are some suggestions for a few basic products.

INSTEAD OF	SUBSTITUTE
Ant killer	Vinegar and water
Drain cleaner	Boiling water once a week
Furniture polish	Three parts olive oil and one part vinegar
Garden pesticide sprays	A mixture of pureed garlic, red pepper, liquid soap, and water to repel aphids; a mixture of baking soda, liquid soap, and water to stop black spot
Houseplant fertilizer	Weak tepid tea solution weekly
Houseplant pest spray	Mild soap and water solution once a week
Mothballs	Cedar chips
Oven cleaner	Vinegar and baking soda
Paintbrush cleaner (for latex paint)	Liquid detergent suds
Paintbrush softener	White vinegar and water
Roach repellent	Bay leaves

Build a towel ladder in the bathroom where space is at a premium. Install two columns of wood from floor to ceiling, and fit dowels between them for hanging towels and washcloths.

Place an over-the-door rack on the back of each of your bedroom doors. Each family member or guest can hang his own towel there, reducing towel clutter and confusion in the bathroom.

TOWELS

Hand-washed knits dry faster when rolled in a towel and squeezed to remove excess moisture. However, laying damp sweaters on towels to dry is not a good idea because the knits and the towels both hold moisture and the knits may turn sour or moldy before they dry. Hang sweaters on a rack to air dry.

Arrange guest towels in an obvious place in the bathroom—espe-

cially hand towels. If they are too artfully or formally displayed, visitors may be hesitant to use them.

Make your own beach towel. Instead of buying an expensive beach towel, make your own with two or three yards of terrycloth. Hem the ends, or sew ribbon around the edge for decoration.

TOXIC PRODUCTS

Use with care. Use home products containing strong chemicals in a well-ventilated area. Wear chemically resistant gloves and, if warranted, a mask and goggles.

Pesticides and fertilizers can be dangerous. Check with your county extension service to find safer methods of controlling pests and helping your lawn to grow.

Play it safe. Use cat litter to soak up spills of toxic products, then put it in a fireproof container until it can be properly discarded.

TOY SAFETY

Keep a child's toys accessible. Toddlers like to get out their own toys, and accidents can happen if they cannot reach them easily. Open plastic bins—inexpensive laundry baskets work well—set on the floor make the best storage containers for a child's toys. Also, avoid toy chests with heavy lids.

Read labels carefully. Many indicate the age a toy is appropriate for, as much for safety reasons as for the child's interest or ability to play with it.

 Watch out for small objects on babies' and toddlers' toys. A cuddly stuffed animal, for example, becomes dangerous if the eyes or mouth or buttons on a garment can be pulled off.

Toilet-roll test. A good way to test if a toy is too small for a young child is to try to put it into a toilet-paper roll, which is about the size of a child's mouth. If it fits inside, it isn't safe.

Wash small plastic toys in the dishwasher, which not only cleans off the excess dirt, but sterilizes toys that often end up in young mouths.

Check old toys for lead paint. Banned in new toys, this toxic substance still shows up in some old toys and hand-me-downs. If you suspect its presence, don't let your child play with the toy.

TOYS

Protect board games. Paint the board with a coat of shellac or polyurethane varnish before you begin playing with it. The game will last longer, and you can clean it easily with a damp cloth. Store the parts in plastic containers.

Recycle the supply. If your child seems bored with his toys, put away some of them for a few weeks. You'll be amazed at how receptive your child will be when they are taken out of the closet.

Buy secondhand mobiles. Most baby's mobiles are used for a short time and seldom receive much handling by babies. Check resale shops for good mobile bargains.

The allure of stacking cups. Once your baby starts to reach for objects, a colorful set of stacking cups makes an inexpensive, durable toy that she will love to play with for hours.

Antique toys have become a booming collectors' market. If you're interested in collecting, magazines like *Antique Toy World* provide schedules for toy shows around the country. Also check out flea markets and auctions.

Antique value. To get an appraisal of an antique toy, take it to a dealer or send a photo of the item to a reputable auction house, which will often provide free appraisal services.

THE STAYING POWER OF CLASSIC TOYS

Today, the toys and games on store shelves dazzle with whiz-bang effects. But while last year's action figure disappears to make room for this year's model, many classic toys remain—continuing, as they have for generations, to fascinate and educate children. You can still make unique images with Colorforms and Etch-A-Sketch, give Mr. Potato Head a new face, send a Slinky bouncing down the stairs, and tell the future with an 8-Ball. The old standards have held up well because they are high quality toys, even without the costly bells and whistles of their contemporary cousins.

HOW TO FIGHT A TRAFFIC TICKET

If you believe you aren't guilty, you should fight a traffic ticket. A conviction stays on your record for three or more years and may raise your car insurance premiums. Here's how to fight a ticket.

▶ *For a serious offense, hire a lawyer. Always consult a lawyer if there has been an accident that involves other people or if your license or your liberty is in jeopardy.*

▶ *Be sure you know the law you are accused of violating. Look up the particular statute at the local library.*

▶ *Check all the information on the ticket. If the police officer made any mistakes, the ticket may be invalid.*

▶ *Ask that the arresting officer be present at your formal hearing. If she doesn't show, your case may be dismissed.*

▶ *Take any reliable witnesses who can back up your story to the hearing.*

▶ *Ask the officer about the time of day of the infraction, the weather, the road conditions, the calibration of her radar, or anything else that might affect your case.*

▶ *If the verdict goes against you, you can appeal. Consult a lawyer before instituting the appeal.*

TRAFFIC TICKETS

Not just for speeders. Don't let aggressive driving habits make you reckless. You can be ticketed for such violations as tailgating, riding on the shoulder, cutting cars off, passing on the right, and running red lights.

Smile! You're on candid camera. In some provinces, using radar to clock speeding vehicles is no longer the sole job of patrol officers. Automated photo radar computer systems have been installed on some major Canadian highways, snapping the picture of your car's license plate should it exceed the speed limit, and then automatically processing your ticket for mailing.

Long-distance drivers who need to know the traffic laws of other regions should invest in *National Motorist's Association Motorist's Guide to State and Provincial Traffic Laws* (608-849-6000; US$9.95). It contains traffic laws for the 50 United States as well as Mexico and Canada.

TRAILERS

The best trailer hitches bolt to your vehicle's frame. Buy one strong enough for the weight it will be pulling. Always err on the side of too much strength.

Let them do it. For a modest fee, trailer rental or recreational-vehicle outlets will hook up your trailer's tail and make sure the brake, turn signal, and side marker lights are in good working order.

Check tie-down straps after towing a short distance. Straps tend to stretch during transport and may need retightening.

To back up with a trailer, hold the steering wheel at the bottom and move your hand to the left if you want the trailer to go left or to the right if you want it to go right. To be extra safe, ask someone to spot for you.

Use a wide-angle mirror to give you a better—and safer—view of your trailer and its load. Look for one at an auto-supply store.

TRANSPLANTING

Transplanting failure with trees and shrubs is usually due to inadequate aftercare. Water weekly in dry weather for the first year after transplanting, soaking the soil thoroughly around the rootball.

Stay put. Some flowers and herbs have sensitive roots that won't tolerate transplanting. For example, balloonflower, celosia, poppies, portulaca, borage, burnet, caraway, chevil, coriander, and dill should always be sown in the spot where they will grow.

Simple seedling tools. Use an old screwdriver to pry seedlings out of a pot, and a sharp pencil to tease apart tangled roots.

Improvised containers. Wrap a 10 cm (4 in.) strip of newspaper around an aspirin bottle, securing side and bottom with tape; slip it off the bottle. Pack a roasting pan full of these containers and fill them with soil and seedlings. Later you can plant them, paper and all.

HOW TO CHOOSE A TRAVEL AGENT

If you want a travel agent to help you find bargains, to guide you to places and lodgings that you will really like, and to advise you about travel logistics that worry you, spend time looking for just the right person.

▶ *Ask friends who travel for names. Satisfied customers are a high recommendation.*

▶ *A travel agent who travels frequently to the places you want to go has firsthand knowledge. It's your firmest guarantee that the agent will book you into the best places.*

▶ *A certified travel counselor certificate, awarded by the Institute of Certified Travel Agents, means the agent has at least five years of experience and has passed tests on the best procedures for serving travelers.*

▶ *The agency itself should have a stock of industry resources for its agents to use, and a good library of literature and videos for you to browse through.*

TRAVEL AGENTS

A good travel agent compares destinations and tour operators, shares the experiences of other travelers, digs for discounts, and passes along useful written materials to help you decide on your trip—all at no charge. Agents are paid by commissions from the companies whose services they book for you.

Do your own homework. Don't rely solely on a travel agent for the latest information. Rock-bottom rates aren't always on the computer, so travel agents can't always go after the lowest fares.

Beware of agencies that try to book clients with only a single airline, hotel chain, or cruise line. They may be getting rebates from the company over and above their regular commission.

TRAVEL FOR BUSINESS

Get plenty of rest. Don't schedule important meetings within hours of your arrival if you are flying across more than three time zones. Instead, arrive the day before and get a good night's sleep in order to be at your best.

Ask for business amenities. Be sure your hotel has room outlets for computers and fax machines, ample work space, and a safe big enough to hold your equipment when you go out.

Send yourself a fax. If you have brought along a portable computer with a modem but no printer, you can get hard copies of your data by sending a fax to yourself at the hotel.

Avoid airport delays by using carry-on luggage. If you are packing a suit or dress, use a garment bag that will hold underclothes and accessories as well. Carry a briefcase big enough to squeeze in toiletries.

Pocket airport guides help you to locate ticket counters, departure gates, baggage claims, and car rentals so you don't have to waste time hunting for them.

Cut entertainment expenses by taking clients out for an elegant breakfast rather than a multi-course lunch or dinner.

TRAVEL FOR SENIORS

Join CARP (Canadian Association of Retired Persons) as soon as you turn 50. You don't have to be retired to take advantage of CARP's group rates for travel and membership discounts on hotels and car rentals. The Association also publishes a newspaper, *CARP News*. Write to them at 27 Queen St. E., Suite 1304, Toronto, Ont., M5C 2M6. Their telephone number is (416) 363-8748.

Senior discounts. Travelers age 65 and over are entitled to a 15 percent discount on Canadian Airlines and a 10 percent discount on Via Rail. All you have to do is ask.

Tell your age. Reservationists don't know you're eligible for senior discounts if they don't know how old you are. Remember to mention a senior discount when you reserve.

Carry proof of age—a driver's license, Medicare card, or other age-related ID—in case you need it to get discounts at hotels, on car rentals, at tourist attractions, or for local transportation.

Learn while you travel. Elderhostel organizes study-travel packages to over 50 countries. Most programs are open to those over 55 (spouses and companions may be younger). For a free catalog, send a postcard with your name and address to Elderhostel Canada, 308 Wellington St., Kingston, Ont., K7K 7A7, or see the home page on the Internet at http://www.elderhostel.org/.

TRAVEL INSURANCE

Protect your investment. When you book an expensive vacation in advance, buy travel insurance to ensure a refund if you must cancel. (Some policies also cover medical costs if illness interrupts your trip.)

Check your coverage. Look at your own health insurance policy to be sure it covers travel abroad. If not, buy one-time insurance that pays hospital and doctor fees and the cost of emergency transportation home. Be sure that pre-existing conditions are covered.

Compare policies. Before purchasing travel insurance from a cruise line or travel agent, look at comparable offerings from independent companies, which may offer savings.

Premium credit cards. Cards that provide travelers insurance or assistance in case of illness may be worth their higher fees.

TRAVEL SAFETY

Don't look like a tourist. Avoid flashing hotel room or rental car keys, displaying convention bags or badges, wearing a camera around your neck, or doing anything else that announces conspicuously that you are a visitor. Try, at least, to appear to be a confident, sophisticated traveler.

Make noise. Carry a whistle or personal alarm on your key chain. Hold it when you are walking at night and don't be afraid to use it if you feel threatened.

Take main boulevards rather than dark, quiet side streets. Keep to the center of the sidewalk, away from alleyways, doorways, shrubbery, or parked cars that could spell trouble. If you cannot avoid potentially dangerous routes, take a taxi—even for only a short distance.

Use a local shopping bag to carry cameras or other valuables (grocery bags are the least conspicuous). Thieves are less likely to go after local shoppers.

TRAVEL TACTICS

Is it the best deal? Advertised bargains are not always the least expensive. Always ask if a lower price is available.

Sold-out flights and hotels may not stay that way. Try again a week, a day, or even an hour later. A good time to call hotels is just past their 6:00 P.M. check-in deadline; you may find empty seats on flights just after midnight when their reservation deadlines expire.

Count up the surcharges. When you compare rates, be sure that all government, hotel, airport, and airport taxes are included. They can add a hefty chunk of change to the cost of your trip.

Avoid mix-ups with look-alike luggage by giving your bags a distinctive appearance. Tie an unusual luggage tag or a piece of colored yarn to your suitcase, or use a colorful luggage "belt" (which can also prevent your luggage from opening accidentally).

Traveling during the holidays? Try flying on the actual holiday, itself, when bookings are often lighter—and cheaper. Take a flight on the holiday morning, and you may even make it in time for Thanksgiving or Christmas dinner.

MONEY UNDER COVER

When you travel, keep money and valuables safe in one these cleverly designed holders: the Eagle Creek waist pouch (center) that slips easily under your clothes, the Eagle Creek belt (right) with a secret area to stash cash, or the waterproof Saf-Sak ankle wallet that keeps valuables dry at the beach. All are sold through travel catalogs and luggage stores.

TRAVELING ABROAD

The lowest airfares to Europe are often on foreign airlines making intermediate stops en route to Asia, such as Singapore Airlines flying from New York to Singapore via Frankfurt or Amsterdam, or Air India flying from New York to Bombay via London. These airlines fill planes on the first leg of the flight, yet leave room for new passengers boarding in Europe.

Avoid high conversion fees when getting cash abroad by accessing your own bank account through ATM machines on worldwide networks such as Cirrus or Plus. The networks have good conversion rates and their fees are lower than the interest charges for cash advances on credit cards. Ask your bank about ATM locations along your route.

Traveler's checks generally receive unfavorable exchange rates abroad. Pay for large purchases with a credit card, which will give you better rates. Save traveler's checks for out-of-the-way places that don't take cards.

Eat like the natives for economical dining in Europe. For example, order small breakfasts and big midday meals in France, and big breakfasts and sandwich lunches in Scandinavia. Ordering foods not common to the region can result in high restaurant and hotel bills.

Health advice for overseas travel, including required immunizations, is available by calling your local passport office or a travelers' clinic at your local hospitals.

Check the consulate. Make sure to note the address and phone number of the Canadian consulate in the city closest to

the overseas destination you are traveling to. You will need to get in touch with them in cases of emergency, such as reporting a stolen passport.

Use up coins before you leave a foreign country. Bills can be converted into Canadian currency, but coins are usually rejected.

TRAVELING ALONE

Plan your days. Read guidebooks and draw up a daily schedule in advance. It will give you a sense of confidence to have a plan when you wake up each day.

Leave a complete itinerary of your trip with a family member or close friend. Include your travel calendar, flight or train information, and the addresses and telephone numbers of the places where you will be staying.

Bed-and-breakfasts, now available even in big cities, have hosts who can supply inside information about the area—and sometimes a fellow guest for company.

Hotels with dining rooms or room service make it unnecessary to go out alone at night in a strange city. Plan to visit special restaurants for midday meals.

Keep a journal. A diary is a solo traveler's friend. It wards off loneliness by giving you a way of "talking" about your experiences, and it provides a memento of the trip.

Don't overload. Juggling packages and luggage when you're on your own can make you an easy target for thieves.

TRAVELING WITH CHILDREN

Small rewards. Encourage good behavior by promising rewards at the end of each day. Suggesting a swim in the hotel pool or a rented movie in the room can give kids something to anticipate.

FINDING GOOD COMPANIONS

If you'd rather not travel alone, you can match up with other travelers in a number of ways.

▶ *The Travel Companion Exchange (P.O. Box 833, Amityville, NY 11701; 516-454-0880) will assist you in finding a compatible person who wants to go places too.*

▶ *Check campus bulletin boards at local universities; students often are willing to split expenses to drive back home for the holidays.*

▶ *A tour operator often will match you with another single traveler who wants to share a room for the trip.*

▶ *Plan a trip with a friendly group such as your bridge club, Sunday School class, or work associates.*

▶ *Associations you belong to—museum or theater subscribers or alumni groups—may sponsor congenial tours.*

Stop often. On car trips, stop briefly every two to three hours to allow kids to use the bathroom and run off their excess energy.

Let children pack and carry their own small bags, complete with pajamas, toothbrush, and favorite toys. They'll be ready for bed at night in no time.

Be prepared. Carry snacks and a thermos of water or juice and have a sweater and a change of clothes handy, just in case there are delays along the way.

Dress kids in bright clothing when you are taking them to crowded places such as national parks, amusement parks, or zoos. A colorful shirt or hat will make it easier for you to spot your child.

Air safety. Your lap is not a secure place for a baby on an airplane. To be safe, pay the fare for an extra seat, then strap the baby in a baby seat into the plane seat. Some airlines permit children under two to occupy a seat free if the flight is not sold out.

Personal scrapbooks. Buy each child a photo album, notebook, or scrapbook—and even a disposable camera—to take along on a trip. Let them take pictures of sights, pick out postcards and other mementos, and write captions for their "vacation books."

JET-SETTING PETS

A small pet will find air travel less traumatic when it is settled into a soft-sided carrier designed to fit snugly under a plane seat. These portable dens, such as the Original Sherpa Bag (left) or the Kartu Bag (right) from Sherpa's Pet Trading Company, are approved by most domestic airlines. Available through pet supply stores.

TRAVELING WITH PETS

Visit the vet. Before you travel with your pet, schedule a checkup to be sure your animal is fit to go. Obtain a health certificate and any documentation of inoculations required by an airline.

Road rules. A pet must be thoroughly car-broken if you plan to take it on an extended road trip. Make your pet feel at home by bringing along its bedding and favorite toys. Give it plenty of exercise before you head out, but to avoid motion sickness, wait at least four hours after your pet has been fed. If your pet starts to salivate heavily, is restless, and throws up, feed it candy or a spoonful of honey to ease its car sickness.

Putting on the dog. Many hotels, motels, and B&B's welcome pets, but be sure to call ahead. For information on pet-friendly lodgings, read the newsletter *DogGone* (561-569-8434; $30 for a one-year subscription) or any of the CAA 'Tours' books.

Lost and found. If you are taking a long road trip with your pet, add a temporary paper tag to its collar with the phone number and address of a friend or relative. Or update the tag daily to reflect your changing lodgings.

Nonstop flights are safer for animals; transfers between planes and unscheduled delays between flights complicate their care.

 Label clearly. Travel containers must be plainly marked "live animal." Tags with your travel itinerary, name, address, and phone number should be firmly attached. Pets should also be clearly identified on a collar.

Avoid bad-weather travel. Cargo compartments aren't climate controlled, so interior temperatures may become dangerously hot or cold when flights are delayed. If you must fly in summer, take a night flight.

A NEW WAY TO PLANT A TREE

It was once believed that the bigger the planting hole and the more enrichment in the soil, the better. Research now suggests that an easier method fosters stronger growth.

▶ *Dig a hole three times as wide as the root ball of the tree and just deep enough so that the root ball top is at ground level (except in poorly drained soils, where a third of the ball should stick up above ground level). Roughen the sides of the planting hole with a garden fork.*

▶ *If planting a container-grown tree, slip out the root ball, score it on all four sides with a knife, and set it in the hole.*

▶ *If planting a balled tree, set the root ball into the hole, cut any twine wrapped around the ball, and roll the burlap down to expose the ball's top half.*

▶ *If planting a bare-root tree, separate the roots and spread them around inside the hole.*

▶ *In heavy clay or sand, mix a modest amount of compost or peat moss into the dirt that will be used to refill the hole (never more than one part enrichment to one part soil). Leave ordinary soil unimproved.*

▶ *Barely cover the root ball with soil. Firm it, then create a 10 cm (4 in.) high berm around the outer edge of the hole and fill the resulting reservoir with water.*

TREES

Bargain or headache? Inexpensive, jumbo-size trees may seem like a bargain at the nursery, but they can turn into a maintenance headache. They are both large and cheap because they grow fast. Within a few years they may outgrow their sites and require extensive pruning.

Stake a newly planted tree that stands more than 1.5 m (5 ft) high so that it has support while its roots get a firm grip. Drive two or three stakes into the ground around the tree and run wires from them to the tree. Thread the wires through short sections of garden hose to protect the trunk, and don't make the wires too tight—a young tree needs to bend to attain its full strength.

Plan for less cleanup by avoiding trees such as sweet gums, horse chestnuts, and mulberries, which drop messy fruits. Look for seedless varieties of landscape trees, such as 'Marshall's Seedless' ash.

TRUNKS

Store extra blankets, linens, out-of-season clothing, and holiday decorations in trunks to free up closets and drawers for items you use every day.

Kindling holder. Place a sturdy old trunk near a fireplace or wood-burning stove as an attractive receptacle for holding wood.

A decorative antique trunk can do double duty as a storage unit and a coffee table, end table, night stand, or bench.

A trunk in a child's room can hold toys, art projects, or clothes. Make sure that the lid has a hold-open brace or an antislam device so the child can't be injured.

Renew the scent in cedar chests by lightly sanding the inside with fine-grain sandpaper. Vacuum well to pick up the particles before replacing the chest's contents.

T-SHIRTS

A classic topper. Men's or boys' white cotton undershirts—crew- or V-necked—make an inexpensive woman's wardrobe staple. Wear them at work under wool or linen jackets, at the movies with slacks and a sweater, and on the tennis court, over shorts.

Poolside comfort. For an easy, comfortable cover-up by the pool, try an oversized T-shirt. Women can find colorful, roomy ones in men's departments.

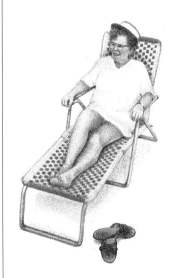

Fun time. Children can personalize their own T-shirts with fabric paints purchased from art stores. Buy white T-shirts. Set the paints up on a well-covered table. Put a sheet of cardboard inside each shirt to keep the paint from going through to the back, and let the kids use their imaginations.

Afterlife. Don't discard old T-shirts. Soft and lint-free, they make great rags for dusting and polishing furniture, washing cars, and general household cleaning.

TUITION

Start early. Save for college tuition by putting aside all your extra income. In addition to a percentage of your salary, you might earmark all cash gifts and any unexpected windfalls for college savings plans.

Don't transfer assets to kids if there is a chance they will qualify for financial aid. Under financial aid, some colleges require a certain amount of family assets to be used for college expenses, but the percentage is higher for assets in a student's name than for those in a parent's name.

Adjust your finances. If possible, avoid taking pension distributions, bonuses, or large income-tax refunds in the base year to be reviewed for your child's financial aid. These items will increase your income level, thus reducing chances for assistance.

If you need financial aid, apply promptly to the school where your child has accepted a place.

Student grants and subsidies are often distributed on a first-come, first-served basis; the earlier you apply the better. You can appeal a financial-aid offer, if you feel it is inadequate to your situation.

Beyond student aid, investigate federal loans not linked to an aid package. Their interest rates can be as much as three percentage points lower than those on private bank loans. Apply through the college financial aid office or at a bank or credit union.

TURKEY

The bigger the bird, the better for feeding a crowd. If your turkey is less than 5.5 kg (12 lb), you'll need 350 g to 450 g (¾ –1 lb) per person; if it weighs more, 225 g to 350 g (½ – ¾ lb) is enough.

Buy turkey breast instead of a whole turkey if your family does not like dark meat. The price is higher, but the actual cost is lower because there is less waste. Boned, rolled turkey roast is not as flavorful as a breast with bones.

For healthier eating, substitute lean ground turkey in any recipe that calls for ground meat. It is less flavorful, but extra spices and herbs can enliven it.

TURTLES

Hold your pet turtle correctly, for its safety and yours. When lifting the creature, place one hand under the stomach and the other on top of the shell. Be careful of the claws, which can injure you.

To care for a turtle, buy two sets of tongs. Use one for food and the other to remove waste; label and store them separately.

Wash your hands after handling your turtle. Even though salmonella-infected turtles are rare these days, new pet turtles should be tested for the disease.

Give your turtle a bath. Turtles get dirty and will likely enjoy a weekly spritzing.

To transport a turtle, put it in a shoe box lined with moist towels to keep it properly hydrated.

RIGHT STUFF

BIG SCHOLARSHIP BOOKS

The cost of higher education is daunting, but many surprising places offer money to pursue academic goals. Scholarship guides list thousands of grants for which you might be eligible—from special grants for undergraduate women studying engineering, to funds for children of parents involved in harness racing. Indices, arranged by field of study, by institution, or by alphabet, help you research the options. Look for scholarship guides in bookstores and libraries.

RIGHT STUFF

TWINS PEEK AND SLEEP

Twin births are on the rise, so parents take note: the Double Delight by Nene Quality Baby Products (below) is a crib to please both parents and babies. It is a space-saving crib-for-two that fits conveniently into a corner and costs less than two baby beds. It is joined by a

Plexiglas separator, so that infants can see each other yet have personal space. Available in specialty baby stores.

TUTORS & TUTORING

Many schools—public, parochial, or private—have programs that match volunteer mentor-tutors with youngsters who need help; increasingly they are sponsored by community businesses and churches. If there is no such program in your district, work with local organizations to start one.

Good time for a tutor. When children change schools, they may have trouble adjusting to the new school curriculum. Talk to teachers about areas of study that are new to the youngsters, and ask about appropriate tutoring aids.

Age differences. For elementary students, educators recommend a combination of in-school and parent tutoring. For teenagers, the most useful assistance is teacher or peer tutoring.

To be a tutor, you need to enjoy working with children. Teacher training is not required—only patience and enthusiasm. Call your local school system about programs. Tutors in reading and basic arithmetic are in particular demand at the elementary school level. In high schools, help is often needed in language skills, math, science, and foreign languages.

Your artistic talent in art, drama, or music may prove invaluable to schools that have been forced to cut back on the arts. Community members can set up and be involved in after-school classes or lessons on a volunteer basis.

TWINS

Newborn twins can wreak havoc on a household. Lessen the disruptions and loss of sleep by getting them on the same schedule as soon as possible. When one baby wakes up, awaken the other and feed them at the same time.

The weaker nurser of twins will have an easier time if the stronger nurser feeds first to get the breast milk flowing.

Different formulas for bottle-fed twins can cause unhappy mix-ups. To keep track of which bottle belongs to whom, slip different-colored rubber bands on them just below the caps.

Be alert to the feelings of other siblings, especially when twins are little. Well-meaning friends often fuss over the twins and forget to notice the other children. Do your best to steer the conversation around to include everyone.

Bonding with other siblings is as important as bonding with the other twin. If your older child is in day care and the facility has an infant room, reserve one space for the twins. Alternate them each week—one twin at the center, where the sibling can look in on the baby and play with her, and the other twin at home with you. When the twins are older, plan outings that pair one twin with a sibling while the other twin stays home with other family members.

For information about having twins or being a twin, write the Parents of Multiple Births Association of Canada (POMBA) at 240 Graff Ave., P.O. Box 22005, Stratford, Ont., N5A 7V6, or call (905) 272-2203. The International Twins Association (6898 Channel Rd. NE, Minneapolis, MN 55432) is also a good resource.

Treat twins as individuals from the start. Refer to them by their given names instead of jointly as "the twins." Give toys and items of clothing that express each one's unique personality. Photograph them separately on occasion (and to avoid any confusion later, write the child's name on the back of each photo).

| U M B R E L L A S   T O   U S E D   C A R S |

UMBRELLAS

Drip dry. If you don't have an umbrella rack, set a guest's wet umbrella outside your door so that it won't damage your floor, or let it dry open in the bathtub.

When choosing an umbrella, try to match the handle size to your hand to make it easy to hold. And remember, natural cloth umbrellas, handsome as they may be, saturate more quickly than synthetics and may leave you damp.

Think small. Invest in at least one sturdy miniature umbrella that fits securely in a briefcase or purse. It will come in handy for surprise showers and for travel.

Safety under cover. Stay alert when walking with an umbrella. Watch out for automobile traffic and avoid oncoming pedestrians and low overhangs. Teach your kids to be careful too.

When commuting, carry a plastic bag in which to stow a wet umbrella; it will protect your clothes and the inside of a tote or briefcase once you are seated.

UPHOLSTERED FURNITURE

Fabric guards. When buying upholstered furniture, take the fabric protection option. Warranteed fabric guards, applied at the factory, pay for themselves in extended wear. (Aerosols that you apply yourself don't bond as well.) When a drop of water no longer beads up on the surface, have new guards professionally applied.

Buy extra fabric when you purchase a new upholstered chair or sofa. If you need to cover a cushion later, the same fabric may be unavailable or from another dye lot, making it noticeably different.

Check out construction details carefully. By law, all materials used in new upholstered furniture must be listed on the label.

USED CARS

Signs of odometer fraud: the dashboard has missing screws, scratches, or a misaligned cover; odometer numbers don't line up; the tires are new (a late-model car with less than 48,000 km [30,000 mi] should have original radials); or the service record is missing (it would show the mileage when maintenance jobs were done).

Avoid classified ads if the price is far lower than other vehicles of the same class, if the seller offers numerous vehicles (he may front for a dealer), or if the same phone number appears in several ads.

Title search. If you question the status of a car's ownership, have a title search done before you put down your money for stolen goods. Contact your local department of motor vehicles.

QUESTIONS FOR A USED-CAR DEALER

Before buying a used car, you need answers to the questions below. If the dealer (or seller) balks, go elsewhere.

◗ *Where did you obtain the car? May I contact the previous owner to talk about the car?*

◗ *Can you confirm the accuracy of the odometer reading?*

◗ *Has the car ever been recalled? Has the car ever been bought back by the manufacturer as a "lemon"? If so, may I see verification that the problem was corrected?*

◗ *What repairs have been done on the car? Do you have the service records? May I see them?*

◗ *Has the car ever been painted? If so, why? Has it been in an accident? Was it ever salvaged? Caught in a flood?*

◗ *Has your certified mechanic inspected it? May I see the results? May I have an independent mechanic inspect it?*

◗ *What warranty comes with the car?*

VACATIONS TO VOLUNTEERING

VACATIONS

Packed to go. Keep nonperishable essentials that go with you on every trip tucked permanently in your suitcase. Include such items as a small sewing kit, a travel clock, a flashlight, a Swiss army knife, a portable hair dryer, and a fully stocked toiletries kit.

Take mini vacations. Studies show that taking frequent three- or four-day trips or long weekends can revitalize you almost as much as longer holidays taken only once or twice a year.

Book a cruise for an easy, stress-free vacation. The advance payment includes room, board, port taxes, and other incidental costs, so you won't have to worry about carrying much cash. You are free to participate in the numerous ship activities or simply daydream in a deck chair all day. Best of all, a cruise allows you to visit many ports of call—yet sleep in the same bed every night.

Don't overdo it. Don't cram so many activities into your vacation that you have no time for rest and relaxation. Be flexible; allow time for unplanned events that can make vacations magical.

VACUUM CLEANERS

Versatile vacuums. Next time you buy a vacuum cleaner, look for the kind that lets you reverse the air flow. You can use it to dry wet boots, defrost the freezer, blow leaves and dirt out of the doorway, and dry hand washables.

 Empty the bag often. Vacuums can't work efficiently when the bag is too full. Even a half-full bag saps up to 40 percent of the machine's cleaning power.

Save wear and tear on your vacuum cleaner by picking up coins, paper clips, staples, hairpins, and other heavy or sharp objects by hand as you sweep. Sucking them into the vacuum cleaner can damage the fan.

Reuse expensive bags. When your vacuum cleaner bag is full, clip off the top, empty out the dirt, staple it closed again, and reuse it. Durable bags can be reused three or four times.

Use a long extension cord so that you won't have to be contin-

---

A TOOL FOR EVERY VACUUM CHORE

Dirt can't hide from these specialized vacuum cleaner attachments from Ideaworks. Clockwise, from top: the Ceiling Fan Vac fits snugly onto fan blades, eliminating dust fallout; the Wacky Vac sucks dust from between computer keys and inside drawers; the Mini Blind Vac cleans fabric, metal, or plastic blinds, four slats at a time; the Lint Brush tidies upholstery and clothing; the Pet Brush grooms your pet and removes shedding hair. These brushes are sold through housewares catalogs and under the Eureka label in retail stores.

ually unplugging and plugging in the vacuum as you work your way through the house. Make sure the cord is the proper gauge for the vacuum cleaner.

VALENTINE'S DAY

A rosy compromise. If you can't afford to send a dozen roses and one just isn't enough, select three, and ask the florist to surround them with sprigs of baby's breath.

Love thy neighbor. If romantic love is not on your horizon this year, invite a few neighbors or friends over for a special Valentine's Day dinner. Decorate your table in non-traditional yellow (the color of friendship) instead of red or pink. Give each guest a chocolate kiss to let him know how much you care.

Instead of icing a Valentine cake, cut a heart out of paper, place it on a chocolate cake, and sprinkle powdered sugar over the top. Lift off the paper, and you'll have a perfect heart design. For a lacy effect, use a heart-shaped doily.

VARNISHING

Prevent bubbles. Don't shake a varnish can before opening it, don't stir it fast when thinning it, and never wipe the brush across the rim (tap it on the inside of the can instead).

Brush varnish on by flowing it instead of dabbing it. Sweep your brush from one end of a panel or section to the other with a single stroke, tilting the handle at a gentle incline from the surface. Don't begin a stroke in the middle of a panel; the brush will leave marks.

Season the brush. Before using a brush, bend the bristles back and forth to dislodge loose hairs. Pull them out, then soak the brush in linseed oil for a few hours. Finally, shake the brush out in a big paper bag, and clean with paint thinner.

ROMANTIC VALENTINE GIFTS

V

Flowers and candy are traditional Valentine's Day gifts, but why not show your special love in a unique way?

▶ *Something indulgent. Give your loved one a gift certificate for something utterly indulgent, such as a massage, a facial, or a day at a spa.*

▶ *Something soft. Buy your partner a gift that feels luxurious, such as a cashmere scarf, soft gloves, or a kitten.*

▶ *Something useful. Instead of slinky lingerie, buy your beloved something useful but fun, like skis or ice skates.*

▶ *Something thoughtful. Instead of a conventional ring, buy an antique charm or locket to mark the day.*

▶ *Something promised. Make a gift certificate, promising dinners cooked for a week or grass cut for a year.*

▶ *Something playful. Treat your love to a day at the circus, the zoo, or the amusement park.*

▶ *Something sweet. Instead of a box of chocolates, bring your loved one a heart-shaped cheesecake—if that is her favorite—or a giant chocolate kiss.*

Varnish surfaces horizontally where possible, to assure a drip-less coat. Turn furniture on its side, pull out drawers, and upend them to avoid vertical varnishing.

Down with holidays. Keep the piece you're varnishing between you and a bright light so you can spot "holidays," or places the brush has missed. The reflected light will help you distinguish the new coat from the previous one.

VASES

Same flowers, different vase. Cluster a variety of vases—short or tall, round or slender, clear or opaque, white or brightly colored. Fill the vases with bouquets of one kind of flower, such as daffodils, tulips, or dahlias.

Improvise vases out of unusual containers. Put yellow daffodils in a blue medicine bottle; arrange lilies in a stainless steel cocktail shaker; put violets in a small creamer. If the vessel is tippy, put sand in the bottom.

Clean a narrow-necked vase by filling it with vinegar, letting it soak for an hour, then scrubbing it with a bottle brush.

VEGETABLES

Cruditees. For hors d'oeuvres, health- and calorie-conscious guests always appreciate fresh vegetables, such as carrots, celery, cucumbers, broccoli, beets, and cherry tomatoes. Make sure any accompanying dip is low in fat.

 Steam vegetables. Get in the habit of steaming—rather than boiling—vegetables. Not only will you lose fewer nutrients, you'll save time since vegetables cook more quickly when they are steamed.

Fool your kids. If you can't get them to eat vegetables, sneak vegetables into recipes that don't normally call for them. Grated carrots and zucchini, for example, can be added to tomato sauces, meatloaf, and muffins with hardly a telltale sign—except for added flavor and texture.

Pure white. To help keep white potatoes and cauliflower from turning gray, add a teaspoon of lemon juice or vinegar to their cooking liquid.

Faux steak. Grill a fresh portobello mushroom and serve it as your "meat" course. Not only is it delicious, it has the flavor and texture of a meaty steak without the fat or calories.

Soupçon. Don't discard the little, tough stems of asparagus, broccoli, cauliflower, mushrooms, or other vegetables. Instead, steam them until they are soft, then puree them for soups or sauces.

PUTTING VEGETABLES UP FRONT

For a vegetable dish to work as an entree, simply substitute hearty vegetables for meat in any number of familiar dishes. Here are a few easy options:

▶ *Basic Vegetable Stew. Stew in a strong broth a melange of your favorite vegetables—squash, carrots, mushrooms, onions, tomatoes, cauliflower. Add beans, pasta, rice, or potatoes to make the stew heartier. Season to taste.*

▶ *Vegetable Pot Pie. Place basic vegetable stew in a casserole dish; top with your favorite pastry dough (store-bought pie crust and puff pastry are the easiest); bake.*

▶ *Vegetarian Shepherd's Pie. Place basic vegetable stew in a casserole dish; top with mashed potatoes; bake, uncovered, until the potatoes are golden brown.*

▶ *Vegetable Lasagna. Sauté "meaty" vegetables such as eggplant, mushrooms, and zucchini; combine them in a bechamel or tomato sauce; layer with pasta and cheeses; bake until bubbly.*

▶ *Vegetable Frittata. Arrange cooked vegetables (including potatoes) in a skillet; mix together eggs, milk, cheese, and seasonings; pour egg mixture over the vegetables; saute.*

VEGETARIAN DIETS

Go for Chinese food when eating out. Chinese menus feature a variety of vegetable dishes, many featuring a prime vegetarian protein source—tofu, or bean curd.

Vegetarian lifestyle. Becoming a vegetarian involves more than eliminating meat from your diet. Important nutrients that come from meat now must be derived from non-meat sources to maintain good health. Study nutrition guides and vegetarian cookbooks carefully to be sure that you are eating a balanced diet.

Complete protein for vegetarians comes from dairy products, soybeans, and combinations of grains, legumes, nuts, seeds, and vegetables that have complementary amino acids, such as dried beans and rice, or hummus (mashed chickpeas and sesame paste) and bread.

Get sufficient vitamin B-12, which is found naturally in animal-based foods but not in vegetables, into a vegetarian diet by eating fortified cereal or by taking a vitamin supplement.

VETERINARIANS

Your friendly vet. Never wait until your pet is sick or injured before finding a reliable vet. Minutes can be vital if your pet has an accident. Get to know your vet, and have your pet checked annually to ensure its health.

Create professional-looking home videos with the Home Video Producer by Videonics. With the Thumbs Up control box (sold separately), you can edit the scenes in the order you want them, and delete the ones you'd rather forget. With the Sound Effects Mixer, you can add voice-overs and music to create an ultra-slick production. Sold at electronics stores.

When you move, take your animal's medical records with you so you won't have to reinoculate a pet unnecessarily when you go to a new vet. (Call the local veterinary medical association for recommendations of veterinarians in the new area.)

Always be there to assist the vet whenever she examines your pet. The animal trusts you and will be comforted by your presence and reassuring voice and will be more willingly restrained by you than by a stranger.

A date for Fido. When you shift to next year's calendar, mark the days for your pets' periodic visits to the vet. Also, flag the days when you should administer heartworm or anti-flea pills. (Some of these medications come with reminder stickers.)

Pay now, argue later, if you have a dispute with a veterinarian. In some cases, a veterinarian can legally keep your animal until you pay your bill. After your pet is safely home, you can pursue your grievance by complaining to the local veterinary medical board, seeking mediation, or suing.

VIDEOCASSETTE RECORDERS

Avoid tape jams in a VCR cassette—just as you do for your audiotapes—by turning the hub with your finger to tighten the tape before putting the videocassette into the machine.

Be kind to your VCR. Don't place it next to a radiator, in bright sunlight, or in an enclosed area without ventilation. If you must stack it on top of the TV, insert blocks at least 12 mm (½ in.) thick under each corner of the VCR so it won't overheat. (Paint the blocks black so that they won't show.)

Prevent wrinkles in your videotapes by rewinding them completely after each viewing and storing them upright on their shortest side. The loaded reel should be on the bottom.

Stop static electricity from damaging your VCR (or TV)—which can happen in an exces-

sively dry, carpeted room—by lightly spraying the carpet with a solution of water and a few drops of liquid dishwashing soap.

VIDEOTAPING

Smooth tracking shots can be taken from a rolling chair or cart, provided you have a smooth path to roll along. Sit securely in the chair or on the cart and have someone push it along the path of the shot.

Panning made easy. To make a smooth pan shot, turn slowly from your waist without moving your feet. Hold the shot for a moment at its start and finish so that the audience has a chance to become oriented.

Stabilizing the camera. Sit astride a chair with your elbows on the chair back, lean on the hood or trunk of a car (but be sure the engine is off, so there's no vibration), kneel on one knee and prop the camera on your raised knee, or position beanbags under the camera, especially on uneven surfaces.

When videotaping children, shoot at their eye level to better capture facial expressions. Keep taping sessions short so that the kids don't get too bored—and look it—or too silly.

VINEGAR

Store vinegar according to type. Plain vinegar goes in the cupboard; its acidity gives it an almost indefinite shelf life. Flavored vinegars retain their taste longer when stored in the refrigerator.

Balsamic vinegar—aromatic and slightly sweet—imparts a piquant flavor. The best is fermented from the juice of sweet white grapes and then aged for as long as 10 years. The longer the vinegar ages, the sweeter and mellower it becomes.

Adapt the oil-to-vinegar ratio in a salad dressing to the strength of the vinegar. A dressing with a mild white wine vinegar would be mixed at a ratio of 3 to 1, for example, while a dressing with a flavorful balsamic vinegar may require more oil and less vinegar. It's really a matter of individual preferences, so taste as you make.

VITAMINS & MINERALS

Think bright colors when you shop for fruits and vegetables. Vitamins C and beta-carotene are found in orange cantaloupes, oranges, carrots, and sweet potatoes and in green broccoli, Brussels sprouts, kale, and spinach. Together with vitamin E, vitamin C and beta-carotene (called antioxidents) repair cell damage and may help reduce the risk of cancer, heart disease, and other ailments.

Save the cooking water when you boil vegetables. It's full of vitamins and minerals that have leached out of the vegetables while they were cooking. Freeze the broth in airtight containers, then use it later to steam rice or to make gravies and sauces.

On a diet? If you consume less than 1,200 calories per day, you may not be ingesting sufficient vitamins and minerals. Take a vita-

Raspberry Vinegar

Vinegars flavored with herbs, spices, and fruits, transform salads from ordinary to extraordinary. Store-bought flavored vinegars are usually expensive while making your own is easy. Try this recipe, customizing it, if you like, with a pinch or two of allspice.

1 In a medium-size, noncorrosive bowl, pile 500 mL (2 cups) of fresh raspberries.

2 Sprinkle on 60 mL (¼ cup) granulated sugar, add 5 mL (1 tsp) of vanilla, and toss.

3 Add 375 mL (1½ cups) white wine vinegar to the berries. Cover and let stand at room temperature for 24 hours.

4 Strain the berries in a sieve placed over a large measuring cup. Discard the berries.

5 Pour the vinegar into a sterilized jar or decorative bottle. It keeps, refrigerated, for 6 months.

min supplement every day while you are dieting.

Take with meals. Vitamin and mineral supplements are absorbed best when taken with food. The exception is an iron supplement, which is more absorbable when taken on an empty stomach.

 Eat a variety of foods within a balanced diet, including plenty of fruits and vegetables, to provide all the vitamins and minerals you require. Pregnant women and people with medical problems may need to take a vitamin supplement.

If you smoke, eat foods rich in vitamin C. Smoking depletes the vitamin in your body. A high intake of vitamin C may help lower your risk of lung cancer.

VOLUNTEERING

Find opportunities for volunteer work at hospitals, nursing homes, schools, museums, and churches. Or go on-line: check out the Internet NonProfit Center (www.non-profits.org/) and the web sites of nonprofit groups in your area.

Research the organization. Call the Better Business Bureau's Philanthropic Advisory Service, which offers guidelines for evaluating local charities.

Narrow your choices. Determine what type of volunteer work most interests you. Doing something you feel strongly about will keep you motivated and increase your personal satisfaction.

Do what you can, even if it's only for an hour or two a month. Tutor a child, read to a housebound person, or make fundraising calls for an alumni group. Most volunteer groups appreciate any amount of time you can afford to give.

WALKING

Do what comes naturally. Walking benefits your health—and you don't have to resort to fancy techniques or revamp your stride. Just speed up your normal walk a bit, and maintain the pace.

Don't like to walk alone? Join a local walking club or recruit friends to form one. Some malls open early for walking groups.

For a challenging workout, vary your routine. Walk up hills or stairs. Try it on sand or in knee-deep water in a pool. Walk backward. Monitor your heart rate so that you don't overdo it.

Take a walk at lunch. Fresh air and exercise clears the mind, loosens up muscles, and energizes you for the afternoon's work.

WALL COVERINGS

Buy extra. Don't count on being able to get more of your wallpaper if you run out before finishing the job. Colors may vary from one shipment to another. Hold on to leftovers to repair future damage.

Textured wall coverings, like burlap, can hide imperfections in old walls and cost less than having walls replastered or repaired.

Paint before papering. It is easier to clean paste off the ceiling and trim than it is to remove paint splatters from wallpaper.

Taking it off. Cloth-backed vinyl paper can often be pulled easily off a wall. If it won't budge, use a chemical remover, an electric steamer, or even a hair dryer to loosen the glue.

IN STRIDE AND ON TRACK

An electronic pedometer can be a useful tool for serious walkers, hikers, and joggers. A basic pedometer, like Sportline Model #342 (left), accurately tracks how far you travel up to 1,600 km (1,000 mi). More elaborate models, such as the Accusplit A210F (center) and Sportline Model #355 Pulse Pedometer (right), also measure stride, pulse rate, and the number of calories burned.

WALL REPAIR

Patch a crack in drywall by making it wider first. Pull a sharp object such as an old screwdriver or a triangular can opener along the crack. Then fill the crack with joint compound and feather the mixture along the crack's edges.

Plug tiny holes in a plaster wall with a paste made of flour, salt, and water. White toothpaste also works well for plugging small holes.

Find a wall stud with a magnetic compass: the compass needle will move when it is attracted by the nails in the stud. The adjacent studs usually will be located 40 cm (16 in.) to either side.

A matching patch. To patch a painted plaster wall in one step, mix some of the same color paint used to paint the wall into the spackling compound before you fill the hole.

WARDROBE PLANNING

Test run. The day before an important event, try on your entire outfit—including undergarments, shoes, and jewelry—to make sure everything fits and looks appropriate. If pieces are missing or don't look good, you still have time to make changes.

Shore up an old wardrobe without spending a lot of money by adding new accessories. A colorful shawl, for example, can revive an old winter coat, an interesting belt can spruce up classic pants, and a pretty tie or scarf can rev up last year's blouse.

A spot of color. Liven up a somber man's suit with a square of bright material poking out of the breast pocket. A colorful handkerchief or small patterned silk scarf is just the right size and weight for the accent you need.

At the end of each season, take your shoes to the repair shop for new heels and soles and patch-ups. Wash or dry-clean all garments before storing them.

Bon voyage! Be prepared for any kind of weather or occasion when traveling. Pack a multiseasonal wardrobe, such as clothes made of lightweight wool. Include items that can be layered—a cotton turtleneck, a sweater, a jacket, and a raincoat with a removable lining—and therefore easily taken off or put on. Pack pieces that are comfortable for daytime wear, but with the addition of a string of pearls, earrings, or a pretty scarf, can double as evening wear.

WASHERS & DRYERS

On the level. To keep a washer or dryer quiet, make sure it is sitting squarely on its site. Using a carpenter's level placed on the machine's top, check the appliance from right to left and front to back to see if it's on a slant. If it is, use a wrench to adjust the feet on the bottom of the machine at the appropriate corners until the level shows that it is even.

Remove mineral buildup from your washing machine by filling the washer with water, adding 250 mL (1 cup) of white vinegar, and letting the mixture run through a complete wash cycle.

EASY DOES IT — A WORKING WOMAN'S WARDROBE

Putting together a different outfit to wear to work each day can seem daunting, particularly for those on a budget or with no extra time. Here are some tips on how to do it.

▶ *Look for versatility. Invest in wardrobe building blocks— such as a classically cut blazer or a pair of wool pants— that will serve as the foundation for many different looks.*

▶ *Choose classics for your building blocks. Update them with trendy accessories: pair a basic black sheath dress, for example, with a leopard-print scarf.*

▶ *Look for seasonless clothes. Buy pieces you can wear year-round: lightweight wools or challis; sturdy cottons, linens, and silks; clothes in neutral colors.*

▶ *Spend your money on quality instead of quantity. A solidly constructed jacket in a lush, long-lasting fabric will give you many years of use.*

▶ *Shy away from fussy or constricting garments. A complicated piece of clothing requiring constant adjustment distracts from the work at hand.*

RIGHT STUFF

To take the work out of washing delicate articles by hand, wash them in your washing machine (on the gentle cycle with warm water), but make sure they are protected by using a mesh laundry bag. Separate your wash, and put cotton knits in one bag, pantyhose in another, lacy lingerie in a third, white linen in a fourth, and so on. Mesh laundry bags are inexpensive, so buying several won't strain your budget. In fact, they'll ensure long life for your most fragile pieces.

Tame those suds. When too much detergent whips up excess lather in your washing machine, just sprinkle salt on the foam to help settle it down.

The colder the water, the more detergent you need to get clothes clean. One sign of too little detergent is the presence of lint on the finished laundry. With enough detergent, lint is retained in the wash water long enough to be washed away in the rinse cycle instead of being redeposited on the clothes.

Speed up drying time for small loads by tossing a dry bath towel in with the wet laundry to help absorb the moisture.

Dryers as humidifiers. You can purchase a special accessory that allows you to vent moisture from the dryer indoors instead of outdoors during winter or when the air inside your house dries out from continual heating. A single dryer load can add more than 3.7 L (0.83 gal.) of water to the air inside the house.

Dryer won't run? Before you call the repairman, make sure you've shut the door tightly. Next check the plug, then the circuit breaker or fuse. On a gas dryer, check the pilot light.

WASTEBASKETS

Fun alternatives to ordinary wastebaskets add to a room's special ambience—an oversize terracotta planter, for example, in a sunroom. (Fit the planter with a plastic insert that can easily be dumped.) In a rustic den, try a peach or apple basket.

Tempt kids into neat habits with amusing wastebaskets. In a young child's room, use a giant, brightly colored, plastic container with a clown face painted on the opening. For an older youngster (or a less-than-tidy adult), place the wastebasket below a small, toy, basketball hoop.

Match a wastebasket to a room's decor with matching wallpaper, upholstery material, or curtain fabric. Measure and cut the wallpaper or fabric to fit the sides of an inexpensive metal waste can, then glue it with wallpaper paste or fabric. Spray a fabric-covered can with a stain guard.

WATCHES

Refashion a watch by switching wristbands. Have styles on hand to use with a variety of outfits or for different occasions. For example, alternate sporty cloth bands with dressy metallic ones. Add a similar gold or silver bracelet on the same wrist with your watch.

Old timer. If you have an antique watch that is too valuable or delicate to wear, consider pinning it on a piece of velvet and putting it in a picture frame, or placing it under a glass cloche on a table, shelf, or mantle.

When you're traveling, tape a spare watch battery to the inside of your toiletries kit or suitcase.

Gentle reminder. If you are chronically forgetful, buy a digital watch with an alarm. Set its beeper to go off whenever you need to make a phone call, for example, or take your medication.

WATER CONSERVATION

Tank trick. Fill a plastic soap bottle or a large soda bottle with water or sand and put it in the toilet tank to save water on each flush. Don't use a brick—it can begin to disintegrate, causing serious plumbing problems.

Fill them up. Wait until you have a large load of laundry or a full dishwasher before you run your appliance; you'll save electricity as well as water.

Cold catch. Does it take a minute for your bathwater to get hot? If so, don't waste the water; instead catch it in a clean bucket and use it to water the plants.

Collect and store rainwater with equipment readily available through hardware stores, garden supply stores, and catalogs. Rainwater is ideal for such non-drinking uses as watering the garden.

WATER HEATERS

Be on the safe side. Don't store any flammable items, such as household cleaners, solvents, paint and paint supplies, or old rags, near a gas water heater.

Prevent scalds—and trim heating bills in the process—by lowering the thermostat of your water heater to 49°C (120° F). Small children and the elderly are particularly prone to hot-water burns.

Stop sediment buildup before troubles arise. Drain your water-heater tank into a pail, pan, or through a hose until the water runs clear. If your home has hard water, drain the tank about once a month; if your home has soft water, do it only two to three times a year.

Noisy plumbing? Try lowering the temperature setting of your water heater, which may be creating bursts of steam that cause the pipes to clang.

If your hot water runs cold, check the pilot light on your gas water heater. If it needs to be reignited, just follow the directions printed on the unit. On an electric unit, check the breaker box or fuse panel.

Water off, power off. Always turn off the power on the water heater if you turn off the water supply to the house. If the gas is left on in a gas-fired water heater, pressure could build up inside the heater and cause an explosion; in an electric unit, the internal elements could burn out and have to be replaced.

WATER QUALITY

Who's responsible? If your water comes from a private well or groundwater source, you alone are responsible for its safety. If your water comes from a public supply, the Environmental Protection Agency (EPA) requires that you be notified if your drinking water doesn't meet safety standards. Don't be too trusting, though. Test the water occasionally on your own just to be sure.

Test the water. You can't judge water safety without a test. Your water can exhibit an unpleasant color, odor, or taste but not be harmful; on the other hand, it can contain toxic ingredients that are both tasteless and colorless. Home water tests for certain toxic elements are available at hardware stores, or you can take a water sample to a lab for a more complete analysis.

Finding a lab. For information on certified labs that can analyze your water, contact your county or city health department or check in the Yellow Pages under "Water Analysis."

A QUICK FIX FOR LEAKY FAUCETS

Even a slightly dripping faucet can waste up to 75 L (16 gal.) of water in a single day. The most common reason for the leak is a worn washer—a defect you can easily remedy.

▶ *Shut off the water under the sink by turning the valve clockwise until it stops.*

▶ *Remove any decorative cap on the faucet handle. Unscrew the handle counterclockwise.*

▶ *Remove the packing nut or lock nut that holds the faucet stem in place, and lift out or twist out the stem.*

▶ *Unscrew the bolt holding the washer at the end of the stem, and replace the washer, using a soft washer for a cold water tap, a harder one for hot. Reassemble the faucet.*

▶ *No washers? For a temporary fix, reverse the old one.*

A SUPPLY OF PURE WATER

If you're concerned about water quality but want neither the hassle of setting up a filter on your faucet nor the expense of buying bottled water, try using a water purifying pitcher which traps water contaminants in an inexpensive, replaceable filter. Brita offers an arrray of pitchers, including the 7.5 L (2 gal.) UltraMax (left) and the 1.8 L (½ gal.) Contour (right), as does Pūr (center). All fit neatly on refrigerator shelves or doors.

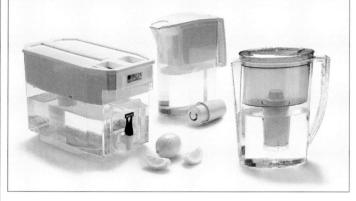

Point-of-use filter systems that treat water at a single tap, such as the one in the kitchen sink, are very practical. Most households don't need filtered water for bathing or laundry. Only 1.8 L (0.4 gal.) of the 227 L (50 gal.) used by the average person daily is for drinking and cooking.

Certified products. Look for the NSF International certification when you choose a water filter. It guarantees that the filter meets the performance standards claimed by the manufacturer. To receive a list of NSF-approved drinking-water treatment units, call 1-800-673-6275.

WAXING & POLISHING

Treat brass like glass. Spray polished brass with a thin coat of window cleaner like Windex and rub lightly. This treatment keeps brass tarnish-free for months.

To maintain the fine finish on wood furniture, apply wax only once or twice a year. Dust it frequently with a slightly dampened lint-free rag coated with a dab of furniture polish.

 Apply polish sparingly. The key to a good shine is more rubbing, not more wax or polish.

Be consistent. If you polish a piece of fine wood furniture with a wax-based product, don't use an oil-based product the next time—or vice versa. Mixing the ingredients may make the finish uneven.

Let it shine. To give newly oiled or waxed wood a lustrous finish, hand-polish the surface with a premixed polishing compound that contains pumice (satin finish) or rottenstone (high gloss).

Combat dampness. Wax finishes often can appear dull and cloudy in high humidity. Remove the clouding by wiping the surface with mineral spirits.

Avoid using lemon oil on high-quality furniture; its harsh kerosene base can damage a fine wood finish.

WEATHER

Buy a weather radio that turns on automatically during a weather emergency, especially if you live in an area that experiences tornados, hurricanes, and other dangerous, fast-moving, weather phenomena. (Make sure your radio comes with an alarm to alert you when it is broadcasting.) Weather radios are available in electronics stores.

Call the airlines before you leave for the airport to make sure your flight is not experiencing weather delays. You'll be more comfortable waiting out the bad weather in your own home or, if you're on vacation, at the hotel.

Weather v. weather change. Sinus, migraine, arthritis, and joint pain sufferers have long believed they are affected by the weather, but studies show that it is changes in weather (an impending storm, for example) that cause the discomfort, not the weather itself (such as long, cold winters.)

Into the wind. When you are at the shore and want to know which way the wind is blowing, look at the seagulls; as they stand on sandbars or piers, they almost always face into the wind.

WEDDING ATTIRE

A nontraditional gown. Save money by buying a dress that's not a traditional bridal gown but still makes you feel like a bride. An elegant ivory suit, for example, or a tea-length gown of cream-colored silk not only is less expensive but can be worn again.

Something old. Instead of spending hundreds of dollars on a new dress, consider wearing your mother's wedding gown or the gown of another beloved relative or friend. You'll have a unique dress that's imbued with sentimental value. Plus, period gowns have cachet, and most can be fitted to flatter the bride.

Rent your wedding dress, and you'll be able to walk down the aisle in a designer gown that might otherwise break your budget. (To find businesses that rent bridal wear, look in the Yellow Pages under "Gown Rentals and Sales.") For a keepsake, buy some other piece of your outfit, such as the veil or gloves.

WEDDING FLOWERS

Decorate with greenery, which generally costs less than floral bouquets. Choose pine boughs in winter and luxuriant ferns in summer. Add white ribbons for color and clusters of candles for effect.

Share the costs of flowers. Is a second wedding scheduled on the same day as yours in your church or synagogue? You may be able to share expenses for church flowers with the other couple. If they agree, get together to go over your selections. You may have to make concessions with regard to color or style, but you'll save a considerable amount of money.

Thank-you presents. Tie gift tags to the flower arrangements that decorate each reception table, designating the flowers to go to loved ones or to those who have helped you in some special way. Donate leftover bouquets to hospitals or nursing homes.

 Buy in-season flowers, which cost less than exotic or out-of-season ones. If your favorite flower is very expensive or is not in season and you must have it, mix it in with other flowers or use it only in your bouquet.

WEDDING GIFTS

How much? When selecting a wedding present, base your decision on what you can afford and on how close you are to the couple, not on how lavishly you are entertained. Nationwide, guests spend $100 to $200 on wedding gifts, more in large cities, less in smaller communities.

Photo memories. Take your camera to the wedding and make a point of capturing a number of charming, informal moments that a formal photographer may miss. As your wedding gift, arrange your pictures in a pretty photo album, or enlarge your best shot and put it into a beautiful frame.

Pool your resources. Get together with several friends of the wedding couple and contribute jointly toward one truly spectacular gift.

Mail thank-you's promptly, ideally the same week that a gift arrives. You don't want to be overwhelmed with the task of writing a huge batch of thank-you notes after the honeymoon.

RIGHT STUFF — SLIP INTO SOMETHING COMFORTABLE

Aching feet can ruin the pleasure of your wedding reception. After you've tied the knot, slip out of tight high heels and into shoes that are fancy yet comfortable. Dance the night away in glittery ballet slippers (left) or circulate for hours at the reception in beaded sneakers (right). Available from the Exclusively Weddings catalog (1-800-759-7666).

WORRY-FREE WEDDING TOASTS

If you're asked to toast the bride and groom, follow these hints to help you carry off this ritual with ease.

▶ *Do your homework. Look through photo albums and read old letters for forgotten details of good times shared.*

▶ *Write it down. If you're nervous or uncomfortable memorizing or ad-libbing your toast, by all means read it.*

▶ *Practice. Take a few minutes in front of a mirror, repeating the toast four or five times so that you'll become so comfortable with it that you almost know it by heart.*

▶ *Don't drag it out. Allow time for other toasts.*

▶ *Don't embarrass anyone or make allusions to past romances. Avoid obscure references.*

▶ *Finale. At the end of the toast, raise your glass to the newlyweds and take a sip. The other guests will follow.*

Make a wedding quilt. If you are handy with a needle and thread, consider making the couple a wedding quilt or, better yet, enlist family members or friends to each make a personal appliquéd square. Be sure to stitch the couple's names and the date of the wedding somewhere on the quilt.

WEDDING INVITATIONS

Save on expenses by not including the second envelope and the enclosure tissue in your invitation. Both are outdated and extravagant traditions that you can easily do without.

Choose a no-frills invitation. Illustrations cost extra, and the more elaborate you make your invitation, the higher the cost. A plain invitation is a classic, elegant choice.

A personal touch. Handwrite your own invitations, particularly if your wedding is going to be small and informal. Or pay a calligrapher to write the invitations.

Buy printed invitations rather than engraved ones. Raised printing, if well done, looks almost as good as engraving and costs about half as much.

WEDDING PLANNING

Decide on a budget—and stick to it. Set a limit on the number of invitees. Remember that each name on the list can add substantially to the total cost.

Read the fine print whenever you contract for wedding services and suppliers. Does the catering bill include extras like coat checkers or bartenders? How much of your deposit is returned if you cancel a reception hall? Also, be sure to negotiate signed contracts with photographers, musicians, and florists.

Church charges. Costs for the use of a church or synagogue can range from nothing to several hundred dollars, depending on where you live, your relationship with the institution, and the size of your wedding. Also, remember to provide a monetary gift for the clergy and any musicians.

WEDDING RECEPTIONS

Affordable reception sites. Not only do most hotels and country clubs charge exorbitant fees, but they often require that you use their equally expensive in-house catering services. Instead, consider renting space in a public or historic building, a local park, a botanical garden, a museum, or a university. The fee for use of such spaces is often minimal, and you can order the food and decorations you prefer at prices you can negotiate.

Single server. Save yourself frustration and hassle by having a packaged reception, with everything supplied by one company—food, wait staff, tables, linens, decorations, drinks. An experienced packager takes the risk out of wedding-day snafus.

Taking the cake. Save big on your wedding cake by having a grocery-store bakery make it.

What about the kids? If you are having a large reception, provide a designated playroom where supervisors can offer videos, games, and food for children. For a small wedding, hire a couple of responsible teens to babysit during the festivities.

WEEDING

Weed when wet. The best time to pull weeds is right after a rainstorm. If the soil is wet, even deep-rooted weeds such as dandelions can be removed with less hassle. If you can't wait for rain, soak the ground with a sprinkler.

Easy prevention. Disturb your soil as little as possible as you garden. Tilling, digging, and hoeing bring dormant weed seeds to the surface. Exposed to light and air, the seeds may sprout.

A newfangled solution. To eliminate weeds from around shrubs, buy a woven or spunbonded plastic cover (often sold as "landscape fabric.") Spread the material over the bare soil around the shrubs and top it with 2.5 cm (1 in.) of an organic mulch such as bark chips. Water, air, and fertilizer can penetrate down to the shrub roots, but weeds can't take hold.

Weeding the path. To eliminate weeds growing in sidewalks, paths, and gravel driveways, drench them with white vinegar. This not only kills the weeds but leaves the soil so acidic that regrowth is stunted. Chlorine bleach or salt will have the same effect.

WEIGHT CONTROL

Change eating habits gradually. Avoid fried foods first, then reduce other high-fat items in

EASY DOES IT

SOLARIZING THE SOIL TO FIGHT WEEDS

You'll get a big head start in keeping your garden weed-free if you purge it of weed seeds and perennial weed roots before you plant. To enlist the sun's heat to do the work, begin preparing the soil in the summer.

▶ *In midsummer, till or dig the proposed garden bed, remove all weed debris, and then rake the soil smooth.*

▶ *Water the soil in the bed thoroughly, then dig a trench 10 cm (4 in.) deep around the bed's perimeter.*

▶ *Cover the bed with thin sheets of clear plastic. Press the plastic sheets down flat, then bury their edges in the trench around the bed.*

▶ *Leave the sheets in place for one to two months, then remove. This treatment should cleanse the bed not only of weed seeds but also of soilborne plant diseases.*

your diet. After a few months, you may even find that foods high in fat, salt, or sugar have lost their appeal to you.

Eating out. Be an informed consumer when ordering in restaurants. If you're counting calories, ask the waiter for a low-cal recommendation. Request that your vegetables be cooked without butter or cheese. Steer clear of cream-based sauces and dressings. Skip the entrees in favor of a hearty soup and salad. Eat slowly and enjoy your food; dining out should be considered a treat.

 Exercise regularly. By making vigorous workouts an integral part of your life, you'll keep unwanted weight off. Schedule your physical activity for the time of day that you're most likely to be tempted to overeat.

Indulge yourself, but only occasionally and in moderation. Vowing never again to touch lasagna

or chocolate, for example, is unrealistic and fosters bingeing.

Think health, not weight. If you follow food-pyramid guidelines and exercise three or four times a week, you'll not only control your weight but lower your risk for heart disease, some cancers, arthritis, and other ailments.

WEIGHT LOSS

Set a realistic goal. Aim for a healthy weight that you have maintained easily in the past instead of attempting to attain an idealized image of beauty.

Pang stoppers. A low-fat diet may at first make you feel hungry every few hours. Counteract your cravings with raw fruits and vegetables, low-fat yogurt, and whole-grain crackers.

Shop from a grocery list, which keeps you from buying impulse items—ruthless diet killers. Stick to the aisles of the supermarket where you find healthful fare such as fruits, vegetables, and breads.

Note your progress. Keep a scale and a tape measure handy to quantify results. Write them down at intervals, noting the dates. It's reassuring to know—even if the change is gradual—that you are progressing.

The limit. You can lose no more than 450 g to 900 g (1–2 lb) of body fat a week. If you crash-diet and the scales show a bigger loss, you have simply given up water and proteins that your body will replace at the first opportunity. Worse, your body will be in starvation mode, which slows down the metabolism. Losing more weight—even on a very-low-calorie regimen—will be even harder.

WHALE WATCHING

Sea-legs savvy. Take a seasickness remedy before going on a whale-watching excursion. To encounter whales, boats often have to travel far out into choppy waters, and many people realize too late that they are unprepared to handle the boat's motion.

Dress the part. Be prepared for fluctuating sea and weather conditions. Wear rubber-soled shoes and dress in layers; a waterproof windbreaker may be required. Take sunglasses and sunscreen.

 Take along binoculars to witness the awesome drama of these huge sea creatures. From far off, you'll be able to distinguish the outline of the whale and perhaps a blowhole spouting. But an up-close view will show the markings that are unique to each whale.

WICKER, RATTAN, & CANE

Mist it. Care for wicker, rattan, and cane by misting it with plain water several times a year. (Let it dry thoroughly before using it.) To prevent cracks from developing, move your furniture out of direct sunlight and away from a fireplace, both of which can dry out wicker. Be sure to bring pieces indoors when the temperature dips toward the freezing point.

Easy fix for sagging. To tighten a drooping cane seat, turn the chair upside down and then wet the underside (except for the chair's rim) with a damp sponge. Let the chair dry for 24 hours or overnight; the cane should have shrunk back into shape.

Protect wicker furniture by painting it with latex paint. Pick cool summer colors or create an antique look by diluting a deep color with water at a ratio of two parts paint to one part water. For this technique, apply the paint solution with a brush, but before it has dried thoroughly, wipe the raised surfaces with a cloth.

Spray-paint wicker furniture inside a large cardboard carton. (Boxes that hold large appliances work well; ask for throwaways from local appliance stores.) Cut off one side of the box and place the wicker piece inside. Work in a ventilated space—outdoors, on a dry, sunny day, if possible.

WEIGHING IN

If you are watching your weight or dieting, knowing the precise size of the portions you are eating can be crucial to your success. A food scale, whether mechanical or electronic, allows you to quickly calculate the weight of food. The EKS Electronic scale (left) measures up to 5 kg (11 lb) and has a large digital display, while The Terraillon 2000 mechanical scale (right) has a magnified display and a handy dish. Food scales are sold through housewares stores and catalogues.

WILDFLOWERS

Ideal soil. A wildflower meadow can be a beautiful, low-mainte-nance alternative to a lawn, but you must keep the soil lean. Never treat the plot with fertiliz-ers, peat moss, or other soil improvements, which encourage weeds, not wildflowers, to grow.

When buying seed, make sure to get your money's worth. Check the contents of prepackaged mixes; many largely consist of fillers such as vermiculite and grass seed. In general, you will need at least 450 g (1 lb) of actual wildflower seeds to plant a 278 m^2 (3,000 ft^2) meadow.

Picking the best posies. Many kinds of wildflowers are particular with regard to the type of climate, soil, sun, and water they require, and are not hardy outside of their native habitat. When choosing wildflowers that are best suited for your situation, consult with your local garden center or con-tact the National Wildflower Research Center (4801 La Crosse Ave., Austin, TX 78739).

WILLS

Sign your will in front of two or three witnesses (depending on provincial requirements). They must watch you sign the will, but they should not include your spouse, a child, or a beneficiary of your estate. A witness with an interest in your estate may throw the will into question.

Videotaping your will signing and reading your will on video-tape can put to rest any suspi-cions that you were not of sound mind when you created the docu-ment. However, a videotaped will may not be valid so don't try to substitute it for a written will.

Separate wills. Spouses should draw up separate wills. Although it is legal to have a joint will, such agreements are difficult to change after the death of one spouse.

HOW TO DRAW UP A SIMPLE WILL

Drawing up a simple will is not difficult, and having one will give you peace of mind knowing that your wishes will be met. Ask your lawyer to check over the will, however; if an error is made, your wishes can be ignored after your death.

Name the province. Laws vary by province, so name your province of residence.

List your spouse. Your spouse generally must be named a beneficiary.

List bequests and recipients of those bequests.

Name an executor to take control of your will and property after your death. Eliminating a bond requirement reduces legal hassles for the executor.

Witnesses should be non-relatives who know you but aren't beneficiaries of your estate. Witnesses sign after you do.

Label it "Will" at the top so that it can be easily recognized. Type the document or use a form (available at bookstores).

List your children. If you don't, questions may be raised about the will's validity—even if they are not granted bequests.

30-day survival. Guard against legal snafus by stating that a beneficiary must survive 30 days.

Dating the will is important, in case you make another one later.

Sign exactly as your name is typed at the top in front of the appropriate number of witnesses.

WILL OF ROBERT P. COLLINS

I, Robert P. Collins, a resident of (city and province), being of sound mind and acting of my own free will, do make and declare this as my Last Will and Testament.

1. I expressly revoke all prior wills and codicils.

2. I am married to Sarah Stone Collins, and all references in this will to my spouse are to her.

3. I am the father of two children, whose names and dates of birth are:
Arthur Collins, born April 6, 1972
Jennifer Collins, born August 15, 1975

4. I give all of my property, real, personal, or mixed, to my spouse, Sarah Stone Collins, with the exception of my share of ownership in the Bull's Run Resort Condominium, lot 2025, in the city of Jasper, province of Alberta, which I give to my two children, Arthur Collins and Jennifer Collins, in equal shares.

If my wife, Sarah Stone Collins, does not survive me for thirty (30) days, then I give all of my property, real, personal, or mixed, to my children, Arthur Collins and Jennifer Collins, in equal shares.

5. I appoint Sarah Stone Collins, my wife, executor of my will. If she is unable to serve for any reason, then I appoint Jonathan Collins, my brother, executor. The executor is empowered to carry out all provisions of this will. The executor shall have all statutory powers available under provincial law. The executor shall not be required to post bond.

This ends my Last Will and Testament.

I subscribe my name to this Will on this (date of signing) in (city, province where signed).

(signature)
Robert P. Collins

On the date stated above, Robert P. Collins declared to us, the under-signed, that the foregoing document is his Last Will and Testament, and asked us to act as witnesses to it. He then signed his name to this Will in our presence, all of us being present at the same time. Now at his request and in his presence, and in the presence of each other, we sign our names as witnesses.

Witness #1 Signature
Witness #2 Signature   (own address)
Witness #3 Signature   (own address)
                            (own address)

Window films keep heat from seeping out in winter and cool air from escaping in summer—resulting in big savings on your energy bills. Window films also cut harsh sun glare, reducing fading and thus lengthening the life of upholstery, curtains, rugs, and carpeting. Some films, such as Gila Sunshine, can be installed by a handy amateur; other styles, such as Vista, should be installed by a professional. Available at home centers.

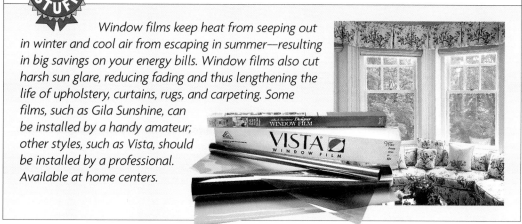

Don't make changes. Marking even tiny changes on your will can invalidate it completely. If you want to make minor changes, draw up a codicil, which must be signed, dated, and witnessed in the same manner as the original.

 A new baby should inspire you to make a will. Select—and get the consent of—a guardian to care for the child and a trustee to look after the child's money should anything happen to you and your spouse. If you already have a will, execute a new one each time you have a new baby or adopt a child.

Last wishes. Write a "Letter of Instruction" separate from your will and mark it "Open In case of death." In it, spell out your personal wishes concerning such details as burial or cremation, a memorial service, and organ donations. Also, list trusts, insurance policies, or other property that contain provisions for survivors apart from those contained in your will. Include any private messages for family or friends that you don't want filed in court with your will.

WINDOW SHADES & BLINDS

Tension control. To tighten the tension on a roller shade, roll it down halfway and take it out of the brackets. Holding the metal piece that goes into the bracket with pliers, roll the shade up by hand and carefully rehang it. To loosen tension, roll up the shade completely, then take it out of the brackets, unroll the shade halfway by hand, and return to its brackets.

Make custom shades to match a room's curtains, bedspreads, or upholstered furniture. Check at home centers or hardware stores for sprays that stiffen heavier fabrics enough to attach to a roller, glues for attaching light-weight fabrics onto ready-made shade bases, or complete kits for making custom shades.

White glove treatment. Wear inexpensive white cotton gloves to dust venetian blinds. Simply swipe the slats with your fingers, and you'll clean both sides of the blind simultaneously.

WINDOWS

Out of window cleaner? Substitute liquid dishwashing detergent mixed with tap water. To avoid leaving a sticky film on the windows, use one capful per 3.7 L (0.83 gal.) of water.

Crosshatch cleaning. Wipe the outside of each pane vertically and the inside horizontally (or vice versa). This makes it easy to tell which side any streaks are on.

Rubbing alcohol sprayed from a bottle also makes an excellent window cleaner. It removes greasy smudges, evaporates quickly, does not freeze (which helps when washing windows in cold weather), and leaves no residue.

Energy efficiency. Consider replacing old windows with new double-glazed ones that have argon gas sealed in the middle as an insulation.

WINDSHIELDS

Remove dried bugs from your windshield and headlights with a plastic mesh onion bag, which is abrasive enough to remove the bugs but soft enough not to scratch the windshield.

Small chips in your windshield glass caused by flying gravel or stones can often be fixed without replacing the windshield. Ask about such repairs at an auto glass shop.

Extend wiper blade life by lightly sandpapering the rubber edge of the wiper to smooth out any nicks. The smoothed edge will clean the windshield better, too.

Winter cleaning. Don't try to clean your windshield of ice and snow with the wipers. Instead, use a scraper and brush and remove snow from the cowl area where the wipers park before turning them on. The wiper motor could burn out working to pull up frozen wipers or to push them down against packed snow.

WINE

 Store wine in a consistently cool, dry place, such as a below-ground cellar. Lay wine bottles on their sides to prevent the corks from drying out and letting air leak into the bottles.

Recap an open bottle of wine with a wine saver, a gadget that forces air out of the open bottle and then reseals it. Look for wine savers at wine and housewares stores. Open bottles of wine usually last a week in the refrigerator.

Buying tip. Most wine vendors offer a discount—generally 10 percent or one free bottle—when wine is purchased by the case (that is, 12 bottles).

Use leftover wine, even if it has gone a bit "off," in salad dressings, where it makes a good substitute for vinegar.

Cooking with wine. Never cook with a wine that you would not drink on its own. Conversely, you need not select an expensive wine for cooking—just a tasty one since the wine's flavor will be enhanced during cooking.

Combine wines after a party if you have several open bottles. Place all the red wine in one bot-

PAIRING WINE WITH FOOD

As a general rule, red wines marry well with hearty foods, such as beef, lamb, and game. White wines go with more delicate dishes, like seafood and chicken. Pork and robust poultry recipes are complemented by lighter reds and heavier whites. The varietal wines suggested here are available under many brand names.

TYPE OF FOOD	TYPE OF WINE	EXAMPLES
Beef or lamb	Full-bodied red	*California:* Cabernet Sauvignon, Merlot, Petite Sirah. *French:* Bordeaux, Burgundy (Côte de Nuits, Côte Rôtie). *Italian:* Barolo, Chianti Classico. *Spanish:* dry Rioja. *Argentine:* Cabernet Sauvignon, Malbec. *Australian:* Shiraz.
Pork	Light-bodied red	*California:* Zinfandel, Pinot Noir, Gamay. *French:* Beaujolais. *Italian:* Bardolino, Valpolicella, Corvo Rosso.
	Full-bodied white	*California:* Chardonnay, Sauvignon Blanc. *French:* Chablis, Meursault, Puligny-Montrachet. *Italian:* Gavi. *Chilean:* Riesling.
Poultry	Light, dry white	*California:* Sauvignon Blanc, Chenin Blanc. *French:* Sancerre or Macon-Villages. *Italian:* Orvieto, Soave, Trebbiano.
	Full-bodied white	*California:* Chardonnay. *French:* Chablis, Burgundy (Meursault, Puligny-Montrachet). *Italian:* Gavi. *Chilean:* Riesling.
Game	Full-bodied red	*California:* Zinfandel, Cabernet Sauvignon, Merlot. *French:* Bordeaux, Burgundy, Rhone (Châteauneuf-du-Pape, Hermitage). *Italian:* Amarone, Spanna, Gattinara. *Portuguese:* Dão.
Fish/Shellfish	Light, dry white	*California:* Sauvignon Blanc, Seyval Blanc. *French:* Pouilly-Fumé, Alsatian Riesling, Sancerre, Muscadet. *Italian:* Pinot Grigio, Orvieto.
	Full-bodied white	*California:* Chardonnay, Johannisberg Riesling. *French:* Macon-Villages, Burgundy (Puligny-Montrachet, Meursault).

WINTERIZING GARDENS

Dehydration from cold winter winds and frozen groundwater poses a threat to trees and shrubs—particularly evergreens. Antitranspirant (or anti-desiccant) sprays, such as Wilt-Pruf, coat leaves and stems to reduce moisture loss. Available in ready-to-use spray (left) and concentrate (right) forms, they are sold through garden centers and catalogs.

Leftover Christmas trees provide a timely and inexpensive mulch for perennial flower beds. After the holidays, scavenge for discarded trees, or ask a vendor on December 26 if you can have leftovers. Cut off the boughs and spread them over beds. This evergreen blanket also protects perennials against winter thaws, keeping plants safely dormant until you remove the boughs in spring.

Winter watering. Water your shrubs during winter thaws to counter the cold-weather dehydration that occurs when winter winds dry branches and soil moisture is locked up as ice.

Double duty. Keep roses from freezing by mounding compost 25 cm (10 in.) deep around the base of the bushes in late fall. Unlike traditional soil mounds, compost mounds won't have to be removed in the spring. Instead, spread the compost around the bushes to prepare them for spring.

tle and all the white wine in another. You'll save the wine, and you may create a delicious blend. Drink it within the next two days.

WINTERIZING YOUR CAR

Antifreeze is most effective in a solution of 50 percent antifreeze and 50 percent water. Never use a solution in excess of 70 percent antifreeze. The freezing point of a stronger solution is actually higher than a weaker mixture, and it will not prevent corrosion in the radiator as effectively.

If you have trouble starting the car in cold weather, your grade of oil may be too heavy. Many car makers now recommend SAE 5W-30 oils for year-round use to improve fuel economy and winter starting. If you use a heavy grade in summer, switch to a light grade in winter.

Check your tires. If the tread is worn, buy new tires before cold weather sets in; you need good traction on slippery roads. Check the tire pressure as the temperature falls. A drop of 5°C (10°F) translates to a 7 kN/m^2 (1 lbf/in^2) loss in tire pressure.

WINTERIZING YOUR GARDEN

Combat sunscald. Young deciduous trees, especially newly planted ones, can be seriously injured by the harsh winter sun scalding the bark of their trunks. To prevent sunscalding, wrap their trunks in autumn with burlap or the paper wrapping manufactured for this purpose (available at most garden centers). A wrap also helps protect trees against nibbling rabbits and mice.

WINTERIZING YOUR HOUSE

OLD SAW **Reduce your heating bill** considerably by using weather stripping. Save as much as 30% on your average heating bill by making sure cold air does not seep in through cracks around windows and doors.

Always remove hoses from outdoor faucets before the first cold snap to prevent fixtures and pipes from cracking and freezing. This applies even to freezeproof faucets that you've turned off.

Keep curtains and shades open on the sunny sides of the house during winter days. Letting in the sun creates passive solar heat, which helps to warm the rooms.

WOK COOKING

Sizzle test. The oil in a wok is hot enough to cook in when a small piece of ginger, garlic, or onion sizzles as it hits the heated oil in the pan.

Hot spot. Cook only in the bottom third of a wok. When feeding a crowd, prepare several small batches rather than one large one.

Buy a flat-bottomed wok if you frequently cook with a wok on a conventional range. The metal rings supplied to steady round-bottomed Chinese woks often position the wok too far from the heat. And placing a round-bottomed wok directly on a gas grid or electric element can be dangerous—the wok may be too unsteady for safe stir-frying with hot oils or other liquids.

Before stir-frying vegetables, cut them on the diagonal. The larger the surface, the quicker a piece will cook. To make sure the slices cook evenly, cut each slice the same width.

No wok? If you don't own a wok, you can stir-fry in a skillet, but you will have to use slightly more oil and cook the food a little longer because of the different shape.

Season your wok before and after each use. You should wipe the wok down with a light coating of vegetable oil each time you cook. When you're finished using the wok, wash and dry it and wipe it down again before storing. Try seasoning it with sesame oil for an Asian touch.

BUILDING A FIRE

To get the full heating benefit of a good woodstove, you need to build a proper fire in it. Here are the steps.

▶ *Start with a base of crumpled newspaper. Lay kindling over the paper in a crisscross pattern that will let air circulate. Add a mix of split logs—soft wood, like pine or spruce, for quick ignition; and hardwood, such as maple or ash, for long burning.*

▶ *Open the damper and warm up the flue by lighting a cone of rolled newspaper and holding it up the chimney. This hot initial flame pushes cold air up the flue, creating an updraft for the fire.*

▶ *Light the paper under the kindling and split logs. The newspaper fire ignites the kindling, and the kindling fire ignites the softwood, which will then heat the hardwood enough to burn.*

▶ *Once the hardwood is burning, add only hardwood logs. Make sure there are plenty of 12 mm (½ in.) air spaces between them; a fire needs air as well as fuel to burn.*

WOODSTOVES

Invest in a new model. Stricter government standards for woodstoves have made 1990s' models far more efficient in burning wood and heating spaces, and far less likely to pollute the air or cause creosote buildup than earlier models. Buying a new stove will ensure safer heating and will pay for itself quickly in fuel economy.

 Safety rules. Before installing a woodstove, be sure you are conforming to local building or fire department regulations regarding the vents, floor protectors, and clearances. Always keep flammable materials and furniture well away from a woodstove that is in use.

Paint a woodstove with enamel spray paint specially made to withstand the high heat. Look for it in hardware and paint stores. Prepare the stove's surface by brushing it lightly with a wire brush and dusting it with a rag dampened with paint thinner.

Rustproofer. At the end of the heating season, wipe a cast-iron woodstove with kerosene to help prevent rust from forming.

WORKING ALONE

Clamps are handy for the person working alone. Buy a supply of clamps in different sizes and shapes. You can use them to hold any number of items together as you mark, mold, or fasten them.

When installing a post, attach your level to the top of it with a bungee or shock cord. This will leave both your hands free to adjust the angle of the post.

The single sawyer. To make solo cutting easier and safer with a table saw, build an outfeed table the exact height as the saw table. Waxing its surface will help the sawn wood slide smoothly over it.

To paper a ceiling by yourself, improvise a high-rise platform to hold the booked (paste-covered and folded) wallpaper while you smooth the other end of the paper onto the ceiling with both hands. Use two stepladders and a wide plank, or build the platform with scrap lumber.

Wainscoting trick. When installing a long board horizontally, prop one end up on a nail tacked into the wall while you fasten the other end. Put the nail slightly above where the bottom of the board will be, so that when the board is nailed in place, it will cover the hole.

WORKSHOPS

Install good lighting, such as a hanging fluorescent fixture, above your workbench and any heavy machine tools. Well-focused light makes your work easier and safer.

 Stand easy. If your workshop has a concrete floor, cover it with old plywood sheets, carpet scraps, or even with flattened cardboard boxes to make standing on it more comfortable.

Install electrical outlets on the front of a freestanding workbench, and you'll always have an outlet handy when you need one. Otherwise, install electrical outlets that hang at a convenient height from the ceiling, rather than on the walls, to minimize the number of extension cords cluttering the floor.

If space is tight, build a fold-down worktable from a solid core door. Fasten one long side of it to the wall with a heavy-duty piano

hinge. Install legs on hinges so that they hang flat against the table when it is fastened up against the wall. Collapsible braces, such as those used on card tables, will steady the table.

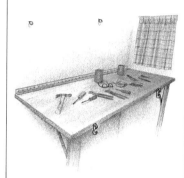

Good storage. Make use of the space between open floor joists in a basement shop ceiling to store long boards. You can use hooks, wooden cleats, or rope slings to hold the lumber in place.

Workshop must. A fire extinguisher marked ABC will put out most types of workshop fires. Keep the fire extinguisher in an accessible place and make sure it's always fully charged.

Work it off. Use a physical workout or a hobby to relieve the stress that comes from worry. Focus on the activity instead of on your concerns.

Reality check. If you are worried, determine whether you can take a particular action to solve a problem. If so, then take the necessary steps. If not, accept that you can do nothing and now you must move on.

Listen up. Be a responsive listener to someone who is worried. Offer support and feedback, but don't become angry if he doesn't follow your advice. Each person must solve his own problems in his own way.

Keep a journal. Write your worries down on paper, together with a description of your feelings concerning your problems. After articulating your anxieties in detail, list ways (as many as you can think of) to resolve them. Sometimes the mere act of describing problems in words stimulates creative solutions.

RIGHT STUFF   A FOOT SWITCH FOR WORKSHOP SAFETY

A foot-operated switch makes many stationary power tools safer and easier to handle by leaving both hands free. You can opt for a straightforward style, like the Reliant On/Off Foot Switch (right), or go for a more elaborate model, like a Delta Lectric Air Foot Switch (left), that comes with a protective guard to prevent accidentally activating the tool. Find foot-operated switches at most builders' supply stores.

XERISCAPING TO ZUCCHINI

XERISCAPING

What is it? Xeriscaping, which got its name from *xeros,* the Greek word for dry, refers to landscaping that requires very little, if any, supplementary water. Such landscaping is built around plants that thrive naturally within a dry area's normal rainfall.

Easy maintenance. After plants in a xeriscaped garden are well established, your watering chores (and your water bills) will be minimal. Put in new plants just before each rainy season. Use mulch to keep the soil cool and moist.

Plant shade trees. Dry areas are hot and forbidding without the cover of trees. Certain evergreens—Scotch pine and holly oak, for example—and deciduous trees—olive and crape myrtle—thrive in dry conditions.

Good annuals to plant in dry gardens include marigolds, cockscombs, African daisies, dusty miller, gazanias, sunflowers, moss rose, and zinnias.

Water booster. Mix an absorbent soil material such as pumice into plant beds in a dry garden. Plant roots will absorb water from the pumice long after the rest of the soil has dried from a rain.

X-RAYS

Limit your exposure by discussing proposed X-ray exams with your doctor or dentist. What is to be gained from the procedure? Is it necessary? Is there an alternative such as a sonogram?

Request a lead apron to cover parts of the body that are not going to be X-rayed, especially in the abdominal and pelvic regions.

Regular mammograms (X-ray exams of the breasts)—are recommended by the National Cancer Institute and most doctors for women over the age of 40. The organization recommends a first regular mammogram by age 40, then a mammogram every two years after age 50. Mammograms use a low level of radiation.

Keep an X-ray card. Whenever you or your child has an X-ray, have the doctor or dentist write down the type of exam and where the X-ray is stored. This can help you avoid having unnecessary repeat X-rays.

YARD SALES

Not enough to sell? Ask neighbors to join in. Use different-colored price tags for each seller. As items are sold, store the tags in the cash box; then divide the proceeds after the sale.

Have change on hand. Start collecting change weeks before the sale until you have amassed a large supply of coins and small bills. During the sale, keep it in a covered box or carry it in an apron with several deep pockets.

IRRIGATING THE GARDEN DRIP BY DRIP

Irrigation systems that water plants in precise amounts reduce water waste. Agrifim, among others, makes xeriscaping equipment that you can tailor to fit your landscape needs. PC Plus emitters (red and green) regulate water pressure over a small plot, which is useful for watering plants located far from a water source. Dial-A-Flow emitters (commonly used on stakes for roses or vegetables) meet changing water needs by converting water from a slow drip to a 75 cm (30 in.) diameter stream (see inset). Sold through garden supply stores and catalogs.

Give away balloons to the kids who come with their parents. The balloons will encourage the parents to linger and browse. The kids may be potential customers too if you've cleaned out the old toys, books, or games in the attic.

Donate the leftovers. Box up anything left from your yard sale and donate it to a local charity or thrift store. You'll get a tax deduction for your donations.

YEAST

Buy yeast in bulk if you bake a lot. Bulk yeast is sold in health-food stores and at some groceries. Look for "dry, activated" yeast. Once you get home, store it in the refrigerator to make it last longer.

 Is it old? Check the expiration date on yeast before using it. You can test, or "proof," it by mixing a little warm (never hot) water and 2 mL (½ tsp) sugar with the yeast. If it fizzes, it is still good.

Dry and compressed yeast can be used interchangeably. 30 mL (2 tbsp) of dry yeast equals a 20 g (⅔ oz) cake of compressed.

HOW TO ORGANIZE A YARD SALE

Advance planning can help to ensure that your yard sale will result in many happy transactions.

▸ *Advertise. Run ads in the daily newspaper and in local shopper newspapers. Post flyers on bulletin boards and on telephone poles. Indicate a rain date.*

▸ *Make a list of things to sell. Go through the closets, cabinets, garage, and attic, so nothing will be forgotten.*

▸ *Mark the house. Put up a big sign (with a bouquet of balloons) where passersby can see it on the sale day.*

▸ *Tag everything with its price. Use masking tape for small items, string tags for clothing, and posters for large items.*

Warm the bowl in which you will be using yeast to create an effective environment for growth. (Just rinse the bowl in hot water.)

YOGA

Take a class. Yoga, which has many forms, can benefit anyone, regardless of age or fitness level. The best way to find a teacher who is right for you is to sample introductory classes (which are often free) offered by yoga centers in your area.

Yoga anytime. After you learn the basics of breathing and postures, you can practice yoga any time and any place. Allow at least 20 to 30 minutes to warm up, go through a routine, and finish with a relaxation period.

It is not a competition. Avoid comparing your ability to that of others in a yoga class, since everyone is at a different level. Work on maximizing your own body's potential. Yoga is not just about acquiring physical skills; its major goal is relaxation and rejuvenation of your mind and body.

Alert your instructor to injuries or sensitive areas on your body. The instructor can then adjust the exercises to make them effective for you without aggravating the problem area.

YOGURT

Thicken yogurt by letting it drain for several hours. Line a strainer with a coffee filter or cheesecloth and set it over a bowl to catch the dripping liquid. Add the yogurt, cover the strainer, and put in the refrigerator. The longer it drains, the thicker it becomes.

Flavorful marinade. Use low-fat yogurt as the creamy base of a healthful marinade for meat or poultry. Season it with Middle Eastern or Indian herbs and spices.

Final touch. Add yogurt to cooked dishes at the very end of cooking. If yogurt gets too hot, it will separate.

ZIPPERS

Pencil it in. Sticking zippers will slide easily if rubbed with lead from an ordinary pencil. The pencil's graphite acts as a lubricant.

Waxing and waning. To ease a balky zipper, rub the teeth with soap, candle wax, petroleum jelly, or lip ointment. Wipe off the residue with a tissue.

Get a handle on it. If the tab of your zipper breaks off, replace it temporarily with a paper clip, a safety pin, or small key ring. (In fact, a key ring can make a stylish ornament on a coat, or an easy-to-pull tab on a child's jacket.)

Shrink it. Before sewing a new zipper with a cotton tape into a prewashed garment, preshrink the zipper. Soak it in hot water for several minutes and let it air-dry.

ZONING

Check local zoning codes before you start any kind of renovation or improvement to your home. These laws regulate what you may build on your property, where you may build it, and how you may use the new or altered structure. Be sure your plans conform to the zoning codes, or be prepared to apply for a variance.

Home business hazard. Many residential communities use zoning codes to prohibit home-based businesses. Before you launch any business such as a day care facility, a word-processing service, or piano lessons, look into the local zoning codes.

In historic districts, modernizing your house can be strictly controlled in every detail by zoning codes, right down to the exact design of the smallest replacement window. Join a neighborhood group that may have identified the resources needed for the authentic renovation work that is required in your area.

ZUCCHINI

Skin deep. Don't peel zucchini or other summer squashes before you eat them. The beta carotene and other vitamins are in the skin.

Zucchini shish kebab. For a fast, tasty supper dish, skewer chunks of zucchini, onion, and lean beef. Marinate the skewers in a low-fat dressing for an hour or more, and cook them over the grill.

Fill zucchini flowers with grated seasoned zucchini, Parmesan cheese, and bread crumbs. Steam the stuffed blossoms briefly and serve with drinks.

 Smaller is better. When it comes to dishes featuring cooked or raw zucchini, select squashes no longer than 15 cm (6 in.) The exception is stuffed zucchini; when stuffed with meat, rice, or other fillings, larger zucchinis hold up better.

Summer crop, winter soup. If you have a bumper crop of zucchini in your summer garden, make a huge batch of zucchini soup and freeze it in individual containers. It will taste delicious served as a winter lunch.

EASY DOES IT — RAISING YOUR OWN ZUCCHINI CROP

If you have a sunny spot in your garden, you can grow an ample crop of zucchini; in fact, if you're not careful, you'll have enough to supply the neighborhood. Here's how.

▶ *Start seeds indoors about four weeks before your last frost date. (Consider bush varieties, which take up less room than vines and don't need staking.)*

▶ *Prepare the soil with plenty of cow manure or other compost, and you won't have to fertilize later.*

▶ *Transplant seedlings to the garden when the soil warms. (You'll pick your first zucchini within a month and a half.)*

▶ *Put aluminum foil under the plants to reflect light and confuse the squash borer moth before it lays its eggs at the base of the stem. If you see any eggs, scrape them off.*

▶ *Pick only male squash flowers to eat (they have no bulge under the blossom). Female flowers produce the squash; the plants won't bear fruit if you pick those.*

▶ *Use black plastic as mulch around your plants in order to conserve moisture and warmth, reduce weeds, and deter most zucchini-loving pests.*

PERMISSIONS

Grateful acknowledgment is given to the following companies and individuals for permission to use their photographs: **Country Estate Polyvinyl Fence**, Nebraska Plastics, Inc., Cozad, NE, p. 128; **Real Fyre Gas Logs**, Robert H. Peterson Company, City of Industry, CA, p. 131; **Edward S. Barnard**, private family photographs; p. 274-275; **Virginia Wells Blaker**, private family photographs, pp. 274-275; **Yamaha PSR520 Portable Keyboard**, Yamaha Corporation of America, Buena Park, CA, p. 276; **Eljer Pull-Out Spray**, Eljer, Dallas, TX, p. 282; **Bell'Oggetti Speaker Stands**, Bell'Oggetti International Ltd., Morganville, NJ, p. 343; **Standesign Speaker Stands**, Melody Audio Ltd., Denver, CO, p. 343; **Kartu Bag and The Sherpa Bag**, Sherpa's Pet Trading Company, New York, NY, p. 377; **Double Delight Twin Crib**, Nene Quality Baby Products, Commerce, CA, p. 380; **Vista Window Film, Gila Sunshine Film**, Courtaulds Performance Films, Inc., New York, NY, p. 397; **Dial-A-Flow Emitter**, DripWorks, Willits, CA, p. 402.

SPECIAL THANKS

Special acknowledgment is given to **Ilise Benum**, editor of *The Art of Self Promotion* newsletter, for help creating the Easy Does It box, p. 200; **Martha Faghani** for designing and making the baby quilt, p. 296; **Sandra Rose Gluck** for developing the recipes for No-Cook Mexican-Style Sauce for Pasta, p. 262, and Raspberry Vinegar, p. 386; **Ruth Perles** for designing and making the dried flower arrangement, p. 110-111; **Grace Young** for her recipe for cooking classic Chinese rice, p. 310; and **Judith Carmel, Linda Ingoia, Claudia Kaplan, Alexis Lipsitz, Harvey Loomis, Ruth Perles,** and **Lydia Tanenhaus** for serving as photographer's models.

CREDITS

The editors thank the following individuals, organizations, and companies for providing products and information that were useful in the preparation of this book: **Accusplit Inc.,** San Jose, CA (pedometer A2110F, 387). **Agrifim Inc.,** Fresno, CA (drip irrigation supplies, 402). **A.M. Leonard, Inc.,** Piqua, OH (scuffle hoe, 151). **American Stationery Co., Inc.,** Peru, IN (personal embosser). **American Yoga Assn.,** Cleveland Heights, OH (meditation tapes, 234). **Arthritis Foundation,** Atlanta, GA (various gadgets, 25). **Arthur Brown and Bro. Co., Inc.,** New York, NY (pens, 265). **Avery Dennison,** Diamond Bar, CA (labels, 210). **Bausch & Lomb,** Rochester, NY (disposable contact lenses, 88). **Big Software, Inc.,** Cupertino, CA (Big Business accounting softwear, 178). **Black & Decker,** Shelton, CT (ScumBuster, 366). **The Bouchard Collection,** Naperville, IL (Reception Sneakers, 392). **Briko,** fine sporting goods stores, (Stinger, 353). **Brita Products Co.,** Oakland, CA (Contour, UltraMax, 391). **Brookstone, Inc.,** Nashua, NH (Smart Key Tracker, 204). **The Business Word/Twins Magazine,** Englewood, CO (information, 380). **CamelBak,** Jackson Hole, WY (Go-Be, 316). **Christine Columbus,** Lake Oswego, OR (Austin House Door Jammer, 181, and SafSak, 375). **Ciba Vision Corp.,** Duluth GA (NewVue, 88). **Colorado Ski Country, USA, Rachel Biederman,** Denver, CO (information, 335, 340). **Comtrad Industries,** Excelsior MN (Recoton wireless headphone and transmitter, 222). **Corel Corp.,** Ottawa, Ontario (Corel Professional Office Suite, 178). **Corning Consumer Products Co.,** Corning, NY (Pyrex Portables, 285). **Cosmi Corp.,** Rancho Dominguez, CA (Label Publisher software, 210). **Delta Int'l Machinery Corp.,** Pittsburg, PA (Delta Lectric Air, 401). **Deluxe Designs,** Lakewood, CO (Easy & Elegant needlepoint kit, 246). **DuPont Co. Fluoroproducts,** Wilmington, DE (non-stick sheets, 90). **The Estate Plan,** Reno, NV (The Living Trust, 290). **Eagle Creek Travel Gear,** San Marcos, CA (Undercover passport carriers, 375). **Elan/Monark Sporting Goods, Inc.,** Burlington, VT (SCX Cap parabolic skis, 335). **Erica Wilson Needleworks,** New York, NY (needlepoint kits, 246). **Evert-Fresh Corp.,** Houston, TX (Evert-Fresh Bags, 140). **Exclusively Weddings,** Greensboro, NC (Reception ballet shoes, 392). **FilmMaster Window Tinting,** Arvada, CO (information, 397). **Fisher-Price Toys,** East Aurora, NY (Wonder Tools Cruiser, 358). **Fisher Space Pen Co.,** Boulder City, NV (pens, 265). **Five Borough Bicycle Club,** a New York City affiliate of Hostelling International-American Youth Hostels (Two-Minute Bicycle Check, 43). **Flex USA, Inc.,** Cincinnati, OH (Flexi 2-5 Compact retractable leash, 104). **Frieda's Inc.,** Los Alamitos, CA (PEAK*fresh* Bags, 140). **Gardener's Supply Co.,** Burlington, VT (bird feeders and Squirrel Prevent powder, 44). **Greater New York Aquarium,** Joe Guzzardo, New York, NY (aquarium supplies, 23). **Harold Import Co.,** Lakewood, NJ (Quickso shrimp cleaner, wide-necked clam knife, oyster knife, 331). **Hayward Pool Products, Inc.,** Elizabeth, NJ (Hayward/Arneson NaviGator in-ground pool cleaner, 354). **The Home Baking Assn.,** Sharon Davis, director, Lincoln, NB (information on baking, 33, 90). **Homedics, Inc.,** Keego Harbor, MI (Back Pleaser Ultra, 232). **Honeywell Consumer Products,** Hagerstown, MD (Enviracaire air cleaner, 169). **The Hoover Co.,** North Canton, OH (Hoover SteamVac Jr., 315). **Hound Dog Products, Inc.,** Edina, MN (Weed Hound, 214). **Ideaworks, Inc.,** Indian Wells, CA (vacuum cleaner attachments, 382). **Interplus Corp.,** Cincinnati, OH (nitril gloves, 329). **Intuit Inc.,** Mountain View, CA (Quicken 6 for Windows, 11). **JB Research Inc./Relaxor,** Bellflower, CA (Ergo massaging chair, 232). **JCA, Inc.,** Townsend, MA (needlepoint kits, 246). **Jogalite,** Silver Lake, NH (Reflective vest, bands, stickers; L.E.D. lights, 303). **JT Products,** Libby, MT (Magi-Cake strips, 58). **King Arthur Flour,** Norwich, VT (Thermohauser Pan Liners, 33, Thermohauser Giant Bread Spatula, 51, EKS Electronic Scale, 395). **Kreepy Krauly USA, Inc.,** Sunrise, FL (E-Z Vac pool cleaner, 354). **The Left Hand,** Bethelhem, PA (left-handed products, 218). **Lefthanders Int'l,** Topeka, KS (Lefthander Magazine, 218). **Levenger,** Delray Beach, FL (Levenger foot rest, 252). **Mag-Nif,** Kearnsville, WV (money sorter and roller, 266). **Magellan's International Travel Supplies,** Santa Barbara, CA (currency converter, 95, Marsona Sound Machine, 337, BioBands & Sea-Bands, 240). **McCormick & Co., Inc.,** Hunt Valley, MD (Bag 'n Season, 312). **Meco Corp.,** Greenville, TN (Porto-Top, 356). **Microsystems Software, Inc.,** Framingham, MA (Cyber Patrol Blocking software, 192). **MIDWEST Home for Pets,** Muncie IN (Puppy crate, 294). **MMO Music Group Inc.,** Elmsford, NY (Music Minus One play-along CDs, 242). **National Organization of Mothers of Twins Clubs, Inc.,** Albuquerque, NM (information, 380). **New York University, Food and Nutrition Program,** New York, NY (Marion Nestle, Carole Gruber, Sharon Dalton, information). **Nite Note,** Irvine, CA (pens, 265). **Nolo Press,** Berkeley, CA (Living Trust Maker, 290). **Old World Innovations, Inc.,** Ellicott City, MD (Hot Bricks, 279). **Oraton Rubber Stamp Co.,** Columbia, NJ (personal embosser, 210). **Pentel of America Ltd.,** Torrance, CA (pens, 265). **Penzeys, Ltd,** Meskego, WI (Coffee Grinders, 344). **PerfectData,** Simi Valley, CA (StatClean spray and wipes, Stat-Free spray and wipes, 346). **Perfect Performance USA,** South Lake Tahoe, CA (Squeezy, 316). **Porter-Cable,** Jackson, TN (Random-Orbit sander, 319). **Powerfood, Inc.,** Berkeley, CA (PowerGel, 316). **Prince Sports Group,** Bordentown, NJ (PrinceGrip Plus lotion and spray, Durazorb overgrip). **Pur Drinking Water Systems,** Minneapolis, MN (Water Filter Pitcher, 391). **Quickie Manufacturing Corp.,** Cinnaminson, NJ (Double Bubble snow shovel, 340). **Reflective Technologies, Inc.,** Cambridge, MA (illumiNITE cap and jacket, 303). **The Reynolds Kitchens,** Richmond, VA (oven bags, 312). **Rubbermaid Office Products Inc.,** Merryville, TN (ComfortTread Plus foot rest, 252). **Salton/Maxim Housewares, Inc.,** Kenilworth, NJ (Wet Reflection, 37). **Sanford,** Bellwood, IL (pens, 265). **Schrader Bridgeport Int'l,** Monroe, NC (Schrader 100 digital pressure gauge, 368). **Serengeti Eyewear,** North Caldwell, NJ (Serengeti Drivers, 353). **Sportline,** Campbell, CA (pedometers, 387). **Sports Street Marketing,** Berkeley, CA (GU, 316). **J. & M. Stearns,** Kent, CT (information on kitchen tools, 207). **Surf Watch,** a division of Spyglass, Inc., Los Altos, CA (Surf Watch, 192). **Terraillon,** Stamford, CT (Terraillon BA2000 mechanical scale, 395). **Tiger Electronics, Inc.,** Vernon Hills, IL (My First Laptop, 358). **Trend Lines, Inc.,** Revere, MA (Reliant On-Off switch pedal, 401). **Jeffrey Tucker,** Philadelphia, PA (information on architects, 24). **Tupperware U.S., Inc.** Orlando, FL (ice cream scoop, 187; Rock 'N Serve, 285). **Ultimate Direction,** Rexburg, ID (Solo water carrier, 316). **Universal Electronics,** Twinsburg, OH (One For All Universal Remote Controls, 305). **Unique Sports Products,** Alpharetta, GA (tennis accessories, 363). **Videonics,** New York, NY (Home Video Producer, 385). **Vistakon,** a division of Johnson & Johnson Vision products, Jacksonville, FL (Acuvue, 88). **Willat Writing Instruments,** Los Angeles, CA (Sensa pens, 265). **Wilt-Pruf Products, Inc.,** Essex, CT (antitranspirant spray, 399).